# Film and Video Synergies: Creation to Delivery

# PROCEEDINGS

138th SMPTE Technical Conference
and World Media Expo

# Film and Video Synergies: Creation to Delivery

October 8-12, 1996
Los Angeles Convention Center
Los Angeles, California

Foreword
Thomas Bentsen

Program Chair
Charles Dages

Editor
Jeffrey Friedman

Editorial Program Coordinator
Marilyn Waldman

**Society of Motion Picture and Television Engineers**
**595 W. Hartsdale Ave., White Plains, NY 10607**

The Society of Motion Picture and Television Engineers,
White Plains, NY 10607



This book was reproduced photographically from original copy submitted by the authors. Statements and opinions contained herein are expressions of the contributors and do not necessarily represent the policies or opinions of the SMPTE.



Printed in the United States of America

ISBN: 0-940690-33-0

**Cover Design: Mathew Kuriakose**

# CONTENTS

Program paper number is shown in parentheses after the paper title.

**Compressed HDTV for Production: The Challenges (An NIST-ATP HDTV Digital Studio Alliance)**



**Special Venues and Techniques**



**Winning in a Global Economy: The Power of Standards**

## Computer-Based Assist for Broadcast



## The Digital Virtual Studio



## Audio: The Widescreen Experience (Film and Video)



## DVD Authoring: A New Technology

## Delivery Systems



## Applications in Production Technology



## Joint SMPTE/ACVL Session: Creating and Delivering on Film



## Additional Papers

# Foreword

Each year, we examine how our industries collide or converge or diverge, and share the results of this interaction. It is a snapshot of the past year and also one into the future. New ways are found to portray the picture, inform of the progress, report the status, exchange information and ideas, and assess the impacts. There is no better forum than the SMPTE Technical Conference.

The 138th SMPTE Technical Conference and World Media Expo, "Film and Video Synergies: Creation to Delivery," is this year's focus on the activities within our industries. Years ago, only two dominant industries — film and television — would have defined these activities, but, as this conference demonstrates, our convergences have produced many derivative technologies that support these industries. As much as we attempt to define the convergences on a macro level, advancing technologies create new industries on a micro level, further redefining and strengthening the convergences, not unlike the way genetic software on a micro level creates new, more robust systems on a macro level.

Now, with this conference, an examination of the derivative technologies is taken to a higher level. New areas — Video Servers, Electronic, Virtual Studios, and DVD — play an ever-increasing and important role in the support of our information industries, so much so that new ones are virtually being formed. As a result of these new areas and the presenters that represent them, this is expected to be the most successful conference to date for the timeliness of the information submitted as a new information age is emerging.

The selection and accommodation of the vast number of exceptional papers submitted for this conference is due to its Program Chair, Charles Dages, and his Session Chairs. This conference, like no other, is distinguished by the breadth and depth of the material presented. Although many of the presenters' names are familiar, many are new to this forum. They represent some new ideas, techniques, and industries that will further expand and enhance our knowledge and use of the new information age.

A warm welcome is given to these new presenters and the industries they represent, as well as to the faithful contributors for their constant and consistent support of these conferences. Thanks go out to all the authors who submitted papers for consideration in this conference.

Special appreciation goes to Marilyn Waldman at SMPTE Headquarters for her untiring efforts to accommodate all of the demands placed upon her to coordinate this conference and this book.

*— Thomas J. Bentsen,*
*SMPTE Editorial Vice-President*

# Improvement of motion judder on converted images by telecine at the TV station

Hajime Sonehara, Yuji Nojiri, Kazuhisa Iguchi, Yukio Sugiura, Hiroshi Hirabayashi
NHK Science and Technical Research Laboratories
Tokyo, JAPAN

## Abstract

Video images converted from films show unnatural reproduction of movement. To correct this, it is necessary to utilize a motion compensation technique which has already been employed for television standards conversion. We modified an existing high-definition television (HDTV) standards converter[1] by adding the necessary functions for motion-compensated film-to-video conversion. To test the practicality of the modified converter, we detected motion vectors on it by using the video signals of images already converted from film by a telecine. Then we interpolated the images using the detected motion vectors to compensate for movement. The result was less unnatural movement and better quality moving images with respect to film-to-video conversion.

# 1 Introduction

Motion pictures are one of the most popular items among for TV audiences. HDTV broadcasting, in particular, conveys the powerful sensation of reality experienced in the cinema directly to viewers at home. It does this on a wall-hanging large-screen receiver which reproduces very clear images. Film-to-video (F-V) conversion is necessary to air movies or filmed programs on television because movies are shot at a rate of 24 frames per second, while television requires a rate of 60 fields (30 frames) per second. In F-V conversion, as detailed in a subsequent section, one film frame is converted into 2 video-signal fields and the next film frame into 3 fields each time. In other words, every 2 film frames are converted into 5 video fields. This is called the 2-3 F-V conversion method and the phase is known as the 2-3 F-V conversion phase. Moving objects treated by this method, however, appear to move unnaturally. Repeated display of the same field of the moving objects makes them look awkwardly. To eliminate this unnatural movement, a motion compensation technique is used for frame rate (F-V) conversion instead of the said simple 2-3 conversion. This technique generates new images in which moving objects have been relocated to correct sample positions with the spatio-temporal geometry. We added some functions to an existing HDTV standards converter[1] to re-convert F-V converted images by a motion compensation process. This smooths out the motion of moving objects in these images. The following are the added functions:

- detection of 2-3 F-V conversion phase, and
- control of the motion vector detection and image interpolation units in the F-V conversion phase.

# 2 Motion judder

Figure 1(a) shows an example of 2-3 F-V conversion where images of 24 frame/sec are converted into interlaced HDTV (1125/60/2:1) signals of 60 field/sec. The first frame of film is converted into the first and second fields of the video signals, and the second frame is transferred to the third, fourth and fifth fields of the video signals, as shown in Figure 1(a). This procedure is repeated thereafter for every two frames of film and every five fields of video signals. This is called the 2-3 F-V conversion phase. The difference between HDTV signals which have been converted in this way and those which have been shot by a HDTV camera is that the output signals of the camera produce different images in every field whereas the converted signals have two or three consecutive fields with the same frame of the filmed images. As a result, moving objects in the converted images look jerky because two or three same images are shown sequentially. This unnatural movement is called motion judder. Motion judder causes degradation of the resolution of moving images. In other words, although the fine parts of a moving object can be seen in images shot with an HDTV camera at 60 Hz, they become unclear under 2-3 F-V conversion. This lowers the picture quality in the moving area of such images. Such quality deterioration would be magnified on an HDTV screen, which is generally watched at closer distance.

Figure 1(b) shows filmed images, including 30 frame/sec. computer graphics, shot at a 1/30 sec. sampling rate and then F-V converted at a 2-2 rate. All of these images, with the same images displayed twice, also produce judder with the moving object overlapped, resulting in picture deterioration.

# 3 Motion compensation

Figure 2(a) shows a typical configuration of HDTV signals converted from 2-3 F-V converted signals. It is assumed that the first field of video signals coincides with the first frame of film. Thus, the second and third video fields should be made from the first and second film frames, while the fourth and fifth video fields should be taken from the second and third film frames. In other words, the motion vectors necessary to compose the second and third video fields should be detected from the first and second film frames and motion vectors for the fourth and fifth video fields from the second and third film frames.

During this procedure, the following should be taken into account if motion vectors are to be detected from video signals converted at a 2-3 F-V conversion phase on an existing HDTV standards converter. The motion detection of existing HDTV standards converters is designed in anticipation of the constant input of different-field images (temporally different images). In this case, however, two or three identical 2-3 F-V converted image signals are input in succession, as shown in Figure 2(a). We therefore adjusted the motion vector detection unit so that it might be able to detect motion vectors between different film frames each time. Also we controlled the image interpolation unit so that it could interpolate images for motion compensation using different film frames each time.

Likewise, Figures 2(b) and (c) show typical charts to compose HDTV signals which are put adequately through a spatio-temporal sampling process from film frames shot at a 1/30 sec. sampling rate. In this re-conversion, we can select 2 sets of interpolation ratio which use motion-compensated frame interpolation. The case shown in Figure 2(b) has interpolation ratios of 0.0 and 0.5. Therefore, either an odd field or an even field is output, as is, from the input film frames. Figure 2(c) shows a case in which the interpolation ratios are 0.25 and 0.75, which implies that the output images are always interpolated.

# 4 Modifying an HDTV standards converter

## 4.1 2-3 conversion timing

We have no standard for recording a 2-3 F-V conversion phase of a telecine on a recording medium. Therefore, there is no way of knowing the conversion phase or timing from a recording medium storing 2-3 F-V converted images.

As may be clear from Figure 1(a), the third and fifth video fields made from the second film frame are the same. In the output signals on a memory-aided telecine (continuous film transport), the difference between the third and fifth fields is completely reduced to zero. In other words, 2-3 F-V conversion timing can be detected by examining temporal changes in the field difference between fields one frame (1/30 sec.) apart from each other.

## 4.2 Motion vector detection

The adapted motion vector detection unit of an HDTV standards converter[1][2] uses a combination of block matching and a gradient method[3]. Figure 3 shows a motion vector detector of the modified HDTV standards converter. The detector detects motion vectors block by block, where a detection block consists of 8 pixels and 8 lines. The block matching method used for the first half of the whole procedure uses using several previously detected candidate vectors. In the second half, detection blocks are transferred by motion vectors chosen in the first half to a new location where the final vectors are detected by the gradient method. The gradient method is used instead of the full-search block matching method for the second half so that even small-scale hardware can detect motion vectors in the order of fractions.

When detecting motion vectors using F-V converted images, one should take account of the fact that many of these images have poor signal-to-noise(S/N) ratios. Such poor S/N ratios are chiefly caused by film's granular noise. Erroneous motion vectors may often be detected between different frames in the stationary areas of F-V converted images because the frame difference is not reduced to zero. We therefore use appropriate processed luminance signals exclusively for motion vector detection to reduce the probability of incorrect vector detection. For that purpose, we modified the pre-filter unit of an existing HDTV standards converter so that the spatio-temporal filter can work on 3 frames of image signals of 2-3 F-V converted images. The pre-filter unit generates luminance signals used for motion vector detection. Since the pre-filter unit has two spatio-temporal filters, as shown in Figure 4 and Figure 5, it can change the spatio-temporal filtering characteristics to generate the luminance signals used for the block matching and gradient methods.

## 4.3 Motion-compensated interpolation

For interpolation, it is necessary to choose two input fields to accord with the odd or even output field, as shown in Figures 2(a), (b) and (c). In the case of an odd output field, the images are interpolated adaptively for motion using the odd fields of different film frames. Detection blocks are arranged in a hierarchy and motion compensation is performed for every 4-pixel by 2-line block. Images are interpolated at every pixel. A spatio-temporal interpolation filter for the moving area, which is used for frame number conversion, uses 2 fields temporally, 2 pixels horizontally and 8 lines vertically. In the stationary area, it uses 2 fields temporally to perform linear interpolation.

# 5 Re-conversion system for film-to-HDTV transfer

Figure 6 shows the configuration of a motion-compensated film-to-HDTV conversion system. As a means for ready realization of motion-compensated film-to-video conversion, we have contrived a method to re-convert images, already F-V converted by an existing HDTV telecine, using an HDTV standards converter adapted for F-V conversion. This is also intended to improve the quality of F-V converted images. The re-conversion system has the following features:

- Removes motion judder caused by 2-3 F-V conversion and improves moving picture quality.
- Requires no modification to existing telecines.
- Enables TV stations to improve the picture quality of videotaped programmes they buy.
- Simplifies the procedure for improving the quality of moving pictures by adding simple functions to an HDTV standards converter or existing TV standards converters.

# 6 Results

We have examined the performance of the motion-compensating re-conversion system using movies and filmed programs, all 2-3 F-V converted, and succeeded in obtaining pictures as good as those of inter-HDTV standards conversion between the Japanese 1125/60/2:1 signals and the European 1250/50/2:1 signals. In the moving area, in particular, the apparent resolution was improved considerably with little judder remaining. This is attributable to human visual properties which make the images look as if they have improved resolution even though their resolution theoretically remains unchanged. The phenomenon was also observed in the stationary areas of images which had been slightly shaken by the film transport mechanism of a telecine. Resolution and S/N ratios actually improved because of the use of a motion compensation technique and the 2-field spatio-temporal interpolation. Fine portions in images hidden by judder could be seen clearly.

We also tested the re-conversion of 2-2 F-V converted images and images generated by computer graphics. The result was reduced motion judder and an improvement in moving picture quality similar to the case of 2-3 converted images. The 2-3 F-V conversion phase was also detected correctly. All in all, the system has thus proved to be useful in practice.

At the same time, the system entails some considerations which are not found in inter-HDTV standards conversion. For example, if an object in motion is simultaneously shot with a 60 Hz HDTV camera and a 24 Hz movie camera, the images of the object recorded on the film move from field to field some 2.5 times farther than those shot with the HDTV camera. This means that if an HDTV standards converter is to be adapted for film-to-HDTV conversion, it is necessary to enlarge its detection window by 2.5 times in order to get the same maximum detection vector value.

Another consideration is that of how to suppress artifacts which are generated by the covered and uncovered background. Since the proposed system has a covered and uncovered background some 2.5 times as large as that in inter-HDTV standards conversion, it allows artifacts to appear in the contour area of the moving objects.

Artifacts can also be an eyesore in scene changes. Since we omitted the processing necessary for scene changes in our converter, two fields of erroneous images made between different scenes are output during film-to-HDTV conversion. The erroneous images can be perceived from time to time depending on the picture patterns during scene changes. This problem, however, will be resolved in the near future with modification of the proposed system by adding a function to detect and treat scene changes, which is already under way.

## 7 Conclusion

Home television receivers already have both large screens and high performance. High-definition television (HDTV) receivers, in particular, have a large and very fine-definition screen which, however, is liable to motion judder generated by 2-3 conversion. This appears as interference more distinctly than on smaller screens. Nevertheless, as stated in the preceding sections, this judder problem has basically been resolved with our adapted HDTV standards converter, which has proved useful enough for broadcasting film-to-HDTV converted programs.

We demonstrated a judder-free film-to-HDTV transfer system at NHK's annual Technology Open House June 1996.

Since our attempt to adapt the HDTV standards converter was directed at the addition of a detection circuit for 2-3 F-V conversion timing, the modification of other conversion control functions or mechanisms was only rather simple. Our next goal is to utilize this technique to improve the picture quality of HDTV movies.

Finally, we would like to thank the Oki Electric Industry Co., Ltd. for cooperating with us in modifying the HDTV standards converter.

## REFERENCES

1. Y.Nojiri, H.Sonehara, H.Hirabayashi, F.Okano, "Motion Vector Detection for HDTV Standards Converter", 135th SMPTE Technical Conference Oct. 29 - Nov. 2, 1993
2. Y.Nojiri, H.Hirabayashi, H.Sonehara, F.Okano, "Motion compensated standards converter for HDTV",International Workshop on HDTV'93, Oct.1993
3. H.Yamaguchi, T.Sugi, K.Kinuhata, "Movement-Compensated Frame-Frequency Conversion of Television Signals", IEEE Transaction on Communications., vol.COM-35, No.10, Oct.1987

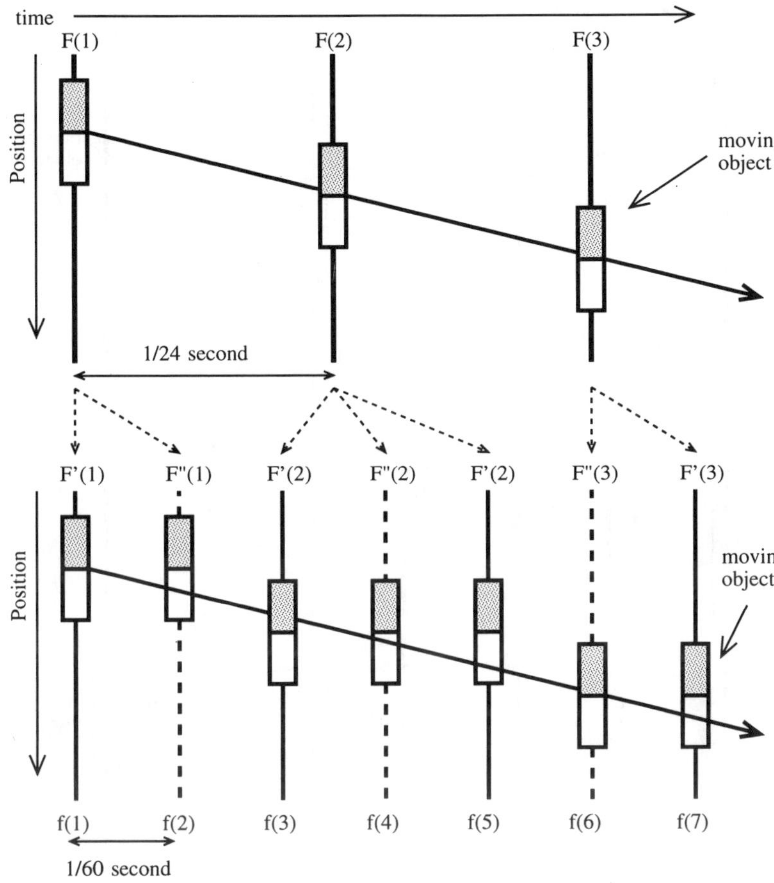


F() : frame of film

F'() : odd field of film frame

F"() : even field of film frame

f() : field of video signals that have been 2-3 converted

Figure 1(a) 2-3 conversion method into normal HDTV signals by a telecine

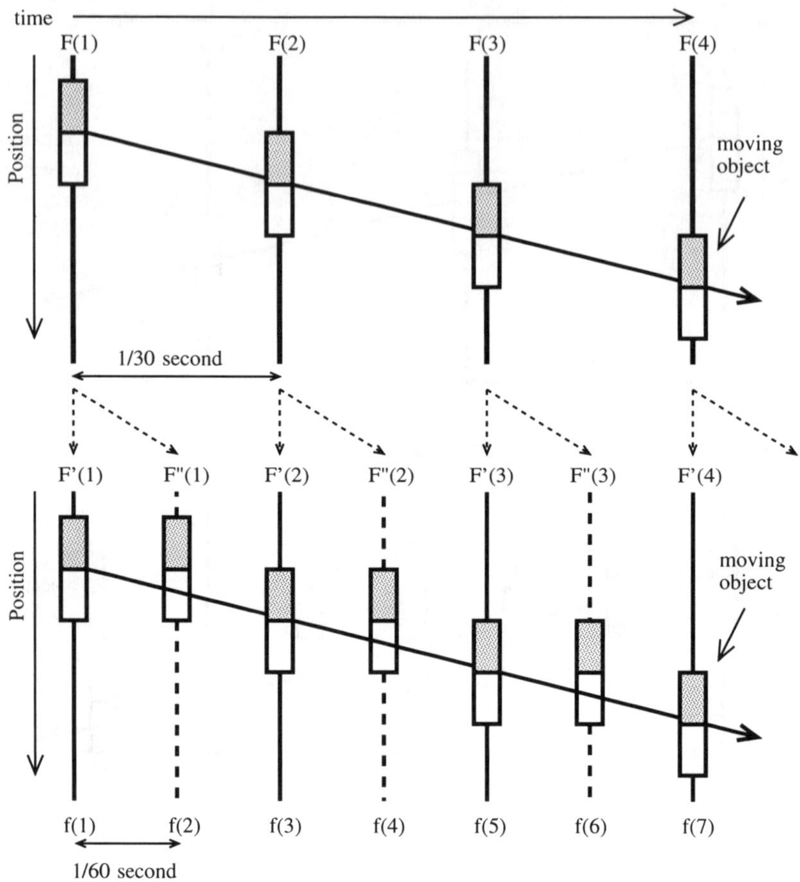


F() : frame of film

F'() : odd field of film frame

F"() : even field of film frame

f() : field of video signals that have been 2-2 converted

Figure 1(b) 2-2 conversion method into normal HDTV signals by a telecine

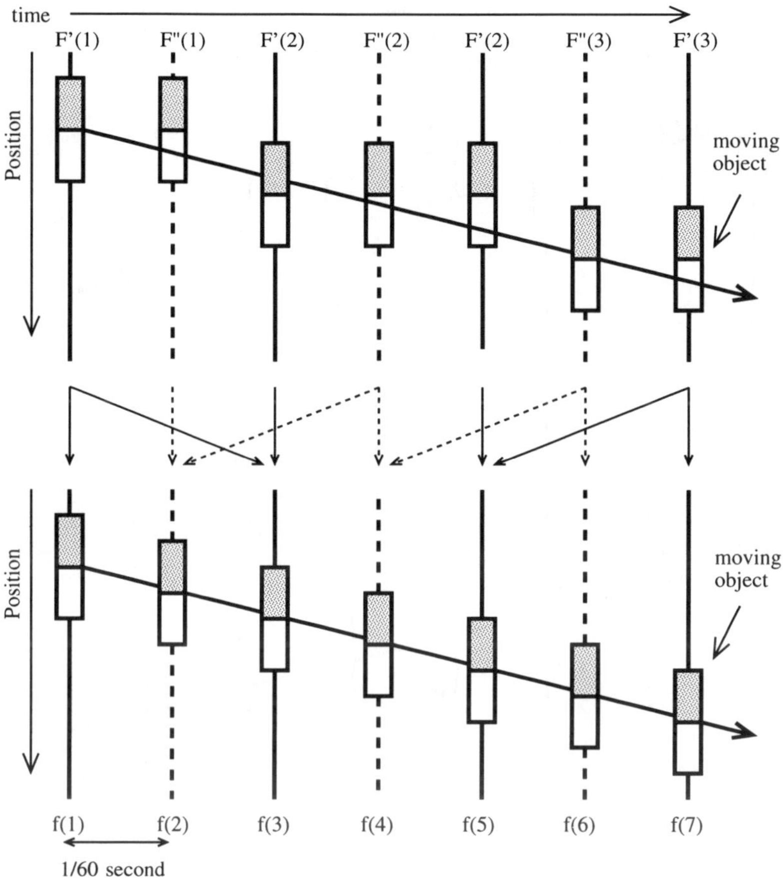


F'() : odd field of film frame that has already been 2-3 converted

F"() : even field of film frame that has already been 2-3 converted

f() : field of re-converted video signals with motion compensated interpolation method

f(2),f(3),f(4),f(5),f(7),··· : interpolated fields with motion compensation method

Figure 2(a) Re-conversion method into normal HDTV signals by the motion compensation technique at 2-3 conversion

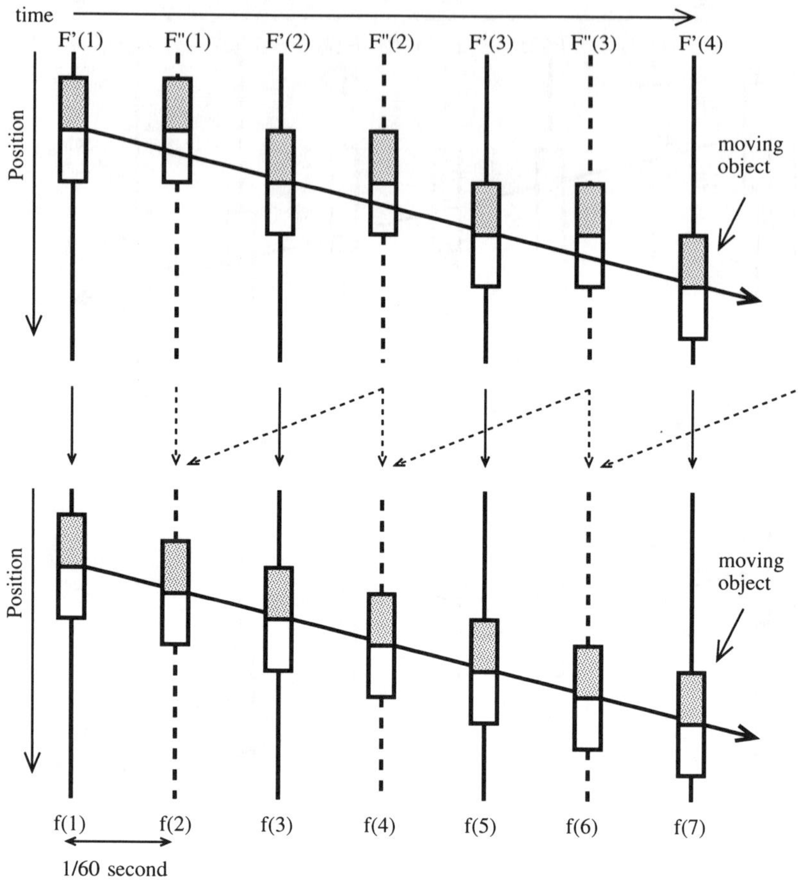


F'() : odd field of film frame that has already been 2-2 converted

F"() : even field of film frame that has already been 2-2 converted

f() : field of re-converted video signals with motion compensated interpolation method

f(2),f(4),f(6),··· : interpolated fields with motion compensation method

interpolation ratio : [ 0.0 , 0.5 ]

Figure 2(b) Re-conversion method into normal HDTV signals by the motion compensation technique at 2-2 conversion

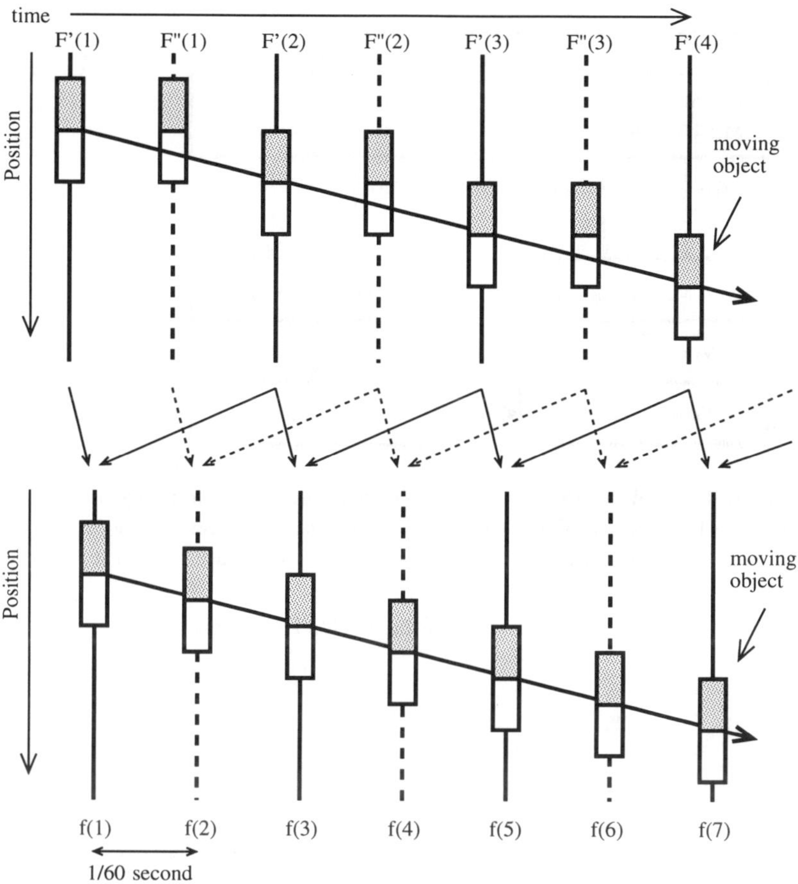


F'() : odd field of film frame that has already been 2-2 converted

F"() : even field of film frame that has already been 2-2 converted

f() : field of re-converted video signals
with motion compensated interpolation method

f(1),f(2),f(3),f(4),··· : interpolated fields with motion compensation method

interpolation ratio : [ 0.25 , 0.75 ]

Figure 2(c) Re-conversion method into normal HDTV signals by the motion compensation technique at 2-2 conversion

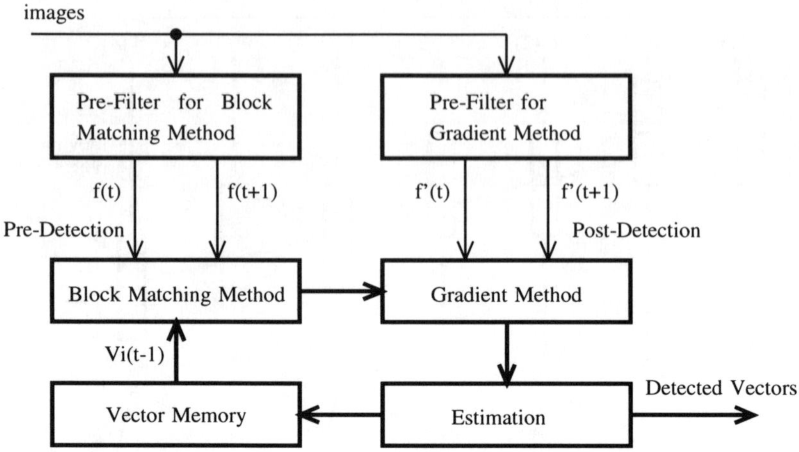


f(t), f(t+1) : luminance signals for motion detection using block matching method
f'(t),f'(t+1) : luminance signals for motion detection using gradient method
Vi(t-1) : previously detected candidate vectors for block matching method

Figure 3 Configuration of the Vector Detector

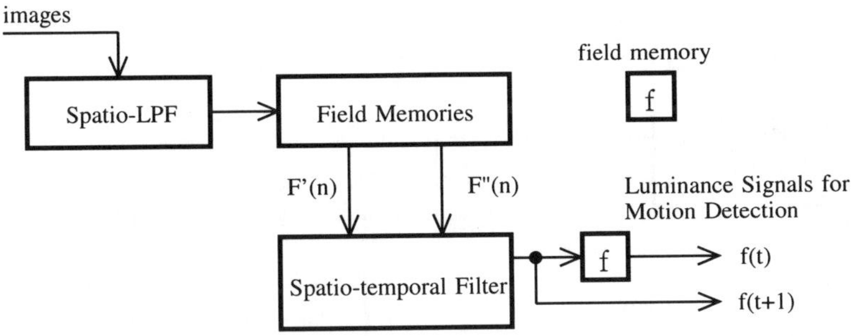


Spatio-LPF : horizontal 13 taps and vertical 13 taps
Field Memories : 3 field memories
Spatio-temporal Filter : vertical 3 lines and temporal 2 fields (a frame of film)
F'(n) : odd field of film frame(n)
F"(n) : even field of film frame(n)

Figure 4 Configuration of Pre-Filter for Block Matching Method

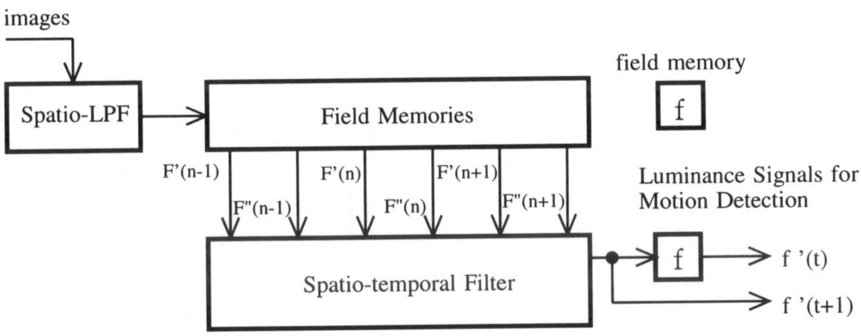


Spatio-LPF : horizontal 13 taps and vertical 13 taps
Field Memories : 5 field memories
Spatio-temporal Filter : vertical 2 lines and temporal 6 fields (3 frames of film)
F'(n-1) : odd field of film frame(n-1)
F"(n-1) : even field of film frame(n-1)
F'(n) : odd field of film frame(n)
F"(n) : even field of film frame(n)
F'(n+1) : odd field of film frame(n+1)
F"(n+1) : even field of film frame(n+1)

Figure 5 Configuration of Pre-Filter for Gradient Method

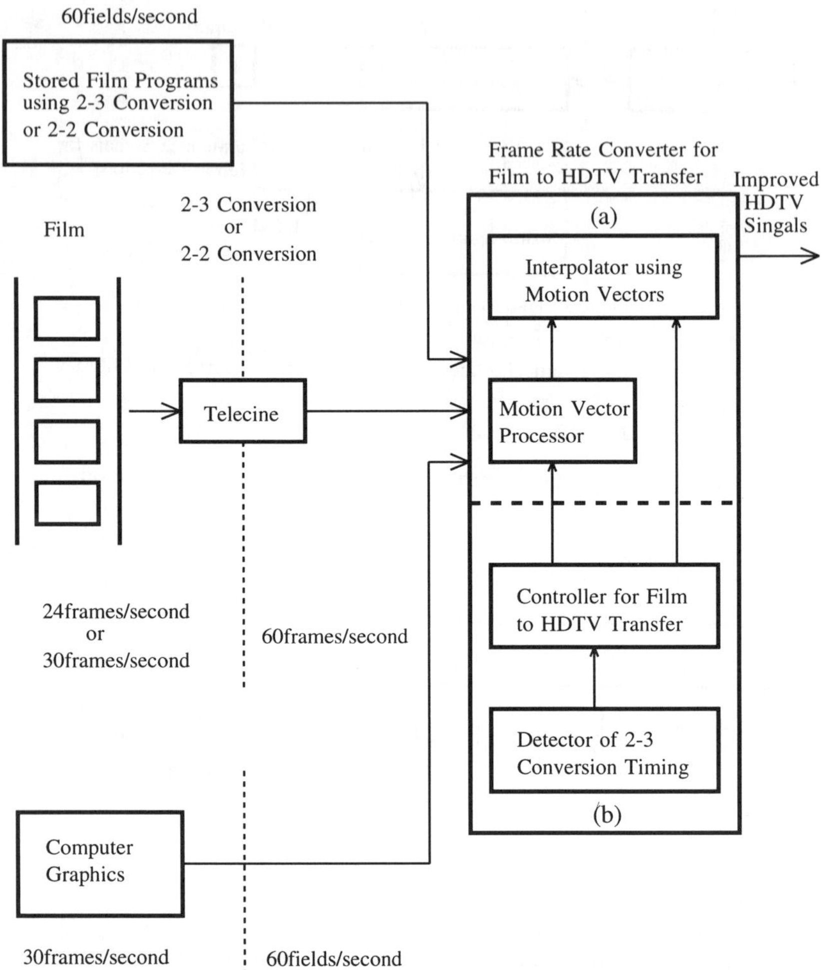


(a) : HDTV Standards Converter
(b) : Additional Functions for Film to HDTV Transfer

Figure 6 Film to HDTV Transfer
Applying Motion Compensated Standards Converter

# The Development of a 1920x1080 Pixel Color CCD Camera Progressively Scanned at 60 Frames Per Second

William E. Glenn & John W. Marcinka
Communications Technology Center
Florida Atlantic University
Boca Raton, Florida

## Abstract

A progressively-scanned video camera is under development using two 1920x1080 CCD sensors (made by Eastman Kodak) with square pixels in a 16:9 aspect ratio. One sensor does not have color filters and the other has color stripe filters. Detail luminance is derived from one sensor; color and low-resolution luminance is derived from the other. The camera output is progressively scanned at 60 frames per second.

If digitized, the output bit rate would be 2.4 gigabits per second. Consequently, subband coding will be used to compress the output to a bit stream that can be recorded on a D-1 or D-5 digital video recorder and still have enough "head room" for post-production processing. This paper will report on the status of the camera development and describe the options for providing good motion rendition without interlace artifacts by using progressive scan.

# 1 Background

Interlaced scanning was invented many years ago as a way of displaying images without flicker at a frame rate of 30 frames per second. The 1/60 second integration time on the face of the interlaced camera was short enough to prevent "motion blur" of moving objects.

Interlace is actually a crude version of 3-D subband coding compression. It updates low spatial frequency information at 60 fields per second but requires 1/30 second to produce detail. Because of the longer integration time of the human visual system for detail information[1], this system works reasonably well. However, it has a large number of artifacts resulting from the compression technique.

The eye frequently scans vertically at the interlace "line crawl" velocity. During this time the field line structure is clearly visible and objects moving at that velocity are displayed with half as many scan lines.

A more objectionable artifact is interline flicker. Detail information near the Nyquist limit of resolution produces a "moiré" beat at low spatial frequencies that flickers at 30 Hz. The visual system has good temporal response for low spatial frequencies. For this reason, computer displays that have considerable information near the Nyquist limit of resolution use progressive rather than interlaced displays.

Interlace was invented before frame stores were available. 3-D subband coding can perform the same function as interlace using frame stores. The detail can be stored at 30 frames per second but displayed at 60 frames per second. This provides the same detail update rate as interlace without the interline flicker and line crawl produced by interlaced scan. The low spatial frequency information can be detected and displayed at 60 frames per second giving the same sharpness for moving objects as an interlaced scan. "Motion blur" that becomes obvious is not just the top octave of detail in the direction of motion. The obvious loss of resolution is typically ten pixels or so. However, a ten pixel blur for 1/60 second exposure becomes twenty pixels of blur for a 1/30 second exposure. For that reason it is important for all spatial frequencies below the top octave to have exposure integration times below 1/60 second. The display, however, for 3-D subband coding must be at 60 frames per second progressive scan. For a detailed analysis showing that the bit rate is the same for the displayed resolution of both progressive and interlaced scans, see reference 2.

Interlace has been a difficult signal to process for compression systems and is a nuisance for electronic video post production. It has been a desire for the computer industry, the compression researchers, and the post-production houses to have a video system that has square pixels, progressively scanned at a 1920x1080 common image format. Displays have long been able to display this format. In fact, active-matrix LCD displays must be addressed at 60 FPS progressively in order to get good motion rendition and high brightness. It is only the lack of a camera and recording device that has limited the transition to progressive scan in the common image format.

The purpose of the current development is to demonstrate that both the camera and a method of recording can be realized. A camera is under construction using two Eastman Kodak sensors. The camera output will be progressively scanned at 60 frames per second. The digital output of the camera with 8-bit encoding would be 2.4 gigabits per second. It is proposed to use a modest amount of compression to allow this signal to be recorded on a standard D-1 or D-5 digital video recorder. This will allow a high quality original image to be recorded for program production. This can either be used directly or scan-converted to lower resolution formats where distribution or recording bandwidths are limited.

## 2 Technical Approach

The camera design uses two Eastman Kodak sensors (KAI-2090 and KAI-2091). These sensors have 1920x1080 square pixels with a 16:9 aspect ratio. They can be scanned progressively at 30 frames per second in the 1080 line mode. Alternatively, they can be scanned two lines at a time to give 540 lines, 1920 pixels per line at 60 frames per second progressive or 60 fields per second interlaced. They are available either with or without color stripe filters.

In this camera, one sensor without stripe filters is used to provide the detail luminance information. It is progressively scanned at 30 frames per second. The other sensor has color stripe filters. It is progressively scanned at 60 frames per second at 540 lines per frame. From this second sensor color information and low spatial frequency luminance information is derived. All signals are stored in frame stores, scan converted to 60 frames per second progressive scan with 1080 lines per frame and added together to give R, G, B signals. A block diagram of the camera is shown in Figure 1.

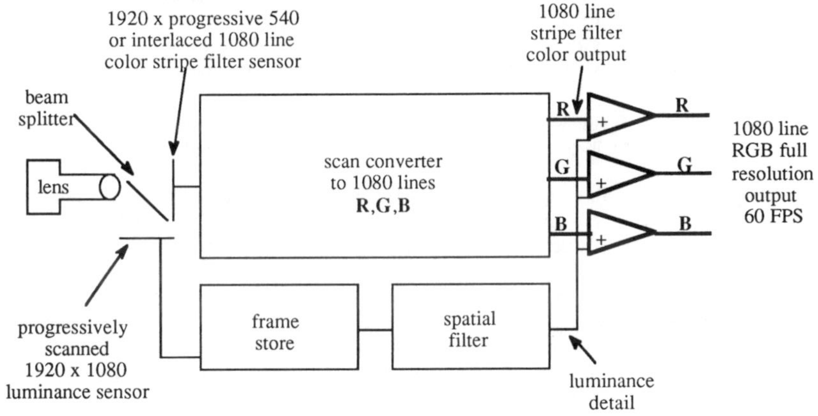


Figure 1. Block Diagram of High-Definition Color Camera

In the output of the camera, everything but the top octave of luminance detail is updated at 60 frames per second. The detail information is updated at 30 frames per second (as it is in interlaced scans, but without the interlace artifacts).

Experiments were performed at 525 lines to compare motion rendition at 60 frames per second with a display that had the top octave of detail at 30 frames per second and the remainder at 60 frames per second. Motion appeared equally good either way. Moving objects appeared sharp and had no visible "judder".

For curiosity, we looked at images from a camera running at 30 frames per second progressive but displayed at 60 frames per second (each frame displayed twice). These images had obvious "motion blur" for moving objects. We then tried progressive scan at 30 frames per second with an electronic shutter set for 1/60 second exposure time; again each frame was displayed twice. In the second case the exposure integration was 1/60 second which gave no "motion blur". However, there was some visible "judder" with a rapid pan of an image. Film has the same artifact. Its exposure time is relatively short at 24 frames per second. The frame is then displayed twice. Cinematographers avoid this "judder" artifact by not panning the camera fast enough to make the judder artifact visible. The Eastman sensor could be used to produce a three-chip camera operating in this mode with the same motion artifacts as film.

For display, the reconstructed output must have the full bandwidth of a progressive scan at 60 frames per second. However, for recording, a much lower bit rate can be used. The detail luminance is already at 30 frames per second. Since this represents 3/4 of the luminance information, the lower frame rate cuts the bit rate considerably. Entropy codes can give lossless compression of roughly 2:1. Using some of the techniques described in two previous papers,[3,4] the compression necessary to lower the recording bit rate to that of a D-1 or D-5 recorder can be achieved.

This camera design has an additional advantage. When color difference signals are transmitted with reduced resolution, the luminance contrast for saturated colors is considerably reduced above the color signal cut-off. It is particularly visible with NTSC transmissions wherever a saturated red appears in a scene. To avoid this artifact, isoluminant color signals should be used. As was described in a previous paper,[5] color difference signals would be much closer to isoluminant signals, if luminance was derived linearly and then gamma corrected rather than derived from gamma-corrected R,G,B signals. The General Electric four-tube color camera that was popular for many years had that advantage, since the fourth tube was used to provide the luminance signal.

The only problem with this technique is that if green is derived in the standard way rather than as described in reference 4, there will be small "Livingston"[6] errors in color. In this camera design only the detail luminance is derived from a separate sensor before gamma correction. The color difference signals can be derived in the standard way from the stripe-filter sensor. These signals will give no color errors with standard decoding. As long as the color signals are not reduced further in resolution by subsequent transmission or recording, the detail above this resolution will not have the contrast degradation in saturated colors. The MUSE transmission system[7] used somewhat similar processing derived from R,G,B sensors and reported a significant improvement in the sharpness of saturated colors as a result.

# 3 Conclusion

A camera is under construction using two Eastman Kodak CCD sensors (KAI-2090 and KAI-2091) that will provide a progressively scanned output at 60 frames per second with 16:9 aspect ratio and 1920x1080 square pixels. The color portion of the camera is operating satisfactorily. Experiments at 525 line scan have shown the validity of the design concept for both the camera design and the compression system needed to give the necessary modest compression ratios that will allow the signal to be recorded on a D-1 or D-5 digital recorder.

# 4 Acknowledgement

The camera is funded by DARPA grant (administered through NASA) NAGW 2753. The authors wish to express their appreciation for the invaluable assistance provided by Mike Richardson, Jim Olson, Fred Strieter, Mike McCreary, Dave Nichols, David Frosini, Charles Stancanpino, Al Bitek, Chris Parks, and Ram Kannegendla of Eastman Kodak as well as Bob Dhein, Al Moreno, Kelvin Moore, J.P. Marcinka, Dave Smith, Pedro Monteiro, Fouad Guediri, Ross Gilson, Barry Rynk, and Petko Dinev of the F.A.U. Imaging Systems Laboratory.

# References

1. V.A. Billock and T.H. Harding, "The Number and Tuning of Channels Responsible for the Independent Detection of Temporal Modulation," ARVO, Investigative Ophthalmology & Visual Science, Annual Meeting Abstracts, 32:840, March 15, 1991.

2. W.E. Glenn, "Digital Image Compression Based on Visual Perception," Digital Images & Human Vision, edited by Andrew B. Watson. (Cambridge: MIT Press, 1993): 63-71.

3. W. E. Glenn, John Marcinka, and Robert Dhein, "Subband Coding Compression System for Program Production," presented at the 136th SMPTE Technical Conference and World Media Expo, SMPTE, Los Angeles, October 1994.

4. W. E. Glenn, John Marcinka, and Robert Dhein, "Simple Scalable Video Compression Using 3-D Subband Coding," presented at the SMPTE Advanced Television & Electronic Imaging Conference, San Francisco, February 1995.

5. W. E. Glenn, K. G. Glenn, and T. L. Glatt, "Logarithmic A/D Converters Used in Video Signal Processing Systems," presented at the 132nd SMPTE Technical Conference, New York, October 1990. Reprinted in SMPTE Journal Vol. 101/5:329-333, May 1992.

6. D. C. Livingston, "Colorimetric Analysis of the NTSC Color Television Systems," Proceedings of the IRE, 42:138-150, January 1954.

7. Yuichi Ninomiya, et al., "An HDTV Broadcasting System Utilizing a Bandwidth Compression Technique - MUSE," IEEE Transactions on Broadcasting, Vol. BC-33/4:130-160, December 1987.

# AN ENGINEERING APPROACH TO CONSISTENT IMAGES:

*Control of video and film image quality in TV Production*


Fred Benedikt — CBC Toronto, Toronto, Canada
David F.E. Corley — DSC Laboratories, Mississauga, Canada
Robert Ross — CBC Toronto, Toronto, Canada



## *Abstract*

*Engineers, video operators, colorists and producers, all share the goal of excellence in television image quality. This paper explores the reasons why some popular and widely used techniques to standardize video and film quality have met with mixed success. A practicable solution is proposed.*

*Previous efforts have, by and large, lacked the precision to ensure consistent high quality images, particularly in regard to tonal range and color. The new system under discussion, while providing production teams with infinite freedom for artistic expression, controls the technical aspects of image quality from camera set-up through the post production process.*

*Using familiar waveform monitoring techniques, the system is comprised of two elements:*

> *a) Optical Signal Generators (OSGs) precision test targets, and*
> *b) a unique portable illuminator.*

*The system, now in day-to-day use in network engineering and studio operations, can provide similar benefits to the production community. A major advantage of using this proven engineering tool through all stages of production is that engineers, operators and production personnel can now all speak a common language.*

*The system benefits film production and scanner/telecine setup. Ongoing tests with major film transfer houses are also discussed.*

## Background

Image inconsistency, particularly scene to scene and program to program color variations, continues to be a dilemma facing program producers and broadcasters. Efforts to address the problem have been either technically inadequate, too time consuming or too expensive.

From the earliest days of motion picture film, test patterns have been used in efforts to control ***image*** quality. Similarly, from the first days of television, signal generators and optical test patterns have been used to control ***picture*** quality. While there are similarities in the alignment practices of the two media, there are also major differences. For a number of reasons, film has been more forgiving than the electronic image. Screened in a darkened theatre, movies have the benefits of human vision adaptability. Film also has a considerably wider dynamic range, and color/density variations can be corrected in the print stage.

This reality has resulted in two cultures. Film production has tended to favour the traditional, less rigorous, subjective approach. Television, on the other hand, having access to signal measuring equipment, has used objective control methods. To satisfy these requirements, two types of test patterns have evolved - front lit reflectance test charts, and rear lit slide transparencies. Both have their benefits and deficiencies:

## Front Lit Test Charts

These are relatively simple to produce and inexpensive, but have three major drawbacks which contribute to and can, under certain conditions, virtually ensure inconsistent results.

**(Fig.1)**

a) surface flare - varies withcamera and lighting angles
b) test image inconsistency - from basic construction materials, surface abrasion nd handling
c) contrast ratio - can vary depending on chart frontal light level

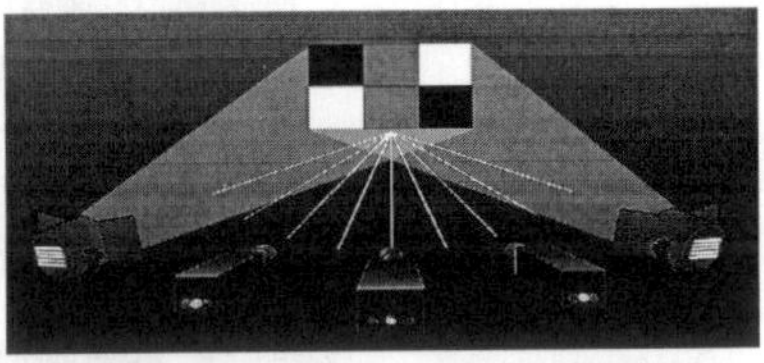

**Figure 1** - Angles of Illumination

The inconsistencies in image quality arising from one or more of the above can be subtle or dramatic, affecting both tonal range and color saturation. The effects are frequently apparent when attempting to match multiple television cameras using a front lit chart. The use of such charts with film cameras can induce similar inconsistencies, which along with exposure, film stock and processing variability are extremely difficult to isolate after the fact.

## Rear Lit Slides

These do not have the flare problems of reflectance charts and are considered technically superior, but do require lightboxes or integrating spheres which traditionally:

a) are awkward and cumbersome to use,
b) often have poor light evenness, and
c) have spectral light characteristics which do not match those of the scene.

This has tended to limit the use of rear lit slides to camera manufacturers, maintenance shops and other specific engineering applications.

A critical point to consider with any test pattern is accuracy and repeatability. Using imprecise material not only limits long term repeatability and consistency, but also the ability to conform to a particular industry standard, i.e. SMPTE or EBU.

## A Practical Solution: **Ambi/Combi OSG (Optical Signal Generator)**

For the industry to realize the full benefit from rear lit test targets as a production tool requires test patterns, evenly lit with scene lighting, which produce signals meaningful to the television system. These principles apply equally to video and film production.

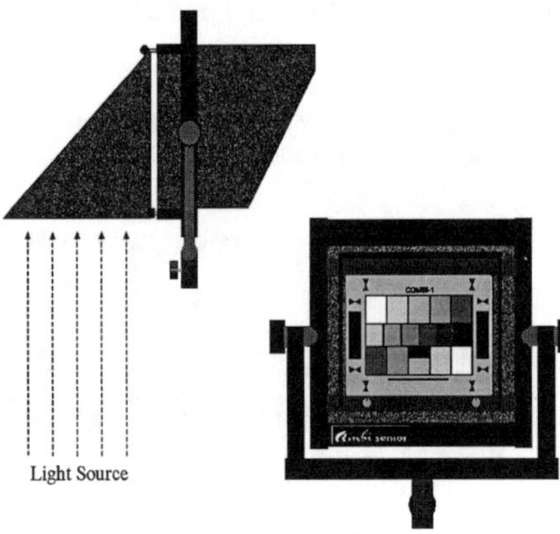


**Figure 2** - Ambi Senior lit from below

Rear lit test targets which produce relevant video signals already existed. The challenge was to design a light weight, portable and sturdy illuminator which would provide even illumination having spectral lighting characteristics which matched those of any production shooting situation. With input from production teams and video engineers, various designs were prototyped and field tested. This work resulted in the Ambi Illuminator. **(Fig.2)** While originally designed for use with ambient light, a dedicated light source matching that of the set is now typically used to illuminate the target.

Ambi's basic components are:

a) a test target holder for Optical Signal Generators (OSGs) including a neutral light diffuser and
b) an adjustable mirror.

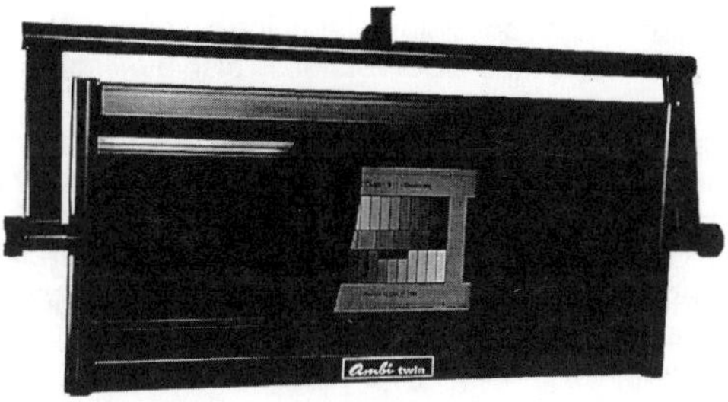


**Figure 3** - Ambi Twin - holds two OSGs

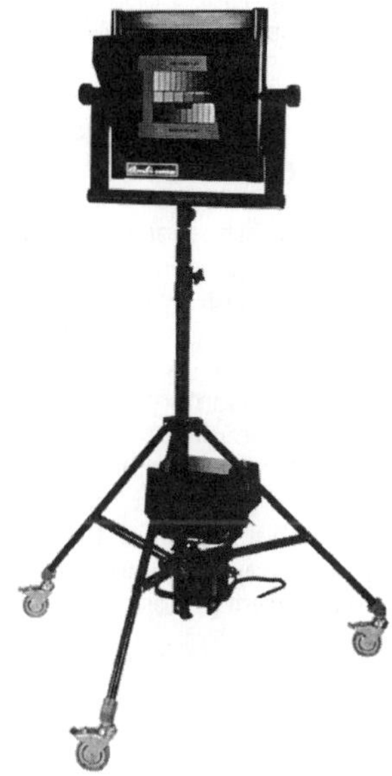

The illuminator's mounting yoke may be rotated, enabling the unit to be hung from a lighting grid. **(Fig.3)** Unlike light boxes and integrating spheres, Ambi's light source is typically 1.5 meters (5 feet) or more from the diffuser resulting in inherently even illumination. A companion stand incorporating a standard 5/8" lamp post at its base enables any appropriate light source to be used. **(Fig.4)** While the Ambi illuminator will accept standard 8x10" test slides, it was specifically designed to provide optimum performance from Combi OSGs.

**Figure 4** - Ambi Senior on stand

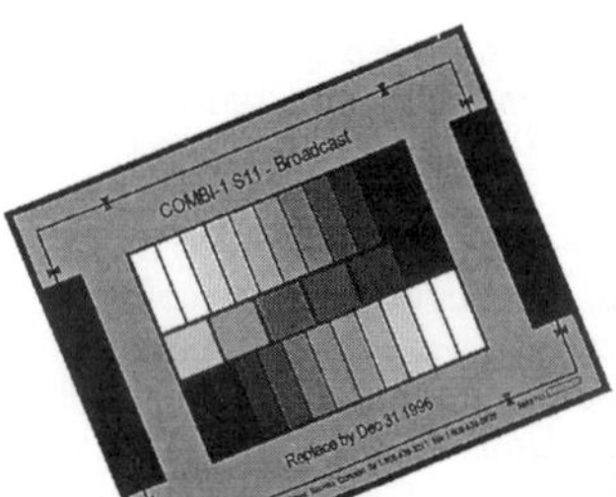


**Figure 5** - Combi-1

## OSG Background

While the design of the illuminator is important, the heart of the system is the test targets, whose precision was vital. Combi OSGs are the latest in a series of test materials manufactured by DSC Laboratories. DSC's first test materials, 35 mm for telecine use, were produced for the CBC in 1966. Studio and ENG camera formats followed later. Early studio camera set-up slides were separate greyscale and color test patterns, bound in glass. One slide was for camera greyscale alignment, the other for adjusting the color matrix to optimize color reproduction

In 1989, an improved color bar was combined with the greyscale and became the first CBC/DSC Combi-1 test target. **(Fig.5)** The luminance and color data provided by this pattern are all that is required for complete and convenient video level alignment.

In the early 1990's Combi-1 became part of CBC's policy for evaluation and acceptance of video cameras to SMPTE colorimetry. A calibrated EBU version is also available.

Combi-1 is produced in both 9 or 11 step EIA crossed greyscale versions, each having six, mid-saturation, vector colors. Individual calibration sheets accompany every OSG. The signals generated are expressed in terms of component RGB levels, composite NTSC levels and CIE L*U*V* color error. For most practical applications, the data sheets are not necessary. The white and cross-over steps have a tight ± 1 IRE tolerance and the optical color bars have minimal color error, typically the CIE L*U*V* RMS color error is < 4 units. For comparison, well matched cameras typically have a spread of about 10 CIE L*U*V* units.

So just as Combi-1 combines several functions to facilitate convenient alignment. Combi-2 provides geometry, resolution and other unique signals for both digital and analogue equipment. **(Fig.6)** Included are: multibursts from .5 to 10 Mhz, linear ramps, zone plates, back focus, smearing/streaking and enhancement patterns.

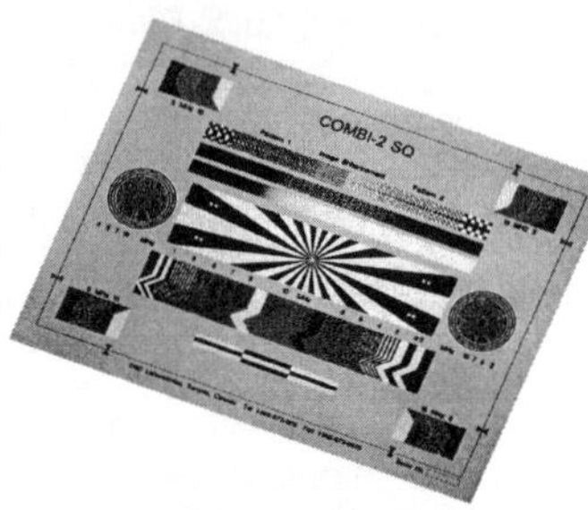


**Figure 6** - Combi-2

## OSG Definition

Both Combi test targets are true calibrated Optical Signal Generators, designed to furnish precise and repeatable electrical signals which are easily interpreted on the standard waveform and vectorscope monitors. This concept has not changed since 1966 and has proven its value over the years.

The manufacturing process and materials used in making test targets are very important. Typically, test charts and transparencies are screen printed, producing an image consisting of thousands of dots. These dots can "beat" with a CCD camera's sensor pixels, creating aliasing or moiré effects. Combi series OSGs are produced on ultra fine grain continuous tone materials which eliminate these problems. The same manufacturing process is used to make custom OSGs supplied by camera manufacturers, such as the Ikegami universal auto set-up pattern for both 16:9 and 4:3 aspect ratios.

In addition to camera manufacturers, the Ambi/Combi System is currently in daily use by broadcasters, rental/service companies and research facilities. Most recently in Atlanta, NBC aligned and matched the cameras used at the Centennial Olympics.

## OSG's - Exploring the New Potential

Well proven in engineering and operational video camera alignment and matching, the Ambi/Combi System's greatest potential is yet to be fully utilized. Present users have all the essential ingredients for additional benefits.

Consider a different use of Ambi/Combi from traditional camera alignment - a production usage. Consider the following evolutionary concept which is a logical extension of the system by: -

a) moving an OSG into the set - as you would a grey card or chart
b) illuminating it with the same type of light as the scene lighting, and
c) recording a few film or video frames before or after a shoot

These three steps capture all the information needed to link the original image with the electronic representation of the image.

Different organizations have different image reproduction goals:- an international standard, accurate color reproduction or a custom look. Once the reproduction objective is established, the alignment tools used must be reliable and consistent. The precision of the Combi test targets, in conjunction with the Ambi illuminator, ensures achieving your image reproduction goal, quickly and effectively.

This alignment provides the mid-point setting from which creative magic can be performed. However *only* a calibrated and precise test target can provide long term repeatability, particularly if the images come from various sources, be they video or film. The system permits film-to-tape, or tape-to-tape, color correction and image matching

By using the method described below along with shooting an 18% grey OSG test target, the cinematographer can control the film image quality and its reproduction on the television system, to any desired image reproduction goal.

The primary step in establishing an image quality control system for motion pictures is the determination of *normal* or correct exposure. Experience has shown that placing the information from an average well lit scene on the optimum portion of the film's characteristic curve, will result in the most pleasing reproduction of the original scene. Where it is placed is established by evaluating the scene's light level using an incident light meter, set to the film manufacturer's suggested exposure index. The Kodak LAD system establishes the optimum position on the curve using an 18% grey patch. Correct placement on the film curve, can be verified by reading the R,G,B negative density levels produced by the 18% Combi OSG.

Once the exposure level has been determined for the set using an incident meter, the light level of the Combi-1 is matched to the scene using a spot meter. A few frames of the Combi-1 pattern are recorded at the head or tail of each camera roll or scene change.

By reading the black and white steps of the Combi-1's greyscale with the spot meter, the Cinematographer now has control over highlight and shadow information in the final transfer. Any scene element having a spot meter reading greater than white or less than the black step will be out of the *normal* video range. Since the OSG is designed to use the same type of lighting as the set, the issue of color temperature is addressed immediately. Once the telecine/scanner is properly aligned using Combi-1's greyscale and color bar data as recorded on the film, image reproduction is standardized and repeatable.

To extend the process further, the Cinematographer can establish a personal reference standard on a carefully controlled roll of film. A section of this exposed and processed original negative could be supplied to the transfer house to be used as a telecine reference and comparison standard. This enables variations in film stocks, lab processing, color temperature and exposure to be monitored. DSC also supplies a negative alignment film produced and processed under controlled conditions.

The Ambi/Combi OSG combination also facilitates control of scenes that are not *average*. By setting up a *standard* alignment a Cinematographer can deviate a set amount to produce a consistent, repeatable special *look*. In conjunction with the spot meter, scene lighting levels and contrast may be set to a desired level and still produce information compatible with the video system. Color balance may be adjusted away from the *average* with reproduction remaining constant even when transferred at different facilities.

The Cinematographer with a firm understanding of the operating philosophy of the Ambi/Combi System has a powerful tool through which to control image quality. The *look* that was so important to establish at the beginning of a production may now be reproduced on a daily basis and becomes independent of the post production facility. Exposure of the original negative can now be carefully controlled assuring the original negative contains adequate density range to enable transfers which satisfy both domestic and foreign markets.

The practicality of the system was proven by running a series of tests as outlined above. These were evaluated, using one of CBC Toronto's Rank URSA Scanners. **(Fig.7)** Based on the satisfactory performance achieved, an additional five tests were shot and supplied to Lab/Transfer Houses across North America for process and transfer.

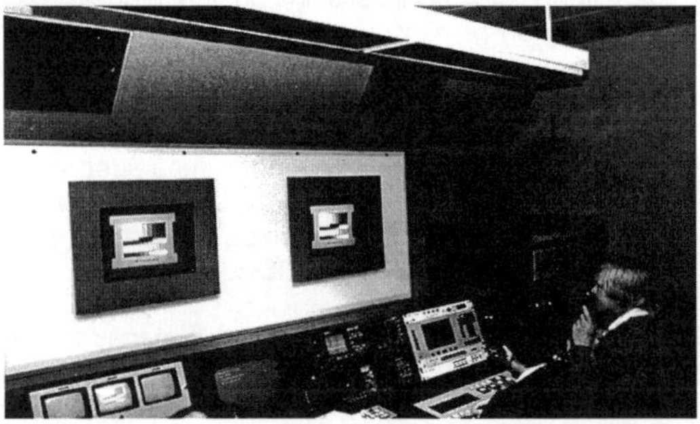

**Figure 7** - 16mm test neg OSG on CBC URSA

On return of the processed negatives the "LAD patches" included in the test exposures were measured. Densitometer measurements and subjective evaluation of the five tests on a CBC URSA indicated that the effect of differences in processing between the five labs was minimal. However, there were major differences in the transfers performed by the different post production labs.

Unfortunately, these tests show that the reproduction of film materials is still plagued with difficulties brought on by the subjective nature of the work and the lack of industrial standards. These results come as no surprise, as this type of variation is well known in the industry and has been documented over a number of years by people such as Zwick et al. While negative processing is well controlled, large variations in image quality can be occur between different post production facilities.

An interesting side note is that a major lab asked to keep a few frames of the Combi-1 negative as it provided an excellent base setting for their scanners. They reported that different film stocks even reproduced better when the scanner was aligned to the Combi-1 negative test film. Clearly these tests demonstrate the industry's increasing need for tighter standards .

## Summary

The Ambi/Combi System was developed in collaboration between DSC Laboratories and the Canadian Broadcasting Corporation and is based on sound engineering and scientific principles. Embracing international standards, it uses conventional waveform and vectorscope instrumentation.

Combi OSGs are multi-function rear lit test targets. Useful not only as camera and telecine alignment tools, but also valuable in film and video production as objective reference standards.

The Ambi/Combi System provides both the precision demanded by engineers with the speed and ease of use essential in difficult production situations. It performs the important function of enabling image quality to be precisely and consistently quantified. The signal information is presented in a familiar manner readily embraced by all working in the television industry.

# THE LOST HISTORY OF FILM FORMATS

Daniel J. Sherlock
Media Technology Consulting
Fullerton, CA

## Abstract

Many stories of the development of some of the various film formats have acquired the status of "legend" which consists of a mixture of truth and fantasy. The development of some of the most famous film formats actually came about as a result of developments in other fields, or in adaptations of other ideas. This paper will present an overview of how this evolution took place for several formats, and will clarify several missing pieces of the lost history of film formats.

The history of film formats reported in much of the media has been filled with many contradictions, myths, and oversimplifications. This is rarely due to some sort of malevolence on the part of the authors. It is usually attributable to the misunderstanding or lack of sufficient information about the format, and the propagation of such misinformation from reference to reference.

A major missing piece in the commonly documented history of film formats has been the acknowledgment of how such formats were based upon other developments, some of which originated decades earlier. Cinerama, Todd-AO, CinemaScope, VistaVision, and polarized 3D processes are all variants of processes that existed prior to 1930. Omnimax (IMAX Dome), Showscan, and the 8-perforation 70m format are also variants of previous formats. Special venue motion base rides based upon projected images have been around since the beginnings of the feature film.

Motion base simulation rides had their origin in 1905 with "Hale's Tours". This consisted of a small auditorium resembling a train car and the viewers would watch the passing of the countryside on a projection screen at the front of the car. To enhance the realism of the simulation, the "train car" shook and rumbled, and fans located on the ceiling enhanced the feeling of motion. One of the operators of "Hale's Tours", Edwin R. Porter, decided to enhance the experience by adding to his facility a film which had a story: *The Great Train Robbery*. Thus, ironically, the feature film business had its beginnings from the special venue business. The "Hale's Tours" simulations were impressive, but the original idea it was based upon was perhaps even more impressive: People were to sit in actual train cars that traveled on a circular track through a tunnel that had projected images on its walls.[1]

The credit for the first simulation ride using motion pictures belongs to an even earlier format: The Cineorama system as presented in Paris, France in 1900. This system is also the origin of mosaiced multi-projector formats and of the wide field of view systems made popular by Cinerama and the Circarama/Circle-Vision 360 systems half a century later. Unfortunately, the Cineorama system had a fatal design flaw: The 10 wide gauge projectors shared the same projection room which was located directly underneath the audience. There was insufficient cooling of the projection booth and the temperatures inside reached levels which posed a serious fire danger with the nitrate film being used. Because of this problem, the exhibit was ordered closed after only 4 days.[2]

The approach of using a single film for wide angle photography began about 1922 with the Panoramica format developed by Filoteo Alberini. It utilized a 70mm film with a pivoted lens (borrowed from the still camera technique) to give about a 60 degree field of view.[3] At about the same time, an American promoter, John Elmes, was also trying to achieve wide angle photography. He first tried synchronizing three cameras together, then two, and then used a single wide gauge camera with a wide image that was printed onto two conventional 35mm strips. The two projectors that were normally found in the projection booth were synchronized together to show the two images side by side. The Widescope format, as it was called, was shown to the public at the Casino theater in New York City in 1926.[4] As it turns out, both Alberini and Elms in an effort to simplify their systems experimented with a horizontally running 35mm format with 10 perforations per frame. The Fearless Super Pictures format promoted in 1929 used the same format but with an optical soundtrack along the bottom of the image.[5]

It is interesting to note that the eight perforation VistaVision format introduced in 1954 was not based upon these cameras. Instead, the first VistaVision camera was a modified Nature Color camera – an additive color format which advanced the film vertically eight perforation holes at a time. The camera was turned on its side and adapted to have one lens expose the entire area. The initial lenses used were designed for Leica still cameras.[6]

The Widescope format also inspired the first imitation large screen format. The Eastman Theater in New York experimented with an enlarging lens on the projector and a larger screen to give an emotional impact similar to that produced by Widescope's larger screen. The technique was successful, and Paramount decided to use it in their theaters under the name Magnascope. Paramount used it on several films, beginning with *Old Ironsides* in 1927.[7]

In 1927 Andre Debrie in France succeeded in synchronizing three cameras and projectors. This format, known initially as Triptique and later as Polyvision, was used for Abel Gance's *Napoleon*.[8] The inspiration for the format was the triptique style used in paintings. Many of the compositions used in *Napoleon*, such as mirror flipped side images, were based upon styles used in these paintings. The format was impressive at presenting a larger and clearer image to the audience, but was complex and expensive to install and present to audiences. As it turns out, the same financial difficulty would plague the three projector Cinerama process 25 years later.

One of the people in the audience in Paris who was impressed by the wide screen was Henri Critien. He had developed an anamorphic lens design which would allow compression of an image in one direction only. His original intent was to use such as lens to permit additive color and 3D formats to use standard cameras. But when he saw the wide screen, he realized that his lens could also be used for a simpler wide screen format. He quickly added patent protection to cover this additional use for his lens. These same lenses would be used 25 years later to photograph the initial CinemaScope films.[9]

----------

The 1920's also saw the development of sound on film processes, driven primarily by the availability of higher quality audio amplifiers. This not only forced the adoption of motorized cameras, it spurred the development of methods to give back the screen width lost to the soundtrack. By going to a wider film gauge, there was the opportunity to go beyond the original 1.33:1 aspect ratio and introduce a larger, wider, and more involving image. These larger film areas were particularly desirable for use in the large movie palaces being built at the time.

One of the first efforts in wide gauge movies in the 1920's was the Natural Vision process developed by George K. Spoor and John J. Berggren. Interestingly, this started out as a 3-D process using a camera with two lenses.[10] After several years of development, the format evolved into a 63.5mm format with a frame six perforations tall. In fact, it was only a little different from the 63mm Veriscope format used to film the Corbett-Fitzsimmons prize fight in 1897.[11] One difference was the addition of a Photophone sound track on a separate 35mm film run through an RCA sound head driven by the same motor as the picture projector.[12] The feature film *Danger Lights* was shown in the process in both Chicago and New York City.[13]

Another early attempt in wide gauge filming was the Magnafilm format used for the Paramount short subject *You're In the Army Now.* Magnafilm was virtually the same as standard 35mm with the same perfs, frame height and running time but used 56mm wide film. The idea was to modify existing projectors for the new gauge. Unfortunately, the demonstration showing in 1929 suffered from a brightness falloff at the edges of the image. This was present in the original image on the film, and the image on the screen was blurred due to the inadequacy of the projection head. The less than enthusiastic response to the demonstration killed the process.[14]

William Fox decided to go one step further and initiated the development of the Grandeur 70mm process. This not only gave the wider image but easily permitted the increase in screen height that made Magnascope popular. Larger rectangular perforation holes and a 0.234 inch pitch were used to maintain the four perforation holes per frame convention. The speed of the film was set at 90 feet per minute to provide adequate sound quality, and this gave a picture frequency of 20 frames per second.[15]

MGM determined that the major benefit of the Grandeur format was in the use of the large negative to reduce the visibility of grain on the screen. They optically reduced the 70mm image to fill the width of a full aperture 35mm frame and used a separate sound-on-disk soundtrack.[16] This allowed the largest film area available with conventional projectors and lenses – something like the Super 35 format in reverse.

Some of the other studios saw the advantages of Grandeur, but William Fox had tight control over the format. Several independent developers all came up with the same approach: A five perf 65mm film frame using standard perforation holes and a standard pitch. This 65mm format was called Magnifilm (not to be confused with Magnafilm) when it was used for the feature film *The Bat Whispers.*[17] It was called the Fearless Super Film format for the camera available from the Fearless Camera Corporation.[18] Warner Bros. developed their own 65mm camera and called the format Vitascope.[19] It was used for the Warner Bros. films *Kismet, A Soldier's Plaything* and *The Lash.*[20] Universal even considered using the format under the name Magnachrome for the short *We-We Marie.*[21] Paramount experimented with a 65mm camera developed by French camera maker Andre Debrie. They also developed a reduction printer to produce 35mm prints from 65mm negatives, similar to what the Realife format did with 70mm negatives.[22] *The Bat Whispers* was processed to allow a 35mm reduction format.[23]

Experience showed that these wide gauge formats needed new projectors rather than retrofitted 35mm projectors. It was also clear that, to be practical, the projectors needed to be able to show both the wide gauge format as well as 35mm since few projection booths had room for both types of machines. The wide gauge formats of 1930 did not succeed due to the cost of theater conversion and the lack of standardization of formats. In 1931, a working group of the SMPE developed a compromise format based upon a 50mm film width.[24] This, it was hoped, would have most of the advantages of the larger formats and yet allow retrofitted projectors to provide an improved image. However, a self-imposed restriction on the number of wide gauge play dates further helped kill the formats. But the equipment would simply lie dormant for their rebirth in the 1950's.

----------

The widescreen boom of the 1950's began with the Cinerama process used for the feature film *This Is Cinerama* in 1952. This film presented, for the first time for most of the audience, the large wide screen with seven track hi-fi stereo from a magnetic sound track. For a time when most films were still in black and white, the overall impact on the audience was overwhelming. It also had something that few formats have had since that time: vection. Sometimes called by some just "the Cinerama effect", it is the sense of self-motion – of foreword movement and rotation – technically known as linearvection and circularvection. This sense of motion was due to the wide field of view in both photography and viewing.[25] As later formats used longer focal length camera lenses and flatter projection screens, this sensation gradually disappeared from the experience of the cinema.

The Cinerama format began as Vitarama, a system that used eleven 16mm cameras and projectors to fill a cylindrical screen capped by a quarter dome. The system was developed for the Petroleum Industry exhibit for the 1939 World's Fair in New York City. But, after a demonstration to some of the people in charge of the exhibit, they felt that the system was perhaps a bit too radical for their purposes and another type of exhibit was used.[26] The original patent for the idea, however, indicates the intent to use fewer projectors and to have directional sound that would move about the screen with the image.[27] The idea to use a louvered screen to reduce reillumination effects came soon thereafter.[28] As Vitarama evolved to the Waller Gunnery Trainer using five 35mm projectors and finally Cinerama using three enlarged aperture 35mm projectors, the screen changed from a dome to a cylinder. This shape allowed the use of simple strips of screen material held taught by hooks and elastic bands, and steadied by guides part way up the screen.[29]

Cinerama was a popular success, and several travelogues used the process as well as two feature films from MGM: *The Wonderful World of the Brothers Grimm* and *How the West Was Won*. To simplify the photographic process, the development of a prototype camera was begun that would photograph the wide field of view on a single 35mm film using a 16 perf horizontal advance.[30] To improve the impressiveness of the presentation in the theater, Super Cinerama theaters were made where an even larger screen filled the entire front wall of the theater.[31] Cinerama was shown in portable theaters in Europe, and was shown on an enormous 60 x 180 foot screen at a Los Angeles suburb drive-in.[32] To help ensure that the three panels were aligned and steady, a system using registration markers outside of each of the images was developed. Photodetectors at the screen would pick up the projected markers and electronically adjust the position of the image in real time.[33] However, the business decision to simplify production and cut the recurring exhibition costs (including multiple projectionists) resulted in the adoption of the use of Ultra Panavision 70 and, later, Super Panavision 70 for the remaining Cinerama productions. A special projection lens was used to maintain focus over the curved screen, and special rectified prints were used to compensate for "screen stretch" at the sides of the image.[34]

The loss of the true 3-projector Cinerama format has been felt by enthusiasts for many years. The sense of vection, the clarity of the image, and the feeling of "being there" was never the same in the later formats. The desire to bring back the original experience resulted in the creation of a Cinerama theater in 1993 at the Pictureville Cinema located at the National Museum of Photography, Film & Television at Bradford, England.[35] The film *This Is Cinerama* continues to show on the first Saturday of each month – at the only public theater in the world that can show the format. That is, until recently. Beginning in August 1996, the New Neon Movies theater in Dayton Ohio began showing the film along with *How the West Was Won* on weekends for a limited time using a specially retrofitted theater.[36] The response to the showings has been very enthusiastic, and there may yet be another permanent theater that will be capable of showing this format.

----------

A key part of the puzzle that allowed the introduction of Cinerama and the other widescreen systems in the 1950's was the introduction of Eastman color negative film. In fact, the introduction of the color film also allowed cannibalizing earlier color cameras for widescreen processes. Besides the first VistaVision camera being derived from a modified Nature Color camera as was mentioned previously, the three-strip Technicolor cameras were modified into 8-perf pull-across Technirama cameras.[37]

Although it may appear to some that Twentieth Century Fox "discovered" the use of wide screen presentation and the advantages of stereo sound only after the success of Cinerama, it was actually the other way around. Fox experimented with a prototype system in the 1940's which used three tracks of optical stereo synchronized with wide film images.[38] It has also been claimed by some historians that Twentieth Century Fox developed the magoptical format, a process where magnetic stripes for stereo sound are included on a print along with a narrow optical track. In fact, the magoptical format was developed by the Motion Picture Research Council. Fox was against the use of such a print since the quality of the narrow optical track was noticeably inferior to that from a conventional 35mm optical track. (Incidentally, the original hope for magoptical prints was to be able to strip the oxide stripes off of the print after first-run showings to reveal a normal size optical track, but this proved to be impractical.)[39]

One "mystery" to some is why the Todd-AO format uses 65mm film in the camera and 70mm film for projection. The answer lies in the fact that Michael Todd wanted to develop a system as quick as possible to convince Rodgers and Hammerstein to allow the format to be used for the motion picture premiere of *Oklahoma!* A 65mm camera and projector from the experiments in 1930 were located and used for the initial tests.[40] The experiments were a success and the process was announced as using 65mm film in the projector with interlocked magnetic sound. In fact, since theater prints were to be step printed anyway, the same long pitch film dimensions were used for both camera and theater prints.[41] The step printing process could compensate for the distortions introduced by the 128 degree bug-eye lens as well as introduce compensating distortions to cancel those introduced by downward projection into a deeply curved screen.[42] Although a technique was developed to compensate for the "horizon sag" on curved screens using anamorphic projection, it was decided to avoid the problems altogether by eliminating the deeply curved screen.[43]

The origin of the early Todd-AO camera has been the source of much confusion. Some have felt that it was a modified version of the 70mm camera used for Grandeur or the Paramount 65mm camera made by Andre Debrie. However, careful comparisons will reveal that it is in fact a modified Fearless Superfilm camera. The Superfilm camera had an aperture that was 0.906 inches (23mm) tall and the aperture was modified to fill the entire area between the perfs.[44]

----------

Simulation experiences utilizing motion bases similar to those used for flight simulation are bridging the gap between film and other techniques to produce the imagery. Several companies have systems that utilize moving seats synchronized with film imagery on large screens. Other systems rely on computer generated imagery to produce the equivalent of a "super video game". One development known as "Driver's Seat" actually used a live video feed from a scale model race car that ran through a race course. The driver of the model car sat in a simulator that could reproduce many sensations including that of flipping the car end over end.[45]

Simulation is just one path for the future of film formats. Large screens, 3-D, in-theater effects, and changing theater geometries are experiencing a renascence. If anything can be learned from the prior history of film formats, it is that future "innovations" will primarily be adaptations of what has been done in the past. And through the creative use of these innovations along with improved technology, we will see a future in film formats that bears a striking resemblance to the glorious days of the past.

REFERENCES


1. Emmanuelle Toulet, *Birth of the Motion Picture*, 108, New York: Harry N. Abrams, 1995.
2. Brian Coe, *The History of Movie Photography*, 52-53, London: Ash & Grant, 1981.
3. Kenneth Macgowan, *Behind the Screen: The History and Techniques of the Motion Picture*, 456, New York: Delta, 1965.
4. _____.,"Wide-Vision Pictures," *New York Times*, 31, November 9, 1926.
5. Grant Lobban, "Widescreen & 3-D Film Formats," Poster Available from British Kinematograph, Sound and Television Society (BKSTS) 67-71 Victoria House, Vernon Place, London WC1B 4DA, England. (No Date)
6. John R. Bishop and Loren L. Ryder, "Paramount's 'Lazy-8' Double-Frame Camera," *American Cinematographer 34*:606, December 1953.
7. Lewis M. Townsend and William W. Hennessey, "Some Novel Projected Motion Picture Presentations," *Jour. of SMPE 12*:348, April 1928.
8. Kevin Brownlow, *Napoleon: Abel Gance's Classic Film*, 159, New York: Knopf, 1983.
9. John Belton, *Widescreen Cinema,* 147, Cambridge, MA: Harvard University Press, 1992.
10. James L. Limbacher, *Four Aspects of the Film*, 86-87, New York: Brussel and Brussel, 1968.
11. Grant Lobban, "Film Gauges and Soundtracks," Poster Available from British Kinematograph, Sound and Television Society (BKSTS) 67-71 Victoria House, Vernon Place, London WC1B 4DA, England. (No Date)
12. L. D. Strong, "Spoor Wide Film Showing," *Motion Picture Projectionist 5*:12, January 1931.
13. Advertisement, *New York Times*, 55, December 12, 1930.
14. James R. Cameron, "The New Wide Film Arrives," *Projection Engineering 1*:26, October 1929.
15. R. H. McCullough, "Grandeur Wide Film System," *The Motion Picture Projectionist 4*:27, April 1930.
16. Rick Mitchell, "History of Wide Screen Formats," *American Cinematographer 68*: 36-37, May 1987.
17. George Turner, "The Magnifilm Enigma," *American Cinematographer 72*:88, May 1991.
18. Hal Hall, "Fearless Camera Company Presents Silent Super-Film Camera," *American Cinematographer 11*:12-14, April 1930.
19. WM. Stull, "Warner Brothers' New Camera," *American Cinematographer 11*:10-11, 30, December 1930.
20. Robert E. Carr and R. M. Hayes, *Wide Screen Movies: A History and Filmography of Wide Gauge Filmmaking,* 187-188, Jefferson, NC: McFarland, 1988.
21. _____.,"U's Wide Film Short," *Variety*, 5, October 29, 1930.
22. _____.,"Methods of Securing a Large Screen Picture," *Jour. SMPE 16*:174-187, February 1931.
23. Scott MacQueen, "A Gathering of Bats," *American Cinematographer 69*:35-36, September 1988.
24. "Report of the Standards and Nomenclature Committee," A. C. Hardy, chairman, *J. SMPE 17*:431-437, September, 1931.

25. Kenneth R. Boff and Janet E. Lincoln, *User's Guide, Engineering Data Compendium*, 31, Wright-Patterson Air Force Base, OH: Harry G. Armstrong Aerospace Medical Research Laboratory, Wright-Patterson Air Force Base, OH, 1988.
26. Ralph Walker, "The Birth of an Idea," in Martin Quigley Jr. (ed.) *New Screen Techniques*, 112-117, New York: Quigley Publishing Co., 1953.
27. Fred Waller and Ralph Walker, "Motion Picture Theater," U.S. Patent # 2,280,206 filed on September 14, 1937, patented on April 21, 1942.
28. Fred Waller, "Screen for Picture Projection," U.S. Patent # 2,273,074 filed on June 14, 1938, patented on February 17, 1942.
29. Fred Waller, "Screen for Picture Projections," U.S. Patent # 2,476,521 filed on September 22, 1947, patented on July 19, 1949.
30. Keith H. Swadkins, "Whatever Happened to Cinerama?" *Cinema Technology 3:*59, July 1990.
31. Special Cinerama supplement, *The Film Daily 122:*4, January 21, 1963.
32. _____.,"Cinerama's Now Showing at Drive-in," *Los Angeles Times*, 18, April 18, 1964.
33. Fred Waller and Willis Robert Dresser, "Apparatus for Locating Images on Screens," U.S. Patent # 2,563,892 filed on December 14, 1946, patented on August 14, 1951.
34. Hikmet Labib Avedis Aghanigian, "Cinerama, Its History and Development", unpublished thesis for Masters degree, University of Southern California Los Angeles, 48, January 1965.
35. John Gainsborough, "The Pictureville Cinema, NMPFT, Bradford," *Cinema Technology 5:*146-147, October 1992.
36. Advertising flyer, New Neon Movies theater, Dayton, OH.
37. Joseph V. Mascelli, "Technirama," *International Photographer 29:*5-7, June 1957.
38. Lorin D. Grignon, "Experiment in Stereophonic Sound," *Jour. SMPE 52:*280-292, March 1949.
39. James Morris, "The Combined Magnetic-Optical Print: A Compromise to End Confusion," *International Projectionist 30:*15-17, December 1955.
40. _____.,"Summary of Current Wide-screen Systems of Photography," *American Cinematographer 36:*655 November 1955.
41. Arthur C. Miller and Walter Strenge, ed., "Film Perforations," *American Cinematographer Manual, Third Edition*, 498, Hollywood, CA: ASC Holding Corp., 1969.
42. Brian O'Brian, "Wide Angle Picture Projection Optical Systems and Screen Apparatus," U.S. Patent # 2,792,746 filed on August 3, 1953, patented on May 21, 1957.
43. John D. Hayes, "Horizon Sag Compensation," *J. SMPTE 68:*697-698, October 1959.
44. Paul Allen, "Wide Film Development", in*Cinematographic Annual*, 188-190, Hal Hall (ed.), vol. 1, Los Angeles: American Society of Cinematographers, 1930.
45. Eric Schine, "The Roar of the Engine, The Glow of the Screen," *BusinessWeek*, October 9, 1989.

# Post Production Synergy of Video and Film with Archival Quality

By: Michael Ostrelich Sr. Staff Image Graphics, Inc.
Lewis Merritt Electronic Engineering Manager
Image Graphics, Inc.

## Introduction

The legacy of humankind is represented by how well we have documented our past achievements and how well they have been preserved. The creative efforts of computer generated cinematography is at risk of deterioration if archival techniques are not applied. A unique technological development has now made it possible to record high resolution cinema imagery directly on archival black and white silver halide film in the post production process as separations for a red, green and blue composite. The application of a high speed electron beam recorder as developed by Image Graphics will create on high resolution silver halide film a permanent archival master interpositive. Motion picture magic will occur when each frame of the 72 black and whites are recorded for one (1) second of imagery. In addition, the versatility of format is almost boundless and the same high resolution can be applied to all motion picture formats including 70mm. The larger venues in particular can take advantage of this technique for a truly spectacular presentation.

## Image Capture

The process begins with an original color image which is usually live camera material. These frames are scanned by high resolution scanners with the red, green and blue filters in place for a digital data file for each separation. A scanner such as a Lensar model number LENZPRO 2001 or an Oxberry model number 6400-20 Cinescan can be used on the 35mm or 65mm frame for the desired number of resolution elements (pixels) that the data storage system will allow or up to 2,671 X 3,675 pixels for 35mm academy or 11,735 X 8,771 pixels for 65mm IMAX. A process flow diagram is illustrated in figure (1). The image capture phase of the process consists of digitizing a color frame into the computer compatible electronic file which is temporarily stored on magnetic tape or can be transferred directly to computer memory. The composite file of a color image is created on the computer monitor so that the image can be manipulated in color by the graphic artist in the image processing phase of the archival development. A summary of the cinema formats and the corresponding digital specifications (pixels) is presented in figure (2).

## Image Processing

The image processing is typically performed at a work station utilizing a Silicon Graphics or a Sun Ultra Sparc computer. The data storage requirements for typical full length feature presentations is shown in figure (3). Usually only a portion of the feature is digitally enhanced

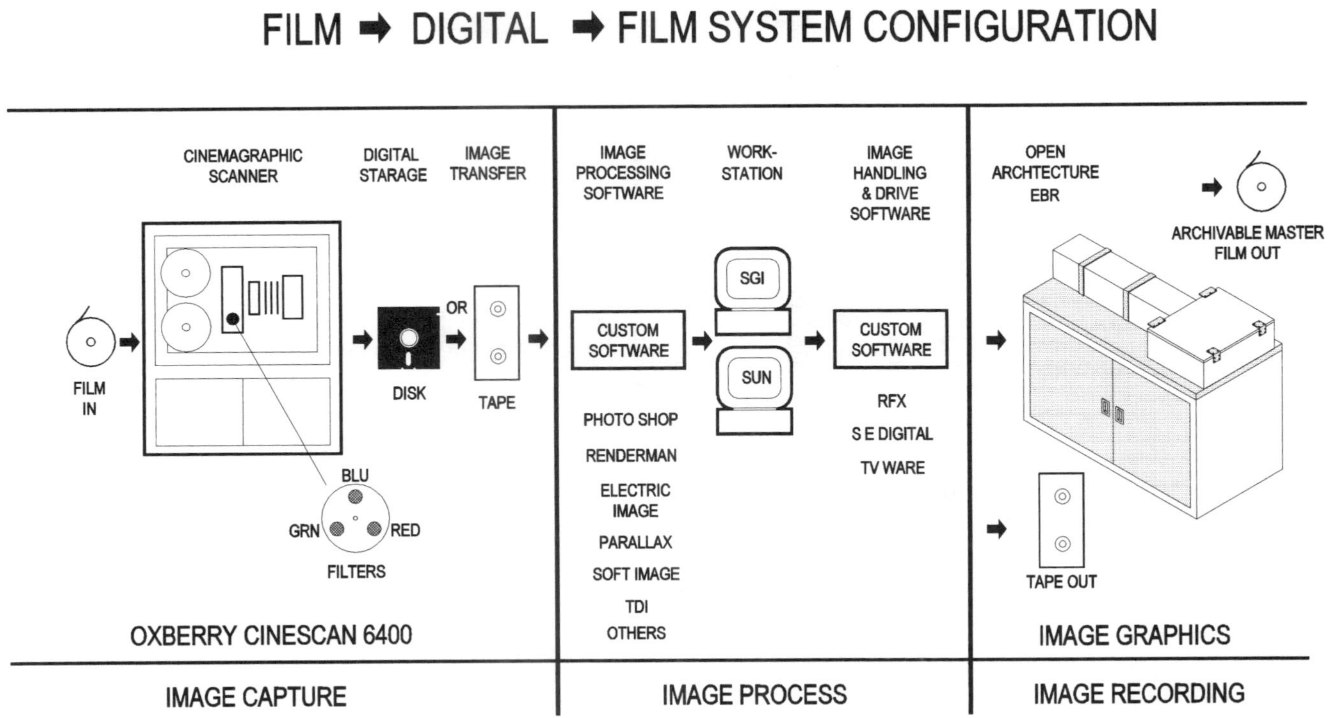


PROCESS CONFIGURATION FOR ARCHIVAL
DIGITAL IMAGE PRODUCTION
FIGURE 1

**Film Formats**

| | | SIZE | |
|---|---|---|---|
| 35MM FILM FORMATS | DIMENSIONS | PIXELS | CINEMA EBR RECORDING TIME (PER SEPARATION) |
| Full Camera Aperture | 0.735" x 0.980" | 3,112 x 4,149 | 0.62 Seconds |
| Academy | 0.631" x 0.868" | 2,671 x 3,675 | 0.47 Seconds |
| Solitare | 0.651" x 0.868" | 2,756 x 3,675 | 0.49 Seconds |
| Super 35 | 0.735" x 0.968" | 3,112 x 4,098 | 0.61 Seconds |
| Cinemascope | 0.735" x 0.868" | 3,112 x 3,675 | 0.55 Seconds |
| Vista Vision | 1.485" x 0.991" | 6,287 x 4,195 | 1.27 Seconds |
| Instrumentation | 0.735" x 0.981" | 3,112 x 4,153 | 0.62 Seconds |
| Anamorphic Sound | 0.732" x 0.864" | 3,099 x 3,658 | 0.54 Seconds |
| Non-Anamorphic Sound | 0.630" x 0.864" | 2,667 x 3,658 | 0.47 Seconds |
| Max. Addressable Area | 1.500" x 1.500" | (Some addressable points outside film area) | |
| 65/70 MM FILM FORMATS | | | |
| IMAX | 2.772" x 2.072" | 11,735 x 8,771 | 4.94 Seconds |
| Other | Not to exceed max. addressable area | | |
| Max. Addressable Area | 3.000" x 3.000" | (Some addressable points outside film area) | |

**AVAILABLE RECORDING FORMATS AND CORRESPONDING RECORDING TIMES**
**FIGURE 2**

## DATA STORAGE REQUIREMENTS FOR FILM

| | 90 MIN FILM | | | 120 MIN FILM | | |
|---|---|---|---|---|---|---|
| FRAME | 50 MBytes | | | 50 MBytes | | |
| # OF FRAMES | 130,000 | | | 173,000 | | |
| TOTAL STORAGE | 6.5 TERABYTES | | | 8.8 TERABYTES | | |
| | XFER RATE | XFER TIME | # OF TAPES | XFER RATE | XFER TIME | # OF TAPES |
| EXABYTE | 1 MB/S | 226 DAYS | 650 TAPES | 1 MB/S | 300 DAYS | 860 TAPES |
| METRON | 1 MB/S | 227 DAYS | 2,450 TAPES | 1 MB/S | 300 DAYS | 3,240 TAPES |
| DD2 | 15 MB/S | 15 DAYS | 197 TAPES | 15 MB/S | 20 DAYS | 260 TAPES |
| SONY ID1 | 32 MB/S | 7 DAYS | 197 TAPES | 32 MB/S | 9 DAYS | 260 TAPES |
| KODAK / GE ID1 | 50 MB/S | 4.5 DAYS | 197 TAPES | 50 MB/S | 6 DAYS | 260 TAPES |

<u>NOTE:</u>

THE ABOVE DATA STORAGE CAPACITIES ARE FOR 35MM FILM
THE FILE SIZE AND CAPACITIES SHOULD BE MULTIPLIED BY 10.5 FOR THE I MAX 65MM FILM FORMAT

DATA STORAGE REQUIREMENTS FOR DIGITAL IMAGE ENHANCEMENT

FIGURE 3

and the storage requirements would be less. The portion of the feature that does not require computer processing can be recorded directly by the cinema recorder onto silver halide film at the archival quality that is desired. The graphic artist today has a variety of software tools that are available for enhancements such as Adobe Photo Shop or RenderMan from Pixar.

The selection criteria is usually based on personal preference or some unique features that are desired. The image data file can be transferred directly to the recorder for output on to film or to a magnetic tape for temporary storage which can be recorded onto film at another time. The IGI cinema recorder is configured with an open architecture, network compatible, computer interface. This approach allows a greater flexibility in accommodating a greater variety of input formats. The video output processing is configured as shown in figure (4) and the data is transferred to the computer controller of the recorder from either a tape drive or the work station computer. The data then goes to the Raster/Vector Generator (RVG-450) which functions as a video adapter for the output recorder. The Raster/Vector Generator controls both the command signals and conditions the digital image data for acceptance by the recorder unit. The RVG 450 uses a standard S bus or PCI computer bus interface and can allow vector or character exposure of areas beyond the normal camera aperture for a variety of frame or job coding.

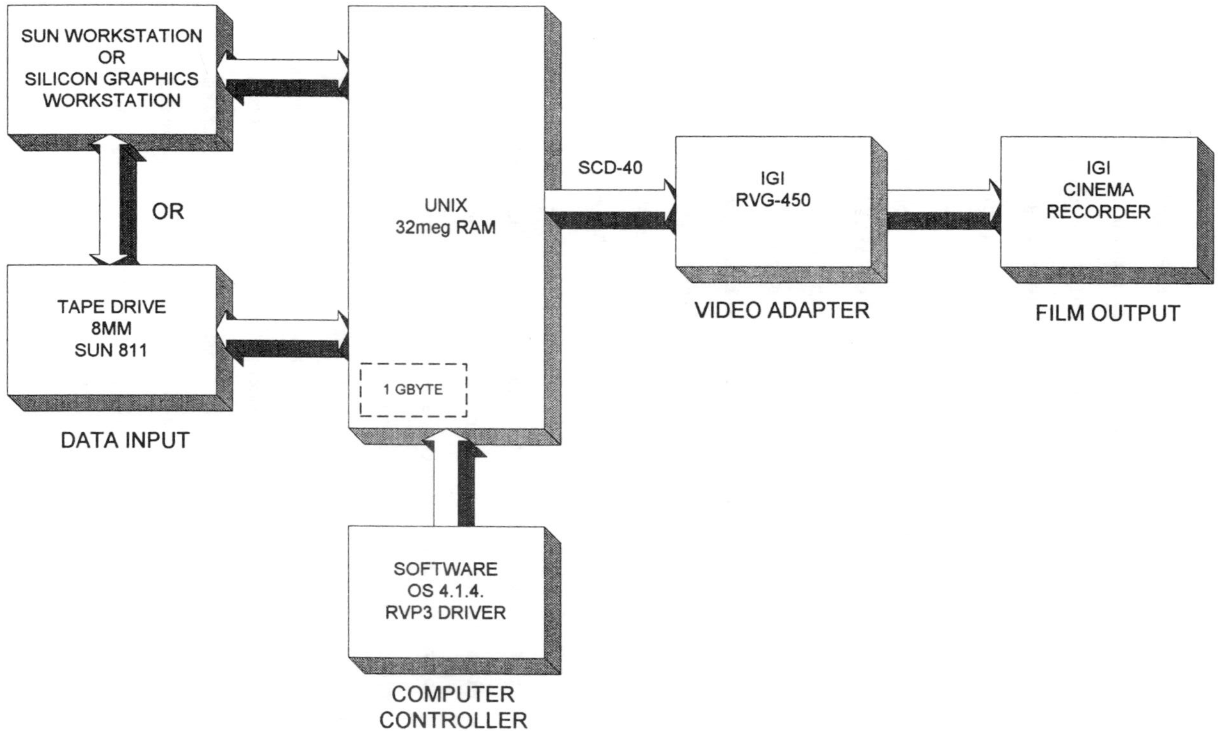


SIGNAL PROCESSING FOR IMAGE RECORDER
FIGURE 4

## Image Recording

The Cinema electron beam recorder (EBR) unit shown in figure (5) uniquely exposes archival, electron sensitive silver halide film with a speed and resolution unmatched by any other recording device. The IGI Cinema EBR can record up to 25 MPixels/second with a 6 micron pixel and a density range up to 4095 levels onto fine grain film having a limiting resolution of 1000 lp/mm. This orthochomatic high resolution black and white film is used to obtain master interpositive red, green and blue separations. The recorder design was developed over many years on several commercial, government and military high resolution image recording programs and the technology is now available for cinematography applications. The unit functions in a manner similar to a CRT type recorder except the beam exposes images on film directly without the degradation of the image caused by the glass face plate and the phosphor coating.

The film is held and advanced by a transport mechanism which is servo controlled with a fixed pin acme type movement film gate for precision alignment of each frame during exposure. This gate is similar to the one utilized by Oxberry in the Cinescan Scanner and has become a standard of performance for the motion picture industry. The film transport can accommodate all the formats shown in figure (2) because the central portion of the gate is on precision guides which allow interchangeability of the film aperture plate. The Cinema EBR is designed for high volume

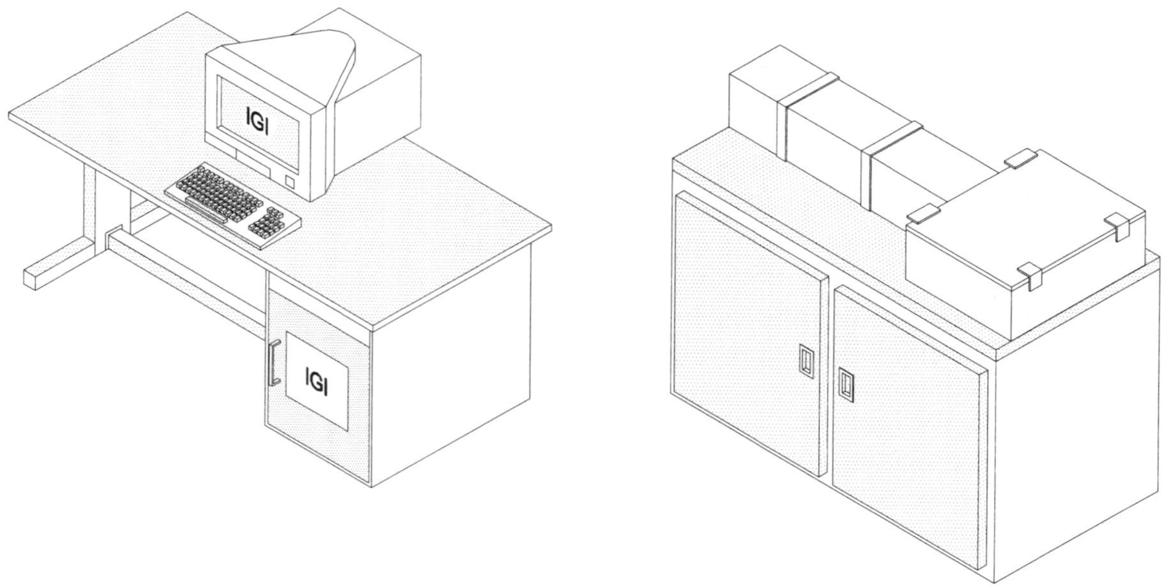


CINEMA RECORDING SYSTEM

FIGURE 5

production. The recording times shown in figure (2) indicate the high rate of exposure which the unit is capable.

Directly creating high resolution black and white interpositives, is an important advantage of the recorder. The final color print is only two (2) generations (image transfers) from the high resolution original archival masters of the recorded digital image whereas with standard production techniques the final print is three (3) generations from the non archival color camera stock. This procedure is illustrated in figure (6). The improvement in print quality is most obvious in the larger venue 65mm format. With silver halide black-and-white film, the recorder can obtain a resolution of 135 lp/m . A practical resolution of 80 lppm was selected for the 35mm and 70 mm cinema formats. This is well beyond the resolution limits of good intermediate color film stocks such as Eastman 5244. The central branch of figure 6 shows the traditional nonarchival laboratory manipulation of the image from the original camera negative to the final print utilizing color interpositive and internegative film stocks. This applies to both optical camera output and to conventional digital film recorders as they typically use the same type camera stocks for the original image recording. The branch at the right in figure 6 shows an alternate laboratory production process used to create an archival film record of the original work. Here the original image from the camera stock is optically

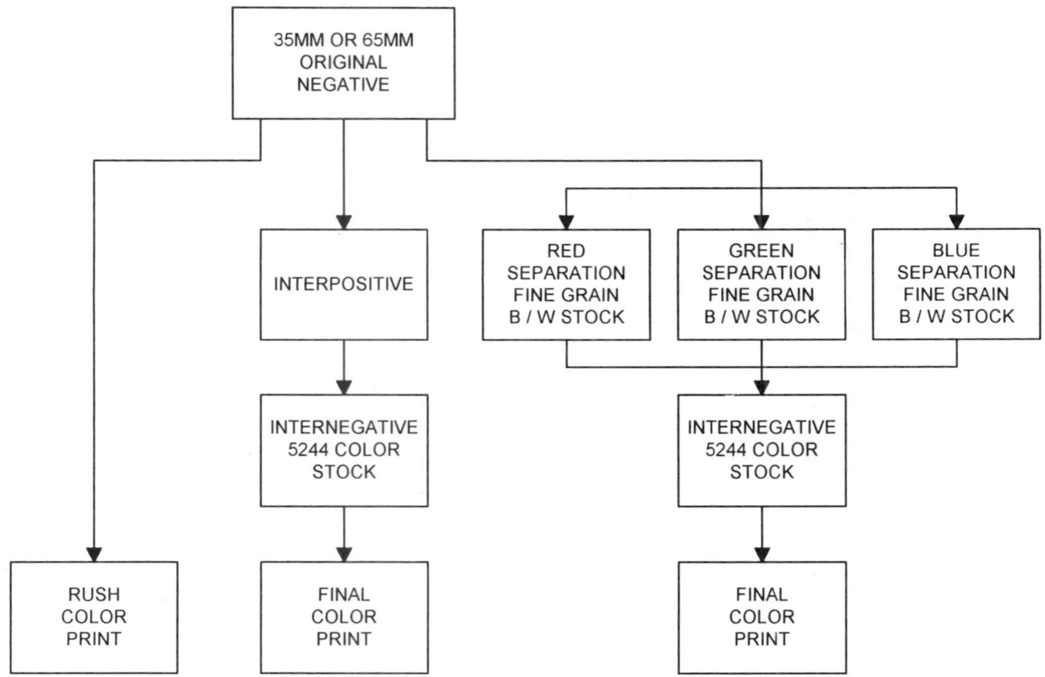


**ALTERNATE PROCEDURES FOR THE PRODUCTION OF COLOR CINEMA PRINTS**

**FIGURE 6**

transferred to a panchromatic black and white film with a separation frame for the three primary colors of the original film. These tri-separations are recorded onto fine grain silver halide archival type of film such as Eastman 5235 or SO-202. The output of the recorder prints the computer images directly as black-and-white separations using a very fine grain Eastman SO-025 film. When processed and handled properly, these films have a storage rating of over 100 years. The technical bulletin in Note 1 has more information on the preparation of black-and white archival separations.

## Print Production

Color internegatives can be constructed from the Cinema recorder to produce the final prints with an optical printer as shown in Figure 7. In the sequential image transfer process, the black and white separations from the original image frame are recorded in a blue, green, red sequence on a single strand of film. When the color separations of the original frames are projected onto a color intermediate stock in a skip step printer, a color filter wheel is used in the optical path to control the separations exposure to the correct color layer of the internegative film stock. In a Technicolor type printer, three separate lengths of film are used with all of the image frames of a like color on a

## SEQUENTIAL IMAGE TRANSFER PROCESS

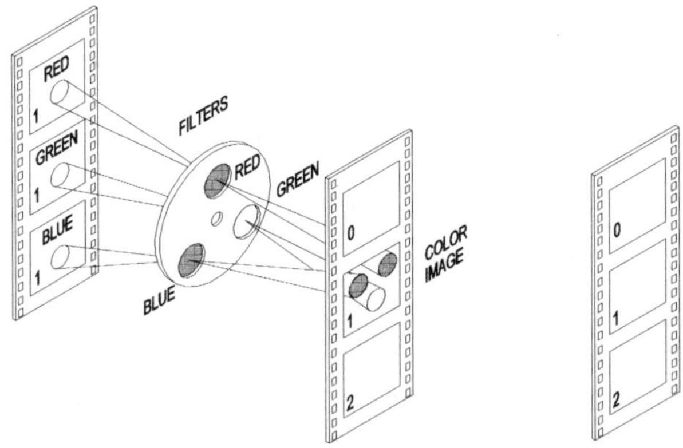


BLACK AND WHITE COLOR SEPARATIONS

STEP EACH COLOR TO SAME FRAME

MASTER COLOR COMPSITE NEGATIVE

HOLD FRAME TO COMPLETE EACH COLOR

COLOR PRODUCTION PRINT (POSITIVE)

## TECHNICOLOR STRIP PROCESS IMAGE TRANSFER

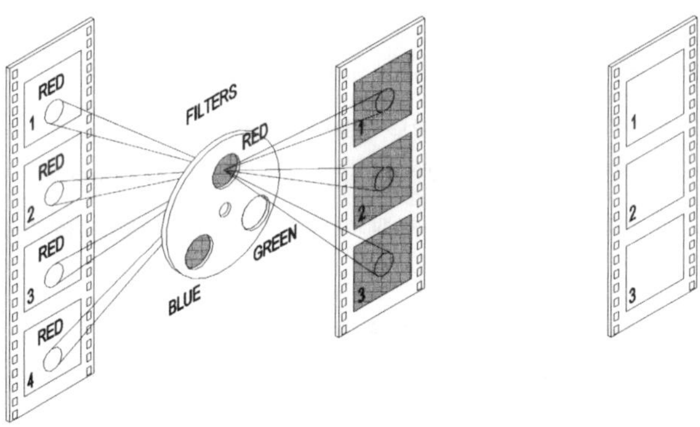


BLACK AND WHITE COLOR SEPARATIONS

STEP ONE COLOR TO CORRESPONDING FRAME THEN REWIND FOR NEXT COLOR

MASTER COLOR COMPOSITE NEGATIVE

STEP EACH FRAME FOR A SINGLE COLOR BACKWIND FOR NEXT COLOR

COLOR PRODUCTION PRINT (POSITIVE)

RESTORATION OF COLOR IMAGERY AND PRODUCTION OF RELEASE PRINT
FIGURE 7

separate length. Again, as the separation film passes through the printer, a color filter wheel is used to transfer the separation image to the correct color layer of the internegative film.

The choice of the printing technique depends upon the printing equipment available to the laboratory as the Cinema EBR can easily output in either format. The computer processed separations that are generated from the IGI Cinema EBR film recorder can be edited into other camera work that has been optically transferred to archival separations. Otherwise, the color internegative is edited directly into the working negatives for producing the final color prints.

Color Management

As the Cinema EBR output has to be matched to other cinematography work, the color management in this recorder system is designed to be flexible and easy to setup. The recorder is capable of recording over a density range of 0.20 DU to 2.6 DU using standard D-96 type developer. This density range is mapped to the incoming video through a 12 bit per color video lookup table system in its computer controller. The desired transfer curve with the necessary gamma for the different color separations is created by entering a table of density AIM points into the computer. These will become the values for the step wedges generated

**by the recorder for calibration. Wedges with as few as 16 steps or as many as 50 steps can be generated by changing the AIM point table entries. After the measured densities from the processed wedges are entered into the computer, the software calculates the recorder's exposure corrections. During the recording process, an exposure remapping calibration system continuously measures the exposure leves at the AIM points and periodically updates lookup tables to compensate for any drifts in the recorder. This calibration process, along with following standard laboratory practices will create color imagery that can be matched to almost any other color work. Additionally, as the dyes in the internegative fade with time or wear out, new internegatives can be created from the archival masters with the proper color balance now and 100 years from now.**

**Note: 1: Kodak Publication No H-1-5235**
**"Eastman Panchromatic Separation Film 5235"**

## Acknowledgements:

The authors wish to thank the engineers and technicians at Image Graphics, Inc. who have contributed to the design of the Cinema recorder and have made this presentation possible.

In addition, we would also like to thank Frank Hauser of Guffanti Film Labs, Bob Brown of RGB Optical, Gordon Harris of IMax Corp., Paul Wainwright of Eastman Kodak and Dr. Alfred Thumim of Oxberry for their valuable assistance, consideration and development efforts which permitted a successful project.

## References:

1. Wreagh Phyllies: "The Computing and Storage Requirements of 4k X 3k Resolutions Being Used in the Film Industry Today." Presented at the 135th SMPTE Technical conference Oct 29 - Nov. 2, 1993 Los Angeles Convention Center Los Angeles, Calif.

2. Braham, Robert: "The Digital Backlot" IEEE Spectrum, July 1995.

3. Sterngold, James: "Digital Studios: Its the Economy, Stupid, The New York Times Business Day, December 25, 1995.

4. Schiffner, Bill: "MGI Helps Bring Toy Story to Life", Photographic Processing, March 1996

5. ANSI/SMPTE 59-1991, "Motion Picture Film (35mm) Camera Aperture Images and Usage".

6. ANSI/SMPTE 215-1995, "Motion Picture Film (65mm) Camera Aperture Image".

# Servers Expectation Versus Reality

Peter A. Dare
Sony Electronics, Inc.
San Jose, Calif.

Over the past four to five years there has been a great deal of interest shown by the Broadcasters in implementing file servers in their operations, with the hope that with such implementation the use of video tape would be dramatically reduced and in some cases eliminated. The enabling technology that made the use of file servers a practicality is video compression. In many cases, the attractiveness of a file server has preceded the thought process of whether or not the system will work and what limitations the system may have. The expectation of many have not been able to be met in reality, the notion that a computer file server can be utilized in the video world has led to many misadventures in the world of video file servers.

The file server is certainly not computational heavy in terms of its demand on any CPU. The basic function of a file server is bandwidth management, simply because we have faster CPU's does not necessarily mean that a file server will automatically be able to handle higher video data rates or wider bandwidths. This misconception is rampant throughout the Broadcast industry. File servers consist of basically two elements, a hardware element and a software element. The hardware consists of some form of hardware controller, disk drives, whether they be in raid configuration, or simply individual drives with video striped across a number of drives, a backplane where the disk drives and controller are interconnected and finally, interfaces to the outside world, either in the form of encoders and decoders, or network interfaces such as FDDI, SCSI or Ethernet. Then there is the software that controls the recording replay, and other hardware derived functions. The software typically is partitioned into a controller or operating system, an application, and finally they may even be a file formatter. Although, in some cases manufacturers have simply chosen to accept the computer industries file format systems, albeit they may not be necessarily appropriate or optimized for the video world. In all likelihood, there are some who feel that a server is a server and that one size fits all. There are key differences between video and ordinary data files, some obvious points to consider are the inputs and outputs, network bandwidth, storage capacity, resource sharing, quality of service, systemization, reliability, fault tolerance, etc., etc. Although file servers offer random access to material by a multi user community this does not necessarily mean that all users may have access to the same material simultaneously. In this respect there are severe limitations particularly as the bit rate of the recorded signal is increased. It is not uncommon for end users when communicating with manufacturers to suggest that any user on the network should have access to same material at the same time. Designs can be formulated to permit such multiple user access, on the other hand the price points and storage capacity of the server increase dramatically when this demand is made.

It is important for end users to clearly define the actual requirements of the server, otherwise their expectations may not be met. The requirements for a A/V server compared to a normal data file server can not be defined in terms of average quality of service. For audio, video, and broadcast applications the server must always deliver a high quality real time signal.

Although hard disk technology is progressing rapidly , in terms of increased speed, density and reliability, and reduced cost per unit of storage, even so the fastest hard disk drive cannot handle the sustained transfer rates required for full resolution uncompressed video. Through a combination of video stripping across multiple disks and video compression, hard disk systems have been made to work satisfactorily in the broadcast environment.

The television signal consumes a large bandwidth compared to ordinary computer data files. A 4:2:2 uncompressed signal operates in the order of 200 Mb/s. Through the use of compression whether it be JPEG or MPEG, the bit rate of the television signal is reduced to numbers that can be handled by hard disk drives. Although as we go into the world of high definition television bit rates in the order of 150 to 600 Mbs can be expected and this will require dramatic improvement in network topology and disk drive transfer rates. It may even be that in the early stages of high definition that we have to revert to magnetic tape as being our primary storage device.

From a hardware perspective, two factors have the most significant impact on the performance of servers and that is hard disk access and network interconnections. The hard disk solution to storage is an attractive solution from the point of view of non linear, or random access, and access to multiple users to the same piece of material providing the number of simultaneous users does not exceed the bandwidth of the system. In the two cases sighted it is expected that disk technology will be expected to achieve far more than simple play out of one program stream, frequent rapid seeking by the disk is required either to support such functions as jogging and shuttling, or to allow continuous simultaneous access to different parts of the disk for a number of users. This requires seek times of several milliseconds to be compensated by fast burst transfers of data into a buffer. Striping a disk (recording data in parallel across a number of disks usually accessed multiple bus arrangements) improves burst transfer speeds but can not resolve the increasing number of seats required as more users attempt to use the same disk or array of disks.

From this figure, it can be seen that the number of channels which can be sourced simultaneously from a server is primarily a function of the seek time, required channel data rate and required response time. The benefit from adding disks to give more input and output bandwidth by striping is limited. In practice the limit is reached when mirroring the original server achieves equal or better efficiency than striping. A number of conclusions can be drawn from this statement; for a given disk technology and required channel data rate, all broadcast servers are limited in the number of users they can serve at one time. This indicates that perhaps distributed hierarchical server architectural may well be more suitable than single server solutions. It should be pointed out that distributed servers are not a panacea either. Software control of distributed servers and synchronization of data can introduce additional complexity. The channel data rate is a primary factor in the economics of hard disk space service, this in turn is determined by acceptable sound and picture quality thresholds for each application. The required response time is also a primary performance factor being a trade off between user controlled response time and the number of supported users.

The cost of the server may well be determined by the specification of the control interface between users and the server. While hard disk access is a key factor, computers and their associated networks also have limits to the performance in terms of both throughput of data and response time to requests. The theoretical performance of a bus, a network, or computer is usually quoted but it is rarely achieved in reality. This apparent loss of performance is caused by the random nature of the events or transactions which share the network and processing resources. In the case of the SCSI fast and wide connection the bandwidth of the system is quoted as 20 MBs. In reality, it is difficult to achieve more than about

12 MBs on a predictable bases. It is for this reason that the industry SCSI Trade Association has introduced Ultra SCSI and the Ultimate Wide Ultra II SCSI Interface.

Improving the bandwidth certainly will permit higher bit rates to be implemented in servers although, the number of simultaneous users accessing the same material does not necessarily improve due to the transfer rate from the disk itself. To optimize the performance of the network connections, computer systems use protocols such as TCP/IP and operating systems to perform automatic scheduling of transactions. This is characterized by the theory of queuing and the effect of relative packet size on the response time.

This chart shows the effect of packet size on systems response time. C has been taken as one which equates to an exponential distribution of packet sizes. This chart shows first how system performance under high loading is reflecting longer response times and secondly how larger packets will also cause a given system to have longer response times. This trend is more probable when large amounts of data are required for each entity, such as a video frame. However, the important observation here is as system loading is by definition dynamic and user dependent response times will vary over a wide range up to a maximum set by the system time-outs when failure will occur. Though systems can be dimensioned with enough performance so that they never reach this point this is not always the most effective solution. In some applications such as video on demand, or video browsing, the architecture of the server is optimized to provide sufficient performance to stream video to multiple clients. In the case of browsing and video on demand applications the bit rate recorder on the server is typically in the order of 1.5 to 5.0 Mb/s. A server designed for browsing typically operates with a special server operating system designed to guarantee sufficient bandwidth to each client over standard link sites such as 100 base T or FDDI.

In the browsing and VOD application the underlying processes are not deterministic in terms of transactions times, the service to user is maintained by buffering data before displaying it as audio and video to the end user. Moreover, this can in turn have an effect on the apparent responsiveness of the system to user inputs. The issue of responsiveness highlights the second fundamental difference between a file server and a A/V server. As mentioned previously, network computer systems are based on messaging concepts which have as their main priority.

a). To ensure that all resources are shared between as many clients as required.

b). To ensure data is transferred and processed reliably.

The speed of response is purely a function of the power and loading the system at any given time, for audio and video applications this type of non-deterministic responsiveness is unacceptable. For the broadcast applications a more general solution to the full range of requirements is necessary. In particular, there is support for a wider range of resources and the real-time and non-real time aspect of the system.

The main points of this diagram are the provision of a fully connected switching (routing in Broadcast terms) system for audio, video, and control data. This provides sufficient bandwidth to ensure that all communications are real-time or faster. Though the switches have a cost associated with their use this should be compared to the cost (and limited performance capabilities) of using network switches for the same purpose.

The complete decoupling of real-time from non-real time aspects of the system, is achieved by replacing the native device driver in a conventional operating system with a media device control protocol. This allows the server and client applications to communicate with general purpose real-time device controllers without placing real-time constraints on the applications themselves.

The provision of task prioritization and resource scheduling functions in the server application to ensure the quality of service is acceptable to all users. Although inherently more complex than the simple file server defined by the VOD applications, the separate real-time interconnection strategy is not more expensive to implement.

The intended application of a video file server can possibly be as follows:

- For video on demand or browsing
- A low bit rate and a high output bandwidth.
- For forward and store of television commercials.
- A relatively low bit rate in conjunction with equal input and output bandwidths.
- Off-line editing where the bit rate is relatively low yet there is a requirement for a high input and output bandwidth to accommodate a large number of users, and for the downloading for a large amount material.
- On line editing in the broadcast environment operates with a bit rate in the order of 15 to 50 Mb/s. The input and output bandwidth must be relatively high in order to accommodate non-real time high speed transfers.
- On-line editing in the post environment requires the use of high bit rate signals an input and output bandwidth that is more or less equal. In the area of news, commercial and program transmissions, the bit rate is likely to be in the order of 15 to 30 Mb/s with a high input and output bandwidth.

In all cases, the functionality of the server must be defined in terms of whether or not there is a requirement for jog, shuttle, picture processing, non real-time load, timecode, real-time control, group of pictures processing or synchronization with other file servers.

While the focus of this paper has been on the hardware limitations, particularly related to network connections and disk transfer speeds, there is an equivalent number of concerns and issues related to the software controlling the file server.

With the limited time available it has not been possible to cover other important issues related to file servers. In particular, fault tolerance, whether or not audio and video files are separate or married, server-to-server transfer protocols, whether or not, it point to point, point to multi point, over LANs or WAN, single or distributed server architectures and their related dependencies and complexities. There is also the issue of the size of the file server and how the material will be purged from the file server, and in what order, when and by whom? Introduction to the file servers in the broadcast environment brings with it a set of new ground rules that must be adhered to otherwise the system will simply choke on the amount of material that has to be stored.

In 1995, the North American National Broadcasters Association, published a booklet on "A 1001 Questions to Ask Before Deciding on Buying a Video File Server." I suspect that more likely the number of questions to be asked, has now been expanded to 10,001, with the conclusion being "Caveat Emptor."

The author would like to acknowledge the assistance of Morgan David of Sony R&D Europe for much of the material presented in this article.

## Servers

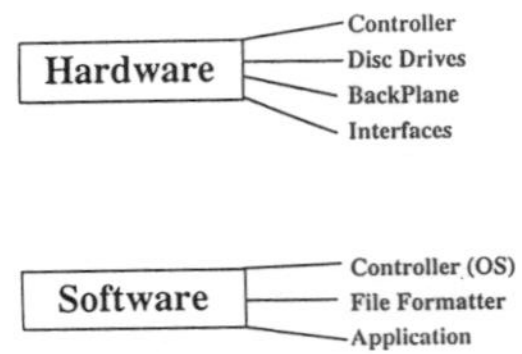


## Servers – Consuming Bandwidth

| | | |
|---|---|---|
| 4:2:2 10 Bits | ≃ | 200 Mb/s |
| JPEG | ≃ | 20 - 40 Mb/s |
| MPEG2 4:2:2P@ML | ≃ | 15 - 50 Mb/s |
| Compressed HDTV | ≃ | 150 - 600 Mb/s |

## Servers – "One Size Does Not Fit All"

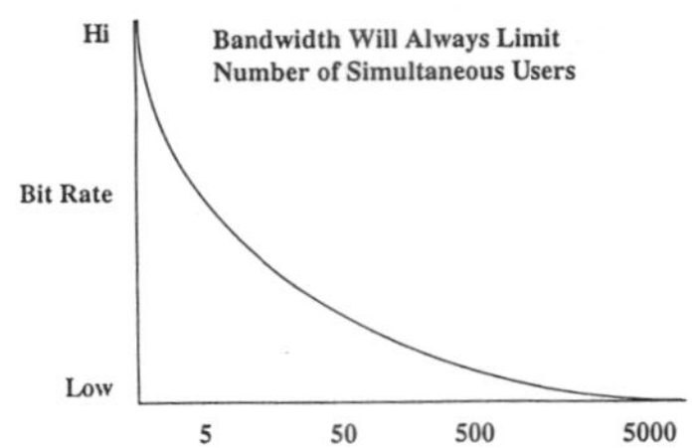


## Servers – Disc Array Performance

$$Nhd = \frac{Rch \times Nch}{Rb} \times \frac{Tc}{(Tc - ts \times Nch \times k)}$$

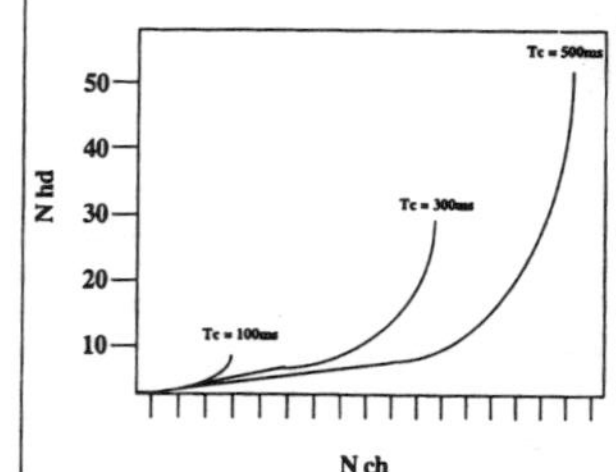


- Nhd = Number of Striped Hard Disc
- RcH = Channel Rate (Mb/s)
- Rb = Hard Disk Burst Rate (Mb/s)
- Tc = Total Cycle Time or System Response Time (ms)
- Nch = Number of Simultaneous Channels or Streams
- ts = Average Hard Disk Seek Time (ms)
- K = Average Number of Seeks Per Channel

## Servers – "Broadcast" Server

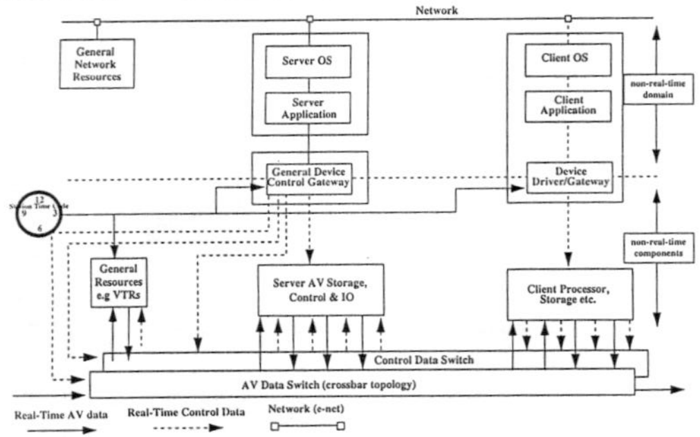


## Servers – System Interface Bandwidth

| SCSI | Bus Width | Mb/s | Max Devices |
|---|---|---|---|
| SCSI 1 | 8 bits | 5 | 8 |
| Fast | 8 bits | 10 | 8 |
| Fast/Wide | 16 bits | 20 | 16 |
| Ultra | 8 | 20 | 4/8* |
| Wide/Ultra | 16 | 40 | 4/16* |
| Ultra 2 | 8 | 40 | 8 |
| Wide/Ultra 2 | 16 | 80 | 16 |

* Single-Ended / Differential

## Servers – "V.O.D." Server

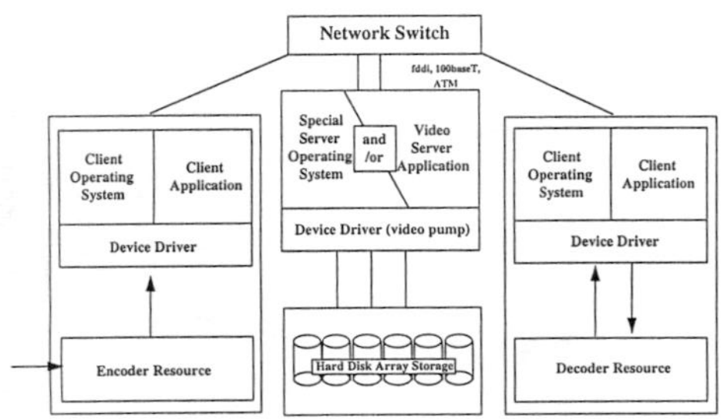


## Servers – Packet Size & Response Time

$$\text{Response Time} = T_{transaction} + \frac{T_{transaction} \times (1 + C) \times \text{System Utilization}}{2 \times (1 - \text{System Utilization})}$$

$T_{transaction}$ = time to transmit one packet

C = squared variance of statistical packet size

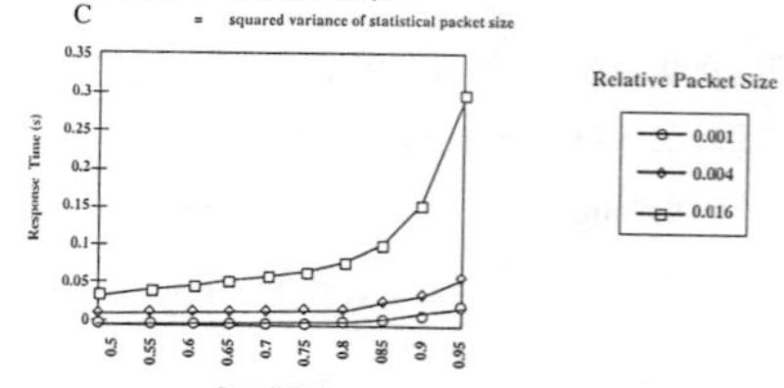


Relative Packet size = (Theoretical maximum throughput of the system / Packet size)

# Media Pool - Flexible Video Server Design for Television Broadcasting

Charlie Bernstein
Senior Product Manager, Storage and Retrieval Products
Philips Broadcast Television System Company
Salt Lake City, Utah, USA

**Abstract**

It appears to be an accepted fact that disk based video storage systems are viable solutions for broadcasters to store and play video in their facilities. One of the more accepted disk based video products in the broadcast facility is the video server. There are various approaches and technologies that manufacturers can use to build servers. All of these design decisions and trade-offs contribute to various video server architectures to address the task of delivering program content and commercials. The Media Pool video server offers a unique architecture and flexibility that leverages disk bandwidth and system modularity to provide a system capable of multiple full bandwidth CCIR 601 streams, system scalability, and standard industry interfaces, protocols to integrate the system into your facility.

A video server is made up of various sub-systems to allow the storage and retrieval of video and audio to and from hard disk in real time. The architecture of each of those sub-systems and the inter-relationship between them have a major impact on the performance of the system in terms of system responsiveness, bandwidth capabilities, and system scalability. In addition, disk array configurations, system timing, internal data transport, data buffering schemes, and disk access algorithms will affect system operation. Providing separate sub-systems that focus on specific tasks allows for increased system performance and more flexible operation.

The Media Pool video server from Philips Broadcast Television Systems Company includes a Storage Sub-System, Input/Output Sub-System, a Video Transfer Sub-System, and a Control Sub-System. The Storage Sub-System is responsible for reading and writing data to and from hard disk drives in real time, perform disk synchronization, and data buffering. The I/O Sub-System (I/O) provides all of the connections to a broadcast facility, similar to the connections found on a Video Tape Recorder. The Video Transfer Sub-System takes care of bandwidth management from one or more storage arrays to one or more I/Os. The Control Sub-System allows for system monitoring, database administration, simultaneous multi-user access, and the support for integrated applications.

Other variables affect the performance of the system. These include system compression techniques, data striping, system bandwidth, and reliability features.

All of these topics and more will be covered in this paper in detail to describe a very effective approach to streaming real-time video from disk based storage to multiple channels in a broadcast facility.

## Video Server Architecture

Most broadcast video servers today have many things in common in their architecture. All servers have major sub-systems that handle storage, video transfer, input/output, and control. Low end systems have taken a more off the shelf computer oriented approach. These systems contain many limitations due to the nature of the components that are used. In general, they were built for computing and not for addressing the problem of streaming real time video data from hard disks. Other vendors have taken a more dedicated hardware approach to solving the problem. Dedicated hardware offers specific solutions that are built to solve streaming video issues and provides greater flexibility and higher performance.

When evaluating the requirements of broadcasters and production houses, careful attention must be made to performance factors of the system. How will the system be used? What bandwidth requirements does the facilities have? How many channels will the facility need? All of these factors impact system architecture, design and performance.

The Philips BTS Media Pool video server combines both off the shelf components and dedicated hardware that makes it a very effective solution for broadcasters. It is a scalable multi-channel system that provides the highest quality video and audio in a facility. Each channel in a Media Pool system is capable of supporting a full bandwidth CCIR-601 uncompressed video stream along with up to two AES/EBU 48kHz pairs of audio. In addition, the server can compress the video stream to leverage economies of scale in storage and bandwidth. The Media Pool is a modular system that can be built in various configurations to meet specific broadcasters needs. The modular architecture offers increased flexibility in video channels, storage capacity, system bandwidth, integrated applications, simultaneous multi-user access, and control alternatives.

The server architecture uses multiple arrays of hard disk technology to provide high bandwidth and high storage capacity. Each array provides a full bandwidth stream of video. The system supports from one to eight storage arrays per system. The Media Pool also provides modular scalable I/O channels. A Media Pool system can be configured starting with a single I/O module up to twelve I/Os in a single system. A system purchased today with fewer than twelve channels can be upgraded with additional channels in the future. Additional drives and arrays can be added to the system to increase system storage. Additional workstations can be added to run Media Pool's integrated applications in a real multi-user environment.

## Media Pool Basics

The Media Pool is divided into the four basic subsystems. Figure 1 depicts the four major components of a Media Pool video server. They are:

**Storage Sub-System** - a shared pool of video, audio, and time code information accessible to all channels in the system. Multiple access of shared files is available with disk based storage systems creating new applications for video storage in the broadcast environment (i.e. multi-cast feeds, time shifting).

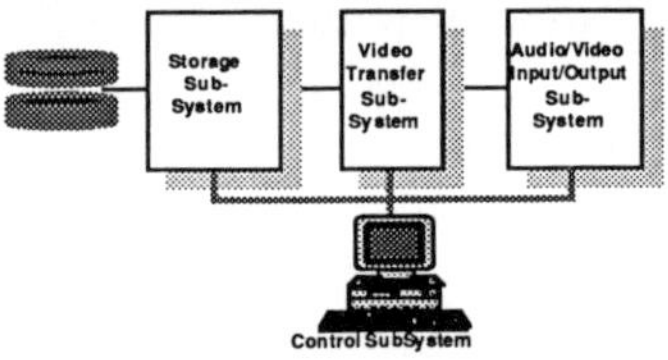


*Figure 1.*

**Input/Output Sub-System** - provides individual access to video files as well as control of streaming video data. It contains interfaces to the broadcast facility similar to a VTR.

**Video Transfer Sub-System** - provides high speed fibre channel switching between various storage arrays and I/O modules enabling the system to provide up to full bandwidth video on multiple channels simultaneously.

**Control Sub-System** - allows for system configuration, media file database tracking, support for integrated software applications, and multi-user capabilities.

# I. Storage Sub-System

Hard disk storage systems have evolved quickly over the past few years. The ability to connect multiple drives as a single addressable storage system has greatly increased the total capacity and sustainable bandwidth of storage via disk. These advances, along with cost reductions in hard disks and RAM, have made video server technology viable today.

Multiple drives connected together as a single storage unit is called an array. The Media Pool can be configured with one to eight storage arrays per system. Each array can contain from ten to forty two drives. This allows for Terabytes of on-line data storage which translates into hundreds of hours of compressed video on a single server.

**RAID Arrays**
There are various options to the interconnection of drives. Some vendors use proprietary algorithms and software to connect drives, others use standard based solutions. One of the most popular and widely used standards based approach to connect drives is the use of RAID - Redundant Array of Independent Drives (also known as Redundant Array of Inexpensive Drives). RAID is a computer industry standard for the connection of multiple drives.

*Table 1. RAID Levels Basic Description*

| RAID Levels | | | | | | |
|---|---|---|---|---|---|---|
| **RAID LEVEL** | **Short Reads** | **Long Reads** | **Short Writes** | **Long Writes** | **Redundancy** | **Notes** |
| LEVEL 0 | Normal | Normal | Normal | Normal | NONE | No protection from any drive failures |
| LEVEL 1 | Faster | Faster | Slower | Slower | 100% | Very expensive due to doubled disk cost |
| LEVEL 3 | Normal | Normal | Slower | Slightly Slower | Excellent | Cost slightly more than no redundancy. Separate drive used for redundancy |
| LEVEL 4 | Normal | Normal | Slower | Slightly Slower | Excellent | Similar to level 3 with block striping instead of byte |
| LEVEL 5 | Normal | Faster* | Slower | Slower | Excellent | Striping plus data protection is spread among all drives |

** Faster when no disk errors occur.*

RAID offers various levels of data bandwidth and data protection. RAID level 0 provides for multiple read and writes simultaneously, as all data is spread to all disks. Unfortunately, if any single drive in the system fails, all data on the system is permanently lost. Some manufacturers use RAID 0 in their systems today, but this is not appropriate for real-time on-air operations. RAID level 1 provides the highest protection, but at a great cost. RAID level 1 mirrors all data of all drives. Since it requires many disks to store a meaningful amount of video, RAID level 1 becomes prohibitively expensive for video server applications.

Along with RAID Level 0, RAID Level 3 and RAID level 5 are also used by server manufacturers today. Both offer economical storage and protection for video data. RAID level 5 provides a higher level of security at the cost of system bandwidth. RAID 5 spreads redundancy data over all drives. If a single drive fails the system will continue to run. Unfortunately, since all data is spread out, it takes longer to access data thus loosing valuable bandwidth for video. RAID level 3 offers better bandwidth capabilities. RAID level 3 can loose a drive and continue operation without bandwidth loss. This ensures that video is uninterrupted.

The Media Pool uses RAID level 3 which provides support for parity protection of data. It uses an additional hard disk to store parity information for the disk array. RAID 3 can support a single disk failure with no data loss and provide high data bandwidth even after a disk has failed.

**Background Rebuilds**

In addition to RAID protection, video servers can also offer automated recovery from failed drives. Background rebuilding of a failed drive ensures that the system will maintain a high level of reliability. Since the server must remain on air to generate income for a broadcaster, it is not practical for a server to be taken off-line to replace a disk. The Media Pool video server has developed system software that provides for the rebuilding of failed disk drives to occur in the background. Since each disk in the server can be removed independently from any other, it is not required to take the server off-line, or unplug any other drives when one fails. The background rebuild is integrated into the system and will not interrupt the recording or playback of video from the server, thus increasing system reliability.

**Disk Bandwidth**

All disk drives used today are SCSI based drives. SCSI, which stands for Simple Computer System Interface, is a standard for the connection of data devices to personal computers. A single disk drive today can sustain about 3MB- 5MB per second. A SCSI bus has a maximum data rate per bus of 20 Megabytes (MB) per second. A full 10 bit digital serial component video signal with audio and timecode takes 270 Megabits per second or 33.75MB/sec.

It takes multiple SCSI hard disks on a SCSI bus to provide up to 20MB/sec. As you can see, even multiple drives on a single bus cannot sustain the bandwidth required for full bandwidth video. There are two approaches manufacturers have taken to solve this problem. First, compression. Using compression, the 34MB/sec video data can be reduced to fit into the less than 20MB/sec data space of the SCSI bus. Second, some manufacturers have used multiple SCSI buses to provide the bandwidth required.

The Media Pool System has taken the latter approach. In fact, the Media Pool uses multiple SCSI buses and multiple arrays to provide and sustain high video bandwidth to all ports. The server supports up to 42 nine gigabyte drives per array. With support for multiple arrays, the Media Pool system is capable of providing multiple full bandwidth streams on all channels simultaneously. Support for full bandwidth and compressed streams allows a user the flexibility to select the video quality they require.

**Compression**

All video servers use some type of compression to provide the required bandwidth on output or provide more economical use of disk storage space. Lower end systems offer a single fixed compression level or a selection of a few fixed compression levels. Offering a single compression level is very easy for the manufacturer. The system will always use the same amount of disk space per second, and have a fixed disk bandwidth requirement on each channel. This may make the system easier to build, but does not provide as much flexibility to the user. Low end variable compression schemes allow for a range of compression usually starting at a high compression ratio and going higher (e.g. MPEG-2 has a maximum data rate of 15 Mbits/sec.).

There are three compression standards being used for server development today: Motion JPEG, MPEG-2 MP/ML, and the emerging MPEG 4:2:2 standard. They are described below.

*Table 2. Compression Comparison Chart*

| Feature | MPEG-2 ML@MP | MPEG 4:2:2 | Motion JPEG |
|---|---|---|---|
| Bandwidth | 1.2Mbps - 15Mbps | up to 50Mbps | 3.5Mbps - Full Bandwidth |
| Trim Video | No | Yes | Yes |
| Compression Type | Discrete Cosine Transform | Discrete Cosine Transform | Discrete Cosine Transform |
| MPEG Encoders* | Yes | Yes | Yes |
| Spacial Compression | Yes | Yes | Yes |
| Temporal Compression | Yes | Yes or No | No |
| Video Quality | Lowest | Higher | Highest |
| Storage Capacity | Low | Higher | Highest |
| Encoder Cost | High | Highest | Low |

** This signal can be decoded and passed through an MPEG encoder for uplinks to satellite.*

There are two ways compression is used to compress a video signal: spacial compression and temporal compression. Spacial compression is used to compress each individual frame. All three compression standards use Discrete Cosine Transform for spacial compression. Temporal compression is used to compress from one frame to another to further reduce the image. Temporal compression throws away like material in some consecutive frames. For example, if the sky is blue in frame 1 and the sky is blue in frame 2, then using temporal compression, only the pixels in the sky that have changed are stored.

**MPEG-2 MP@ML**
MPEG compression uses spacial and temporal compression to reduce storage requirements. Spacial compression is accomplished with DCT as mentioned above. Temporal compression is accomplished using three types of frames: I frames, P frames, and B frames. I frame are index frames and are similar to frames stored in Motion JPEG. They contain the entire frame (compressed). P and B frames use temporal compression and motion estimation to predict what the next frame will be.

Although MPEG requires less space, there are some limitations it creates. First, the cost of an MPEG encoder today is greater than that of a motion JPEG encoder. Even though there is cost savings in disk space, additional cost is added to the encoder. The second issue is video quality. In MPEG, the higher the compression ratio, the farther the distance between I frames. If a scene change occurs between I frames, the quality of the image will degrade until the next I frame appears. This is because you do not have all the information for the whole frame when the scene changes until the next I frame is played. The third issue effects cutting material in MPEG. Since you may not have all the information at the edit point in the video (not on I frame boundary), it takes more processing and intelligence for a video server to cut two streams together. It is possible to edit two MPEG transport streams together on frame boundaries on output, but additional processing and bandwidth is required to read the previous I frame and all the frames between it and the current frame. This is not a simple feat for some video servers where bandwidth is a premium. The maximum data rate of MPEG-2 ML@MP is 15Mbps.

**MPEG 4:2:2**
MPEG 4:2:2 is similar to MPEG-2 ML@MP in that is supports an MPEG transport stream and uses I, B, and P frames. MPEG 4:2:2 differs in that it allows for higher bit rates and supports an I frame only mode (no temporal compression), where media can be cut on frame boundaries.

**Motion JPEG**
Motion JPEG supports full variable compression. Motion JPEG, which compresses video on a frame by frame basis, allows the system to support limited editing capabilities, not currently supported with MPEG-2 MP@ML compression. Video recorded onto the server can now be trimmed and manipulated on a frame basis without concern for loss of video quality or the requirement of additional bandwidth or processing.

The Media Pool video server uses Motion JPEG compression and supports variable compression from full bandwidth video up to 50:1 compression selectable by the user on a frame by frame basis. It uses a separate mezzanine board to support compression requirements of the system. The compression mezzanine card can be replaced in the future to support other compression algorithms, like the emerging MPEG-4:2:2 standard being established.

**Motion JPEG and MPEG Compatibility**
Since all of these compression algorithms use DCT for spacial compression of each image, interchanging between MPEG and JPEG is not a concern. A Motion JPEG server can be used to feed an MPEG encoder for uplinks to satellites without concern for artifacts. The two compression algorithms are compatible.

Today, Motion JPEG offers the most flexibility for video server users. MPEG based solutions are viable for video servers offering higher compression with some limitations.

**Scalability**
The key to the Media Pool's Storage Sub-System is its scalability. Multiple drives and multiple arrays allow for storage and bandwidth management. Using compression, storage capacity can be increased and bandwidth shared. Flexible storage capacity and flexible system bandwidth are the result of the scalable architecture of the Storage Sub-System.

## II. Input/Output Sub-System

There are a range of choices developers can make to interface to a server. Using an off the shelf architecture, video server manufacturers require PC based video cards. These cards are limited in physical space and data bandwidth due to the limitations of PC industry standards and the low data rates the buses support (ISA about 8 MB per second). Higher end systems have developed system specific I/O Sub-Systems that perform the task of playing and recording video into the server. The Media Pool video server has dedicated hardware developed for this task. The server's I/O Sub-System provides Serial Digital Component video output on all channels. Since all video information is stored in the server digitally, and the industry is migrating to the digital domain, it makes sense to provide a digital signal to a broadcast facility from a server. It ensures the best quality video & audio will be provided from the server, and it provides support for the digital future.

The Media Pool I/O, known as the VR-7000, contains all control and inputs, outputs required for a broadcast facility. The VR-7000 supports CCIR 601 Serial Digital Video input and output. There are two selectable video inputs and a single video output with dual connections for support of E-E mode operations during recording. The VR-7000 contains two AES/EBU (48kHz 24 bit) digital audio stereo pair inputs and outputs per I/O. The I/O supports LTC time code, and General Purpose Inputs and Outputs for interfacing to a Master Control Switcher or other trigger devices. The VR-7000 contains a Fast Wide SCSI interface for data transfer to storage libraries. The board also supports RS-422 ports for control via the Beta Control Protocol and the Video Disk Control Protocol for automation system support. LAN based control is also provided.

Each I/O houses a separate Audio Mezzanine and Compression Mezzanine. Either board can be replaced to support other audio or compression standards. A Motion JPEG based I/O, could be converted to an MPEG based output with a board swap. The Media Pool can support from one to twelve I/O Sub-Systems, or Channels, in a single server.

The modular architecture of the I/O Sub-System allows a system installed today to be upgraded in the future with additional channels or new compression algorithms. This provides customers with flexibility and investment protection not offered in other systems.

## III. Video Transfer Sub-System

The Video Transfer Sub-System can take on various forms. At the low end, standard PC based buses can be used to distribute video signals to multiple I/O ports. At the high end, high speed links can be switched to create multiple channels of I/O. The use of separate high speed links to transfer data from storage arrays to the I/O modules is preferred. It provides the system with the horsepower needed to serve high bandwidth applications or can be used to cut the bandwidth into smaller units for distribution to many I/Os.

In the Media Pool, this sub-system is comprised of a gigabit matrix switch, called the Data Transport Commutator. Signals between the Array Sub-System and I/O Sub-System are switched very rapidly over a matrix fibre channel switch to allow the system to provide up to full bandwidth digital serial component video for each I/O simultaneously. The timing of the switch is regulated by system software in the I/O Subsystem and the Control Subsystem, allowing for flexible bandwidth allocation and support for multiple data formats. The ability to provide this bandwidth allows the Media Pool various architectural options. These include full bandwidth output for high quality video applications, system modularity, bandwidth allocation management, and variable compression.

**Data Striping**

In order to gain the benefits of multiple disk drives and multiple arrays to provide maximum bandwidth to all I/Os in the system, data striping is used. Striping of data is performed by the data transport commutator and array electronics and allows video from a single file to be placed on all disks of the system (Figure 2.). This is an important feature of the server, as it allows each I/O to be connected to a different array at any time and still get simultaneous access to the file it is playing.

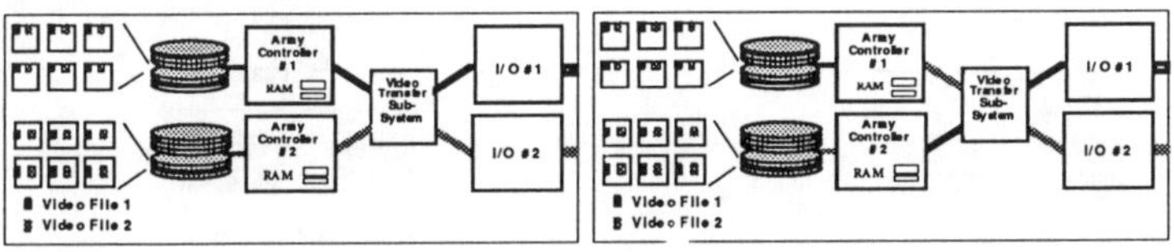


2a 2b

*Figure 2. Media Pool Data Striping*

In Figure 2a, I/O 1 is reading Video File 1 from the drives in array 1 while I/O 2 is reading Video file 2 from Array 2. In Figure 2b, the Video Transfer Sub-system switches the connection and I/O 1 reads the next block of Video File 1 from Array 2 and I/O 2 reads the next block of Video File 2 from Array 1. All video is read into RAM buffer so that when the I/O is ready to get video from the array, the video is ready to be transferred. Figure 3 depicts the connections between I/O subsystems and Array subsystems and the switching concept.

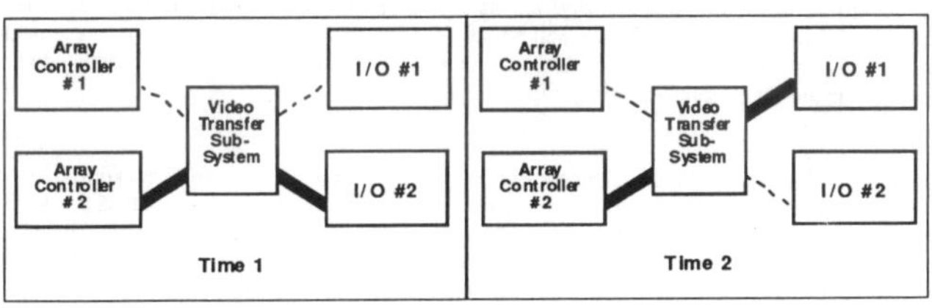


*Figure 3. Media Pool Connection Diagram*

**Simultaneous Access of Media Files**

The Media Pool's RAM buffer allows for simultaneous access of video from the same file at the same time. Blocks can be read into the buffer separately in the background, and once the buffer is full, you have multiple virtual copies of the file. By adding more arrays and more I/Os and allow switching to occur very rapidly (gigabit rates), and you can see that each I/O can get access to any file from any and all arrays simultaneously.

**Full Bandwidth Video and Bandwidth Allocation**
The Media Pool arrays are capable of providing full bandwidth digital serial component video with 2 AES/EBU stereo pairs of audio, LTC time code track, and full preservation of the vertical interval on each I/O. This bandwidth can be broken up into smaller segments to allow for increased system modularity. By providing bandwidth allocation management software, and variable compression, the storage system can now be leveraged by multiple I/O channels.

For example, if a user needs two full bandwidth channels, the Media Pool server can be configured as shown in Figure 3a below. The two arrays can support two full bandwidth channels as configured. This is referred to as a symmetrical system. In Figure 3b, you can see that the system can also be configured with more I/Os than arrays; known as an asymmetrical configuration. In this case, the total bandwidth of the combined arrays is divided among the four channels. The full bandwidth signal is compressed (in this case 2:1) and striped across both arrays. The Data Transport Commutator provides the appropriate bandwidth allocation and switching for all four channels.

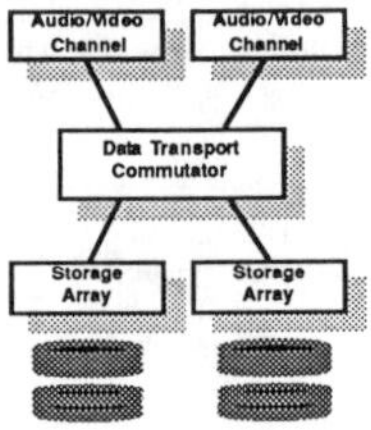

3a. Symmetrical System

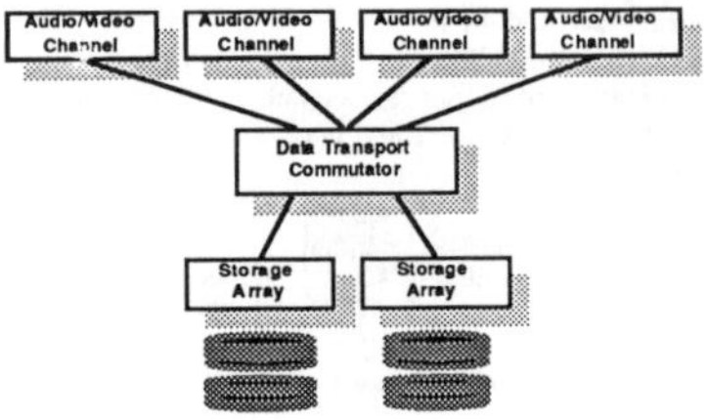

3b. Asymmetrical System

*Figure 4: Media Pool Configuration and Bandwidth Management*

The Media Pool system is very modular and can be configured in many combinations of channels and arrays. This modular approach allows broadcasters to build a system that meets their needs and also allow for expansion of the system in the future.

**Media Pool Configurations**
The Media Pool is capable of seventy four different configurations (up to twelve channels and eight arrays per system). Almost any combination of one to eight arrays can be combined with one to twelve channels with some minor limitations. Additional configurations will be added in the future. Each array can be connected to up to four I/O modules in a system. This is referred to as a four to one fan out. This allows a facility to leverage a few storage arrays with multiple channels when compression is used.

**MPS Series Media Pool Systems**
Although the Media Pool video server can be configured in any of seventy four configurations, there are a smaller number of configurations that most facilities require today. As a result, Philips has created the MPS Series Media Pool Systems. Each Model in the MPS series is pre-configured and includes all I/Os, arrays, drives, cables, and RAM buffer a customer needs to integrate a video server into their facility. There are ten MPS series families and twenty models available. The table below depicts the configurations available in the MPS series.

*Table 3. MPS Series Media Pool Configurations*

| Series | Model #s | Channels* | Arrays* | Workstations | Drives | Min Storage | Storage @ 8:1 |
|---|---|---|---|---|---|---|---|
| MPS-2100 | 2110, 2112 | 2 | 1 | 1 | 10 - 42 | 57 Mins | 28 Hrs |
| MPS-3100 | 3110, 3112 | 3 | 1 | 2 | 10 - 42 | 57 Mins | 28 Hrs |
| MPS-4100 | 4110, 4112 | 4 | 1 | 2 | 10 - 42 | 57 Mins | 28 Hrs |
| MPS-4200 | 4220, 4224 | 4 | 2 | 2 | 20 - 84† | 114 Mins | 56 Hrs† |
| MPS-5200 | 5220. 5224 | 5 | 2 | 3 | 20 - 84† | 114 Mins | 56 Hrs† |
| MPS-6200 | 6220, 6224 | 6 | 2 | 3 | 20 - 84† | 114 Mins | 56 Hrs† |
| MPS-6300 | 6330, 6336 | 6 | 3 | 3 | 30 - 126 | 172 Mins | 84 Hrs |
| MPS-7300 | 7330, 7336 | 7 | 3 | 4 | 30 - 126 | 172 Mins | 84 Hrs |
| MPS-8300 | 8330, 8336 | 8 | 3 | 4 | 30 - 126 | 172 Mins | 84 Hrs |
| MPS-8400 | 8440,8448 | 8 | 4 | 4 | 40 - 168 | 229 Mins | 112 Hrs |

* Note: Larger Media Pool systems are available.
† Note: Some drive configurations may not be supported by all systems

## IV. Control Sub-System

The Control Sub-System in the Media Pool is comprised of one or more UNIX based workstations running X Windows. UNIX was chosen because it is one of the most reliable operating systems available today. The workstation was chosen so that the controller would have enough horse power to drive multiple channels concurrently. The Media Pool system controller is responsible for initiating system booting, system configurations, compression level setting, system monitoring, media file database administration, and running the server's integrated applications. The System Controller communicates to the other sub-systems in the server via an internal communications network. The System Controller contains software applications for system administration, commercial insertion, and Record/Playout. Additional workstations can be added to allow for simultaneous Multi-User access.

**Multi-User Capabilities**

The Media Pool supports multiple workstations in a single system. Each workstation can run one or more applications or protocols allowing multiple users to operate and use the Media Pool system simultaneously. This is a very important distinction, as the operations within a broadcast facility, though fairly basic, are very repetitive and time consuming. By allowing for multiple simultaneous access to each channel of the system, broadcasters can increase operational efficiencies and reduce operational costs. Now there is lower idle time as conflict for resources is reduced.

**Media Pool Integrated Applications**

There are currently four integrated applications, and three integrated protocols available for the server. The applications provide integrated functionality that takes advantage of tightly coupled control and high end features. The protocols provide the server with an open system approach, so the system can be integrated into the facility with other devices and also to allow for custom application development by broadcasters and other vendors. The four applications are SPLASH, System Administration Application, Stream, VTR Emulation Application, DiskCart Cart Emulation Application, and DiskCache Broadcast Facility Application. The protocols supported are BVW-75 serial control protocol, Video Disk Communications Protocol, and PoolNet native Media Pool Protocol.

**SPLASH**

The main interface to system administration and system configuration is a software program called SPLASH (Software Package for Logical Administration of System Hardware). SPLASH allows a systems administrator to monitor system activity, initialize and boot the system, and configure the system and its integrated applications.

SPLASH allows a user to create Media Pool "Instance" files. An instance file in the Media Pool server is a configuration file for a specific application or protocol and can be assigned to a specific operator. Multiple configuration files or instances can be created for each I/O, but of course only one instance can be run per I/O at a time. For example, if a broadcaster has a four channel Media Pool with two arrays, two of the channels can be configured as instances for dubbing spots and another two for commercial spot insertion. The instance scheme we have described allows for very flexible configuration management and usage of the pool.

**STREAM Record - Playback Software Application**
The STREAM record/playback application emulates the transport functions of a video tape recorder. Stream runs on the native Media Pool workstation and provides the ability to record, playback, stop, pause, cue, shuttle, set variable compression, and create spot files on a Media Pool system. E-E mode is supported as well as external GPI triggers. Stream supports the ability of clicking in the time-line to go to specific frames in a video file, and also supports setting cue points for easy navigation though the media file or spot. Stream has the ability to remotely control a tape machine for easy loading of material.

**DiskCart Cart Emulation Software Application**
The DiskCart Spot Playback application provides a complete integrated cart emulation application for the video server. DiskCart runs on a native Media Pool workstation and provides the capability to create or import playlists, control event playout and monitor the system.

DiskCart can import a playlist from external traffic systems or create one in the playlist editor. The editor supports drag and drop capabilities to add or delete events. The application supports multiple event types including Absolute Timed events, Externally Triggered Events, or Follow Events. External events can be controlled via a General Purpose Interface from Master Control or an automation system. DiskCart supports real -time on air playlist editing, and the ability to nest playlists, insert break lines, comment lines, or delete events. All events are moved to the as played log for reconciliation later.

**DiskCache Broadcast Facility Application**
The DiskCache broadcast facility application offers seamless integration of the Media Pool video server into an existing broadcast facility. DiskCache provides the Media Pool with cart machine functionality along with integrated control of other devices. DiskCache offers automatic control of dubbing material into the Media Pool server from multiple devices and can control the Media Pool and other devices for recording and playback for air. DiskCache can also control routers and switchers or master control.

**External Protocol Support**
The Media Pool also supports a number of control protocols for external control of the system. BetaCP is a RS-422 Beta protocol emulation. Using BetaCP, a channel of Media Pool can be controlled like a VTR. Video Disk Communications Protocol (VDCP) is a protocol developed for interfacing to Automation system. Broadcast facilities can control a Media Pool via the Louth or Alamar automation systems by using the VDCP protocol. Finally, PoolNet is the native control protocol of the Media Pool. PoolNet can be used for custom applications and integration of third party devices. PoolNet has been used by Philips for development of integrated applications. DiskCache uses PoolNet to control the Media Pool.

**Time Delay**
The Media Pool is very capable of supporting Time Delay or Time Shifting applications. Currently using an automation system, the Media Pool can record satellite feeds into a broadcast facility, via automation, can be scheduled for playback at a later time. After the video has played the automation system can delete the files from the pool. In the future, additional applications and functionality will allow the creation of third party applications and integrated applications to allow for new time delay features, such as destructive playout.

**Archiving Solution**
Using the Media Pool's I/O Sub-System SCSI data port, new applications have been developed to connect medium and long term storage devices to the server. Otherwise known as near-line storage, files can be moved to an archive device from the server and brought back when needed. Video is transferred as compressed data which offers a number of advantages. First, since the data is compressed going out and coming back into the server, there is zero data loss (also known as generation loss). Also, when data is compressed, it is possible to transfer

information at greater than real-time speeds. Since the Media Pool can begin playing while a file is still being recorded onto the pool, or transferred from archive, it is possible to start playing a file stored on the archive before it is completely transferred. This allows for flexible on air operation, when a file is needed for a last minute schedule change.

**Summary**

The Media Pool video server architecture uses independent sub-systems, variable compression, and integrated applications to provide a flexible solution for storing and serving professional video. The system offers flexible configurations, system scalability, and support for multiple full bandwidth video streams. A Media Pool system configured today can be upgraded in the future with additional storage, bandwidth, channels, and users.

Todd Roth

VP of Research and Development
ASC Audio Video Corporation

ABSTRACT

Video Servers: "Shared Storage" for Cost Effective Real-time Access

The architecture used in defining a video server has been traditionally based upon the hierarchical storage model of a computer network. This model was typically specified as independent workstations with local storage connected via a high performance network to a more powerful server configured with a larger bank of remote storage. While supporting a large number of workstations or channels, this approach suffered the drawback of high costs and limited real-time availability to media. The channels are only able to offer real-time access to media on local storage (availability to media on the remote storage being limited by availability of the network), while incurring the cost of the server computer as well as the additional overhead of having material stored in multiple locations.

The shared storage approach to building a video server is a result of a different way of looking at bandwidth. This approach starts by defining the bandwidth of a single drive to be the maximum video channel data rate, and the bandwidth to the storage interface to determine the amount of channels. The shared storage video disk recorder model typically involves a high performance, real time storage interface such as Small Computer System Interface (SCSI) and a lower performance inter-channel synchronization /communication mechanism. The model for this is the multi-channel video disk recorder where each channel acts as an independent device with dedicated storage bandwidth. By virtualizing to storage, a well designed system allows the total number of channels to be equal to the storage bandwidth divided by the maximum channel bandwidth.

With the advent of combined, advanced storage platforms such as SSA and Fibre Channel (FC), integrating support for multiple initiators (VDR channels) and targets (storage devices), the topology for an advanced multi-channel "centralized media / distributed access" video server can be realized. FC with the advantage of its diverse supported topologies, will lead to a radical change in the modeling of future video distribution systems. Fibre channel both increases network bandwidth to 100 MB/sec ( 200 in the future) and supports both fabric, point-to-point, and arbitrated loop interconnections. The immediate benefit is a resulting five- fold increase in storage bandwidth by moving from SCSI (fast/wide) to fiber channel arbitrated loop (FC-AL) and the corresponding increase in channel capacity. A 30 channel VDR in itself is a major breakthrough in product capability, while the increase in supported devices to 127 alleviates the total storage restriction. This combined with a clever implementation of RAID (intrinsically supported under FC-AL) eliminates the need for an external RAID controller.

The evolution of disk drives from being simple devices on an independent "storage-only" bus, to being self sufficient targets on an advanced multi-purpose network marks the start of a new paradigm in the design of distributed computing systems. Understanding and incorporating this new design approach into multi-channel VDR systems will pave the way toward the goal of an integrated digital broadcast environment.

1.0 INTRODUCTION

1.1 Bandwidth Requirements

The relatively high-bandwidth requirements of digital video compared to the lower bandwidths of digital computer networks (see fig. 1.1) has confined separate video signals to separate wires, whereas on the computer side multiple users can share resources over a single network.

Figure 1.1

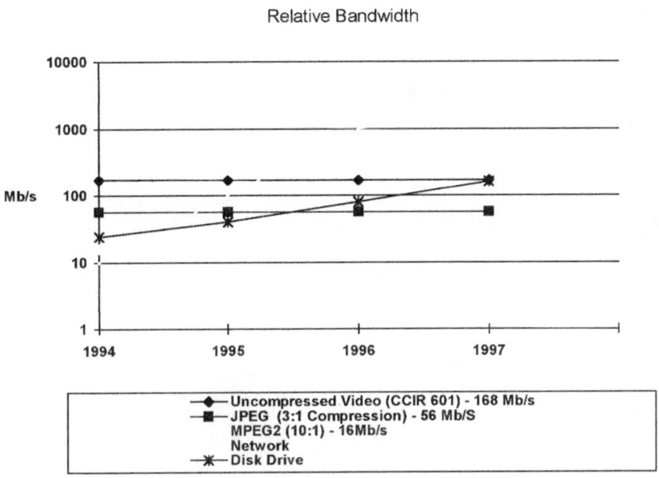


As figure 1.1 shows the bandwidth available over high-performance computer network and computer disk drives have been growing rapidly, while the bandwidth of video for different compression technologies has remained constant. A video server designed to simply leverage performance off improvements in computer industry has a built-in path for growth.

1.2 Hierarchical Storage (Server - Workstation)

Early development (when disk drives roughly equaled the performance of video streams) of video served systems had to concentrate on getting around the bandwidth restrictions. Video servers architectures originally were based on hierarchical storage techniques and centralized network topographies. This potentially caused substantial delays in the availability of material while the server had to copy video data from central to local storage for real time playback. This process limits the availability of the video material to the time the available network capacity takes to move the data to local storage (see fig. 1.2). The advantage these systems offered was higher and more flexible channel capacities. The disadvantages included:

- Increasing latency as the number of channels are increased .
- System bandwidth being the lesser of server, storage, and network bandwidth.
- High vulnerability to component failure, many single points of failure.
- Higher system cost, money wasted on local storage.

Figure 1.2 - Hierarchical Storage Model

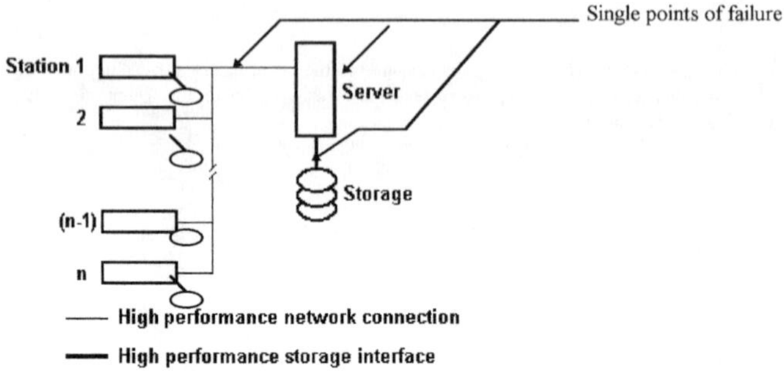


The inherent lack of real-time responsiveness makes integrating hierarchical storage model video servers difficult to near impossible in the time-critical broadcast environments.

1.3 Shared Storage (Peer - Peer)

The multi-channel video disk recorder (VDR), fig. 1.3, typically involves a high performance (real time) storage interface such as Small Computer System Interface (SCSI) and a lower performance inter-channel synchronization / communication mechanism to supervise the management of the "shared storage". A well designed system allows the total number of channels to be equal to the storage bandwidth divided by the channel bandwidth. In broadcast applications multi-channel VDR usually has fewer than 6 channels, but offers real-time access to any material since the storage is, in a sense, local to every channel. This system has intrinsically lower cost and lower complexity since no server platform nor multiplicity of material is required. The major drawback being a sacrifice in the number of potential channels due to storage bandwidth as well as the limitation of the amount of supported devices to 8 or 16. The latter restriction can be mitigated by adding external hardware such as RAID controllers and LUN expanders.

Figure 1.3 - Shared Storage Model

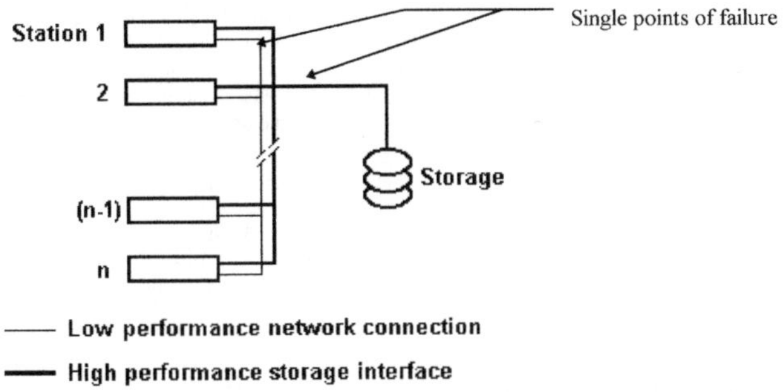


In broadcast applications, multi-channel video disk recorders usually have fewer than 6 channels, but offer the real-time responsiveness the hierarchical servers lack.

## 2.0 THESIS: "Virtualizing" the Server

As storage systems become more advanced the multi-channel VDR will obsolete the hierarchical server. In order to keep up with the growing storage bandwidth the "server" will need to increase in performance at twice the rate of the storage system or become the bottleneck of the system. Fibre channel by providing a 1Gb/sec interface and allowing network interconnection will allow the multi-channel VDR to grow into a loosely coupled multiple processor environment that finally "virtualizes" the server and relegates hierarchical storage to the single role of interfacing to archival systems.

## 2.1 A Fibre Channel Based Solution

Fibre channel supports multiple simultaneous topographies as well as interconnection and communication protocols. Point-to-point, arbitrated loop (AL) and fabric are the names that describe the topographies in order of ascending sophistication. As shown in fig. 2.1, the FC-AL multi-channel VDR supports a fault tolerant ring of independent channels.

Figure 2.1 Fibre Channel Multi Channel VDR

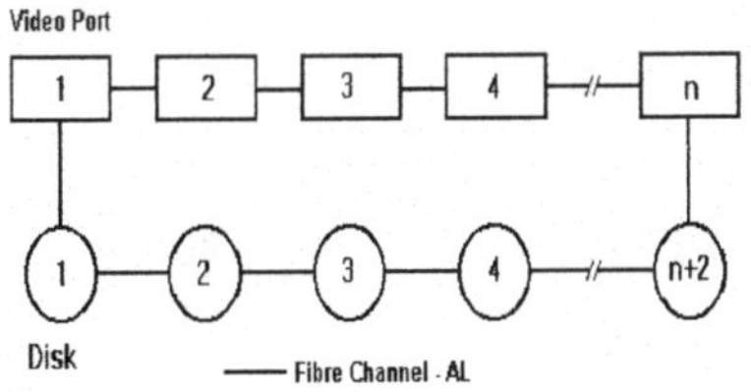


The fiber channel system provides 1 Gb/s of "system-wide" bandwidth connecting up to 127 devices. Designed to be used as a foundation for RAID based fault tolerance, an arbitrated-loop can be used to configure a group of disks into a large and flexible array.

2.2 Loosely Coupled Multiple Processors For Redundancy

By taking advantage of fibre channel's ability to detect the loss of a resource and reconfigure itself to continue to function, the storage management functionality can be distributed among the VDR channels. If the channel changing the media (i.e. via recording) were to fail drastically, the fibre AL would shunt out the failed resource and report its loss. Having been continually receiving the location data for the data that has been recorded, the next VDR in the loop would assume the responsibility of insuring the integrity of the data on the disk.

2.3 Raid In, Extra Hardware Out

By taking advantage of the performance of the fibre channel connection, RAID can be implemented by solely using the distributed resources on the loop. First data is broken down into N equal chunks, where N equals the number of data drives dedicated to the logical stripe. As the data passes through memory, a parity chunk is created and appended to the end of the stripe as shown below:

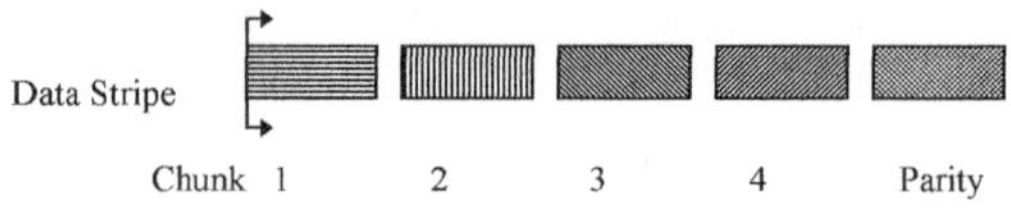


Since multiple video channels are contending for the same set of storage, synchronization must be maintained to avoid conflicts. Conflicts can occur if multiple channels try to access the same drive concurrently (access bandwidth would be limited to the bandwidth of the individual drive). However since the channels are synchronized via a timing protocol running on the same FC loop, this situation can be prevented via a mechanism we designed for our Virtual Recorder (VR) called "Offset Data Striping"(see fir. 2.3).

Figure 2.3 Offset Data Striping

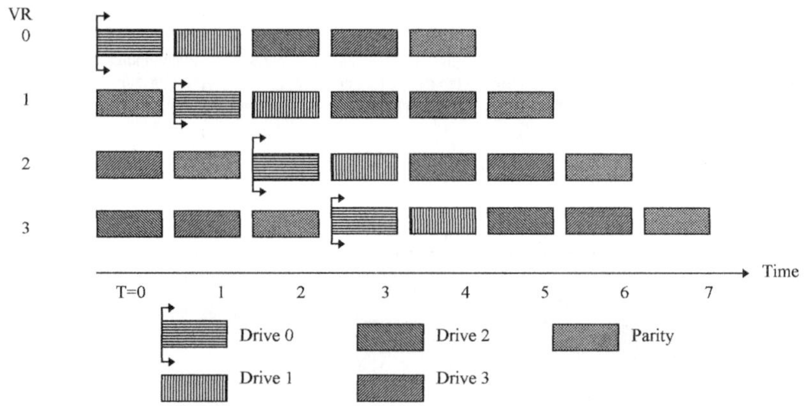


During a given time slice T=0 VR 0 is starting to write its data at drive 0, VR 1 is reading its parity data, VR 2 is writing its stripe on drive 3, and VR 3 is starting its reading on drive 2. This process avoids bottlenecks at the drive level.

## 3.0 FACTS AND SPECULATIONS - FIBRE CHANNEL AND VIDEO

As described earlier, fibre channel - AL is the most versatile high - performance storage interface to be developed. As a replacement for SCSI, FC-AL is the best solution available. However the other fiber channel topographies and protocols should not be overlooked.

### 3.1 Fibre Fabrics

The second topography, called a fabric, is a point-to-point switching interconnection, similar to a telephone company switch. The amount of ports connected to a fabric is limited to 24 bit addressing (over 16 million); loops and fabrics may be connected together to form an expandable distributed network with a nearly infinite amount of virtual interconnections.

### 3.2 Fiber Channel Layers

Along with these versatile topographies, fibre channel also uses a hierarchical layer approach toward different levels of interconnection. These layers are called services and range from FC-0, the physical interconnection which can be copper or optical to FC-4, the upper level protocol layer where different software command sets can be mapped.

It is both the lowest (FC-0) and uppermost layers (FC-4) that have the greatest implications upon using fibre channel as the foundation for a shared storage video server.

FC-0 allows for a combination of both optical and copper interconnections to be combined within a facility. This allows for the use of low cost copper connections where distances of up to 25 meters are adequate. The cabling is simply twinax using a low noise / capacitance DB 9 connector. This interconnection method supports the full bandwidth of fibre channel and is ideal for the short distance requirements of environmentally controlled machine and computer rooms.

Longer distances (up to 10KM) can be achieved using single mode fiber and longwave laser physical interconnection. Networks using these connections can be spread out over several nearby buildings or production vehicles, again with no sacrifice in bandwidth.

FC-4 standards allows for both network and channel (typically storage) protocols to coexist and be concurrently transmitted over the same physical interface. Among the channel protocols supported are:

- Small Computer System Interface (SCSI)
- Intelligent Peripheral Interface (IPI)
- High Performance Parallel Interface HIPPI

While on the network side the supported protocols are:
- Internet Protocol (IP)
- ATM Adaptation Layer (AAL5)
- Link Encapsulation (FC-LE)
- IEEE 802.2

## 4.0 ANSWERS AND MORE QUESTIONS

Shared storage video server systems benefit directly from advances in storage technology. Fibre channel advances on the horizon include doubling the bandwidth to 2Gb/sec as well as the expansion of the supported topologies and addition of more layer options. By relying on loosely coupled multiple processors, and RAID data protection the servers also benefit from higher levels of failure tolerance.

REFERENCES


1. Feit, Sidnie, TCP/IP Architecture, Protocols and Implementation, McGraw-Hill, New York, 1993

2. Winch, Robert, Telecommunication and Transmission Systems , McGraw-Hill, New York, 1993

3. Advanced Micro Devices, Ethernet/IEEE 802.3 Family World Network DataBook / Handbook, Advanced Micro Devices, Inc., Sunnyvale, 1994

4. The Fibre Channel Association, Fibre Channel: Connection to the Future, The Fibre Channel Association, USA, 1994

# Automated Video Indexing for On-Demand Retrieval from Very Large Video Libraries

H. D. Wactlar, A. G. Hauptmann, M. A. Smith, K. V. Pendyala
Carnegie Mellon University, Pittsburgh, PA

D. Garlington
ISLIP Networked Information Technologies, Pittsburgh, PA

## Abstract

The Informedia Digital Video Library project is implementing full content search and retrieval from digital video, audio and text libraries. This is accomplished through the utilization of integrated speech, image and language understanding technologies for their automated creation and exploration. Image processing analyzes scenes, speech processing transcribes the audio signal, and natural language processing determines word relevance. Together, these generate a meaningful index into the video content. Segment breaks produced by image processing are examined along with the boundaries identified by the natural language processing of the transcript to partition the video library into sets of segments, or "video paragraphs". Automating these techniques into a unified collaborative system enables us to include and search through vast amounts of video data in the library.

## 1. Introduction

The Informedia™ Project at Carnegie Mellon University [1,2,3,4] has established a large on-line digital video library, incorporating video assets from WQED/Pittsburgh, BBC produced content from the Open University (U.K.), and broadcast news. The project is creating intelligent, automatic mechanisms for populating the library and allowing for its full-content and knowledge-based search and video segment retrieval. The library retrieval system can effectively process natural language queries and deliver relevant video data in a compact, subject-specific format, based on information embedded with the video during library creation.

Our approach utilizes several techniques to enable content-based searching and segment retrieval. Content is conveyed in both the narrative (speech and language) and the image. Only by the collaborative interaction of image, speech and natural language understanding technology can we successfully populate, segment, index, and search diverse video collections. This approach uniquely compensates for problems of interpretation and search in otherwise error-full and ambiguous data sets. We start with a state-of-the art, speaker independent, connected speech recognizer which will automatically transcribe video soundtracks. The resulting transcript is then processed through methods of natural language understanding to extract subjective descriptions and subsequently mark potential segment boundaries where significant semantic changes occur [5]. Comparative difference measures are used in processing the video frames to mark potential segment boundaries. Source information about camera cuts, object tracking, speaker changes, timing of audio and/or background music, and change in content of spoken words is also automatically detected and recorded.

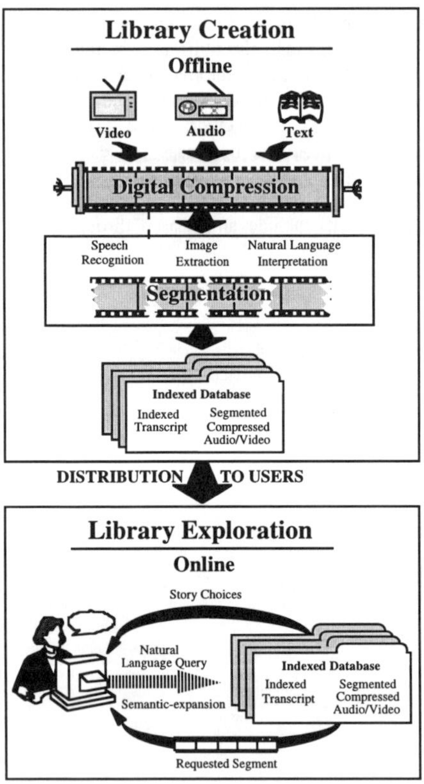

**Figure 1:** Informedia System Overview

Segment breaks produced by image processing are examined along with the boundaries identified by the speech and natural language processing of the audio and transcript, and an improved set of segment boundaries are heuristically derived to partition the video library into sets of segments, or "video paragraphs" [6]. Another innovative concept is the implementation of "video skimming". This enables an accelerated viewing of the key video and audio sequences without the perceptual disturbance of simply speeding up the frame rate and audio, thereby creating a video abstract that conveys the essence of the content in 5 to 20% of the time.

Users are able to explore the Informedia library through an interface that allows them to search using typed or spoken natural language queries, select or browse relevant document segments retrieved from the library and display the material on their PC workstations. Figure 1 provides an overview of the library creation and exploration phases of the system.

## 2. Component Technologies for Video Indexing

Library creation deals with the accumulation of original content in all media, ancillary information, transcription, segmentation and indexing.

There are three broad categories of technologies we can bring to bear to create and search a digital video library from broadcast and unedited video and audio materials [6]. Figure 2 shows the result of analyzing a video clip by various speech, language and image understanding techniques.

2.1. *Text processing* looks at the textual (ASCII) representation of the words that were spoken, as well as other text annotations. These may be derived from the generated transcript, from accompanying notes or from the closed-captioning that might be available on broadcast material. Text analysis can work on an existing transcript to help segment the text into paragraphs. An analysis of keyword prominence allows us to identify important sections in the transcript. Other language based criteria are still being evaluated. For example, the concept of semantic connections between text portions may also be exploited for segmentation. We currently use two main techniques for text analysis:

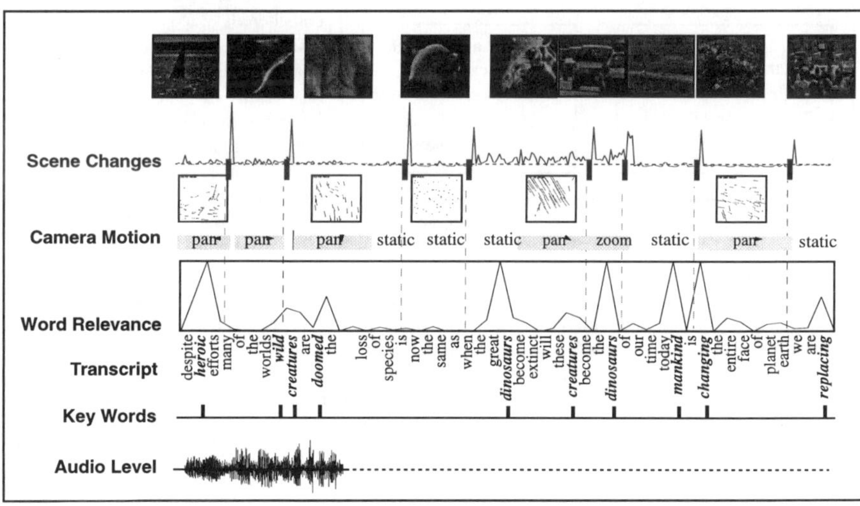


**Figure 2:** Combined technologies for video indexing and segmentation.

1. To identify and rank the contents of a particular segment, we use the well-known technique of TF/IDF (term frequency/inverse document frequency) to identify critical keywords and their relative importance for the video document [7]. Word relevance, plotted in Figure 2, is each word's frequency in a particular script divided (normalized) by a measure of its frequency in a broader context. Thus if a word that seldom appears in an entire video appears frequently and densely in a section of that video, it signifies the word's relative importance in that segment.

2. If we have a complete transcript available from the closed-captioning or through a human-augmented transcription, we can exploit natural "structural" text markers such as punctuation to identify content boundaries.

2.2. *Image analysis* looks at the images in the video portion of the MPEG encoded stream. This analysis is primarily used for the identification of scene breaks and to select static frame icons that are representative of a scene. Image statistics are computed for primitive image features such as color histograms, and these are used for indexing, matching and segmenting images [8]. Using color histogram analysis, video is segmented into scenes through comparative difference measures. Images with little histogram disparity are considered to be relatively equivalent. By detecting significant changes in the weighted color histogram of successive frames, image sequences can be separated into individual scenes. A comparison comparison between the cumulative distributions is used as a difference measure. This result is passed through a high pass filter to further isolate peaks and an empirically derived threshold is used to select only regions where scene breaks occur. Using only the histogram difference, we achieve 90% accuracy compared to human analysis of the same video stream. Figure 2 shows the disparity plot (second row) and the resultant scene breaks with the first frame from each scene (first row).

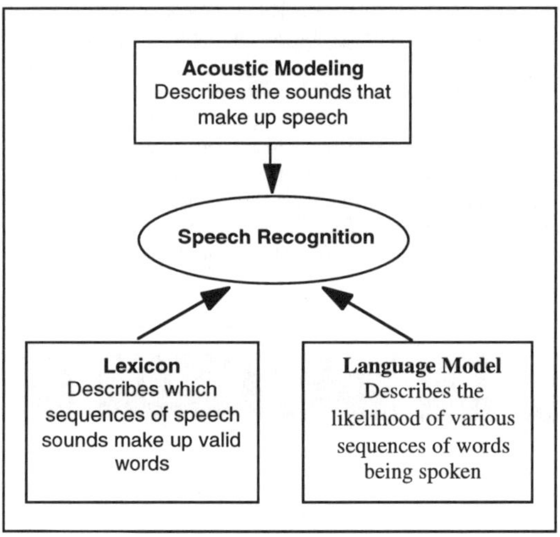


**Figure 3:** Knowledge sources used in speech recognition.

Optical flow analysis is an important method of visual segmentation and description based on interpreting camera motion. We can interpret camera motion as a pan or zoom by examining the geometric properties of the optical flow vectors (Figure 2, third row). Using the Lucas-Kanade gradient descent method for optical flow, we can track individual regions from one frame to the next. By measuring the velocity that individual regions show over time, a motion representation of the scene is created. Drastic changes in this flow indicate random motion, and therefore, new scenes. These changes will also occur during gradual transitions between images such as fades or special effects.

2.3. *Speech analysis* provides the basis for analyzing the audio component of the video content. To automatically transcribe the content of the video material, we principally use for American English content the Sphinx-II system, a large-vocabulary, speaker-independent, continuous speech recognizer created at Carnegie Mellon [9]. The speech recognition process addresses three knowledge sources: acoustic modeling, pronunciation modeling and language modeling (see Figure 3).

The Sphinx-II system uses semi-continuous Hidden Markov Models to model context-dependent phones (triphones), including between word context. The recognizer processes an utterance in 3 steps: It makes a forward time synchronous pass using full between word models, Viterbi scoring and a trigram language model. This produces a word lattice where words may have only one begin time but several end times. The recognizer then makes a backward pass which uses the end times from the words in the first pass and produces a second lattice which contains multiple begin times for words. An A* algorithm is used to generate the best hypothesis from these two lattices. The language model consists of words (with probabilities), bigrams/trigrams which are word pairs/triplets with conditional probabilities for the last word given the previous word(s). The language model was constructed from a corpus of news stories from the Wall Street Journal from 1989 to 1994 and the Associated Press news service stories from 1988 to 1990. Only trigrams that were encountered more than once were included in the model, but all bigrams and the most frequent 58800 words in the corpus were included [10].

The speech generated transcripts have word error rates ranging from 10% in a lab environment and 20% for studio recorded narration to over 50% for some documentary soundtracks. These error rates result from various conditions besides out-of-vocabulary words, including accents and non-English words, music and non-verbal noise mixed with speech, and multiple signal-to-noise ratios.

## 3. Video Segmentation and Indexing for Subsequent Retrieval and Summarization

When the system responds to a query it needs to determine how much content and context to display -- where should the video clip start and where does it end? This is partly determined by the content of the user query, but is also dependent on natural segments within the video which we call "video paragraphs". In the ideal case, a video paragraph starts at the natural boundary of the relevant content and ends whenever the video moves to a different subject.

The Informedia library creation phase will use three different levels of segmentation for a video. The first and generally largest segment shows the video paragraph, which consists of a series of related scenes with a common context. The second level of segmentation identifies a single scene on the video within the video paragraph. Finally, within a single scene we also need to be able to select a representative frame icon for static displays.

### 3.1 Video processing sequence

The following steps are performed during library creation by a coordinated suite of programs:

1. *Digitize the video and audio data into MPEG-1 compression formatt.* Our current library creation process starts with a raw digitized video tape or live broadcast. Using relatively inexpensive off-the-shelf PC-based hardware we can compress video and audio to about 540 MB/hour of video in MPEG-1 format. The audio component of the MPEG stream is compressed to about 80 MB/hour.

2. *Create a time-aligned transcript from speech recognition and/or closed-captioning.* The audio portion is fed through the speech analysis routines, which produces a transcript of the spoken text. Some of the broadcast content also has closed-captioning text available. However, the closed-captioned data, if available, may lag up to 25 seconds behind the actual words spoken and have a word error rate of approximately 15%. These timing problems and inaccuracies in transcription are especially glaring when the broadcast is "live". We use speech recognition in conjunction with closed-captioning, when available, to improve the time-alignment of the transcripts. To create a time-aligned transcript from closed-captioned text, the speech recognizer output is aligned against the closed-caption transcript words using a standard dynamic programming algorithm based on orthographic match. Through this alignment each word in the closed-captioned transcript is assigned a time marker derived from the corresponding word in the speech recognition output. For the broadcasts that are not closed-captioned, we use a transcript generated exclusively by the speech recognition system. The vocabulary and language model used here approximate a "general American news" language model. These were based on a large corpus of North American business news from 1987 to 1994 [10]. In addition, transcripts or closed-captioning text maybe obtainable for the video data. If there is a text transcript available during library creation, speech recognition helps create a time-aligned transcript of the spoken words and aids precise segmentation of the broadcast into paragraphs. The library index needs very specific information about the start and end of each spoken word, in order to select the relevant video "paragraph" to retrieve and to find individual words within the story.

3. *Segment audio boundaries.* To allow efficient access to the relevant content of the data, we need to break up the video broadcasts into small pieces or stories. To answer a user query by showing a half-hour long presentation is unsatisfactory. Transitions between speakers and topics are often marked by silence or low energy areas in the acoustic signal. Similarly, music is often initiated (or terminated) or its volume adjusted at scene transitions. Such breaks and effects can be detected using modified signal-to-noise ratio computations on the audio spectrum to compute signal power. These transitions indicate potential acoustic "paragraph" breaks (Figure 2, bottom row). This is the first pass at segmentation. If a closed-captioned text transcript is available, we use structural markers such as punctuation and paragraph boundaries to identify stories. If only a speech recognition generated transcript is available, we use acoustically determined paragraph boundaries of silence in the audio track.

4. *Segment images by scene breaks and select key frames*. Image analysis is primarily used for the identification of breaks between scenes and the identification of a single static frame icon that is representative of a scene. Image statistics methods are used to describe primitive image features such as color histograms, and their time functions. These are used for indexing, matching and segmenting images.

5. *Index all stories*. The keywords and their corresponding paragraph locations in the video are indexed in the Informedia library catalogue. An inverted index is created using a modified version of the Pursuit search engine [5]. To obtain video clips suitable for viewers, we first search for keywords from the user query in the recognition transcript. When we find a match, the surrounding video paragraph is returned using the timing information derived from speech recognition.

### 3.2. Video Summarization

Another use of the combined technology is the development of the "video skim" [11]. By only displaying significant regions, a short synopsis of the video paragraph can be used as a preview for the actual segment. Time compression rates as high as 20:1 make it possible to "skim" large amounts of data in a short time. Based on the transcript automatically created from the audio track, keywords are extracted based on the word frequency/inverse document frequency weightings, and separated from the audio track. Significant image frames are identified through the use of the various image understanding techniques which interpret camera motion and object presence. The identified subset of image and audio information is combined to produce the skim with only a small number of selected regions displayed at normal viewing speed.

The same keyword extraction techniques are used with higher relevance thresholds to automatically generate a one-line title for each video paragraph. These are associated with the single frame representative icon and aid the user in narrowing their selection for full video viewing.

## 4. Conclusion

We are currently using these techniques to create digital video library collections suitable for full content retrieval. The current test library contains 300 hours and will expand to over 1000. While some of the steps are not yet fully integrated, each one has been shown to work independently, and several of the techniques are fully integrated within the Informedia system. The Informedia digital video library is a working system that provides a baseline capability which routinely processes content in two to twelve times real-time (depending upon number of networked processors applied in parallel) with speech word error rates ranging from 20% to 65%. Nevertheless, retrieval experiments have demonstrated recall rates to be 80%-90% of those achieved from a perfect transcript of the same content. Further work will focus on improved integration for higher performance processing and improvement in the underlying accuracy of the recognition and segmenting processes through dynamic language models, automated scene characterization and semantic inference.

## Acknowledgment

This material is based upon work supported by the National Science Foundation under Cooperative Agreement No. IRI-9411299. Any opinions, findings, and conclusions or recommendations expressed in this material are those of the authors and do not necessarily reflect the views of the National Science Foundation.

## References

1. Christel, M., Stevens, S., & Wactlar, H. "Informedia Digital Video Library," Proceedings of the Second ACM International Conference on Multimedia, Video Program. New York: ACM, October, 1994, pp. 480-481.

2. Stevens, S., Christel, M. and Wactlar, H. "Informedia: Improving Access to Digital Video". Interactions 1 (October 1994), pp. 67-71

3. Christel, M., Kanade, T., Mauldin, M., Reddy, R., Sirbu, M., Stevens, S., and Wactlar, H.","Informedia Digital Video Library", Communications of the ACM", 38 (4), April 1994, pp. 57-58.

4. Wactlar, H.D., Kanade, T., Smith, M.A., and Stevens, S.M. "Intelligent Access to Digital Video: Informedia Project," IEEE Computer, 29 (5), May 1996, pp. 46-52.

5. Hauptmann, A. G., and Smith, M., "Text, Speech, and Vision for Video Segmentation: The Informedia Project," AAAI Fall 1995 Symposium on Computational Models for Integrating Language and Vision, Cambridge, MA: MIT, November 1995, pp. 90-95.

6. Mauldin, M. "Information Retrieval by Text Skimming," Ph.D. Thesis, Carnegie Mellon University. August 1989. Revised edition published as "Conceptual Information Retrieval: A Case Study in Adaptive Partial Parsing, Kluwer Press, September 1991.

7. Salton, G. and McGill, M.J. "Introduction to Modern Information Retrieval," McGraw-Hill, New York, McGraw-Hill Computer Science Series, 1983.

8. Zhang, H., Low, C., and Smoliar, S. "Video Parsing and Indexing of Compressed Data," Multimedia Tools and Applications 1(March 1995), pp. 89-111.

9. Hwang, M., Rosenfeld, R., Thayer, E., Mosur, R., Chase, L., Weide, R., Huang, X., and Alleva, F., "Improving Speech Recognition Performance via Phone-Dependent VQ Codebooks

10. Rudnicky, A., "Language Modeling with Limited Domain Data," Proceeding of the 1995 ARPA Workshop on Spoken Language Technology, in press.

11. Smith, M., Kanade, T., "Video Skimming for Quick Browsing Based on Audio and Image Characterization," Carnegie Mellon University technical report CMU-CS-95-186, July 1995. Also submitted to PAMI Journal (Pattern Analysis and Machine Intelligence), 1995.

# BITSTREAM TRANSCODING IN THE STUDIO

by

**Bhavesh Bhatt and Christopher Ward**
*David Sarnoff Research Center*
*CN 5300, Princeton, NJ 08543*

## Abstract

One of the benefits of carrying video in the studio as compressed bitstreams is the great flexibility in trading off various compression parameters to optimize the bitstream for the task at hand, For example, when live switching is required, we may require frequent I frames and thus a high bit rate, but when the bit rate must be low, as when distributing video by satellite, the I-frame density must be reduced. Thus there is a need for studio devices that perform this bitstream transcoding. This paper will examine the requirements for bit rate transcoding and possible cost/performance enhancements that may be achieved in such devices.

## 1. Introduction

Transcoders are used to maintain compatibility among the many different MPEG-2 studio formats, video formats, and video frame rates [1,2]. Within a compressed digital studio there will be transcoders for audio only, video only, or for a combination of audio, video and data. The transport of integrated audio, video and data is provided for by the MPEG-2 Systems specification [3,4]. Control, the other input to a transcoder, is not provided by MPEG-2 (although a control specification is provided for storage media devices [5]) but may be conveyed either using aux data or a separate channel.

Typical activities required of transcoders are bitrate transcoding (e.g. from 360 Mbps to 19.2 Mbps), picture size transcoding (e.g. from 1920x1080 to 1280x720), picture format transcoding (e.g. from interlaced to progressive) and picture frame rate transcoding (e.g. 29.97 frames per sec. to 30 frames per sec.) Other types of transcoding can be easily imagined. Usually the term "format converter" is used instead of "transcoder" when the transcoding unit permits picture size, frame rate, and interlace to change . In addition, transcoders that must process all types of payload (audio, video and data) must also ensure that the audio, video, and data alignment at the output is the same as that of the input. I.e. a transcoder should be considered a filter in a bitstream. With this large number of parameters to be contemplated, the number of combinations that are required of a transcoder are truly daunting.

Section 2 illustrates that by restricting the services to be provided by particular transcoders this task may be greatly reduced. Section 3 then demonstrates some cost performance tradeoffs that may be realized by taking this approach.

## 2. Services to be Provided

Although the number of parameters that may be used to perform an arbitrary transcode is large, from a cost perspective it is more economical to provide a family of transcoders. Members within this family provide specialized functions while using common components. Limiting the functions that a transcoder has to deal with permits significant savings by removing unnecessary levels of decoding and re-encoding within specific units. Additionally, using common components amortizes design effort. Examples of transcoder specialization within a studio are: a transmission transcoder, a intra-studio transcoder , an NTSC to HDTV transcoder and a HDTV to NTSC transcoder. These are described in greater detail below.

### *2.1. HDTV TRANSMISSION TRANSCODER*

A HDTV transmission transcoder is needed to allow over-the-air transmission of audio, video, and data from an HDTV studio. This transcoder accepts as input audio, video, and data in a studio format and generates a correctly aligned transmission format audio, video, and data stream at the output.

#### 2.1.1. Input Format

The studio format in the context would be MPEG-2 4:2:2 @ High profile encoding using either all I-frames or an alternating I P format. These formats are favored because of the ease with which video segments can be spliced together. However, these encoding schemes require a significant number of bits to encode the frame if the picture quality is to be preserved. This in turn results in high bit rates for real time video transcoding. 350 Mbps is not considered an unreasonable studio transport rate.

#### 2.1.2. Output Format

For transmission, the compressed MPEG-2 bitstream must be compliant with ATSC Digital Television Standard (A/53). [6] This format uses MPEG-2 parameters N=15,M=3 to give a transmission bit rate of about 19.2 Mbps. This data rate may be transmitted over a single 6 MHz channel using 8-VSB modulation.

### *2.2. INTRA-STUDIO TRANSCODER*

The Intra-studio Transcoder is a device that is used to change the digital representation of the input to meet arbitrary transmission and transport requirements. The transcoder is required to deal with a multiplicity of encoding formats and data rates and as such may be considered a generalization of the Transmission Transcoder. It is expected that the picture format (size and frame rate) is the same for transcoder inputs and outputs, but the representations are different.

#### 2.2.1. Input Format

The input would be a compressed bit stream with any of the standard MPEG-2 studio profiles and levels.

#### 2.2.2. Output Format

The output would be in a user specified studio profile and level, GOP structure, bit rate, and chroma format.

### 2.3. NTSC-HDTV TRANSCODER

An NTSC to HDTV Transcoder converts a standard resolution NTSC video stream into one of the two ATSC Digital Television Standard (A/53) supported video formats. This transcoder would convert aspect ratio, frame rate and image size. Clearly the complexity of this transcoder is significantly greater than the previous case.

#### 2.3.1. Input Format

The input form would be NTSC, the input resolution would typically be CCIR-601 in component form.

#### 2.3.2. Output Format

The output would be one of the many standard MPEG-2 profiles and levels presently used. Output video format and aspect ratio may also be under operator control.

### 2.4. HDTV-NTSC TRANSCODER

The function of this device is to allow simulcast of NTSC video and ATSC Digital Television Standard (A/53) HDTV video. The compressed MPEG-2 video at ATSC Digital Television Standard (A/53) profile is input to this transcoder and the output will be a scan converted (re-sized) NTSC baseband video. This transcoder will accept both audio and video streams and generate a composite output.

#### 2.4.1. Input Format

The input to the transcoder is ATSC Digital Television Standard (A/53) profile.

#### 2.4.2. Output Format

The outputs of the transcoder will be of standard NTSC/M resolution in either analog (SMPTE-170) or digital (serialized SMPTE-125) format.

## 3. Transcoder Design Considerations

By using a several special purpose transcoders it is possible to make cost/performance tradeoffs in the design process. Figure 3-1 shows a variety of transcoder configurations that are able to capitalize on common hardware components. For example, the High Bitrate (HB) Decoder is a common feature of all transcoders (and dedicated studio picture monitors also). Notice that the transmission transcoder and intra-studio transcoder do not need an image resizer unit whereas the video format converts do.

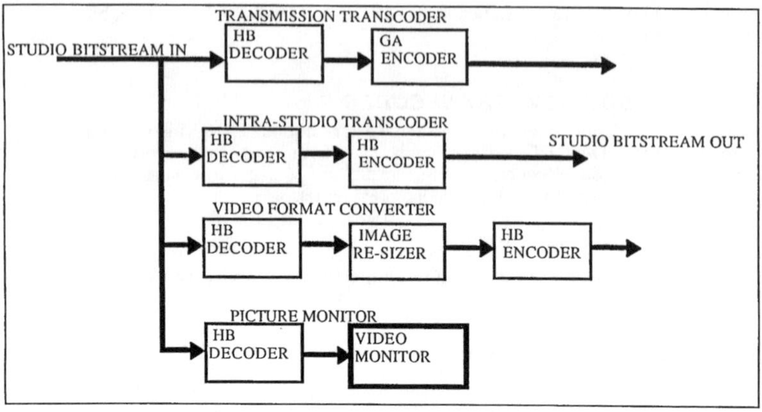


**Figure 3-1. Use of common components in transcoder designs.**

A more detailed diagram showing the major components in the video format converter is provided in Figure 3-2. The first step in the process is to extract the appropriate video stream from the MPEG-2 transport stream (not shown). The video stream and system clock are then provided as input to the High Bit Rate MPEG-2 Decoder which results in analog (YUV) output, this is then passed to a pixel domain processor. The output of the pixed domain processor is then re-encoded.

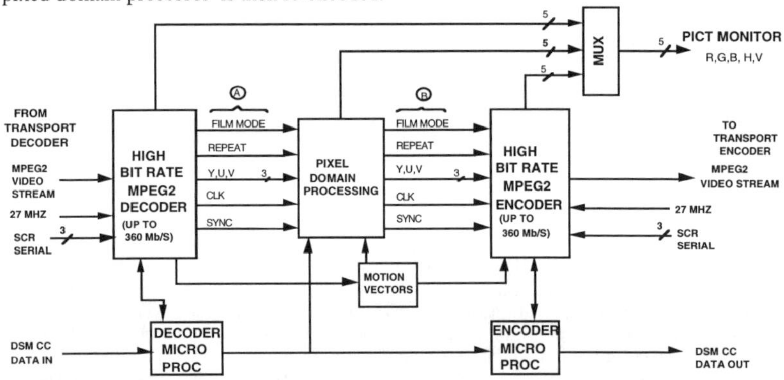


**Figure 3-2. Overview of format converter design.**

Notice that Figure 3-2 includes a control path (indicated generically as "DSM-CC DATA") and that motion vectors obtained from the decoder are used in the re-encoding process. The output video stream would then be remultiplexed into the outgoing transport stream for delivery to another studio component.

## 4. Conclusions

This paper has presented a variety of applications for which transcoder technology would be appropriate and has outlined the requirements associated in using these transcoders. It is expected that a video stream may pass through several transcoders between the time it enters the studio and the time it is transmitted. The paper has also illustrated that by selection of core functionality, a common hardware realization is possible. This permits cost optimizations to be made based on cost/performance tradeoffs.

## 5. References


[1] *Information Technology—Generic Coding of Moving Pictures and Associated Audio: Video - ITU-T Recommendation H.262.0/ISO/IEC 13818-2 International Standard.* I(MPEG-2 Video). ISO/IEC JTC1/SC29/WG11/N0905,N1120,N1121. Jan 1995.

[2] Isnardi, M. A., "MPEG-2 Video Coding: A Tutorial Approach," David Sarnoff Research Center, 1996.

[3] *Information Technology—Generic Coding of Moving Pictures and Associated Audio: Systems-ITU-T Recommendation H.222.0/ISO/ 13818-1 International Standard.* (MPEG-2 Systems). ISO/IEC JTC1/SC29/WG11 N0801rev. Apr. 1995.

[4] Isnardi, M. A., "MPEG-2 Systems: Tying It All Together," David Sarnoff Research Center, 1996.

[5] *Information Technology—Generic Coding of Moving Pictures and Associated Audio: Digital Storage Media Command and Control - ISO/IEC 13818-6 Draft International Standard.* ISO/IEC JTC1/SC29/WG11/MPEG95/N1100. Nov. 1995.

[6] Grand Alliance, "ATSC Digital Television Standard (A/53)," David Sarnoff Research Center, 1995.

# Network-Centric Computing in a Studio Environment

Ruud M. Bolle, James Janniello and Baiju Patel
IBM Watson Research Center
Hawthorne, N.Y.

**Abstract**

As the evolution of the digital studio progresses, video content distribution and production will increasingly be aided by the capabilities of network-centric computing. The technology being developed today will enable collaborative production, searching, and sharing of video content among studios and production houses, television networks and affiliates.

We will review IBM's Digital Library and ATM Network efforts in digital video production. Digital libraries provide the ability to maintain and to access large video libraries. We will describe new technologies for searching video libraries based on both spatial and temporal video content.

Today, separate digital networks enable the operation of broadcast studios and provide content distribution to the viewer. We will describe the application of mechanisms within tomorrow's ATM networks that offer studios an integrated communication environment for content sharing, both within studios and across large geographic areas. The integration of digital network and library technology gives rise to a seamless studio environment for video content production, sharing, and searching.

# 1 Introduction

Network-centric computing, while not a new concept, is in the process of developing new solutions to many recurring problems. In the broadcast / production studio environment, this technology can create a seamless studio environment where accessing, sharing and creating video content can be efficiently performed and managed. It enables greater reliability, security and copyright protection.

The economics of producing news stories as well as entertainment programming demand the use of efficient production processes and reuse of existing video content. Both of these require easy access to large video libraries cataloged in a flexible yet inexpensive fashion. Digital libraries with advanced querying capabilities provide the means to automatically index and search video content. For instance, closed-caption information can be used for keyword searches. When closed-caption is not available, speech recognition can be used to generate transcripts and to create speech-based indexes into video content. Eventually, this will lead to speaker identification, where a query of all segments containing a particular speaker can be searched for.

All of these elements will lead to the efficient production of news stories and segments. For the production of entertainment content, an image based search may be more appropriate. Today, query by image content [1] (QBIC) enables the searching of video shots for a particular color, texture or shape. These mechanisms are being enhanced to search for particular objects and scenes. Once located, advanced mechanisms for browsing will provide for quick random access of candidate videos. Automatically, frames will be grouped into shots, shots into segments and keyframes displayed in a timeline. In addition, graphs illustrating the temporal relation between shots and segments will provide a compressed view of the video on a single screen. Together, this technology will revolutionize the production of new video content.

Querying and browsing video libraries from remote locations will also be possible with the ATM / Digital Library technology. This will provide for the immediate sharing of video content between networks and affiliates, studios and production houses. Distribution of video over terrestrial links will offer alternatives to satellite distribution and, with the family of bit rates available in SONET, will facilitate the transmission of both low-resolution and high-quality video.

Today, studios utilize many different networks to perform day-to-day operations. Video, audio, intercoms and LAN traffic all travel over separate networks. This increases the size of the underlying infrastructure, increases maintenance costs and complicates the design of fault-tolerance. ATM networks, however, provide connectivity for all of these traffic types over a single network infrastructure. It also provides the security and availability required by long-distance carriers, while offering the economies of scale of the computer and telecommunication industries.

ATM can provide seamless connectivity to TELCOs, affiliates, studios, content providers and end-users. While the statistical multiplexing attributes of an ATM network are often viewed as unsuitable for a studio environment, this is principally due to the fact that ATM is traditionally configured and operated to fill the needs of a voice-based public network. In actuality, an ATM network can be designed and managed so as to provide the latency and loss specifications required in a studio environment.

Finally, reliability, fault-tolerance, fault isolation, copyright protection, security, user authorization, archival, network management and database management will all become more readily realizable in an ATM / Digital Library environment.

In this paper, we will focus on Video Querying and the underlying support required from the studio network, servers and the database management. We will begin with a detailed discussion of the concept of video querying and will then describe the requirements and architecture of the Video Query System.

# 2 Video Search and Digital Libraries

The digital form of video allows processing of the data to generate appropriate data abstractions that allow for flexible video database organization and enable content-based retrieval of video. That is, just as today's large text databases can be searched with text queries, video databases will be able to be searched with combined text and visual queries. Possibly short video clips can be retrieved from longer sequences in large databases based upon some sort of organization of the linear time-oriented structure of the video and, more interestingly, based upon the semantic video content. For the latter case, an example of video content is the presence of an object in the video. The semantic content of video can also be dynamic or motion-based, i.e., the appearance or disappearance of objects, and actions or interactions of objects.

The area of video on demand (VOD) has addressed the issue of efficient video retrieval and rapid video viewing for a number of years now. The emphasis of VOD is on mechanisms for accessing video data, typically stored on tertiary storage devices, where the amounts of data can be quite enormous. Rather than linear viewing of video, VOD systems provide the ability to filter out unwanted information while retrieving video of interest.

Rowe et al. [2], by surveying a variety of users, characterized the types of video queries that are needed and identified indexes that should be associated with the video data to satisfy the queries. These indexes are:

1. Bibliographic Data. This category includes information about the video (e.g., title, abstract, subject, and genre) and the individuals involved with the production of the video (e.g., producer, director, and cast).

2. Structure Data. Video (and film) can be described by a hierarchy of movie, segment, scene, and shot where each entry is composed of one or more entries at a lower level. A segment is composed of a sequence of scenes and a scene is composed of a sequence of shots [3].

3. Content Data. End-users want to retrieve videos based on content. For example: 1) sets of keyframes representing key images in a video (e.g., frames with each actor, or a sequence that depicts the major segments and scenes); 2) keyword indices built from sound track/closed caption; 3) object indices that indicate entry and exit frames for each appearance of a significant object or individual.

Until recently, most of the video has been annotated solely by hand by meticulous pre-viewing of the video. Research in video data modeling has been centered on proposing video abstractions or video objects that offer enhanced textual descriptions to the segments of video beyond visual content [4, 5, 6, 7]. Our research efforts are focused on the automatic generation of annotation information and on the process of video query – i.e., what a particular video query might actually look like.

## 2.1 Video Structure

The fundamental unit of film and video is a shot. The content of a shot depicts the continuous world action captured by a single camera between some start and end point. Hence, a shot presents an image of an interval of space-time.

The importance of the shot as the fundamental video quantum has been realized by many researchers and the computational detection of video shot boundaries has gotten much attention. Shot boundaries often can be detected by automatic schemes that analyze the variations in visual primitives [8, 9, 10, 11].

An observation made by various researchers [12, 13] is that the representation of a video shot as a single still image could be a significant step toward the video indexing problem. Assuming there is no independent motion (only camera motion) in a shot, then by finding the transformation between subsequent frames, the frames can be "pasted" together into a larger high-resolution image. If there is independent motion, the moving object(s) have to be segmented from the background and the high-resolution image of the background can still be reconstructed – along with images and trajectories of the moving objects [12, 14, 15, 16, 13]. A simpler way to obtain a single image to represent a shot is the selection of a keyframe or, if there is much motion and action in the shot, the selection of multiple keyframes. Hence, a video shot is represented by one or more images, and in this fashion, the problem of video query is reduced to the problem of image query where one can rely on traditional image search engines (e.g., [1]) to retrieve video.

Now, an hour of video is typically composed of hundreds shots and hence the number of images that represent a video library will rapidly increase with the size of the library. Searching large video databases that contain a large quantity of video amounts to searching large image databases. For example, a video database of 100 hours (four days of continuous broadcasting of one TV station) is represented by some 50,000 images. Hence even a small number of hours of video already pushes the capabilities of image search engines in terms of the size of image database that can be searched. We will discuss alternate techniques for representing video for query purposes.

The medium of film and video has at least two levels of discontinuity. One of these levels is the frame to frame discontinuity which is psychophysically unperceivable; the other level is the shot to shot transition. This latter discontinuity is optionally unperceived and if the psychological conditions are not favorable it is all too perceivable. A video is built up from shots to form a story. A shot is an image of continuous space-time. Groups of shots are concatenated in sequences to form a depiction of a three-dimensional event which is continuous in time – such a concatenation of shots is referred to as a *scene* or a *story segment*. A video, in general, consists of multiple segments where beyond the segment discontinuity there may or may not be continuity of time, the story can move to a different place or the story moves all together to a different time and place. Either way, the continuity of time is not what is really important, what is important is if there is continuity of meaning, i.e., does the story continue in the new video segment. This is perhaps the most challenging aspect of automatic video annotation, *finding the underlying discontinuities of meaning.* Or, equivalently, establishing from shot to shot whether there is a continuity in the meaning or the subject of the video. Here what needs to be defined is a meaning of the meaning of video or, at least, computational measures that express something related to the meaning of video.

As is discussed in [17], this is not such a daunting task as it originally may seem to be. Once video segmentation based on meaning or subject has been achieved, one is left with video data that deals with a particular subject and is uninterrupted by video segments about different subjects such as commercials. Such data can represent very short video sequences like a news item in the evening news. The task of automatic video annotation then is one of finding high-level interpretations, *not* of the individual shots but of collections of shots and possibly of the video as a whole. It seems apparent that in order to find these higher-level interpretations, between-shot computations – computations on frames or pixels from two or more different shots – are initially more important than within-shot computations. After all, it is the relation or lack of relation between two shots that we need to compute which can only be achieved by computations on data that belong to different shots. This will allow for re-discovering the story structure and associating semantic meaning to sequences of shots, thereby explaining large amounts of data without expending too much computational effort. It will also allow for the grouping of shots that exhibit the same meaning and identifying shot breaks where there is a discontinuity of meaning.

Of course, within-shot data processing is an important aspect of automatic video annotation and video retrieval too. Here the complete arsenal of computer vision techniques, both static image analysis (on keyframes) and dynamic image analysis (on the whole or part of the shot), could potentially be applied. The purpose of this is two-fold. First of all, search keys can be developed from shots which can then be used in video queries to search for individual shots. The simplest example is where a keyframe is extracted from each shot and image search techniques (e.g., [1]) are used to retrieve shots. More involved keys can be constructed using motion analysis on the shot sequence [18], and relating the shots by discovering syntax through motion picture grammars.

As is described in [17], high-level video processing techniques can make use of the syntax of video to compute semantic meanings. Techniques have been developed for dissecting the video into segments – i.e., re-discovering the underlying video structure – both for hierarchical and graph-type video representations. Further, high-level models can be fitted to the video to detect dialogues-type video where there is repetition in shot type. Statistical models allow for detection of discontinuities in meaning, for example, commercial detection. We will not be describing these techniques in this paper; rather, it is the use of these techniques that enable visually based queries.

## 2.2 Video Query

Of course, the prime concern of any video query station is that a query is natural and easy to formulate, that the user interface assists in a user-friendly way in the query formulation process, and that the query results are presented in an organized and sensible fashion. A second concern, and probably of equal importance, is that the search is performed quickly. Finally, it is important that in a network-centric environment the search results are readily viewable and browsable. At any given time during a search the intermediate search results should be accessible from the query station interface and it should be possible to direct search results to, say, the production server or nonlinear edit workstations.

Video, being the rich source of information that it is, should be searched in such a fashion that the candidate list is brought down to a manageable size and duration as quickly as possible. Various search keys can be used – text, static visual cues (image), dynamic visual cues – and the use and the presentation of these cues to the system may very well effect the search performance of the query station. Therefore, the query engine should use the cues in the proper order and the user interface should prompt the user for the appropriate cues if they are not presented in the order that narrows down the search as fast as possible.

Two completely different types of queries can be expected from the end-user:

1. The user may have seen a particular piece of video and simply wants to retrieve it for viewing or reuse. The keys for such a search are based upon the memory of the user.
2. The user may only have some vague idea of what it is that she or he is actually looking for. Here the keys may more loosely describe what the user actually intends to find.

In either case, one could attempt to define what it would mean for a retrieved video to be appropriate to the query. For the first case, a candidate can only be appropriate if it is the particular video clip or the candidate has the clip embedded in there in some form. The second case, 'appropriateness' is less clear a concept and it may be something best left up to the user. However, even without a proper definition, the issues involved in query performance can be discussed. We do not consider this to be a topic of this paper; the terms and methods used in the data retrieval area that capture system performance can be found in [19].

We view a video query as an iterated sequence of *navigating, searching, browsing,* and *viewing.* Each of these phases may require different types of annotations and a different level of indexing into the actual video clip. There are, however, common visualization and viewing operations that are needed at every stage of the video query process. We will cover in some detail what we envision the different stages of the query process to look like.

*Navigating.* This is the stage at which the user (or the query engine) decides which category of video is to be searched. Video can be classified into categories such as, say, news, sports, entertainment, etc. Other categorizations, of course, are possible. We could assume that such a categorization of the video is available, which could create problems for certain video items. What category should, for instance, news about a sporting event belong to – to the category of *news* or the category of *sports.* Then certain videos will have to be classified into multiple categories or the burden could be put upon the user to select multiple categories on which a search should be performed. This is a problem where automatic video categorization (combined textual and visual categorization — a new area of research) may bring some answers. We will not dwell on this topic any further here.

*Searching.* Once the category of video to be searched has been selected, the individual video items within the particular category can be indexed. The result of this search is a list of candidate videos that in some sense are constrained by the video query. The ultimate goal of the search is to make this list as short as possible without missing the video of interest.

It is obvious that text should be the first search filter since every piece of video has some text associated with it. Moreover, many advances have been made in the area of text retrieval that should be applied in this arena. So, a video query interface definitely needs some sort of text input field, be it parametric text or free text — or both. Here all the advances that have been made in recent years in the area of text retrieval should be brought to bear. The reader is referred to [19].

Consider the following scenario. Let us suppose a user enters the keywords *Clinton* and *investigation* in the input frame on the user interface. Then the resulting (simplified) candidate list might look something like this:

| | *Hits:* 254 *Time:* 8.4 hours | |
|---|---|---|
| ⋆⋆⋆ | Clinton confronts D'Amato | 15.4 min |
| ⋆⋆⋆ | Financing an open-ended fishing license | 45 min |
| ⋆⋆⋆ | Hearings extended no further than April 3 | 10 min |
| ⋆⋆⋆ | Democrats prepare investigation filibuster | 23 min |
| ⋆⋆⋆ | With elections nearing, Democrats had enough | 17 min |
| ⋆⋆⋆ | ................. | |
| ⋆⋆⋆ | ................. | |

Of course, the interface should be much more graphical and thumbnail images giving some indication of the visual content of the individual hits should also be displayed. But the basic idea is that this particular query has produced 254 video clips of a total duration of 8.4 hours. Incidentally, the ⋆⋆⋆ rating in the first column is an indication of how well the particular hit satisfies the query, i.e., how relevant the particular candidate item is to the query. Note that even in this early stage of the search process, the end user will want to have access to all the video — 8.4 hours. This, consequently, puts a burden on the network and servers since this material can be distributed all over the studio and can reside in tertiary storage.

At this point of the inquiry, the user may feel that this is still too much material and may, for example, enter the additional keyword *Arkansas*. The resulting hit list could then become:

| | *Hits:* 109 *Time:* 4.7 hours | |
|---|---|---|
| ⋆⋆⋆ | Little Rock continues | 31 min |
| ⋆⋆⋆ | Clinton confronts D'Amato | 15.4 min |
| ⋆⋆⋆ | Financing an open-ended fishing license | 45 min |
| ⋆⋆⋆ | High-stake implications of simmering | 10 min |
| ⋆⋆⋆ | With elections nearing, Democrats had enough | 17 min |
| ⋆⋆⋆ | ................. | |
| ⋆⋆⋆ | ................. | |

Still 109 hits of total duration 4.7 hours, which surely may be too much time to spend for the user to watch linearly. But, again, if needed, random access to this video should be possible.

At this point in the search there may be a problem. The amount of text that is associated with the individual video clips in the video database is probably very unbalanced. Some video may have only two or three keywords associated with it stemming from traditional alpha-numeric database technology, while other video may have the script, closed-caption, or speech transcript available. So, further text querying may not narrow down the candidate list much further.

It is here that visual cues are important. At first glance, this may seem quite a difficult thing to do — what are the visual properties that can be extracted from video that will bring down this candidate list to manageable size? What one would like to have here is the ability to do data mining on the visual properties of the candidate, i.e., some sort of visual data mining. One would like to interactively constrain visual and other attributes of the candidates and in this fashion narrow down the candidate list.

One attribute of a candidate in the list, that may not have that much to do with the visual content, is the actual clip length. The ability to order the candidates by length will be valuable because that gives some indication of the content – e.g., documentary versus news clip. Also, as discussed above, the shot is important as the elementary unit of video. The distribution of lengths of the shots of a candidate clip, by the very nature of a shot, is an indication of the type of programming that is represented by the candidate clip. Short shots indicate fast moving footage like news and action movies, longer shots, on the other hand, indicate drawn-out programs like senate hearings. As is described in [17], local shot length distribution can be used to detect, e.g., commercials. Next is to look at other attributes than time that are associated with shots. Fairly simple representations of shots can be used to already compute fairly complicated syntactical video properties. For example, a color histogram of a keyframe turns out to be a powerful representation of a shot. Between shot comparison of these histograms, allows detection of video syntax that has semantic meaning. This includes portions of videos that contain dialogues as discussed in [17] and structural video organization like scene structure [17]. It is this type of semantic labeling of large amounts of video that will be important in the search on visual content. It is the rediscovery of visual video structure, possibly augmented with semantic annotation.

What surely should be possible during the search phase of a video query is that all candidates are browsable in some sense. It should be possible to get good high-level overviews of the candidate's visual content. This is something we will discuss next when we cover browsing. Ideally, one should also have random access to *any* point of *any* video in the candidate list during the search phase.

*Browsing.* The result of the search phase is a series of video clips. The total duration of these clips could still be quite long, possibly a couple of hours of video. No matter what length the actual candidate list may be, the user should have the capability to view video in a nonlinear fashion and, if possible, be able to get an overview of each candidate video that fits on a minimal number of screens. What is needed for the latter is something called *visual summaries* of videos, or *video visualization*, if you will.

Visual summaries are a very important facet of the video query process, and it certainly deserves a lot of attention. The problem is to derive mappings of the video data, which is a streamed, three-dimensional object, to a two-dimensional display. This has to be done in such a fashion that the underlying structure and content of the video is obvious to the viewer. The video structure is, of course, related to the semantic video content and semantic video interpretation may be associated with visual summaries. Ideally, of course, a visual summary would be keyframes of the video – as few as possible – that adequately depict the story and the story line. This involves automatically finding the semantically most important frames, i.e., those frames that represent turning events in the video. Again, this involves thorough high-level automatic semantic interpretation of the video, something that cannot be expected in the near future (given the current state of the art).

However, even with today's technology, a good start can be made in this area. As discussed in [17], the scene structure of, for example, sitcoms can be rediscovered using agglomerative clustering [20] of shots represented by color histograms of keyframes. This allows for graphical representations of the scene-scene-scene structure of video in terms of the shot-shot-shot structure. One such representation is a directed graph where nodes in the graph represent similar shots, fully connected subgraphs then represent scenes of the video. Other representations of the scene structure can also be envisioned – for example, hierarchical representations.

The look of visual summaries will depend very much on the video domain, i.e., the genre of video. Sporting events do not have a structure in terms of scenes. A natural segment for a team ball sport may be a period of time where the ball is in the possession of one of the teams, and segment breaks occur where the ball changes possession. Graphical representations that both display the sequence of events and allow random video access to any point of the game are what is needed here.

*Viewing.* First of all, the traditional functionality of today's VCRs should be available in the viewing phase. That is, *Play, Pause, Fast Forward, Reverse,* and *Variable Play.* (Reverse and variable play will be quite difficult to implement if the video is MPEG compressed.) Further, capabilities like semantic fast-forward should be available in the viewing phase. The user should be able to skip forward (or backward) to frames, shots, or scenes that she or he gives some semantic description of.

What is important to note about video query is that it may not be necessary to view all search results at the highest resolution. The burden on the network can be diminished by allowing for lower resolution display of intermediate search results. This means, however, that the servers and other legacy storage devices should be able to stream video out at reduced resolution. Certain end-users may want to view multiple video streams simultaneously at the query station interface. Probably only the high-end query stations should be enabled to perform such functions since it will involve multiple MPEG decoders in a single query station. Finally, some query station users may want the ability to view only sub-windows of high-resolution high-quality video. This will be particularly important when searching for video that is to be used for nonlinear editing operations like roboscoping.

A few last words about image search for video query. We see image search to be useful in the later stages of the search phase, and in the browsing and viewing phases. Then the amount of video in terms of hours will be of manageable size, maybe in the tens of hours. The number of images that then represent the shots, if each shot is represented by a keyframe, will be in the thousands. This is about the number of images where still reasonable search results can be expected using image search. Moreover, the type of images that represent the keyframes will be sufficiently constrained such that it is less likely that unpredictable and unreasonable results will occur, such as, asking for a shot of a beach and getting a shot of the desert in return.

# 3 Video Query System

A Video Query System should be a flexible and efficient environment for locating video content stored at either a local or remote location. The accessible information should include text, graphics, video and audio. It should be possible to execute searches based on any of these information types. Security should be provided to prevent access by any unauthorized users and provisions should be made to produce some type of billing information.

The system should support all prevalent video formats including NTSC, PAL, HDTV, MPEG-2, etc. It should be possible to browse through candidate material at various resolutions and bit rates and to obtain one or more thumbnail images of candidate videos. The system should also be capable of randomly accessing any candidate video. In addition, it should be possible to search for and view several videos simultaneously.

An architecture to fulfil these requirements has been created based upon the Digital Library architecture. This architecture consists of three major components. First are the Video Query Stations, or clients in our network-centric model. Some of these stations will be located within the studio and connected via the campus network, others will be located at remote sites and connected by dedicated links and still others may be connected via the internet. Second are the servers which contain the video content and the library directories. In our Digital Library environment, the video content is stored on the Object Servers (OS) and the directories are stored on the Library Servers (LS). Finally, there is the network, which interconnects the Video Query Stations, the Servers, the other devices in the studio and the outside world. The next section describes a typical video query session. The subsequent sections describe the Digital Library and ATM Network architectures and describe how they support the video query operation as well as the other activities within the studio.

## 3.1 Video Query Scenario

A video query session would typically begin with the entry of some keywords at a video query station (client) and, possibly, the selection of a navigation category (sports, news, movie, etc). The client would then transmit the query to the Search Manager (SM) on the Library Server. After executing a search through an preexisting index of keywords, the SM would return to the client a candidate list. If appropriate, the candidate list would include a ranking indicating the relevance of each particular candidate with respect to the query. If the candidate list is too long, the user would have the option of entering additional keywords to narrow down the list.

Once a candidate list is established, the user could then request some bibliographic or other parametric information on one or more of the candidates. The client would request this information from the Library Server using an Item Identification number which was included in the candidate list. Of course, this can also be accomplished interactively by clicking on the candidate. Once the server returns this data, the client can request an inventory of all information associated with the candidate. This could include a text abstract, the video itself or, possibly, the closed caption track for the video. In the Digital Library environment, this is called the table of contents and the candidate is referred to as the document.

If the user wishes to access any of the items in the document, he issues a command from the client requesting the Library Server to open the document. The LS then performs an access rights checks to insure the user has authorization to view the content and, if approved, sends the client a handle for addressing this query. The client may then request a "read" of data from the Object Server. This request is first processed by the Library Server and then forwarded to the Object Server. As the OS streams data/audio/video to the client, the client may continue to submit new requests for additional items in the document, or may simultaneously begin a new query.

### 3.2 Digital Libraries

The Digital Library environment consists of a Library Server and one or more Object Servers. The Library Server, sometimes called the Index Server, contains a DB2 Relational Database which maintains the indexing information for objects stored on the system. This information may contain bibliographic information, indexes to videos based on speech transcripts (obtained form closed caption text or from speech recognition), thumbnail keyframes, etc.

The Object Servers physically warehouse the objects (audio and video shots, segments and stories) and maintains the system managed storage. They are responsible for streaming tens or hundreds of simultaneous streams of data to clients in the system. To accomplish this, they need to communicate with other servers, clients and the outside world. They need to transport a variety of media types at many different bit rates and priorities. In most cases, they also require guaranteed service and error-free transport. In the next section, we describe a solution for these networking requirements.

## 4 Studio Networks and ATM

A broadcast / production studio presents one of the most demanding environments for a campus communication network. The studio is composed of a multitude of devices communicating using many different types of digital media. The media types include video, audio, graphics, and data while the devices include cameras, microphones, video monitors, digital storage devices, editing and splicing stations and on-air interfaces. At any time, many concurrent media streams are being transported from one device to another as the activities of storing, processing and transmitting the data progresses.

The video query process itself is perhaps the most demanding operation in the studio as the characteristics of the data needed varies widely. The Query station requires the network to transport data (queries and candidate lists), audio, video at various resolutions and frame rates and, possibly, voice for intercom connections. The streams require bandwidths ranging from several Kbps to several hundreds of Mbps. Some of the streams are real-time; others non-real-time. Some can tolerate loss and delay while others can only tolerate very small delay and/or must be lossless. On the positive side, the studio is a small, relatively well controlled environment where most of the delays in the network are the result of the processing and buffering (there is practically no delay in transmission due to small distances). Moreover, the entire studio can be controlled as a single entity and thus, can have much better management compared to a generic distributed system connected by a large public network.

The digital studio also cannot exist as an island by itself. It needs to be able to successfully receive live feeds from the outside as well be able to exchange information with other studios. Thus, the networking architecture for the digital studio should be suitable for communications with the external world.

## 4.1 Network Requirements

Besides the Video Query station, a typical studio may have several hundred digital devices including small lightweight portable intercoms, large editing stations, digital library servers, monitors and on-air interfaces. Each of these devices poses a different constraint on the network. For example, the hand-held device requires limited bandwidth and relatively few streams and thus, should have a relatively simple network to reduce its size, cost and power consumption. Alternatively, the large digital library servers need to supply media on demand and must be able to handle many different media streams, each with possibly different communication requirements. In such cases, the network connectivity to the digital libraries must be fairly sophisticated.

There are also several media formats being used today and the number is growing rapidly with advances in technology. For example, Query Stations and studios in general may have to support MPEG, H.261, HDTV, NTSC and uncompressed video today. The bandwidth required for H.261 is in the hundreds of Kbps range while uncompressed video requires hundreds of Mbps to over 1 Gbps. Similarly, there are several audio formats that need to be supported. Highly compressed audio may require 5-10 Kbps while uncompressed multichannel audio could approach several hundreds of Kbps bandwidth. Based on the compression technology and the application, a media stream will have different loss, delay and jitter requirements. For example, a highly compressed video stream is able to tolerate very little loss and the effect of any loss may be felt over a large number of subsequent frames. On the other hand, the uncompressed video can tolerate relatively higher loss because of the redundancy in the video itself. In many cases, even though the loss of data may be unnoticeable, it may still be required that the transmission is lossless. Similarly, the video sent to the digital library may require no loss, even at the cost of higher delay.

When switching video in a studio environment, it is also required that all transitions between video streams be frame accurate and seamless. In the analog world, this is easily accomplished by synchronizing all video sources to a single station clock. Thus, all access switching points in each of the video streams (frame boundaries) are in alignment. In the digital world of compressed video, however, it is difficult, even undesirable, to synchronize the switching access points of all video sources as this would make inefficient use of the network bandwidth. In addition, it may be desirable to multiplex several video streams over a single transmission link. Both of these situations require the video streams to be realigned after the switching point. Thus, either the network switch or the receiving device must perform this synchronization.

In addition, there is also a need in the studio to connect with external resources such as other studios for the sharing of information or for the reception of live feeds. These external communications may include remote interviews, video distribution to affiliates or the browsing and sharing of videos between studios. Here, care must be exercised to insure the wide-area network meets the requirements of the media being transported.

Therefore, a well designed network for digital studio will have the following characteristics:

- Support a large number of devices (e.g., up to 1000).
- Support high bandwidth per stream (up to 1.2 Gbps).
- Support low delay/jitter (as low as 10msec).
- Support fairly low loss/lossless transport.
- Support compressed and uncompressed video formats.
- Support video synchronization (station genlock).

## 4.2 Why ATM?

Asynchronous Transfer Mode (ATM) [22, 21, 23, 24, 25] is the internationally agreed upon technique for transmission, multiplexing, and switching in a broadband network. ATM is a ITUT standard for broadband ISDN (B-ISDN). It is designed to support the integration of high quality voice, video, and high speed data traffic. To the end-user, it promises to provide the ability to transport connection-oriented and connectionless traffic at constant or variable bit rates. It allows for allocation of bandwidth on demand and intends to provide negotiated quality of service. The broadband networking solution based on the *Asynchronous Transfer Mode* (ATM) [21, 22] has been continuously gaining momentum as the solution of preference for the next generation of networks capable of integrating various types of traffic (audio, video and data) on a single network. In order to transport such diverse types of traffic, an ATM network uses *Quality of Service* (QoS) contracts that potential users of the network negotiate prior to their admission (or, permission) into the network.

Quality of service refers to a set of performance (or, quality) constraints that, if the network is able to meet them, then the network end-user will consider its interaction with the network satisfactory. During a QoS negotiation, the end-user notifies the network of its QoS expectations and of the statistical characteristics of its traffic. The network will process the information provided, and it will accept or reject the new end-user based on the current utilization of the network and the availability of enough resources to accommodate the new traffic, e.g., buffer capacity in intermediate nodes.

## 4.3 ATM Network Topology

A typical ATM network is composed of several interconnected ATM switches. Each switch has an internal interconnection fabric (e.g., crossbar or multistage networks), temporary storage buffers and ports. The ports are attached to the communication links as shown in figure 1. The simplest form of an ATM network is a switch where the devices that need to communicate with each other are directly attached to the ports. The ports are not required to be of the same media, and they do not need to support the same bandwidth. A larger network may be built by interconnecting the ports of different switches. Thus, an arbitrarily large network may be constructed by interconnecting a large number of switches.

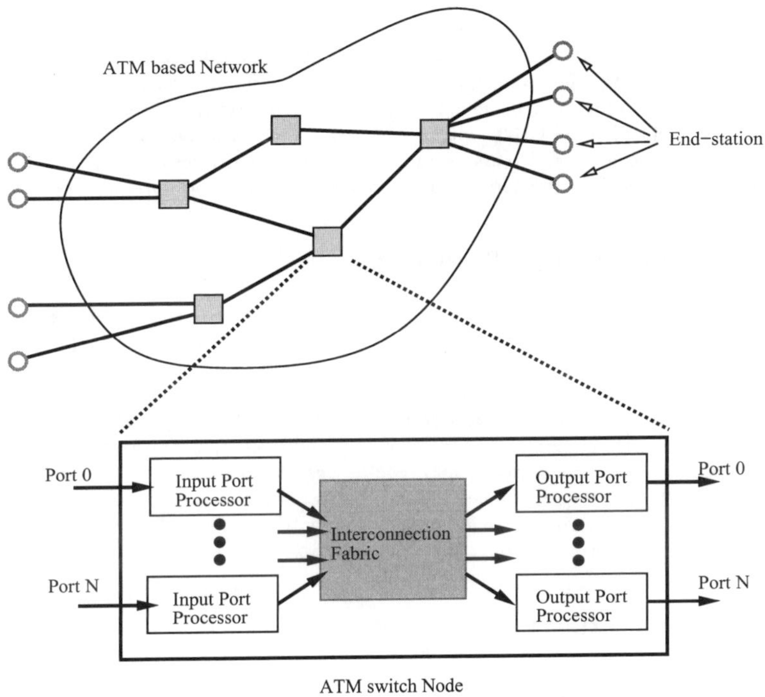


Figure 1: An ATM Network.

Consider a specific example of a digital studio design as shown in figure 2. Here, we have a Library Server with a high bandwidth link capable of supporting sessions with hundreds of clients and many individual Object Servers. Some of these servers may be providing HDTV at relatively small compression ratios (SONET OC-12 links) while others are providing broadcast quality compressed HDTV at 20 Mbps (25 Mbps links). Intercoms may be directly connected to our low bandwidth (25 Mbps) ATM switches or, if desired, multiplexed together before feeding a 25 Mbps link. Monitors, Editing and Preview stations are connected to different switches depending on the video formats they are intended to support. Our external communications will most likely be provided by SONET OC-3 links at present, as these will support both satellite communications and will provide a quality of video suitable for some applications which utilize terrestrial links (e.g. browsing). As one may observe, this network is highly overengineered. A studio may choose not to populate the unused ATM ports. Moreover, if it is observed that the link between switches is heavily loaded, an additional link may be added between them. Similarly, if there are more editing stations to be added, more OC-3 switches may be added. Finally, when the bandwidth requirements grow over several years, one may deploy OC-48 swiches and connect high-end devices to that switch directly while continuing to use the existing networking infrastructure.

## 4.4 Compressed Video Switching

The nature of compressed video will often mean that there is an interdependence between sequential frames. This may be due to the interframe compression and/or, as is the case with MPEG video, the need to embed clocks in the video stream to synchronize the video decoder with its encoder. In either case, whenever a switchover from one video stream to another is executed, the two streams must be spliced together if a seamless output stream is desired. In the case of MPEG compression, this requires retimestamping both the clock references and the presentation time-stamps. It also requires the alignment of the appropriate splice access points in each of the input video streams. As stated previously, it would be inefficient to perform any type of frame alignment prior to the switching point. These operations can, however, be easily performed within the output interface of the network switch.

## 4.5 Communication Protocols

There are a number of suitable protocols for handling the end-to-end communications within the studio. For the communications that cannot tolerate losses, such as certain control messages and non-real-time traffic, TCP/IP is an excellent candidate. TCP/IP has been widely used for data communications, and it provides reliable data transfer and reacts well to the congestions within the network. For the real-time traffic (e.g., live feeds and on-air interfaces), RTP/IP (real-time transport protocol) may be a good choice. Finally, the devices with minimum computational resources may use ATM Adaptation layers (e.g., AAL-1 or AAL-5) to meet their communcations requirements. When directly using AAL protocols, the QoS parameters must be appropriately selected to ensure that loss, delay and bandwidth requirements are satisfied.

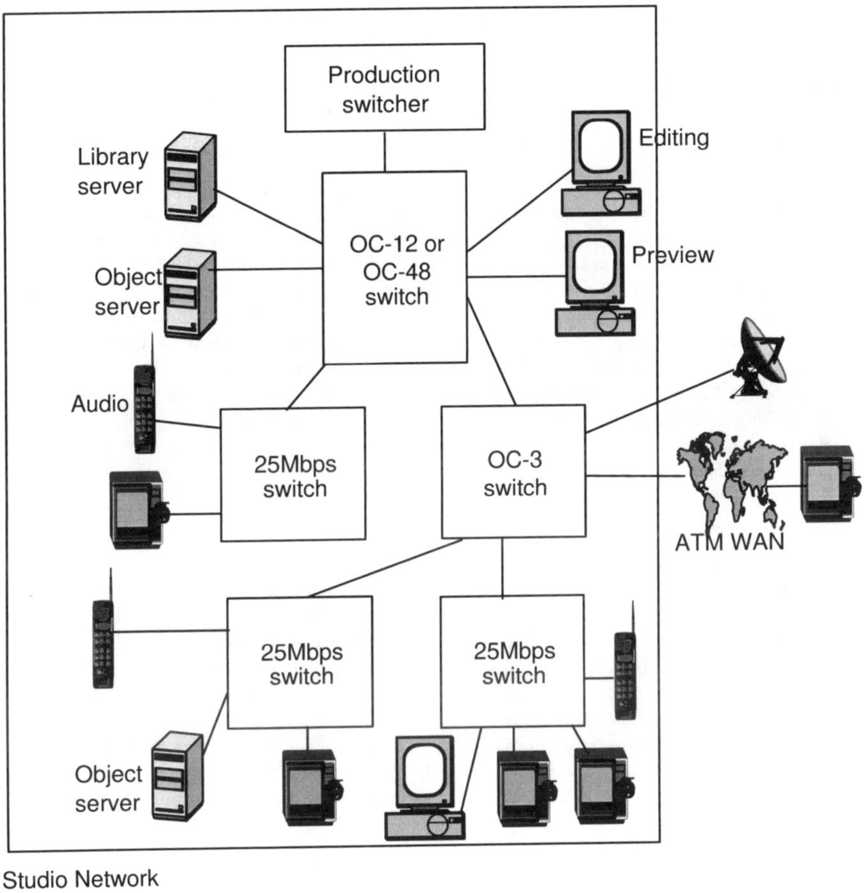


Figure 2: An Example of an In-studio ATM network.

## 4.6 Network Delay

In some ways, delay and jitter are equivalent because, if an estimate on jitter is known, the jitter can be converted into delay. Consider an example where the end-to-end delay is estimated to be one millisecond and the jitter is 100 microseconds. In that case, the initial 100 microseconds worth of data is buffered at the destination node prior to transmission to the application (e.g., a media player). Thus, when cells arrive with a jitter of 100 microseconds (delay of 1.1 milliseconds), there is still sufficient data in the buffer to make the jitter transparent to the application. Since all the data is going through the jitter buffer, effectively, the application sees end-to-end delay equivalent of 1.1 milliseconds. Therefore, in what follows, we will consider delay only.

One of the significant components of delay in a large network is that of transmission delay (bounded by the speed of light), which can be on the order of 10's of milliseconds across a continent. However, a studio is a local area network where all the devices are in close proximity to each other, and therefore, propagation delay is negligible. The main source of delay and jitter is contention for an output in the switch which results in buffering delay. Therefore, if the buffering delay can be kept small, the end-to-end delay may be well within ten milliseconds. There are a few key observations to be made while considering cell delay and jitter: 1) Not all the media streams have the same cell delay and jitter requirements. 2) It is possible to negotiate cell delay and jitter for each media stream. Therefore, a carefully designed negotiation scheme will ensure that the media streams that need low delay and jitter are satisfied. 3) The ATM network allows for flexibility to add more links and switches and thus, if the network is not able to meet the delay and jitter requirements, it is fairly easy to add more capacity to the studio ATM network.

It has been shown extensively in the literature that if a switched network is operated above 60% to 70% capacity, the delay and jitter increases rapidly. Therefore, an in-studio network should be designed to operate under 70% load. To better understand the buffering delay in a switch, consider an ATM switch at OC-3 rates (155Mbps). At this rate, the transmission time for an ATM cell (53 bytes) is less than 3 microseconds. Thus, if the switch has output cell buffer of 100 cells/port, it takes the switch 300 microseconds to empty the entire cell buffer. If the connection is going through 4 switches, each with a 100 cell buffer and each with enough traffic to completely fill up the cell buffer, the overall buffering delay is still little over 1 millisecond. We have already observed that the transmission delay is very small in a studio. Thus, overall delay can be kept very small within a studio.

## 4.7 Network Loss

Much work has been done to create algorithms which optimize network resources to maximize throughput while maintaining satisfactory levels of packet loss and delay. This is especially challenging when dealing with a large number of network switches where a complete model of the network traffic cannot be maintained. In a studio, however, a more complete picture of the network traffic can be computed. In this case, bandwidth can be allocated in such a manner as to eliminate packet loss due to congestion for particular packet streams. For instance, a video stream to be recorded by a video server can be directed to a route where there will be minimal contention for network resources. A video browsing session, on the other hand, may be multiplexed with other traffic which can tolerate packet loss. This low priority traffic can be managed in such a way as to not interfere with the higher priority traffic.

# 5 Summary

The technologies we reviewed in this paper will all prove to be significant assets within the broadcast / production studio environment. Although each of them is an area of study unto itself, we have presented them together since an understanding of all these technologies is required to create a truly seamless, practical digital studio. Through our participation in the NIST HDTV Broadcast Studio project, our goal is to demonstrate the integration of these technologies in a complete end-to-end solution for Advanced Television Systems.

# Acknowledgments

This work is funded in part by NIST/ATP under Contract Number 70N1NB5H1174 - HDTV Broadcast Technology. We would like to acknowledge the NIST Technical Program Manager Ms. Florina Hoffer.

# References

[1] W. Niblack, R. Barber, W. Equitz, M. Flickner, E. Glasman, D. Petkovic, P. Yanker, C. Faloustos, and G. Taubin, "The QBIC project: Querying images by content using color, texture and shape," in *Storage and Retrieval for Image and Video Databases*, vol. SPIE 1908, pp. 13–25, 1993.

[2] L. Rowe, J. Boreczky, and C. Eads, "Indices for user access to large video database," in *Storage and Retrieval for Image and Video Database II, IS&T/SPIE, Symposium on Elec. Imaging Sci. & Tech.*, Feb. 94.

[3] G. Davenport, T. Smith, and N. Pincever, "Cinematic primitives for multimedia," *IEEE Computer Graphics & Applications*, pp. 67–74, July 91.

[4] R. Weiss, A. Duda, and D. Gifford, "Composition and search with a video algebra," *IEEE Multimedia*, vol. Spring, pp. 12–25, 1995.

[5] E. Oomoto and K. Tanaka, "OVID: Design and implementation of a video-object database system," *IEEE Transactions on Knowledge and Data Engineering*, vol. 5, pp. 629–643, Aug. 1993.

[6] S. Hibino and E. A. Rundensteiner, "A visual query language for identifying temporal trends in video data," in *Multi-Media Database Management Systems*, 1995.

[7] R. Jain and A. Hampapur, "Metadata in video databases," in *ACM SIGMOD*, Dec. 1994.

[8] B. L. Yeo and B. Liu, "Rapid scene analysis on compressed videos," *IEEE Transactions on Circuits and Systems For Video Technology*, vol. 5, pp. 533–544, Dec. 1995.

[9] H. Zhang, A. Kankanhalli, and S. W. Smoliar, "Automatic partitioning of full-motion video," *Multimedia Systems*, vol. 1, pp. 10–28, July 1993.

[10] A. Nagasaka and Y. Tanaka, "Automatic video indexing and full-motion search for object appearances," in *Proceedings of the IFIP TC2/WG2.6 Second Working Conference on Visual Database Systems*, pp. 113–127, Sept. 30-Oct. 3 1991.

[11] F. Arman, A. Hsu, and M. Chiu, "Image processing on compressed data for large video databases," in *Proceedings of First ACM International Conference on Multimedia*, pp. 267–272, Aug. 1993.

[12] L. Teodosio and W. Bender, "Salient video stills: Content and context preserved," in *ACM Int'l Conf. on Multimedia*, 1993.

[13] Y. T. et al., "Videomap and videospaceicon: Tools for anatomizing video content," in *ACM INTERCHI*, pp. 131–136, 1993.

[14] S. Mann and R. Picard, "Virtual bellows: Constructing high quality stills from video," in *ICIP*, 1994.

[15] R. Szeliski, "Image mosaicking for tele-reality applications," Tech. Rep. Technical Report CRL 94/2, DEC Cambridge Research Lab, 1994.

[16] H. Sawhney, S. Ayer, and M. Gorkani, "Model-based 2D&3D dominant motion estimation for mosaicking and video representation," tech. rep., IBM Almaden Research Lab, Dec. 1994.

[17] R. Bolle, B.-L. Yeo, and M. Yeung, "Video query," *IBM Journal of Research and DEvelopment*, 1997.

[18] R. Bolle, Y. Aloimonos, and C. Fermuller, "Video representations," in *Proc. Second Asian Conference on Computer Vision*, pp. 24–28, Dec. 1996.

[19] I. Witten, A. Moffat, and T. Bell, *Managing gigabytes: Compressing and indexing documents and images.* New York, NY: Van Nostrand Reinhold, 1994.

[20] A. K. Jain and R. C. Dubes, *Algorithms for Clustering Data.* Prentice Hall, 1988.

[21] The ATM Forum, "ATM Traffic Management Specification," Version 4.0, Printice Hall, expected 1996.

[22] The ATM Forum, "ATM User-Netowrk Interface Specification," Version 3.0, Printice Hall, 1993.

[23] T. Kowk, "A Vision for Residential Broadband Services: ATM-to-the-Home", *IEEE Network*, pp.14-29, Vol. 9, No. 5, Sept/Oct. 1995.

[24] S. Dixit and P. Skelly, "MPEG-2 over ATM for Video Dial Tone Networks: Issues and Strategies", *IEEE Network*, pp.30-41, Vol. 9, No. 5, Sept/Oct. 1995.

[25] David Feldmeier, editor, *IEEE Network*, Vol. 10, No. 4, July/Aug. 1996.

# Controlling the Virtual Broadcast Studio

**Ken Guzik**
**Technology Development Group**
**Sun Microsystems, Inc.**
**Menlo Park, CA**

## Abstract

The shift from broadcasting video stored on tapes to entirely digital video stored on high speed servers allows for a dramatic change in the nature of controlling studio operations. The architecture of the studio shifts from a web of directly connected mechanical devices to a community of computers and peripherals that are linked together by a high speed wide area network. The job of managing studio operations becomes one of controlling these networked resources which enables the creation of a "virtual" studio where individuals can control the entire broadcast process from geographically independent locations.

## Introduction

The fusion of digital video technology, high speed wide area networks, and digital file servers allows us to view the future of television broadcast studios very differently than we do today. As computer and network technologies have advanced in both sophistication and performance, our understanding about the possibilities that the application of these technologies can provide has also grown. Digital networks are no longer used simply as a mechanism for communication between computers, but are capable of transferring data fast enough to make the real-time distribution of high quality video data to a wide audience a reality. The ability to store, access, control, and move large volumes of digital data reliably across great distances at very high speed gives us the tools with which we can build the types of services necessary to manage and run a broadcast studio. In addition, through the use of network distributed object software models, we can build studios that are very flexible to change, and highly adaptable to new technologies with a minimum of effort or disruption. To understand how we can use these new technologies to design a more efficient broadcast studio, we first need to look at the current state of the art in studio architecture and examine its drawbacks.

The architecture of today's broadcast studio can be viewed as a complicated web of electronic and mechanical devices connected together by miles of cabling and numerous switches. Because of this complexity, studios exhibit a number of problems that must constantly be addressed. The most apparent and costly of these is that of maintaining the enormous bulk of cabling and switches upon which the studio is built. While this is generally not a problem with smaller studios, it becomes an increasingly more pressing issue as the studio matures. As studios grow and new components are introduced, cabling must be added to connect it to the existing studio devices. In most cases, reusing cabling may not be an option as the current studio operations often cannot be interrupted. As the studio matures and the equipment in the studio undergoes enhancement and change, the job of maintaining and managing this ever increasing mass of wiring requires a significant effort. Over time, even matching a given cable with its function can be a difficult task. In addition, the dependence that existing studio devices can have on their particular position in the web can create serious problems when cabling is removed, or when the web topography changes. The end result is much of the studio technologies that are in use today is both costly and difficult to change. Hence, the deployment of new technologies into a studio requires a great deal of time and effort to ensure that the studio remains in a properly working state. As we can see, reuse of existing technologies when introducing new ones cannot be accomplished easily with existing methods.

Another problem with current studio architectures are the physical limitations placed on the equipment in the studio. Since adding new cabling to a studio represents a significant amount of effort and cost, new devices are generally placed where they are easiest to wire. While studios have adapted their current operations to accommodate these constraints, planning for future technologies whose physical requirements are unknown becomes a difficult task. The result is that adoption of new technologies can be slowed significantly because of pressures to conserve valuable studio real estate. In addition, personnel that use or manage the studio devices are generally located where it is most economical to deploy them. Often, this will mean that studio workers must be located within close proximity to the devices they manage. The overall result is that people and equipment tend to be located within the studio where they physically make sense rather than being grouped together where their functions are logically beneficial. This becomes a very important benefit when we look at how an all digital, networked studio is operated.

**Object Systems**

Before we examine how to use new networking technologies to solve the problems of the current studio architectures, we need to explore some of the basic concepts. We've eluded to using an idea known as the "network distributed object model" to solve many of our problems. Let's look closely at some of the basic concepts embodied by this model. For interested readers, the specific model we've chosen is CORBA[1], but other models exist and the concepts are the same.

One of the more useful and exciting methodologies to come along in the computer science arena is that of object oriented programming. The basic idea behind this concept is that software services are provided in terms of individual building blocks (classes) that have the ability to perform all of their logical operations on themselves and the data they contain. A simple example of this is a VCR class, that contains basic information about a tape deck such as the format of the tape it accepts (Figure 1). In addition, it also provides several operations that will control the basic functions of the tape deck. Each instance of this class, known as an "object", contains its own specific copy of the data. That is, in this case each instance represents a different physical device. For example, if I have two tape decks that accept tapes of different formats (say D1 and Beta), I can create two instances of class VCR, one that represents and controls the D1 tape deck, and the other that controls the Beta deck. This notion of objects containing their own data and the operations that can be performed on that data is known as "encapsulation". When looking at how object systems can link together to perform complex tasks, this idea becomes critically important.

Aside from the benefits of data encapsulation, another important attribute of classes is their ability to inherit functionality from other classes. This idea is known as "subclassing" and can be illustrated very simply by looking at a our example class, the VCR class in Figure 1. As we've described, instances of this class store information about the specific tape device and provide control of the tape decks basic functions. So the tape format information and the control operations encapsulate all of the "attributes" of the class. As you can see in Figure 1, we have created a second class, the Timing VCR Class, that inherits all of the attributes of the VCR class, but adds an additional bit of functionality that starts and stops the VCR at specific times. In this case, the subclass does not replicate the attributes of its ancestor, but inherits them at no extra cost and only needs to provide the new functionality. One could extend this idea and create subclasses of the Timing VCR Class that add yet more functionality. With each successive subclass, only the new attributes need to be provided - everything else is inherited from the ancestor classes. This ability to add and change functionality without replication of effort is what makes object oriented methodologies so compelling. The functionality of existing classes can be augmented without duplicating it by simply adding in the desired operations. In a complete system implemented using this methodology, this means that new functionality can be added to existing systems with very little effort and without risk of breaking the current functionality.

1. Common Object Request Broker Architecture developed by the Object Management Group

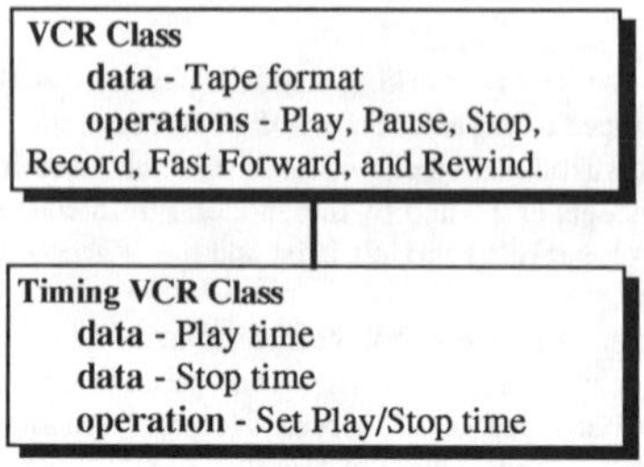


*Figure 1*

To complete our basic understanding of object systems, we can extend our view just a little further and see how objects can not only contain static data as part of their attributes, but also other objects whose functionality they need. With the ability to both inherit functionality from existing classes, and to use the functionality of existing objects, we can build very large and complex systems that are easily maintained, easily enhanced, and flexible to change.

Another common, and very useful feature of many object systems is a mechanism that allows objects to "observe" the state changes of other objects. An example of this might be a Monitor object that watches the VCR class so that when the tape starts to play, it automatically turns itself on to display the output. In this case, the monitor will request notification of state change events in the VCR, which will in turn broadcast these events to its observers when the changes take place. The key here is that the VCR does not need to know anything about the objects that are observing it, or even the number of objects interested in its state changes. It simply has to broadcast a notification using a standard mechanism that is part of the object system, and all of the observers will receive the appropriate events. As we will see later, this a very powerful concept in that it allows us to add new objects to the system that can interact with existing ones without their knowledge and without disruption of the current system activities.

Now to complete the picture, we'll need to extend our ideas about building object systems just a bit further and explore the notion of a distributed object system. In the examples illustrated above, we drew a picture of a closed system in which all of the objects reside within the same physical environment - i.e. a single computer workstation. However, we can open up this model and envision a system where objects reside on computers anywhere on the net and are still accessible to all other objects and software clients. We can accomplish this by creating a 'registry' of objects on the network that knows the location and capabilities of all objects in the system. When a client wants to subclass an existing class, or wants to use an existing object, the registry will provide them with the information necessary to access their attributes. If the registry allows objects and classes to be registered with information about their nature, i.e. a "Monitor" type, or a "Tape Deck" type, then we've created a system where the presence of an object or class on the system can be queried when needed, and the client need not have any prior knowledge of the specific makeup of the network. An example of where this is useful is an application that wants to pipe the output of a tape deck to all the monitors in the studio. The client retrieves the object controlling the specific VCR it wants to play, asks the registry for all of the currently registered objects of type "Monitor" and instructs the tape deck to output to those devices. While this is a very simplified view, it gives a general idea of how most network distributed objects systems work.

Now that we understand some of the basic technologies we can use to develop system architectures, let us see how we can apply them to the next generation of studio design. We can directly apply the ideas of network distributed objects to the broadcast studio if we view all of the studio devices as network objects. That is, devices such as tape decks, monitors, video file servers, cameras, network routers, and even transmitters will all implemented as network citizens that provide well know operations to control their functions. We described above the example of sending output from a VCR to a studio monitor as a simple case of this general idea.

**The Networked Studio**

In a studio designed around a network distributed object system (hereafter simply called a networked studio), all physical devices are attached to the network either by containing the necessary software within themselves, or by attaching themselves to a computer 'proxy' that is on the network and is able to control its functions. In each of these cases, a software implementation of the object that controls the device is present on the network and registered with appropriate information about its nature. A practical example of this is a tape deck that is attached to a computer through an RS-422 connection, which in turn is attached to a network and implements all of the functions of the "Tape Deck" object. If a client wants to start the tape deck playing, he queries for the specific tape deck object and invokes the Play operation. Figure 2 shows a graphic of the network with a variety of devices connected to it. Notice that objects are viewed the same way on the network whether they represent real physical devices, or are purely software objects such as a playlist editing application.

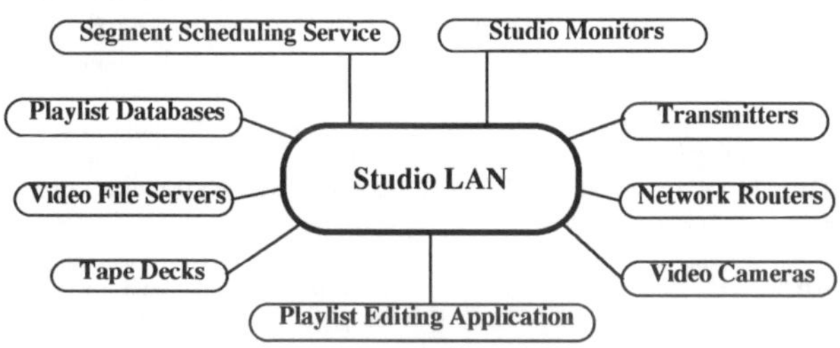


*Figure 2*

As an exercise in mapping our knowledge of the networked studio to real studio operations, we'll use the network objects shown in Figure 2 to describe a simple scenario. Shown in the diagram are a playlist editing application that allows modification of currently scheduled playlists; a playlist database that stores the content information for all of the video segments in the playlists; a segment scheduling service whose task it is to ensure that a given video segment is broadcast at the scheduled time; a video file server that stores all of the studio's video segments; a network router that routes the video signals to the transmitter; and the transmitter itself. The diagram is somewhat simpler than what we would see in an actual studio, but it illustrates the point of network objects cooperating together to accomplish a task. In this case, the task will be to change a commercial segment in a currently airing playlist. The flow of network operations to achieve this is as follows: the playlist editing application connects to the network, finds the playlist database object, queries for the playlist contents, and displays a graphic showing the playlist. Through the application's user interface, the user swaps out a commercial that is set to air in a few seconds with a different one.

The playlist application invokes the operation in the database object to make the appropriate change. Upon detecting the change, the database finds the segment scheduling service object and instructs it to ready the new commercial for air. The segment scheduling service then finds the video file server object and requests that it compute the time it will take to ready the new commercial for air. It enough time is available, it sets a timer which when triggered causes the service to create a connection between the video server and the router, and instructs the server to send the commercial's video data. The router then sends it to the transmitter and the broadcast is accomplished. This example illustrates how components in the studio interact with each other to accomplish a specific task. In the complete studio, there will be many of these kinds of operations occurring simultaneously to handle all of the studio's functions.

Before we look at how the networked studio solves many of the current studio problems, we should explore more fully the concept of connecting to a network. In the simplest case, connecting to the studio network means a computer with a network adapter running the necessary network software that is attached directly to the network cables. However, a network connection can also be made by connecting an outside network, such as a corporate Intranet or even the Internet, to the studio by means of a network gateway. Or, a connection can be through a satellite link that connects to the network via a computer workstation. Or, it can even be a connection over a telephone line to a modem that is attached to the network. So, the idea of connecting to the studio network can take a variety of forms. In general, devices in the studio only require a network presence to be legitimate network citizens. However, from a practical standpoint, they also require a connection with the appropriate performance characteristics to be effectively perform their tasks. For instance, a video file server requires a very high bandwidth, very predictable connection to reliably transfer video information with sufficient quality. However, an application that manages a playlist database needs only the performance of a modem connection since the amount of data transferred from the application to the database is relatively small. These varying degrees of performance requirements allows us some freedom to design the studio network topography in ways that are both effective and economical. It also opens up the possibilities of accessing the network through any number of avenues. What is beginning to evolve is the idea that the studio is no longer defined by the physical space it takes up, but by the accessibility of its network entry points. This is the underlying concept behind the notion of the "virtual studio".

Now, we're ready to look at how the problems with existing studio technology can be solved using our networked studio model. As we described at the beginning, existing studios suffer greatly from the complexity and sheer mass of the cabling that interconnects all of the studio devices. As a result, the introduction of new technologies into the studio is generally done with great care and expense since the addition of new devices to the complicated web of connections can disrupt other studio devices whose dependencies on the network topography may not be completely known. In a networked studio however, we've seen how the addition of new objects can be done with relatively little impact to the overall system since the new technologies can be built directly on top of the old without effecting their functionality. In the case that new objects provide completely new functionality and do not inherit from existing ones, they can guarantee that their presence will be completely invisible to the existing system by adding themselves to the network registry as a type not currently known to the network. Hence, new technologies can be added to the studio network and their functionality tested fully without risking disruption of the current studio operations. Its easy to see that the cost of developing and deploying new studio devices and network services can be reduced dramatically over their current costs. In addition, since the functionality of every object on the network is well known ahead of time, and objects share a great deal of functionality, the time and cost to track studio problems and implement solutions is likewise reduced.

As we described before, one of the primary artifacts of a networked studio is that the boundaries of the studio are not reflected in the physical location of the studio devices, but in the access points to the network. The implications of this to developing studio operations can be quite remarkable. In the current studio environments, workers whose jobs involve dealing directly with physical devices are generally required to work within close proximity to those devices. The personnel whose jobs are linked to the operations of those workers are likewise constrained to work near them, and hence, close to the devices as well. The cascade of job related dependence dictates much of the way that studio real estate is used. In many cases, workers are physically grouped together more because of the nature of the studio landscape than their logical needs to work together. In the networked studio, the physical location of a given device is not generally relevant. So decisions about where a person should work, or where a device should be located can be made based on economic principles rather than the physical layout of a building. One practical implication of this is that physical devices such as video file servers or tape backup drives are not required to take up valuable real estate in the studio itself, but can be moved to a less expensive location, perhaps across town or even across the country, and tied directly back into the studio network. This frees up studio real estate for any desired purpose such as additional soundstages, or more personnel. What is important in these examples is that studio personnel can be grouped together based on their logical working relationships rather than physical constraints.

### Studio Automation

Another significant benefit of the networked studio is the ease with which many studio operations can be automated. In the example above where we describe controlling the playout of a commercial segment, much of what occurs in the process is a sequence of cascading operations where a change in the state of one object automatically invokes a response from another. In many cases, the response is invoked not by directly calling the object, but is done using the event notification mechanisms described earlier. For example, in the commercial play out example, rather than the playout database calling directly to the segment scheduler service to schedule the commercial, it can simply broadcast a change notification to its observers and let them deal with it as they see fit. In this case, the segment scheduler service observes the database and watches for these changes. When it receives a notification that a commercial segment has been added, it responds by scheduling it. In the same way, we can add any number of services to the network that respond to a wide variety of events to perform whatever actions we need. A practical example might be a service that notices when a commercial has been aired and automatically sends electronic mail to the client to let them know about it. The possibilities for creating new applications that can automate a large number of studio tasks without requiring changes to the system provides us with a vast amount of extensibility and flexibility that we are unable to achieve with current studio technologies.

### Security

We have demonstrated how the networked studio is readily extensible in its functionality and easily accessible by the wide variety of network connection options. One of the potential problems with both of these attributes is that of network security. In one case, unauthorized people need to be prevented from accessing the network in order to protect the studio's proprietary information. In another, we must ensure that malicious services that can disrupt the studio operations are not allowed to operate within the system. Both of these issues have been the focus of much study in the computer community for many years, and methodologies and protocols have been developed in the computer industry that provide for extremely secure access to network resources. These services are currently available in most modern commercial network systems and discussion of their specifics is beyond the scope of this discussion. However, in addition to these well known network security services, a number of distributed object systems have also implemented their own security models that augment this functionality and provide secure access at the object level. In these cases, security services take into account more issues than simply a user name and password. In some systems, objects are stamped indicating their origin or author and security models have been developed that require a client to be authenticated as "trusted" before it can invoke the operations of another object[2]. The notion of an object being trusted can take on a variety of meanings, but in general it refers to an object of known authorship or origin that is assured of not being malevolent. Beyond this, an object can also allow for varying levels of access to its operations and data depending on how well trusted the calling client is. For example, an object may provide some functionality to all objects, while other operations can only be accessed by well know clients. As we can see, a great deal of technology is available to ensure that access to the network and to the network objects occurs only by authorized personnel, and that malicious services will not be allowed to operate within the system that can disrupt studio operations.

### File Servers

One of the most important artifacts of the networked studio is that video data no longer primarily resides on video tapes, but is stored and maintained on high speed file servers. While the network model can be adapted to operate virtually any type of physical device, the key to the success of the network studio lies in the file server's ability to store very large amounts of video data and to deliver that information fast enough to enable the transmission of high quality video in real time. By using high bandwidth networks such as an OC-12/OC-48 ATM network, a single video file server can handle multiple U.S. Grand Alliance HD video/audio streams simultaneously. The specific configurations of the file servers and networks that handle this type of data flow are covered in numerous other papers and are beyond the scope of this discussion. However, with viable streaming server technology, we can take advantage of many other benefits that provide the networked studio with significant value. The first such benefit is that video servers can provide very high reliability. By taking advantage of the redundant storage technologies such as RAID arrays, and the current technologies embodied in fault tolerant computer systems, we are able to provide file servers that can deliver extremely high levels of reliability under even the most adverse conditions. While catastrophic mechanical failure can occur in any system, the possibility of such a failure can be reduced to levels well below that of current studio devices. In addition, recovery from such a failure can be handled automatically by the network services, so that downtime is minimized and the studio can be back on air quickly and requiring a minimum of support personnel. Another significant advantage is that video data is available from a single source and can be accessed by multiple clients simultaneously. One of the many implications of this idea is that multiple play out streams can be created simultaneously for a single source, allowing play out to different destinations at varying times. In addition, access to video source material by multiple clients for editing and browsing can be provided from the source directly without requiring copies. If copies are desired, however, they can be made simply and quickly without disrupting clients that may be currently accessing the video data. And finally, perhaps the greatest benefit comes in the ease of managing the video data in the studio. Finding, displaying, editing, copying, and removing of source material can be done using a single computer workstation from anywhere on the network. In addition, administration of access privileges for any video source material can be accomplished with equal ease. As we can see, the management of video data in the networked studio no longer requires the administration and cataloging of tapes or other physical media, but is done by simply

---

2. CORBA and Sun Microsystem's Java™ are examples of systems that use this security model.

managing files on the network video servers.

## Conclusion

As we have seen, the networked broadcast studio provides a faster, more reliable, more flexible, and more easily maintained system than is currently used in the television industry. When all of the studio information is stored digitally, and all of the studio devices are connected by a digital network, then managing the operations of the studio simply involves managing the movement of the data, regardless of whether that data is video, audio, or any other type. This powerful and simple idea allows us to produce the next generation of broadcast studio that is more efficient and more economical than is possible to achieve using the technologies that are in place today.

## Acknowledgments

This paper is one in a series presented by the HDTV Broadcast Technology group as part of the NIST Advanced Technology Program, Cooperative Agreement Award No. 70N1NB5H1174. We would like to express our thanks to NIST and to our program manager, Ms. Florina Hoffer for making this project possible.

## References

1 "The Common Object Request Broker: Architecture and Specification - Revision 2.0", July 1995, Object Management Group, Inc., Framingham, MA

2 ISO/IEC 13818-6 IS, "Coding of Moving Pictures and Associated Audio, November 1995

3 "OMG White Paper on Security - Issue 1", April 1994, OMG Security Working Group

# A New Approach to Transporting Program Content

Paul Donaldson & Fred Huffman
MCI Communications
Richardson, Texas

## Abstract

The distribution of program content to broadcasters, cable headends, satellite uplink sites and between production studios is a high-volume and cumbersome process requiring immense resources. Today, content distribution is largely conducted via satellite circuits and physical tape. In certain cases, the element of time becomes important enough that physical movement of videotape is not even considered an option. Technological advances in the development of lower-cost, higher-powered computing and digital processing devices are finding wider use in the creation and delivery of programming. With server-based (digital) content storage, delivery becomes a matter of moving bits; however, digital program content transport requires payload bit rates from 20 Mbps to 270 Mbps. Existing electronic, network-based content delivery systems are limited in capacity, signal performance and flexibility. Leveraging advanced terrestrial digital networks holds the promise of removing these limitations. This paper will describe the development and envisioned uses of a unique Network Interface Device (NID) that is expected to make content transport via advanced common carrier (ATM and SONET/SDH) communications networks as easy as making phone calls.

# 1. Introduction

To begin, we should say that MCI's business is services, not physical products. The only items manufactured by MCI, per se, are phone bills - lots of them. The contents of this paper might lead the reader to conclude otherwise. In the instant case, our objective is to contribute a transport access device to the National Institute of Standards and Technology (NIST) Advanced Technology Program (ATP) - the "HDTV Broadcast Technology" project.[1] The intent of MCI's contribution is the development of a Network Interface Device (NID) to demonstrate the technical feasibility of transport services over a communications network.

This paper is about the transport of program content among producers and users of that content required for ultimate delivery to homes for consumption by the national viewing and subscription audience. It is not about program content creation or end-link distribution. By program content we mean, full-motion video and high-quality audio information as delivered on film, video tape and live, real-time communications media.

Looking at the "food chain" of program content, we see three distinct processes: content creation, content assembly and end-link distribution (See Figure 1.1).

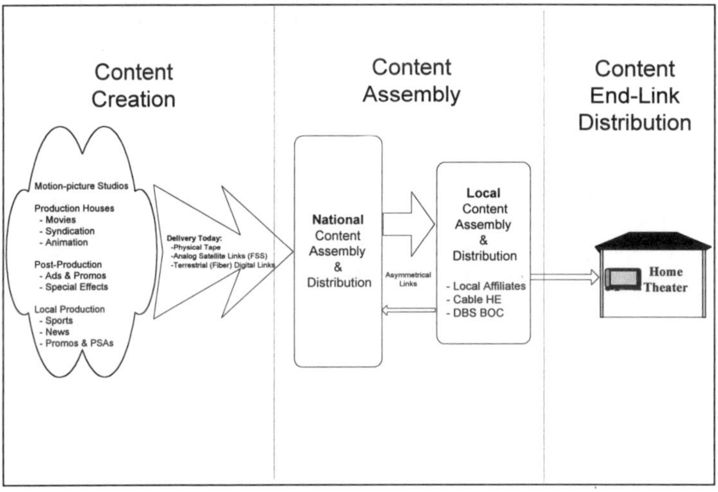


**Figure 1.1 Program Content "Food Chain"**

Program content movement occurs two ways; physical movement of magnetic storage media or over communications links. Change has been technology enabled and is likely to continue. As the national viewer/subscriber audience adapts to change, the source and amount of program content is likely to change in response to market demands and economic forces.

### 1.2 Changes In The Landscape 1975 -1995

In 1975, there were just under 1000 television stations on air in the US. By 1995, the number totaled 1,520.[2] In 1975, there were four major "networks." Today there are more than 100 "networks" delivering programming to the national audience through the television stations. Cable systems numbered less than 5,000 in 1980; today we have tens of thousands of cable head-ends, SMATV and other end-link transmission pipes reaching the national television audience.

Direct Broadcast Satellite (DBS) television arrived on the scene in 1994 producing yet another requirement for acquisition and transmission of high-quality content. Regional and national sports and other specialized programming production forms hundreds of hours per week of content sent to the national audience. Distance learning and other uses of high-quality video and audio are emerging.

TV Homes have grown from around 60 million[3] to more than 90 million. In 1975, most homes had one television set; today the number ranges from 1-9. VCR's were essentially non-existent in 1975; today the average household is likely to own several. A movie rented at the local grocery store or pharmacy has become an item we can't get along without. A trip to the big movie rental store for a supply of weekend movies is not unusual for many of us. The demand for high-quality program content has never been greater and continues to grow. Historically, television has migrated from monochrome to color and, more recently, to DBS/MPEG-2. The quality hurdle continues to ratchet up with High Definition Television (HDTV) on the horizon.

### 1.3 Postulating a Business Opportunity

We see that existing programming distribution networks are primarily satellite-based and inherently limited in terms of picture quality and information transfer rates. There is a lack of diversity, alternate routing or backup service. The general nature of services available today is half-duplex, dedicated private lines. Would not a switched service offering that enables program content movement between creators and wholesale users of that content be viable?

Today's public communications network service providers' (formerly "common carriers") businesses are built on a technical infrastructure consisting of three basic elements: switching, transmission and network management or back office systems. This infrastructure together with customer equipment (telephone or personal computer) makes up the physical platform enabling today's communications industry. This infrastructure has value. Leveraging that value, i.e. finding a way to incrementally provide more services using existing infrastructure, seems logical and financially attractive.

For example, the MCI network is built around a core business that supports point-to-point voice and data calls - "telephony." Each call uses a 64 kbps channel on a shared transmission facility. This service is enabled by major switches at transmission network nodes in each of the areas where the traffic is concentrated. There are more network elements ("peers" to the 64 kbps switches) that support dissimilar "peer" services. Examples of this type of service include the Internet, specialized data services and a Virtual Integrated Services Network where specialized service sets are delivered to unique customer requirements not met by any of the other services.

MCI's network and competing networks undergo constant change. The change is driven by customer demand and enabled by technological development implemented incrementally into existing network infrastructure.

Given the above, we believe a reasonable business opportunity can be postulated. MCI's contribution to the NIST ATP "HDTV Broadcast Technology" project[1] is to design and deliver a NID that will provide traditional private line services, and enable new switched services for the "new" digital television industry. We see that the basic segments of the entertainment industry have complementary issues:

| ENTITY | ISSUE |
|---|---|
| Content Creator: | "How do I deliver content to the DBS Operator Uplink Site, or cable head end, or TV station transmitter site?" |
| Broadcaster Cable Operator: | "How do I provide content at an economically attractive cost?" |
| Advertiser: | "How can I get my commercial in front of the appropriate audience at the right time to support time-to-market sensitive product and service offering promotion." |
| Network Services Provider: | "How do we leverage the business infrastructure? |

It is these issues we hope will be addressed by the NID and provide a new means of transporting entertainment content between the program content producers, television broadcasters, cable and DBS operators, ultimately providing viewers and subscribers with greater choice and diversity of programming. The capabilities envisioned would permit program content to be transported across networks and tracked by owners and users with the ease and simplicity of ordinary telephone or video conference calling.

A popular view of the NID is that it may further enable the "Virtual Studio", a concept whereby creative producers, editors and assemblers can collaborate and work together in physically different locations as effectively as they could in the same room.[4]

# 2. Communications Network Architecture

## 2.1 Existing State of Network

From a strict communications network service provider viewpoint, the infrastructure in place is limited in its ability to support shared use of the assets among a diversity of service offerings (See Figure 2.1). Clara (the hamburger lady) would ask: “Where’s the video?” The answer is, “It’s in there somewhere.”

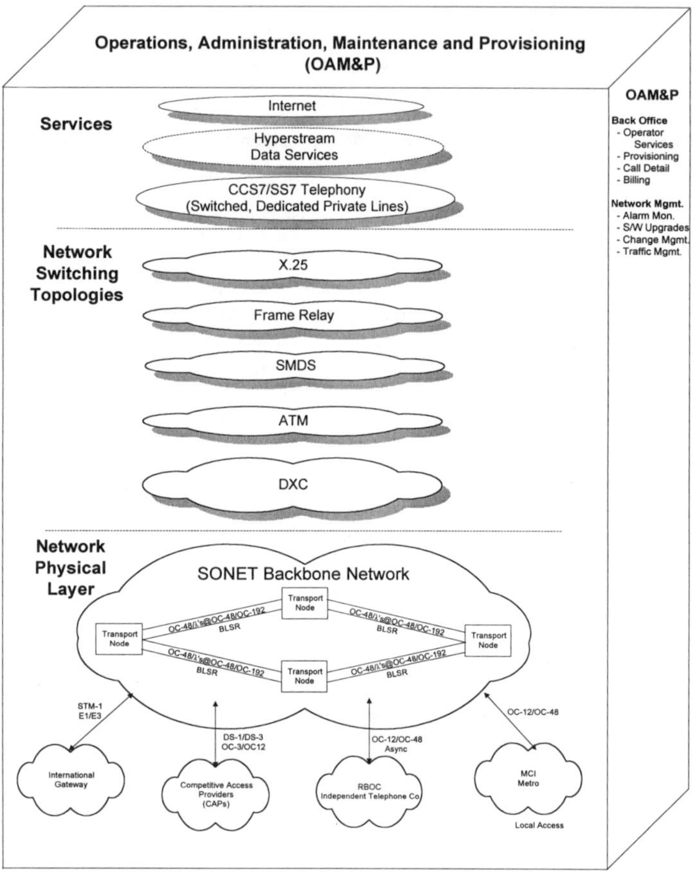


**Figure 2.1 Network Service Provider Architecture**

Today's communications networks are primarily comprised of DS-3 (45 Mbps), meshed links generally running east-west or north-south between major population centers. These networks, however, are migrating from DS-3 to OC-3/OC-12 (155/270 Mbps) links. At link terminations in major population centers, large switches switch 64 kbps channels that enable dial-up telephony. Generally, the use of the transmission capacity is loaded and managed so the links between the switches operate at 50% capacity with normal traffic loading. The service provided is the core business. It deserves a high level of protection in event of failure of a single backbone link. This is a competitive fact of life - the service is delivered, or the customer goes elsewhere.

## 2.2 Network Changes & Developments

The basic architecture of the global public transmission network is migrating from meshed links to hybrid networks of both meshed links and rings. Early examples of Synchronous Optical NETwork/Synchronous Digital Hierarchy (SONET/SDH) rings are under construction in the Atlantic (TAT-12/13) and Pacific (TPC-5) oceans. Partially operational today, they are expected to become fully operational by the end of 1997. Transmission facilities of similar design have appeared in major metropolitan areas around the country and it's believed that this type of architecture will proliferate as the communications industry changes in response to recently inaugurated legislation. Eventually, one can reasonably speculate that regional ring-based transmission networks may appear, interconnecting the metropolitan rings. As the national network infrastructure evolves, a more homogenous structure will provide greater opportunity to utilize idle backup transmission capacity.

Improvements in speed performance per unit of fiber transmission capacity have been dramatic in recent years and are expected to continue (Figure 2.2) .[5]

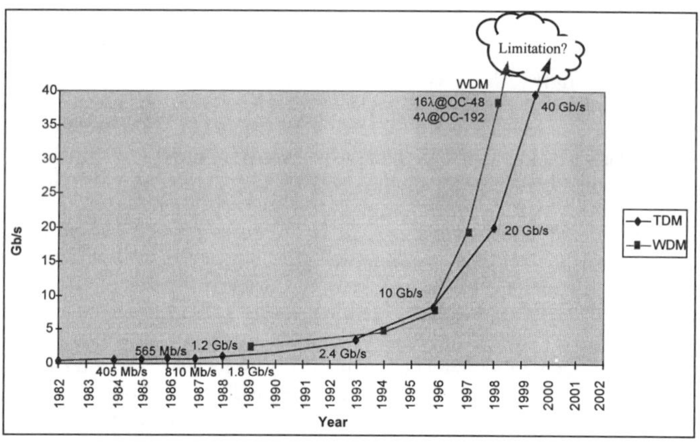


**Figure 2.2 Bandwidth Growth**

10 Gbps (OC-192) links have been operational and carrying live traffic within the past year. Experimental and development work at 40 Gbps and above is known to be underway in numerous labs.

Continuing development in this area is expected to continue to drive unit cost lower. Improvements in the capacity per unit of optical component increase the amount of bandwidth available for new services. This in turn reduces the service providers unit cost, paving the way for more competitive pricing in the marketplace. As improvements in capacity per unit of transmission network have improved, costs have dropped just as dramatically (Figure 2.3)[5].

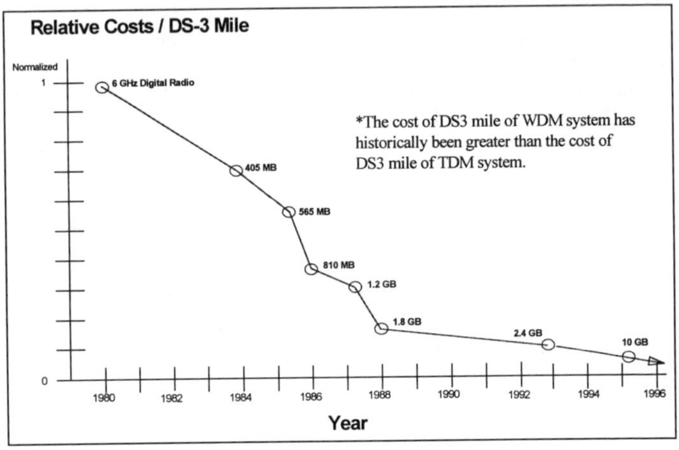


**Figure 2.3 Bandwidth Costs**

Improved digital compression such as MPEG-2 at higher speeds and other techniques known to be underway are likely to add to the opportunity for improved, lower cost services available to the content creation and distribution community.

On the switching side of the network, change is also taking place. Classical CCS7/SS7 signaling-based services are not likely to disappear. But proponents of Asynchronous Transfer Mode (ATM) techniques continue to make progress and enable new services. It is our belief that ATM over the SONET/SDH transmission plant represents an opportunity to enable switched program content transport services, leveraging existing network infrastructure. ATM switching as a peer to existing CCS7/SS7 64 kbps switching will increase the amount of available bandwidth far beyond the capability of existing narrowband digital network based services. This in turn provides greater utilization of a given amount of fixed transmission capacity, further improving overall network efficiency.

# 3. Network Interface Device

## 3.1 Design Rationale

The ultimate purpose of the NID is to interface the HDTV Studio/Operations Center with high-speed ATM and SONET/SDH digital network services. Existing programming distribution networks are satellite-based and inherently limited in their ability to transmit higher, multiple bit rate signals envisioned in future HDTV production and operations. For example, the raw, uncompressed signal produced by cameras and other signal generating devices is around 1.2 Gbps. Compressed rates are being pursued in an attempt to bring the acceptable, studio-quality bit rate down to 270 Mbps (or perhaps 155 Mbps) for recording, editing, production and distribution around the inside plant. Satellite bandwidth is primarily analog and development of specialized modems will be required to obtain these high data rates. Even with these new modems, the data rates will be limited to around 90 Mbps. This is a technical barrier to transmission of production quality of 270 Mbps signals outside the production center. In addition, satellite networks do not have intelligent network switching and inherent interoperability required for highly-automated transport of program content.

Another major technical barrier in the distribution infrastructure is a lack of ability to selectively distribute material to individual stations, cable headends, or DBS uplink sites. The number of unique paths is limited to the number of satellites times the number of transponders available. "Occasional service" is available, but more often than not, demand exceeds supply, particularly on occurrence of major national or global events such as the Olympics, or disasters such as the World Trade Center and Oklahoma City Federal Building bombings.

Today, physical transport of content by physical shipment and handling of magnetic tape is by far the dominant transport mechanism. **Without some means of effectively moving production-quality material electronically, the industry will be relegated to continued transport via physical movement of magnetic tape.**

The NID concept will provide access to intelligent network switching and transmission facilities at speeds up to 270 Mbps. These capabilities will enable point-to-point and point-to-multipoint transport of program content on demand between production centers; between production centers and broadcast, cable and DBS program transmission sites; and between remote field production (news) sites where access is available. The service envisioned will make transport of program content as simple and easy as making a phone call. Lower bit rate (less than 270 Mbps) program content , stored on servers, could be transported faster than real-time (faster than the normal bit rate of the streamed content). Advertisers with access to the network and program content servers can select audiences based on fine grain demographics to the individual broadcast, cable or DBS program transmission point. End-point transmission system operators (broadcast stations, CATV systems, DBS operators) can gain access to wholesale program content program content servers on an automated basis. Faster than real-time transmission will enable the end-point transmission operator to make program content available using smaller, lower cost program content servers.

The NID will provision the collection and storage of call detail information satisfying administrative, billing, operations and maintenance requirements. Various levels of interoperability between the studio/operations center and the network will permit automated transport of content over the network, simultaneously collecting details about network usage and content transported. For example, a live program originating at one location may be transported across a network to multiple distribution points, or a program content server at one location may connect to a counterpart at another location and transfer content for editing or direct transmission. This value-added function permits the network owner/operator to perform administration, operations and maintenance functions.

### 3.2 Key Design Assumptions

Design planning for the NID includes the following key assumptions:

1. Electrical or optical interface to the network in accordance with current and emerging ITU Recommendations covering ATM and SONET/SDH services.

2. Use of Asynchronous Mode Switching (ATM) with ATM Forum UNI 3.1 switched virtual circuit provisioning will be *technically viable.*

3. Picture quality and audio fidelity acceptable to the *customer* while transporting high-quality content in real time will be achieved.

4. Network monitoring and modeling techniques will be developed to allow network service providers to plan, provision and manage network capacity where the network is simultaneously transporting classical telephony content and high-quality program content.

Use of standards-based interfaces will allow existing multi-service bandwidth to be leveraged by traditional private line program content services and new switched services. ATM technology is beginning to show enough maturity to be considered a technical platform capable of supporting a long-term, commercially-viable business in switched broadband program content services (See Figure 3.1).

The NID design and development project for HDTV content will address these issues in an effort to provide dynamic, high-quality content transport services.

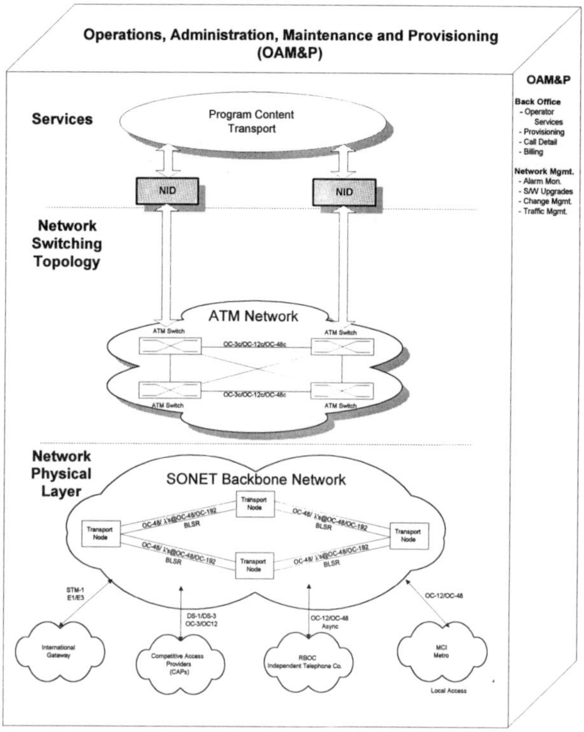


**Figure 3.1 Program Content Services Network Architecture**

### 3.3 Concept Design

A high-level functional diagram of the NID is shown in Figure 3.2. The primary concept is based on an ATM multiplexing or concentrator device having a mid-plane interconnection design with communications network interfaces and studio interfaces to support planned HDTV standard interfaces and existing CCIR-601 digital video. Additional capabilities are planned to support legacy signal interfaces to support current communications needs and to assist in the transition from analog to digital and from standard definition digital to high definition digital technology.

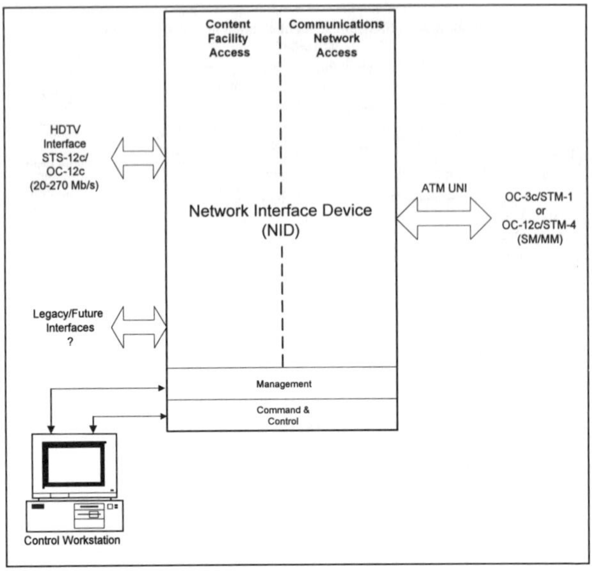


**Figure 3.2 NID Functional Block Diagram**

A local control workstation is specified to provide the customer the ability to quickly and easily set-up and tear down high-bandwidth communication connections. It will also provide some maintenance, administration & provisioning control of external communication links. For example, the customer can setup a communications link first by "dialing" the appropriate number (e.g., NSAP Encoded E.164 format[6]) of the desired entity (distant studio, server, broadcast facility, etc.). Next, the customer can specify the required bit rate and ATM Quality of Service (QoS) parameters.

In the case of recorded, or stored content, the customer can establish the desired delivery speed level of service - real-time, faster than real-time, or slower than real-time. The choice of service level would be based on the customer's minimum requirements and/or on cost considerations. For example, if the customer wished to receive program content that was not immediately needed, or time sensitive, a request for transport delivery "when possible" could be specified. The transport provider could then potentially offer this transport service at a lower cost and stream the content when there is available capacity identified by traffic management.

After the call is established, the customer can then monitor the transmission performance with various metrics (i.e., Cell Delay Variation, Cell-Loss Ratio, bit errors, etc.).

## 4. Technical Issues and Challenges

MCI has identified several important technical issues and challenges to providing program content services. These include:

1. The existing network was designed to handle time division multiplexed voice and data content. The data rate (channel) increments are DS-0 (64 kbps), DS-1 (1.5 Mbps) and DS-3 (45 Mbps). Newer standards-based designs are in the early stages of implementation and operations. The data rate requirements for real-time program content basically begin at DS-3 rates and require OC-12 rates ($\geq$ 270 Mbps) to support uncompressed CCIR-601 and HDTV compressed program content. Molding the emerging network design to deliver classical private line, and newer switched program content services is not a trivial exercise.

2. In practice, high bit rate transport of high-quality program content over ATM switched networks has not been fully validated (i.e., handling real-time traffic capacity under peak traffic conditions). Development of ATM traffic modeling and network testing of high bit rate (HDTV content) transport is required.

3. How to migrate service as technology changes once a design approach has been selected.

4. How to maintain security of communications access (i.e., server access) and program content during transport.

5. How to provide network management integration of program content transport services.

6. How to define Quality of Service and measure picture quality and sound fidelity.

## 5. End-to-End Network and Service Verification Testing

MCI's development of a NID includes the development of test procedures and performance measurements to characterize the ability of terrestrial fiber and satellite-based transmission networks to reliably transport digital HDTV signals at rates from 20 Mbps to 270 Mbps. This effort is intended to validate the design of the NID and associated switching and transmission facilities. It will also characterize performance and interoperability of server-to-server transfer of content. The planned test network is shown in Figure 5.1.

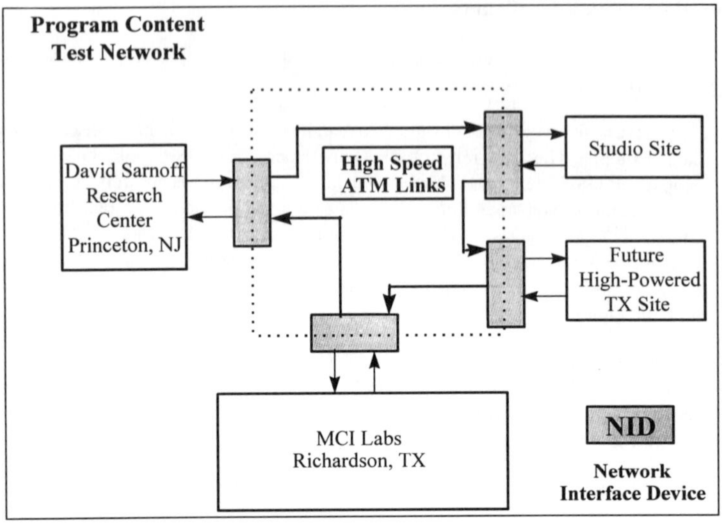


**Figure 5.1 Program Content Transport Test Network**

The major testing requirements will be to evaluate the prototype and final version of the NID. It will be necessary to make sure that various HDTV signals can be successfully transported into and out of the network using the NID at access and egress points in the network. One of the early characterization exercises will measure performance of two NID's connected back to back by a network simulation tool. The network simulation tool can provide a connection with controlled network impairments while tests are conducted and results recorded to produce a reference benchmark characterization. Once the reference benchmark is complete, then the network simulator can be replaced with a real network segment and end-to-end network performance can be measured. The network segment can be either terrestrial fiber or satellite links.

Once the NID and network are characterized, then signals can be transported from the HDTV Studio/Operations Center to broadcast transmitter sites, DBS uplinks and cable headends for transmission to HDTV receivers. For example, MCI believes it will be necessary to conduct tests to prove the feasibility of transporting material from a program content server at one location to a program content server at another location. MCI will require a program content server to be located at the Labs in Richardson for the purpose of characterizing and proving performance of server-to-server interoperability across the network. MCI also believes it is necessary to include end-point transmission link testing over CATV facilities and plans to use its CATV Simulation Lab.

The ability of the network to set-up and tear down calls in response to a NID request for service will be verified. This will include collection of call detail records from which administration, operations and maintenance activities can be performed by MCI's network operations and back office accounting functions.

Since a key assumption in the NID design is the use of an ATM switching network architecture, there are numerous performance concerns that require investigation and resolution. We are aware of similar work underway that deals with assessing performance of ATM (AAL-5) transmission of program content. This work is described elsewhere in a report attributed to Deutsche Telekom AG and ZDF.[7]

We see several critical ATM performance measurements and their impact on program content (especially video) which must be carefully evaluated and considered.

1. Delay
2. Jitter
3. Lost/dropped ATM cells (Cell-loss ratio CLR)
4. Random bit errors in ATM cell header
5. Random bit errors in ATM cell payload

It will be necessary to evaluate the quality of the transported real-time program content. This is somewhat difficult because of the lack of objective quality assessment tools. *MCI is actively seeking objective measurement tools to evaluate program content technical quality.*

Lastly, effective ATM traffic modeling is important to insure that the effects of peak traffic loading does not impact the quality of end-to-end service offered to the users. Such testing has been suggested by Deutsche Telekom and ZDF.[7]

## 6. Business Challenges

The first and foremost business issue for MCI is how to provide competitive program content services. Today, transport services for program content are primarily point-to-point, dedicated communications services that are quite expensive and inflexible for many customers. Exacerbating the problem for HDTV, the minimum data rate requirement is the 20 Mbps rate for an end-link Grand Alliance (GA) signal. This will require a DS-3 facility over the standard telephony links. Higher data rates of 155-270 Mbps (OC-3c, OC-12c) will be required for studio-quality HDTV. The cost of high bit rate communications links (i.e. DS-3, OC-3c) is considered prohibitive by many potential customers in the program content industry.

MCI's planned NID will be modular for flexibility in choosing only necessary bandwidth access. Also, the choice of using ATM network technology is expected to provide switched transport service and cell multiplexing for bandwidth efficiency leading to reduced transport costs.

Backbone communications network bandwidth costs are dropping as bandwidth is increasing. However this has not been the case with "last mile" access links. These costs remain relatively high and in many cases commercially prohibitive. It is expected, however, that the 1996 Telecommunications Act, which opens up local competition, will lead to reduced access costs.

MCI also must determine tariffing, or pricing, plans for providing high-bandwidth program content transport services. The provisioning and maintenance methods of the services must also must be defined and validated for flexible and competitive service offerings.

## 7. Conclusion

In conclusion, we believe technology to permit affordable, cost-effective transport of high-quality digital program content through emerging communications networks is on the horizon. We expect to demonstrate a operating NID during the next 24 months. When combined with ATM switching and SONET/SDH transmission services, it will deliver classical, dedicated program content transport service as well as a new set of switched transport services. We welcome comments and suggestions on the work outlined herein.

## 8. References & Acknowledgments


1. Hoffer, Florina, National Institute of Standards and Technology (NIST) Advanced Technology Program (ATP) , "HDTV Broadcast Technology," Cooperative Agreement Award Number: 70N1NB5H1174, Gaithersburg, MD, September 1995.

2. Broadcasting & Cable Yearbook, Washington, DC: Broadcasting & Cable, 1996.

3. Bower, Robert T., "The Changing Television Audience in America," New York: Columbia University Press, 1985.

4. Mills, Karen, "Video on the Run: Eliminating Geography as an Obstacle to Production," *millimeter*, March 1995, pages 131-140.

5. Liu, Shoa-Kai, "TDM vs WDM," Dallas, TX, Supercom Conference, June 27, 1996.

6. Alles, Anthony, "ATM Internetworking," Cisco Systems, Inc., May 1995.

7. "ZDF Conducts ATM Field Trial for Video and Audio Purposes," SMPTE Journal, April 1996, pages 226-227.

## Using Intelligent Nodes and Fiber Optics to Control the Next Generation of Digital Television (DTV) Transmitters

by
Mark A. Aitken
and Gerry Wawrzeniak
COMARK

### 1. INTRODUCTION

When faced with the fact that the requirements for transmitting the Grand Alliance DTV signal are different from that of today's standard, many opportunities for improving the "State of the Art" exist. COMARK has taken such an opportunity to design a transmitter uniquely matched to the new standard, as well as other requirements broadcasters have requested.

Product costs will be more important with the DTV transmitter than normal since the revenue stream that it will produce for the station will lag the initial installation of the system. Keeping product cost and support cost in mind infers the need for an advanced remote control and automated fault analysis system.

This paper will describe a system that is being created at COMARK based on these realities. In the context of that, the general features of that product will be detailed as well.

### 2. NTSC TO DTV DIFFERENCES

Today's UHF NTSC transmitter is required to deliver high peak and average power. The power levels in the market today are generally between 60kW and 240kW peak. The average power varies with the picture content and places a varying load on both the AC power line and the internal components of the transmitter.

This power hungry NTSC system typically demands large water cooled tubes and support systems, as well as large RF transmission line structures. The floor space that these systems occupy can be significant and expensive. Some modern transmitters that use IOT tubes are capable of providing good DTV service but have not been optimized for DTV service.

The DTV signal is significantly different from that of NTSC. From the receiver end, the DTV signal is at a constant average power at a level that is about 12 dB below the peak power of NTSC, for equivalent coverage. Industry analysis, taking into account fade and noise margins, estimates many DTV transmitter power requirements to be 12kW average in many station situations. This is well below the 80kW average power levels found in a 120kW peak NTSC transmitter. The peak power of this 12kW average DTV signal would then be about 50kW. (It should be noted that this peak power occurs less than 1% of the time. The NTSC peaks occur about 10% of the time.)

The differences in the two systems (NTSC and DTV), when addressed, present the designer with some very interesting technology solutions.

## 3. IOT - THE TECHNOLOGY CHOICE FOR DTV

A new "DIGITAL" version of the IOT (IOTD150R) was introduced by EEV at the '96 NAB. This compact tube, under final development, is based upon an analog unit available that is rated for 20kW in combined 10dB aural/visual NTSC service. This tube has undergone testing and it has been confirmed that it will support 50kW peak and 12kW average powers when amplifying DTV signal formats. Most importantly, it is AIR COOLED.

The linearity of the IOT is well proven in NTSC service where it consistently provides -60dB or better intermodulation performance in combined 10dB aural/visual service. This is fully 6dB better than any other current technology at the system level. The IOT, in a COMARK transmitter, is the device that has been used for over two years in Charlotte NC to prove the Grand Alliance DTV system.

The IOT was introduced to the industry in 1986 by COMARK and Varian as the Klystrode®. COMARK and Varian received an EMMY award for their work pioneering the Klystrode® and its transmitter in 1991. Early success with the tube was later marred by production problems at Varian that slowed its industry acceptance. The first Klystrode® transmitters were put into full time broadcast service at Georgia Public Television in 1989 and are still providing reliable operation today. In 1991 EEV introduced an improved IOT that rapidly gained industry wide acceptance. Early problems with the EEV IOT were traced to gun stability and input cavity dielectric strength issues. By 1994 these problems were largely solved. Today there are over 250 tubes in service and another 100 under contract in over 20 countries. Tubes manufactured after mid 1993 show a Weibull life analysis of 37,500 hours. This means that by 37,500 hours 2/3 of the tubes shall have died. From the same data, the hours per failure were 28,500 hours. By December 1995 there were at least 61 tubes (30.5%) still operating with more than 15,000 hours and more than 22 tubes (11%) still operating with greater than 25,000 hours. To date not a single tube has exhibited a failure from "old age".

From the above data clearly the IOT has fulfilled the initial promise of "klystron like life". Thus, the reliability of the IOT is certainly proven in NTSC actual field service. Since we have no way of measuring statistically the DTV life we can only speculate that it will be at least as good as that of its NTSC service.

There are good reasons to believe that DTV service will be much easier on tubes and systems than NTSC. These reasons include the constant average power of DTV that will eliminate the temperature cycling that NTSC picture changes induce. Another reason is that the peak power duty cycle demands of DTV are less than 1/10 the demands of NTSC. These factors certainly will extend the lifetime of the IOT. The cathode capacity of the IOT is virtually the same as a klystron. Thus we might hope for close to 50,000 hours or more from an IOT in DTV service. 50,000 hours represents almost 6 years of life at 24 hours a day. DTV may not be transmitted daily for 24 hours in the early years so that the initial installed IOT could very well last till a viable solid state solution (in this 50kW peak domain) emerges over next several years.

The new IOT available from EEV is AIR COOLED and this eliminates a vast set of problems that would be part of many other solutions. IOT's are available from at least two sources, with more sources tooling up to bring a product to the market. This will insure consistent product supply and price stability into the DTV future.

## 4. CONTROL SYSTEM

Conventional wisdom in transmitter design and packaging dictates that all of the transmitter functions be tied together by hardwire harnesses and multipin connectors. Once that is accomplished, a central control logic system (today it's solid state, possibly computer based) is used to direct the sequence of events and protect the transmitter.

The wire harnesses and their associated connectors are one of the major sources of field problems. They are also a major cost driver in the manufacturing process. Therefore, if the wire harnesses and connectors could be eliminated the DTV transmitter would be less costly to build and more reliable in the field. It would be a bonus if the new system would be able to provide diagnostics and "work arounds" automatically.

COMARK's new DTV transmitter will NOT use wire harnesses and will provide automatic fault detection and operational fall-back conditions.

### DISC™

Commercial building control systems and the telephone network have something in common. Both are adopting a new technology to control their operating functions. They are fitting control nodes that contain computing capability right at the point that is controlled. These control nodes carry discrete digital addresses that are controlled from a central processor. The individual nodes are programmed to fit the specific function that they are to perform and can adjust their parameters to the local conditions. They can also be commanded to change their role as a result of instructions received from the central processor. Each node contains internal self calibration instructions as well as monitoring and reporting capabilities.

COMARK calls its adaptation of this technology "Distributed Intelligent System Control" or DISC™ for short. The Man Machine Interface (MMI), which is GUI (Graphical User Interface) based, and the overall system architecture is shown in **Figure 1**. The MMI allows the use of a standardized interface to control the system, and the use of a GUI allows users to select pictures and depictions of that system with which he/she is familiar. Additionally COMARK has added the enhancing capabilities of a CD drive and Modem in the MMI computer. This can be used in supplying context sensitive help and instructional materials with a wide variety of text and descriptive pictures to guide the user. (Schematics, Parts, Maintenance operations, etc.) COMARK support personnel will Interactively be able to assist users in operation and maintenance of their system. This is truly a revolution for the end user.

DISC™ uses a central (redundant) processor at the system level, to monitor and instruct the intelligent nodes placed throughout the system. The nodes have discrete addresses and are communicated to by a daisy chained pair of fiber optic cables (**Figure 2**). Thus, there are no longer conventional wire harnesses and a minimum of multipin connectors remain. All parameters are calibrated automatically at their source before being transmitted to the central processor. As an added level of redundancy, these communications channels are monitored and provide "weak link" detection functions.

The use of fiber eliminates any EMI/RFI and common mode problems in the control system. It also allows direct control of high voltage functions without the need for isolation transformers or the like.

For example, the bias and filament voltages of the IOT can be monitored and adjusted by simply sending the correct command to the intelligent node that is actually floating at the high voltage level. The central computer and the metering circuits do not have any high voltage involvement.

Other advantages of this DISC™ system are listed below;

1. No complex and unreliable inter-wiring harnesses and connectors.
2. No calibration potentiometers for meters or comparators. Measurements are designed to be accurate since they are developed inside the intelligent node and are absolute and presented in digital code to the central controller.
3. No common mode signal problems. Each measurement is made at the voltage it is measuring.
4. Absolute records maintained on all measurements and adjustments.
5. Automatic calibrations on command from the central controller.
6. Adjustments to all operating parameters are made as digital commands to the intelligent nodes.

One singular advantage of the DISC™ system is that controlling all the transmitter's functions is accurate because it is not an analog system. The internal intelligence of the control points and their discrete address allows the system to be controlled and adjusted without needing physical access to the actual controlled point. This feature not only allows for a much more precise control platform, but it creates the ability to change operation of the transmitter and all or any of its internal parameters by "log-on" verified remote control.

With the addition of a sophisticated touch screen display system and diagnostic software, it is possible for the operator to remotely control and analyze all aspects of his system, and provide an active network environment for the needs of more complex systems (**Figure 3**). This meets the objective of reduced operator involvement with the operation of the DTV transmitter. In many cases, factory support and repair or work arounds can be done without actually traveling to the transmitter site.

It should be noted that critical protection systems are backed up with hard wire controls as an absolute protection for the tube and hardware.

The technology that is behind the DISC™ system is used extensively in commercial building control systems, telephone network control and now "fly by fiber" aviation systems. It is even incorporated into modern commercial aircraft control systems. It is therefore about time that the transmitter takes advantage of a modern digital solution to control and monitoring.

## 5. SPECTRUM CONSIDERATIONS

The DTV spectrum will be very crowded. It is expected that the output from a DTV transmitter must be closely controlled for out-of-band energy. **(Figure 4)** shows the spectrum mask that may be applied to the DTV transmitter. A critical requirement is the reduction of the out-of-band energy. The nonlinearity inherent in any power amplifier that is operating efficiently creates intermodulation products that fall out-of-band. This is one reason why intermodulation performance of the power amplifying device is so critical. The current analog and/or digital predistortion technology that is applied to NTSC systems will not be able to meet the out-of-band energy requirements of DTV without the addition of a high power output filter, as seen by a typical transmitter output spectrum **(Figure 5)**.

Output filters are large and expensive components. Thus it would be desirable to eliminate the filter if at all possible. In the process of eliminating the filter it would also be a bonus if the in-band performance of the transmitter was enhanced.

COMARK, in conjunction with the David Sarnoff Research Center (SARNOFF), is developing a new kind of Digital Adaptive Predistortion (DAP) technology that will provide intermodulation product reductions of over 30dB **(Figures 6 & 7)**. This huge reduction of nonlinearity effects will vastly improve the in-band transmitter performance AND eliminate the need for a large and expensive output filter. In addition, the system is fully automatic/adaptive, and does not require operator intervention. The days of tweaking numbers of linearity control adjustments are eliminated with this system. Thus, the criterion for minimizing operator involvement with the transmitter is achieved. In addition, the cost in man-hours for setting the transmitter up initially and as an ongoing requirement is eliminated. That meets the low cost criteria set for the new generation of dedicated DTV transmitters.

## 6. CONCLUSIONS

DTV is a breakthrough technology that will become the standard terrestrial transmission system in the 21st century. The early implementation of DTV may be impeded by the lack of a receiver population that will generate a revenue stream to the station. This paper has described the reasons for choosing a technology that meets today's requirements. Those requirements are low purchase cost and operating cost, reduced operator involvement, reliable long term service and reduced risk of early obsolescence through flexibility in design.

The DTV service demands new solutions. This paper describes such a solution for the DTV transmitter and a new control architecture. The product is the COMARK Advantage TV product.

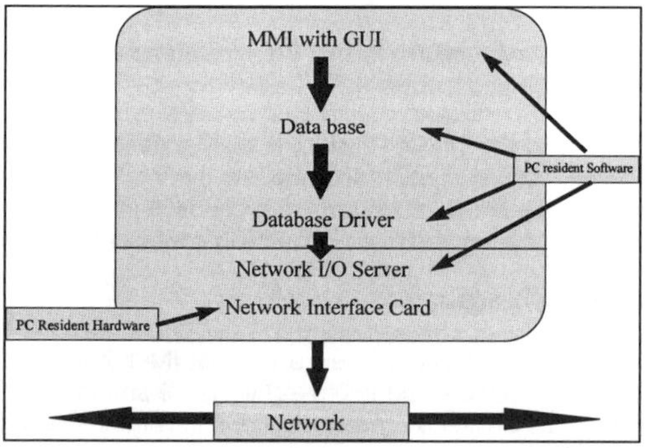


Figure 1

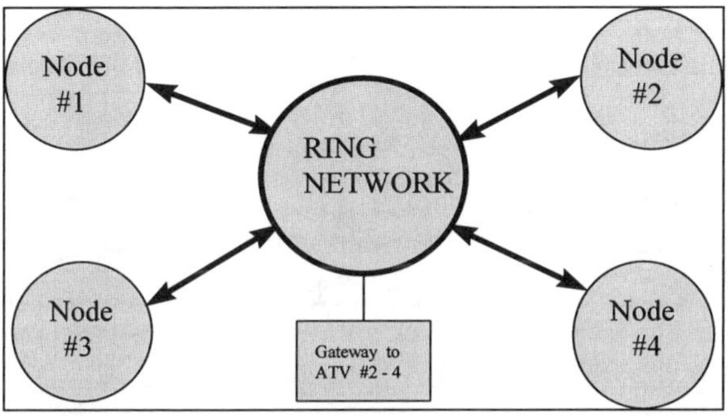


Figure 2

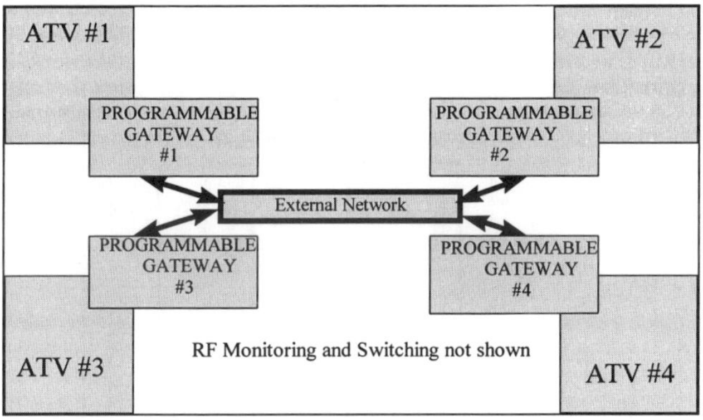


Figure 3

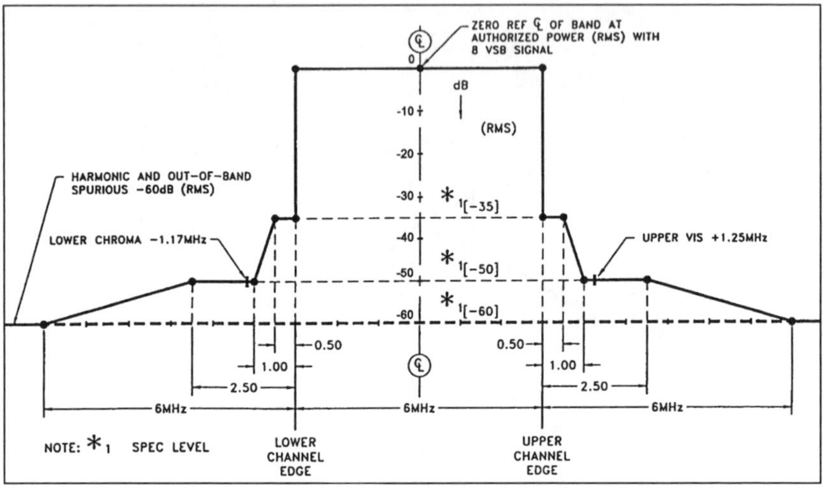


Figure 4

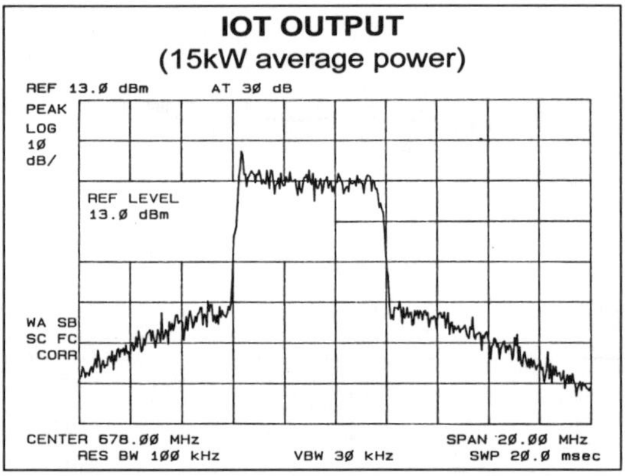


Figure 5

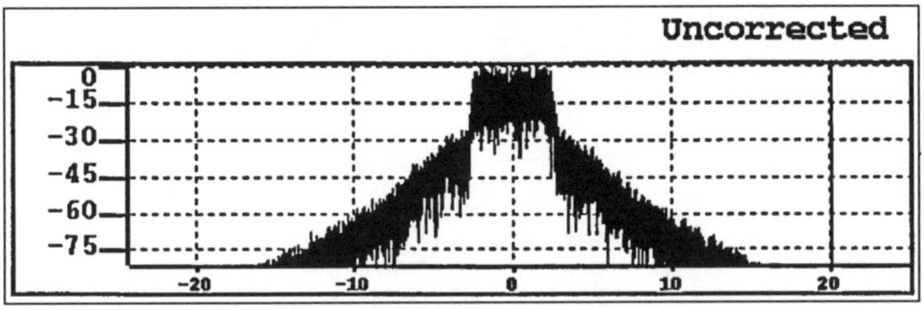


Figure 6

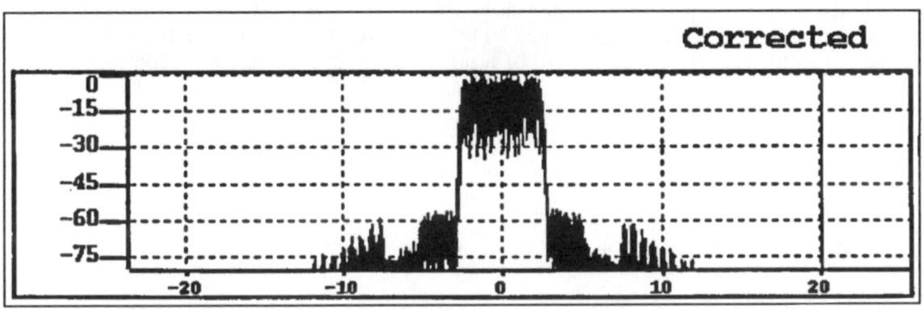


Figure 7

# METHODS FOR EVALUATION OF DIGITAL TELEVISION PICTURE QUALITY

William Y. Zou
Public Broadcasting Service
Alexandria, VA

Philip J. Corriveau
Communications Research Centre
Ottawa, Ontario

## Abstract

With the emergence and proliferation of digital video compression in television systems, there is an increasing requirement for effective methods to evaluate picture quality. In this paper, we describe traditional and novel objective and subjective test methods. We review standard methods to subjectively evaluate picture quality, outline their limitations and suggest ways to change these subjective methods. In addition, we also discuss research into objective methods that employs perception-based models with easily measurable parameters that could give a high degree of correlation with subjective evaluation methods. Finally, we draw some conclusions about the types of research needed to further the development of methods for picture quality evaluation.

## Introduction

Improvements in technologies, particularly the use of digital compression techniques, the concatenation of diverse transmission media and a changing viewer environment, are demanding that broadcasters ensure that the quality of service is adequate and meets expectations. One problem the industry faces today is how to evaluate a new generation of artifacts.

Digital television systems introduce unique artifacts which are visibly different from those in existing analog television systems. In order to study the effect of these new artifacts on television picture quality, new approaches and methodologies may need to be developed. This paper will discuss the objective and subjective evaluation of artifacts and the problems digital television systems introduce. We will discuss a link between objective and subjective evaluation techniques. Finally, we will present some conclusions with respect to the types of research needed into methods of evaluating picture quality.

## Picture Quality Assessment

There are two ways to evaluate the quality of a video signal. The first is by using objective measurements, while the second involves subjective assessments. Recently, a novel approach of combining objective and subjective methods has emerged. In the following sections, we will examine both traditional and more novel methods for picture quality assessment.

### Traditional Objective Method

Traditional objective measurement of television signal quality is performed by measuring physical parameters such as signal amplitude, timing and signal-to-noise ratio. To characterize the linear and non-linear signal distortions from signal transmission and processing, specially-designed static test signals are inserted into the video and analyzed at reception. The advantage of using static test signals is that they yield numerical values which have been correlated with subjective picture quality. The standard test signals and measurement procedures are defined in the standards such as NTC-7 and EIA RS-250.

With the introduction of digital signal processing into television, the traditional test waveforms were unable to accurately predict the signal distortions. Therefore new test waveforms have been developed specifically to characterize digital video signals. For example, to explore quantization noise a ramp signal is used instead of the staircase signal to measure non-linear distortions. The situation is even more complex with digital video compression where signal impairments are dependent on picture content. Therefore, traditional methods are unable to measure the perceptual picture quality; they can only measure the analog front and back ends of the system.[1]

### Perceptual Coding in Video Compression

The key principles behind video compression are (a) the removal of redundancies (spatial and temporal), and (b) the elimination of irrelevant information, i.e., information that is not visible to the Human Visual System (HVS). Perceptual coding, which exploits the properties of the HVS, has been employed in various video compression standards such as MPEG-2. Typically, this is done in the video pre-processing and quantization stages. In pre-processing, the source signal is filtered and sampled to reduce the information which is not visible to the HVS. This includes chroma conversion, chroma subsampling, and signal transformation. In the quantization stage, the bit allocation process allocates bits according to the perceptual importance of the various coefficients, therefore shaping the quantization noise into the perceptually less important areas. This can be accomplished by varying the relative step-size of the quantizers for the different coefficients. For example, low-spatial frequency coefficients must be quantized finely, while the less important high-frequency coefficients may be quantized more coarsely.

## Impact of Using Compression on Objective Quality Measurement

The use of digital video compression has a direct impact on objective quality measurement. Static test-signal waveform measurements fail with compressed video. First, the objective of designing a compression algorithm is not to replicate the original signal waveform as closely as possible, but to yield a perceptually equivalent approximation of the picture. Secondly, because of the constraint of bandwidth/bit rate, the resulting compressed picture quality is highly content dependent. In other words, if stressful source material (in terms of spatial detail and motion) is used, artifacts would be more visible and subjective picture quality would be degraded. In addition, the subjective picture quality is not a linear function of compression ratio or bit rate. Furthermore, unique digital transmission artifacts such as blocking, error strips and freeze frames make assessment of video quality more difficult for digital systems than for analog systems. In addition, the time-varying nature of these impairments further complicates quality assessment of digital systems. For example, digital artifacts may be short-lived and the quality of a digital transmission may fluctuate more than that of an analog transmission.

## Designing New Objective Measurement

New methods were proposed to remedy the inadequacies of traditional objective tests for compressed and digital television signals. These can be grouped into three categories: 1) using synthetic dynamic test signals and analyzing them to measure the dynamic performance of compressed video, 2) performing distortion measurement to assess how well the compressed video replicates the original, 3) using natural video test scenes and analyzing a set of features that correlate well with subjective picture quality. The first approach is an extension of the traditional objective test methods that use signal waveforms. The second one is based on fidelity comparison. The third approach, called perception-based objective measurement, to be discussed later in the paper, aims to bridge objective and subjective quality measurement and leads to a new direction for compressed video quality assessment.

### Dynamic Test Signal Measurement

To assess the dynamic performance of video compression systems, new time-variant test signals have been designed. Examples are signals to measure edge busyness, slope overload, dynamic nonlinearity, temporal response and dynamic response measurements.[2] There is also a need, to examine the loss of picture quality due to compression. New ideas such as measuring step-response rise time for image blur, step-response jitter for edge busyness, peak-to-peak signal to minimum quantizing error for rise time of a moving edge for temporary image blur, and maximum noise amplitude for a "dirty window" effect were proposed.[3] Using newly developed multi-dimensional test signals such as zone plates, new measurements of resolution,[4] zone-plate loading,[5] noise loading[6] and dynamic noise[1] were also proposed. The industry has not yet widely accepted or used these new methods. The missing ingredient in these methods is that the HVS is not incorporated; there is no link between the measured objective values and the related subjective picture quality.

### Distortion Measurement

In image and video coding, the root-mean-squared error (RMSE) and peak signal-to-noise ratio (PSNR) are widely used as a measure of distortion. These metrics are popular largely because of their analytical tractability. However, a global measures such as these cannot predict the perceptibility of distortions. Spatially localized and time-varying distortion is far too complex to be summarized by a global distortion measure.[7]

Bit error rate (BER) has long been used for data communications. For digital transmission, BER measurement is effective to assess the integrity of the transmission system. In digital television systems, transmission errors manifest themselves as freeze frame or block distortions. The relationship between error rate and subjective picture quality is further complicated by the error concealment scheme at the receiver. Like RMSE, error rate does not accurately predict the perceptual impact of transmission errors.

## Subjective Quality Assessment

Subjective assessment of picture quality attempts to quantify the response of the HVS to selected images. This is done by having viewers rate the subjective quality of images using pen and paper tests or computerized tests. Recommendation 500[8] of the International Telecommunications Union, Radiocommunications Section (ITU-R), defines guidelines and procedures for such tests.

The recommended testing procedure for subjective quality assessment is the double-stimulus continuous-quality scale (DSCQS) method. In this method, a 10 cm graphical scale is divided into five equal intervals. In the middle of each interval the following quality terms are associated from top to bottom (Excellent 100-80, Good 79-60, Fair 59-40, Poor 39-20 and Bad 19-0). The 10 cm scale provides a "continuous" rating system to help reduce quantization errors in viewer responses. Selected test sequences are presented twice in pairs sequentially in time to allow for first viewing and then evaluating. Sequence duration is usually 10 seconds although variation from 5 to 15 seconds is not uncommon. Viewers are instructed to assess the quality of both the reference and test picture, though they are unaware of the order of presentation for each trial. A maximum of 30 minutes of constant viewing is suggested in order to avoid having the effects of fatigue and boredom introduced to the results. This does not mean that a total test has to be limited to 30 minutes. If a design calls for more than 30 minutes of viewing, there should be a break between sittings.

Recommendation 500 provides detailed specifications for viewing distance, display parameters and viewing environment. But it leaves certain design factors unspecified, and it is the experimenter's responsibility to choose the levels of these factors. The two most important factors that are left up to the experimenter's discretion are selection of video sequences and viewer characteristics (expert, non-expert, age, etc.). Clearly, these factors cannot be set in advance and are unique to the requirements of each evaluation.

It is well known that the quality of the output image from a CODEC is significantly influenced by the criticality of the video sequence. Thus, the selection of appropriate image sequences is an important process. One of the first considerations is that material be chosen from several sources. For example, material should be drawn from film, video and computer graphics. This is important because film material tends to be less stressful on a CODEC than a video. Both moving and still sequences should be used, with some motion sequences containing scene cuts and fades in order to assess CODEC performance. The practice of taking a subset of ITU-R accepted sequences and a set of sequences representing regular programming has proven to be useful.

Generally, non-expert viewers are used to evaluate image quality. Non-expert viewers are people who have no prior professional or extensive personal experience in dealing with video display systems or devices. These viewers are recruited through a reliable source and screened for normal or corrected to normal visual acuity, normal contrast sensitivity and normal color vision.

Below, we review a variety of improvements that have been proposed to the methods described in Recommendation 500. Suggestions for changing the design of the rating scale, duration of sequences and overall viewing environment have been made.

## Quality Rating Scale

The Double Stimulus Continuous Quality Scale is a 10 cm line that corresponds to numerical ratings between 0 and 100. Viewers evaluate the subjective quality of images using scales with the assistance of associated word indicators. These indicators (Excellent, Good, Fair, Poor and Bad) currently break the continuous scale into five equal 20 mm sections. Some researchers state that interpretation of the descriptors, may lead viewers to divide the scale into psychologically unequal sections. For example some may rate Good and Excellent closer in perceived quality than Good and Fair. Viewers have in the past been asked to write the adjectives beside a numerical scale but it was impossible to conclude whether the adjectives were truly equidistant. To complicate the issue further the concern of language translation becomes a factor. Extreme effort was taken by the ITU-R to select adjectives that are easily translated from English but other researchers such as Kees Teunissen suggest alternate scale design. Kees Teunissen suggests a 10 term scale rather then the current 5 term scale.[9] This concept is illustrated in Figure 1, where both the current and proposed scales are sketched.

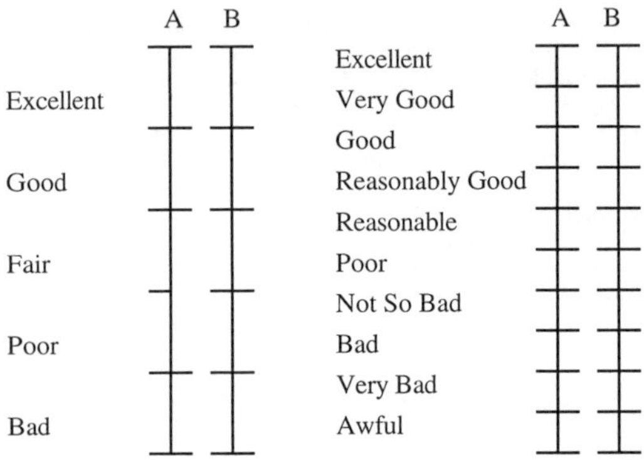


Figure 1 Proposed changes to ITU-R DSCQS

However, the addition of more descriptors to the current scale creates the possibility of increased confusion. Doubling the number of adjectives associated with the rating scale increases the complexity of the judgment task. For example, non-expert viewers may tend to become distracted from the actual task of evaluating picture quality if there are too many categories to distinguish between. Research should be performed to fully evaluate the implication of changing the current scale and to ensure that any scale used achieves the intended task.

The simplicity of the quality scale lies in the fact that viewers are asked to evaluate quality for both a reference and test sequence. This provides the experimenter with raw mean scores for both reference and test sequences. For example, the rated quality of the reference could be 85 out of 100 and the quality of the test could be 65 out of 100. From this it can be determined that the difference is -20 (Test Score - Reference Score). When interpreting quality data, this difference measure is one of the more interesting facets. The distance between stimuli is a very useful tool when determining the quality of a system and some other methods do not allow for this comparison. Rather than asking the viewer to determine the difference between the reference and test, the easier task of evaluating individual quality is requested. The difference data is then extracted using the above described method. This allows the experimenter to first examine the stability of scores given to reference sequences, and then extract difference data. However, one study questioned the ability of the continuous scale method employed in quality tests to yield difference information.[10]

## Test Sequence Duration

Current testing methods use 10 second sequence segments. Viewers are asked to evaluate the overall quality of each 10 second segment. Presumably each viewer attempts to average their impression of the quality over the duration of the sequence. However, Digital artifacts that are short-lived and temporally spaced may not be captured by a 10 second segment. It might be more appropriate to increase the duration of test sequences to properly evaluate these time-varying artifacts. An experiment was performed to evaluate an increased duration of the image sequences to 30 seconds. It was found that subjects were strongly influenced by what they saw in the last section of the sequence (a recency effect). For example, if a sequence had an artifact in the first 15 seconds and then recovered to be a better quality, a subject would assign a high score. On the other hand, if a visible artifact occurred in the latter part of the sequence, the viewer would lower the rated value. It was observed that subjects formed a weighted temporal average of the instantaneous quality variations during the sequence, giving maximum weighting to the part of the sequence seen most recently.[11] This effect can lead to a difference in rated quality of about 10 points on a scale of 100, or half a grade on a scale of 5. It is clear from this result that viewers form an averaged value of perceived quality.

The problem of averaged image quality ratings could be overcome by increasing the sequence duration and sampling viewers more frequently. This principle was applied to a study where the sequence duration was increased and a sliding scale was used for continuous assessment of image quality. The mechanical scale sampled the position of the slider every second. This experiment demonstrated that it was possible to measure the quality in a continuous and reliable manner.[12] The notion of continuous rating over a longer duration has lead to a proposal by T. Alpert and J.P. Evain called the Single Stimulus Continuous Quality Evaluation Method (SSCQE). This method based on work undertaken by groups associated with the European MOSAIC project was reported at the HDTV '96 conference. The SSCQE has been designed to allow for the evaluation of picture and service quality over a wide range of areas. This method allows for subjective evaluations in conditions near to the 'home' environment. Assessors are asked to evaluate the quality of long sequences (20-30 minutes) with content representative of the service being provided. The votes are collected continuously (twice per second) from sliding devices that each assessor can manipulate during the entire test session. This allows for the interpretation of the entire program stream and for a better evaluation of time-varying impairments.

With these new methods of evaluation, the number of sampled points gathered increases by a factor of more than 20. Of course, the reporting and analysis of this additional data causes its own difficulties. However, the ability to analyze sectional data will be gained. In theory, these methods will allow for a better understanding of time-varying impairments and a true sense of overall subjective quality for longer program material.

## The Viewing Environment

In order to ensure the reliability and repeatability of test results, viewing conditions are carefully described in ITU-R Recommendation 500. However, some researchers[13-15] feel that these conditions do not reflect those of a typical 'home'. For example, factors such as viewing distance and display size, ambient lighting and display parameters may differ in the 'home' than those specified in Recommendation 500. Deviations between the 'home' environment and Recommendation 500 are not a serious problem, provided that the condition of the viewing environment are at least as critical as the 'home' environment. In this situation tests conducted under Recommendation 500 will always guarantee a satisfactory performance in the 'home'.

### Viewing Distances and Display Size

Currently, the recommended viewing distance is 3H (3 times the picture height) for HDTV and 5H for all SDTV systems (NTSC, PAL and SECAM). It is known that the seat position that viewers chose can vary from the distance specified in the recommendation. One study found that by using larger HDTV displays, there is increased convergence of the desired (currently used) and the preferred (chosen by viewers) viewing distances. Essentially, the finding is that with increased monitor size, the viewers are not likely to move farther from the display, but to remain in the same seating position. This could be attributed to the fact that with increased resolution, the line structure is less visible. Thus a viewer can sit closer to the set even at 3H without perceiving the line structure. Based on this work, a display size and distance of 3H could be standardized for laboratory use that would keep both the preferred and desired distances relatively equal, and ensure critical viewing conditions.

### Ambient Lighting

For most viewing conditions the ambient lighting in the 'home' tends to be quite low. For example, to fully enjoy the effects of a movie, most viewers will reduce the amount of light in the room. The light level specified in Recommendation 500 is quite low and probably very close to that of the average 'home'. Ambient lighting conditions provide an environment in which a viewer's attention is not drawn away from the display. This allows for viewers to evaluate image quality without being distracted by other stimuli.

### Display Parameters

Luminance, contrast and resolution interact in varying proportions to result in a perceived level of image quality. With changes in monitor technology, such as increased peak luminance, the current Recommendation 500 specifications may need to be revised to higher values of these parameters.

## Correlation Between Objective and Subjective Methods

Subjective quality assessment plays such an important role in both analog and digital television environments. However, subjective evaluation is both costly and time-consuming which has motivated researchers to explore objective measurements that are correlated with the perceptual characteristics of the HVS. This goal leads to the development of perceptual models.

Applying knowledge of the HVS to television design and test methodologies is a difficult and challenging art. For example, in digital compression systems, knowledge of the HVS has been applied to the design of coding parameters with the goal of hiding the artifacts introduced by compression and coding.

With the advances in the knowledge of the HVS, new methods for making correlation between objective and subjective measures are emerging. These new methods rely heavily on perception-based modeling.

### Perception-based Objective Measurement

In theory, perception-based objective measurement can quantify the subjective quality of a digitally compressed picture without having human subjects rate the picture. Perception-based methods compare a pair of images/sequences, usually natural video scenes, to predict the visibility of the difference similar to subjective method. A reference measurement is made on the input (source) signal and an identical measure is made on the output of a system under test. The parameters (feature statistics and comparison) are defined as combinations of an input measurement with a corresponding output measurement according to explicit formulas. The selection of parameters is based on the HVS. Such formulas produce results that effectively quantify the comparability of the input and output measures. In general, analysis can include measurements that quantify information in the time and/or the spatial-frequency domain.

It should be noted that an additional complication arises from the use of natural scenes since the severity of compression artifacts is a function of both the system and the picture content.

## Selection of Objective Features

The success of assessing compressed video relies on the selection of an appropriate set of features which can be measured and used to characterize video information. To model the HVS, features can also be extracted in the spatial, temporal and chromatic domains. Researchers have found that the features which incorporate HVS processing lead to higher correlation with subjective scores performed by human observers.

### Spatial-frequency Domain

Luminance transitions, which define edges are an important feature in HVS modeling. As discussed earlier, perceptual coding in video compression occurs at the quantization stage. High-frequency spatial components are often eliminated for the purpose of data reduction. Loss of spatial-frequency might result in blurring or smearing. Coarse quantization may introduce blockiness into the picture. The perceptual block distortion is a result of false spatial-frequency components or edges introduced by compression. Therefore, spatial features are good indicators of the amount of spatial information or edges in the compressed picture.

Various edge detection schemes such as the Sobel, Roberts and line edge detectors (filters) can be used to extract spatial information. Another approach is to compute the local entropy of the neighborhood of each pixel.[16] The histogram of each neighborhood is generated and the entropy is then computed. Pixels of interest are those for which the value exceeds a specified threshold. Unlike convolution techniques that depend on region contrast to detect edges, the local entropy operator does not. Therefore, very faint edges found in low contrast images will be detected just as edges with higher contrast.

### Temporal Domain

Like in the spatial domain, redundancy in the temporal domain can be reduced if not completely eliminated using motion estimation and compensation. However, the limitations of search range, accuracy, bit rate and the selection of Group of Picture (GOP) affect coding efficiency and subjective performance. Artifacts such as temporal noise, blockiness and jerkiness result from compression in the temporal domain.

The temporal features are indicators of the amount of temporal changes, or degree of motion, in video scenes from one frame to the next. Temporal features can be measured by the inter-frame difference energy.

### Feature Statistics and Comparison

The use of natural video scenes for objective picture quality measurement raises the issue of how to deal with the variation of measured values due to the constant change of picture content and the dynamic performance of compression systems. Using statistics provides the best way to characterize features from different frames at different times in a sequence. The primary statistics of these features can be the mean and the standard deviation of the pixel values across a frame/field. To better present the distortions caused by compression and other signal processing, the ratios of input and output features can be calculated based on various comparison functions. Some proposed functions include maximum and minimum (over time) of the log ratios, maximum and minimum (over time) of the error ratios, root mean square (over time) of the error ratio, peak signal-to-noise ratio, minimum (over time) of the peak signal-to-noise ratio and root mean square (over time) of the peak signal-to-noise ratio.[17]

## Perceptual Models for Picture Quality Assessment

The basic approach of developing perceptual models is 1) the selection of a set of features which can be objectively measured, 2) the establishment of a model which can simulate the HVS for the processing and analyzing of the selected features. By processing individual features, perceptual models can predict not only specific attributes but also global picture quality.

Development of perceptual models has two major obstacles. First, the HVS[18] is extremely complex and not fully understood. Secondly, complex models are expensive to implement, and also time consuming for real-time applications.

In general, a simple HVS model can be viewed as having several levels, one of which is the peripheral level.[19] Most of the peripheral level can be described in signal processing terms such as filtering, sampling and coding. More specifically, the current understanding of early vision can be characterized by modules diverting a common flow of information into specific areas such as color, motion and shape detection. For video quality assessment there is another high level process that sits on top of the HVS. This is the process that a human uses to make a quality judgment. For example, the HVS might be able to detect an impairment but the human judgment might not consider it significant enough to influence the quality decision.

Perceptual model were first developed for machine vision, target detection and photograph analysis. Recently, perceptual models for color video and compressed video including HDTV picture quality assessment, have been studied. Various systems have been proposed and implemented for different applications.[20-25] These systems in general select spatial and/or temporal features, which are extracted by filtering, and manipulate these features through processes such as squaring, averaging, weighting, and normalization. To some extent, these processes simulate some functions of the HVS. The last stage is to detect and construct numerical results or graphic maps.

Using numerical indexes is convenient and compatible with traditional subjective methods. The most popular quality indexes are the ITU-R quality and impairment scales. Other scales such as Just Noticeable Difference (JND) are also used for quality measurement. One JND corresponds to a 75% probability that an observer viewing two images multiple times would perceive a difference. JND's can also be plotted as a map showing the probability, as a function of position on the images, that an observer would be able to detect differences between the images. By averaging JND values, a single mean JND value can be generated for image quality.[24]

### Example of Perception-Based Objective Measurement System

Wolf et al proposed a perception-based objective measurement system developed for video and television signal.[25,26] They developed an automatic video quality measurement system which is composed of two sub-systems: one for source and one for destination. By extracting a set of features that can be used to predict perceptual video quality changes, an objective quality estimate of the system performance can be obtained by comparing the source and corresponding destination features. The system is based on both spatial and temporal features using the Sobel filtered image for spatial domain and the motion difference image for time domain analysis. In order to produce an single score/index of picture quality performance, a formula composed of a set of spatial and temporal features is determined using two subjective test experiments.[27] Experiments were carried out on CODECs operated at 56 kbps to 1.5 Mbps for videoconferencing and 45 Mbps for program contribution. They also include channel impairments such as burst errors. The system had a 0.92 correlation with the subjective scores.[28] However, the database did not include a critical range of MPEG-based compression systems operating at bit rates between 1.5 and 20 Mbps. This bit rate range is believed to be the operation model for the future digital television service including HDTV. Based on the algorithm, a computer system was developed to perform the quality rating as well as distortion measurements. The system allows the user to view video side-by-side with plots of measurement results on the computer display.[29]

## Conclusions

For quality monitoring and performance evaluation of digital video, perception-based as well as objective measurements are essential. Practical and efficient methods and equipment must still be developed. It should be noted that, so far, no perceptual model is able to replace subjective methods for picture quality assessment. Even the most sophisticated models are unable to discriminate between two or more similar systems.

One key component for perception-based objective measurement as well as subjective evaluation is the establishment of standard test material to be used in all the laboratories. Some sequences have already been accepted by the international community (as found in the 'Test Materials to be Used in Subjective Assessment' - ITU-R Document 11/6-E)[30] but these sequences lack the ability to address some of the current issues. The largest hurtle to clear is the ability to choose sequences that evaluate digital artifacts and represent typical viewing material.

The search for a universal objective measure of picture quality will fascinate researchers for a number of years to come, and the link between the subjective and objective measures will take longer. However, the constant march of technology will drive us to our goal regardless.

## Acknowledgment

The authors wish to thank S. Wolf of NTIA/ITS for reviewing the paper and providing valuable comments. The authors also wish to thank, Lew Stelmach, Andre Vincent and Metin Akgun of the Communications Research Center for their efforts in reviewing and commenting on this paper.

## References

1. W. Y. Zou, "Performance Evaluation: From NTSC to Digitally Compressed Video," SMPTE Journal, Dec. 1994.

2. Technical Report 16: "DS-3 Transport for Contribution Application of System M-NTSC Television Signal - Analog Interface and Performance Objectives," Committee T1-Telecommunications, May, 1991.

3. Report 1206: "Methods for Picture Quality Assessment in Relation to Impairments from Digital Coding of Television Signals," Reports of the CCIR, 1990, Annex to vol. XI - part 1.

4. E. S. Kohn and G. W. Beakley, "Resolution Testing of An HDTV CODEC with Moving Zone Plates," 134th SMPTE Technical Conference, Toronto, Nov. 1992.

5. G. W. Beakley, C. R. Caillouet, E. S. Kohn and J. L. Van Pelt, "Testing of a Digital HDTV CODEC Through the NASA Communications Network," 1992 HDTV World Conference Proceedings, NAB, April 1992.

6. G. W. Beakley and E. S. Kohn, "Transmission of Compressed Digital High-Definition Video Through the NASA Communications Network," Proceedings of SPIE Conference, San Diego, July 1992.

7. P. Teo and D. Heeger, "Perceptual Image Distortion," 1st. IEEE Intl. Conf. on Image Proc., vol. 2, pp. 982-986, Nov. 1994.

8. Recommendation ITU-R BT. 500-6, "Methodology for the Subjective Assessment of the Quality of Television Pictures," ITU-R 1974-1994.

9. K. Teunissen, "The Validity of CCIR Quality Indicators Along a Graphical Scale," SMPTE Journal, vol. 105, No. 3, March 1996.

10. B. L. Jones and P. R. McManus, "Graphic Scaling of Qualitative Terms," SMPTE Journal, November 1986.

11. R. Aldridge, J. Davidoff, M. Ghanbari, D. Hands, and D. Pearson, "Recency Effect in the Subjective Assessment of Digitally-coded Television Pictures," Rapport No. 1071, Proceedings of the MOSAIC Workshop Advanced Methods for the Evaluation of Television Picture Quality, Institute for Perception Research, Sept. 11, 1995.

12. R. Hamberg and H. de Ridder, "Continuous Assessment of Perceptual Image Quality," Rapport No. 1071, Proceedings of the MOSAIC Workshop Advanced Methods for the Evaluation of Television Picture Quality, Institute for Perception Research, Sept. 11, 1995.

13. M. Ardito, M. Gunetti and M. Visca, "Preferred Viewing Distance and Display Parameters," Rapport No. 1071, Proceedings of the MOSAIC Workshop Advanced Methods for the Evaluation of Television Picture Quality, Institute for Perception Research, Sept. 11, 1995.

14. M. Ardito and M. Gunetti, "The Impact of Display Parameters on the Quality Perceived by the Viewers," IEEE 1995.

15. S. Rihs, "The Influence of Audio on Perceived Picture Quality and Subjective Audio-video Delay Tolerance," Rapport No. 1071, Proceedings of the MOSAIC Workshop Advanced Methods for the Evaluation of Television Picture Quality, Institute for Perception Research, Sept. 11, 1995.

16. J. Barba, P. Fenster, H. Jeanty and J. Gil, "Edge Detection in Cytology Using Local Statistical Properties," SPIE vol. 974 Applications of Digital Image Processing XI (1988).

17. ANSI standard T1.801.03-1996, "Digital Transport of One-Way Video Signals - Parameters for Objective Performance Assessment.

18. R. A. Young, "Oh say, can you see? The physiology of vision," SPIE vol. 1453 Human Vision, Visual Processing, and Digital Display II (1991).

19. J. Lim, "*Two-dimensional Signal and Image Processing*," Prentice Hall, 1990.

20. C. R. Carlson and R. W. Cohen, " A Simple Psycho-physical Model for Predicting the Visibility of Displayed Information," Proc. Soc. Infor. Display, vol. 21. pp. 229 (1980).

21. P. C. Teo and D. J. Heeger, "Perceptual Image Distortion," Proceedings of the First International Conference on Image Processing, vol. 2 pp. 982-986, Austin, Nov. 1994.

22. H. Hamada and S. Namba, "A Study on Objective Picture Quality Scales for Pictures Digitally Encoded for Broadcast," IEICE Trans. com vol. 177 B No.12, Dec. 1994.

23. J. A. Saghri, P. S. Cheatham and A. Habibi, "An HVS-Based Image Quality Measure," SPIE vol. 974, Applications of Digital Image Processing XI (1988).

24. J. Lubin, "A Visual Discrimination Model for Imaging System Design and Evaluation," David Sarnoff Research Center, Feb. 1995.

25. S. Wolf, "Features for Automatic Quality Assessment of Digitally transmitted Video," NTIA Report 90-264, US Department of Commerce, June, 1990.

26. A. Webster et al., "An Objective Video Quality Assessment System Based on Human Perception," SPIE Human Vision, Visual Processing, and Digital Display IV, vol. 1913, San Jose, CA, Feb. 1993.

27. S. Wolf and A. Webster, "Objective and Subjective Video Performance Testing of DS3 Rate Transmission Channels," ANSI T1A1 contr. No. T1A1.5/93-060, April, 1993.

28. N. B. Seitz, S. Wolf, S. Voran and R. Bloomfield, "User Oriented Measures of Telecommunication Quality," IEEE Comm. Magazine, vol. 32, No. 1 Jan. 1994.

29. C. P. Cressy and G. W. Beakley, "Computer-based Testing of Digital Video Quality," IS&T/SPIE's Symposium on Electronic Imaging Science and Technology, San Jose, CA, Feb. 1994.

30. Draft temporary document "Test Materials to be Used in Subjective Assessment" - ITU-R Document 11/6-E, 1996 sessions.

# Thorough Control System™: a method of color-accurate and contrast consistent film transfer to video dailies

**Y.Neyman, S. Riviére, H. Sisko**
**Gamma and Density Co.Inc.**
**Studio City, California**

## Abstract

The "Thorough Control System"™, from Gamma & Density Co., establishes a method to help cinematographers arrive at the "look" they desire during a film-to-tape transfer session and maintaining artistic and technical control over their images. The system begins on the set and establishes standards of communication with the telecine colorist in the film-to-tape transfer process. Now, instead of subjective and debatable opinions regarding images, the cameraman and telecine colorists are speaking a common language.

The key element of the system, the Gamma=IC Cinematographer's Control Chart, has one distinguished feature that sets this chart aside from any other charts: the idea of connecting brightness of the scene with scientifically calculated IRE unit equivalents printed right on each corresponding gray field. This chart creates a proper connection between the brightness of the scene and luminance of the electronically converted film signal. With the use of the system, the telecine colorist is able to transfer dailies with accurate and consistent contrast, color, and tone renditions. This continuity in dailies takes the guesswork out of the transfer set-up process.

# 1. Introduction. The contemporary cinematographer's technical environment in the film and TV industries.

This is the age of video dailies. Almost 70% of processed negatives never see the light of a printer. Therefore the quality of video dailies has become one of the most important technical and creative problems for cinematographers to overcome. The following outlines the source of problems which affect the quality of images during the film-to -tape transfer:

In the traditional film negative - positive process, assuming the exposure is correct and the film stock is not defective, there are only a few ways the quality of filmed images could become corrupted.

- Defective negative processing.

An unlikely event in any reputable modern lab.All negative stocks of all manufacturers are processed until a specific contrast (gamma) of the negative is achieved. The universally accepted gamma of color negative film is g=0.55, The standard gamma for black and white film is g=0.65.

- Faulty color timing of dailies.

Strict technological regulations have been put in place to insure that with proper exposure and accurate negative processing the final images will be seen exactly how they were designed by the knowledgeable Director of Photography. This control is imperative for the correct processing of answer prints, which determine the ultimate "look" of the film. If the print stock destined for dailies does not go through extremely rigorous sensitometric control, the colors and densities of dailies prints can vary.

While the negative-positive process utilizes tightly regulated, controlled, interdependent and measured parameters, the film-to-tape transfer process has somewhere between 12 and 43 different non-standardized parameters.

IRE, chrominance level, PEC, tele-cine GAMMA, gain, enhancement, etc. These are a few of the many parameters which affect quality of the transfer and images on tape.

Some of the parameters and units of measurement differ among various manufacturers of equipment designed for the film-to-tape transfer process. The one common denominator for all manufacturers is the use of IRE units for the measurement of the intensity of the video signal (See Illustration #1).

Until now there has been no relationship established between the terminology of the traditional film negative-positive process and the film-to-tape electronic transfer. GAMMA & DENSITY Co., has done research in the field of motion picture and television technology in order to establish such a relationship, and to create the tools for optimum quality printing and film-to-tape transfers.

One goal was to create film-to-tape transfer standards for controlling contrast, latitude, and color rendition. These standards will allow cinematographers to control the quality of the video image with the same degree of precision they are used to when using print film.

# 2. The Thorough Control System (T.C.S.)™ .How the GAMMA=1 charts give the cinematographer control over the quality of film and video images

As a result of our research, "GAMMA & DENSITY Co.", designed the "Thorough Control System (T.C.S.)™". This system enables the preservation of the artistic and technical integrity of the original negative throughout the various stages involved in post production and distribution. The system carries control through the "traditional" negative-to-print process, the tele-cine transfer from negative to tape, and is capable of controlling the transformation of images using machines such as Cineon, Domino or other special effects. It also allows control for video dubs, broadcasting, or images that are beamed via satellite the world over.

The key to the Thorough Control System T.C.S.™ is the series of GAMMA=1 charts and their implementation.

## 2.1 Areas of application:

a) the film-to-tape transfer (use GAMMA=1c and GAMMA=1t)

b) negative -positive process (use GAMMA=1c and GAMMA=1p)

c) color and tone correlation between different image setting systems (use GAMMA=1c and GAMMA=1t)

d) color monitor adjustment (use GAMMA=1t or GAMMA=1t+)

The Thorough Control System T.C.S.™ is based on reciprocity of three variations of the GAMMA=1 charts and their interdependent values:

1. The chart for cinematographers is called GAMMA=1c
2. The set up loop chart for tele-cine adjustments is called GAMMA=1t
3. The set up loop chart for print color timing is called GAMMA=1p .

Charts GAMMA=1t and GAMMA=1p are complimentary to the chart for cinematographers GAMMA=1c. The GAMMA=1c is the only chart the cinematographer needs for use on the set. The other two charts exist only on exposed set-up loops for use by the tele-cine colorist (GAMMA=1t or GAMMA=1t+) or print timer (GAMMA=1p).

The use of a combination of charts in the GAMMA=1 system is indispensable to the process of making conscious and rational technical adjustments while creating high quality video images. All three charts include similar elements but each chart is designed for specific use due to the special requirements of each respective process.

# 3.A Look at the Charts. A description of the different elements on the GAMMA=1 charts.

The series of all GAMMA=1 charts are similar in their key elements. (see illustration #2)

The key elements of all three charts include:

1) 7 field gray scale;

2) Exposure Latitude strip;

3) 24-color strip;

4) 3 linearly blended strips of Easily Recognizable Colors

The first element represents a sequence of seven gray fields with various coefficients of reflectance. Each field is printed with its assigned IRE number. The Numbers are 10 IRE, 15 IRE, 20 IRE, 30 IRE, 45 IRE, 60 IRE and 90 IRE respectively. The exact IRE information is crucial for setting proper contrast (GAMMA). When each field is set according to its value on the wave form monitor (see illustration #3), the result is correct contrast for the video image.
The 45 IRE mark corresponds to 18% neutral gray reflectance - the standard control in professional exposure systems.

The 10 IRE mark and 90 IRE mark correspond to the useful range of the negative to be transferred to video. (see illustration#4). While the absolute range of the video transfer from negative lies between marks 7.5 and 100 IRE , the Thorough Control System T.C.S.™ uses 10-90 IRE. Our research indicated a need to leave room for possible adjustments during the final "on-line" transfer of the negative.

The second element represents the Exposure Latitude Strip of the chart. This element permits on-the-spot analysis of important characteristics of your film stock such as contrast and latitude. It also allows for the comparison and analysis of various negative and print stocks. The exposure latitude strip consists of 14 fields. Each field is equal to a 1/2 stop difference in exposure.

The red numbers represent the numerical order of the fields.

The green numbers represent the increase or decrease of exposure in 1/2 stop increments.

The yellow numbers work in conjunction with the green numbers to calculate the contrast ratio. The formula is: subtract the lowest distinguishable field's green number from the highest distinguishable field's green number. The resulting green number will be next to the yellow number which indicates the contrast ratio. If, for example, we can only distinguish the difference between fields #3 (green 1) through #13 (green 6), then the absolute increase of difference in exposure will be 6 minus 1, or 5 F-stops. Next to the green 5 is yellow 32. This indicates that in this particular case the combined latitude of the stock and print or the stock and tape will be only 1:32 or 5 F-stops.

The blue numbers represent elements of the Exposure Latitude Index, and quantify the increase or decrease of difference in exposure from neutral 18% gray. Field #9 represents 18% reflectance and equals 45 IRE. This field represents KEY EXPOSURE (the exposure determined as correct for the scene). All the fields above the KEY EXPOSURE are darker and represent various degrees of

shadows, and all the fields below key exposure are lighter and represent various degrees of highlights. These numbers are a practical way to express the Exposure Latitude Index of the image. Let's say that 11 distinguishable fields can be seen on the monitor or screen. The first signs of distinguishable differences begin in field #3 (black) and also in the #13 (white) field. Field #3 corresponds to the blue designation -3.0 F.-stops and field #13 corresponds to the blue designation +2.0 F.-stops. This means that for all practical purposes you are working with a brightness range for the visually important information (reflected readings) somewhere between 3 stops below and 2 stops above your key exposure. This indicates that the particular stock or system or process has an Exposure Latitude Index -3.0/+2.0.
With the introduction of the Exposure Latitude Index numbers, cinematographers, timers and colorists now have a powerful tool of analysis for the comparison of different stocks and systems.

The third element is a 24 field color spectrum designed to compare the color sensitivity and color bias of different stocks. By numbering each segment of the color chart, the colors can be compared not only by verbal description, but also using the assigned numbers. This feature is designed to facilitate communication between the cinematographer and the tele-cine colorist and/or the timer-colorist.

The fourth element includes three optical wedges or linear blends - skin tone, blue sky and greenery . Research indicates that while the human eye can distinguish between thousands of different colors and hues , only a few colors exist that people readily agree on and experience practically every day. As a new element of the Thorough Control System, the GAMMA & DENSITY Co. Inc. " introduces Easily Recognizable Colors (E.R.C.) - skin tone, blue sky and greenery.

The cinematographer can choose, according to her/his taste and technical specifics, any area from the color wedges for use as a reference point for color adjustments. This will also help in communications with the tele-cine colorist and timer colorist. Selected numbers from the color strip can be noted for future reference and control of the E.R.C. optical wedges during the transfer and/or printing process. (The skin tone used is a sample for the purposes of reference and is not intended to represent all skin tones)

## 3.1 Differences between the charts:

The gray scale, E.R.C. bands, numbered color fields, and Exposure Latitude Index described above are identical for all GAMMA=1 charts. Each chart has differences in design and composition specific to the processes they are used for. (see illustrations #2-a/d)

The chart GAMMA=lc has an additional Information Area that helps the tele-cine colorist or timer colorist to know the specifics of the particular scene or shot. The information area consists of three spaces to put the specially designed magnetic instruction labels.

The index SET UP FOR could be labeled for different choices when color correction must be done according to the neutral-gray tone of the chart, the GRAY label is used. The labels CORAL , SUNSET, DAY, NIGHT can be used to indicate to the timer immediately that this scene or shot contains special color and tone adjustments which are not to be "corrected" out.
The indexes FILTER, FILM, STOCK MANUFACT. (manufacturer) are self-explanatory. Your chart comes with 40 information labels.The chart GAMMA=1t (on a film loop) includes an additional gray strip below part 1 (10-90 IRE strip), which is equal to 45 IRE or 18% gray. This strip helps the tele-cine colorist to make the first step in adjusting the tele-cine machine by placing this line across 45 IRE mark on the wave form monitor .

The GAMMA=1t (on a film loop) chart includes a red strip below the 45 IRE gray strip designed to

enable the tele-cine colorist to set up the color red on the vectorscope. Extensive testing determined that the red we are using is the closest possible color to any of those used for reference on a vectorscope. (see illustrations #2-b,c) By setting the red reference, the rest of the colors will be aligned according to the spectral sensitivities of the particular film stock.
The chart GAMMA=1p (on a film loop) has 3 additional rectangular areas that correspond to 10, 45 and 90 IRE respectively. These areas enable the lab timer to measure the control densities of the positive images (see illustration 2-d). By using the GAMMA=1p loop, the lab timer colorist, the cinematographer and the tele-cine colorist now have a reference for communication.

# 4 - Methods of Practical Use. How to use the GAMMA=1 charts.

## 4.1 Control Strips.

The negative control strips of charts GAMMA=1t and GAMMA=1p are produced by GAMMA & DENSITY Co. for every negative, positive, intermediate, and low-con stock commercially available. They are photographed under laboratory conditions according to the specifications of each stock.

The Thorough Control System (T.C.S.)™ is based on using the exposed GAMMA=1c from the processed negative shot on the set and matching it to the same stock negative control strip with the GAMMA=1t and/or GAMMA=1p. The tele-cine chart and print chart are designed specifically to decrease the set-up time and increase the accuracy of adjustments for tele-cine colorists and print timers respectively.
The T.C.S.™ system in no way limits the creative abilities of the cinematographer. Used from the set throughout all aspects of post production, the GAMMA=1 system should allow for greater creative control as the principles involved will have better communication and more precise information to work with.

The GAMMA=1t tele-cine control strip with the GAMMA=1c chart can also be included as a part of the head leader in the "prep-for tele-cine" procedure . This will help to adjust luminance and chrominance levels at once for the whole roll, and later will help the print timer to establish a starting point for his timing of the same roll during the production of the answer print.

## 4.2 Set Up of the Tele-cine Machine

The cornerstone of the system is the proper set up of the IRE values of the tele-cine machine in relation to the negative and/or positive densities. These values are universal and do not depend on the manufacturer of the machine or from the video encoding standards (NTSC, PAL, SECAM, etc.).

The GAMMA=1 Total Control System™ works with all tele-cine machines and all color-correction systems. Not only will it decrease the set up time in a supervised transfer, it is the perfect solution for unsupervised transfers.

Using the tele-cine and color correction controls, the colorist will adjust the PECs, gain, gamma, and color controls to match the marks on the control film loop of the GAMMA=1t chart to the corresponding numbers of IRE on the waveform monitor. (see illustration #3)

Enclosed is an outline of the steps a tele-cine colorist will use to achieve proper adjustment using the set-up control strip GAMMA=1t. It is the only part of this manual legal to copy for the purposes of giving it to your tele-cine colorist.

### 4.3 Using the chart GAMMA=lc on the set.

1. At the beginning of the day, expose the greeting on the back of your GAMMA=lc chart to prepare your tele- cine colorist to be ready for adjustment.

2. Shoot the GAMMA=lc chart full frame and expose it at speed for approximately 5-10 seconds. It is our recommendation that when possible, you shoot your chart at the same F-stop you use for shooting the actual set or scene. The source of illuminance for the chart should be "pure white "- 3200°K or 5500°K. according to the stock you are using, and be evenly illuminated without any glare or dark areas.

Your chart on the negative will then match the image of the control strip in the transfer session. This will assure proper contrast and color for your dailies, and indicate potential problems with the exposure, film, processing, or tele-cine equipment.

It is our recommendation that you re-shoot your chart for every set or scene that has a different look. This will insure the maximum potential from the image transfer of your negative to video tape .

For scenes lit for visual effect, i.e. sunset, we recommend that you shoot the chart twice.

First you shoot GAMMA=1c under normal, i.e. 3200°K or 5500°K light conditions then by using the magnetic labels, attach label "GRAY" next to "SET FOR".
Then implement whatever you do to achieve your intended effect (i.e. amber or 1/2 CTO gel on the lights to create a sunset look), and shoot the chart a second time, after applying the pre-printed magnetic label SUNSET next to SET UP FOR on your chart. This will indicate to the tele-cine colorist that the set is lit with warm "sunset" light intentionally, and it should not be "corrected" out of the scene.

## 5 -Technical Specifications. Requirements for film negative to be transferred to video tape.

### 5.1 Density Range

One of the most important advances created by the GAMMA & Density T.C.S.™ is the ability to judge the exposure quality of the negative using IRE designations.

The differences between print film and video tape create what is essentially a different range of densities that can be reproduced on each respective medium. As you can see from the graph (see illustration #4), only part of the negative's entire range of densities can be printed to have positive densities in which details can be distinguished in the highlights and shadows.

Even less of the negative's range of densities will transfer to video tape. The graph shows that a negative destined for print allows the cinematographer to place important details of the scene up to 3.5 F-stops below the KEY exposure and up to 3.5 F-stops above the KEY exposure, or in terms of T.C.S.™, the useful Exposure Latitude Index is -3.5/+3.5 F-stops

As of now, video technology limits the exposure latitude of a negative destined for video transfer. For video, the useful latitude is less than film. While the information might be on the negative, nothing that transfers below 7.5-9 IRE. will be reproduced on video and nothing that transfers above 100 IRE will be reproduced on video. It is possible to adjust the gamma and compress the image, but doing so (unintentionally) can cause a loss of detail and compromise the quality of the image.

## 5.2 Determining the Exposure Level of the Negative During Tele-cine

In the negative-positive process the cinematographer could determine the exposure quality of the negative by a combination of printing lights needed for properly looking (timed) print dailies. Because each printing light has 50 possible settings, every lab is theoretically supposed print the LAD negative density on the same combination of printing lights of 25R-25G-25B. But in real life every lab (for reasons too numerous to be explained in this manual) achieves the same result in printing from the same LAD negative by different combinations of printing lights unique to their lab. Generally 6 to 8 printing lights, depending on the color sensitive layer of the negative film , are equal to 1 F-stop of exposure.

When a cinematographer processes dailies at a lab, he/she receives a lab report that the negative of scene 100 was printed on lights 36-35-25, and scene 101 was printed on lights 48-47-37. Immediately he/she knows that scene 100 is normally exposed but scene 101 was overexposed approximately 2 F-stops.

Until now when a negative is transferred to video tape for video dailies the cinematographer loses the opportunity to evaluate the exposure qualities of the negative. This is especially problematic if the project is also going to be printed for theatrical release as well as video.

For the first time ever GAMMA & DENSITY Co. introduces a system for accurate translation of IRE units into printing light equivalents. When using the GAMMA=1c Chart and the TCS™, 1 printing light is equal to 2 IRE units. Diagram (illustration#8) shows the relationship between 45 IRE on your GAMMA=1c chart as exposed on the set, and the same 45 IRE field on the GAMMA-1t negative control strip. The difference between IRE levels on the two charts can be stated in the traditional timing light equivalents.

Example: After setting the 45 IRE field of the GAMMA=1t negative control strip on the 45 IRE mark on the wave form monitor, the tele-cine colorist will put your camera negative on the tele-cine machine and roll to the GAMMA=1c chart. If the 45 IRE field from your negative falls on the 65 IRE mark, it is fair to say that your negative would have to be printed about 10 printing lights higher than the LAD printing numbers from any lab. (see illutstration #6 above) The cinematographer immediately knows the negative is overexposed and can take the steps necessary to correct the problem (assuming it is unintentional).

# 6.Setting up the Location Monitor.

One of the worst problems with the use of video dailies is the inconsistency between video monitors. We strongly recommend using a professional quality monitor to obtain the best possible rendition of the image. We also recommend using a well maintained professional grade video player, preferably Beta SP and at least 3/4 inch.

## 6.1 Professional Monitor Set Up

With SMPTE color bars showing, set the monitor to blue only. This will turn the color bars on the top 2/3 of the screen into four blue and three black bars.

1) Using the hue or chroma phase knob, adjust until the center and right black bars are exactly the same. This should also result it in the two center blue bars being the same.

2) Use the chroma or color knob to make the second from the left left blue bar perfectly solid. Return screen to full color.

3) At the bottom right of the screen are three dark areas. One of the areas is divided into three vertical bands (they should be visible by turning the brightness knob all the way up). In this area, the left band represents 3.5 IRE, the middle band 7.5 IRE, and the right band 11.5 IRE. Adjust the brightness level until you can just distinguish between the right (11.5 IRE) and the center (7.5 IRE) mark. The 7.5 IRE band and 3.5 IRE band should both be solid black and indistinguishable from one another.
4) The second feild from the bottom left represents 100 IRE. Using the brightness knob, carefully adjust this field to the point where any turn down will result in a visible decrease, but any turn up gives no visible increase.

Note: If the tube has an inherrent shade problem, it will probably be most apparent in the black areas.

## 6.2 Using a Consumer Monitor

Regardless of the monitor used, we have included a special table for measuring the fields of the GAMMA=1 chart from the screen. (see illustration #7) While we intend this process to be helpful, we cannot guarantee exact results due to the variation of monitors or television sets used in the field.

These measurements can be done with a spotmeter using EV numbers. Set your spotmeter to ASA 100 and the time of exposure to 1/50 of a second.

| | | | | | |
|---|---|---|---|---|---|
| IRE | 10 | 20 | 45 | 60 | 90 |
| EV | 1.9 | 2.6 | 6.4 | 7.5 | 9 |

The monitor set-up procedure should be done using the image of the control strip GAMMA=1t or GAMMA=1t+ only, recorded at the head of each day's dailies, as was described in chapter 4 and included in the instructions for tele-cine colorists. After setting the monitor to the gray scale, use the color fields and E.R.C strips of your GAMMA=1c chart recorded on the tape to adjust the color as close as possible.

# Thorough Control System™: a method of color-accurate and contrast consistent film transfer to video dailies

**Y.Neyman, S. Riviére, H. Sisko**
**Gamma and Density Co.Inc.**
**Studio City, California**

## Illustrations

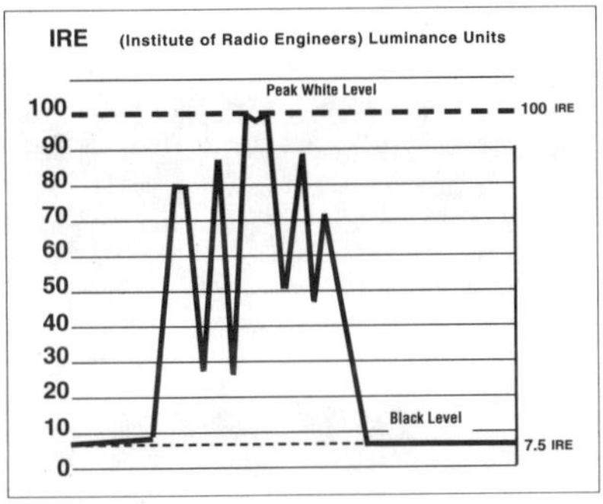


*Illustration 1. Video signal on waveform monitor*

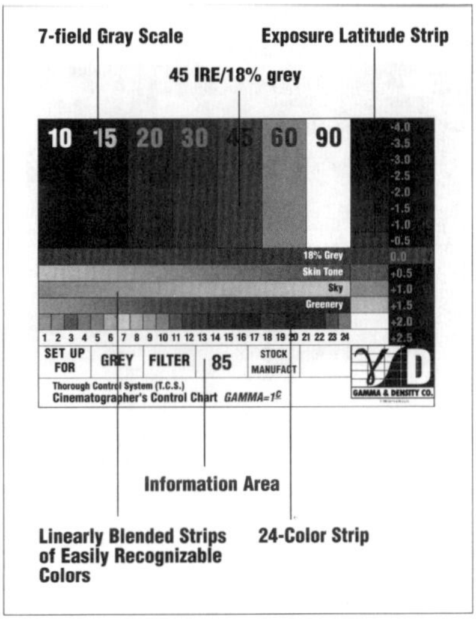


*Illustration 2-a.* ***Gamma=1c*** *Chart*

# Thorough Control System™: a method of color-accurate and contrast consistent film transfer to video dailies

Y.Neyman, S. Riviére, H. Sisko
Gamma and Density Co.Inc.
Studio City, California

## Illustrations

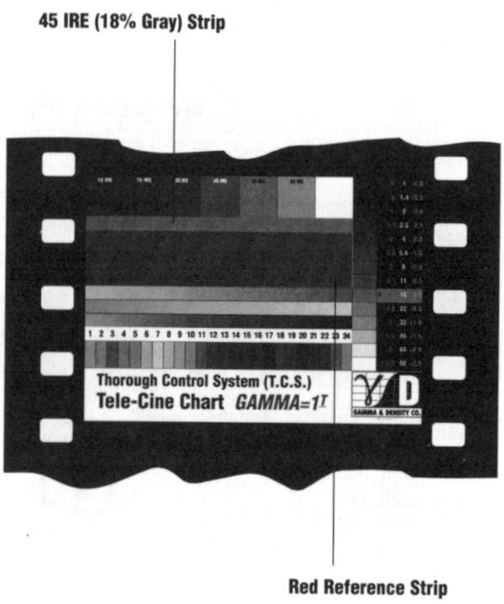


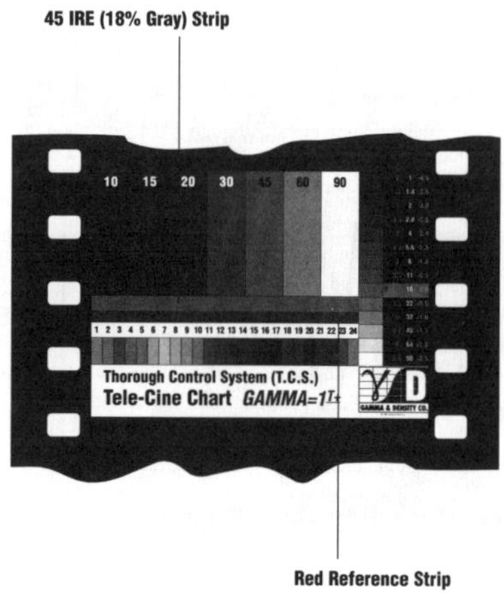


*Illustration 2-b.* ***Gamma=1$^{T}$*** *Set up Loop*

*Illustration 2-c.* ***Gamma=1$^{T+}$*** *Set up Loop*

# Thorough Control System™: a method of color-accurate and contrast consistent film transfer to video dailies

**Y.Neyman, S. Riviére, H. Sisko**
**Gamma and Density Co.Inc.**
**Studio City, California**

## Illustrations

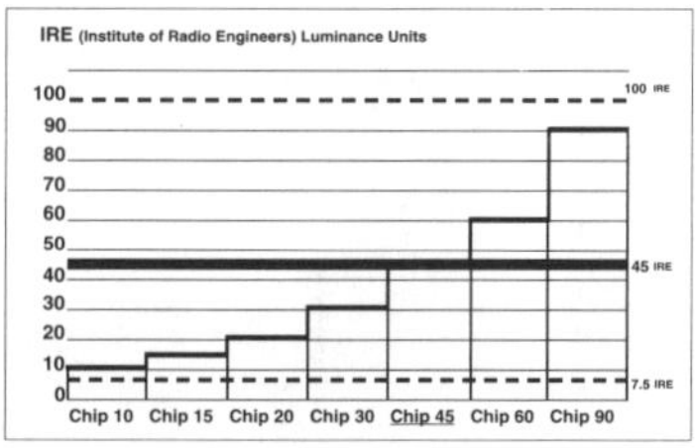


*Illustration 3. 7-field Gray Scale on Waveform Monitor*

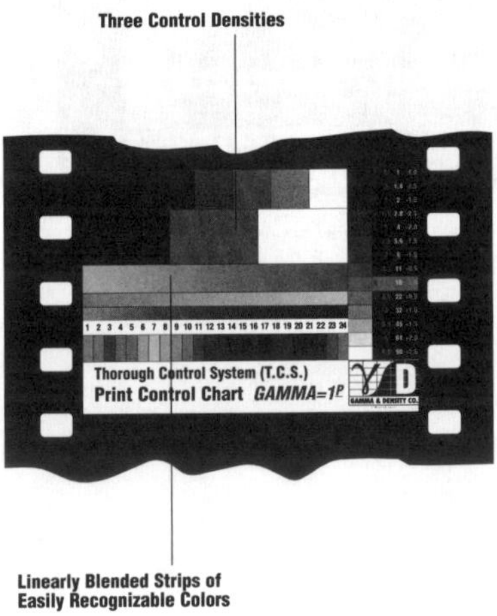


*Illustration 2-d.* ***Gamma=1P*** *Set up Loop*

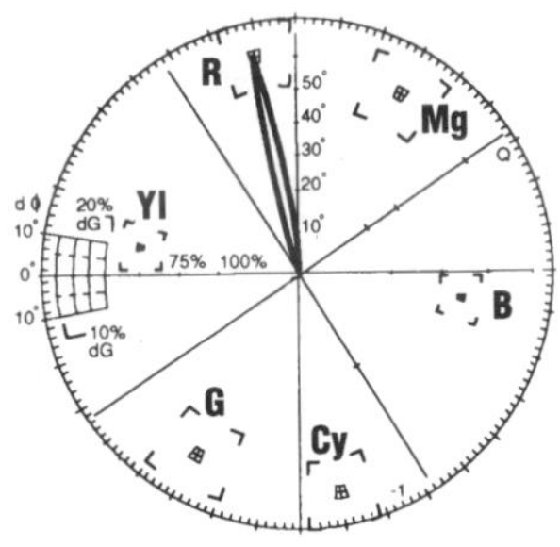


*Illustration 4. Red Strip on GAMMA=1P Set up Loop set in Red Fine Adjustment Box on Vectorscope*

# Thorough Control System™: a method of color-accurate and contrast consistent film transfer to video dailies


**Y.Neyman, S. Riviére, H. Sisko**
**Gamma and Density Co.Inc.**
**Studio City, California**


## Illustrations

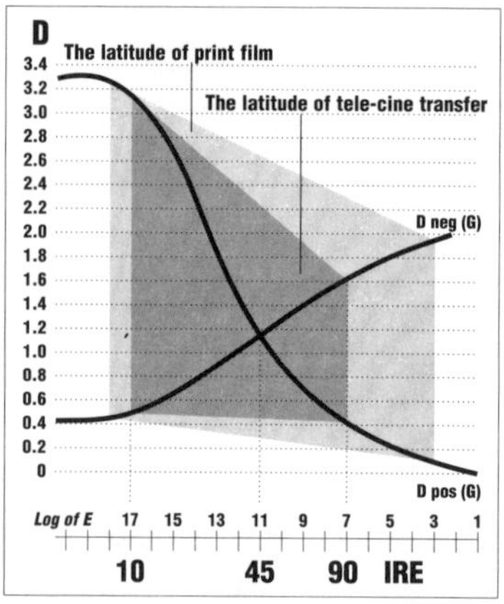


*Illustration 5. Useful range of the negative densities for negative-positive and tele-cine processes.*

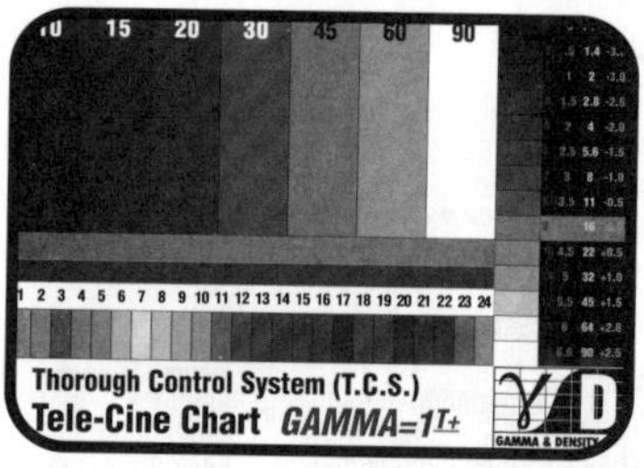


*Illustration 7.* ***Gamma=1*** *on location monitor*

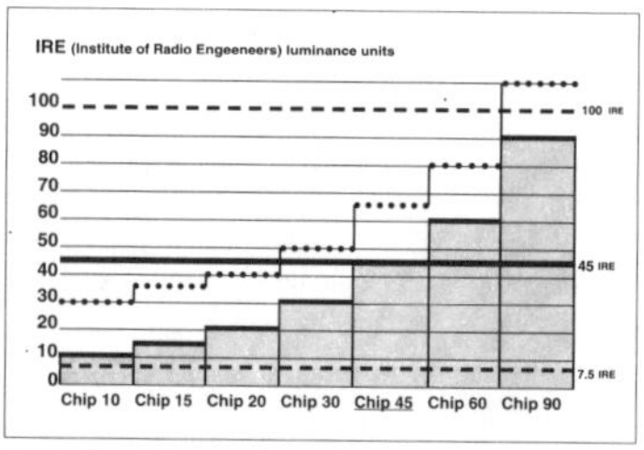


*Illustration 6. Comparison of normal and overexposed negatives showing 7-field Gray Scale on a waveform monitor*

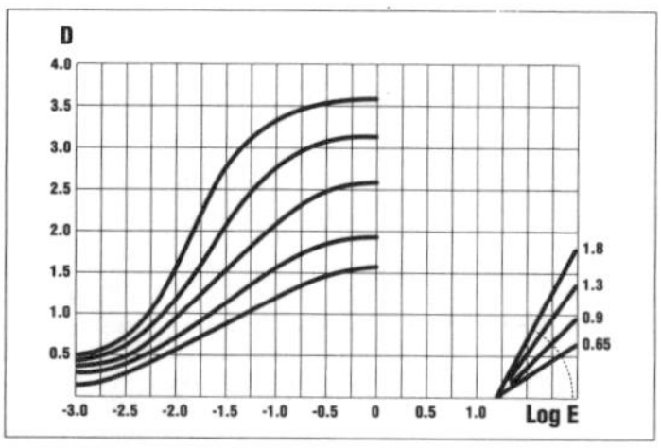


*Illustration 8.*

# Twelve bit acquisition, the next step in digital broadcast cameras

Jan van Rooy and Rob Voet
Philips Broadcast Television Systems
Breda, The Netherlands

## Abstract

CCD image sensors are capable of delivering at least 600% of linear video to the signal processing. This headroom is needed to reproduce large scene contrasts in a convincing way on displays not capable to handle these large contrasts.

Today's cameras have 10 bit A/D conversion in the video path. This calls for some form of non-linear analog processing like (pre-)gamma or (pre-)knee to handle these 600% signals.
This weakens the well known arguments of better accuracy and stability for these digital cameras: non-linear circuits like knee, gamma and whiteshading multipliers are not the most accurate and stable analog circuits.

The move to 12 bit A/D conversion in the camera allows digital videoprocessing with sufficient dynamic range, and all non-linear processing in the digital signal path.

This also opens the way to reconsider processing, given the new possibilities of the digital domain.
Examples will be given in the paper. Some items that will be addressed are : dynamic pixel correction, automatic skin contours and a new digital highlight compression with improved color fidelity.

The architecture of a 12 bit camera, the Philips BTS LDK20P will be explained in the paper, together with the algorithms used.

# 1. Introduction

In the book Digital Television[1] published in 1990 the following statement can be found:

*"At the time of writing there has not been a pressing requirement to produce a digital processing channel for use in television cameras since analogue techniques have a perfectly adequate performance"*

As television standards have not changed since 1990 the above statement still holds today, but technology has advanced to a degree that using digital signal processing (DSP) in cameras becomes attractive.
So digitalization of the broadcast chain finally has reached the camera, after first being introduced in postproduction and studio recording. The main reasons for this relatively late introduction of digital cameras are:

- The wide dynamic range of the camera signal : 80dB at the CCD sensor
- The tight power and space budget of the portable camera
- The adequate performance of analog processing in cameras

The digital state of the art addresses these challenges:

- Availability of 12 bit low power video A to D converters
- Availability of low voltage sub micron processes for integration of signal processing in ASICs
- The ability to introduce attractive digital features, and some specific advantages of digital over analog realizations. This pushes performance to a level higher than adequate.

Based on a generic camera processing channel this paper will deal with the subjects of quantisation and dynamic range in chapter 2.
The practical realization of a digital camera, based on a chipset jointly developed by Philips BTS and Thomson Broadcast Systems will be explained in chapter 3. Features like digital highlight compression, pixel correction, skin contours will be explained in chapter 4.

# 2. The camera video processing channel

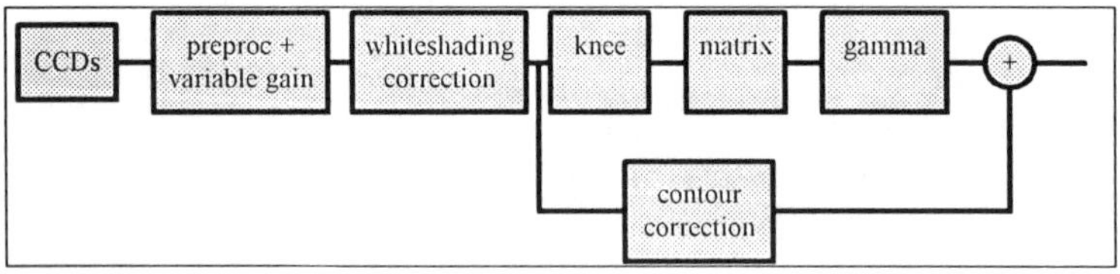


**Figure 1**

In fig.1 a video processing channel is depicted.
For non camera experts a brief summary of the functions:
There are three channels of processing, red, green and blue (RGB)
The preprocessing/variable gain stage removes the reset noise and sets the gains in the RGB channels to adjust sensitivity of the camera (gainswitch) and to correct the individual channels for color temperature (painting, white balance).
White shading correction compensates for non uniform distribution of light across the sensors. This is done by multiplying the videosignals in R,G and B with non-linear correctionsignals.
Higlight compression, or 'knee' compresses the video signal from a typical 600% of video into a 100% range. The gamma correction transforms the signal from a 'linear in luminance' signal to a 'linear in perception' signal (which happens to be a signal suitable to drive CRT's).
Somewhere in the video chain a matrix is used to correct the colors and contour correction is used to correct and enhance the horizontal and vertical sharpness of the picture.
The input signal of the processing is the CCD signal with a dynamic range of well over 80 dB (in case of the FT17 DPM sensor as used in the LDK20P). This dynamic range is reduced in the variable gain stage to about 76 dB. The knee circuit compresses this dynamic range to about 60 dB by mapping the 600% video range on a 100% range. The initial gain of the gamma correction amplifies the noise near black , leaving a dynamic range in the post gamma signal of about 50dB.
As dynamic range gradually decreases from sensor to output in the videoprocessing chain, digitalization of the signal requires less bits going downstream in the processing.

## 2.1 Digital and analog strengths

A comparison of analog and digital techniques for video processing gives the following:

- Delays, and especially line delays are very difficult in analog techniques. Line delays require the use of modulation/demodulation ultrasonic transducers and trimmed glass delay lines. In digital systems delays of an integer number of clock cycles are relatively easy once the signal is digitized , and can be accomplished within the processing ASICs.
- Non linear operations like highlight compression and gamma correction can be achieved with a much higher precision in the digital domain. It is possible to design adequate analog circuits, but they always will have some temperature drift and inaccuracies, as they rely on the temperature dependent nonlinear characteristics of diodes, transistors or FETs.
- Mathematical operations like multiplication, division, median filtering and maximum/minimum operations are far more accurate in the digital domain, and easier to realize. This opens the way to a new kind of video processing that was impossible in the analog domain.
- Signal processing noise in the analog domain is a matter of physics, in the digital domain it is a matter of using a sufficient number of bits.
- far less presets and adjustments: cameras are easier to produce with better quality and reliability

Aren't there any drawbacks for using digital videosignals in cameras?
Yes there are:

- With the IC processes of today digital processing consumes more power than a state of the art analog processing.
- Digital transmission is less effective in bandwidth than analog transmission. In the case of triax cameras the signal must either be compressed, or the maximum triax length must be drastically reduced for digital triax.
- Development of digital ASICs is expensive.
- Anti alias filtering is needed for digital processing.

## 2.2 A/D converters and dynamic range: Why 12 bits?

Mapping the digital and analog strengths to the video channel described in 2.1 leads to the following observations about the added value of digital signal processing:

Preprocessing: Basically sampling and subtracting signals with a short subpixel time delay, best to be done analog
Variable gain stage: No special advantage for digital realization, just gains
Whiteshading: multiplying video with a time varying correction signal: best to be done digital
Highlight compression: non linear operations; best to be done digital
Gamma correction: non linear operation, best to be done digital
Contours: many delays: best to be done digital

The number of bits required in various stages of the signal processing chain has already been covered in an earlier presentation.[2] The use of a 12 bit A to D converter allows a video processing chain in which all non linear signal processing is done in the digital domain, because digitalization can be done before white shading correction. This is not possible with 10 bit A/D converters. Cameras with 10 bit A to D converters always have analog pregamma and/or preknee circuits to compress the signal to a lower dynamic range .
An added difficulty for 10 bit cameras is the headroom that has to be reserved for highlights. This leads to a coarser quantisation of the 0-100% video range. To illustrate this a 10 bit quantisation scheme of a 600% video range[3] is compared to a direct 12 bit quantisation (fig2.). The headroom needed in the 10 bits case results in 438 quantisation steps in the normal video range, compared to 672 steps in the same range for a direct 12 bit conversion.
Digitizing the signal at an early stage with 600% of dynamic range allows the use of more sophisticated schemes for highlight compression. This will be further explained in section 4.1. It also allows the use of a wide dynamic range signal as a source for image enhancement.

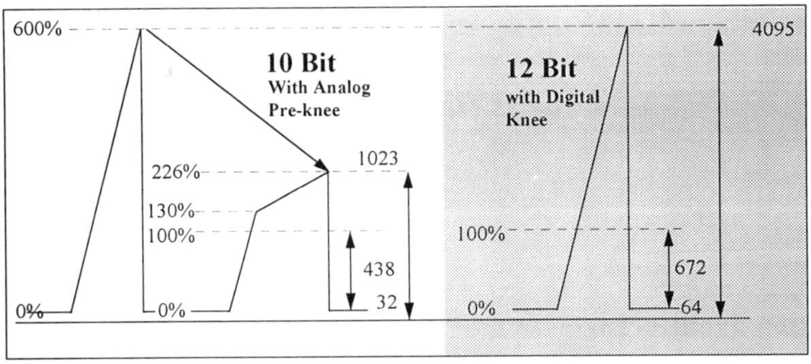


**Figure 2**

# 3. The LDK20P digital camera

The LDK20P is a one piece portable triax camera. The camera is developed to benefit from the advantages of digital processing, but is compatible to the existing Philips BTS equipment. Digital processing enables extended controls like a digital matrix with "360 $^{0}$" control range . The matrix is switchable to pre or post gamma correction. The camera offers a wide range of generic gamma curves including CCIR, SMPTE240 and three BBC gamma definitions, with additional faders for variable gamma (master,R,B).
Aperture and contour correction are combined using two dimensional FIR filters.
The contour circuit can accept wide dynamic range signals up to 600% of video to allow for sufficient detail in the highlights.

## 3.1 concept

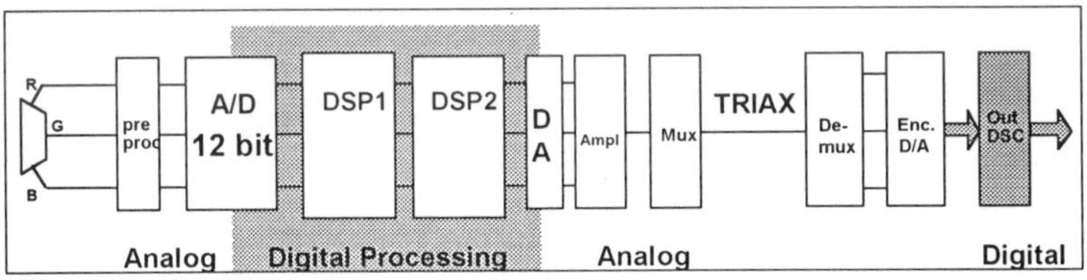


**Figure 3**

The basic concept of the video chain is depicted in fig 3. In this concept the individual strengths of analog and digital processing are maximally used.
Preprocessing is mainly sensor signal processing and gain control. These functions can easily be done in analog processing. All nonlinear functions like highlight compression, gamma correction, and delay intensive functions like contour processing are done in the digital domain in this concept.
The triax system is analog, as this is more efficient in bandwidth and can accommodate more than 2400 meter of triax. The output of the camera can be RGB analog, YUV or serial digital according to SMPTE259M.

## 3.2 video architecture

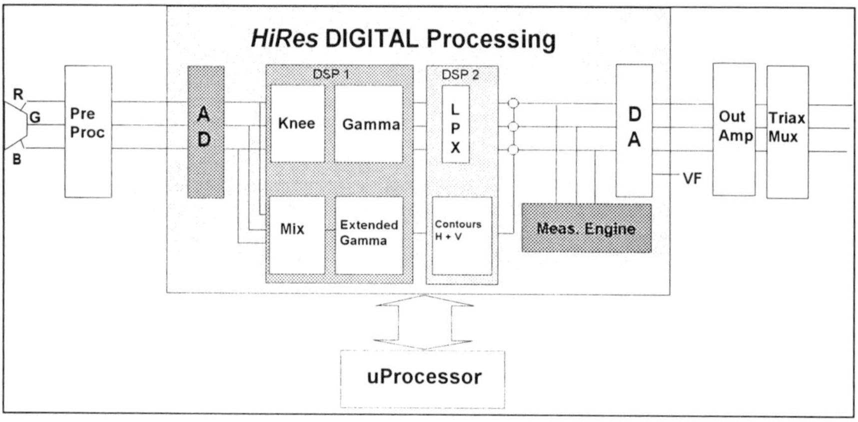


**Figure 4**

Fig 4. zooms in on the processing channel in the camera. A/D conversion is done in 12 bits. The first ASIC in the chain (ASIC A) handles mainly the transfer curve (knee, gamma), whiteshading and color selection for the skin contours. ASIC B takes care of the 2D filtering like contours and has leaking pixel correction and output formatters. The D/A conversion in the LDK20P works with 2x oversampled signals at 36 MHz.
The viewfinder channel is separated from the output channel, carrying its own contoursetting. Both ASICs have an integrated measurement engine. This circuit probes and evaluates the signal at several points in the ASICs. It acts as an intelligent interface between the relatively slow microprocessor and the high speed signal path. The measurement engine is used for diagnostics and camera automatics.

# 4. Digital advantages

Once the video signal is digitized, operations can be performed on the signal which are impossible to do analogue, or at least are considerably more inaccurate or complicated.
This chapter focuses on a number of applications in the LDK20P camera, of which especially the method of highlight compression only can be done in a 12 or more bit quantised digital signal. Dynamic pixel correction and skin contours are examples of algorithms that might be done in the analog domain , but are considerably easier and more accurate when performed digital.

## 4.1 Highlight compression: trucolor knee

### 4.1.1. Background

Cameras for film and video have the non trivial task to capture scenes with a contrast ratio of sometimes more than 1000:1 in a convincing way for displays often not exceeding a 50:1 range. Film has it's toe and shoulder to compress this range. Most present video cameras have similar transfer characteristics, the linear part of the gamma curve is the toe, and three tracking knee circuits in the color channels compress the signals to form the shoulder of the curve.

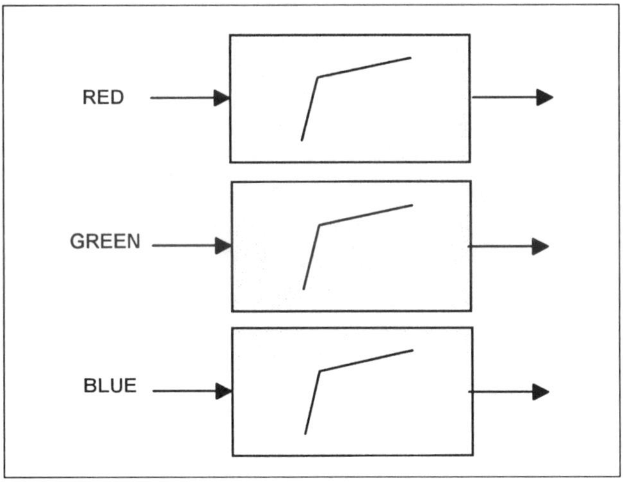


**Figure 5**

Fig 5 depicts a conventional highlight compression or 'knee' function in a camera. Above a certain point, the kneepoint, the video gain in the R, G and B channel is diminished to accommodate a larger dynamic range within the 100% video range at the output. Compressing highlights inevitably means making a trade off. The need for compression stems from the fact that it is impossible to display the full range of luminance from the original scene. Therefore the luminance of the signal needs to be compressed, but quality of the compression scheme is also determined by the way color hue and saturation are handled.

For the conventional knee circuit of fig.5 hue and saturation in colored scenes change with compression[4]. On top of that the compression curve in the Y signal is different for each color. Compression for colored signals begins as soon as the maximum of R,G and B reaches the kneepoint. The corresponding Y signal will always be lower than this maximum, so the kneepoint in Y is lower than the kneepoint value.
In fact, there are 3 separate kneepoint (when R,G and B respectively reach the kneepoint) and 3 extra bends in the Y signal when R,G,B reach the clipping level.

Saturated colors tend to receive more compression than desaturated colors or grayscales. As a pathological case it can be mentioned that for instance fully saturated blue never will reach more than 11% in luminance, no matter what overexposure is used.

### 4.1.2 Design of a digital highlight processing

Highlight compression has to compromise in one or more of the properties luminance, hue or saturation of the signal. The availability of 600% uncompressed videosignals in the digital domain enables the use of more sophisticated algorithms, and a fundamental rethinking of highlight compression. We have to provide an optimum path for all colors from black to peak white in order to fully exploit the dynamic range of the display. The image on the CRT has to be a convincing representation of the scene before the camera.
In the digital domain it is possible to calculate color information for every pixel on an individual basis. It will be possible to optimize for constant hue, controlled saturation and/or better luminance relationship between colors.

Compressing the upper part of the luminance curve is the obvious way to go, as we don't want to change anything in the normal exposed parts of the scene. As luminance goes up, the color space becomes more limited, so desaturation will be necessary. There is no principal reason to change hue.

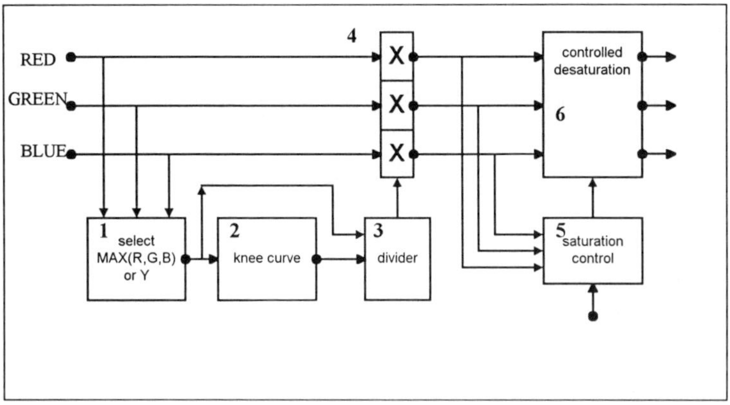


**Figure 6**

Fig. 6 shows a simplified model of highlight compression as is implemented in the LDK20P ASICs. The real implementation is somewhat different to optimize for minimum silicon area.
In block 1 of fig. 6 a single channel representation of the RGB signal is made. This can be either the maximum of R,G,B or the luminance signal Y derived from the RGB signals before knee, depending on the application. This single signal receives its compression in a knee circuit, fitted with a manually controllable, or adaptive knee circuit (block 2).
The ratio of the compressed signal and the input signal of the knee circuit (calculated in block 3) is the gaincontrol for the R,G and B channels in block 4.
As R,G and B are multiplied with the same factor, the output of block 4 is a compressed RGB signal with correct hue and saturation, but with its luminance compressed. This change in luminance Y is according to the compression curve of block 2, if Y is selected as input in block 1.
If the maximum of (RGB) is selected, the kneepoint in Y will be the kneepoint of block 2, multiplied with Y(R,G,B)/MAX(R,G,B). So the compression in Y in that case is depending on the color of the input signal.
A compression scheme like this, with the MAX(R,G,B) as selection for compression has already been implemented in cameras in an analog form[5]. However, the use of videomultipliers and dividers makes this implementation rather complicated and vulnerable to noise and tolerances.
After compression in this first stage, R,G or B still may reach levels above 100%. Of course it is possible to clip above 100% in the RGB signals, but this leads to unwanted hue changes.
Therefore block 6 is a desaturation circuit in which controlled desaturation of the signal takes place, to fit the colored signal in a range up to the user selectable desaturation level without hue changes.

### 4.1.2 Evaluating performance

For evaluating the effect of compression on colorimetry the CIE 1976 UCS diagram[6] is useful, as u' and v' are independent of luminance.. The length of the vector from the point (u',v') to the white reference ($u_0$',$v_0$') represents the saturation *s*, the angle of the vector is a measure for hue *h*.

Deviations of the compressed signal can be given with *ds* and *dh* :

$ds=100*(s-s_{100\%})/s_{100\%}$ and $dh=h-h_{100\%}$ (degrees)

$s_{100\%}$ and $h_{100\%}$ are the saturation and hue in the u' v' diagram for normal exposure.
ds=-100% means that no color is left.

For the color dependency of the luminance compression the factor *dl* can be defined as the percentual difference in compression of the colored signal and of the grayscale signal with the same luminance Y:

$dl= 100*(y_{uncolored}-y_{colored})/y_{uncolored}$

Color dependency of luminance is a measure of 'luminance fidelity': how much luminance relationships between colors gets distorted by the highlight compression.

To evaluate knee performance *ds,dh* and *dl* are calculated for three situations: the conventional kneecircuit of fig. 5 (=*RGBknee)*, the LDK20P trucolor knee acting on MAX(RGB) signals (=*TrcolNAM)* and the LDK20P knee acting on the Y signal (=*TrcolY)*.
Calculations are made for the EBU colors.[7]
An overexposure of 5, a kneepoint of 60% and a gain above the kneepoint of 0.2 has been assumed for all situations.

| | | NOMINAL YRGB | | | | RGBknee | | |
|---|---|---|---|---|---|---|---|---|
| | | Y% | R% | G% | B% | dl | ds | dh |
| **EBU/CAM 01** | Dark skin | 11 | 18 | 8 | 6 | -12 | -32 | 11 |
| **EBU/CAM 02** | LIght skin | 39 | 59 | 32 | 24 | -2 | -66 | 5 |
| **EBU/CAM 03** | Light grayish red | 32 | 48 | 26 | 23 | 0 | -62 | 0 |
| **EBU/CAM 04** | Light yellow green | 30 | 27 | 37 | 6 | -3 | -28 | -6 |
| **EBU/CAM 05** | Light bluish green | 29 | 15 | 35 | 38 | 0 | -60 | 0 |
| **EBU/CAM 06** | Light violet | 32 | 37 | 26 | 53 | 0 | -60 | 1 |
| **EBU/CAM 07** | Foliage | 13 | 10 | 15 | 5 | -9 | -15 | -8 |
| **EBU/CAM 08** | Medium red | 24 | 56 | 10 | 10 | -11 | -64 | -3 |
| **EBU/CAM 09** | Medium green | 41 | 18 | 58 | 11 | -4 | -56 | -4 |
| **EBU/CAM 10** | Medium blue | 21 | 12 | 19 | 57 | -1 | -69 | -1 |
| **EBU/CAM 11** | Dark red | 8 | 17 | 3 | 4 | -16 | -19 | -1 |
| **EBU/CAM 12** | Dark green | 19 | 8 | 27 | 5 | -12 | -30 | -6 |
| **EBU/CAM 13** | Dark blue | 7 | 4 | 5 | 21 | -11 | -32 | -3 |
| **EBU/CAM 14** | Medium yellow red | 47 | 91 | 33 | 8 | -14 | -57 | 32 |
| **EBU/CAM 15** | Medium purple | 22 | 30 | 14 | 43 | 0 | -67 | 0 |

**table 1**: *The 15 EBU , together with the errors in luminance (dl), saturation (ds) and hue (dh)*

Table 1 gives the EBU colors with their nominal YRGB values (Y%,R%,G%,B%), together with the dl, ds and dh of the conventional knee circuit . Table 2 shows the performance of respectively the trucolor knee with Y based compression and the one with MAX(RGB) based compression. Desaturation is on for the trucolor knee, with the desaturation point set at 100%.

| | | TrcolY | | | TrcolNAM | | |
|---|---|---|---|---|---|---|---|
| | | **dl** | **ds** | **dh** | **dl** | **ds** | **dh** |
| **EBU/CAM 01** | Dark skin | 0 | 0 | 0 | -25 | 0 | 0 |
| **EBU/CAM 02** | Light skin | 0 | -73 | 0 | -19 | -22 | 0 |
| **EBU/CAM 03** | Light grayish red | 0 | -53 | 0 | -20 | 0 | 0 |
| **EBU/CAM 04** | Light yellow green | 0 | 0 | 0 | -10 | 0 | 0 |
| **EBU/CAM 05** | Light bluish green | 0 | -1 | 0 | -14 | 0 | 0 |
| **EBU/CAM 06** | Light violet | 0 | -60 | 0 | -23 | -2 | 0 |
| **EBU/CAM 07** | Foliage | 0 | 0 | 0 | -14 | 0 | 0 |
| **EBU/CAM 08** | Medium red | 0 | -76 | 0 | -39 | -9 | 0 |
| **EBU/CAM 09** | Medium green | 0 | -70 | 0 | -16 | -19 | 0 |
| **EBU/CAM 10** | Medium blue | 0 | -70 | 0 | -44 | -7 | 0 |
| **EBU/CAM 11** | Dark red | 0 | 0 | 0 | -23 | 0 | 0 |
| **EBU/CAM 12** | Dark green | 0 | 0 | 0 | -22 | 0 | 0 |
| **EBU/CAM 13** | Dark blue | 0 | -3 | 0 | -33 | 0 | 0 |
| **EBU/CAM 14** | Medium yellow red | 0 | -96 | 0 | -24 | -63 | 0 |
| **EBU/CAM 15** | Medium purple | 0 | -53 | 0 | -33 | 0 | 0 |

**table 2:** *Errors dl,ds and dh for trucolor knee acting on the Y signal and on the MAX(RGB).*

The difference between the conventional highlight compression and the trucolor knee is clear from the tables: the hue change which is present in the conventional kneeRGB is eliminated. If the situation TrcolY is chosen the color dependency of luminance compression is also eliminated. The compressed picture is consistent regarding luminance differences between colors. However, desaturation is considerably more in the case of TrcolY versus TrcolMAX, and comparable to the desaturation in the RGBknee.
The TrcolMAX knee optimizes for color hue and saturation, at the cost of luminance fidelity. With the same settings of kneepoint and slope more of the highlighted parts remain visible.

The optimal settings of highlight compression are dependent on the application.
The optimum can be either 'diminish' highlights and concentrate on showing as much as possible from the highlighted parts of the scene, or transferring the 'impression of highlights' within the picture, more or less in the way 17th century painters did on their very limited display dynamic range by using white paint: allowing the colors to desaturate to allow a higher contrast.
The TrcolMAX knee diminishes highlights, compression in luminance for colors is quite strong, and saturation is preserved to its maximum, improving recognizability of objects.

The TrcolY knee respects the luminance relationship between colors and can be used to give the impression of highlights in the scene.
In situations where the highlighted parts carry important information, diminishing highlights will be the best choice. For example: with shadow and bright sunlight across the field of a football stadium shirts of players are more easily recognizable if saturation and hue is retained.
In a situation where the highlighted part in itself is not so important, but conributes to the scene composition, giving an impression of highlights will probably be the best strategy. Highlighted parts of the scene really appear as highlights.

## 4.2 Dynamic pixel correction

A problem associated with all kinds of CCD sensors is the appearance of leaking pixels in the sensor. When leaving the factory, all cameras have very tight specifications regarding the absence of leaking pixels, but during the lifetime of a camera pixel errors occasionally occur. These pixels can be time varying, temperature dependent, and can even disappear and reappear after some time.
As the sensors are the most expensive part of the camera and cannot be replaced in the field, a pixel correction circuit is advantageous, both for economical and technical reasons.
Several manufacturers have introduced a pixel correction device in their camera, mostly based on stored data about the address of the leaking pixel. At least one automatic pixel corrector has been published[8] relying on a off-line measurement of the video signal with the lens capped.
Detecting leaking pixels in this way doesn't account for the temperature dependence of these pixels and does not correct for new leaking pixels.
It is therefore desirable to have a fully adaptive leaking pixel corrector. To avoid unwanted effects on the signal this pixel corrector has to be very selective.

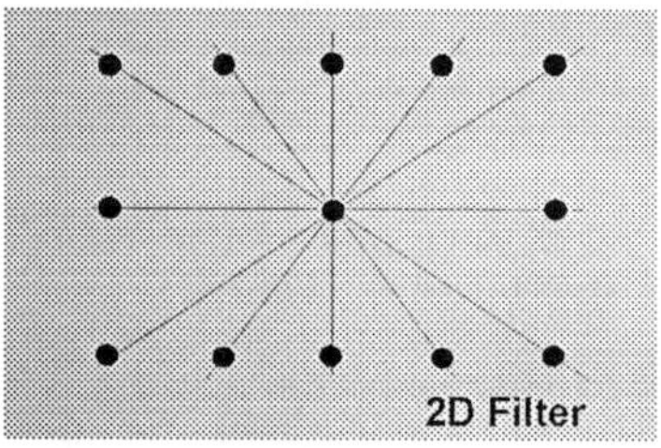


**Figure 7**

In a Philips BTS patented pixel corrector the pixels have to pass a severe examination to qualify as a leaking pixel. First of all in every color channel the pixel is compared to the average of a couple of neighboring pixels on a number of diagonals, as depicted in fig.7.
If the value of the center pixel is higher than the maximum of these averages plus the permitted picture deviation, then the pixel might qualify as a leaking pixel. To avoid false alarms, the result of each color channel is compared. If more than one color channel reports a leaking pixel on the same spot then the pixel is likely to be a part of the scene. If a pixel occurs in one color channel only, it is detected as a leaking pixel and will be corrected to the maximum average of the diagonals plus the permitted pixel deviation. For measurement purposes, like acceptance tests, the pixel corrector can be switched off.

## 4.3 Automatic skintone contours

To my knowledge the first reference to skin contours is an RCA patent in 1984[9].
The general idea of diminishing contours in areas with skintones to provide an "electronic make-up" was presented , with an application operating on the I vector in the NTSC system.
The idea was never implemented by RCA, but surfaced in several cameras in the late eighties.

The Philips BTS implementation of a skin contours circuit with automatic tint detection got an Emmy Award in 1994. There were several additions to the original idea :

- the system works for all colors, not only skintones, but also for grass, etc...: It can efficiently clean up a bad football field, or can be used to diminish the load for MPEG coders trying to code large areas of detailed single colored backgrounds
- Target colors can be selected automatically by pointing at the object and simply running the automatic detection function.
- Two independent colors can be selected
- The color detection circuit operates on chromaticity rather than chroma. This means that the selection of a color is constant over a wide range of light and f-stops without readjusting.
- As detection is before knee, the range even is extended to the highlighted areas. Gamma, matrix and knee can be freely manipulated without altering the selection.

Selected colors can be shown with a zebra signal on the viewfinder output, and/or by showing them as the only colored objects in a monochrome background in the output signals.
The skin contours system is implemented in the LDK10 and LDK10P as an analog circuit .
However, as lots of video multipliers and comparators are being used, it works even better in a digital camera like the LDK20P.

## 4.4 Digital matrix

The matrix corrects the colorimetry of the camera. Fixed matrices and factory settings found in cameras are often the result of careful measurements of calibrated test charts, and calculations to obtain a matrix with minimum errors. As matching between cameras is important, the calculated coefficients have to be implemented accurately in the camera. This is the reason that analog Philips BTS cameras normally have matrix resistor networks with relative tolerances of 0.1% to reach that level of accuracy.
On the other hand there is a need for variable matrices.
Digital processing allows a variable matrix with an excellent accuracy and repeatability.
In the LDK20P processing a full 6 coefficient "360 $^{0}$" matrix is implemented, to be used pre- or post-gamma, with a wide range for the coefficient. For example, is possible to monochrome the matrix, put in a sepia effect with gamma controls , and still keep the original color selection for reduced contours.

## 4.5 Extreme settings

Controls for gamma, knee, white clippers for analog cameras used to have separate controls in the color channels. This was needed to trim out the tolerances associated with analog processing. In digital processing the need for trimming individual channels is eliminated. However, the LDK20P is equipped with individual controls for gamma and white clippers and has a very wide range in matrix coefficients. The camera can now serve as an artistic tool, a first stage in postprocessing. Examples of settings are:

- Colored monochrome: matrix set to monochrome, color midrange levels with individual gamma to obtain the effect of old photographs or B/W film.
- Use skin view to monochrome the scene with the exception of one or two selected objects

# 5. Conclusion

The introduction of 12 bit A to D converters suitable for video signals enables the introduction of the digital LDK20P camera with all non linear videoprocessing in the digital domain, and the maximum use of digital techniques in the signal path. The advantages of incorporating all non-linear processing within the digital domain are a better accuracy and controllability, giving way to an easier and more reproducible setup of the camera and more artistic freedom to the operator. Twelve bit A/D conversion allows more steps in the 100% video range and a wider digital dynamic range compared to 10 bit solutions. The camera is not only acquisition, it is also a first tool for postprocessing starting at 600% videosignals.

---


**references**

[1] C.P. Sandbank (ed) :'*Digital Television'* John Wiley & Sons 1990 ISBN 0 471 92360 5

[2] J. van Rooy, B.Botte et al: '*Requirements for digital signal processing in broadcast cameras'* Symposium Record 19th International Television Symposium Montreux 1995, p212-218

[3] L.Thorpe and A.Takeuchi: *The all digital camcorder* SMPTE journal, january 1996 p18

[4] H.Blom et. al. *Adaptive highlight compression in today's CCD cameras",* SMPTE journal , march 1992 p135

[5] J.P.Lacotte, et. al "*Towards full quality CCD studio cameras: the last steps,"* IBC conference 1988

[6] CIE pub. nr 15.2, 1976

[7] EBU tech 3237-E, 1983.

[8] B.Botte "*Digital automatic pixel correction in new generation CCD Broadcast cameras"* IBC conference. 1992 p474

[9] Robert N. Hurst *Independent fleshtone contours"* US pat no. 4,506,293 ( 1984)

# Distributed Digital Post-Production

Christopher C. Woollard,
University of Greenwich,
London, England.

## Abstract

It is now possible to use powerful general purpose computer architectures to support post production of both video and multimedia projects. By devising a suitable portable software architecture and using high speed networking in an appropriate manner, a system has been constructed where editors are no longer tied to a specific location. New types of production, such as multi threaded interactive video, are supported. Editors may also work remotely where very high speed network connection is not currently provided. An object oriented database is used for the comprehensive cataloguing of material and to support automatic audio/video object migration and replication.

## Introduction

Today, nonlinear post production systems are available from many sources at a very wide range of prices. Organisations wishing to acquire such systems are faced with a plethora of decisions and compromises. Many of these questions relating to video program production have been summarised [Turner 94]. At any point in time, we find ourselves limited by our budget and the state of developed equipment within this. To complicate matters, our industry is currently in a stage of unprecedented technical change, indeed a position analogous to that which has persisted in the computer industry for many years. It may be concluded that some of the factors revolving around a very high rate of change within the computer industry also apply to us:

Adoption of 'Standard' techniques.

Preservation of skills across hardware and software upgrades.

Migration from single to distributed systems.

Underlying technologies evolving at very high rate.

What we propose here is an 'open' architecture intended to support video and multimedia productions by effective team effort. It is capable of evolving with time to support new kinds of productions, which will become possible with developments in distribution and exhibition technologies. For us, this system has application within the context of a large

UK University offering programs at various levels within what are currently regarded as the video and multimedia fields.

## A Distributed Architecture

It has been our aim to produce an object oriented, location transparent architecture to support AV and Multimedia productions. Some of the component technologies necessary to support this, such as object databases, are relatively stable and available. Others, such as the video hardware itself will inevitably require updating. It is therefore necessary that the system support direct migration. Essentially, it does so using the Object paradigm, which is well established within the software engineering community [Goldberg 83].

Currently the underlying hardware comprises the following:

> 10 Bit, 2x Oversampled 4:2:2 video encoding conforming fully to the CCIR-601 standard. Component / Composite / S-Video and D1 input output. RS-422 VTR control.
>
> Variable JPEG intrafield compression (for the edit environment)
> MPEG-1 for Multimedia CD authoring.
>
> Multiple 4.3 Gbyte AV disks, minimally two per edit station. Dual SCSI channels per edit station dedicated to video support.
>
> 1-8 track 16 bit 44.1/48KHZ audio.
> ATM network provision.
> 17" or greater computer monitor plus separate video monitor per edit station.
>
> Special purpose 35/70mm film support. Multiple modified Cinemeccanica Victoria 8 projectors for special large format film project [Woollard 97].

In hardware terms, ambitious architectures such as the IBM POWER system [Epstein 95] or indeed high end industry standard products from vendors such as AVID lead us to conclude that a certain minimum level of investment must be made. Our current implementation is illustrated in Figure 1.

Currently, 133MHZ and 150MHZ Pentium processors are primarily employed throughout the system augmented by a single Sparc 20 based station. Video processors support either 720 x 576 or 1250 x 1024 non-interlaced displays. The genlock timing settings may be altered to synchronise the system to an external reference signal in order to synchronise with other equipment.

In order to support the real time constraints imposed by broadcast quality video, dedicated video AV disks are employed. It is not necessary that all video be resident at a particular edit station in order to work with the material, but the overheads imposed by any general purpose operating system on the system disk(s) alone would greatly complicate video buffering design.

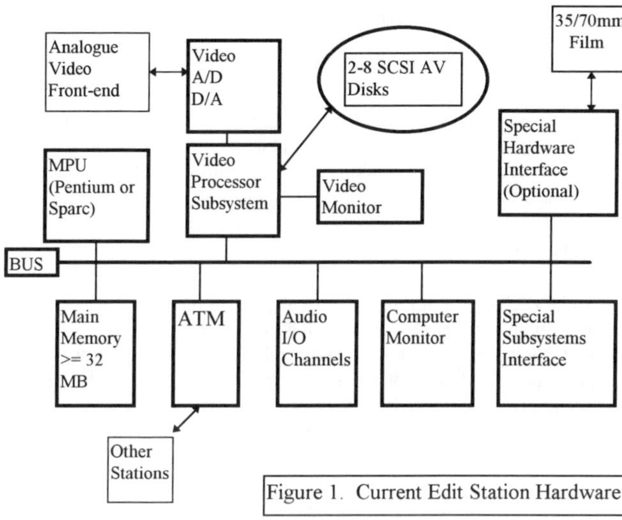


Figure 1. Current Edit Station Hardware

Each video segment is treated by the software as an object. An access path to remote video objects may be established via the high speed network. If very high speed access to remote objects is not possible for any reason, the system will resort to object migration which obviously may impose delays. In this case, the system will assemble a 'working set' of clip objects on the local AV disks prior to editing. The granularity of the working set is tuneable, typically comprising an entire small video project or that portion of a large program currently being edited. The derivation and maintenance of the working set is automatic, analogous to the page table maintenance within computer operating systems [Singhal 94].

## The Network

In order to satisfy real time video access across the network, an ATM solution has been adopted [Mandeville 95]. We have found that some care must be taken when selecting a suitable switch architecture for real time video networking. ATM switches may be categorised as time division switches and space division switches. The first of these uses a time division backplane bus capable of transferring N cells, where N is the number of input ports, within a single cell arrival time. Each input port controller is assigned its own cell time to transfer a cell over the bus. The input controller appends the required output port number to the head of the cell and this is used by the output controllers to decide whether a specific controller should read and buffer the cell. With the space division switch however, the switching hardware comprises a matrix of interconnected switching elements that collectively provide a number of parallel alternate paths through the switch. Those switches employing a delta switch matrix have been found to offer adequate real time performance at a cost lower than fully connected switches.

At present, our typical data rates for broadcast video transfer between edit stations with the current JPEG compression is 5 Mbytes per second and around 1.5 Mbytes per second when working on reduced resolution productions for multimedia. Our current network configuration is illustrated in Figure 2.

## Real Time Software

Object orientation in itself does not directly support the real time software design development and testing essential to a project such as this. Throughout the development of both network and edit station, we have taken a radically different track with regards to implementing the required real time software. We have adopted a portable tuning method based upon synthetic perturbation tuning. This involves (1) prototype code for the network or edit station code object under development P, (2) measurement of the response to be improved such as the run time of P, (3) mathematical methods from the statistical design of experiments, (4) standard synthetic methods of delay imposition into program P. Initially, a starting set of test locations are inserted into the program object under development. These cause logging information to be gathered in real time by a special item of hardware connected directly to the system bus.

This hardware has been supplied to us by the National Institute of Standards and Technology (NIST) and comprises the MultiKron 1.2 toolkit [Mink 94] to whom we are indebted.

The software tuning process is as follows:

1. Select suspected performance locations, called factors, in program P. Each location can receive a factor treatment via a perturbation (typically, a delay), or remain untreated.

2. Insert standard perturbations in treatment patterns over the factors. This will generate numerous treated versions of the program. Order these randomly.

3. Run each treated version of the program and record its response. This is a trial. Repeated runs should use a fresh randomisation order.

4. Analyse the measured responses with a linear response model. This typically employs the analysis of variance. In some circumstances, a linear response surface is inappropriate, here more informal methods suffice.

5. Assess step 4 and select those effects that appear significant relative to noise. Significant effects correspond to either single or multiple factor interactions to which the program is sensitive. Unimportant factors are dropped and new factors added.

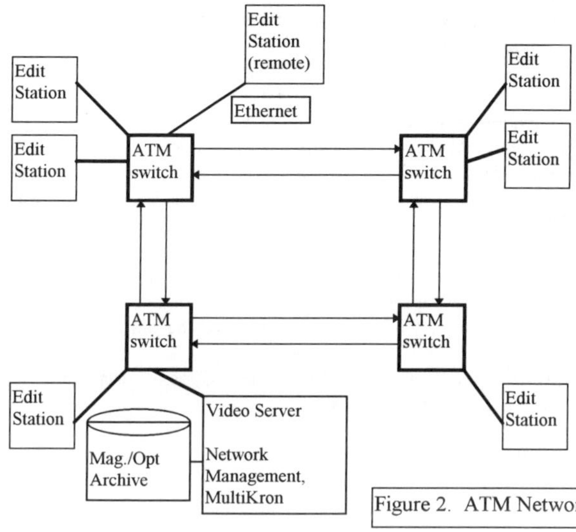


Figure 2. ATM Network

6. Repeat steps 1-5 as needed. Analysis proceeds in cycles of refinement.

7. Improve sensitive factors for program P. Return to step 1 as necessary.

Essentially then, the use of direct hardware assistance, in the form of the MultiKron hardware, has enabled us to a) measure and b) improve all real time critical aspects of the system critical for the video objects.

A workable software architecture for what is after all a distributed real time high performance computing system must provide a suitable environment for what are demanding applications even without the complication of the network. System attributes are used to define precisely the operating environment required for all code objects used to implement the system.

This system implements each video clip as an object. Essentially, when a video object is opened at some edit workstation, the complete environment required to support that object must first be successfully established.

The operating system will decide on one of two possible object location strategies:

.Leave object in present location and access via the network.

.Migrate object to location of processing.

These decisions are made dynamically. Whenever an object is created, certain performance related attributes will be inherited from its parent object. For example the attribute defining required I/O to its permanent storage device. This information will be updated periodically during the life of the object. With this example, the attribute value may decrease substantially if the object is rendered to lower resolution and frame rate for multimedia use.

If the system decides it cannot support remote access to the object, such as if an edit station is connected by a low speed ethernet, then object migration is employed. Here the system must pause while a copy of the object is made on the edit stations local AV disk.

Ultimately, the system may fail an object open in which case the user is informed of the operating requirement that cannot be met.

By keeping detailed statistics automatically, the continued development of the edit software can be done in such a way as not to exceed the current abilities of the hardware base.

It has been observed that some users find certain changes in system performance acceptable whilst others do not. We have found that some editors will accept substantial delays when opening or closing projects but will not accept rendering delays during the edit session. The balance between greater hardware expenditure and delays imposed by the system during the edit process can be changed radically without compromising the system software.

With a multi user networked edit suite, the simultaneous use of objects must be provided. For example, the establishment of a clip library available to all (as copies) but editable only under strict security control should be easy to establish. Fortunately by providing a distributed shared object environment the logic needed for this has already been put in place.

## Multi Threaded Productions

Supporting networked conventional video post production is for many sufficient for now. Soon however, technologies such as DVD and powerful personal computers will enable consumers to experience our work in a nonlinear manner as well. We therefore anticipate this development by enabling multiple pathways to be defined during the edit process.

For example, when editing a production, the editor edits the material so as to show the experience of all of the key characters as separate story lines. The viewer then has the ability to jump between these story lines dynamically, as well as to jump forwards or backwards in time as they do today with conventional video.

These concepts are in their infancy at present, but it is important that any multimedia oriented production system be capable of supporting such work and be easily extensible so as to produce material for specific user delivery systems as they are developed. As of today, we support story line multithreading. The system is currently being extended to investigate the use of the database record of clip content and an Artificial Intelligence inference engine to 'customise' video delivery to the historic preferences of individual 'viewers', performing a dynamic personalised edit.

## Archiving

Initially, RDAT tape was used as an archive device. This is essential in any practical system in order to maintain adequate edit working space on the distributed collection of AV magnetic disks. Unfortunately, the nature of an archive is that work may be left for many months before it is required, when it must be retrieved in tact. This is an important point, as from the viewpoint of the computer systems, video productions are a collection of very large computer files. Loss of any part of these files can be quite catastrophic, not at all the relatively minor event of an analogue tape dropout. Problems were experienced with reliability when tape was employed in this manner and stored without use for a long period.

The archiving reliability problem has been solved by moving to (for the present) magnetic optical disk storage. Such was the reliability of this system, that provision for automatic object migration to and from the backup server has been implemented. This was a simple task to implement on top of the existing object migration algorithm supporting migration between the AV disks of the edit stations. The increased storage capacity and sophisticated error correction provided for DVD [Immink 96] indicates a likely upgrade path for the archive storage component of the system.

## User Interface Issues

At present we offer to the user a conventional time line based edit screen accompanied with a separate monitor for the viewing of clips and sequences of finished work. Sound is available through either headphones or monitors, two channel or Dolby Surround currently supported. Migration to AC3 or MPEG audio will be made when the European decision for DVD has been made.

As every item presented to the user is also strictly implemented as an object, a certain degree of user configuration of the interface is possible and encouraged. Again, statistics gathering via attribute histories is being used to gain some information on the suitability of various interface options. For example, we know that multimedia authors will accept an additional low resolution reduced frame rate software window as an alternative to the external monitor. Editors working with conventional video most definitely cannot use such a feature.

An interesting variation on conventional interfaces to nonlinier edit systems has been to provide a virtual reality view rather than simply moving to larger and larger computer screens. Here, the amount of detail that can be presented to the editor at any one instant is in fact less than that of the conventional monitor. The ease with which head and hand movements can be used to navigate the display however (via a VR glove) does present interesting alternatives. We have found that repeated expanding and contracting of the timeline is an activity often performed and expressed by editors to be a barrier to intuitive work when working with conventional displays. Head movement combined with finger selection of a virtual zoom control makes navigation of the timeline far more natural. The quality of current VR headsets is such that multimedia editors often use this interface for all of their work. Video editors however, must still rely on the external monitor for certain tasks (those involving a quality judgement of the entire video image). With either approach, one very valuable feature is the ability to zoom the display to view portions of the image in detail. It has proven possible to support the editing of high resolution material using conventional video monitors or the VR headset.

## Object Library

There is growing interest within the industry to go beyond the ability to attach notes to captured clips, one example being the SONY DV notion of capturing keyframes on cassette and subsequent down loading to the nonlinier system. Other possibilities include cut counting [Tonomura 94], camera movement logging and brief audio descriptions. Some information may therefore be gathered automatically. Most probably some, such as recorded descriptions of a scenes content and worth, will always rely on human judgement and remain subjective.

We have decided to provide an object oriented database within which editors may define attributes of interest and attach (via objects) some support for the automatic analysis of content. Presently this is limited to spatial temporal analysis of clips. The analysis and cataloguing of the clip database is treated as a separate background task, partially performed during digitisation (for the obvious textural descriptions etc.) and partly performed when the system is idle (for the highly computationally expensive frame by frame analysis). These techniques are of course also applicable to audio clips and other multimedia based objects, such as still images.

To achieve the aims above it is essential to have considerable flexibility to dynamically define and modify the database schema, for the object class definitions and the inheritance structure of the class lattice. Only in this way can we directly support the many different types of categorisation needed by different editors, video and multimedia. For example, we hope soon to add a 'firewire' interface to support DV. Additional object classes and object instances may then be added to the database design to support that particular product optimally.

## Video Object Sharing

Key to effective distributed video post production is the effective sharing of video objects throughout the system. Possible architectures include:

Access to objects stored on a central server. Here edit stations are only used to temporarily store objects, while they are actively being used. Copies may be shared for 'library' objects. The server is used as the sole permanent repository.

Distribution of objects throughout system with access paths established via the network whenever remote use of objects is required. This technique minimises movement of objects around the network, but implies performance problems should an edit station posses objects used by a number of other stations.

Object migration and replication. Here, a combination of object relocation and controlled copying is used to manage the resource usage within the network. It is the technique adopted by us and concerns itself with:

> Minimising the impact of remote object accesses at an edit station.
> Migration of objects so as to locate objects where most likely to be used.
> Use replication to reduce object migration overheads when resources (primarily disk space) permits.

This object sharing technique was devised and optimised by experimentation using the MultiKron kit to solve the associated real time critical problems. As the budget for hardware development of the edit stations was limited, use of very highly parallel disk I/O subsystems was not possible. It was found that remote (i.e. other edit station) access to video objects stored on an active (in use) edit station must be handled so as to impose no delay to that edit station during work of a time sensitive nature (i.e. most edit activities). Each edit station builds a working set of objects on its local disks prior to editing, maintaining and updating this throughout the edit session.

The migration algorithm takes advantage of the locality of reference amortising the cost of migration over remote access to the migrated data. Care has been taken to avoid thrashing, where objects frequently migrate between stations while servicing only a few access requests. Tuneable parameters [Fleish 89] are used to enable stations to calculate the duration for which they can possess shared objects. This allows a station to make a number of accesses to the item before it is migrated. The size and usage statistics of video objects are used to drive the migration algorithm.

Objects used in a 'read only' mode are replicated if the space is available for them at the station requesting their use. The replication technique found suitable for video objects is the concept of a quorum for operations on replicated objects [Woollard 88]. A quorum for an operation is defined to be any set of station operating systems whose co-operation is adequate to execute an operation on the object.

Quorums are divided into two parts: A transaction manager executing an operation reads from an initial quorum and writes the result to a final quorum. Operating systems are the controllers of the disk video object storage resources for differing versions of the video objects throughout the network. They implement version counts for the various object copies they hold.

To read an object, the operating system reads the versions from an initial quorum of sites, returning the object with the highest version number to its client (the edit station). To write to an object, the operating system first reads the version numbers from an initial write quorum of edit stations, it then creates a new version of the object with a version number greater than any it has observed and writes out the new version to a final write quorum of edit stations.

This object replication scheme imposes two constraints on object operations by edit stations. Firstly each final quorum for write must intersect each initial quorum for read. Secondly each final quorum for write must intersect each initial quorum for write. The first constraint ensures that each read request will observe the effects of the most recent write. The second constraint ensures that each new version created by a write request will have a greater version number than its predecessors. As a consequence, each read quorum must intersect each write quorum and each pair of write quorums must intersect.

## Conclusions

It has been demonstrated that a portable post production system can be built capable of migrating easily to future hardware platforms. This was demonstrated in the move to the Sun Sparc environment, which was accomplished in less than one working week. It is important to protect those to whom these technologies are but a tool, from the rate of change now present within this industry. We believe portable object oriented architectures to support all aspects of audio, video and multimedia production are now possible and offer a means of preserving the investment production organisations are making in their material and personnel. By the adoption of appropriate implementation algorithms, these systems can be made adaptive to widely varying types and size of program projects. We propose that this paradigm is the most natural for supporting integration of new requirements and technologies as easily as possible into the work of production organisations.

## References

1. R. R. Turner, "1001 Questions to Ask Before Deciding On a Nonlinear Video Editing System", SMPTE Journal March 1994.

2. A. Goldberg, D. Robinson, "Smalltalk-80: The Language and its Implementation", Addison-Wesley, 1983.

3. C. C. Woollard, "70mm Sound Restoration (Parts 1 & 2)", Image Technology, Journal of the B.K.S.T.S. Vol. 78 Numbers 6 & 7, 1996.

4. D. A. Epstein et al, "The IBM POWER Visualisation System: A Digital Post-Production Suite in a Box", SMPTE Journal March 1995.

5. M. Singhal, N. Shivaratri, "Advanced Concepts in Operating Systems", McGraw-Hill Series in Computer Science, 1994.

6. R. Manderville, "ATM Monitor", Data Communications International, June 1995.

7. A. Mink, "Operating Principles of MultiKron II Performance Instrumentation for MIMD Computers", Draft Publication, U.S. Department of Commerce, Technology Administration, NIST, Gaithersburg, MD 20899.

8. K. A. S. Immink, "The Digital Versatile Disk (DVD): System Requirements and Channel Coding", SMPTE Journal August 1996.

9. Y. Tonomura et al, "Structured Video Computing", IEEE Multimedia, Fall 1994.

10. B. D. Fleisch, G. J. Popek, "Mirage: A Coherent Distributed Shared Memory Design", Proceedings of the 12th ACM Symposium on Operating System Principles, Operating Systems Review Vol. 23 No. 5 December 1989.

11. C. C. Woollard, "A Network Object Oriented Operating System", University of Essex Ph.D. Dissertation 1988.

# High Speed Data Recording: Digital VTRs Find New Applications

John Krooss
Viewgraphics Inc.
Mountain View, Calif.

Philip Livingston and Stephen Mahrer
Panasonic Broadcast & Television Systems Company
Secaucus, N.J.

Abstract:

Entertainment production, be it cinema, television or even "game" software is turning increasingly to computer generated or manipulated information. Computer processing and digital manipulation has permitted the creation of images otherwise impossible, the production of effects not otherwise practical, and correction of innumerable image defects large and small. Given this combination of voluminous data and expensive hardware, the industry faced a dilemma: How to "move" jobs in and out of a facility quickly so the equipment could be made available to other clients and projects.

Existing small format data recorders generally have proven unsatisfactory for these purposes due to the limited data rates and media size. Current digital videotape recorders are now capable of data rates well in excess of 200 Mbps (25 MBps). Unfortunately, some recorders incorporate data compression rendering them only suitable for traditional video. Other video formats have been customized and re-purposed for data recording, but these machines are no longer applicable for video recording.

As the boundaries between the computer and video worlds blur, users need multi-purpose solutions for both fast data storage of non-rasterized image information and high quality conventional video storage. Full bit rate uncompressed digital video recorders can provide the desired performance capabilities for both video and high performance data recording, allowing dual purpose use of the same transport and cassettes.

Panasonic developed the D-5 (uncompressed 10 bit ITU-R601) VTR format for high-end video post production, and it has met with wide acceptance. The Viewgraphics (Mountain View CA) "Dataview" is a VME interface device developed to allow large data files to be recorded on unmodified D-5 VTRs and to allow video to be input as data into platforms like the Silicon Graphics Onyx and Challenge. This paper describes the D-5 format, the Viewgraphics Dataview adaptor, and data recording on videotape.

## Introduction:

Film and production companies employ high-end UNIX based computer systems today to generate and manipulate film and video images. These modern computers, with their phenomenal processing power and ever increasing speed can release the user from the traditional production constraints and permit the realization of images and special effects that until now were only dreamt of. Such obvious benefits have resulted in a tremendous increase in the use of computer graphics, and their ever more cost-effective applications now extend to the realm of everyday production and post production.

Fast computers are very efficient at numerically intensive operations such as morphing or the performing of multi-layer compositing. However, they all suffer from an increasingly important deficiency - bit rate transfer limitations to peripheral data storage devices. In addition, the file sizes for video, image creation, and manipulation can be voluminous. For example, 10 bit HDTV, 1080 active lines (V) by 1920 pixel (H) requires about 1.25Gb/sec (155.2MB/sec), and film scanned as RGB at a typical 2048 x 1526 sampling requires some 2.25Gb/sec (281MB/sec). Large film clips used for multiple layer compositing thus impose mammoth storage requirements with enormous attendant time delays to transfer data files to an archive tape media.

Users need to get multi-Gigabyte files in and out quickly, not only to back-up work in progress but to shift jobs in and out of the facility rapidly. Standard data recorders linked to such computers has provided very low bit rate transfers, typically in the low Mb/s range in the early days up to several MB/s today. Using such low bit rate data recorders created a problem whereby the computer could perform the required image processing in mere minutes, but hours were then required to transfer the same images to a data recorder. While the data was safe and secure, the time spent transferring the data to tape resulted in enormous inefficiencies. Expensive equipment was idle, no new project could be undertaken, and the wasted time and money parsing out a few megabits per second to a data recorder negated the benefits of the system's high speed and its attendant high cost.

The required solution is obviously faster storage! However, fast data recorders are frequently built to service a specific application; some are semi-custom and often military. Most are cost prohibitive. Nevertheless, at the same time advances were being made in image computing, digital videotape recorders were improving despite the staggering data rates required to record video and the users' desire for ever-smaller media. For example, conventional ITU-R601 component 4:2:2 with 10 bit resolution requires about 210Mb/sec (26.2MB/sec). A simple and attractive alternative for data storage would be to use a conventional "broadcast" digital videotape recorder, with its significantly lower purchase cost, and provide it with a direct interface to the computer's memory. That solution has been implemented and wiil be described.

The Dataview SDA-21 is a very cost effective solution for high backing up and restoring large amounts of digital data using conventional digital videotape recorders and videotape as the media. Since its availability last year, Dataview has provided digital film producers with a much needed breakthrough throughput volume. Just recently, Dataview made it possible for Pacific Ocean Post in Santa Monica to establish a new mark for sheer volume of digital film used in a single production ("Independence Day"). Over the course of six months Pacific Ocean Post completed more than 200 visual effects which required the scanning and recording of 12.8 Terabytes (1 TB = 1,000GB) of film resolution data.

## Modern Videotape Recorders

Today's digital videotape recorders can provide payloads in excess of 100+ Mb/sec and feature industry standardized digital I/O and control schemes. These modern videotape recorders are basically divided into two categories; full bit rate (uncompressed) recorders, and those using some form of video compression. This difference is crucial. Compressed videotape recorders cannot record external data due to the inherent use of video compression in the format. Uncompressed videotape recorders may be considered rasterized "bit buckets", providing high speed data recording capability with numeric transparency. Table 1 shows standard uncompressed videotape formats in use for recording data. While most modern videotape formats provide more than adequate error correction for video and audio recording, additional or secondary error correction (ECC) beyond that done within the VTR is usually required for data recording purposes.

Note that the more modern formats have significantly improved post error correction bit error rate (BER) performance. As witness to almost a decade of progress, the D-5 format often exceeds the D-1 format by a 100,000:1 margin in error rate with a much increased useful payload. The 238 Mb/s payload of D-5 is a 25% increase over D-1's 190 Mb/s.

| Format | Format Bit Rate | "Useful" Payload | BER After ECC | Max Rec Time | Cost $ |
|---|---|---|---|---|---|
| D-1 (19mm) | 220Mbs | 190Mbs | $10^{-6}$ | 90 min | $125k |
| D-2 (19mm) | 125Mbs | 90Mbs ** | $10^{-9}$ | 208 min | $75 |
| D-3 (1/2") | 125Mbs | 90Mbs ** | $10^{-11}$ | 245 min | $50 |
| D-5 (1/2") | 300.6Mbs | 238Mbs | $10^{-11}$ | 124 min | $75 |

Table 1. ** Note: These figures are for NTSC D-2 and D-3 VTRs. PAL VTRs of both formats have format bit rates of about 20% higher.

The formats shown in Table 1 are conventional videotape recorders. As such they expect to be fed with very specific, steady and fixed data rate signals. There is no "flow control" in video. It is therefore a relatively simple matter to bit map the computer data into the digital input signal of the VTR. In this manner the data rate is kept constant and the de-mapping of the recorded data is equally easy to accomplish upon playback. The extra error correction mentioned above is also often added at this step.

## The Interface Solution: Dataview SDA

The Viewgraphics Dataview SDA is a single board VME card designed to be inserted into a graphics computer system to support two primary functions. The SDA allows the computer to archive data to industry standard digital video recorders, and to connect digital video inputs or outputs directly to the computer system. In the data mode, Dataview permits users to selectively backup and restore computer data files between their host computer system and the digital video recorder operating as a high speed "bit bucket". The SDA also includes both secondary error correction (ECC) and a read after write (RAW) circuit to insure data integrity. In the video mode, Dataview provides real time video connectivity to serial digital video equipment. It provides a full bandwidth path for the video between an external device (usually a DVTR) and the host computer system memory, i.e. the computer system can be used to capture or output component serial digital video. In addition the SDA can be configured with expanded buffer memory providing up to 20 seconds of video storage on the board., and two Dataview adapters can be ganged together to facilitate 4:4:4 interfacing.

The Dataview adapts an industry standard D5 VTR for use as a high speed, high capacity data tape recorder. With Dataview, users can store up to 125Gigabytes on a single tape cassette, and can transfer data at speeds above 17MBytes/sec. This phenomenal capacity and speed allows backup or restoration of the entire contents of a large disk array in minutes instead of hours or even days. By striping together multiple D5 tape units, data rates in excess of 100 Mbytes/sec can be achieved and, by using the Panasonic M.A.R.C. robotic system, the multiple machines can have access to hundreds of tapes.

The Dataview adapter was designed for production environments, and a key objective was to insure reliable operation independent of host computer configuration and I/O performance. Because the host computer is not normally a real-time system, there may be occasions when it is difficult if not impossible for the computer, no matter how powerful the configuration, to continually input or output video data streams. By utilizing an on-board interface buffer, the Dataview SDA continues to receive data during these brief periods and thereby relieves the host computer system of the demanding requirement of a real-time response. As long as the host computer can sustain the full bandwidth transfer rate on average over time, the Dataview SDA can provide real-time video input and output as well as data transfers at the limit of the component serial digital interface.

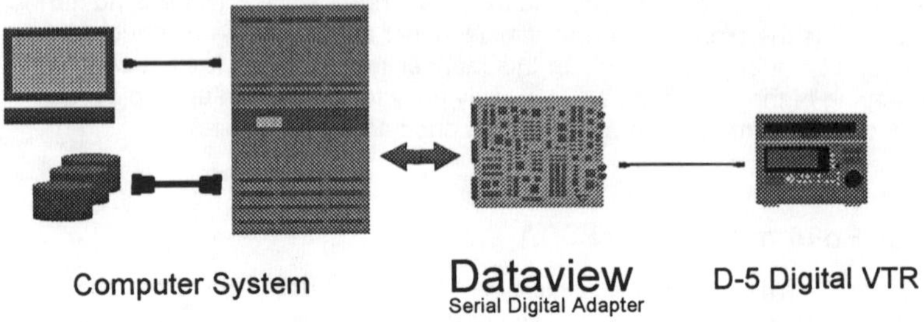


A detailed block diagram of the Dataview SDA is shown below:

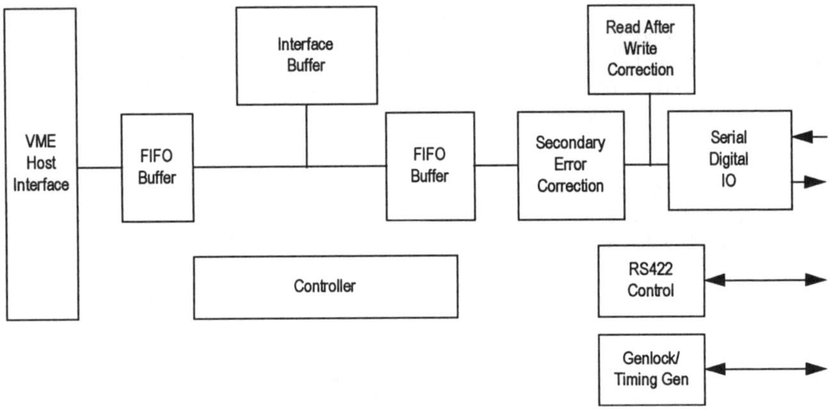


The Dataview SDA can sustain a data transfer rate of 17.5MB/sec to a D5 VTR directly from host computer memory. This can be maintained without interruption for the full duration a D5 cassette (124 minutes maximum). Similarly, in the 4:2:2 video mode, rates above 20MB/sec can also be sustained (full uncompressed digital video). In order to maintain that this high data rate to and from the storage device connected to the host computer, the device must be able to transfer data to and from host memory at a similarly high sustained data transfer rate.

The file systems of most servers are not able to sustain the necessary data transfer rate. Care must be taken by the system integrator to insure that not only is the raw hardware performance available, but that the file system of the server is sufficient for the task, such as the XFS file system from Silicon Graphics. For those file systems that can transfer data at an average of 20MB/sec, the ability of the adapter to buffer data on board has the effect of allowing the host computer to keep up the transfer at a high rate even if the connected storage device can only sustain high data transfer rates for short periods of time.

***Table 2*** shows the data transfer rates of the Dataview SDA in different modes of operation. In the data modes, data is written to tape with added ECC data into the active range of a 4:2:2 video frame.

| | DOD5 525 VTR | DOD5 625 VTR | Video 10 bit (4:2:2) Y, R-Y, B-Y |
|---|---|---|---|
| Number of Bytes/Line | 1260 | 1260 | 1800 |
| Number of Lines/Frame | 486 | 576 | 486 |
| Tape Rate Frames/Sec | 30 | 25 | 30 |
| Transfer Rate Mbytes/Sec | 17.52 | 17.30 | 25.03 |

**Table 2** Transfer rate of the Dataview SDA in different operational modes

| Tape Capacity for different sizes of D5 cassettes (Gbytes) | Data On D5 525 VTR | Data On D5 625 VTR |
|---|---|---|
| Medium Cassette (12 minute) | 12.32 GB | 12.17 GB |
| Small Cassette (23 minute) | 23.61 GB | 23.32 GB |
| Medium Cassette (33 minute) | 33.88 GB | 33.46 GB |
| Medium Cassette (48 minute) | 49.27 GB | 48.67 GB |
| Medium Cassette (63 minute) | 64.67 GB | 63.87 GB |
| Large Cassette (94 minute) | 96.50 GB | 95.30 GB |
| Large Cassette (124 minute) | 127.29 GB | 125.72 GB |

**Table 3** Data capacity for different D5 cassette sizes

The Dataview SDA can handle files up to 4GB in size when in use to backup a normal UNIX file system, the file size limit imposed by UNIX. However, when used with an XFS file system from Silicon Graphics, much larger files up to the capacity of a tape, approximately 127GB for a 124 minute D5 cassette, can be stored. ***Table 3*** shows the capacity of different sizes of D5 cassettes in each *DATA* mode.

The Dataview employs a proprietary Data On D5 (DOD5) encoding / decoding scheme for storage of date on tape. Additionally, it utilizes its capabilities for secondary error correction (ECC), data block checksum (DBC) and read-after-write (RAW) functions to guarantee data integrity. The data mode capabilities of the Dataview allow it to provide high-speed, resolution independent, digital video or image file backup and retrieval.

Another key feature of the Dataview Adapter critical to the post production process is direct file access. In contrast to other data tape devices, Dataview permits users to access individual files stored on the tape directly by sub-directory and file name. This feature greatly speeds production throughput and simplifies systems integration.

A comprehensive API is provided to allow custom development. Viewgraphics has over one dozen developers, including industry leaders Kodak and Discreet Logic who have easily integrated their programs with Dataview.

## The Data Recording Solution: The D5 Component Digital VTR.

The first digital VTR format, the 19 mm D-1, made its debut in 1987, followed by D-2 in 1989, finally making digital recording technology a viable alternative to that of analog. Rapid developments in technology prompted development of a half-inch digital composite VTR format which could be implemented in a camera recorder similar to half inch analog component, and D-3 made its debut in 1991. However, the world fully expected to enter the era of high definition television in the late 1990s, and this has created a demand for component signal based systems that facilitate editing and flexible format conversion with high resolution.

Since this transition to component recording was envisioned by the developers, notably Matsushita and Nippon Hoso Kyokai (NHK, the Japan Broadcasting Company), the D-3 composite format was created to not only satisfy the present demand for a cost-effective composite format, but to also form a base or platform for a component format. D-5 realizes full-bit component recording with full production features and is based on the D-3 format and technology.

While D-5 has been created on the D-3 platform, there are significant differences. In the D-5 format, the linear tape speed is twice that of the D-3 format in order to maintain the same track pitch as D-3 while still doubling the number of recording channels from 2 to 4. The number of digital signal processors, recording and playback amplifiers, rotary transformers, and heads are also approximately doubled - D-5 VTR has 18 heads while a D-3 VTR has 10 heads. It is thus possible to record digital component signals whose video data rate is about twice that of digital composite signals. The maximum recording time of the D-5 format is two hours (half the four hours of D-3).

As was previously described, two different methods have been conceived for new digital component VTRs. One is full-bit recording, and the other is Bit Rate Reduction (BRR) recording. Since D-5 is a full bit rate (uncompressed) format, it is not only appropriate for the 525/60 and 625/50 Standard Definition Television (SDTV) systems, but can be extended to high definition television (HDTV) recording using a 4:1 compression adapter, and to true digital data recording as well.

### Data Capacity

The D-5 format consumes 21.2 $cm^2/s$ of recording media with input data rates of 270 Mb/s (10 bit) or 288 Mb/s (8 bit), as compared with 25.0 $cm^2/s$ for D2 (143 Mb/s 8 bit) or 54.3 $cm^2/s$ for D-1 (216 Mb/s 8 bit). This allows up to two hours of program material in a single large cassette (1237 m of tape). This two hour program length equals approximately 127 GB of data storage, or about 100 GB payload per cassette.

**D-5 Specifications**

| | |
|---|---|
| Scanner Rotation | 90/1.001 Hz |
| Tracks per Rotation | 8 |
| Track Azimuth Angle | ± 20 degrees |
| Drum Diameter | 76 mm |
| Helix Angle | 4.9 degrees |
| Wrap Angle | 178.11 degrees |
| Total Average Data Rate | 300.6 Mb/s |
| Channel Bit Clock | 133 MHz (7.5 nsec) |
| Shortest wave length | 0.64 mm |
| Tape Consumption | 7.6 $m^2$/hr |

# D-5 Footprint

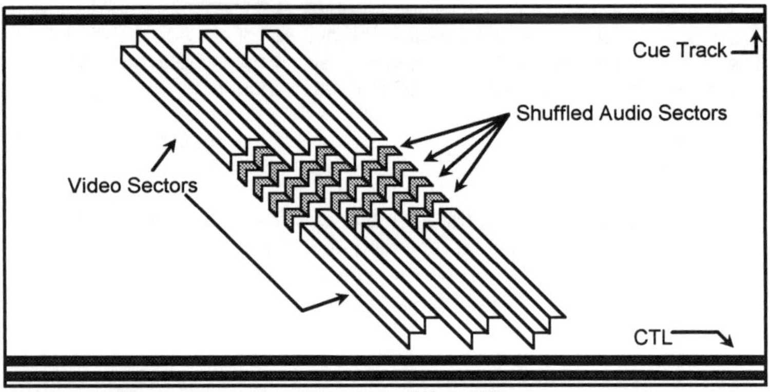


**D-5 is a 4 Channel Recorder, CH0, CH1, CH2 & CH3**
**Track width is 20 um**
**Rotary Erase is standard**
**Audio sector shuffling is used**
**Drum rotation is 5400rpm (525)**

Figure 3 Show the D-5 Tape Footprint for One Field of Recording (525)

**8 Bit/10 Bit Signal Processing**

The D-5 VTR accepts two types of digital component signals: 18 MHz sampling with 8-bit quantization, and 13.5 MHz sampling with 10-bit quantization. In the 13.5 MHz mode, the 10-bit samples are reformatted to 8-bit samples, creating new 8-bit words from the aggregated 2-bit "difference" in word length. At the same time, the bit rate is changed to 18 MHz in the 10-bit to 8-bit conversion process in order to achieve efficient and identical processing regardless of input signal.

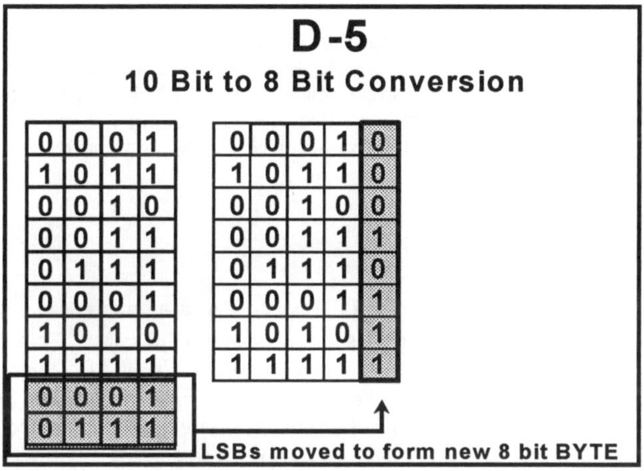


**Figure 4. 10 - 8 bit Data Mapping Used in D-5**

At 13.5 MHz, each active line contains 720 samples of Y and C to be recorded, but 48 samples are added to each, making them equal 768 samples. These 768 samples undergo the same channel and segment distribution as that for 18 MHz signals. The four components $Y_E$, $Y_O$, $P_B$ and $P_R$ are distributed evenly to all channels and video segments, and each video segment of each channel is comprised of 32 samples in 525/60 mode, or 24 samples for 625/50 mode. The 10-bit words are divided into the eight most significant bits and two least significant bits; the two least significant bits from four samples are collected together to make one 8-bit pseudo-sample. To assure potential errors are largely contained within a single pixel, the two least significant bits of the $Y_E$, $P_B$ and $P_R$ samples of a single pixel are placed into the same 8-bit pseudo-sample. (This philosophy is repeated in channel and segment distribution.) The two least significant bits of the $Y_O$ sample are placed into pseudo-samples, separated by

16 samples (for 525/60) or 12 samples (for 625/50) in each video segment. Through this process, 32 bytes (525) or 24 bytes (625) of 8-bit data are assembled from the two least significant bits for each video segment in each channel. Distributing this data evenly into four outer codes for each video segment results in 8 bytes (525) or 6 bytes (625) each, and adding these to the "eight most significant bit" group of 32-bytes (525) or 24-bytes (625) data yields 40 bytes (525) or 30 bytes (625) of 8-bit data, which is the same as that for 18 MHz. After intra-subsegment shuffling, processing is performed in the same way as for 18 MHz signals, eliminating the need to greatly increase the hardware for field memory and error correction to 10-bit and yet maintaining full-bit recording.

Clearly, this formatting allows the remainder of the processing to function on 8-bit data at 18 MHz (one of the two signal formats accepted) and minimizes the difficulty of handling two different input signals while passing the full 10-bit 13.5 MHz signal. What may not be so clear is the contribution this makes to using D-5 as a data storage device and the robustness of the internal error correction scheme due to the cosited data.

**D-5 Video Data Arrangement**

In D-5, the three cosited pixel samples (Y, $P_B$ and $P_R$) are handled as a single group and are written to the tape in the same sync block if at all possible. This is preferable because any erroneous sample(s) of the three cosited Y, $P_B$ and $P_R$ samples result in only a single pixel error in the image, whereas three erroneous samples of distributed Y, $P_B$ and $P_R$ would result in three pixel errors. Therefore, as much as possible, each group of cosited samples is placed into one sync block in D-5.

The outer Reed-Solomon codeword of 120 data bytes and 8 check bytes can correct up to 8 bytes of error. The inner codeword is either 85 data bytes (in 525/60) or 76 data bytes (625/50), with 8 check bytes attached, and can correct up to 4 bytes of error.

**D-5 Tape / Format Interchange**

D-5 is typical of most modern tape formats in that the tape path is carefully designed to be stable and repeatable. In this way tapes from other VTRs maybe played with confidence knowing that there will be no marginality of data recovery. Head to tape interfacing is very stable due to D-5's low tape tension (<30G). Head wear and tape life are also greatly improved over earlier formats.

**D-5 Bit Error Rate**

D-5's powerful ECC combined with its stable and robust tape path help provide a very low post ECC bit error rate. D-5 BER with the ECC off can be compared to D-1 with its ECC active. When both formats are working as designed, D-5 produces a post ECC

BER of about $10^{-11}$, about a $10^5$ improvement over D-1. D-5's proven track record of superb reliability, low BER, and very useful 238Mb/sec recordable payload provide a very useful format not only for conventional 4:2:2 component graphics, but also in conjunction with the Viewgraphics Dataview as a high speed data recorder to back up today's high speed graphics computers.

**Conclusion:**

Archiving of computer data on digital video tape allows graphic and image manipulation users to realize the full potential of their investment in computer technology. With Dataview's diverse set of operational modes and D-5's cost-effectiveness, speed and reliability the computer graphics and film production process can retain the high throughput methods and rapid job shifting once reserved only for video production. At the same time, the system benefits from the dual nature of the Dataview adapter, acting as both a high speed data and video storage/retrieval interface. By combining speed, capacity and economy these two new technologies will forever break the bottleneck that now exists in computer based production.

# A Unified Hybrid Recorder:

## *Combining Hard Disk Drives, Betacam SX, and Analog Betacam*

*I. Sato, K. Hyodo, C. Golson, and J.P. Creignou*
*Sony Electronics, Inc.*
*San Jose, Calif.*

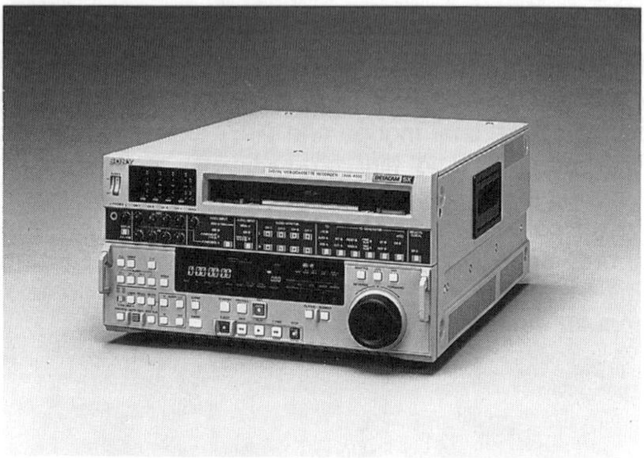

***Figure 1: Sony Betacam SX Hybrid Recorder - DNW-A100***

## Introduction

Digital video and signal compression technologies have created an increasing demand for high performance, efficient systems with the promise of streamlined operations and increased productivity. The transition of the broadcast industry to an all-digital environment for the creation of television news programming and television broadcast operations poses some unique challenges. For a new system to satisfy these requirements, the core design imperative has to incorporate novel networked system concepts, and the best of contemporary digital compression technology with an efficient total video and audio data rate that supports higher quality than that of current analog ENG systems.

Based on the 4:2:2 digital component signal format, this new high-end digital system streamlines the production of broadcast news programs to service the existing analog NTSC delivery services, but also fully anticipates the imminent 4:2:0 MPEG-2 SDTV digital U.S. broadcasting standard. At the same time, recognizing that U.S. broadcasters must transition at their own pace – oftentimes in incremental steps spanning years – the introduction of new technologies dictates a system approach that assigns equal importance to maintaining compatibility with the vast majority of existing analog Betacam equipment.

The following document describes the operation of the Betacam SX Hybrid Recorder, a unique component of the Sony Betacam SX family specifically aimed at bridging today's analog environment to tomorrow's digital future. Several examples of the applications where this new type of editing machine will be found are also presented.

## System Concept

The idea of a Hybrid Recorder (HBR) originates from the duality of addressing the needs for nonlinear systems and their inherent benefits while preserving present investments in tape libraries and people's expertise. It introduces a unique new concept in video technology: a high performance nonlinear recording system that incorporates both digital videotape and digital recording to hard disk drives. The implementation of this concept is realized in a HBR, that is, the Sony DNW-A100--a single five rack unit component.

This self-contained one-half inch videotape recorder/player operates in the MPEG-2 4:2:2 Profile @ ML digital video compression system. This compressed video signal along with four channels of uncompressed audio and other control data constitute the Betacam SX signal format which is laid on tape. The Hybrid Recorder downloads Betacam SX videotape recordings to the built-in hard disk drives (HDDs) at up to four times normal play speed. The internal HDDs facilitate standalone, full resolution, nonlinear disk-based editing.

The HBR provides high-speed multiplexed video/audio/data Input and Output through a Serial Digital Data Interface (SDDI), and it can play back one-half inch analog Betacam or Betacam SP (i.e., oxide or metal particle) videotapes which can also be digitized in real time to the Hybrid's HDDs.

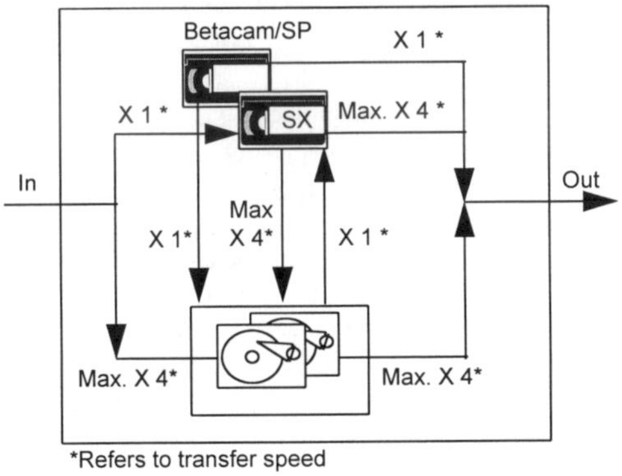


*Figure 2: Betacam SX Hybrid Recorder (DNW-A100) Signal Flow*

### *System Interconnections*

To ensure interconnectivity in today's evolving broadcast equipment environment, the Hybrid Recorder provides a comprehensive set of signal Inputs and Outputs (I/Os). For analog interfacing, outputs for component video with four channels of audio (two selectable monitoring channels) are standard with three composite outputs (one composite output can display superimposed character data). Optional component or composite video input is also available. Digital interfacing is done through a Serial Digital Interface (SDI) I/Os (Baseband, real-time 4:2:2 as defined in SMPTE 259M).

Transfer of audio and compressed video data at real time or faster than real time is done through the SDDI output. There is an optional SDDI input. An AES/EBU audio interface is also available as an option which replaces the standard analog audio I/O.

A SCSI-2 interface is provided to expand the disk storage capacity by attaching additional storage units. For example, a 68 GB storage capacity array may be added for an additional 6.4 hours of HDD operation.

### *525/59.94 or 625/50 Line System Switchable*

The HBR's great versatility allows it to be used in both 525/59.94 and 625/50 component systems by providing dual standard component analog, SDI, and SDDI digital I/Os. This greatly facilitates the exchange of tapes between crews traveling around the world by switching between 525/59.94 and 625/60 operation. Prerecorded analog tapes can only be played back in their respective 525/59.94 or 625/60 standard machines.

In addition, a composite PAL signal is available at the output of the 525/59.94 machine, for monitoring purposes only, when replaying a 625/50 recorded videotape. (In a similar manner, the 625/50 machine offers a monitor quality NTSC output.)

### *MPEG-2 4:2:2 Profile @ Main Level (MPEG-2 P@ML) Video Compression*

The Betacam SX family of products adopts the MPEG-2 422 Profile @ ML video compression standard. This new standard represents a major achievement by meeting all the requirements necessary to operate in demanding broadcast environments--from television news, to program and commercial production and playout.

4:2:2 video is maintained within the compression system ensuring high picture quality throughout the processing chain. This is especially important when including effects, chroma keying, and multi-generation processes. Furthermore, the entire 507 lines of the active video frame and Vertical Blanking Interval are carried through. This gives the broadcaster access to embedded signals such as VITC, Closed Captioning, and VIRS.

By utilizing the spatial redundancy within the video frame and the temporal redundancy between frames, the MPEG-2 style compression system can achieve a higher picture quality for the same bit rate as compared to Intraframe-only compression systems, such as JPEG.

As an implementation of the MPEG-2 4:2:2 Profile @ML, Betacam SX adopts a two-frame Group Of Pictures (GOP) consisting of only an Intraframe (I) and a Bi-directional (B) frame at a raw video bit rate of 18 Mbps. Four uncompressed audio channels at 16 bits per sample and 48 kHz sample rate result in an additional 3.072 Mbps of raw bit rate.

### *Serial Digital Data Interface (SDDI)*

SDDI is employed to facilitate point-to-point transport of the compressed video and audio data. The data carried by the SDDI bitstream represents compressed data, and it shares the same mechanical, electrical, and synchronization syntax of the SDI interface as defined in the SMPTE 259M standard.

It is important to note, that since SDDI is designed to carry bitstreams representing various compression systems, only equipment using the same compression system can freely exchange data without the need for transcoding between the different compression schemes.

SDDI is used to transfer Betacam SX encoded signals at up to four times normal speed. Also, the SDDI interface can share existing SDI routing and any switching equipment which does not decode the embedded video or audio data. SDDI has been submitted to SMPTE for a Standards proposal and has now been published for comments.

## Hybrid Recorder Videotape Transport

### *Betacam SX Footprint*

A videotape system used in Broadcast operations must be robust in order to endure the rigorous physical environment of the ENG application, as well as repeated play, and high speed shuttle. It must also allow for long-term archiving. The half-inch videotape footprint of Betacam SX is designed to meet those criteria with its wide 32 micrometer (**μm**) track pitch. In addition, the low signal bit rate translates into a long recorded wavelength of 0,74 **μm** giving additional headroom for the Carrier-to-Noise ratio needed to replay the on-tape signal. This additional headroom is used in several ways to make the transport even more robust. For example:

- Playback head width is increased which improves tracking performance.
- A high ratio of redundancy is applied to audio and video data for better Error Correction Coding (ECC) which means that a typical drop-out (videotape scratch) or momentary head clog will be completely recovered with no effect on the output picture or sound.
- Wear-resistant material is used for the rotary heads to give extended head life.
- Proven metal particle tape technology in a economical new format

| Robustness of Format | Betacam SP | Digital Betacam | DVCAM | Betacam SX |
|---|---|---|---|---|
| Magnetic property | Oxide/MP | MP | ME | MP |
| Videotape thickness | 14.5 μm | 14.5 μm | 7 μm | 14.5 μm |
| Track pitch | 80.5 μm | 22 μm | 15 μm | 32 μm |
| Min. Rec. λ | 0.9 μm | 0.69 μm | 0.49 μm | 0.74 μm |
| ECC V | N/A | 22.7% | 19.2% | 42% |
| Redundancy A | N/A | 122.2% | 71.7% | 159% |
| Tape Speed | 118 mm/s | 96.7 mm/s | 28.2 mm/s | 55.9 mm/s |
| Drum Rotation | 29.97 Hz | 89.91 Hz | 149.85 Hz | 74.925 Hz |

*Figure 3: Format Characteristics*

### *Multi-Tracing System*

The Hybrid Recorder employs a multi-tracing system utilizing two sets of staggered rotary heads to allow the playback of the RF waveform even in the extreme case where the track on the videotape is not straight. The playback head is wider than the track and because the second head is offset to the side, the second head can replay the skewed part of the track. This unique system eliminates the need for sophisticated dynamic tracking.

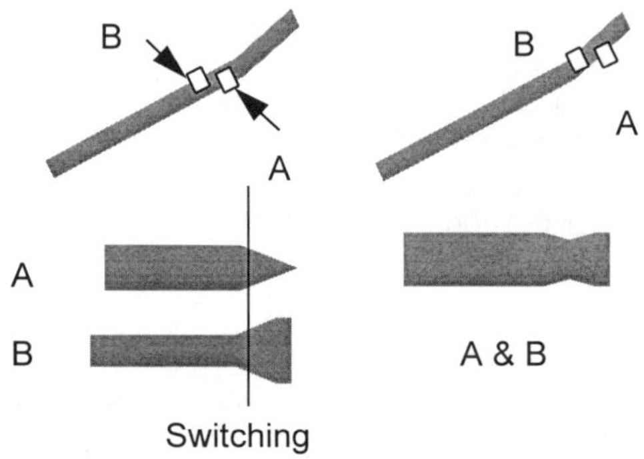


*Figure 4: Multi-Tracing Concept*

Furthermore, thanks to the multi-tracing system, high speed playback of the videotape is also performed reliably.

### *High Speed Videotape Playback*

Betacam SX recorded tapes can be played back at up to four times normal speed for video/audio material transfer to the internal HDD, or output through the SDDI interface to a server, for example.

This is accomplished by increasing the longitudinal videotape speed and using four sets of playback heads to capture all the required data. This method does not require an increase in the rotational speed of the drum which remains at 74.925 Hz in the 525/59.94 system. The results are good transport stability during high speed mode with less overall wear of the scanner.

### *Betacam SX Videotape*

The Betacam SX HBR uses a new lower cost metal particle videotape for digital recording which has an equivalent running cost to current oxide videotape.

This new advanced videotape technology utilizes ultra-fine metal particles (Hi-Packing™ Technology) giving a high carrier-to-noise ratio and a strengthened binder for high videotape stability as proven in BCT-MA type videotape used with Betacam SP. While this new videotape is particularly suited for Betacam SX format recording, the current Betacam SP metal particle tapes (the BCT-MA and UVW-T type tapes) may also be used reliably for recording and playback. The analog Betacam oxide-type videotape is only used for the playback of prerecorded material.

As the Betacam SX's normal linear videotape speed is half that of Betacam, longer duration recordings of up to 180 minutes may now be achieved for full length programming, live remotes, or sporting events.

Videotape cassettes come in two sizes, a small "S" cassette with up to 60 minutes record time and a "L" large cassette for up to 184 minutes of operation.

## Disk Sub-System

The DNW-A100 Hybrid Recorder is equipped with two built-in HDDs which provide 90 minutes of record playback time. This record time can be expanded incrementally up to 6.4 hours by connecting additional HDD storage units to the SCSI-2 port.

The internal storage combined with an external RAID 3 level HDD storage array, gives a higher protection of the A/V data which is a significant benefit for on-air application. With this added array, it is also possible to replay fully edited programs while simultaneously recording source material. Simultaneous recording mode and playback is also done with the internal HDD with assembled scenes that have no audio/video split.

### *Simple Edit and Full Edit Modes*

Independent editing of the video and all, or any, of the four audio channels is available on the Hybrid's HDD. This operation requires access to multiple files and restricts certain functions like simultaneous recording and playback of a programmed sequence.

To maximize functionality, the HBR introduces two main modes of editing:

- The *Simple edit* mode which is used when the video and audio material of each scene is kept together throughout the edited program (no audio split from the video). The benefit of this mode is that it is possible to perform simultaneous recording of a source signal while editing by previewing a Program, or playing out a Program or Master file.
- The *Full edit* mode is used when any video or audio channel material is edited independently, as in an audio channel insert. In this mode, simultaneous playback of a Program while recording is only possible with the optional external hard disk drive array connected.

## *Edit Accuracy*

The Hybrid Recorder uses a dual decoding method. Frame-accurate editing accomplished by switching at the transition between each edit point is made in the decoded baseband domain.

The edited Program of the HBR may always be played out in real-time or recorded back to the disk, or on videotape with complete frame accuracy.

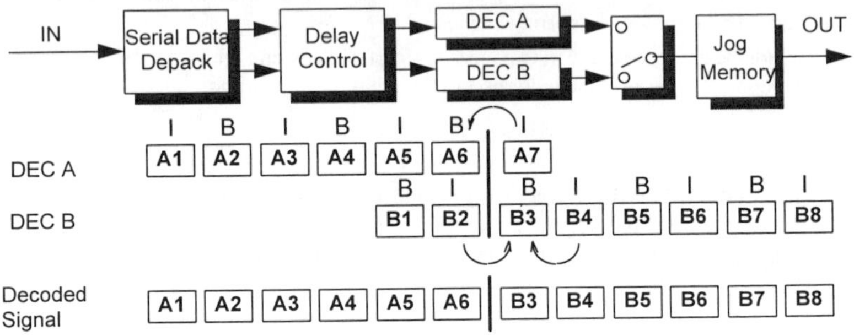


*Figure 5: Dual Decoder System*

## *Frame Switch/GOP Switch*

While the HBR is capable of frame-accurate editing with full picture quality, it may also be desirable to directly playout the *Simple Edit* mode Program at high speed (2X normal speed) before first recording it on the disk or videotape. This is useful when feeding the Digital Satellite News Gathering system, for example.

In this case, the Group Of Picture (GOP) switch mode is used to enable the 2X transfer at the SDDI port. In this mode, the edit accuracy becomes plus or minus one frame as the encoded bit stream is switched at a GOP boundary. The Bi-directional "B" frame at the edit point is treated as a Predictive (P) coded frame resulting in unnoticeable changes in the picture. If not in *GOP switch* mode, the HBR is then in the *Frame switch* mode with frame accurate editing.

It should also be noted that any programmed sequence or *Program* can always be recorded back to the videotape or disk as a *Master* file for high speed playback.

| | Frame Switch | GOP Switch |
|---|---|---|
| Simple Edit | 4 X | 4 X |
| Full Edit | 3 X | |

*Figure 6: Master File Record/Playback Maximum Speed*

| | Frame Switch | GOP Switch |
|---|---|---|
| Simple Edit | 1 X | 2 X |
| Full Edit | 1 X | |

*Figure 7: Program File Maximum Playback Speed*

### *Jog Playback Mode*

The HBR utilizes a ring buffer called "Jog Memory" which stores multiple frames of past and future decoded frames. This method allows the HBR to replay video and audio at a variable speed within the range of +/- 1 normal speed.

## Shuttle Playback Mode

### *Videotape Shuttle*

In shuttle mode, the video head crosses several tracks resulting in bursts of data picked up randomly. Since a video frame is encoded by blocks of 16 (H pixels) X 16 (Lines), the HBR can scan the videotape at up to plus or minus 75 times normal speed and still capture entire video blocks for the decoding process. The result is a mosaic picture on the video monitor made of 16 X 16 blocks of different adjacent frames. The picture in shuttle is recognizable at up to +/- 75 times normal speed.

### *Disk Shuttle*

The data on the disk is read in blocks containing entire Group of Pictures (GOP), with the buffer memory managing the played out frame sequence to achieve the desired playback speed. At higher than normal speed, some frames are skipped, while complete frames in between are decoded and displayed. This eliminates the mosaic type effect seen on the shuttle videotape playback. Playback in shuttle from the disk is possible at up to plus or minus 100 times normal speed

## Editing Functionality

The most innovative aspect of the Hybrid is its ability to combine various editing methods from the most simple control panel editing to the more sophisticated and specialized applications using a dedicated controller. The main appeal of the front control panel editing is the straight forward approach that gives the user the comfort of familiar VTR-like control with the added flexibility and speed of the disk operation.

Exploiting the features of the HBR, a number of nonlinear controllers are targeted at specific applications with a specialized Graphical User Interface (GUI). For example, there is a field editor based on a laptop configuration with scripting and Good Shot Marker capability. Additionally, there is a "live" editing system, with two overlaid video windows in order to simultaneously monitor the incoming feed to mark the highlights and prepare, or to replay a sequence with motion animation on the other window. Even a studio editing workstation will be able to use the HBR as local storage.

In the disk file system, an A/V recording on the HBR disk is called a *Master* file. There can be up to 256 Master files of any duration. Once recorded on the HBR disk, Master files may easily be browsed by using the Index function to skip from file to file, similar to skipping between the songs of an audio CD player. Master files are recorded back-to-back sequentially as shown in Figure 8.

An edited sequence is called a *Program* and it is composed of a selection of any portions of chosen Master files. The Program by definition is not a recording on the HBR disk, but rather it exists as a list of In and Out points or markers referring back to the original material of the Master files. The Program can be revised in many ways with no danger of altering any of the original Master files. Once a Program is completed, it can then be played out, recorded back to disk as a new Master file, or to videotape for archival. A Program may contain up to 1000 events.

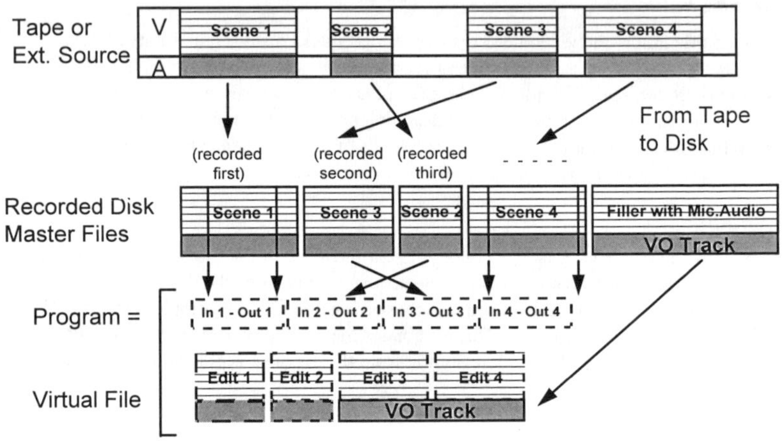


*Figure 8: HBR Files and Program*

### *Control Panel Edit Process*

Editing from the Hybrid Recorder's control panel is very much like machine-to-machine editing with conventional VTRs. You simply select the source such as "Tape"; Mark the In and Out points of the material; Switch to "Recorder", set the Record In point, and press "Auto Edit". (See Figure 9)

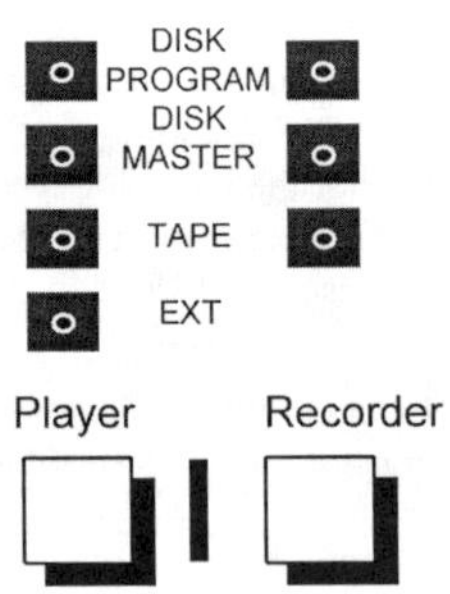


*Figure 9: Source and Destination Selection*

### *Disk Editing Process*

The editing process consists of recording Master files onto disk by selecting scenes from a source videotape, either from the HBR or from an external VTR. Trimming, rearranging, overlaying, or inserting new scenes are then performed to create a Program. The created Program can then be played out or recorded back to SX videotape for later high speed transfer or archival.

This represents only one of many possible methods, as the HBR also allows a Program to be built directly from the source videotape to disk (as it is commonly done in machine to machine editing) creating an edited sequence as you go.

Yet another method consists of recording the entire source videotape to disk as a first step, and then creating a Program exclusively utilizing the disk. In any of the above cases, the Program may always be revised by changing the desired events at any point.

### *Multi-Event Memory*

When selecting the scenes from the source videotape, each scene can be recorded sequentially to disk, or a multi-event memory may also be used to memorize a series of scenes (Maximum 100 scenes). This allows to execute a "batch" recording of the corresponding Master files to disk. A Feed Auto Edit function will transfer the selected scenes from a Betacam SX videotape to the disk at up to four times normal speed resulting in notable time savings. The Master files recorded onto the disk have excess A/V material recorded before the In point and after the Out point to facilitate later trimming of each scene.

### *Overlay and Insert Mode*

The HBR supports both *Overlay* mode where the new material is overwritten to replace existing material or *Insert* mode, where the new material is added by sliding the existing material to the side. When audio split editing is performed at the control panel, the Overlay mode is always selected to avoid loss of "lip sync".

### *Revising a Program*

When creating a Program, the Auto Edit function saves the list of In and Out points that define the edited program to disk. In this way, the edited Program may be recovered in case of a power failure or user error. Any event from the Program may be recalled and revised by changing the In and Out points, inserting a new scene, or reordering the existing scenes.

### *Videotape Controlled by Conventional Edit Controllers*

The Hybrid Recorder can be controlled as a videotape player by conventional linear edit controllers to play source Betacam, Betacam SP, or Betacam SX tapes. Assemble editing on a Betacam SX videotape is only available from the HBR's control panel.

## Typical Applications

The following applications for the HBR have been suggested based on current broadcast operations, but it is easy to imagine that in our evolving environment, users will soon discover even more uses for this unique and versatile tool.

### *Integration in Current Edit Systems with Videotape Playback*

Current edit suites can immediately benefit from Betacam SX recorded material on videotape because the HBR can be controlled as a source deck to replay Betacam, Betacam SP, or Betacam SX videotapes.

### *Standalone Editing*

The Hybrid Recorder is the most natural application to replace two VTRs in a machine-to-machine editing configuration. The HBR's front control panel gives simple access to the non-linear editing functions for quickly assembling cuts-only stories.

### *Nonlinear Editing Workstation*

The primary benefit of today's disk technology is clearly demonstrated in the nonlinear editing application. A nonlinear edit system has typically limited storage capacity and must therefore be connected to a high capacity A/V server system or to a videotape recorder for downloading and uploading the finished program. The Hybrid Recorder is used for both local disk storage and videotape program material uploading and downloading in a variety of editing configurations from simple cuts-only workstation to fully-configured nonlinear edit systems with effects.

### *Digital Satellite News Gathering with 2X Transfer Speed*

Using the high-speed transfer capability of the Hybrid Recorder, a reporter in the field can edit the story using the HBR. As soon as the program is completed, the story can be played out at two times normal speed back to the station through a satellite uplink or microwave transmission realizing significant cost savings and maximizing transponder time allocation.

### *Live Events with Simultaneous Recording and Editing*

When used in conjunction with the Sony DLE-110 "Live Editor", the Hybrid Recorder can be used to simultaneous record the live feed to its HDD (and to the videotape for backup or archival) while instantly recalling highlights for replay.

Variable speed effects are also available, including learning a Dynamic Motion sequence, for later replay. While the live feed is still being recorded, a sequence of highlights may be assembled as a Program that can then be played out at any time.

A protection mode allows the user to save selected events so that in case the disk fills up and more capacity is needed, recording over the old material is done without destroying the protected events.

### *Time Shifting or Program Delay with Endless Loop Recording*

Network time shifting is easily accommodated using the simultaneous recording and playback capabilities of the Hybrid's HDD. During this operation, a videotape can also be recorded for backup or archival. Protection of chosen events is also available to prevent overwriting the selected events. Only Master files are recorded in this mode.

### *Field Editing with Portable Editor*

A laptop computer-based portable edit controller is used for on-line editing in the field. The videotape and the disk are controlled by the user who can also perform a quick scan of preselected scenes from the videotape by detecting and highlighting corresponding stamp pictures.

A batch transfer of the highlighted scenes can also be executed at four times normal speed from the Betacam SX videotape to its internal HDD. This application, which is designed for journalists "on-the-go", also features scripting synchronized to video for voice-over and directing notes.

### *On-Air Playback*

The random access capability of the disk with the additional videotape playback for last minute story insertion make the Hybrid Recorder an excellent candidate for play-to-air. In addition, the optional extended storage unit can provide the protection of a redundant disk array system.

### *Server Feeder with High Speed Transfer*

The four times transfer speed capability of the HBR is specially suited to feed A/V servers at high speed through a SDDI interface.

## Conclusion

The Betacam SX format presents the clear prospect of efficient picture coding with high picture quality for the demanding infrastructure of a modern all-digital broadcast facility. The Hybrid Recorder is a key component to this new digital facility, but more importantly, it provides a practical path between today's analog-based infrastructure and tomorrow's digital world.

# Surviving in the Format Jungle

Jim Wheeler
Tape Archival and Restoration Services
Belmont, CA

## Abstract

This year is the 40th anniversary of the Ampex Quadraplex videotape recorder introduced in 1956. The quad format dominated for over 20 years, until it was finally replaced by the helical format. Now, thousands of Quad tapes are sitting on archive shelves, but only a few quad machines exist in a few special facilities.

Since the helical videotape recorder was first introduced in 1962, there have been an average of about two new videotape formats per year. About half of these obtained some degree of popularity and half ended up on the format floor. This abundance of old tape formats is a major problem for anyone with old videotapes with no machines to play them on. As a member of the engineering team that developed the Ampex VR-660 in 1962 and several other Ampex videotape recorders since then, I have closely followed the development of videotape formats. A chart of about 40 of the more popular videotape formats is presented.

The problem of equipment obsolescence is a major problem and is magnified at a large Archive, like the Library of Congress. Recently, the Library of Congress held hearings at three cities in the U.S., at which they heard from national archives, regional archives, production studios, broadcasters, educators, and technology experts on the topic of "The current status of American Television and Video preservation". At these hearings, several people voiced their concern about the problem of dealing with the continual birth and death cycle of videotape formats.

SMPTE Study Group V16.09 "User Requirements for Automated Storage and Retrieval" was formed in December, and members have expressed their concern about the format problem and that something should be done about it. Possibly, this SMPTE Group could work with archivists to specify a universal archival format.

## I - Introduction

For most of you, the new videotape formats introduced at NAB each year are exciting technological advances. But, for a person responsible for preserving the information recorded on videotapes, growth in the number of formats is a constant headache.

Archives commonly have vast numbers of videotapes in ten to twenty different formats, but their budgets support equipment to play only a few of the formats. In other words, archivists cannot play all of the tapes in their collections, and they usually don't even know what is recorded on many of their tapes.

A national awareness of this problem is needed in the video industry and I am here to inform you of the issues facing videotape archivists.

## II - Obsolete formats

Figure 1 gives you an idea of how many videotape formats exist in archives today. How would you go about finding the equipment to play tapes made on all of these formats? That is the question archivists face all the time. Overwhelming, isn't it?

The good news is that there is someone who is collecting old videotape recorders and making them usable again. My good friend Jim Lindner at VidiPax in New York City is dedicated to helping archivists copy their old tapes to a new format. To my knowledge, he is the only person in the world doing this on a large scale. Jim Lindner also has the problems of finding technical manuals for the old equipment and locating technical people who can maintain the equipment properlv.

I have been immersed in videotape formats for 34 years. My first project as a design engineer at Ampex was the two-inch helical, and that was in 1962. As you can see by Figure 1, that was the start of the Format explosion.

There is no sign that this explosion in the number of formats will die down in the foreseeable future. At NAB-96, the DV formats were being pushed by Sony and Panasonic, and JVC was pushing Digital-S.

## III - Tape Formats Suitable for Archiving

D1, D2, D5 and DCT may be good archival formats, but they are too expensive for budget-conscious archivists.

I recommend digital over analog for archives because it provides the ability to monitor error rate and to make copies with no loss in image quality.

I advise against formats that use ultra-thin tape. The 10 μm tapes are more susceptible to damage, and recovery of the data is more difficult after damage occurs.

I recommend against using a format with compression. For an archivist, compression is a potential disaster. After many years of storage, some of the key bits could be missing and cause an entire table to be missing or jumbled. Another problem with compression for archival tapes is that archival material should never be altered, and compression is a form of alteration.

## IV - The Main Tape Archival Problems

All of the archives I have visited over the past 20 years have inadequate budgets and cannot properly care for the material they have.

Aside from this budget problem, the two main problems faced by archivists are:

**Obsolescence of Formats:**

An example of an obsolete format is quad. When was the last time you saw a quad machine? Well, many archives have quad tapes but no quad machines. Maintaining a quad machine is very difficult because of the many electrical and mechanical adjustments and because of lack of replacement parts.

Recently, CBS-Hollywood completed the transfer of 32,000 quad tapes to a new format. Out of 32,000 tapes, only two were unplayable. That says something about the durability of the quad format. This is a rare example of management deciding that the old material was valuable and funding the money and the resources to save it.

**Deterioration of Tapes:**

Most tapes manufactured in the period between about 1970 and 1990 were made with a binder that is not stable. This problem with polyurethane binders wasn't known until Ed Cuddihy at the Jet Propulsion Laboratory discovered that binders break down at high temperature and/or high humidity. Since Ed Cuddihy published his paper in the *IEEE Journal* in 1982, most tape manufacturers have developed a more stable binder for their product.

Because of potential liability problems, tape manufacturers are reluctant to discuss the binder issue. Engineers who have any concern about the long-term stability of the tapes they are now using, should ask the manufacturer tape service engineer if the particular tape has an archival-quality binder.

## V - Report by Library of Congress

In March, the Librarian of Congress, James H. Billington, held three public hearings for the purpose of receiving input about the condition of American television and video preservation efforts.

As a result of these hearings, the Library of Congress has formed three task forces to make recommendations about preservation of the U.S. television heritage. These task forces will complete their reports by the end of this year. I am one of the six people serving on the Preservation Task Force.

These reports will be very important in clarifying and resolving the issues faced by videotape archivists worldwide.

## VI - Conclusion

The present system of storing our television heritage on multiple videotape formats for later retrieval is not working. The Library of Congress report will provide guidance and may recommend a solution. Once the Library of Congress report is published, I foresee SMPTE and AMIA (Association of Moving Image Archivists) working together to resolve the mess our videotape archives are in today.

# Figure 1 VIDEOTAPE FORMATS

| | Professional | Industrial/Educational | Consumer |
|---|---|---|---|
| 1956 | Ampex 2" Quad | | |
| 1960 | Ampex Quad Low-Band Color | | |
| 1962 | Ampex 2" Helical (First popular helical) | | |
| 1963 | Ampex Quad High-Band Color | Sony 2" | |
| 1964 | | Sony 1" | |
| 1965 | | Ampex 1" (SMPTE A) | |
| 1968 | | IVC 1" | |
| " | | Sony 1/2" | |
| 1969 | | EIAJ-1 1/2" | |
| 1970 | | Phillips 1/2" VCR (1st Cassette) | |
| 1971 | Ampex Quad Super High-Band | *Sony 3/4" U-Matic | |
| 1973 | IVC 2" Helical | | |
| 1975 | Bosch 1" (SMPTE B) | | Sony Betamax |
| 1976 | Sony 1" | * JVC VHS | |
| " | Ampex 1"(A Format with Slo-Mo) | | |
| 1978 | *Ampex/Sony 1" (SMPTE C) | | |
| 1983 | Panasonic M | | |
| 1984 | Sony Betacam | | 8 mm |
| 1986 | * Panasonic M-II | | |
| 1987 | * Sony Betacam-SP | | |
| " | * D1 [1] | | * S-VHS |
| 1988 | * D2 [2] | | ED-Beta |
| 1989 | | * Hi-8 | |
| 1992 | * D3 [2] | | |
| " | * DCT [1] (Compressed) | | |
| 1993 | * D5 [1] | | |
| " | * Digital Betacam [1] (Compressed) | | |
| 1995 | | * DVC [1] (Compressed) | |

* In common use in 1995

Notes:
1. Component Digital
2. Composite Digital
3. The dates are when the product was first publically available.
4. In the years 1962-1975, about 30 to 40 Industrial/Educational formats came and went. Only the more popular formats are listed here.
5. All formats are Helical except when noted as Quad (1956-1971)

# TOWARD A UNIVERSAL DATA FORMAT FOR THE PRESERVATION OF MEDIA.

Dave MacCarn
WGBH Educational Foundation
Boston, MA.

**Abstract**

There is a significant need for a Universal Preservation Format (UPF), designed specifically for digital technologies, that can store compound content (not only media itself but also information about it) so that the content can be accessed easily both today and into the indefinite future. The UPF could break the bond between the recording format and the machine through which the format is accessed.
This paper points out some existing technology that could be used, and is intended to provide a basis for industry discussion toward producing a universal preservation format.

**Introduction**

> Film, video and sound recordings are vital components of our collective memory... This vast source of information, inspiration and creativity—the most known contemporary archive of our society—is threatened. ...[W]e are losing large parts of our recorded past."[1]

According to a recent Library of Congress report, video materials in the public and private sector are estimated to exceed several hundred thousand recorded hours. The same report judges the amount of feet of news film and other film used to record television programming to total in the several millions.[2] Much of this historical material is in danger of being lost.

> [T]he preservation of television and video materials faces enormous obstacles, in particular, the vulnerability of videotape to adverse storage conditions, abusive handling, and technological obsolescence.
>
> William T. Murphy, Coordinator
> Report on the State of American
> Television and Video Preservation
> In a letter dated January 16, 1996

Technological obsolescence, in particular, has hindered the preservation of film and video materials by contributing to the enormous expense of accessing stored materials. The standard format for recording television programs has taken several forms over the past fifty years, including kinescope, 2″ videotape, 1″ videotape and digital tape. As the standard for recorded programming continues to evolve, the equipment used to access materials produced in earlier formats has become increasingly difficult to find and, accordingly, more expensive to use.

Archivists and industry members have addressed the problem by transferring older formats to digital tape, thus attempting to maintain the quality of the original material. However, this costly process simply puts off—rather than solves—the preservation problem. The enormous and rapid changes taking place in digital technology have resulted in a veritable explosion of formats. Thirteen different digital tape formats are available at present (D-1, D-1 SP, D-2, D-3, D-5, D-6, Digital Betacam, Betacam SX, Ampex DCT, Consumer DV, DVCAM, DVCPRO and Digital S) with several more in development (for High Definition Television.) With the format wars heating up, many of these formats may soon become obsolete, making them unsuitable for preserving media information. In addition, digital non-linear editing systems have internal proprietary media formats.

From an archivist perspective this is a nightmare. On one side of the room you store the tapes and on the other side the tape machines and spare parts.

As with the videotape materials produced during the last fifty years, technical obsolescence may make digital formats that are common today inaccessible tomorrow. **There is a significant need for a Universal Preservation Format (UPF), designed specifically for digital technologies, that can store compound content (not only the media itself but also information about it) so that it can be accessed easily both today and into the indefinite future.** What is not being stated is that we need a universal acquisition format.

This thinking is reflected in a national plan for redefining film preservation put forth by the Librarian of Congress in August of 1994, . As one of his eight recommendations, he suggested that:

> [the new electronic technologies] are already transforming film access but archives should insist that certain stringent criteria be met before new technologies are adopted as preservation media.[3]

Paul Messier, Conservator of Photographs and Works on Paper for the Boston Art Conservation, also called for the establishment of criteria for assessing digital video as a preservation medium in a paper that he presented at Playback '96: A Round Table on Video Preservation. His suggested criteria were adapted from those suggested for still images by Basil Manns, Research Scientist at the Library of Congress in his article "The Electronic Document Image Preservation Format." These "criteria" anticipate the technical specifications necessary for the selection and description of data to be preserved through a UPF. However, to date, no further action has been taken within the field of archives.

**Use of existing technology**

Why can we address this problem now? Along with the surge of digital formats are technologies that are designed to handle digital media of all types. Apple Computer's "Bento Specification"[4] and Avid Technology's "Open Media Framework Interchange Specification"[5] are both media technologies that approach the UPF concept .

**Bento**

Apple Computer's "Bento Specification" is the underlying technology of Apple Computer's OpenDoc Standard Interchange Format.[6] Bento is a specification for storage and interchange of compound content. Bento defines a standard format for storing multiple different types of objects and an API to access these objects. An object container is just some form of data storage (such as a file.) This storage is used to hold one or more objects (values) and information about the objects (metadata.) Bento containers are defined by a set of rules for storing multiple objects, so that software that understands the rules can find the objects, figure out what kind of objects they are, and use them correctly.

Bento objects can be simple or complex, small (a few bytes) or large (up to $2^{64}$ bytes, approximately $2^{27}$ hours of D-1 video.) Bento is designed to be platform and content neutral. so that it provides a convenient container for transporting any type of compound content between multiple platforms. The Bento code currently runs on Macintosh, MS DOS, Microsoft Windows, OS/2 and several varieties of Unix.[7]

**OMF**

Avid Technology's "Open Media Framework" (OMF) Interchange, now a standard format for the interchange of digital media data among different platforms, has adopted the use of Bento containers. Additionally, the OMF format encapsulates all the information required to transport a variety of digital media such as audio, video, graphics, and still images, as well as the rules for combining and presenting the media. The format includes rules for identifying the original sources of the digital media data, and it can encapsulate both compressed and uncompressed digital media data.

OMF Interchange provides for a variety of existing digital media types and the ability to easily support new types in the future. A single OMF Interchange file can encapsulate all the information required to create, edit, and play digital media presentations.

While OMF Interchange is designed primarily for data interchange, it is structured to facilitate playback directly from an interchanged file when being used on platforms with characteristics and hardware similar to those of the source platform, without the need for expensive translation or duplication of the sample data. OMF Interchange provides for the development and integration of new media and composition types.[8]

The International Multimedia Association (IMA) recently released their Recommended Practice for data exchange which is also based on Bento and OMF.[9] The Society of Motion Picture and Television Engineers (SMPTE) is currently voting on a similar Recommended Practice which uses a subset of the IMA Recommended Practice. However, to date, no one has explored the use of these technologies as a <u>preservation</u> container.

**Bento and OMF as a Preservation format**

Preservation requires the handling of many different recording formats—such as 2" videotape, 1" videotape, D-1, D-2, D-3, and others—which can be thought of as having data types (4:2:2, $4f_{sc}$.) Although Bento allows for any data type, the OMF Interchange and the recommended practice by the IMA only define a <u>minimum</u> number of data types (e.g. TIFF, RGBA and AIFF). By adding <u>additional</u> standard data types (e.g. CCIR 601, 4:2:0, 4:1:1, etc.) to the Open Media Framework Interchange and IMA's Recommended Practice for data exchange, a new Recommended Practice would result in a storage container format that will be able to encompass all present recording forms and allow for all future forms. In moving from the raw recording format (e.g. videotape) to a data tape (or other media) format that incorporates the UPF, the number of formats that archivists need to preserve will be substantially reduced. The UPF breaks the bond between the recording format and the machine through which the format is accessed. In addition, since the UPF can be used not just for videotape but also for text, still image and other digitizable or data materials, commercial technology manufacturers will be able to extend the usefulness of media created on their products.

The storage and retrieval of media could be handled by a so called "media compiler" (figure 1.) This media compiler would then remove the acquisition format from the archive requirement. One has to acknowledge that there will always be a format that media has to be stored on and that this format will always become obsolete at some time. The UPF does not solve this problem. But, it does allow the archivist to choose a format best suited to their needs and one that they feel has the best long term storage potential(one storage manufacturer has created a 50TB near-line storage system using D-3 tape.[10])

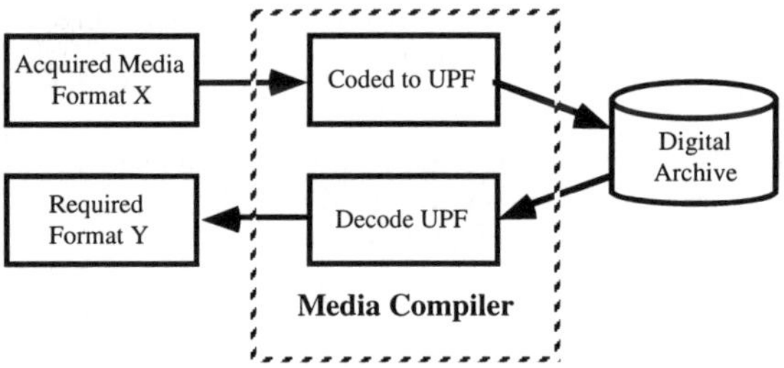


figure 1.

Additional header information that defines the formats stored in the UPF could be included. In archival terms, it may be necessary to record these definitions to provide decoding of the original material.

**Summary**

Clearly, it is time to bring together technology manufacturers, archivists and standards organizations to advance the creation of a Universal Preservation Format that fits the needs of all.

The goal of the Universal Preservation Format is to produce a Recommended Practice that, if adopted, would benefit a broad range of users of archival records—including archivists and technology manufacturers, distributors and producers—by making it efficient, cost-effective and relatively simple to access records originally created in (or transferred into) a variety of digital formats.

Remember that we are talking about an universal archive format and not a universal acquisition format.

Bento and it's use by OMF and the IMA is a good step toward a Universal Preservation Format.

**Acknowledgments**

Mary Ide, Archivist and Director, Media Archives & Preservation Center, WGBH Educational Foundation, Boston, MA.

---

1 From Fading Away: Strategic Options to Ensure the Protection of and Access to Our Audio-visual Memory. Task Force on the Preservation and Enhanced Use of Canada's Audio-Visual Heritage, National Archives of Canada, June 1995, p.i.

2 Library of Congress, "Redefining Film Preservation: A National Plan" August, 1994.

3 Redefining film preservation: a national plan; recommendations of the Librarian of Congress in consultation with the National Film Preservation Board [coordinated by Annette Melville and Scott Simmon]. August 1994. Recommendation 3.7.

4 Bento Specification, Copyright © 1993, Apple Computer, Inc. [retrieve at: ftp://cil.org/pub/cilabs/tech/bento/]

5 Open Media Framework Interchange Specification, Copyright © 1995 Avid Technology, Inc.[retrieve at: http://www.avid.com/omf/]

6 Open Doc underlying technologies [see: http://dev.info.apple.com/du/intro_to_opendoc/iod4_underlying_technology.html]

7 Bento Specification. [see 4]

8 Open Media Framework Interchange Specification.[see 5]

9 IMA Technical Working group, data exchange, IMA 950701.1, p. 2.ii. [retrieve at: http://www.ima.org/forums/imf/de/]

10 Storage Technology Corporation [see: http://www.stortek.com/StorageTek/redwood1.html]

# CCIR 601 , Future File Image
# or
# The Last Universal Video Standard?

Peter Owen,
Quantel,
Newbury,
Berkshire , UK.

## Introduction

The fundamental nature of television standards has changed little in the first 60 years of broadcasting. The elegant solutions designed in the research laboratories of the twenties and thirties still endure to this day providing hundreds of millions of viewers with good images on economical home screens and programme makers with economical solutions to acquisition an production. Whilst two of the original 405,525, 625, and 819 line scanning standards have since fallen by the wayside, 525 and 625 are still going strong and are set to be with us for at least the next twenty years ( so hopes the author and many millions of others who have recently bought new home receivers ! ). The ingenious aspect of those early standards was to incorporate a form of image compression which traded off spatial resolution for temporal resolution on moving scenes. This trick of using 2:1 interlace for the line scan / field scan relationship made the home receiver and studio camera not only technologically possible but also economised on channel bandwidth and in one step eliminated large area flicker and doubled the temporal resolution compared to the 24 frames per second of the cinema.

Since the scanning standards in the home and in the studio were and mostly still are identical, definition and standardisation of signals throughout the production chain was in the analogue era a process of cloning and refining by groups of industry experts brought together under the wing of organisations such as the ABU, EBU, SMPTE etc. which then forwarded the results of their deliberations to national organisations such as ANSI or world organisations such as ISO or the CCIR.

Today's studio cameras, video recorders, post production technology and playout still function to the principles laid down when video recording was very much a non real time film based technology.

The transition to digital began in the seventies when the economics of digital processing made digitally based systems viable for broadcast television applications. Many differing sampling techniques of the analogue signal evolved precluding digital interconnection of equipments. But all the sampling schemes followed the raster sequence of the analogue sources in order to maximise image transparency and real time throughput.

Meanwhile in the computer arena image based applications were beginning to emerge ,based upon diverse source and display 'standards'. Like their broadcast counterparts digital image between differing systems was impossible.

After much study, the broadcast community defined image sampling standards which were independent of the colour encoding method for the home receiver, and developed inter - equipment digital connections based upon familiar co-axial technology thus preserving the real time nature of image delivery. In the new digital domain the CCIR 601 sampling standard and the CCIR 656 interface standard not only fitted well with the present but incorporated headroom for future extensions and applications. Today CCIR 601 is *the* image sampling standard. Although based on the early interlaced scanning principles of its origins, it is today used with progressive and interlaced images and now finds acceptance as a standard image size in computer files, scanning arrays and compression techniques such as MPEG and DVC.

Meanwhile the computer community faced in some ways a greater challenge of harmonising the diverse display 'standards' and image sizes and file formats. Unlike the broadcast community where real-time source to screen requirements had demanded simplicity, even the task of harmonising computer image origination sizes was a non starter. Agreement of the source scanning trajectory was confused, many starting at the top left whilst the mathematicians who prefer their X,Y, 0,0, start of scan at bottom left. In terms of colour RGB samples could be pixel sequential, line sequential or even frame sequential.

In order to simplify exchange of diverse sources file formats such as TIFF were developed which unlike the broadcast approach of rigidly defining the images allowed not only the storage and exchange of images but also carried with it attributes of the image such as size, aspect ratio, copyright, scanning sequence, history, and any other parameter attached to the tags. Using such an approach the receiving device could prepare it self to accept and if necessary, reorder or process the image data in preparation for the application.

This contrasting situation of the television standardisation and computer file standardisation clearly reflects the needs of the respective industries. But as broadcast expertise moves into the computer industry and computer technologies find application in television, can a situation be reached where broadcast technology can take on board some of the flexibility of file formats or will the computer and associated network speeds increase such that inspite of the lack of mandatory image sizes definition, computers will provide the same throughput as today's broadcast technology ?

## Files or Frames ?

The fundamentally different approach to storage and transport of images described in the introduction demonstrates the emphasis placed upon real time operation demanded by broadcasters. This real-time continuous frame after frame approach is also extended to the physical means of image transport and storage, both of which must have sufficient bandwidth or data rate to deliver images on time and in phase with other sources at the destination.

With the introduction of the standardised time code, two or more VTR sources could be synchronised to the exact frame.

Transporting data other than the image is a recent development and possibilities now exist of transmitting compressed data faster than real time over serial digital carriers. Many organisations have developed digital equipment control commands carried in the redundant blanking periods of the television signal , but few of these can be classed as standards. Latterly through the auspices of the SMPTE and EBU, working groups have studied the inclusion of data to accompany the digital images. Multitrack audio can now also run synchronously alongside digital images in the CCIR 656 serial digital real-time standard

Contrast this situation with that of files and file storage.

Offering greater flexibility, files provide extended facilities treating sampled and digitised audio and video as data or a sequence of numbers. Other information can ( and often must ) be carried along with the data.
Data storage and delivery hardware have no awareness of real time operation delivering data rates from a few KB / sec to many GB / sec, often mixing technologies and data rates from source to destination. Given these variables it is today impossible to guarantee real time delivery to the frame, second minute, minute or sometimes the hour.
The concept of frame synchronisation has only been recently understood as broadcast standards knowledge becomes incorporated into compression formats. It is hoped that as network bandwidths, disc data rates and processor speeds continue to increase, transporting files will be as fast as transporting video frames. In reality this unlikely, the restriction not being the hardware technology but the lack of agreement across file formats, operating systems and networking standards. Undoubtedly standards exist in each area but such is the open philosophy of computing and networking that the goal of transporting any file from any source to any processor in real time is clearly unattainable.
This real-time need may or may not be necessary.

## Real-time or Non Real-time ?

Today it is difficult to imagine CCIR 601 operating in non real-time. With one or two notable exceptions, CCIR 601 based acquisition, post production, presentation and playout operate in real time. For acquisition and playout real-time is mandatory. Not too many years ago all screens in the television production chain also displayed true real-time images; today diverse approaches to editing offer less than or greater than real-time with screen refresh rates bearing no relationship to the original capture rate.
The choice depends on the accuracy and precision required at the time. News editing and shot listing it is said requires little temporal or spatial accuracy. On the other hand final conforming and high end commercials require high quality and interactive workstations. Editing can take advantage of compression whereas post production tolerates little of the redundancy of compression algorithms.
In terms of image quality, preserving the full CCIR 601 sampled data throughout the production chain guarantees transparency from source to screen. The standard was developed with quality in mind. Although this is becoming the norm in broadcast technology, no computer solution can match the performance of dedicated CCIR 601 hardware.
Real-time in computers is often achieved today through the adoption of compression, a technique which may or may not be allowable.
Using CCIR 601 preserves source quality, but real-time, full image size demands hardware which is tuned to the standard. The processors, discs and interfaces are optimised to the standard, but interfaces with the computer world allow the import, and sometimes export of non standard size images.
Before investigating the relationship between image standards and recording hardware, a brief review of the structure of image files is required.

## Image and Graphics files.

The " Encyclopaedia of Graphics file formats " ( ISBN, 1 - 56592 - 058 - 9 ) lists over one hundred different file formats. Over forty are suitable for bitmapped or sampled images. some can truly be described as standards, being open to all, and having been registered with ANSI, ISO, ITU etc. Others are de facto standards which are recognised by their commercial dominance.

Most are related to specific platforms of PC, MAC, or the UNIX operating system. A few are platform independent.

To accommodate the wide application of computer files, information beyond that of image data must be carried alongside the bitmap.

All file structures follow the common approach of : -

Header, followed by
Data.

Here the commonality ends.

The header may be text describing the following data e.g.: -

Horizontal pixel count
Vertical pixel count
Origin, (top left, bottom left, centre etc. )
Bits per pixel
File data, image locations etc.
Colour information
Pixel order ( pixel, line or frame sequential colour )
Space for additions ( future changes , enhancements )
An unique number identifying the file type
Byte order
Etc. etc.

The requirement to read the header information before reading the pixel data is mandatory. This information prepares the receiving device such that the order of the data is correctly sequenced and correctly mapped into the computer ready for the subsequent application. If the requirements defined in the header are complete, correct and matched by the necessary supporting hardware or software, all is well. Often mismatches occur preventing correct loading of the data, faulty or slow functionality. Supporting software modules can be written to supplement the header information (fine in the research laboratory but not in a broadcast environment ).

One detail of header data relates particularly to CCIR 601. Most bit mapped files assume square pixels. CCIR 601 samples are not, especially so the colour difference samples which are distinctly rectangular, hence the non standard variations to CCIR 601 using 720 x 540 or 768 x 576 samples per luminance frame.( The television derived HDTV standard was modified to include a square pixel 1920 x 1080, 16 x 9 aspect ratio ).

It is beyond the scope of this paper to evaluate the pros and cons of the various file formats suffice to say that all are unnecessarily complex for the exchange of images in broadcast and post production.

In terms of the CCIR 601 specification, the term standard cannot be applied to the diverse nature of computer file bitmaps.

## Recording Hardware

The consequence of these contrasting approach to image standards is nowhere better illustrated than in the digital tape recorder, the tape cassette and the formatting of information on the tape. Data recorders reflect in a linear fashion on the tape the Header / Bitmap structure of files, This is supplemented by directory and sync. information. which is required on all tapes.
Although today's digital video recorders and tape formats allow some data to be added to the video and audio information, the recorders and video tape do not require header information. format Image parameters such as

- Horizontal pixel count
- Vertical pixel count
- Origin
- Colourimetry
- Aspect ratio
- Bit depth
- Frame rate
- File format

are all predetermined in the standardisation meetings. Knowledge of these parameters is embedded into the recording hardware. Details of how data is laid on the tape, error correction and error concealment is mostly a matter for the manufacturer.
Unlike data tape, directory information is presently carried as a hand written list along with the tape. Some variants of the DVC formats include solid state memory attached to the cassette, a perfect solution to rapid access to on tape material. This must be a superior solution to the data tape directory which is inaccessible, easily damaged if placed at the start of the tape and is wasteful since the length of the directory space is indeterminate.
Once of the obvious benefits of incorporating header information outside the video recorder (i.e. at during the format standardisation process), is that the recorder becomes a self contained device not requiring transfer if data to a workstation for viewing.
The benefit of data recorders is the flexibility to record more or less any type of file. Not requiring any knowledge of real-time, many tape formats are available, some standardised, some not. Increasingly tape transports originally designed for digital audio or digital video are being adapted or re - engineered as data recorders. Many types exist, the numbers of data recorder formats probably exceeds that of video tape formats, both analogue and digital.
High end data recorders are direct descendants of video recorders, but are inevitably slower due to the file handling requirements.

## File size

As discussed previously, many computer files, TIFF, TARGA etc. can accommodate almost any size of image. Originally necessary because of the disparate requirements of users, particularly those in the printing industry who traditionally use file sizes related to the final printed image.
This flexibility is unnecessary in the broadcast world where absolute definition of image resolutions is well understood and real-time hardware can maintain the full file size throughout the programme making chain. Inevitably inputs from images at resolutions beyond that of CCIR

601 are to be occasionally expected. But if the situation was to develop where an anarchic approach to image size was the norm, then production and transmission would inevitably suffer in terms of quality and economics.

Working at resolutions inappropriate to the end product results in :-

- Loss of quality due to repeated resizing of images. (decimation or pixel replication as used on computer screens is unacceptable )
- Over complicated transmission technology.
- Inefficient use of tape and disc recording technology.
- Unnecessary copying of data between storage media.

On the other hand the image size of 720 x 576 or 720 x 473 is well matched to today's and tomorrow's home screens. As computer processing improve, non square pixels should become a non issue.

Working to fixed image sizes has simplified the traditional problems of television production not only in terms of image quality but for example at the edges of the image where the tolerances of analogue blanking made accurate butting up of two images a tedious or unpredictable process.

In terms of hardware benefits the fixed file size of CCIR 601 simplified the design of very high performance digital video recorders and image recorders whose performance cannot be matched by so called resolution independent hardware.

## Conclusion

Working to the well defined image standard of CCIR 601 brings to the television production process benefits of simplicity, and hence quality and productivity. Today via our NTSC and PAL home receivers, the vastly improved quality of graphics, commercials and film transfers is clearly seen. In the era of digital to the home, the results will be even more apparent.

Whist the 601 standard is often related to broadcast hardware it should be equally at home as a standard bitmap within computer file formats. Taking the pragmatic approach to image sizes would undoubtedly lead to improvements in speeds of processing and data transfer in the computer world.

But to truly mimic the efficiency of this broadcast approach, the computer community could consider the design of a **very simple** file format, addressing **only** the exchange of CCIR 601 images, perhaps with associated audio, leaving room for some supporting information.

# Database Applications for Server-Centered News Production

Stevan Vigneaux
Avid Technology, Inc.
Broadcast Products Group
Tewksbury, Massachusetts

## Abstract

A completely integrated television news production system, which produces video, audio, and text for news programs will require comprehensive and flexible database management tools. The purpose of this paper is to examine the various needs for database management, describe a potential set of features, and define the operational procedures likely to be encountered in a server-centered production system complete with robotic near-line storage.

The paper will examine issues surrounding the use of multiple separate databases and how they are linked and kept synchronized. Database redundancy and administration will be reviewed along with an analysis of the key responsibilities for the database administrator/librarian. The paper will consider the major elements of database customization on a per-site basis.

## Introduction

The age of the server-centered video production system is here, as is evidenced by product offerings from a number of major broadcast suppliers. Some of these systems are currently deliverable, one vendor has put multiple installations on the air starting with April of 1995, while other "systems" are still prototypes or technology demonstrations. The importance and magnitude of the server business within the broadcast community has even drawn in suppliers whose background has been in the computer industry rather than broadcast. However one examines it, the evidence is incontrovertible, the server-centered video production system is here to stay and video is just one of the multiple forms of media with which broadcasters must contend. As these video-oriented systems become ever more tightly linked to traditional text-based newsroom computer systems, true multimedia news production will arrive. And as it does, so will the need to partner with those non-broadcast suppliers mentioned above.

The advent of server-centered multimedia news production systems brings a wealth of benefits and a number of new challenges — one of which is managing the vast amounts of data contained within the server's storage subsystem. A server-centered production system without state of the art cataloging capability will soon be overwhelmed by the sheer number of media elements and the incredible rate of change of those elements.

## What Is A Video Server?

The term "video server" has been applied too broadly in many cases. Depending on the vendor, a server might be a simple disk-based VCR emulator or a system capable of supporting multiple client workstations with simultaneous access to a shared central library of audio and video. The following definitions are offered in an attempt to bring some clarity to the situation:

### *Video-On-Demand Server*

Designed almost exclusively for delivering video to the home, this type of server usually contains highly compressed video and supports many simultaneous streams without any editing capabilities. A potential application could be found in the browsing capability of multimedia news production systems.

### *Playback Server*

Primarily intended for commercial record and playback applications (replacing automated tape libraries and jukeboxes), this type of server provides high-quality video and audio with high reliability. Editing is not provided since the application does not require it.

### *Production Server*

Intended as the center of a video production system, a production server supports recording, editing, and playback either directly or via attached client workstations. It further supports:

- the creation and storage of database information
- the management, control, and command information related to playlists,
- and configuration data for the clients.

The presence of these additional capabilities, especially editing and database management, is a critical difference between a production server and a playback server.

It should be noted that one way to create a pseudo-production server is to use video outputs from a playback server as sources in a traditional editing system. The edit controller treats the server's outputs as if they were VCRs. The server's video is first decompressed and then flows through a small video switcher. It is then re-compressed for storage back in the server. This model uses two playback channels out of the server and one record channel to achieve. While it mimics the same capabilities of a true client-server architectures, it does not come close to the level of efficiency.

These three different types of video servers are designed for very different applications. Distinguishing between them is critical to clear discussion and evaluation.

## "Multimedia News Production System" Defined

One of the buzzwords of the last few years has been "multimedia." It seems that every vendor of computers or consumer and professional audio/video equipment has a multimedia offering of some type. It also seems there are more questions on what to do with this technology than there are answers.

Millions of homes contain multimedia PCs. Several publishing corporations have launched major business efforts into multimedia only to find a dearth of returned revenue and even fewer profits. However, multimedia's current non-success (as opposed to failure) in some areas hinges more on the lack of suitable applications, rather than on a fundamental weakness or shortcoming in the technology itself. When multimedia technology is applied to television news production there is near-perfect alignment between its capabilities and the user's needs.

Rather than dealing with just one medium, such as text-only newsroom computers or video/audio-only video servers, a multimedia news production system unites all relevant media types into an integrated whole. A multimedia news production system allows its users to work with text, audio, video, graphics, and composition data as a single coherent entity and process. This stands in stark contrast to today's systems where text is processed on a text-based newsroom computer system and the video and audio are handled in separate systems. It also contradicts the fact that a news story is clearly a combination of text, the script, and video. The development of multimedia production systems for television news will dissolve that technology-enforced separation and allow news production to become a single integrated process. This integrated production process will result in improvements in operating efficiency, of course. But, far more important and noticeable will be the dramatic improvements in process and quality as the artificial separations between cameramen, editors, reporters, graphics artists, etc. disappear.

There are eight predominant data types in a multimedia news production system:

*Video/audio*
This describes what most people think of when they say "video." It is really video with audio and is typically that which comes in over satellite or on field tapes. Most, though surely not all, video has audio along with it.

*Audio*
There is also a separate world of audio-only. Some audio-only media elements exist in what is usually considered the world of television. Voice-overs or announce tracks are examples. The majority of audio-only is in radio, the more venerable forerunner of television and a major product of many of the world's leading broadcasters.

Further, even when discussed in regard to video production, audio is often captured and processed separately. In a facility which produces both television and radio, the audio which came in with video is often "floated off" to serve as cuts for radio news.

*Graphics*
Graphics are in one sense a form of video, but they deserve recognition as a separate media type because both their use creation process are also very different. Graphics include captions (lower thirds), full screen stills, and "over-the-shoulder" elements created by a range of character generators and paint systems.

*Animations*
Also a form of video, animation is genuinely different from video captured on camera. Animations are a creation rather than a reproduction. They display that which never was.

*Text*
Wire service data and locally-created scripts are only two forms of text media which a multimedia news production system must accommodate. E-mail, memos, word processing documents and web pages are rapidly becoming important in the production effort. Some documents, such as those formatted using HTML, contain more data than just text. Additional information includes hypertext links to other web pages, embedded spreadsheets or graphics, etc. This data must be stored in an "intelligent" form and not only as text.

*Command and control data*
The command and control data includes: playlists; automated archiving and media management policies, machine control commands, and composition data necessary to reconstruct, on the fly and in real-time, the video sequences created by the editing workstations.

*Meta data*
Meta data is "data about data." Meta data describes the data which has been stored. For example, meta data about a piece of video might describe the time and date of original capture, copyright holder, and the photographer's name.

*Ancillary data*
Any information outside the above categories which can be expressed and stored as data falls under this category. One example would be spreadsheets.

In such a system there are five major components:

*Text-server, database engine and client workstations*
The text-server and database engine form the heart of the traditional newsroom computer system. This portion of the multimedia news production system receives wires service text, stores it, performs database operations on it, such as creating queues and performing searches, and provides the infrastructure capabilities like word processing, machine control, etc.

The client workstation is a desktop computer optimized for operation in a multimedia news production environment. In addition to basic essential features such as word processing and an operating system, it will include a decoder for the compressed browse video and playback capabilities for this video along with audio and graphics.

*Online video MediaServer, database engine and client workstations*
This major system component performs the video and audio functions which equate to those described above for the text subsystem. The online MediaServer and its client workstations record the incoming audio and video into the server's RAIDed hard drive storage subsystem, provide database capabilities for cataloging and searching, and provide access to the media for the client workstations. The record, edit, and playback client workstations, networked to the MediaServer, perform the actual tasks of recording, editing, and playback from the server's storage.

*Browse Video MediaServer and database engine*
The Browse Video MediaServer is dedicated to providing very highly compressed lo-res video and audio to the journalist's desktops. Audio and video enter the system either through the online MediaServer's client workstations, the most common entry method, or through dedicated digitizing workstations connected directly to the Browse Video MediaServer. When the browse video comes in through the online MediaServer it is linked to the online media through their respective databases.

The Browse Video MediaServer is accessed via the network to which the journalist's workstations are connected. The lo-res video and audio, running at less than 2 Mbps, passes across the network and is decoded to view-able video via on-board processing within the workstation.

*Data network*
The data network is the information highway for the system. It actually consists of at least two individual networks:

*Journalist network*
The network serving the journalists is a general purpose data network. Data traffic levels run, as mentioned above, under 2 Mbps for video and very much less for text-only. Depending on implementation specifics the browse video may be streaming in real-time or downloaded to the journalist's workstation much faster than real-time for offline viewing.

*Online network*
This network carries high-resolution compressed video (lightly compressed when compared to the browse video) at data rates typically in the range of 30 Mbps. All work is in real-time and streams off of the RAIDed drives attached to the MediaServer. The network must function at very high-speed because of the high data rate of the video/audio and the fact that the video and audio are, by their very nature, time dependent (isochronous).

*Command and control network*
In some implementations a third network may be used for command and control purposes. This network would also be a general purpose data network.

*Archiving subsystem*
The archiving subsystem is essential to the system because online storage alone will not meet the needs for long-term storage of massive amounts of media. The archiving system may be driven and controlled by the database system(s) in each individual component listed above.

## The Role of the Database in Server-Centered News Production

In one sense, server-centered news production is not new at all, nor is the use of high-powered database technology. Newsroom computer vendors such as BASYS (purchased by Avid Technology in September 1994) pioneered this approach many years ago though available technologies limited the application to text.

Newsroom computer systems make use of central databases to store and track textual elements including wire copy, scripts, character generator data, and program rundowns. Newsroom computer systems' databases were designed to achieve the equally critical goals of high throughput, fast response time, ease of use, and reliability. The database capabilities of newsroom computer systems have evolved continually and dramatically since their introduction. For example, newsroom computer systems now include much faster and more comprehensive search capabilities and some even search using "fuzzy logic" which successfully finds information on "Bill Clinton" even if the user accidentally types in "Bill Klinton."

The catalog system built on a database engine has always been the core of text-oriented newsroom computer systems. Database engines will be just as important in the new world of multimedia server-centered news production systems which add video, audio, and graphics to text and thereby produce a truly integrated and complete news production system.

The database has always been much more than just the fundamental enabling technology of newsroom computer systems. It is also, in a manner of speaking, the front end, the operating controls of the system. Journalists use the database capabilities to search for and sort text media, to organize the search results into coherent sub-categories related to different projects or aspects of a particular project. The database stores playlists and is involved in all phases of machine control including character generator text loading and controlling tape or disk playback systems.

## Distinctions Between Text-Only and Multimedia Systems

There are three significant differences between the database applications for text-only newsroom computer systems and those of true multimedia news production systems:

*The amount of data to be cataloged*
A single page of text rarely exceeds 5 Kbytes, whereas compressed video ranges from 50 Kbytes for low complexity frames to 200 Kbytes for more complex ones. One hour of compressed video with four channels of audio averages around 10 Byte, the equivalent of two million pages of text at 5 Kbytes per page. Storing hundreds of hours of video requires multiple terabytes of storage, all of which needs to be cataloged and managed.

*Multiple media types*
Instead of storing text data only, multimedia news production systems will also store audio, video, graphics, and composition data, the information which links the individual media elements into a continuous stream for playback of edited stories. It is probable that other data types such as spreadsheets or word processor documents will also be linked into the system's database for completeness.

*Media relationships*
In a text-only news system it is standard practice to keep multiple copies of the same text for each incident of use. If two journalists prepare separate scripts which coincidentally use the same two lines of text from the same wire story, then those two lines of wire text are stored separately in each script thereby doubling the storage. However, the modest capacity increase (less than 200 bytes for the two lines in each script) is inconsequential.

The multimedia environment is dramatically different due to the far greater requirements of video storage. If the two journalists mentioned above also each used the same 10 seconds of video/audio and the system forced duplicate storage then each stored incident would be approximately 40 Mbytes. If such duplication occurred a dozen times per day the monthly penalty would approach 30 Gbyte.

While this amount of redundancy might be acceptable for offline storage because of the low cost-per-gigabyte of data tape cartridges, it is clearly unacceptable for online use due to both the considerable cost of RAIDed online hard drives and the reduction in unique capacity caused by storing duplicate media.

Thus, the database applied to a multimedia production system must allow multiple uses of a single piece of media, such as video, without forcing duplication which would unnecessarily waste online storage. Further, the database must be implemented in such a manner as to prevent that video clip, as an example, from being deleted from the online library until all users who have laid claim to it have released their reservations thereby freeing it for archiving or deletion.

*Multiple databases*
Multimedia news production systems are likely to use multiple databases for two compelling reasons:

*Independent systems*
A significant percentage of potential system purchasers will either not be able to or not desire to change to a multimedia news production system all at once. Instead, they will stage their implementation. Separate databases will facilitate purchase of the major separate system elements at different times.

*Task optimization*
A multimedia news production system will have some degree of segregation among its key tasks and major components. Thus, separate databases, each optimized to separate and different tasks, has value to, as two examples, minimize search time within the text database or allow media relationships to be tracked in the video media database.

*Data integrity*
Separate databases allow each major subsystem's data to be stored locally thereby protecting it against the catastrophic failure of any single element.

A multiple database implementation provides the benefit of product separability but it incurs the potential penalty of synchronization and communication between the databases. It is clear that the users need a global view of the entire system's data. Creating a news story and/or program is a multimedia project involving audio/video, text, and more. The journalists will want to search wire service text and then find video to match. Or, they may need to update an old story and need to see what resources are in house, whether they be graphics, animations, audio-only, audio with video or text. Moreover, having identified the various media items they need, they must create a structure which allows those items to be played out and perceived by the audience as a single integrated package.

Therefore, knowing that the users connected to the text media database must also know about audio/video media on the MediaServer's database and vice versa, there are three possible implementations which provide this capability:

*Master central database*
A master central database, either actual or virtual, would contain all the data from each of the independent databases. All transactions would be posted into the individual databases and then communicated to the central database. The advantage of this implementation is simplicity on the search side, one search of one database. However, writing data to the databases is less efficient since each transaction needs to be posted twice, once to the independent database and a second time to the central database. Similarly, transactions on the central database need to be reported back to the independent databases. Further, synchronization issues arise if any one of the databases is disabled for a period of time while transactions continue to occur on the central database.

*Cross-database communication*
In this approach each database application must be capable of querying the others. A search applied to one would trigger a search on the others which would, in turn, report their results to the primary inquisitor. Thus, a search by a user nominally connected to the text-server's database would trigger parallel searches on the online and browse video servers databases by their applications. There is no synchronization issue this way though the complexity of each independent database increases because of the requirement for it to communicate with the others.

*System-wide searches across databases*
A third approach is to have the client search engines capable of working independently across multiple individual databases. When implemented in this manner there is no need for synchronization of the data in the multiple separate databases though the links between them

must be synchronized. Access to the databases is assigned to the client workstations which can each be empowered as required. Thus, a text-only workstation could be provided which did not access all the databases while another workstation could perhaps be configured to access text and browse video.

## Workflow in a Multimedia Production System with a Database

Workflow and process management are not terms most broadcasters use. Workflow tends to be thought of in terms of a factory and process management as related to a chemical plant. The truth is, broadcasters have always planned their workflow and managed their processes. Broadcast workflow and process management practices have developed in each facility over many years and are, in many cases, more implicit than explicit. How things are done, who does them, in what order they are usually done, and the communication related to each one are all parts of the corporate heritage, each new staff member trained by an existing one.

Workflow and process management are usually the domain of the assignment desk and executive producer. They manage and control the production of each individual newscast as well as the day's overall work and preparation for the next day. The pressures of getting to air combined with living in a near-constant state of change make planning an ad hoc process at best in most stations. Likewise, process management usually means spraying water on the tallest flames first rather than being able to take time to understand and document the process so it can be readily understood, communicated, analyzed, and improved.

The transition to a server-centered multimedia news production system provides the opportunity to study and, if appropriate, modify workflow to optimize benefits from server-centered multimedia production and to incorporate and improve process management. An integrated multimedia news production system will have the database system at its very core, just as text-only newsroom computer systems do today. The database system will be used to catalog media but that will only be a small portion of its total value and importance to news production.

A typical workflow would include:

- Capture, storage, and automatic basic cataloguing of media
- Search and access functions
- Processing (editing video, writing scripts, etc.) and revisions
- Archiving

Workflow in such a system starts with automatic cataloging of all incoming media-based linked or embedded metadata, as is common with wire service text, or other information such as knowing that a video feed was recording from router source 17 and that this is always the feed from city hall. Time and data stamping will likewise be automatic as will information identifying the workstation through which the media entered the system and the user who was logged in and initiated the recording. The automatic catalog data is basic and should be supplemented by user-entered descriptive information which further describes the media.

The need for browse quality video drives the use of a separate server devoted to holding and providing access to that highly compressed digital video. Normal operation will be for browse and online recordings to be made simultaneously and in parallel. In order for work performed on the journalist's workstations to be passed back to the online media, the database must link these clips to each other and maintain that relationship during digital copy and move operations, especially when media is moved from the online storage to either a near-line automated library or offline.

Once the audio, video, text, or other media has entered and been cataloged into the system, the users have universal and immediate access to it. The database's search tools can be used to find material relevant to the task at hand. The database can constantly monitor incoming material and build a queue which notifies the user of additional available media. The journalist can create a script which would be cataloged and stored using the database and which may include reference links to relevant audio, graphics, stills, or video. The journalist could have browsed the lo-res video clips returned by the database search right on the desktop workstation used for creating the scripts to which that video is then linked.

The video portion of the story can be edited, based on the guidance in the script, using an online editing workstation connected to the online video server. The user would use the database to select the desired script and then open it which would automatically establish the links between the lo-res clips and the online versions. Clips which are currently not online could be automatically moved to online status and the editor notified of their availability by the database which tracks their status. Additional material can be searched for using the editor's access to the database and retrieved from the near-line and offline libraries as needed. The finished story would be cataloged into the database, perhaps by something as simple as dragging the story's on-screen icon into a folder on the workstation's screen, and be immediately available for viewing on any other workstation or playback to air. One result of cataloging the finished story would be to update the database which would, in turn, change the status of that story in the program's rundown from "being edited" to "ready for air."

In parallel with the above, the producer would be creating a rundown for the program and the assignment manager delegating staff and facilities.

The finished story, consisting of any combination of video, audio, text, graphics, etc., could easily be posted to the station's Internet web page using a separate server dedicated to that purpose (the separate web server provides increased security and segregates the web traffic load away from the actual broadcast production system). Better yet, it could be posted complete with the links to the media elements used in its creation. The web viewer would be able to see the video, hear the audio, and read the script. If the viewer wanted more information he could follow the embedded links to the original wire service copy, see some of the unused source video, or perhaps link to a spreadsheet detailing some statistical element of the story. This in-depth publishing to the web is possible because the database was used in the research, established the links between the media elements, and maintains them when the story is published to the web.

At day's end, or any other determined time, clips, scripts, wire service data, graphics, and any other media elements can be automatically or manually moved to a near-line archive with additional catalog data attached if desired. All these media elements remain in the database and can be search for and displayed as the result of a search with their status being indicated as near-line or offline. Retrieval can be automatic and might even be pre-arranged for "anniversary media." American broadcasters might want to automatically stage back to online status the Kennedy assassination media every November while British broadcasters might also stage video, audio, and scripts on C.S. Lewis that week since he died the same day as President Kennedy.

The database is the foundation of every step in the production process. It is used to store, catalog, manage, control, and structure every aspect. It is obviously critical that the database be designed for this demanding task.

### User-Based Database Design Customization

When researching possible database structures it soon became apparent that no two broadcast facilities could be expected to agree upon a common set of criteria. In fact, it is common for users within a facility to have great difficulty agreeing on the correct structure for a database to serve their shared needs. Thus, customization is a critical requirement of any database system which expects to be broadly accepted and implemented.

There are three areas where customization is essential:

*Data fields*
Each facility has unique needs. Some are as simple as the distinction between defining the people who run the field cameras to be: photographers, photogs, cameramen, camera operators, or shooters. Five terms for the same role. are more common than not.

Beyond the fairly simple, though often hotly contested, issue of what to name a particular field there is the issue of which fields to provide which goes directly to two other questions 1) which data is truly useful and 2) which data is perhaps useful but not worth the time to gather and enter it?

Designing a database is not a task to be taken lightly, decisions made during the design phase may have ramifications for many years in the future. Data not gathered and entered for the first six months of operation because it was not requested is most likely impossible to ever recover and input later. Contrariwise, data not entered because the time involved was onerous is equally lost yet for an even more regrettable reason.

It is probably obvious that only the end user can properly design the database for a particular facility. Consultation with appropriate experts will surely guide and assist the definition process but the basic wisdom and experience to define each broadcaster's unique needs and desires can only come from within.

*Required versus optional data entry*
Database designers have a tendency to want to make every data field mandatory entry. If the user does not enter data then progress is prohibited. There are two major problems with this. The first is that people quickly realize that satisfying mandatory entry text fields requires little more than a swipe across the keyboard. The mandatory entry requirement does not require intelligent data, just text. So, people quickly learn to stroke the keyboard and move on thereby defeating the requirement (though it should be noted that data validation techniques applied at entry time can force text or numeric data in a particular field or restrict numeric entry to phone number format). The second drawback to mandatory data entry is that it imposes a potentially significant operating speed penalty by consuming time for data entry when the user is trying to get the piece to air.

Collecting data is good, collecting too much data or collecting it in a way that actually slows down operations is not. It is disruptive. However, having said that the following ought to be considered. Sometimes slightly slowing down operations at one stage to speed them up dramatically at another may be a wise tradeoff. Mandatory data entry should not be dismissed simply because it adds a few seconds to every edit session or recording. The decision ought to be made in light of the total production process. Those extra seconds spread over individual edit and record sessions could potentially pay enormous dividends when searching for critically needed media in later years.

*Screen layout*
While it may initially appear trivial screen layout is far from insignificant. The layout of the screen can greatly affect both data entry time and the intelligibility of that data when subsequently read back.

*Client customization*
Another aspect of customization is the need to tune the system to the particular user and/or workstation type. A text-only remote workstation needs no ability to view and work with video or graphic media elements. Similarly, some individuals will have different privilege and access levels than others and the database must provide for this.

Once the initial database configuration is established there is but a single guarantee which can be offered, it will be changed. Repeatedly. One consideration for a database implementation is how it deals with changes such as deleting, adding, or re-naming data fields. If any change in the database destroys existing data that presents the genuine risk that media relationships will be lost because the fields upon which they have been built are eliminated. Thus, customize-ability is only one requirement users ought to have for their database. The second is data integrity during changes.

## Data Integrity

Once it has been gathered the database information must be protected. Losing it would bring the system to its knees by making it impossible to find the media.

Two major strategies are available for protecting the database data. The first is RAIDed storage. It serves the purpose but imposes a fairly high cost penalty. Further, the RAID system can never be taken offline because it is the only repository for the database data. Mirroring is the second, and generally preferred, approach to protecting the information in the database. Mirrored drives provide double the data access bandwidth when both are operating properly and drop to one-half that bandwidth when one fails. Service is easier because one drive can be taken offline briefly because the other remains online meeting user's needs. If one drive fails the other continues to provide full service though with slower response time due to the drop in aggregate bandwidth. The offending drive can be replaced and rebuilt while normal, though reduced bandwidth and slower response time, operation continues on the single undamaged drive. The data should be automatically backed up to offline storage such as a data tape or optical disk for even further protection.

## Administration

Any media library needs some degree of administration, a server-centered digital one will be no different. Most facilities will likely choose to appoint an administrator or librarian who will be responsible for the modest level of administration which a well designed system will require. Some of the key tasks which will fall to the librarian will include:

*Storage space allocation*
The system will not have infinite space, therefore, the available online storage capacity must be allocated to assure that, for example, the sports department does not fill it all with football games nor that the weather department does not consume the entire system's capacity with storm footage. Again, the database is the key.

The librarian/administrator will research the needs of the production staff, storage capacity will be assigned based on the research. Allocation specifics are likely to change periodically based on the dynamics of news gathering. During major sports playoffs more space would probably be assigned to that department and online allocations to other departments reduced.

*Archiving policy*
Without a clear and well-enforced archiving policy the system's online storage will fill rapidly thereby placing significant constraints upon operations. The archiving policy, derived from research within the department, must specify how material may remain online before being automatically archived, how the owner of that media will be notified before the media is moved from online status, and what procedures must be followed to retain the media online.

A similar policy will be needed to address near-line to offline transitions where media is removed from the automated robotic archive. The policy must address how and where the removed media is retained and how it should be retrieved to online status.

The archiving policy might even require each media element to be approved before archiving in order to verify the worthiness of the item and to assure hat it has been cataloged in such a manner as to facilitate eventual retrieval.

*Database quality assurance*
Garbage in garbage out is an ancient truth in the computer world. It applies with a vengeance to databases. If every story about the President of the United States is cataloged solely as "Clinton" the returns from a search will be so copious as to be unusable. In order for the database to actually provide the power it offers the users must provide a reasonable set of information for each and every media element. Much of this will come from the associations of completed video stories with scripts whose text can be searched and link back to the video. The same is true for voice-overs and announce tracks, stills, graphics, etc.

As mentioned above, it is not difficult for the users to "cheat" the data entry process (though well designed content trapping can help greatly). The librarian would do well to spot check data entry from users to verify the usefulness of their input.

## External Access

One often mentioned benefit of powerful database capabilities linked to a server-centered multimedia production system is external access to the data — not external access solely for employees of the company, but access to non-staff members. One aspect of that access was discussed above — web publishing. One of the greatest benefits of the web is the relative ease with which a firewall is established to protect data which the broadcasters does not want to make available to the general public. But, what about data which might be sold or shared between broadcasters or other media organizations? Though a detailed analysis of this area is beyond the scope of this paper two key issues merit mention:

*Security*
A broadcaster's media is such a valuable asset, access is not to be given lightly nor without assurance that those given access will either be responsible in their use or be prohibited from any damaging actions. The database and the media must be protected through high-reliability security which regulates both access itself and privileges once access is granted.

*Billing*
One way to exploit the value of the media is to sell, rent, or even barter it. The famous "Zapruder" footage of the Kennedy assignation has produced revenue for years. A station may choose to sell media permanently or rent it for a limited period. Or, the station might exchange it for a return favor in the future, which might turn out to be far more valuable than cash payment now.

## Criteria for Selecting a Database Engine

*Industry standard*
The engine should be a broadly supported one or, better yet, an official industry standard-for a number of reasons including: long term supportability, availability of interfaces, availability of applications, availability of administrators, etc. The selected database engine must support industry standard APIs such as SQL or an equivalent in order to easily provide external access to the data.

*Multiple data types*
The database engine should have an underlying architecture capable of handling multiple data-types including all those listed above in the section on media types. Further, the system must be extensible to new media types or combinations of media types.

*Scaleability and extensibility*
The database must be scalable to accommodate a wide range of system sizes. Typical news production systems range from under fifty workstations of all types to several thousand in a few facilities.

*Top level application*
The quality of the Asset Management application which runs on top of the database is the ultimate determinant of the suitability-to-task of the underlying technology. It is this top level with which the users must contend every minute of every day. It is the top level application which will either succeed or fail to fully exploit the incredible power of a database coupled to a multimedia news production system.

## Conclusion

A high-powered and well designed database system is the essential and enabling core of a multimedia news production system. The database ties together all the individual components of the system, allows cataloging and finding media elements and the relationships between them. A great percentage of the production system's power, flexibility, reliability, and capability will depend upon careful and thorough implementation of the system's database. The broadcast industry will benefit greatly from continued developments in commercial database technology already in use and those on the near horizon.

## Author's Note

The author wishes to thank the following Avid colleagues for their assistance in preparing this paper: John Chapman, Larisa Fay, Massimilliano Gaspari, Ben Golub, Richard Hennessy, and Adrian Scott.

=====

About the author: Stevan Vigneaux is director of broadcast industry marketing for the Broadcast Group within Avid Technology, Inc. of Tewksbury, Massachusetts USA. His responsibilities include: market analysis along with product requirement research and specification for Avid's Broadcast Group. Immediately prior to this position he was responsible for product development and marketing of Avid's NewsCutter editor and the Digital News Gathering server-centered news production system. Prior to Joining Avid, Stevan was product marketing manager for Production Systems Products (digital switchers, effects, stillstore, editor, router, etc.) for Sony Broadcast's U.S. operations. Stevan has also been chief engineer for two television stations and has served on several SMPTE and NAB committees including chairing the Time and Control Code Working Group. He holds a bachelor of science degree in electrical engineering from Boston's Northeastern University.

# *A Common Information Structure for Broadcast Applications*

**Jerry Boetje, David Collier**
**Sony Electronics, Inc.**

**Defines an information structure which independently captures the compositional and representational aspects of broadcast scheduling and material management.**

## *Abstract*

This paper defines an integrated data structure supporting the management of events, material, media, and playback resources. The structure supports any number of levels of abstraction for dealing with the complexities of modern broadcast, editing, and newsroom applications. The structure separates the compositional aspects of broadcast operations (the pieces that make up a program or story) from the representational aspects (the material that manifests the specified compositional pieces). As such, it differs significantly from other industry attempts to provide a unified data structure[1] which do not separate the programmatic intent from the actual material which implements that intent. The data structure is a simple, two-level information structure where the levels are similar to each other, creating a recursive structure for operating within the commonly accepted abstractions of the industry such as rundown, event, story, program, pod, schedule, and channel as well as new abstractions that meet the needs of an increasingly complex industry. Sequencing constraints may be applied to elements in a time-independent manner. In addition, this two-level recursive structure is independently applied to both the compositional and representational aspects, supporting a rich expressiveness for planning, operating, and reporting the actions of a complete broadcast operation.

1. For example, the Open Media Framework Interchange (OMFI) created by AVID Technologies.

## Introduction

Computers are ubiquitous in today's broadcast industry. Automation systems provide frame-accurate control of equipment; non-linear editors assemble material without the restrictions of tape-based linear systems; traffic systems deal with the complexities of scheduling commercial and spot play; computer graphics systems create new video effects and illustrations; news systems edit scripts, tie them to clips, and provide searchable archives. However, the increasing prevalence of these independently designed computer-based systems does not automatically guarantee the smooth integration of these systems into a coherent, unified broadcast operation. On the contrary, we more often find that these systems cannot "talk" to each other without creation of specialized "gateways" which attempt to translate among systems. The analogy to the hardware world is as if there were no RS422, SDI, or CCIR601 standards but at least everyone was using the same kinds of wire. A customer's only alternative is to purchase "single-vendor" systems which support their own internal dialects and usage conventions, forcing the customer to discard their investment in existing applications.

If we step back and examine these integration problems from the perspective of computer science, we find that there is no unifying model for integrating and managing the information and intent contained in these various systems. Much of this is, of course, historical. Computer systems were introduced over many years to handle different aspects of a broadcast plant. And before computers, each area of broadcast had its own set of terminology whose meaning is very context-dependent. For example, the terms material, media, clip, spot, pod, element, and event all mean more-or-less the same thing depending on the specific operational context. Similarly for the terms break, event, edit, and transition. Depending on context, the same word (event) can be used with such different meanings as "thing to play" or "play a thing". With this historical semantic stew as background, a necessary step for further integration is to discover a common information structure and processes which unify all of the informational and operational aspects of general broadcast systems. This paper proposes such a structure.

The concepts and processes proposed in this paper are grounded in the worlds of both broadcast video and computer science. From computer science, work in knowledge representation and planning systems provided the theoretical foundation. Sony's long and continuing involvement with all aspects of broadcast video provided the equally necessary practical insights. Much of the early work leading to this paper found its way into Sony's Transmission and Automation Systems (STAS) debuted at NAB96.

## Approach

We first introduce the concepts of the information structure, showing the relationships among scheduling, composition, and representation. These concepts are demonstrated by using several common situations encountered in a broadcast plant to show how different aspects of the model are used to handle each. Following the examples, we discuss some of the model's computational properties, and provide an object-oriented description of the model. The paper concludes with a discussion of future work based on this model and a set of appendices providing additional technical information, a glossary of broadcast terms and their meaning in the context of the data model, and a bibliography of related work.

## *Definitions*

**Constituent**

A constituent is the umbrella category for the types of data structures in the model. All constituents share certain attributes and behaviors. In object-oriented terminology, constituent is the abstract superclass of the model's components.

All constituents have the following attributes:

**ID.** A globally unique identifier which may be used to reference or retrieve the constituent from anywhere in the system.

**Name.** A human-readable designation for the constituent.

**Temporal Specification.** A specification of the starting, ending, and duration values.

**TrackSet.** A set of tracks defined by the constituent. The Track Set can have any number of tracks of any number of types.

There are three specializations (types) of the fundamental constituent. Each specialization models the behavior of one aspect of broadcast systems. For purposes of composition, each type can be composed from other members of that type.

**Element**

Elements are a special type of constituent used for scheduling actions such as play a clip, trigger a GPI, start an effect, or choose among alternatives. Elements are different from other constituents in that they are not bound to specified times but may be organized in a time-independent manner. This is particularly important for implementing the specification and handling of live events, default actions, and alternative choices. Elements can be represented by Material.

**Material**

Material is a kind of constituent that represents the actual signals or specific action that should play. For example, material may be the signal in a turnaround feed or the content of a syndicated program. In a digital sense, it is "the bits" without regard to where the bits are stored or where they come from. A material may also be a specification for a trigger action ("Take") although the specific GPI line, for example, is not specified. Material may be represented by Media. Material may also be non-A/V data such as Conditional Access data or scripts destined for a teleprompter.

**Media**

Media is the constituent which represents the physical manifestation of material. It can be magnetic tape, files on a hard disk, an incoming signal feed, a GPI trigger line, or any other physical representation of material.

### Constituent Variables

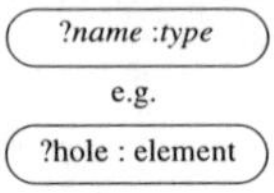


**FIGURE 1. Variable Naming Conventions**

A constituent variable is a kind of placeholder constituent which can be bound to a real constituent at a later time. There are three types of constituent variable corresponding to the three types of constituent. Constituents can only be bound to variables of the same type. Constituent variables have neither compositions nor representations. Constituent variables are bound to constituents via association relationships where the relationship is defined as equality.

The naming convention for constituent variables is *?name :type* where name is a user-chosen label and type is one of element, material, or media.

Constituent variables, in addition to substituting for a single constituent, can take the place of a list of constituents. This is indicated by concatenating the '[]' symbol to the end of the variable's type indicator. Such a constituent variable can take the place of any number of constituents of that type. The next section illustrates how constituent variables can be used to construct common, re-usable patterns of broadcast elements.

### Constituent Relations

Constituents may relate to each other in several different ways. A constituent relation is a three-way relationship among constituents such that the relation is defined between two constituents and that relation is valid in the context of a third (which may be one of the pair). The presence of the context constituent may introduce dynamism into the information structure in that, for some situations, the meaning of the structure at any point can be completely determined only by knowing how that point was reached in traversing the structure.

There are three different ways in which constituents may relate to each other.

- Composition

  This relation defines the set of subcomponents of a constituent and may provide additional information such as time base or track mapping. Composition defines a child-parent, part-to-whole relationship. A composition is defined in the context of the parent constituent.
- Representation

  This relation defines how a constituent may be manifest by another constituent. The second constituent contains sufficient information and data to completely manifest the intent of the first constituent. Representation defines an equality relationship in time and track sets. A representation is defined in the context of the constituent whose representation is being defined or a compositional ancestor of that constituent.
- Association

  This relation defines arbitrary ordering relationships among constituents of the same type. Usually, associations are created between sibling constituents but are not restricted to siblings. The context of associations is usually the parent of the siblings involved. It may be an ancestor constituent of the siblings in the data structure.

**Mapping.** Constituent relations define two distinct mappings between constituents. One relationship, time base transform, defines how to transform between the time specifications of each constituent. A second relationship, track set transform, defines how to select and merge tracks of one constituent into the tracks of the containing constituent. The time base transform is reversible (can go in either direction). The track set transform may not be reversible. For example, the track set transform may specify a mix-down of four audio tracks into one.

### Composition

A mapping of a set of (one or more) constituents into another as parts of a larger whole. For example, a pod has several elements composed into it. A composition provides a complete definition for the construction of a constituent from other constituents of the same type. The composed constituents are "contained by" the parent constituent. A contained constituent's as-composed duration will be less than or equal to the duration of the containing constituent. The composition must supply mapping functions for the time base and track sets of each constituent into the parent constituent.

**Context.** The context of a composition is the parent constituent of the composition. This is the simplest of the context specifications in that it is independent of any dynamic behavior. The definition of the composition does not depend on how the parent constituent was reached in traversing the structure. This means that a compositional structure, no matter how complex, forms a finite-state machine - the simplest of all computational models. A resulting property of the composition structure is that it can be statically analyzed for completeness and consistency.

**As-composed duration.** The composition of several constituents into a larger whole has the property that the combined duration of the constituents, as mapped to the parent, equals the as-composed duration of the parent constituent. It follows that, since the context of a composition is the parent constituent, the as-composed duration is dependent only on the specific composition without regard to structure traversal.

**Containment.** Containment refers to the ability of one constituent to use another as a portion of its content. The data model enforces a containment restriction that constituents can contain only constituents of the same general type.

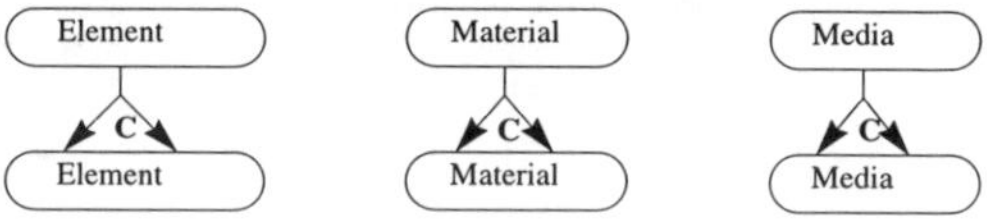


FIGURE 2. **Constituent Containment Relationships**

### Scheduling Hierarchy

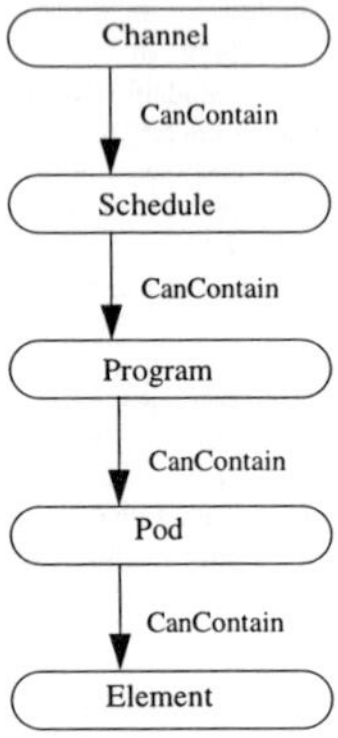


FIGURE 3.
**Containment Hierarchy**

Scheduling constituents are arranged in a hierarchy defining what kind of constituent can contain another. The hierarchy is defined by current broadcast conventions of terminology and usage and is not a fixed requirement of the data model. The implication of the hierarchy is that a scheduling constituent at some level can contain constituents of that type and ones lower in the hierarchy. For example, a pod can contain elements but not programs.

**Element.** An element is the lowest level of scheduling component. An element can contain only other elements. This situation occurs for example in the specification of an editing sequence, a particular grouping of related spots such as a donut, or a choice of alternative elements.

**Pod.** A pod is a grouping of short-form elements (spots) into a commercial break.

**Program.** A program is a grouping of long-form elements and pods into a broadcast segment (typically an hour or half hour). Programs are also known as rundowns in news operations.

**Schedule.** A schedule is a grouping of programs, pods, and other elements into a meaningful broadcast unit such as "Prime Time" or "Morning News". Day schedules are often built from other schedules.

**Channel.** A channel is a grouping of schedules and other subordinate elements into a continuous stream of input or output. Channels may be grouped into other channels. For example, in a multi-channel facility, a transmission channel may be formed from several different facility channels during a broadcast day.

### Representation

Constituents can be represented by other constituents. For a constituent to represent another means that it has the property of being able to manifest the intent of the represented constituent. For example, a tape cassette is a media which can represent a material constituent.

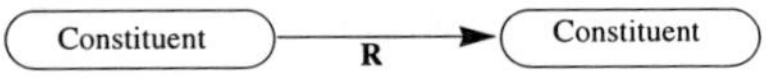


FIGURE 4.
**Basic Representation**

In this model, a constituent may be represented by one other constituent not of that type. The restrictions are illustrated below. Note that the representation relation is transitive. That is, an element can be represented by a material which is in turn represented by a media. It is correct to assume that the media can represent the element.

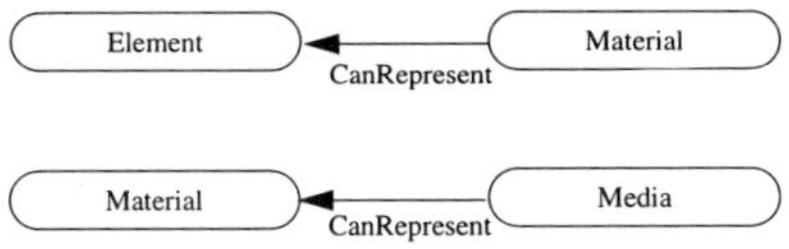


**FIGURE 5. Representation Relations**

**Context.** The context of a representation is the "represented" constituent or one of the represented constituent's ancestors in the composition hierarchy. Unlike composition, this context specification is dependent on the dynamic behavior of the structure-traversing algorithm. In other words, the definition of the representation does depend on how the represented constituent was reached in traversing the structure. This means that the traversing algorithm must at least implement a form of push-down automaton (a finite state machine combined with a stack) – the next level of complexity beyond a finite state machine. A resulting property of the representation structure is that it can be statically analyzed for completeness and consistency.

**As-represented duration.** The representation of one constituent by another has the property that the duration of the representing constituent, as mapped to the represented constituent, equals the as-represented duration of the represented constituent. It follows that, since the context of a representation may be anywhere in the represented constituent's composition hierarchy, the as-represented duration is dependent on the traversal history of the information structure.

**Association**

An ordering relationship between a pair of constituents, usually used in the context of a composition to provide relative ordering information between sibling constituents in the composition. For example, three elements are composed together where the first two are audio-video elements and the third is a GPI trigger. While the composition defines that all three make up the parent, associations are used to specify that the GPI element and the first a/v element start together (the GPI triggers the first element) and the second element starts sometime after the first (e.g., an offset voice-over). Note that associations are independent from any time base specifications.

**Context.** The context of an association is the parent or ancestor constituent of one of the associated constituents. It is recommended practice that associations be used between constituents of the same type in order to avoid significant computational complexity.

**Mapping.** Associations define only ordering relationships between constituents, hence they do not support the mapping functions of the other types of constituent relations.

**Proxy Relations**

Any constituent can have at most one composition and one representation. However, it is also necessary to accommodate the possibility that some constituents might have alternative compositions or multiple representations. Alternative compositions occur in elements when there are alternative possible actions in a playlist, for example, following a live event. Multiple representations occur in elements where there may be several materials which represent the element (see "News @ 11" on page 9) or in material where there may be multiple tapes ("clones") that each store a copy of the desired program. The model handles this situation by introducing the concept of a proxy relation.

**Definition.** A proxy relation is a container for a set of possible relations of the same type. The proxy appears to any client to be a constituent relation in terms of the methods and attributes it exports. However, in addition to the contained relation set, the proxy also carries a set of rules for determining at runtime which relation, if any, is appropriate. A proxy relation is owned by the creating constituent. It is this constituent which specifies the selection rules for the proxy.

Proxies which have not calculated a constituent relation to return are said to be "unresolved". Proxies may be resolved dynamically during active traversal of the structure or at any other appropriate time.

**Context.** The context of an unresolved proxy is the creating or owning constituent. The context of a resolved proxy relation is the same as that of the selected relation.

**Selection rules.** The rules may be implemented as a computer function, a set of logic rules, a pattern for a pattern-matching algorithm, or any other computable entity.

**Restrictions.** It is possible to have proxies for compositions and representations. Associations may not have proxies. A proxy is created by an uncomposed constituent, the parent constituent of a composition, or a represented constituent.

## *Unified Information Structure*

The general structure is a set of three compositional (recursive) hierarchies (element, material, media) linked via representations. Movement downward in the hierarchy

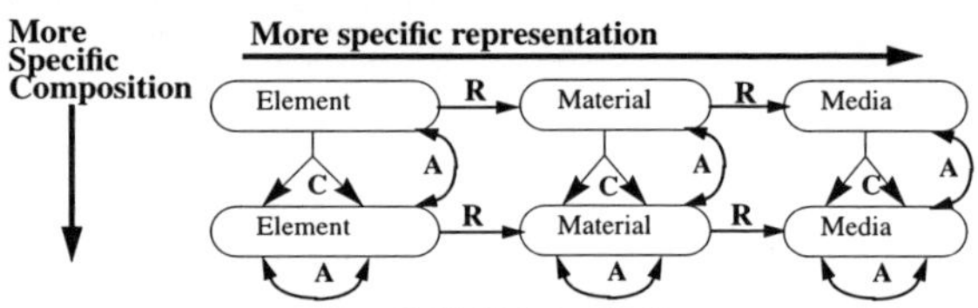


**FIGURE 6. Unified Information Structure**

reveals progressively more detail of the formation of a constituent. Movement to the right increases the detail of the manifestation of a constituent in time and physical reality. Associations enforce ordering constraints on constituents of the same type. Associations may cross multiple levels of composition to connect arbitrary constituents. Associations may also relate constituents not in the same compositional structure.

# *The Examples*

This section presents and discusses several examples and how they illustrate the model.

**News @ 11**

**Description.** News @ 11 is a spot consisting of three video segments: a lead-in (upcoming news broadcast later), a teaser (brief clip of a lead story), and a close (tune in at 11pm). This spot is played typically four times per hour during prime time every day. On one particular day, a breaking news story arrives at 10:05pm and will be the new lead story on the 11pm news.

**Problem.** How to change the News @ 11 spot to reflect the new lead story prior to the 10:26pm airing of the spot?

**What this illustrates.** This example is used as a standard to introduce several important features of the model: basic terminology, composition, multiple scheduling (re-use), and representation.

**Composition.** The News @ 11 spot has the following element composition:

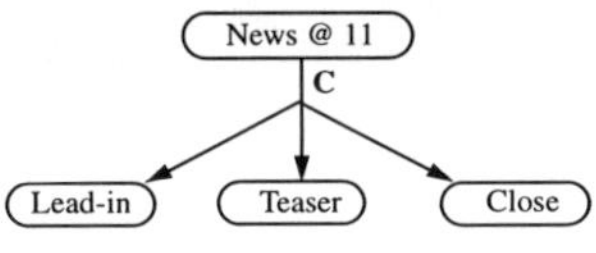


FIGURE 7. **News @ 11 Composition**

There is an implicit left-to-right play sequence of elements.

**Representation.** Prior to 10:05pm, the News @ 11 spot has the following representation structure:

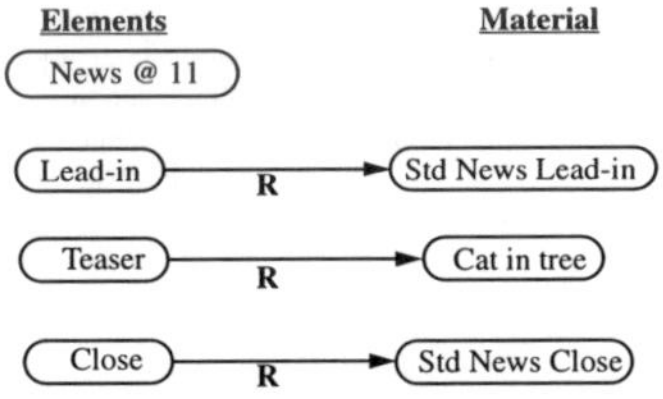


FIGURE 8. **News @ 11 Representation - 1**

There are two interesting features of this representation set. First, the News @ 11 spot itself has no representation. Hence any search algorithm seeking to locate a representation of the main spot must assemble the representations of its constituents at runtime. Specifically, to play the News @ 11 element the automation system must locate the elements Lead-in, Teaser, and Close and play their individual representations in order.

**Duration.** The News @ 11 spot has three durations: as-scheduled, as-composed and as-represented. The first may be specified for planning purposes. For example, this may be planned as a 20 second spot. The second and third are derived, and the values depend on the respective durations of the component spots. The as-composed duration is derived from the scheduled durations of the elements Lead-in, Teaser, and Close. The as-represented duration is derived from the durations of the representing materials. Usually the values of all three durations are close but are not required to be exactly the same.

**Multiple use.** The News @ 11 spot is obviously used in a number schedules. It is run every day and several times each day. Scheduling this spot is equivalent to composing it into other, higher-level element structures. The following illustrates what this might look like:

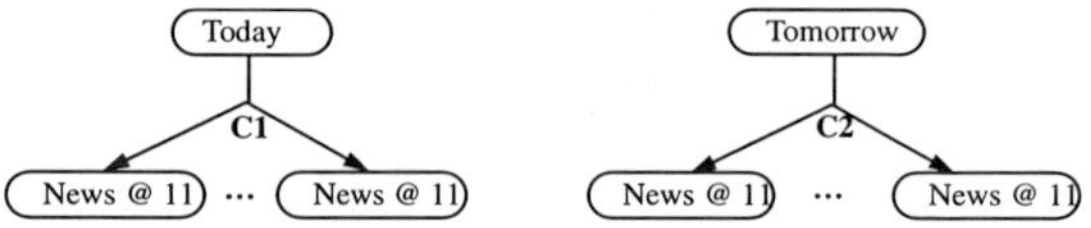


FIGURE 9. **Scheduling News @ 11 Elements**

Each mapping of News @ 11 into another element provides a unique context for the News @ 11 element. There are two direct implications from this mapping requirement. First, any structural change made to the News @ 11 element will be directly and immediately reflected in all uses of the element. Second, each unique context can be the context for a representation of News @ 11 or for its subordinate elements, implying that in every place it is scheduled to execute, it may have a different representation based on which schedule (day) it is composed into.

**Multiple representations.** There is another technique for providing News @ 11 with different representations: the use of proxy representations. Unlike specifying representations in the context of a composition, proxy representations specify multiple representations in the context of the element it represents. A proxy representation allows an element to maintain multiple possible representations with the choice made at runtime. In the specific example, the Teaser element is defined to have a proxy representation so that it can maintain multiple representations. Initially, of course, it has only one in our example.

**The scenario.** Finally we have defined enough of the model's features to construct a scenario that addresses the problem of changing the News @ 11 spot at the last moment.

At 10:05pm a news team arrives with footage of a breaking story with more audience value than the current cat-in-a-tree story. An editor calls up the stored footage for the News @ 11 promo (assume it is stored on a RAID server) and finds that the spot is in three segments. Since the Lead-in and Close will not change, the editor only needs to prepare new material to represent the Teaser element. From the new footage, she edits a new segment of about the same duration as the Teaser's scheduled duration and stores the new segment as an additional representation in the Teaser's proxy representation. Elapsed time 15 minutes:

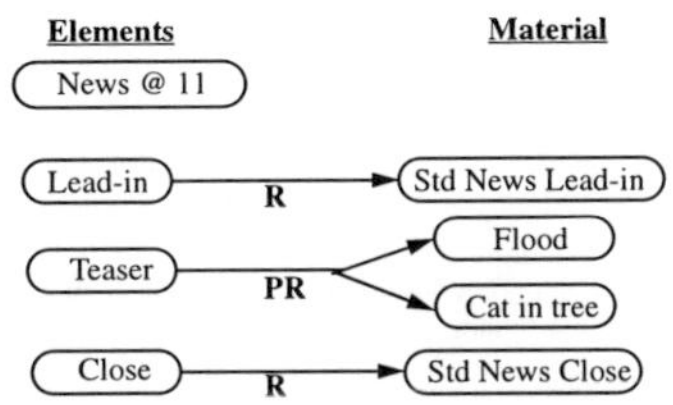


**FIGURE 10. News @ 11 Representation - 2**

A few minutes later, the automation system prepares the news @ 11 spot to run. It calls up the representations for the three component elements. There is a single representation available for each of the Lead-in and Close elements in the context of the Today playlist. However, for the Teaser there is a proxy. The Teaser element asks its proxy representation to select an appropriate representation. This proxy contains the selection rule that picks the most recently created representation and therefore returns the new clip just created by the editor. At 10:26 the promo runs with the new Teaser clip.

It's important to notice that because of the knowledge built into the information structure of this plant, only one person, the editor, had to take an action to change the execution of the spot. This edit did not involve changing the definition of News @ 11 so the scheduling department wasn't involved. And there was no change to the running playlist (the scheduled spot remained the same) so the operator didn't have to take any action. This simple example illustrates the model's ability to bring together broadcast automation, commercial insertion, and editing into a unified operation.

## Donut

**Description.** A donut is a commercial insertion specification between two spots, one of which is composed of two segments. The donut plays the first segment followed by the second (unrelated) spot followed by the second segment.

**Problem.** How to specify this arrangement as a standard pattern for re-use with different second spots.

**What this illustrates.** This example introduces the concepts of element variables and binding.

**Composition.** A donut has the following composition:

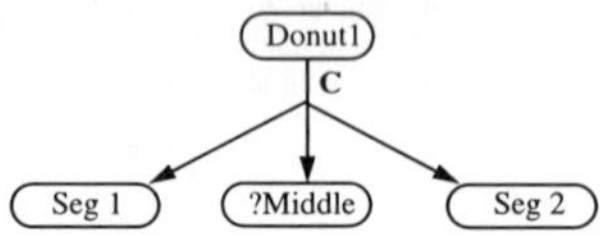


FIGURE 11. **Donut Composition**

The donut illustrates the use of an element variable in a composition pattern. This pattern specifies that Seg 1 plays followed by one other element followed immediately by Seg 2.

**Representation.** The specific representation is unimportant to this example. It is worth noting that the runtime representation of the variable element is determined by the choice of representation made by the element to which the variable is bound at runtime.

**Association.** The Donut1 element can be composed into any schedule just as any other spot. However, the binding of ?Middle is created by an association between ?Middle and the schedule element the broadcast programmer (or Traffic system) wishes to place between the two segments. This association specifies that the interval relationship is equality, therefore the new element can be substituted for ?Middle. The context of the association, which determines the active binding, is the element the donut is composed into. So this same pattern could be re-used in any number of other places with a different binding context in each. The following figure illustrates the association binding.:

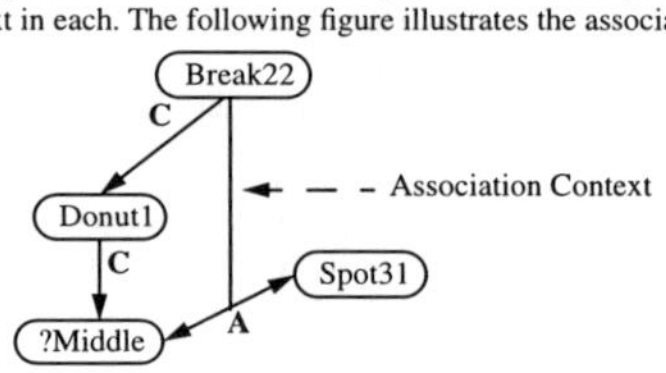


FIGURE 12. **Donut Composition**

By this pattern, during the execution of Break22 when Donut1 is invoked, Spot31 plays between Seg 1 and Seg 2 of the donut. Notice that Spot31 is not specifically composed into Break22 which may have binding implications for any representations or element variables contained within Spot31.

**Bookend**

**Description.** A bookend is similar to a donut except that the specification states that the first segment plays at the beginning of the commercial break and the second segment terminates the commercial break. There can be any number of spots in between the two segments.

**Problem.** How to specify the indeterminacy that the second segment ends the break no matter how many intervening spots.

**What this illustrates.** This example illustrates the use of Interval Algebra and its capability for expressing ordering relationships without requiring either exact or approximate time values. It also demonstrates the use of element types in scheduling.

**Composition.** A bookend has the following composition:

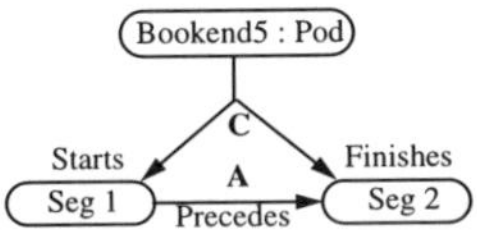


FIGURE 13. **Bookend Composition**

This structure is similar to the donut example but with some subtle differences. The first is that the type of the parent constituent is not the general element but is defined to be a pod, restricting the use of this pattern to compositions (schedules) where pods can be contained. The second is that there is an association relation defined between the child elements of the pod restricting their permissible ordering relations.

And finally, the structure defines specific interval relations which must exist among the various elements. The Starts relation between Seg 1 and its parent means that no other element can come between the beginning of the pod and the beginning of Seg 1. Similarly the Finishes relation between Seg 2 and the pod means that nothing can come between the end of Seg 2 and the end of the pod. These restrictions are implied but not enforced in a donut pattern. In addition, the use of the Precedes relation between Seg 1 and Seg 2 means that there is an indeterminate gap between the two which will be filled by other spots.

Use of these interval relations makes explicit and visible the semantics of the bookend pattern. As in the case of the donut, this allows an automation system to retain the semantics and aid the transmission operator when changes are made to a schedule. The conventional playlist, for example, would not explicitly indicate that Seg 1 must start the pod and the Seg 2 must end it or the contract is violated.

**Live event**

**Description.** The live event is the classic, hard-to-handle situation in broadcast. Most current broadcast systems depend in one way or another on the specification of time. But live events do not have exact time specifications (particularly duration) making it difficult for operators to manage. An operator will often find that they must continually update an estimate of the end time of a live event in order to keep the automation system from improperly cutting off the event or running long and not switching properly. The automation system itself must have complex, special-case "ripple rules" for understanding how to propagate time changes to downstream events.

**Problem.** How to specify the handling of live events where there is an incomplete time specification, and how the live event affects downstream events without resorting to special-case logic.

**What this illustrates.** This example expands the use of Interval Algebra and shows how to relate the derived endpoint (start/end) relations to SOM/EOM specifications. The example also shows how manual triggers can be treated as just another kind of element within the model and not handled as special attributes of events.

**Composition.** The following diagram shows the composition of a live event followed by a filler event of indeterminate duration followed by an event with a hard start time.:

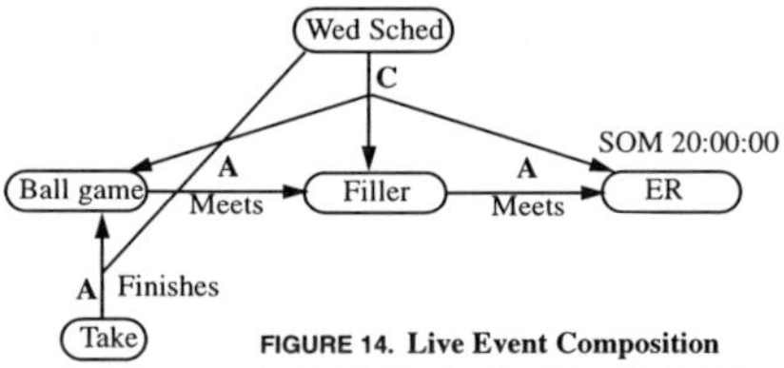


FIGURE 14. **Live Event Composition**

The use of the Meets relation in the two associations defines that, whatever the time values are, Filler starts exactly when the Ball game ends and that the Filler ends exactly when ER starts. Only the ER start time is defined in the schedule. The Finishes association between the Ball game and the Take element defines that these two element complete at the same time. Since we know that Take is manifest as a GPI without showing it here, we can infer correctly that the Ball game event is ended by the Take element.

From this, the automation system knows that it must maintain Filler in a ready state for the end of the Ball game which will occur when the operator presses the Take button. It can also trivially update the expected start time of Filler since it is always now. The system also knows the ending time of Filler (20:00:00) and can continually update the expected duration of Filler. However, if the Ball game is still running at 20:00:00, the system must switch to ER since it has a defined start time.

While this is a simple example, extending it just slightly creates situations that time-based automation systems find difficult. If the Ball game were followed by a series of events each defined to autofollow the previous one, a conventional automation system would require an approximate specification of the end time of the Ball game so that it could calculate the start times of each succeeding event. Having calculated these times, as the Ball game goes on, the automation system must continually ripple the time changes through the playlist according to its built-in set of "ripple rules". These rules must, among other conditions, recognize and differentiate between calculated start times (soft starts) and specified start times (hard starts). The one-time calculation of endpoint sequences from the interval relations produces a simple dependency chain which renders general rules unnecessary.

## Alternates

**Description.** Broadcast playlists or newsroom rundowns often contain alternates which an operator can choose at different points during operation. Often the alternates have different duration from each other and from the primary. This example combines a live event followed by a choice of alternatives followed by a fixed time event.

**Problem.** Specify this combination of live event, alternates, and fixed time event. Determine during the course of the live event which of the alternate playlists are still viable, i.e. there is enough time remaining before the fixed time event to initiate the alternate.

**What this illustrates.** This example builds on the live event example, showing the specification of alternates by use of proxy compositions and how the resulting endpoint relations can be used to prune the list of alternates. It also shows the use of disjunctive (logically or'ed) interval relations

**Composition.** The following figure modifies the previous example to show the compositional structure of alternates in a schedule. This also illustrates a two-level composition structure. The Take element is eliminated from this example for clarity.

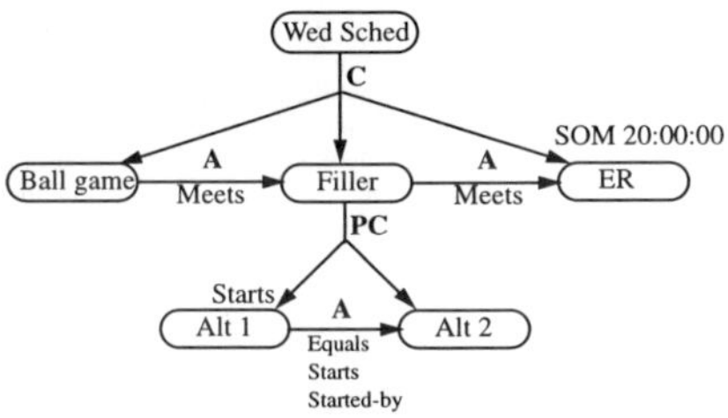


FIGURE 15. **Alternates Composition**

In this example, the first layer of composition behaves exactly as it did in the previous example. However, the definition of the Filler element has a different kind of behavior. By using the Proxy Composition to define Filler, we have explicitly stated that there are two entirely different ways, Alt 1 and Alt 2, to define Filler and that the choice will be made at runtime. In this case, the Filler element does not specify a scheduled duration; it's as-composed duration will be taken from the duration of the chosen element.

The set of interval relations within Filler defines how the two alternatives relate to each other and to their parent. Here Filler and Alt 1 are defined to start at the same moment. But Alt 1 and Alt 2 have a relation between them even though only one will play. This disjunctive relation specifies that both will start at the same time, but when one ends bears no relation to when the other would end. This captures explicitly the specification that the two elements may have very different durations. The runtime choice of Alt 1 or Alt 2 creates an equality relationship between Filler and the chosen alternative, defining at runtime that Filler ends whenever that alternative ends. And since the end time of Filler is known (20:00:00 by deduction from the hard start of ER), the alternative ends at that time also.

While this seems overly complex, in practice the processing of the interval relations is no harder than for any other composition. And the creation of the endpoint dependency sequence yields a surprising benefit. If the durations of Alt 1 and Alt 2 are known (as is usually the case), then, as the automation system monitors the progress of the end of the Ball game and updates the expected duration of Filler, it can automatically prune alternatives that can no longer be completed.

Alternatives appear in other broadcast operations under different names. Alternate playlists are common in scheduling. News stories in a rundown often have alternate versions which are chosen at runtime. Each of these can be handled in the same way.

## As-Run Log

**Description.** All systems must provide a log of exactly what material played and at what times. This example demonstrates how as-run logs are constructed in the model.

**Problem.** Given a schedule, construct an as-run log from the execution of the schedule.

**What this illustrates.** This example shows how to construct new material and media representations which define exactly what was broadcast.

**Composition.** The previous examples presented compositions of scheduling elements. Creation of an as-run log is performed by creating compositions of material and media as a result of executing the specified schedule composition. The following diagram shows a simple schedule composition with basic material and media representations.

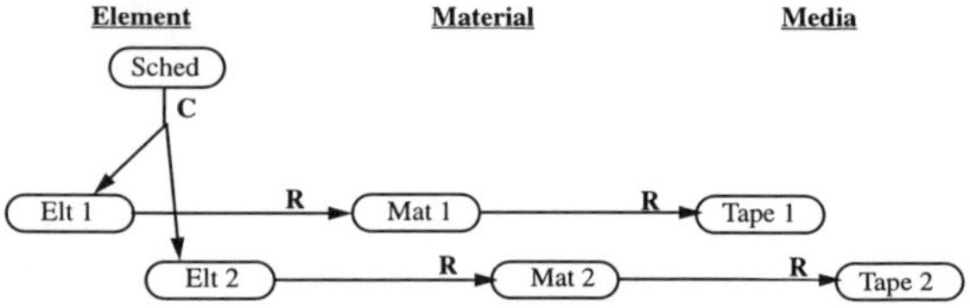


FIGURE 16. **As-run Log Initial State**

As-run log creation starts with the execution of the parent element Sched. The automation system first creates a new Material representation for Sched. The new Material will by definition be the combined as-executed signal. The system also creates a new Media representation for the new Material. This new Media might be a router crosspoint or switcher where the Material signal is manifest as a whole unit.

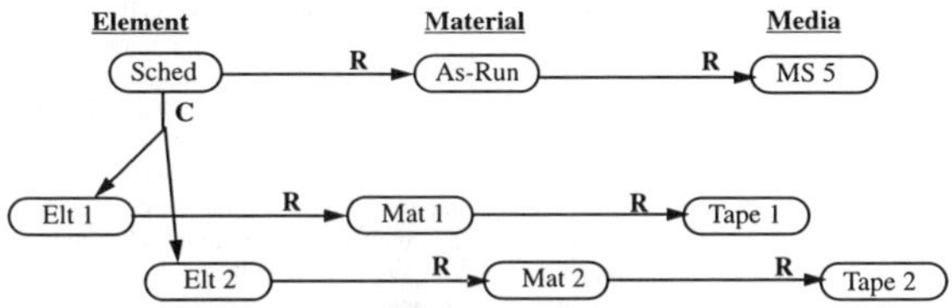


**FIGURE 17. As-run Log at Start of Sched**

At the start of Elt 1, the automation system creates new compositions on the As-Run material and the MS 5 media. These compositions map Mat 1 and Tape 1 to their respective parent constituents. The time base mappings of the compositions reflect the exact SOM/EOM of the child material and media.

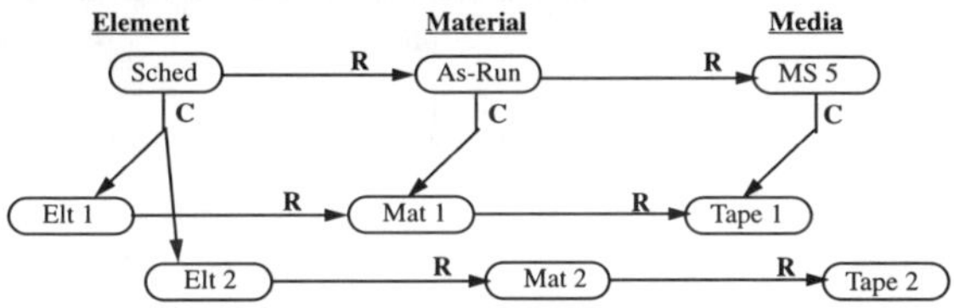


**FIGURE 18. As-Run Log at Start of Elt 1**

At the start of Elt 2, the automation system completes the material and media composition structures. As each element finishes, the system performs any additional accounting such as recording the actual EOM values in their respective compositions.

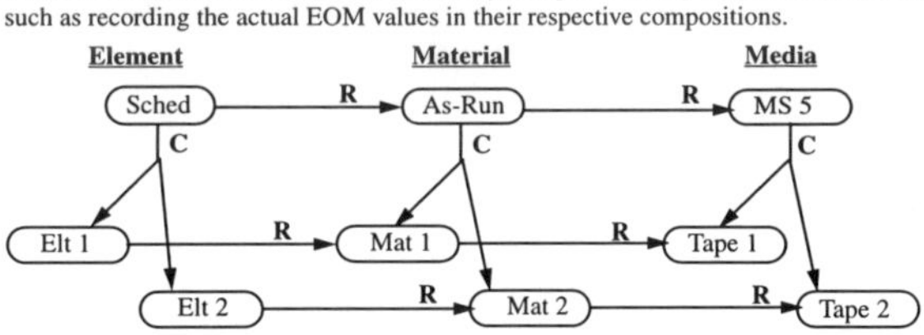


**FIGURE 19. Completed As-Run Log**

To produce conventional as-run logs, a system walks the tree rooted at the As-Run Material constituent. The tree-walk can be any search algorithm the visits the desired nodes in the correct order. For example, to list only the individual low-level constituents and the media which manifest them, the search visits all the leaf nodes of the Material tree and lists the corresponding Media nodes. To list the complete structure, the walk would be an in-order traversal of all nodes in the tree.

The creation of an as-run log via composition in the material and media domains is the same procedure which woiuld be used to conform an EDL with the exception that physical recording media would be used instead of ephemeral devices such as routers. To create an EDL, a system creates the composition structure of the material and media prior to conforming the composition into a new media and material.

## *Object-Oriented Description*

**Objects and Relations**

The following diagrams present a set of object classes which can implement the semantics of the model and a depiction of the relationships among instances of those classes.

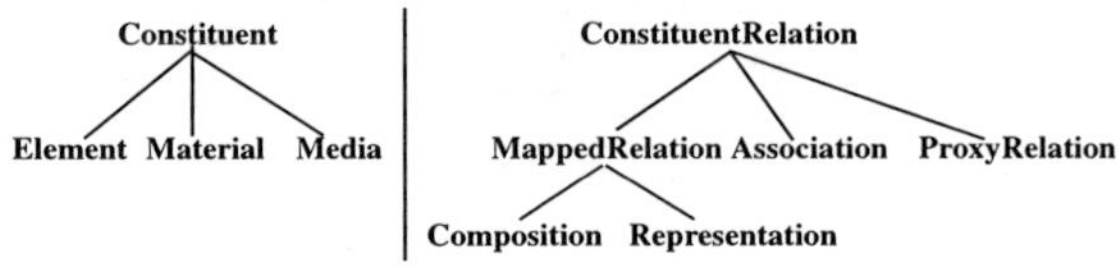


FIGURE 20. Class Hierarchies

The Proxy class is a special subclass of ConstituentRelation designed to be a container for instances of Composition or Representation classes. The Proxy class adds support for runtime selection from among a list of other relations.

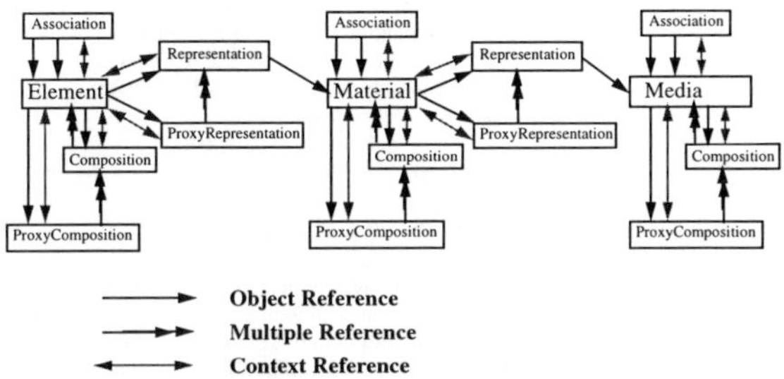


FIGURE 21. **Object Instance Relations**

## Persistent Storage

This object format is designed to be stored in a persistent object storage system defined by the SMPTE Recommended Practice: Edit Decision Data, which conforms to the Bento container file format.

## Future Work

One future area of research are the design of a High-level Broadcast Programming Language which carries the semantics of this model but is more approachable on a human level. A second, companion task is the design of a Virtual Machine (VM) which could execute the model. Once defined, it is possible to create compilers and interpreters for such a language and VM combination. Such a VM could form the basis of a new generation of automation systems.

## Conclusion

This paper has presented a brief look at an innovative information structure which captures the semantics of various broadcast operations into a single, unified system. The structure is both powerful in its expressive capabilities and simple to create, traverse, and manipulate. It provides a unifying terminology that supports integration of disparate, computer-based, broadcast systems. It is mathematically well-defined leading to fewer implementation special cases and behavior that is predictable and can be modeled. While we do not claim sufficiency for this model in terms of being all things to all broadcast, we believe that this model or one of at least the same level of expressiveness is a necessary foundation for unifying the web of broadcast complexity.

**Authors**

The authors are employees of Sony Electronics, Inc. in San Jose, CA. They can be reached electronically at

jboetje@sec.sel.sony.com
david@sec.sel.sony.com

## *Bibliography*

[1] Allen, J. 1983, Maintaining knowledge about temporal intervals. *Communications of the ACM* 26(11):832-843.

[2] Allen, J. 1991, Temporal reasoning and planning. In *Reasoning about Plans*, ch. 1. J. F. Allen, H. A. Kautz, R. N. Pelavin, and J. D. Tenenberg, eds. Morgan-Kaufmann, San Mateo, Ca., pp. 1-67

[3] Nebel, B. and Bürckert, H., 1995, Reasoning about temporal relations: a maximal tractible subclass of Allen's interval algebra, *Journal of the Association for Computing Machinery*, 42(1):43-66

[4] Ladkin, P. and Maddux, R., 1994, On binary constraint problems, *Journal of the Association for Computing Machinery*, 41(3):435-469

[5] van Beek, P. 1992, Reasoning about qualitative temporal information, *Artificial Intelligence,* 58:297-326

[6] Vilan, M. and Kautz, h. 1986, Constraint propagation algorithms for temporal reasoning. *Proceedings AAAI'86*, 377-382

[7] Macworth, A. 1977, Consistency in networks of relations, *Artificial Intelligence*, 8(1):99-118

[8] Bessière, C. 1996, A simple way to improve path consistency processing in interval algebra networks, preprint from *Proceedings AAAI'96*

## *Glossary*

**Constituent.** The basic building block of the data model. It can composed and be composed from other constituents. It can represent and be represented by other constituents. It can be associated with other constituents. It has a finite, non-zero, but possibly indefinite duration. It contains a possibly empty set of tracks.

**Element.** A kind of constituent used for the scheduling of other elements. It may compose and be composed from other elements. It can be represented by an element or by a material. An element is conceptually the simplest of the schedulable constituents.

**Material.** A kind of constituent used for the representation of elements and material. It may compose and be composed from other material. It can be represented by a material and by a media. Material is conceptually the intended signal (analog, digital, control, etc.) but is not the physical medium carrying the signal.

**Media.** A kind of constituent used to manifest material. It can compose and be composed from other media. It can represent material. Media is conceptually the embodiment of material.

**Constituent Relation.** A mapping of one constituent to another. There are three types of constituent relation: composition, representation, and association. The first two constituent relations may define mappings of timings and track sets.

**Composition.** A mapping of set of (one or more) constituents into another as parts of a larger whole. For example, a pod has several elements composed into it.

**Representation.** A mapping of one constituent to another where one constituent provides the data needed to support the intended execution of another. For example, when a system attempts to play a material, the representation of the material (a media) contains the desired signals which manifest the material.

**Association.** A mapping between two constituents which defines the relative ordering of the two constituents. For example, one might come entirely before or just meet the start of the other. Associations are commonly used to define relative orderings between sibling elements in a composition, but may be defined between any two constituents of the same type.

**Binding.** An equality relationship established between a pair of constituents. More specifically: 1) an equality between a constituent variable and a constituent of the same type (see "Constituent Variables" on page 4), or 2) an equality between a constituent and its representation. In the first case, the relationship is an Association where the stated relationship is equality and the context of the relationship is defined at the point in the composition structure where the binding becomes true. In the second case, 'binding' is a synonym for 'representation' (see "Representation" on page 6).

**Pod.** A kind of element. Used primarily to group spots (commercials, promos, PSAs, etc.) into collections that play in a station break.

**Program.** A kind of element. Used to group long form segments and pods into a larger grouping such as "Star Trek: The Next Generation" played at a regularly scheduled time.

**Schedule.** A kind of element. Used to group programs, pods, and other elements into longer segments such as "prime time".

**Rundown.** Same as a Schedule but used in newsroom operations

**Channel.** A kind of element. Used to group schedules, programs, pods, and other elements into continuously broadcast segments. The time base of a channel is always physical or "wall" time.

**Event.** A specific composition of one element into another. Usually refers to the lower level compositions in a schedule tree such as the start of a pod or the start of a segment of long-form material.

**Track.** An indivisible material which can only rendered on a specific type of hardware, for example, video, audio, closed-caption, control, or data. There may be multiple separate tracks in a material, but tracks themselves cannot be decomposed. Tracks are usually named with a leading type identifier followed by a number if there are several of the same type. For example, V (video), A1 (audio track 1).

**Track Type.** The generic type of hardware required to render a track, for example video, audio, closed-caption, control, or data. Under this model, any number of track types can be specified corresponding to the resources needed to render the signals.

**Track Set.** A collection of tracks.

## *Appendix A - Review of Interval Algebra*

Interval Algebra provides a mathematical framework for manipulating ordering relationships between finite segments of time (intervals) without requiring actual time values for the start, end, or duration of an interval. Since all material in the broadcast industry has bounded duration, the mathematics of Interval Algebra can be applied to the scheduling of broadcast events. This section reviews the basic elements of the Interval Algebra. More specific information can be found in [2],[5],[6].

### Purpose of Interval Algebra

The aim of Interval Algebra is to discover the maximal set of ordering relationships among the starts and ends of the intervals. In other words, to calculate the ordered sequence of starts and stops for the events in a broadcast schedule. The ordered sequence includes the groups of start and stop points which happen at the same time (events that autofollow or events such as GPIs which trigger other events). It is also possible to compute multiple possible sequences given some sets of relations. These frequently occur in broadcast event lists as alternative sets of events which will be chosen at run time.

### Intervals

**Interval** is the term given to a finite segment of time, regardless of whether the interval specifies exact time values. The formal algebra defines an interval to be a pair of **endpoints**[1], $(X^-, X^+)$, which can have real values and $X^- < X^+$. Intervals are **instantiated** by assigning values to the endpoints of the interval.

In video, clips are bounded segments of video containing one or more **frames**. Frames are counted using a mechanism called **timecode** which approximates real values of time. The first frame of a clip is the **SOM** (Start Of Message); the last frame is the **EOM** (End Of Message). From historical convention, a single-frame clip is defined such that SOM = EOM. So for purposes of matching the Interval Algebra correctly, the following definitions hold: $X^- = \text{SOM}$, $X^+ = \text{EOM} + 1$.

### Interval Relations

**Basic Interval Relations.** To be useful, Interval Algebra must do more than just provide a definition of intervals. The strength of Interval Algebra lies in defining how intervals relate, and how to manipulate those relationships.

1. In broadcast terms, the start and end of a clip or event.

There are 13 possible atomic relationships between any two intervals, X and Y. Note that most of these relationships occur in converse pairs such as "precedes" and "follows." Table 1 on page 24 shows this set.

**Table 1: Interval Algebra Relations**

| Interval Relationship | Symbol | Pictorial Example | Endpoint Relations |
|---|---|---|---|
| X precedes Y | < | xxx | $X^- < Y^-,\ X^- < Y^+,$ |
| Y follows X | > | yyy | $X^+ < Y^-,\ X^+ < Y^+$ |
| X meets Y | m | xxxxx | $X^- < Y^-,\ X^- < Y^+$ |
| Y met-by X | mi | yyyyyy | $X^+ = Y^-,\ X^+ < Y^+$ |
| X overlaps Y | o | xxxxx | $X^- < Y^-,\ X^- < Y^+$ |
| Y overlapped-by X | oi | yyyyy | $X^+ > Y^-,\ X^+ < Y^+$ |
| X during Y | d | xxxx | $X^- > Y^-,\ X^- < Y^+$ |
| Y includes X | di | yyyyyyy | $X^+ > Y^-,\ X^+ < Y^+$ |
| X starts Y | s | xxx | $X^- = Y^-,\ X^- < Y^+$ |
| Y started-by X | si | yyyyyyy | $X^+ < Y^-,\ X^+ < Y^+$ |
| X finishes Y | f | xxx | $X^- > Y^-,\ X^- < Y^+$ |
| Y finished-by X | fi | yyyyyy | $X^+ > Y^-,\ X^+ = Y^+$ |
| X equals Y | ≡ | xxxx | $X^- = Y^-,\ X^- < Y^+$ |
| | | yyyy | $X^+ > Y^-,\ X^+ = Y^+$ |

**Disjunctions.** The 13 atomic relations define most of the usual specification of event sequencing in broadcast such as **meet** (autofollow) or **starts** (trigger). But there is limited expressive power in using just the atomic relations. The full algebra allows for all of the disjunctive combinations of the atomic relations such as <**precedes** or **meets**> (may or may not be a gap between the events). These disjunctive relationships express the complex orderings that exist in broadcast operations such as alternate or parallel playlists. There are a total of 8192 ($2^{13}$) such combinations including True (the relationship is unspecified) and False (there is no legal relationship).

**Tractable Subset.** There is a computational problem inherent in using most of the full Interval Algebra. Solving a complex set of disjunctive relationships to produce the sets of implied legal orderings is an inherently hard problem.[1] Obviously, this makes using the full algebra impractical. However, it is possible to keep the computation from becoming excessively long if the specifications only allow for a using a subset of the total set of relations. There is a **maximal subset**[2] [3] consisting of some 868 relations which reduces the computational load to polynomial time.[3] Fortunately, this subset is also powerful enough to express the needs of the broadcast industry.

## Binary Constraint Propagation

Given any set of intervals (clips), users only specify a few of the pairwise relationships among the members of the set. A trivial example is a set of clips in a commercial break where a user specifies which clip starts the break, which one ends it, and the sequence of other (autofollow) events in between. What is missing are the relationships between non-adjacent clips in the sequence. In order to correctly and completely specify the end-point sequence for this example, it is necessary to determine all of the unspecified relations as well.[4] Fortunately, Interval Algebra can use a simple algorithm, binary constraint propagation (BCP) [4], for filling in the blanks.

The algorithm for BCP is very simple. Organize the intervals into a matrix where the matrix entries are the interval relations between pairs of intervals. Any entry that is unspecified is set to True (no specified relation). This matrix has certain properties that make it possible to use a simple algorithm to close the relations[5]. First, the diagonal entries are all equality (interval X equals interval X), and the entry for any given row/column is the converse of the entry for the corresponding column/row (interval X **follows** interval Y implies interval Y **precedes** interval X). So the interval relation matrix is triangular with the equality on the diagonals.

Given these conditions, the matrix can be closed in polynomial time by repeatedly squaring the matrix until no entries change. A table lookup is performed in place of an arithmetic multiplication and the results are intersected instead of arithmetically added. Because of the nature of the matrix, the algorithm is guaranteed to terminate. Because of the subset chosen, the algorithm executes in polynomial time.[6]

The result of the closure operation is the full set of interval relations among all of the intervals. However, there is also interesting practical information which comes from the computation. Any remaining entries of True in the matrix mean that the user-specified

1. Technically, the problem is NP-hard which means that computing the solution takes time exponential in the number of intervals. It is easily possible to produce a set of relationships which would take days or weeks to solve.
2. Maximal means as big as possible. It does not however imply unique. However, this subset is both maximal and unique [3].
3. A polynomial time algorithm executes in a time which is proportional to the square, cube, or other such exponent of the number of intervals. Such algorithms execute in seconds instead of the days required by an exponential algorithm.
4. This is called the transitive closure over the set of relationships.
5. This operation produces the transitive closure of the constraint matrix. In other words, it will deduce all of the possible interval relationships that exist among the set of intervals. The closure is mathematically complete.
6. In practice, the algorithm terminates after 3-4 passes.

set of interval relations is incomplete and cannot be turned into a complete schedule. It also shows exactly which pairs are in doubt. If any entries are False,[1] then the user has specified an inconsistency in the relationships which must be corrected before the schedule is complete.

**Use of Other Algorithms**

There are other algorithms in the literature which can be used to provide a solution to the specified matrix. The principal alternative to BCP is Path Consistency (PC) [7],[8]. The distinction is that PC will find a single correct sequence of endpoints through the matrix where BCP will find all of them. The completeness of BCP makes it the preferred technique for video and broadcast since it calculates all of the possible paths including alternates and can identify any unspecified relationships. PC is useful during dynamic operations such as a user manipulating a schedule via a GUI where it is important to quickly determine if there is a feasible solution to provide feedback without having to calculate all of the side-effects.

**Endpoint Sequencing**

The final operation is to reduce this relation matrix to a sequence of endpoints (SOMs and EOMs). This sequence will be a list of the endpoints in the order needed to satisfy the interval relations. Note that some members of this list may be a cluster of endpoints denoting simultaneity. For example, events in an autofollow mode will create (EOM, SOM)[2] pairs to show that one starts exactly when the other one finishes.

Creating the sequences is a two-step process. The interval relation matrix is converted to a matrix of endpoint relations by a lookup process on each entry (one interval relation yields 6 endpoint relations). This matrix can then be topologically sorted to produce the final sequence. Note that the sort should take account of possible bifurcations in the endpoint relations[3] and may produce multiple sequences. Multiple sequences imply points of departure for alternate schedules where a run time choice is made. It may also be that multiple schedules converge back to a single endpoint which implies a re-joining of the schedules. In practice, both steps are reduced to one, requiring only a single traversal of the interval relation matrix.

## *Appendix B - Recursion in Data Structures*

In programming, recursion is defined as a process where the a function performs an action on the first part of the process input and then invokes itself on the rest of the input. The canonical example is the factorial function which multiplies its input by the result of applying the factorial function to the input minus 1. The technique is extremely

1. Note that the matrix squaring operation must terminate on any pass where a False value is detected. Otherwise, the entire matrix will end up in a contradiction (all entries False) and the most specific contradiction will be lost.
2. Remember that the convention is that the end of a clip is really at EOM + 1. The notation in this example is sloppy, since the real value pair should be EOM+1, SOM.
3. Such bifurcations are indicated when the endpoint relation is unknown ("?') in the literature. An unknown relation between a pair of endpoints means that the algorithm cannot determine whether one comes before the other or the two are simultaneous.

powerful when handling complex operations since it means the programmer only needs to program for the case of one instance of a problem and then use recursion to handle the rest.

A recursive data structure is one which is designed to be processed by a recursive algorithm. The simplest example of such a structure is a list; a corresponding algorithm would process the first element of the list and invoke itself on the rest of the list. For example, if the input is a list of numbers, a recursive algorithm to add up all the numbers in the list would look like:

```
SumList : (input theList)
    if not empty(theList)
        return FirstElement(theList) + SumList(RestOf(theList))
    else
        return 0
```

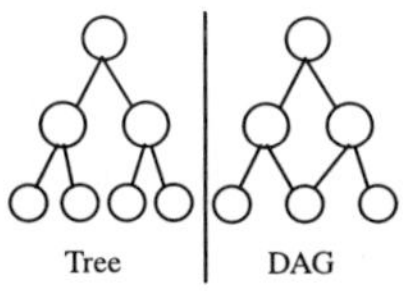


**FIGURE 22.**
**Recursive Structures**

Note that it's important to provide a termination condition for the recursive process just as it is for the more familiar iterative processes.

Many other data structures can be processed by recursive algorithms. The most typical are trees and directed acyclic graphs (DAG) although many others may be used. All share the property that to perform an operation on the whole is equivalent to performing the same operation on the constituent parts.

Because of the basic simplicity and transparency of recursive algorithms, it is advantageous to find a recursive data structure that will correctly and completely model a particular problem domain. A useful starting point is to examine the problem domain for constituents which can be composed from other constituents of the same type. The figure to the left illustrates a basic two-level recursive structure which can applied to a number of situations in broadcast video. For example, in editing, a finished piece is built from a number of smaller pieces of the same type (video clips). In broadcasting, a schedule is made from programs and pods; pods are made from spots, etc. News rundowns are made from stories which themselves may have alternate versions of the same story. All of these may be defined by a two-level, recursive data structure.

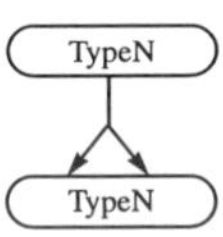


**FIGURE 23.**
**2 Level Structure**

Having started with a basic recursive structure (which will rarely fully capture the complex reality of the problem), it is possible to extend this model with additional recursive structures. These structures progressively combine the various aspects of the problem domain into a more complex structure which retains the underlying local simplicity of the recursive structure. For example, the following structure can define very complex relations among different components while remaining simple to process.

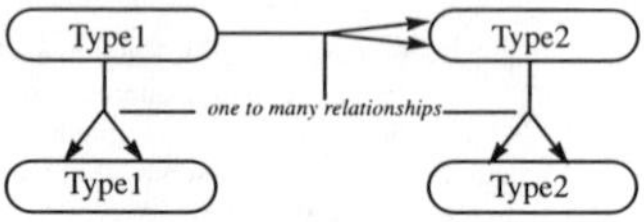


**FIGURE 24. Complex Recursive Structure**

While this picture seems deceptively simple, it's complexity becomes apparent after realizing that Type1 children can have relationships to any of the Type2 entities (parent or child) and that in either case, parents and children of either type can appear many times in different levels and different branches. The complexity can be further increased if there is a type relation between Type1 and Type2. For example, a Type2 may be a kind of (ako) Type1 meaning that they share some attributes and behaviors and may be used interchangeably in some operations. But underneath, the basic structure is extremely simple leading to simplicity of implementation.

A familiar example of the combination of simple recursive structures and recursive algorithms are fractals. Fractals have the property of being "self-similar", that is, a subpart of an entity looks very similar to the larger entity and this is true no matter how far the entity is divided. A branch of a tree is similar to a tree; a rock is similar to a mountain. Each of these can be described by the correct combination of recursive data structures and algorithms. In an entirely analogous way, the behavior and appearance of broadcast systems can be described by a combination of self-similar structures.

# The Professional Video Industry Needs a Standard, Over-The-Top Digital Audio/Video Expansion Bus

Alain Legault, Vice President - Product Development
Janet Matey, Marketing Manager
Matrox Video Products Group
Dorval, Quebec, Canada

## Abstract

The use of economical, general-purpose PCs in demanding professional video applications like nonlinear editing, graphics creation, animation recording, 3D rendering, video-on-demand and commercial insertion continues to grow. In these applications, specialized PC adapters are typically used to handle the massive processing requirements for transporting natural data types in real time. Commonly used sub-systems include: video I/O, video processing (DVE-mixing), video compression/decompression (codec), audio I/O, audio processing (EQ-mixing), mass storage interface, network interface and video-in-a-window console display. Although it is possible to accomplish some of these tasks with host CPU software and a single highly integrated adapter, most professional systems require more than one adapter.

How to connect these multiple video adapters together inside a PC is a question that system integrators have been wrestling with for many years. The problem is essentially one of data rate considering that:

- a single ITU-601 4:2:2 digital video stream = 21 MB/sec. (32 MB/sec. with key bus 4:2:2:4)
- eight 48 KHz - 16-bit audio tracks = 768 KB/sec.
- motion-JPEG compressed digital video stream at Betacam quality = 6 MB/sec.

This paper examines the limitations of commercially available busses in these demanding broadcast video applications, proposes the Movie-2 bus as a high-performance open-architecture standard that overcomes these limitations, discusses the Movie-2 bus in detail, and finally, presents a model of a typical nonlinear editing platform as an example of system-level Movie-2 bus implementation.

## The Bandwidth Problem

Through the use of specialized adapters, economical general-purpose PCs can be used in demanding professional video applications like nonlinear editing, graphics creation, animation recording, 3D rendering, video-on-demand and commercial insertion. Systems designers must provide the system bandwidth to handle the massive processing required to transporting natural data types in real time. The problem is essentially one of data rate considering that:

- a single ITU-601 4:2:2 digital video stream = 21 MB/sec. (32 MB/sec. with key bus 4:2:2:4)
- eight 48 KHz - 16-bit audio tracks = 768 KB/sec.
- a motion JPEG compressed digital video stream at Betacam quality = 6 MB/sec.

Commonly used sub-system adapters include: video I/O, video processing (DVE-mixing), video compression/decompression (codec), audio I/O, audio processing (EQ-mixing), mass storage interface, network interface and video-in-a-window console display. Although it is possible to accomplish some of these tasks with host CPU software and a single highly integrated adapter, most professional systems require more than one adapter. For example, a nonlinear editing system may require a codec card, a videographics card, a 3D DVE unit, an audio processor, a console display and mass storage and network interfaces. (Figure 1)

How to interface these multiple video adapters together inside a PC is a question that system integrators have been wrestling with for many years. Of course, the ideal solution is an open architecture that leads to a wide variety of different price/performance solutions from multiple vendors.

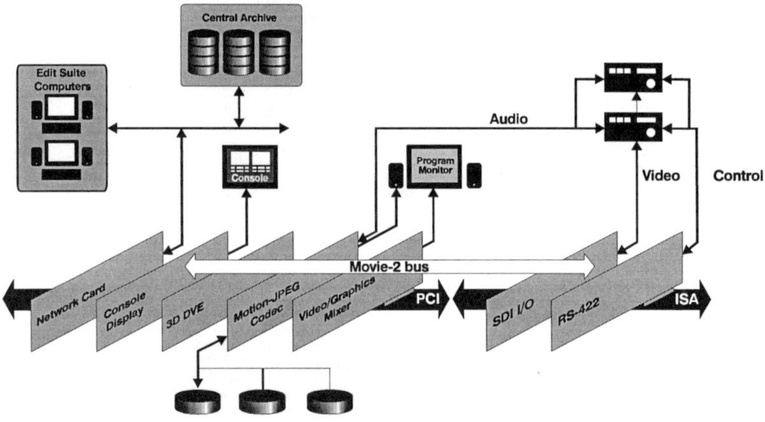


*Figure 1 - Typical PC-Based Multi-Adapter Nonlinear Editing System Configuration*

# Exploring the Alternatives

There are two ways to deal with digital video data types – through the system host bus and through a dedicated bus architecture.

## Host bus interfaces

Digital audio and video data can be communicated through the system host bus, but with this approach the bus bandwidth needed by the video stream(s) must be shared with the other common host-CPU activities such as interfacing with the system hard disk controller (SCSI or IDE), the graphics display device (GUI) and the network interface controller (NIC). Where the bus bandwidth is insufficient to handle the demands placed upon it, normal application response time diminishes and/or the video stream breaks. (Figure 2)

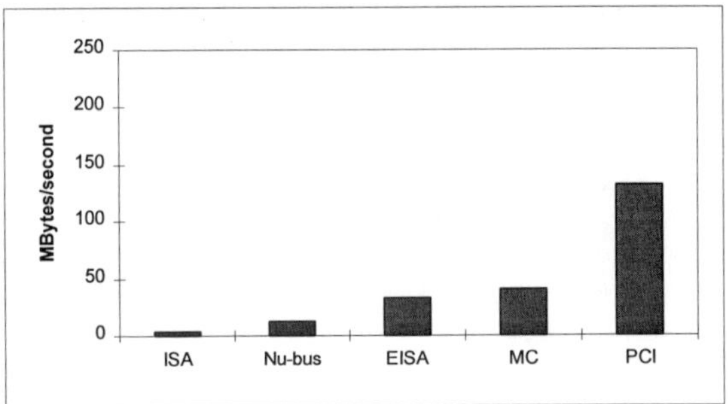


*Figure 2 - Maximum data throughput of various commercial busses*

***ISA bus***
ISA is clearly useless for professional video applications. Bandwidth is insufficient for uncompressed video or even high-quality compressed video data. Products using ISA can only communicate digital audio data over this bus.

***Nu bus, EISA and MicroChannel***
Nu bus, EISA and MicroChannel (MC) have been used successfully by a number of vendors over the last 5 years to send compressed video and audio data between adapters. EISA and MC even have enough bandwidth theoretically to accommodate a full, uncompressed digital video stream interface. In practice unfortunately, there is not enough bandwidth left for the rest of the application, which kills system performance.

The market is now demanding realtime A/B roll systems, lossless 13 MB/sec. compressed data streams, multiple audio tracks, powerful mass storage, high-performance graphics controllers and LAN interfaces. Clearly, these busses aren't good enough anymore.

***PCI bus***
At first glance, the advent of PCI bus with its 132 MB/sec. throughput would seem to be the perfect solution. A number of video chipsets are becoming available that can send uncompressed digital video information over PCI. Rather quickly, however, video equipment manufacturers found PCI's limits. Here's why:

Although the theoretical speed of PCI is 132 MB/sec., the effective bus bandwidth ranges between 40 and 80 MB/sec., depending on the chipset used on the motherboard and various PCI implementation factors. In addition, fast disks, high-resolution desktop displays and fast network cards require incremental bus bandwidth, leaving less bandwidth available to video adapters.

PCI transfers data by grouping the data into packets. Different agents alternately take control of the bus every 10 to 30 μsec. (depending upon their latency times) leaving enough time to transfer only a small data packet (approximately 3000 bytes) until the next transfer. Because video is synchronous, video data needs to be fed continuously. The higher the quality of the video and the more simultaneous streams involved, the more difficult maintaining continuity becomes. This inherent incompatibility creates substantial hurdles for those who want to interface professional-quality video through PCI. To integrate the bus design, manufacturers must devise complicated interfaces that require ASIC technology, FIFOs and buffering. The result is longer development cycles, greater expense and higher risk.

It has become clear that PCI can be used successfully to interface video adapters for some multimedia applications, but it is not ideal for professional video systems.

## Expansion busses

The alternative to commercial general-purpose busses are dedicated, over-the-top expansion busses. A few alternative proposals are available in the marketplace including VGA FC, VAFC, VMC and Movie-2 bus. (Figure 3)

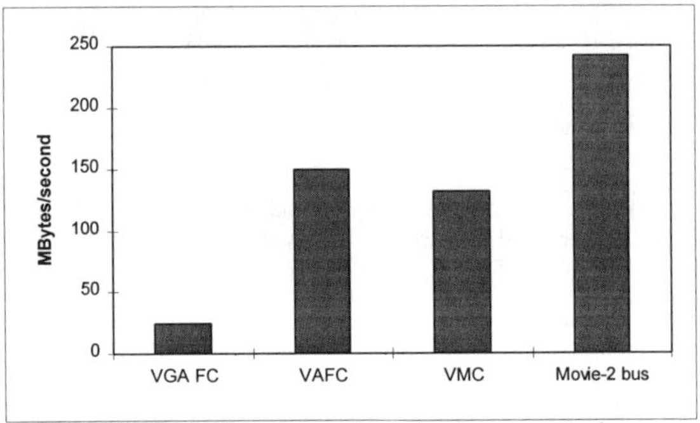


*Figure 3 - Maximum data throughput of various expansion busses*

***VGA FC -- VGA feature connector***
VGA FC, the first over-the-top expansion video bus used in PCs, is limited to 256 colors, has only one video bus and no audio support. It is of no use for professional video applications.

***VAFC -- VESA Advance Feature Connector***
VAFC is an enhanced version of the VGA FC. It offers the ability to interface 32-bit RGB with alpha or YUV without alpha, but still is limited to a single video channel and provides no audio support. Its primary application is in computer graphics.

***VMC -- VESA Media Channel***

VMC is closer to the needs of the professional video marketplace. It interfaces multiple video streams over a unified bus, similar to PCI. Video can be 32-bit RGB or YUV, and there is enough bandwidth for designers to implement an alpha channel and support for audio. When it was initially proposed, VMC generated some interest, but it has not garnered many adherents because, like a PCI interface, it is complicated and costly to implement. In addition, since both VMC and PCI exchange data through packets, some of the same problems exist in this area as well. Systems designers ask, "If PCI and VMC accomplish the same task, in much the same way, why design the same solution twice?"

***Matrox Movie-2 bus***

The broadcast and professional video industries have standardized on the ITU-601 specification. Virtually all video chipsets, board-level products and systems adhere to the 601 standard. This specification defines the video timings, the frequency of operation and the video data format needed to communicate digital video information. The Movie-2 bus has been designed around the ITU-601 standard. Because the Movie-2 bus was defined for demanding professional video applications, it uses synchronous parallel D1 as the native video data format. Movie-2 features an uncompressed, 10-bit video bus architecture. These characteristics ensure a simple and inexpensive implementation for board designers.

The Movie-2 bus carries eight digital video busses, six digital key busses and four serial digital audio busses for a constant data bandwidth above 242 MB/sec. -- almost three times the effective bandwidth of PCI! (Figure 4)

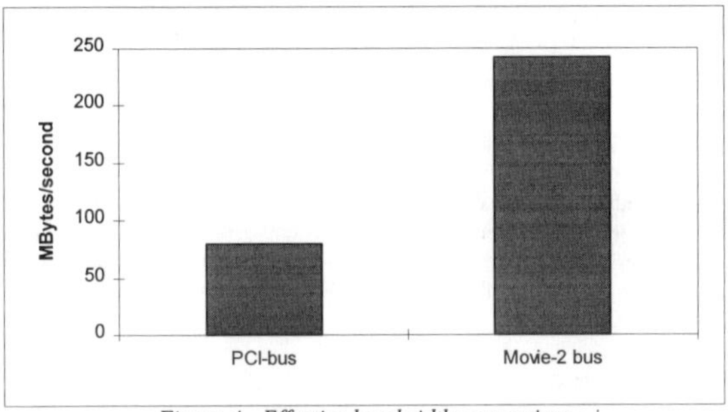


*Figure 4 - Effective bandwidth comparison*

# The Movie-2 Bus Solution

The Movie-2 bus is an over-the-top expansion bus consisting of two high-density, right-angle connectors -- CON 1 and CON 2 -- on the top edge of adapter cards. (Figure 5) CON 1 has 90 pins and CON 2 has 70 pins. Movie-2 bus compliant audio/video adapters interface to each other through an over-the-top, passive printed circuit board (PCB) that connects to CON 1 and/or CON 2, depending on the adapter's function in the system. PCI, EISA or ISA video adapters can use the Movie-2 bus.

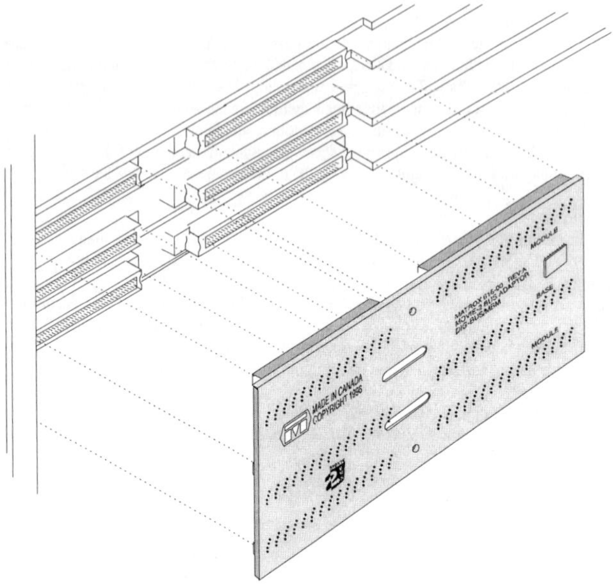


*Figure 5 - Passive PCB interconnects Movie-2 bus compatible adapters*

CON 1 is used to provide video input and video output busses to/from a digital video mixer card, for example. CON 1 also provides master reference synchronization signals. CON 2 is used to interface with an optional video effects card (for example, a 3D DVE generator). The connector provides the busses to send and return video and key signals from the DVE. CON 2 also provides the same master reference synchronization signals as CON 1.

CON 1 and CON 2 (Figure 6) carry the following information:

- 8 independent ITU-601 8 or 10-bit uncompressed digital video busses in YUV 4:2:2 (parallel D1)
- 6 independent ITU-601 8-bit key busses
- 8 tracks serial digital audio data (AES/EBU and S/PDIF compatible)
- $I^2C$ Philips device control bus and other general purpose control signals
- Video and audio timing reference signals

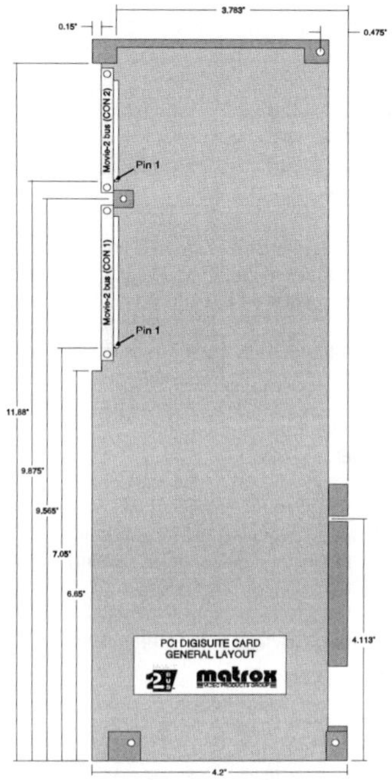


*Figure 6 - Mechanical positioning of Movie-2 bus connectors CON-1 and CON-2*

From a video timing point of view, a video adapter on the Movie-2 bus can be either a slave or a master agent. Only one master agent is allowed at a time. Typically, the video I/O board that is genlocked to the studio reference generates the master signals on Movie-2 . The other adapters are slaved to the Movie-2 master.

From an audio timing point of view, there is always a master audio reference card, with any other audio devices slaved to it. The maximum number of audio cards is three: one master, one slave input and one slave output. To allow proper synchronization between audio and video streams, the master audio reference clock must be locked on the video reference. Thus, the audio system is slave of the video system.

## Movie-2 bus functional specifications

Eight video busses and six key busses carry the uncompressed digital video information between the Movie-2 adapters, in sync with the master video reference signal. The main time base uses the 27-MHz video clock. These busses are bi-directional, under software control, to ensure flexibility in the bus operation. Probably the best analogy is to picture the bus as a very compact digital D1 video router.

***Video bus format***

Video busses carry time-multiplexed data with a standard encoding of 4:2:2 in the form:

$U_0,Y_0,V_0,Y_1,U_2,Y_2,V_2,Y_3....$

Note that the $U_1$ and $V_1$ values are not used in the 4:2:2 coding scheme.

- Y is the luminance signal encoded in ten (10) or eight (8) bits. If the data is encoded in 10 bits, then the black level is 64 and the white level is 940, giving 877 discrete values. The corresponding ITU-601 8-bit value is derived by using the 8 most significant bits.

- U corresponds to $C_b$ and V to $C_r$ (naming alternatives are B-Y and R-Y). If data is encoded in 10 bits, the zero level is 512. The lower level is 64 and the highest level is 960. There are thus 897 levels available. As with Y, using the 8 most significant bits conforms to the ITU601 specification.

The video is conveyed at 27 MHz time multiplexed in the above order. The parameters are as follows:

- Y at 13.5 MHz, U and V at 6.75 MHz
- the first sample of each active line is U
- number of active luminance samples is 720
- there are 360 color-difference samples per line

The following eight video busses can be found on the Movie-2 bus:

- I0, I1 and I2 — video input/output between video adapters
- MAIN — typically the main video output (program)
- PREVIEW — typically the preview video output of the video mixer
- LOOPOUT A and B — typically the front and back face video for 3D DVE
- LOOPIN — typically the processed video output from 3D DVE

***Key bus format***

Key busses carry data with a standard encoding of 4:0:0 in the form:

$Y_0,Y_1,Y_2,Y_3....$

Only luminance data is carried on this bus. The parameters are as follows:

- 256 quantization levels are available
- code 0 is the black level and code 255 is the peak white level
- number of active samples per line is 720
- sampling frequency is 13.5 MHz

The following six key busses can be found on the Movie-2 bus:

- I0KEY, I1KEY AND I2KEY — key busses associated with I0, I1 and I2 video busses
- KEYIN — key bus associated with the LOOPIN video bus
- KEYOUT — KEYOUT time-multiplexes the key bus associated with the LOOPOUT busses and the main video output (2 key busses)

***Audio bus format***

Audio busses serially carry digital audio samples coded using standard two's complement binary integers. The serial word length must be 16 or 32 bits. Data samples are transferred using the most significant bit (MSB) first. Multiple audio streams can be time multiplexed together on one bus. One serial data line can time multiplex eight audio tracks. Two different methods of time multiplexing are possible:

*Continuous multiplexing*

Each audio sample (S) is time multiplexed in a sequence from stream 1 to stream N without interruption.

S1,S2,S3,S4...SN,S1,S2,S3,S4...SN...

*Burst multiplexing*
Each audio sample is time multiplexed in a sequence from stream 1 to stream N. A delay can occur between the transmission of each sample sequence.

S1,S2,S3,S4...SN (delay) S1,S2,S3,S4...SN (delay) S1,S2,S3,S4...SN (delay)...

The following audio busses can be found on the Movie-2 bus:

- SDATAIN two audio input busses transmit audio data from the input card to the master card
- SDATAOUT two audio output busses transmit audio data to the output card from the master card

## Movie-2 bus synchronization signals

The master adapter on the Movie-2 bus generates the video and audio signals.

***Video Signals***

- 27 MHz clock
- 13.5 MHz clock
- clock qualifier to identify U/V samples from Y samples
- horizontal sync
- vertical sync
- field signal

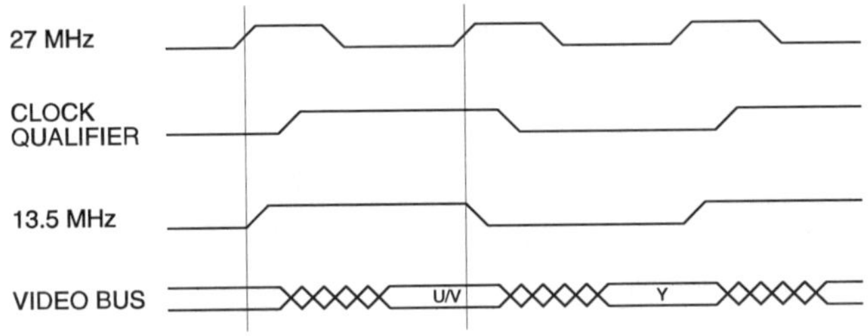


*Figure 7 - Horizontal line video timing*

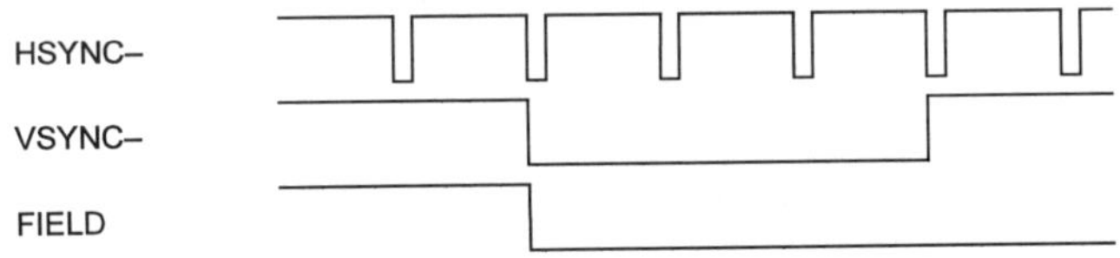


*Figure 8 - Vertical line video timing*

**Audio Signals**

- audio sampling clock
- in 48 KHz audio applications, the audio sampling clock will have a frequency of 12.288 MHz
- frame sync to define each sample's MSB position

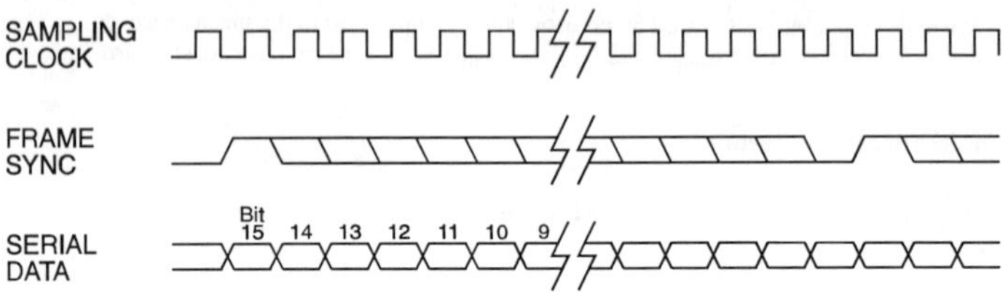


*Figure 9 -- Timing of the transfer of one audio sample (S1)*

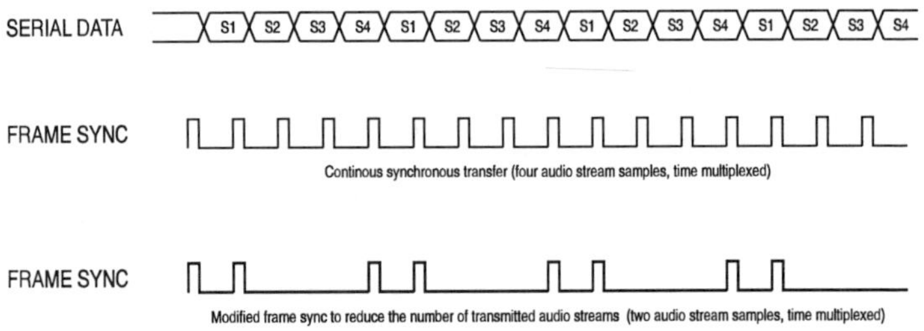


*Figure 10 -- Timing of the transfer of a complete audio stream sequence*

## Typical Movie-2 bus nonlinear editing system implementation

The modularity of Movie-2 bus makes it easy to combine different vendors products to create system-level digital video solutions like nonlinear editing systems, virtual VTRs, MPEG-2 video-on-demand servers, live video switchers, commercial insertion systems, CATV barker channels, animation/paint/CG workstations and compositing systems. For example, products from Matrox Video Products Group, Pinnacle Systems and Miranda Technologies – all built around the Movie-2 bus – can be used to build a hardware platform for third-party nonlinear editing applications. Such a system would include a Matrox DigiMix – digital video/graphics mixer with 2D DVE, a Matrox DigiMotion – motion JPEG codec/digital audio mixer/Fast-20 SCSI controller, a Pinnacle Genie – 3D DVE unit, and a Miranda DigiLinx -- serial digital (SDI) I/O board. (Figure 11)

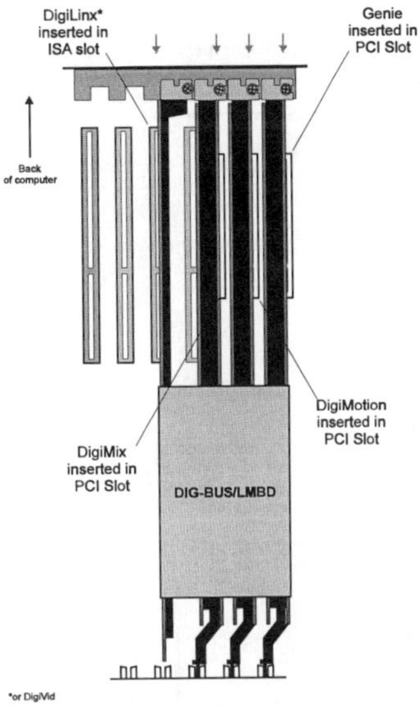


*Figure 11 - Top view of Movie-2 bus in a four-card NLE configuration inside a PC*

Data flow over the Movie-2 bus in such a system is as follows: (Figure 12)

- Three video inputs are sent from the DigiLinx SDI I/O board to the DigiMix video mixer using I0, I1 and I2.
- The program and preview outputs from DigiMix are sent to DigiLinx using MAIN and PREVIEW.
- DigiMix interfaces with the dual codec DigiMotion over I1 and I2. These bi-directional busses allow two streams to be sent back and forth for record and playback.
- A key signal can also be played back using the I1KEY bus on DigiMotion.
- The Genie 3D DVE board interfaces with the DigiMix through five video busses.
- LOOPOUT A and LOOPOUT B transmit front and back face video layers to be processed along with a key fill using KEYOUT.
- The transformed video image is sent back to the DigiMix through LOOPIN and KEYIN.

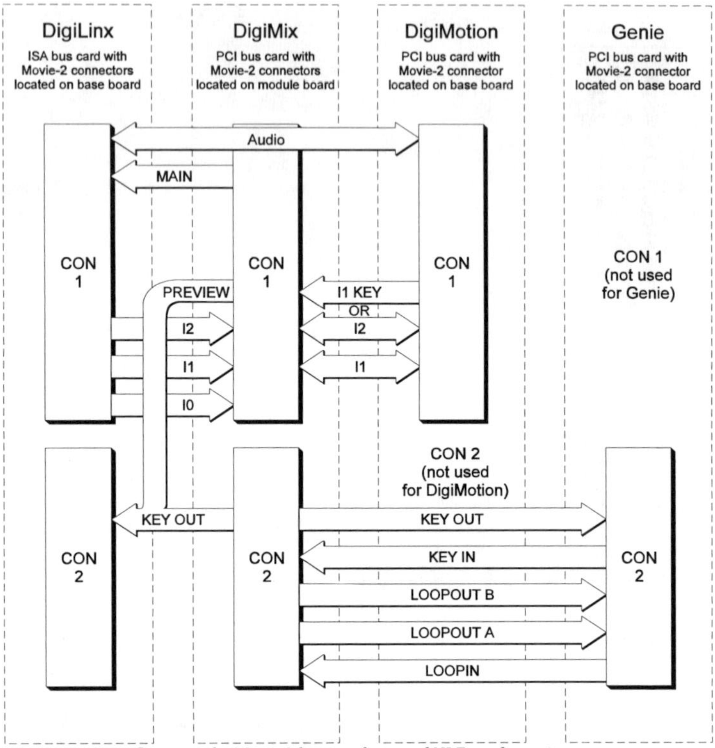


*Figure 12 - Data flow over the Movie-2 bus in a four-card NLE configuration*

# Conclusion

Movie-2 bus is the only open-standard, high-speed PC adapter interconnect that meets the needs of the professional video industry. Movie-2 bus overcomes bandwidth problems experienced by designers of broadcast-quality digital video systems who must use multiple adapters in a PC. It is a simple, inexpensive bus to implement and provides the high-performance and modularity that system integrators need. Its widespread adoption in the video industry provides a way to quickly incorporate different digital video building blocks from many different vendors into a complete system.

# PC-Based Open Architecture Standards: An Overview

Alain Legault, Vice President - Product Development
Janet Matey, Marketing Manager
Matrox Video Products Group
Dorval, Quebec, Canada

## Abstract

Hardware and software enabling technologies are now firmly in place for the migration to economical PC-based digital video solutions in many areas of the professional video industry. The move from "black boxes" to PC-based open systems is well underway . It began in the late 80's with nonlinear editing systems, and now PCs are becoming ubiquitous in all segments of the video industry from content creation, through post-production, to broadcast delivery.

There are many benefits inherent in using PC-based technologies in video system designs. The widespread use of PCs in other applications makes them cost-effective. They offer significantly smaller system size and power requirements than traditional 'dedicated-box' architectures. In addition, intelligent control over the entire video application is provided by the computer. Perhaps the greatest PC benefit is modularity and multi-vendor interoperability of hardware and software through open standards.

This paper provides an overview of some of the important enabling technologies for PC-based open architecture in professional video applications including PCI-bus, Movie-2-bus, Advanced ASIC technology and IEEE 1394 on the hardware front; and Windows NT, ActiveMovie and OpenDML software extensions on the software side. It directs the reader to sites on the World Wide Web where further information on these topics can be obtained.

# Introduction

The desire to use economical PCs in professional video applications continues to grow. Hardware and software enabling technologies are now firmly in place for the migration to PC-based digital video solutions in many areas of the professional video industry. The move from "black boxes" to PC-based open systems is well underway. It began in the late 80's with nonlinear editing systems, and now PCs are becoming ubiquitous in all segments of the video industry from content creation through to broadcast delivery. For example, PC- based solutions can be found in all of the following applications:

- Content Creation
  - Character Generators (CG)
  - Graphics
  - Video Paint
  - 3D Animation
- Post-Production/Editing
  - Nonlinear Editing
  - Live Video Switchers
  - Visual Effects/Compositing Systems
  - Virtual VTRs
  - Digital Disk Recorders (DDR)
  - Animation Recorders
  - Closed Captioning and Teletext Systems
- Broadcast/Delivery
  - Time Delay Systems
  - Commercial Insertion Systems
  - Instant Replay Systems
  - CATV Barker Channels
  - Video-on-Demand Servers (VOD)
  - Near Video-on-Demand Servers (NVOD)
  - Interactive TV
  - M-JPEG to MPEG Transcoders

**The benefits inherent in PC-based systems are many:**

- cost-effectiveness based on large-volume, mass-market use
- significantly smaller system size and power requirements
- intelligent control over the entire video application provided by the computer
- inherent networkability of PCs
- hardware/software modular interchangeability
- multi-vendor interoperability through open standards

**Important enabling technologies for PC-based open architecture in the video industry include:**

- Hardware
  - PCI Local bus
  - Movie-2-bus
  - Advanced ASIC technology
  - IEEE 1394
- Software
  - Windows NT and 95
  - ActiveMovie multimedia architecture
  - OpenDML software extensions

# PCI Local Bus

The advent of the PCI bus, with its high-performance features, low-cost implementation, cross-platform flexibility and plug n' play ease of installation, has been a real boon to professional video products vendors.

## Performance

- 33 MHz clock speed
- 32-bit time-multiplexed address/data bus
- peak bandwidth of 132 MB/sec
- data bursting allows read and write at full-PCI speed (132 MB/sec with 0 wait states)
- linear burst mode reduces the need to send addresses in data streams and ensures that the bus is continuously filled with data
- low access latency guaranteed for realtime devices
- arbitration scheme allows multiple master PCI adapters in a system
- concurrency capability ensures that the host processor continues to operate while a PCI adapter is mastering data over the bus

## Cost

- highly integrated PCI chips substantially reduce glue logic cost and card real estate
- low interface pin count

## Flexibility

- processor independent – Intel, MIPS, DEC Alpha, PowerPC
- platform independent – widely adopted in the market by Intel, Apple, DEC, SGI
- wide availability of adapters

## Plug and Play

- auto-configuration capability ensures that users can install cards without manually configuring jumpers, DIP switches or interrupts
- configuration registers describe the system resources required for each adapter – memory space, interrupts, I/O space and power
- upon power-up, PCI adapters are configured according to the configuration registers eliminating conflicts

The PCI bus was originally proposed by Intel Corporation in late 1991. In 1992 the PCI Special Interest Group (SIG) was established by leading computer industry companies to monitor and enhance the development of the PCI architecture.

Additional PCI-bus information can be found on the World Wide Web at http://www.pcisig.com.

# Movie-2 Digital Audio/Video Over-the-Top Expansion Bus

In professional video applications like nonlinear editing, graphics creation, animation recording, 3D rendering, video-on-demand and commercial insertion, specialized PC adapters are typically used to handle the massive processing requirements for transporting natural data types in realtime. Commonly used subsystems include: video I/O, video processing (DVE-mixing), video compression/decompression (codec), audio I/O, audio processing (EQ-mixing), mass storage interface, network interface and video-in-a-window console display. Although it is possible to accomplish some of these tasks with host-CPU software and a single highly integrated adapter, most professional systems require more than one adapter. For example, a nonlinear editing system may require a codec card, a videographics card, an audio processor, a console display and mass storage and network interfaces. (Figure 1) Movie-2 bus is an open-standard, digital audio/video, over-the-top expansion bus that allows system designers to interface various PCI, EISA and ISA adapters together to build virtually any broadcast digital video application.

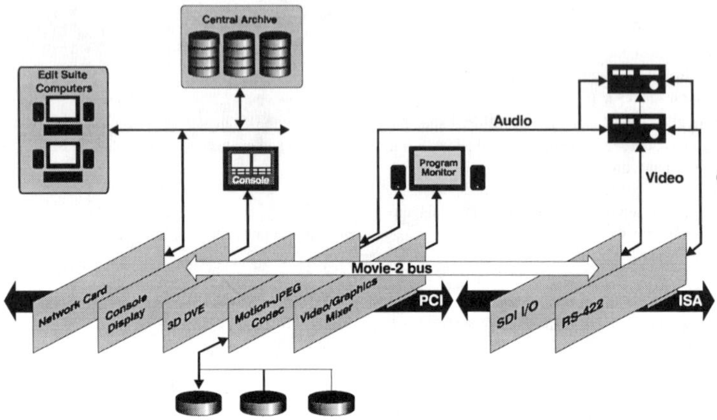


*Figure 1 - Typical PC-based multi-adapter nonlinear editing system configuration*

Movie-2 bus is designed to overcome bandwidth problems experienced by system designers who must deal with the facts that:

- a single CCIR-601, 4:2:2 digital video stream = 21 MB/sec. (32 MB/sec. with key bus 4:2:2:4)
- eight 48 KHz, 16-bit audio tracks = 768 KB/sec.
- a Motion-JPEG compressed digital video stream at Betacam quality = 6 MB/sec.

The Movie-2 bus carries eight independent, 10-bit CCIR-601 uncompressed digital video busses, six digital key busses and four serial digital audio busses for a constant data bandwidth above 242 MB/sec. – almost three times the effective bandwidth of PCI! Moreover, it accomplishes this feat without penalizing system performance, leaving the host PCI-bus free for all its other system activities like graphical user interface refresh, hard disk access and network interface.

Movie-2 bus allows simple, inexpensive implementation using minimal card real estate which is an important consideration given that PCI cards are small and that the number of PCI slots is limited in most machines. (Figure 2)

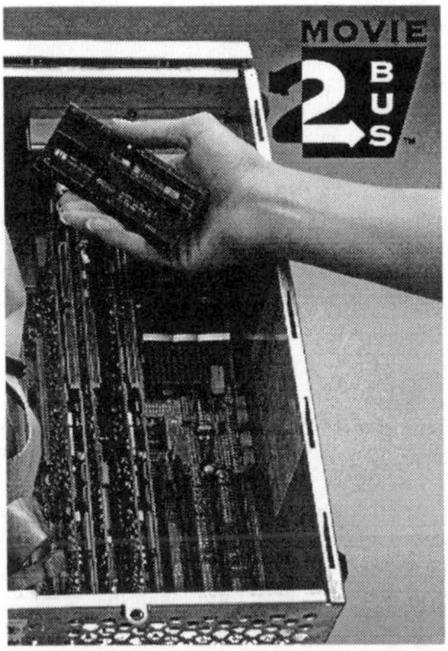


*Figure 2 - Passive PCB interconnects Movie-2 bus compatible adapters inside a PC*

Additional information about Movie-2 bus can be found at http://www.matrox.com/video.

# ASIC Design Advancements

The space restriction on PCI-bus cards requires board designers to develop ASICs that implement system-level functionality. New technology advancements are now available to ASIC designers to provide the high level of integration required to fit complex functionality onto PCI-bus cards. The ASIC enabling technologies include: high-level design description languages like VHDL, logic synthesis software tools like Synopsis Design Compiler and high-density silicon like 0.5 micron meter CMOS process. ASICs with the complexity of more than 250,000 gates and 350 I/O connections provide system-level functionality (i.e. a complete digital video mixer) on a single chip.

Additional information about advanced ASIC design can be found at http://www.lsilogic.com.

# IEEE 1394

IEEE 1394 is an open hardware and software serial digital interface standard for transporting data at 100, 200 or 400 megabits/sec (Mbps). Its use in the new generation of DV/DVC digital camcorders and VTRs makes it of interest to the professional video industry. IEEE 1394 specifies two types of data transfer: asynchronous, as is typically used in computer applications; and isochronous, which provides guaranteed data transport at a pre-determined rate (25 Mbps in the case of DVC). The isochronous feature of 1394 is important in time-critical delivery of multimedia data streams as it eliminates the need for extensive data buffering. IEEE 1394 was designed to address the consumer electronics market, so it is inexpensive and simple to use. The interface is a thin serial cable that supplies serial data along with power. Because power is in the serial cable, live insertion and plug and play are supported. In addition, there is no need for terminators, device IDs or elaborate set up. Up to 63 devices can be connected on a 1394 bus.

Apple Computer was the originator of 1394 in the late 80's. In 1994, the 1394 Trade Association was formed by leaders in the electronics, computer and consumer products fields to support the technology. It now includes more than 50 member companies. In 1995 the 1394 specification was formally adopted by IEEE.

Additional information about IEEE 1394 can found at http://www.1394ta.org.

## Windows NT

The Windows NT operating system architecture (Figure 3) provides the system performance needed in professional video systems. The features that make it ideal in this environment include true 32-bit architecture, realtime responsiveness, preemptive multi-tasking, multi-processor support (i.e. dual or quad Pentium) and the high-performance NT file system (NTFS). As an added benefit, NT offers multi-platform support (Intel, Power PC, DEC Alpha, MIPS). In addition, NT 4.0 incorporates the Windows '95 user-friendly interface. NT is a robust operating system that can perform in the most demanding applications. In fact, it that has obtained the C2-level security certification of the U.S. Government.

The NT file system provides the features needed in professional video applications. Its 64-bit structure allows files size to be virtually unlimited ($2^{64}$ Bytes). This feature is important given the fact that ITU-601 video files, by definition, are very large (21 Mbytes/sec). NTFS also allows multiple hard disks to be configured in software stripe sets to provide overall throughput that is the sum of the throughput of the individual hard disks minus some overhead. NTFS splits the digital video data stream into chunks of data and writes them in a round-robin fashion to each disk in turn. This facility lets system designers use relatively inexpensive drives, rather than expensive hardware RAIDs, to provide the throughput necessary to record and play back 601 video in real time.

The architecture of Windows NT is very modular offering a high level of inherent openness. Each important subsystem -- storage, network, peripheral interface, graphics/ multimedia -- provides a common interface to the operating system kernel independent of the specific technology used. For example, storage device options include SCSI, SSA, and Fiber Channel; networks interfaces include Ethernet, Fast Ethernet, ATM and FDDI; peripherals interfaces include IEEE-1394 FireWire and Universal Serial Bus USB; and multimedia and graphics APIs include ActiveMovie, Direct3D, and OpenGL.

Networking is an integral part of Windows NT and is implemented in a client /server model using NT Workstation for the clients and NT Server for the server. Workstations can access files on the server and on other workstations transparently, as if they were stored locally.

Additional information about Windows NT can be found at http://www.microsoft.com/NTWorkstation

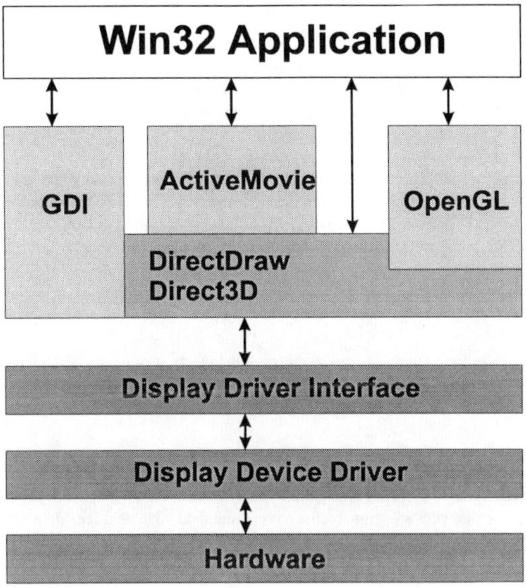


*Figure 3 - Windows operating system architecture*

# ActiveMovie Multimedia Software Architecture

ActiveMovie is a multimedia streaming architecture for Window NT and 95, that delivers high-quality video playback, while exposing a flexible, extensible and future-proof set of interfaces upon which digital video applications can be built. It replaces multimedia streaming services and APIs provided by Microsoft in previous versions of the Windows Software Development Kits (SDK) such as Video for Windows (VFW) and MCI.

ActiveMovie overcomes all of the limitations of VFW. The improved audio/video file format that was originally proposed by OpenDML has been incorporated in ActiveMovie. High-performance I/O throughput is ensured by the new data streaming architecture. Driver models now have a consistent Application Program Interface (API). They support more data types and are modular, leading to a high level of software/hardware interoperability. System-level, accurate synchronization for all media types is provided and ActiveMovie API is identical for Windows 95 and Windows NT minimizing the work required for software developers to support both operating systems.

## ActiveMovie Data Types

ActiveMovie allows the system designer to define a wider variety of data types than was possible under VFW. For example, in the Matrox DigiSuite implementation of ActiveMovie, the following multimedia data types are defined:

- Digital video data from various types of codecs – Motion-JPEG
- Digital audio data – PCM WAV
- Digital video F/X control attributes – 2D or 3D DVE attributes
- Digital audio F/X control attributes – EQ, mixing and panning
- Graphics and still images – 32-bit RGB-Alpha images
- Scroll and crawl of graphics overlays and titles – Inscriber scroll and crawl files
- VCR control – RS-422 Sony Betacam protocol control

The ActiveMovie data streaming architecture allows the optimal, timely interchange of all of these data types. There are three major benefits to the data streaming approach. Data throughput is maximized by the ability to use large data buffers (more than 64 Kbytes). CPU intensive memory copying operations are eliminated by the use of shared memory buffers. System-level synchronization is ensured through the use of time stamps on all data streams.

## ActiveMovie Filters

A filter is an object that performs a single task in a multimedia system. For example, in a complex subsystem such as the Matrox DigiMix digital video mixer, individual filters perform such tasks as background and wipe generation, chroma keying, layer priority selection, proc amp adjustments, 2D DVE, etc.

More complex functions can be performed by interfacing multiple filters together to act on a specific data type. Filters are connected together by interfaces called "pins" in ActiveMovie terminology. Different types of ActiveMovie filters can either provide, transform or consume data. These three functions are accomplished using the following:

- Source filters
- Transform filters
- Renderer filters

A source filter provides data such as digital audio, digital video or graphics to other filters downstream. Alternatively, it can provide control information such as video and audio keyframes. For example, a data source filter would typically perform functions such as an AVI file reader, WAV audio file reader and title animator. A source filter can get its control information from a file or from interaction with the user via a user interface device like a scroll bar or fader control. A source filter typically has only an output pin.

A transform filter accepts a data stream at its input pin, performs a transformation on the data and provides the processed data to its output pin. For example, in Matrox DigiSuite, the video codec, the 2D DVE processor, the audio equalizer and the Movie-2 bus interconnect are just a few of the many hardware-assisted transform filters.

A renderer filter is responsible for consuming the processed data and relaying it to a presentation device such as a video display or a speaker. The renderer will ensure presentation of each media stream at the correct time, based on the system-level synchronization mechanism. In Matrox DigiSuite, for example, the "correct time" is defined as presentation of each media stream accurately synchronized at the video field level. Typically, a renderer filter has only an input pin.

## ActiveMovie Pins

Two types of pins are defined in ActiveMovie: shared memory buffers and implicit hardware connections. Shared memory buffer pins are used whenever a filter interfaces to another through the use of computer memory. Hardware connections are made when a filter employs hardware acceleration. Because pins are standardized for a given data type, a shared memory buffer pin can be easily replaced by a hardware connection without affecting the interface with the application software. This transparency between hardware and software allows the same application to easily migrate from software-only operation to a higher-performance level using hardware accelerators.

## ActiveMovie Filter Graphs

A multimedia system requires the connection of multiple filters to accomplish system-level functions. A representation of the multimedia system is called a filter graph. (Figure 4) Filter graphs are customized connections performed between many filters in order to accomplish a specific task.

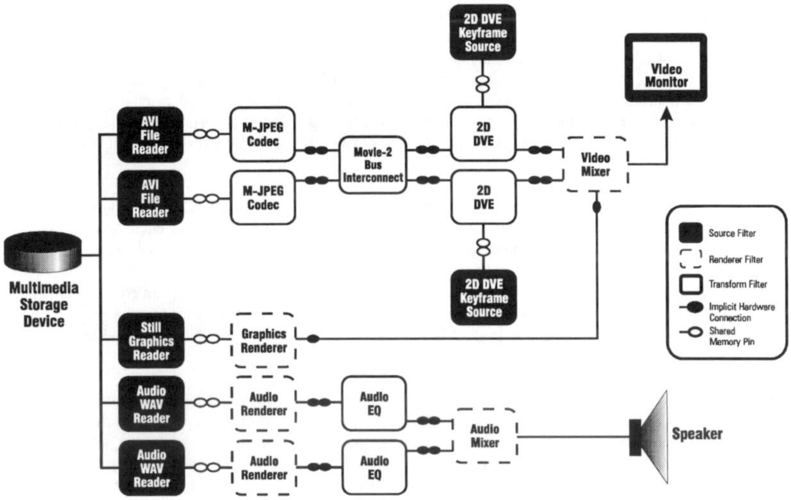


*Figure 4 - Simplified example of one DigiSuite filter graph*

In order to establish a connection between the input pin of one filter and the output pin of another filter, a negotiation of data type takes place. A connection can be established between two filters that share the same data type (i.e. Motion-JPEG digital video) but cannot be successfully established between two inconsistent data types. This prevents feeding a digital video stream into an audio equalizer, for example.

### System-Level Synchronization

The goal of system level synchronization is to present all streams of data to the presentation device in a timely manner. The system designer must decide what the timebase or reference clock will be for his application. For example, in Matrox DigiSuite, the timebase is the video field (60/sec. NTSC, 50/sec. PAL) so the reference clock is derived from the hardware vertical synchronization signal provided by the DigiSuite video card. In the film industry, a system designer would likely choose a reference clock of 24 frames/sec. The rendering filters for all the data streams in the multimedia system must be controlled by this single reference clock.

Additional information about ActiveMovie in the professional video arena can be found at http://www.matrox.com/videoweb/actmvwh.htm.

## OpenDML Software Extensions to ActiveMovie

ActiveMovie 1.0 is primarily designed for MPEG playback and Internet applications. Because of its extensible nature, however, it is also an important enabling technology for high-performance professional applications. Some developers have already demonstrated that ActiveMovie provides realtime multi-stream capture and playback of digital video, audio, video F/X, audio F/X, graphics and animations in a field-accurate and synchronized manner. This is the functionality required in professional video applications. To standardize various vendors' approaches to these functions, the OpenDML consortium is working with Microsoft to define the features of ActiveMovie 2.0 and develop standard APIs for extensions needed in the video industry.

OpenDML is a video industry consortium established in early 1995 and is made up of more than 100 companies with the mission to make Windows the platform of choice for professional video applications. The first project undertaken by the OpenDML group was the definition of enhancements to make the Video for Windows AVI file format more useful for professional audio/video/film applications. The enhanced file format specification was released by OpenDML in November '95 and has been incorporated by Microsoft into ActiveMovie. The new file format defined improvements to Video for Windows for greater interoperability, maximum throughput, larger file sizes, lower overhead and greater editing and random-access capability.

To maximize its usefulness in professional applications, ActiveMovie requires additional extensions. The active members of OpenDML have established a Device Driver Workgroup that has taken on the task of identifying, studying and recommending these extensions to the rest of the industry to ensure full interoperability between vendors, one of the major benefits promised by the ActiveMovie architecture. The extensions will also significantly ease the process for software developers of supporting multiple hardware platforms.

The general goal of the Device Driver Workgroup is to standardize the various media types needed for professional video applications: digital audio, digital video, video effects descriptors (2D DVE, 3D DVE, transitions, chroma key, luma key, alpha key), audio effects descriptors (volume control, EQ, pan, mix, soft cuts, reverb, echo, etc.), animation and graphics. The Workgroup is also identifying a standard API for various filters: DVEs, mixers, codecs, etc. Since ActiveMovie 1.0 is a playback tool, a capture model is also needed. Finally, the Workgroup is identifying a standard common functional subsystem (called a "filter graph" in ActiveMovie terminology) that will allow software developers to program application software independently from hardware functionality. Common filter graphs for audio and video subsystems are being defined. The initial proposal for the video subsystem model is an A/B roll switcher with graphics downstream keying, DVE and proc amp control. (Figure 5) The audio mixer subsystem features a variable number of tracks with pan, mix and EQ. (Figure 6)

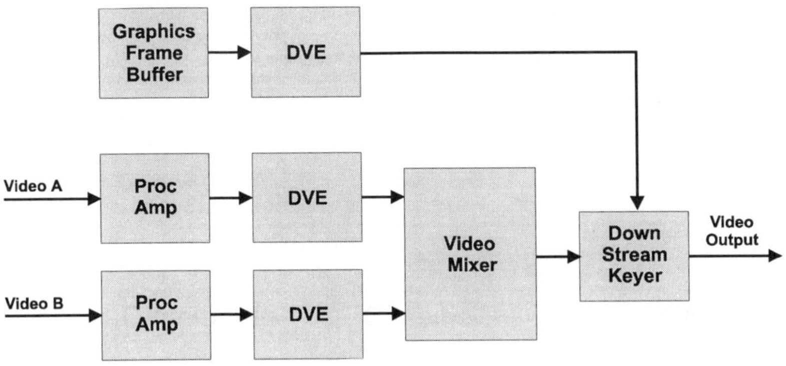


*Figure 5 - OpenDML video switcher model – A/B + Graphics*

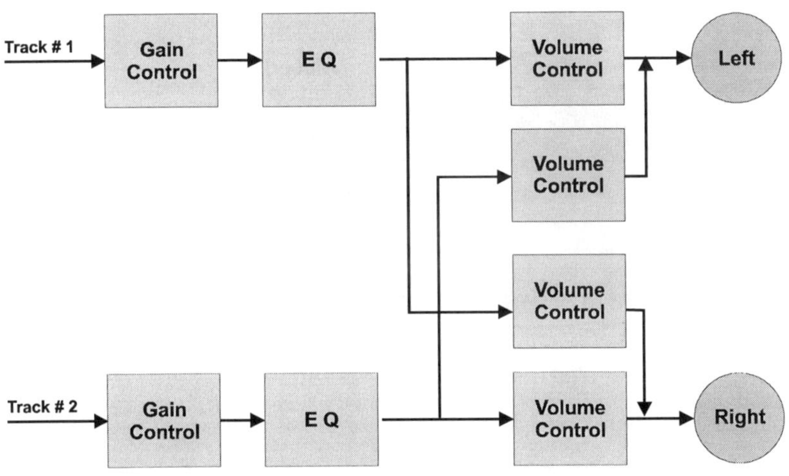


*Figure 6 - OpenDML audio mixer model*

One important use of the extensions to ActiveMovie is the seamless playback of cutlists with effects in real time on all types of data streams. (Figure 7) This is particularly important for nonlinear editing applications. In realtime NLE applications, the enhanced AVI file format provides fast access to individual frames within an AVI file and it also allows the definition of input and output trim points. ActiveMovie provides the streaming architecture and support for all media types – audio, video, video F/X, audio F/X, graphics and animations.

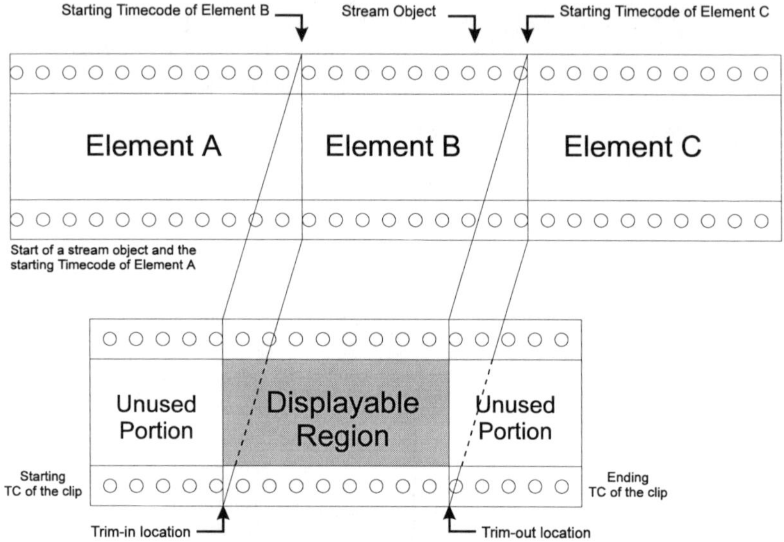


*Figure 7 - Video stream cutlist*

Additional information about the OpenDML consortium can be found at http://www.matrox.com/video.

# Conclusion

Designers have access to a number of open-standard hardware and software technologies that allow them to take advantage of economical PCs when developing digital video solutions in many areas of the professional video industry. Some of these important enabling technologies include PCI-bus, Movie-2-bus, Advanced ASIC technology and IEEE 1394 on the hardware front; and Windows NT, ActiveMovie and OpenDML software extensions on the software side. Most of the leading hardware and software companies in the professional video marketplace are committed to PC open architecture. All the elements are in place to take a giant step toward multi-vendor interoperability within the next six months and significantly enhance the capabilities of products being announced and delivered in 1996 and beyond.

# Broadcasting and Processing of Program Guides for Digital TV

Stephan Hartwig, Thomas Rautenberg, and Tilman Bollmann
NOKIA-Multimedia Network Terminals
Bochum, Germany

Keywords:
Digital TV, Service Information, Electronic Program Guide

## Abstract

From the consumer's point of view the transition from analog to digital TV comes in two flavours, quantity and quality. First, the number of services increases significantly and second, there are new service types to come. Paper TV-guides with their linear and non-hierarchical presentation of program information are unlikely to assist any longer in service- and program event selection. Instead, Electronic Program Guides will provide an interactive user interface offering comfortable and fast program browsing functions.

Unlike in the computer world, the desired schedule information will just virtually be served from a local random access data base, but will mostly be fetched from the current transmission. Caching techniques will be applied, which are, however, restricted due to the lack of sufficient local storage media. This makes the development of transmission, processing and buffering strategies a difficult task, bearing in mind that users expect fast and random access, whereas the service provider wants to keep the transmission bandwidth allocated for this type of data as small as possible.

Starting with an outline of the DVB Standard for Service Information and an example EPG, this paper will analyse SI transmission schemes and SI caching and processing strategies. Typical hard- and software constraints of consumer Set Top Boxes are taken into account.

## 1. Introduction

We currently experience a major breakthrough for digital TV Services throughout the world. Although it is widely accepted that digital TV is just a necessary step towards interactive digital services, it will be the key application in the first years. The main achievement of digital TV as it is today is not primarily image quality, but new services as NVOD, PPV and last but not least the Electronic Program Guide (EPG). This interactive graphical user interface is to replace the old-fashioned TV-magazine by providing fast and clearly arranged schedule information about all services in the network. In Europe the transmission of this schedule information has been standardized as part of the so-called Service Information (SI) [1]. Unfortunately, some difficulties still have to be overcome until decent EPGs will run smoothly on consumer Set Top Boxes (STB). An attractive program schedule contains several megabytes of program information even for just one or two weeks of schedule and service providers feel uncomfortable with the idea of sacrificing a significant part of their video bandwidth "just" for schedule information. The STB manufacturers, however, want to provide what customers expect: fast random access to any schedule information and sophisticated browsing functions. If the schedule information is not constantly repeated with sufficient repetition rate, consumer STBs will have to cache information in advance. Keeping in mind the memory limitations of low-cost consumer STBs, we conclude that just a small part of the schedule can be kept in cache. Furthermore, it is unlikely that the schedule of all services is sent on every channel. Caching information about all services would require tuning to different transportstreams which is not a good idea if the customer watches a movie.

These are just some of the problems to be solved. The purpose of this paper is to analyse some strategies for SI transmission schemes and SI processing in the STB in order to provide a basic functionality of the EPG with reasonable response times. Chapters 2 starts with a discussion of typical SI request patterns caused by user interaction. A short outline of the SI Standard is presented in chapter 3. Based on this, chapter 4 and 5 analyse useful SI transmission schemes as well as SI caching and processing strategies on the STB side, taking into account typical hard- and software constraints of consumer STBs.

## 2. Typical requirements for an Electronic Program Guide: An example

The presentation of program events in TV-magazines is mainly focussed on the two familiar concepts of channel and time. Only the latter is a natural criterion; the logical ordering of events into channels is a leftover copied from the technical implementation of analog TV transmission. More suitable program guides will abstract information content from information media offering a more intuitively access to program information [2]. Surely, the selection of events by category (e.g. "Movie") is more natural than selection by service. Moreover, the user interface will hide complexity where possible. The technically important concept of a transportstream, for example, should not be introduced to the user. This design goal is not always easy to fulfil, since if information of certain service is requested it might make a difference in response time whether this service is on the actual or another transportstream.

In the following, an example program guide is analysed (see **figure 1**). This EPG is a joint development of NOKIA, UI-Design, and Beta Digital for the German DF1 digital service. The EPG has two modes, the Viewing Mode and the Guide Mode. In Viewing Mode, the user can select services and request information about the current service and the present and following event as well. This information is displayed as an overlay on the current movie, i.e. the respective data has to be fetched from the current transportstream. In Guide Mode, the whole screen is under control of the user interface, which will - if necessary - tune to different transportstreams to acquire the information requested.

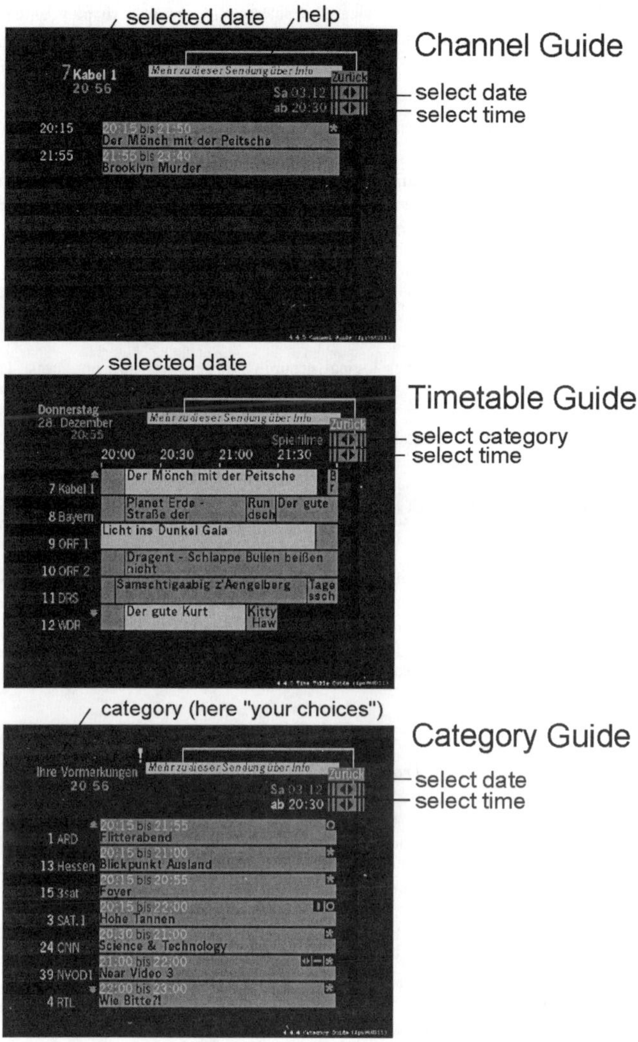


***Figure.1:*** *Screenshots of the Service, -Timetable, and Categroy Guide*

The EPG supports three modes of schedule browsing, the Service, Timetable, and Category guide. In each of these modes, the date-time interval of interest can be chosen. In the *channel guide*, the event schedule for a selected service is presented. In the *timetable guide*, the EPG lists all events for a selection of 6 different services. Events belonging to the selected category are highlighted. The *category guide*, finally, lists all events of a given category (movie, sports, etc) without specifying any services. In each of these menus, an event can be selected in order to display extended textual information about the event or to mark it for later viewing or recording.

## 3. The DVB Standard for the transmission of Service Information

The transmission of event schedule information has been standardized as part of the DVB Service Information (SI) [1]. According to this standard, the data is transmitted in MPEG2-private sections [3]. Addressing and finding this information in the transportstream is based on the Packet-Id (PID) in the MPEG packet header and different fields in the Private Section syntax, among others the table_id and table_extension_id. The entire SI consists of different tables, the most important ones beeing the NIT, BAT, SDT and EIT:

- *Network Information Table* (information about the networks and physical transmission parameters of the different transportstreams, like frequencies, modulation types, etc).

- *Bouquet Association Table* (provides logical grouping of services into bouquets. This table is optional)

- *Service Description Table* (contains information about all services in the network like transportstream, service- and service provider name, service type, etc)

- *Event Information Table* (describes the program events in terms of starttime, duration, category, textual description).

In NVOD, services and events are just timeshifted copies of each other. In order to save bandwidth, these are efficiently coded by using so-called reference services and reference events.

It is important to note that just the EIT presents by far the biggest portion of the SI. Without going into the details, a simple estimate for the amount of data is

$$nBytes = nTransportstreams \cdot \frac{nServices}{Transportstream} \cdot \frac{nEvents}{Day \cdot Service} \cdot nDays \cdot \frac{nbytes}{Event}.$$

If the data is packed efficiently into sections and MPEG-packets, the corresponding bitrate depends mainly on the repetition rate used to cyclicely repeat the data.

$$Bitrate = nBytes \ x \ Repetitionrate \ x \ 8.$$

Clearly, this bitrate has to be multiplied by the number of transportstreams, if every transportstream should contain the whole EIT. In chapter 5 different strategies to distribute the SI among the transportstreams of a network are discussed. In order to get an impression of the amount of information, let´s assume an example network with 10 transportstreams carrying 8 services each. Each service presents 40 events per day, which are described by an average of 300 bytes. A one week-schedule would then amount to 6.7 Mbytes of schedule. Let´s further assume we want to guarantee a modest response time of 10 seconds disregarding any time needed for processing, tuning and acquisition, this would result in a bandwidth of more than 5 MBit/sec. This makes clear, that once we talk about large networks, transmission and reception of SI have to be jointly optimized, considering potentials and restrictions of transmission- and terminal equipment.

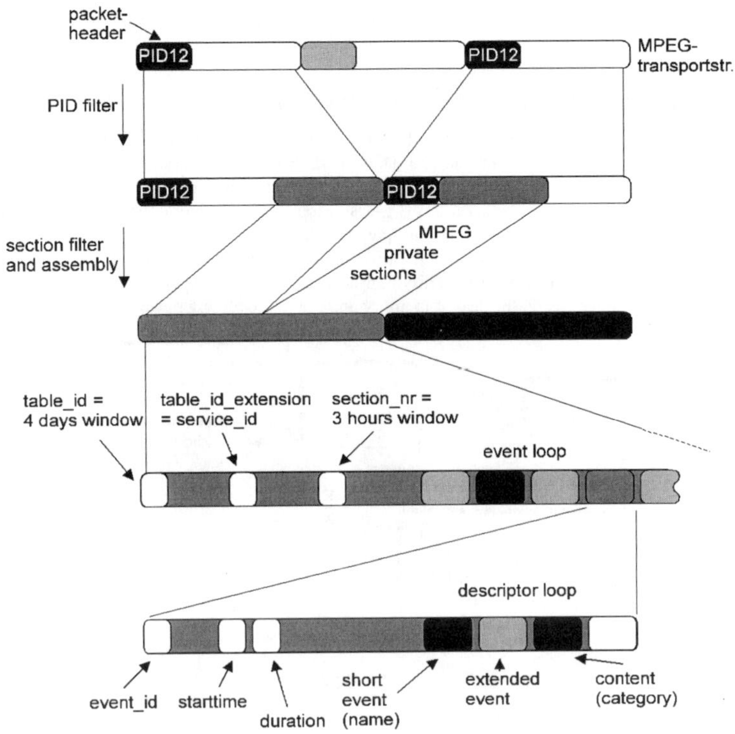


*Figure.2: Coding of event schedule information in the DVB -SI: The Event Information Table*

**Figure 2** outlines the addressing of event information. First, the tuner has to tune to the respective transportstream. This will carry MPEG2 transportstream packets 188 bytes each. EIT sections are just found in packets with PID 12h. The EIT sections can have any length from 18 to 4096 bytes. In most cases, they do not fit into one single packet and have to be assembled out of many subsequent packets. Inside the sectionheader, the *table_id* specifies a four-day interval and eight successive sectionnumbers cover a three-hour time interval (starting from "today midnight"). The *table_extension_id* specifies the corresponding service. Different sets of table_ids are used to distinguish between the events (services) transmitted the actual transportstream (tableId 50h, 51h, ..) or some other transportstream (60h, 61h, ..). Another field, the *versionnumber*, is increased every time the information for the corresponding service and four-day period is updated. This will at least happen every midnight since the table_ids and sectionnumbers refer to "last midnight". Two more table_ids are reserved just for the present and following event.

Once we have found that the section describes the requested service and date-time interval, the data portion of the table contains the event description. Every event starts with a header (event_id, starttime, ..) followed by an arbitrary number of descriptors. These descriptors in turn are identified by their first byte called the *descriptor tag*. One important descriptor is the *content descriptor* (tag 54h) which associates a category/subcategory with the event, like "Movie/Western" or "News/weather report". The *short event descriptor* (tag 4dh) containes the event name and optionally a short textual description (e.g. episode name of a dayly soap), whereas multiple *extended event descriptors* (tag 4eh) can be cascaded to contain textual description of any length.

## 4. Processing MPEG Private Sections in the Set Top Box

**Figure 3** shows how the data is processed in the STB. If the requested data is not transmitted in the current transportstream, the STB has to tune to the desired channel. Of course, this is just possible in the Guide Mode (unless the STB has two tuners). The analog signal is demodulated (QPSK or QAM) and is almost error-free ($10^{-11}$ according to DVB specs.) after foreward error correction. The resulting MPEG2 transportstream is fed into the demultiplexer, which queues the respective data into pre-allocated portions of the System RAM (queue buffers). Third, the data is further filtered, formatted and reinserted into the system RAM. The ability to process SI is mainly dependent on three factors: 1. the functionality of the demux, 2. the size of memory and 3. the processing power of the main micro.

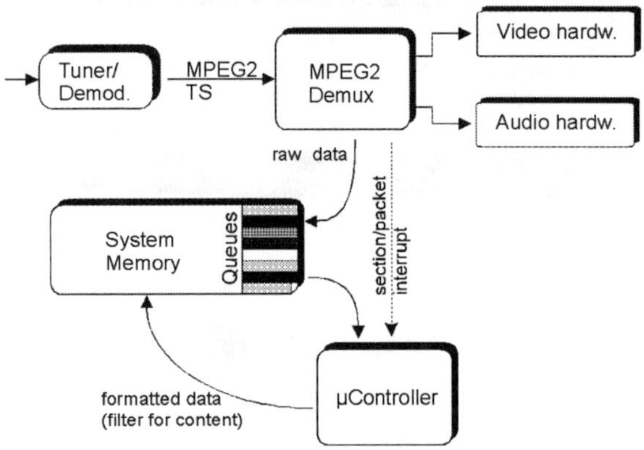


***Figure.3:*** *Processing of SI in the STB*

All MPEG2-demultiplexers filter at least on PID level, but advanced components support filtering of private sections specified by table_id, table_id_extension and versionnumber. The latter concepts lead to a significant reduction of processing load of the main micro. A demux might support simultaneous filtering on one or more queues, where each filter, specified by a set of different parameters (PID, table_id, ..), stores its data into a different queue buffer. Once a data unit (MPEG-packet or section) has been completed in the queue buffer, an interrupt is raised and the main micro has to process and filter the data.

Depending on the number of parallel requests, large portions of the system memory have to be allocated just for buffering. In general, queuing and processing is done successively and not simultaneously, since the bursty nature of the data signals does not generally allow immediate processing of the incoming data. Furthermore, the execution of higher priority tasks might block the SI-filtering process. In the worst case, the queue buffer will have the size

$$queue\_bytes = n\_services \cdot n\_hours \cdot \frac{8 sections}{3 hours} \cdot \frac{4 kBytes}{section},$$

taking into account that eight sections cover three hours of schedule and the maximum size of a section is four kByte. For the Timetable Guide, for example, and a time interval of six hours this amounts to almost 400 kBytes of memory. Clearly, this example is based on a very pessimistic estimate and usually a smaller amount of memory will suffice, but always taking the risk that not all data can be collected at once. If filtering is just done on PID level, a powerful micro is needed to perform online-filtering on the entire EIT-data, coping with burst rates of up to 40Mbit/sec.

Especially the Category Guide is very demanding, since all services of the network have to be scanned. If the SI-data is processed only after all desired sections for a service have been received, acquisition time can become rather long, since just a limited number of services can be scanned at a time. Disregarding the processing time, acquisition time becomes

$$reponsetime = \frac{n\_services}{n\_filters \cdot repetitionrate}.$$

System response can become very slow, since the EIT is unlikely to be repeated more often than every 10 seconds (rate=1/10). In case of PID filtering the whole EIT has to be scanned. In this case, the number of services and the specified time interval only affect the amount of data that has to be copied during the scan.

If not the entire SI-Information is found on every transportstream, even more delays due to queuing and processing have to be taken into account, since the STB will have to tune to the respective transportstreams. Disregarding any restrictions due to memory and available number of queuebuffers, the delay time will be approximately the repetition interval times the number of transportstream to be tuned. An Example: Category search is performed looking for western movies on the whole network containing 8 transportstreams and each transportstream contains just SI for its own services. Since there is no a-priory knowledge about which services might provide such movies, all transportstreams have to be tuned to. For a repetition rate of 20 seconds, the time for collecting the complete category´s schedule will - in the worst case - amount to 160 seconds, not even considering tuning delays, processing times and other overhead. This makes the EPG less usable than a common TV-magazine.

Obviously, an EPG with decent response times definetely requires look-ahead caching of schedule information. Caching, however, is not an easy task for various reasons: 1. Low-cost consumer STBs are unlikely to have enough memory to store several days of schedule. 2. Caching is mainly to be done in the viewing mode. Once the EPG is in guide mode the information should already be available and the demux is busy reacting on users requests anyhow. In Viewing Mode, however, just data of the current transportstream can be collected.

*High- and low level caching*

Two types of caching can be applied: High- and low level caching. In low level caching, the data is cached in the raw private section format, whereas high level caching implies storage of formatted data in compressed or uncompressed format. Both techniques have their advantages. Low level caching is recommended if just part of the sections´ data is of interest. The protocol overhead of the private section syntax is rather small so that the representation in raw format is quite effective. Furthermore, version monitoring and updating of information is easy in raw format, since versionnumbers are associated with (sets of) private sections. Another advantage is that the software layers doing the search and extraction are the same no matter whether the information comes from cache or directly out of the transportstream. Candidates for low level caching are the NIT, BAT, SDT and the EIT for the present and the following event.

Whenever just part of the sections´ data is of interest, high level caching becomes more efficient. If for example just all event names, starttime, duration and categories are to be cached, low level caching would be very inefficient. Moreover, protocol parsing is done just once for every data unit and not for every request.

## 5. SI Transmission Schemes

### 5.1. Bursty vs. smooth transmission

For a fixed size of queue buffer memory, bursty transmissions increase the risk of buffer overflow leading to delays or even data loss due to timeouts in the system. If the demultiplexer is filtering on section level, the burstiness of the data received also depends on current filter settings. The most demanding request is the category search, where every filter is setup to collect a small consecutive number of sections of a different service. The sections should be ordered in a way to minimize the probability of bursts of matching sections. This can be achieved by grouping sections belonging to the same service, i.e.

$$S_{11}, S_{21}, S_{31}, ..., S_{12}, S_{22}, S_{32}, ..., S_{13}, S_{23}, S_{33}, ...$$

if Smn is section m of service n. Certainly, this strategie is not optimal for the Channel Guide where it might be desirable to cache a longer time intervall for a single service. In this case, however, the whole queue buffer can be used for this single service.

### 5.2. Distribution of the data among transportstreams

*a) All SI in every transportstream*

If the whole SI is included in every transportstream of the network, every event information can be retrieved without channel changing. Furthermore, caching of event information in viewing mode is possible. Unfortunately, the bandwidth required increases with second power of the number of transportstreams. Consequently, this method is just suited for small networks or schedules covering just a small time interval.

*b) All SI in one single transportstream*

Once switched to the guide mode, the STB can immediately tune to the channel including the SI data signal and find any data requested. This method strongly reduces the bandwidth required, but makes caching of event information in viewing mode almost impossible, unless the STB is by chance tuned to that transportstream. Depending on the SI bandwidth, one or more video services might have to be sacrificed on the corresponding transportstream to provide the required SI-bandwidth. Both in a) and b) bursty transmission becomes likely.

*c) SI for a service is just found on the corresponding transportstream*

From the service provider´s point of view, this is certainly the most economical way of transmitting SI. Response times, however, will be awfully slow as explained in chapter 4. Caching in Viewing Mode is almost impossible. Due to the low SI-bandwidth on every transportstream, STB with no SI-filtering supported by the demux, might profit from this approach.

*d) Hierarchical transmission of short- and extended event information (***figure 4***)*

This strategy is a compromise between the approaches a) and c): Short event infomation just containing start time, duration, category and the event´s name is transmitted for every event on *every* transportstream, whereas all descriptors for an event are just found on the *corresponding* transportstream. The additional overhead compared to scenario c) is small. Furthermore, the repetition interval can be increased, since this will just affect the speed of caching but not the final response time. A simple example: Including just the short event- and content descriptor, the amount of data to transmit is about 45 Bytes/event assuming a 20 character event name. For 80 Services and 40 Events per day a one-week schedule would amount to about 400kBit/sec if a repetition interval of 20 seconds is selected. Without considering any savings due to compression and NVOD referencing every event consumes about 30 bytes in the cache (after formatting) resulting in less than 670kBytes of memory.

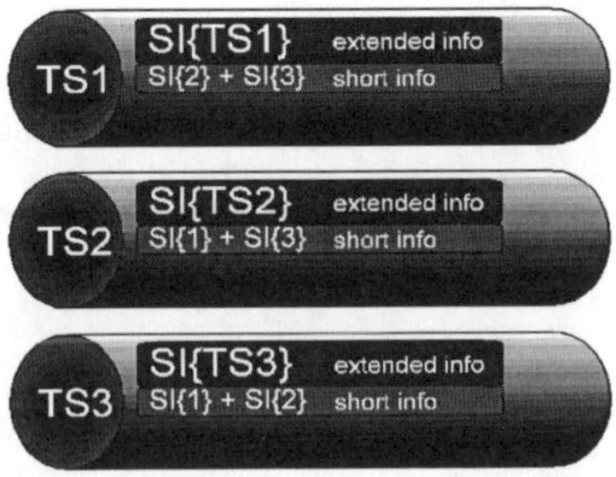


***Figure.4:*** *Hierarchical transmission of SI*

Obviously, this transmission strategy is well suited for high-level event caching. Assuming that the average user will stay in Viewing Mode for a few minutes, there is enough time to cache short event data before going into Guide Mode. In the Guide Mode, the movie´s name and its category can be displayed with almost no delay. Just a small number of events can be displayed on the screen for further selection. While the user will move the cursor to select an event for further information, caching of this information for all events currently displayed can start in the background ( **figure 5**).

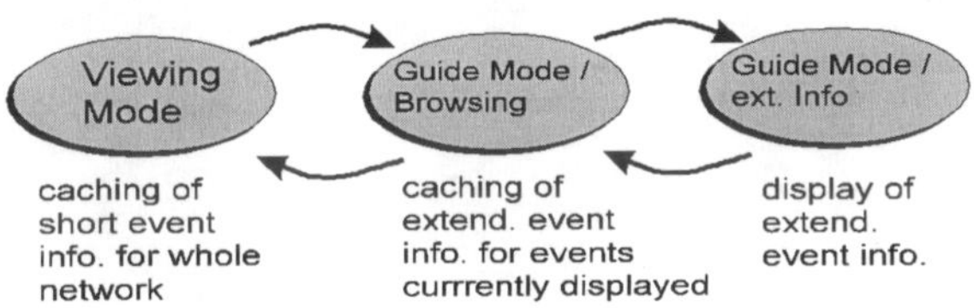


***Figure.5:*** *caching of SI in the STB*

The above solution is well suited to reduce SI bandwidth and allows reasonable response times while keeping the memory requirements in the STB rather low.

## 6. Conclusions

The standardization of Service Information was an important step in the European DVB project. Although some general guidelines for the transmission of SI have been published as well, the final transmission and processing strategies will depend on the actual technical constraints. The main goal is to optimize response times while accessing SI in the user interface. A few transmission techniques and their impact on bandwidth and processing have been discussed. It appears that a hierarchical transmission - short event information on all transportstream and extended event information just on the corresponding transportstream - seems to be a suitable candidate for program guide distribution for large networks and a variety of consumer STBs.

**References**

[1] ETS 300468, "Specification for Service Information (SI) in Digital Video Broadcasting (DVB) Systems"

[2] R.L.W. Cooper et al.,"A User Interface For Multichannel Television", IBC 1995

[3] MPEG2 International Standard: ISO/IEC 13818 parts 1-3

*Acknowledgements:*

*The authors represent just a small team of a large Mutimedia-Terminal software project involving more than 40 engineers in Sweden, Germany and Finland. The authors want to thank all their colleagues for their friendly cooperation and support both in the project and the paper presented. The "look and feel" of the user interface presented is specified and owned by BetaDigital, Gesellschaft für digitale Fernsehdienst mbH. Responsible for the content of this paper are the authors alone.*

# A Virtual Studio– Set System of High Speed and High Functional Performance Realized with Dedicated Hardware

Ryu Watanabe
NHK (Japan Broadcasting Corporation)
Tokyo, Japan

Akio Nishimura
Matsushita Electric Industrial Co., Ltd.
Osaka, Japan

## Abstract

NHK and Matsushita Electric Industrial Co., Ltd. have jointly developed a virtual studio– set system adopting the CG generation dedicated hardware based on their unique architecture. The newly developed system is characterized by its high speed, high functional performance, and its low cost, space– saving and low power consumption.

This paper describes the details of the development of this system, its functions and performance characteristics, together with how it is operated in the actual studio program production.

# 1 Introduction

For the image production in the TV studio, it is conventionally practiced to build up a studio-set which resembles quite close to the actual object. However, such studio-sets require high cost of manufacture, and their storage cost and space requirement are also problems. Moreover, the time required for building up the studio-set and setting the lighting for the same set is considerably long and the studio-set is sometimes a problem also in respect of the studio work time. Furthermore, once built-up, the studio-set requires much time for its repair if required, and studio-sets which can be realized actually are limited. That is, their flexibility in operation and performance is limited.

On the other hand, the three-dimensional computer graphics (CG) technology has made progress and made it possible to generate high-quality CG images in real time (at 60 fields/second). Then, many attempts have been made to produce studio-set images by CG, in place of manufacturing studio-sets actually, and combine these images with the images actually taken in the studio. This is the virtual studio-set concept, and to be sure, the CG generated studio-set has the following merits which can solve the problems of the above-mentioned actual studio-set.

(1) The program production cost can be reduced.
- It is not necessary to manufacture and arrange studio-sets actually.
- Studio-set storage cost and storage space are not necessary.
- It is easy to reuse studio-sets by changing their arrangement.
- It can substitute for remote outdoor setting.

(2) A variety of performance effects can be obtained.
- It is possible to represent unreal space, etc. for which it is difficult to manufacture studio-sets with the actual object.
- It is possible to allow a narrow studio to look as if it were a wide space.
- It is possible to move the studio-set as an animation.

(3) The studio work time can be reduced.
- The time for building up studio-sets is not necessary, and repair and position change can be done easily.
- The lighting for actual studio-sets is not necessary.

However, TV stations must send out programs one after another every day, but only for few of these programs, vast cost and time can be given to each frame in the image production as in the motion picture production. In the studio operation of TV stations, it cannot be permitted to produce those programs only which require much time for the post-production processing. On the other hand, the quality of CG images which can be generated in real time is limited. Thus, from a compromise between the image quality and the production cost, the CG studio-set system has not been introduced on a full scale. NHK has made many investigations from many years ago on what systems should be constructed in order to utilize the merits of CG studio-sets to the full. This has led to introducing the virtual studio-set system which will be explained in the following sections.

## 2 Progress of Technology for the Image Synthesis in the TV Studio

There are a few alternatives proposed for studio–sets, and what has been used for most long is, of course, the chroma key. This means is an important technique which is used with almost no exception in the keying signal extraction from the images actually taken in the studio even in the newest CG synthesis systems. However, in the case of plain chroma key synthesis, the background images are not in interlocking with the actually taken images, and changing the camera angle of view results in unnaturally affected images.

In order to resolve this drawback, NHK developed "Synthe–Vision" in 1988. In Synthe–Vision, the background signals are extracted and synthesized from HDTV size images in real time in interlocking with panning, tilting , zooming and focusing camera information. Thus, in any sense, the background images are two–dimensional. The program production making use of Synthe–Vision was reported on the SMPTE Conference of 1995. (At that meeting, it was referred to that a virtual studio–set system will be introduced in the conference of 1996.)

In the program production by Synthe–Vision, the background images are constructed with the CG images in addition to the actually taken images. Of course, in that case, the CG images are made originally as three–dimensional and then changed to two–dimensional by advance rendering. This method is advantageous in that, because of no real time rendering performed in the studio, the quality of the CG images can be improved up to any desired degree if it is possible to spend the CG production cost and the rendering time as amply as required. However, any three–dimensional effect such that hidden portions show up cannot be obtained by changing the camera position.

Then, the next phase desired is to develop a system in which the background images are the very three–dimensional by CG and the real time rendering in interlocking with the camera angle of view is performed. NHK has already developed such a three–dimensional CG synthesis system using the general–purpose graphics workstation, and it is used in the election report programs, etc. However, the depth position at which the actually taken images can be synthesized is fixed and the CG images are limited to either one, background or fore ground. Therefore, the depth synthesis in its true sense that the camera subject may go around to the front or back of CG images, cannot be realized. Moreover, for the reason of the cost, the multi–camera system cannot easily be adopted and its use is limited to special programs, etc. Then, what is undertaken to be developed and introduced is the virtual studio–set system which is presented this time.

## 3 Details of the System Introduction

The reason why it is difficult to judge as to whether the CG studio–set system is to be introduced or not is that it is difficult to calculate the promising cost merit of the introduction of this system. However, as described above, NHK has used Synthe–Vision for daily operations including live broadcasts. In these operations, many experiences were accumulated to produce CG studio–sets at a cost of about 1/10 of that required for manufacturing the actual sets. As a result, it was judged that the cost–effectiveness could be further improved if any system equivalent in cost to Synthe–Vision could be used to provide three–dimensional synthesized images. And it was then decided to construct a new CG studio–set system in a studio separate from the Synthe–Vision studio.

However, it was judged that there is no promising cost merit which may justify the construction of a new dedicated studio, and it was decided to install this new CG studio–set system in any existing studio. As this studio, CT–415 Studio (about 330 $m^2$) was selected. It is located in the vicinity of and is slightly wider than the Synthe–Vision studio (about 230 $m^2$). Apparently, the area comparison of this selection is contradictory to the CG studio–set concept that a narrow studio can look as if it were wide. But, the decision was based on a consideration that, in order to develop those programs which allow the three–dimensional CG images to be displayed effectively, it will be better to have an ample area for the camera to go around freely. However, only one of two horizont cyclorama faces was painted uniformly in blue ready to be used for synthesis operation at any time so that the studio may be used not only for the synthesized but also for the general programs.

The switcher provided in CT–415 Studio is a digital switcher for NTSC signals, and the VTR used in this studio is also a composite VTR (D–3). If it is necessary to use a component VTR in the same studio, it was decided to bring it there separately.

In the matter of programs, it was decided to start the introduction of the new system by shifting into this system those of the programs produced by Synthe–Vision of which the performance effects can be further improved by combining them with the three–dimensional CG images. By verifying these programs, it will be possible to develop new three–dimensional synthesized programs.

Based on the way of thinking about the system introduction mentioned above, the criteria for the selection of the new CG studio–set system were specified as follows.

(1) In order to insure the cost merit, the system price should be equal to or below that of Synthe–Vision.

(2) For the daily studio operations to be performed smoothly, this system should have at least all of the Synthe–Vision's functions.
For example:
> Function of defocusing to CG.
> Function of HDTV size two–dimensional image synthesis.
> Permitting use of at least three–camera, and if possible, four–camera systems. (In the case of a single Synthe–Vision, cut–switching only is permitted.)

(3) In order to make the performance effects distinct as compared with Synthe–Vision, this system should be complete in the depth synthesis function so that the camera subject may go around to the front and the rear of the three–dimensional CG image.

(4) The Synthe–Vision programs use high–definition CGs of at least 80,000 polygons (the smallest triangles constructing the CG geometry). It is difficult to generate similar numbers of polygons in real time by the present state of technology. Therefore, even if studio–sets are built up with the three–dimensional CG images, it is impossible to maintain the quality if a

considerably high definition texture mapping technique (that is, a technique of separately preparing high-definition patterns and designs and pasting them to the CG model) is not used in combination. Thus, on the assumption that HDTV size textural patterns are used for two walls, the floor and the ceiling, the texture memory capacity should be more than 24 Mbytes.

(5) For the Synthe-Vision programs, a maximum of 6,000 polygons for CG animation are synthesized by plain keying. On the assumption that the quality should be maintained and for the background CG images, the polygons of a number thrice as large as for CG animation are necessary, the CG generating capability per field should be more than 24,000 polygons.

(6) In order to insure smooth shifting from Synthe-Vision programs, and moreover, in provision for such a case where, for any reason, the Synthe-Vision studio cannot be used, it should be possible to draw images by reading magneto optical disks (MO) for the data of Synthe-Vision.

(7) The pan heads, lenses, data collection devices, data cables, etc. for Synthe-Vision should be realized as compatible with this system as far as practicable, so that the spare parts may be used in common for both systems.

(8) This system is installed as an addition in the existing studio, and as such, it should be of space-saving and low power consumption type.

(9) For this system to be usable also for live broadcasts, the system manufacturer's support should be available at any time during 24 hours.

Based on these criteria, several companies' CG studio-set systems were investigated by comparison. All these systems have already attained the level of practical use and are based on the general-purpose graphics workstation (ONYX by SGI, etc.). The greatest consideration for these systems includes cost and image drawing speed, but these two subjects trade off with each other and cannot be satisfied simultaneously. Then appeared a proposition to develop any high-speed dedicated hardware for the parallel processing of CG image drawing.

In the case of cascade-connectable small-sized and inexpensive dedicated boards, the number of boards can be selected according to the quality requirement and available budget and space and the extensibility is high. Further, if these boards are used with the multi-camera system, they may be used in such a way that each camera may be allocated with its required number of boards, and if only one camera is used for recording, all the boards may be used for high-speed drawing. In this method of use, there appears a possibility that the polygons of a number as large as 80,000 can be addressed in real time in place of by advance rendering in the conventional practice.

Based on such dedicated hardware concept, NHK and Matsushita Electric Industrial Co., Ltd. have developed this system. The features of the new system are explained in more detail below.

## 4 Features of This System

This system consists of three CG generators. Each CG generator consists of a main body shelf plate of 620 mm in height and a power supply shelf plate of 180 mm in height. The main body shelf plate has CG generating boards, a texture/intensity mapping board, a moving picture texture DVE board, a depth key generating board, etc. mounted on it. Each CG generator is connected with a personal computer which has a built-in hard disk as an independent controller. Three controllers in total are connected through a network with an operation terminal. Each component apparatus will be described in the following sections and here, the features of the system as a whole are described.

### Features of CG generator:

(1) Each CG generator shelf plate is designed to be compact so that it may be accommodated in a single half-rack. CG generators and controllers, each three, and an A/D and D/A conversion shelf are accommodated in two 2m racks.

(2) The image drawing speed is 2,000 polygons/field on average per CG generating board. In the shelf plate configuration at this time, a maximum of 12 CG generating boards can be mounted, and so, the image drawing speed in total is 24,000 polygons/field. If, in the future, it becomes possible to use all these boards in the one-camera system, it may be 72,000 polygons/field.

(3) Precise intensity calculation by the Radiosity method is carried out during CG shading, so that subtle shades may be represented. When it is said that this system has a CG image drawing capability of 24,000 polygons/field, this value refers to intensity-mapped and texture-mapped polygons.

(4) When each CG system is fully equipped with 12 CG generating boards, the power consumption is as low as about 1 kW.

(5) When each CG system is fully equipped with boards, the cost is lower than that of Synthe-Vision.

(6) Each CG generator uses camera sensors to collect camera panning, tilting, zooming, focusing and iris information. The panning and tilting data are obtained by counting the output of a rotary encoder mounted in the dedicated camera head. The lens data to be received may be either a voltage value or a rotary encoder output.

(7) Each camera sensor is provided with an interface to take in the camera position information (front and back, right and left, height) in real time. In this respect, although camera tracking cannot be done at the present time, in order to permit the camera position to be changed in real time when a crane camera is installed, the crane data output software is under development.

(8) After the camera information is taken in, the CG images of the camera angle of view are generated and output with a delay of two frames. In correspondence to this timing, the actually

taken images are also delayed by two frames inside the CG generator.

(9) The CG generator shelf plate contains the DVE board to take in externally live transmission images, VTR images and other SMPTE 259M component signals, and these images can be converted into any form and mapped as the moving image textures. They can be treated in quite the same manner as the ordinary still image textures. By using this function, for example, any form and any number of image transfer monitors can be arranged at any place in the CG space. Since these moving images are output with a delay of 1 frame, it is normally not necessary to give special attention to the lip synchronization.

(10) In this system, the iris information is also collected, so that the defocusing taking into account the CG image depth may be applied according to the focus position and the camera field depth. This defocusing is a combination of that applied inside the texture by software and that applied to the portion including the edge of the CG model by hardware.

(11) Plural CG studio–sets can be loaded previously and switched later between different CG studio–sets during the vertical interval. The number of CG studio–sets which can be loaded simultaneously varies with the contents of the CG studio–sets, and usually, it is determined by the texture memory capacity of 24 Mbytes which is the upper limit.

## System Features:

(1) To each of three cameras, an independent CG generator is connected, and in the event that one of these CG generators fails, this system can be operated with the two remaining cameras. Moreover, the synthesized images of each of the three cameras can be monitored of the broadcast quality at all times. Further, the respective synthesized images are input to three cross–points in the studio switcher, so that any processing, such as dissolve, wipe, DVE, etc., can be performed freely between these synthesized images.

(2) Each of these CG generators and controllers has an input portion for the image signal (SMPTE 259M component) and camera information for three cameras, and the allocation of camera and CG connections can be changed freely. In this respect, the present system is constructed not to produce contradictions to tally and return images to be returned to the cameras.

(3) Each CG generator can select the camera, with which it will operate in interlocking, from three connected cameras during the vertical interval according to the tally information supplied from the studio switcher. This function permits each CG generator to operate with three cameras (for cut–switching only) and so, this system can operate with up to 9 cameras.

(4) The CG system judges automatically as to where in the CG space the depth synthesis position of the actually taken image should be placed. That is, based on the information from the magnetic sensor mounted on the camera subject (as measured 20 times per second), the distance of the camera subject to the camera is calculated. The calculated result is used to judge as to which of the actually taken image and the CG model comes in front for each pixel.
If the CG model comes in front, the keying signal to extract the actually taken image for the

pixel is generated. (This is called "depth keying signal".) The magnetic sensor is a commercial product and here, its description in detail is omitted.

(5) Each CG generator has three systems of image outputs (SMPTE 259M component), and two frames delayed actually taken images, CG images and depth keying signals are output. By inputting these signals to an external chroma–key synthesizing device, the three–dimensional synthesized images are obtained. Thus, the camera subject can move freely to the front and the rear of the CG image. This system is constructed also to be able to output the actually taken images, CG images and keying signals (composite keying signals for background and fore ground) selected by means of the studio switcher for the purpose of post–production processing.

(6) The chroma–key synthesizing board can be mounted also in the CG generator shelf plate, and if any external chroma–key device is not used, the three–dimensional synthesis can be made internally and the resulting synthesized images can be output.

(7) Three–dimensional CG animation characters can be treated simultaneously with the CG studio–sets. Three CG generators are synchronized to prevent contradictions from being prodded in the movements in animation between them. The movements in animation can be realized not only by reproducing the previously specified movements, but also as those movements controlled in real time by external devices (data glove, keyboard, mouse, etc.) operation.

(8) On the camera side, a remote control terminal is provided so that the cameraman may adjust the synthesized images finely. This means is effective in the event that the performer's movement have become different between in rehearsal and at the take, and the CG position (front and back, left and right, height) and the camera panning, tilting, zooming and defocusing with respect to the CG can be adjusted in real time. However, in the camera operation, it is to be noted that if the adjustment is too large, a contradiction may result in relation to the actual take (especially in the case of zooming adjustment).

(9) The remote control terminal for the cameraman is provided with 6 memories to store the adjustment results. Thus, if the camera position is determined in advance up to 6 places and the corresponding CG positions are kept in memory, then it is permitted to move the camera for shooting from different angles at the take. (This is not real time tracking.)

(10) Images can be drawn by reading data from the magneto optical disk for Synthe–Vision. In this case, it is possible to select the location to which the HDTV size texture is to be pasted, such as a plate, a part of a cylinder or a part of a sphere.

## 5 Hardware Configuration

The hardware configuration of this system is explained in the following sections.

## 5.1 CG generator

The CG generator has been developed aiming the following objects.

(1) It should be easy to insure real time image generation.

(2) The delay time in processing should be suppressed to within 2 frames.

(3) The texture/intensity mapping should be able to be used flexibly.

The CG generating board, which is to perform image generation by parallel processing, is constructed with 4 general-purpose micro processors and an ASIC dedicated for graphics processing. The texture mapping and intensity mapping intended to improve the reality of CG images are performed collectively on the texture/intensity mapping board. The texture capacity can be up to 96 Mbytes. However, at the present state, it is 48 Mbytes, 24 Mbytes of which are intended for intensity mapping.

The CG generation architecture adopted in this system is called "Merge and Map Architecture". Its feature is that the mapping processing is performed after the hidden face elimination processing. It becomes necessary to store the mapping information for each pixel, but the mapping processing for hidden faces is unnecessary and mapping paralleling is no longer required. This is a great advantage. Therefore, in each CG generation board, all kinds of processing prior to mapping are completely paralleled.

The hidden face elimination processing is performed as follows. CG generating boards are connected in series with each other and, in any stage, the results of processing obtained in all preceding stages are compared and synthesized with the depth information obtained in that stage, and the resultant information is sent to the subsequent stage in the relaying system until the final results are obtained. Mapping is performed on these final results only. In order to reduce the buffer capacity for the hidden face processing, buffers are restricted to 1 scan line only and are synchronized for each scan line to be processed. This is called "Scanline Z-buffer Method".

## 5.2 Controller

The controller controls the CG generator so that it generates CG in the field timing in accordance with the camera information taken in at the intervals of 1/60 second from the camera sensor. For the real time processing, a personal computer running on an OS for real time operation is used. The controller also controls the static load distribution between CG generating boards of the CG generator.

## 5.3 Operation terminal

The operation terminal is a personal computer running on Windows NT. It controls 3 systems of CG generators by means of GUI (Graphical User Interface) based operation tools and performs switching of CG studio-sets, animation start-up, etc. and tally input/output processing, as well. Further, the operation terminal is connected with various animation control devices (data glove, etc.) and a magnetic sensor.

## 6 Software Configuration

The software configuration of this system is explained below.

### 6.1 Scanline Z-buffer renderer: SZ

In order to generate CG images in real time, coordinate transformation, perspective transformation, clipping, and packet formation for the delivery to CG generation dedicated ASIC are performed. Load distribution processing is performed dynamically by 4 processors in the CG generating boards, so that the dispersion of processing time between the processors may be absurd.

### 6.2 Rendering data Distribution controller program: RD

In order to distribute the dispersion of load between the CG generating boards statically, data allocation is determined when CG set data is loaded and it is sent to each CG generating board.

### 6.3 Virtual Studio Execution controller program: VSE

In synchronism with the vertical synchronization signal, the camera information is taken in from the camera sensor and delivered to SZ on each CG generating board. When CG set data is loaded, commands are given to SZ and RD to start data reading. Moreover, register renewal for the operation specification of dedicated hardware in the image section, etc. is done.

### 6.4 Graphical User Interface program: GUI

Software to operate this system. The basic functions of this program include switching of CG studio-sets, animation start-up, manual control of CG positions and depth synthesis positions, etc. Further, in order to address switching of plural CG studio-sets within one program, it performs setting and editing of scenarios to specify these plural CG studio-sets to be used.

### 6.5 CG set data Conversion tool: CGC

Geometry, texture and lighting information, modeled by commercial three-dimensional CG modeling software "SoftImage" or "3D-Studio", are collectively converted into the internal data of this system. Radiosity calculation is also processed by this tool.

## 7 Flexibility in Operation and Operating Procedures

The ordinary operation is performed at the main operation terminal in the sub-control room and also at the TD terminal mounted in the switcher console. The main operation terminal is a DOS/V personal computer and runs on Windows NT. It is provided with GUI so that the operation may be performed without being conscious of this OS. The TD terminal has a thin-layer liquid crystal display of touch-panel type and is provided with GUI which is the same as in the main operation terminal, except that the main operation terminal is operated by mouse and keyboard operation.

In order to facilitate the selection of CG studio-sets to be used, reduced scale pictures obtained by rendering each CG are displayed on the GUI display. The operation terminal is added with the functions equivalent to the remote terminal used by the cameraman. The decision as to whether the fine adjustment of CG positions during the take is to be done by TD or by each cameraman is made according to the circumstances. However, some basic rules should have been determined in order to prevent erroneous adjustments from being made by simultaneous performance at both.

The flexibility in operation in the studio is as described so far. Then, the operating procedures in the CG modeling stage are explained below. For the programs using this system at present, CG studio-sets are produced by means of modeling software called "SoftImage". In consequence, at present, conversion software to convert the data of SoftImage into the data structure of this system have been prepared. For other modeling software (such as "3D-Studio"), conversion software will be prepared in succession.

For the conversion, the magnification of size, the kind of shading (Constant, Gouraud or Radiosity) and the brightness can be specified, except that animation is limited to Gouraud shading only.

For the use of this conversion software, it is assumed that it is installed in the terminal in which SoftImage is installed. How the CG data after conversion is rendered in this system can be confirmed while selecting the angle of view on the screen of the terminal. By this advance confirmation, it is permitted to minimize the cases there the CG data is repaired after it is brought into the studio. As a rule, the converted CG data is brought in the form of DAT or MO into the studio.

## 8 Effects in the Program Production

It is in August, 1996, that this system started the studio operation with the CG studio-sets produced, not for demonstration, but for broadcasting. Therefore, it is still impossible to decisively evaluate what studio-sets are best suited for this system.

There are still no complete three-dimensional CG sets produced actually for the programs. At present, it is the main practice that the floor, the wall faces and the ceiling are built up three-dimensionally and the high definition textures are pasted to them. However, even this practice alone is successful in producing a feeling of depth different from Synthe-Vision.

Moreover, in order to make use of the great advantage of this system that animation characters can be synthesized three-dimensionally, the production of new three-dimensional CG characters is also under investigation.

Further, in the future, in order to produce complete three-dimensional CG studio-sets, it will be necessary first to get sufficient understanding of the persons concerned with CG design about the performance effects of these three-dimensional CG studio-sets.

## 9 Summary

It has not been a long time since this system started the operation, and its functions are still not made full use of in the actual program production. However, this system, which has been realized as a full-scale virtual studio-set production system with three-dimensional CG and usable daily with the three-camera system, will as such probably be the first system in the world. For the time being, it will be actively utilized for producing dreamy studio-sets for children programs and overseas-imaged studio-sets for language learning programs, etc. Further, various propositions from the program side have begun to appear for the future.

Moreover, several plans are proposed to introduce this system in any studio narrower than the studio in which it is installed, so that the studio may look as if it were wider. A great advantage of this system is that the number of CG generating boards suited for the intended purpose and the budget can be selected in introducing this system.

The subjects left in the future are as follows.

(1) Development of camera position detecting methods and addressing to handy cameras.

(2) Expansion of the measuring region of the depth measuring magnetic sensor.

(3) Development of techniques to synthesize plural camera subjects in different depth positions.

(4) Improvement of GUI (such as addition of the present angle-of-view range to the CG reduced images).

(5) Simplification of the initial setting method for the camera-CG positional relation.

(6) Simplification of the lens calibration (measurement of lens characteristics) method.

(7) Improvement of the polygon processing capability by paralleling the CG generating boards between shelf plates.

Many of these subjects may be common to almost all of the CG studio-set synthesis systems rather than specific to this system. It is expected that, by solving them, CG studio-set synthesis systems will be further developed.

# Developing New Program Production Techniques using the "Virtual Set" and the Motion Capture System at NHK

**Yoshikazu Taoda, Seiji Kunishige, Toshiyuki Sakamoto, Akira Suzuki**
Broadcasting Engineering Department
NHK ( Japan Broadcasting Corporation )
Tokyo, JAPAN

## Abstract

The practical usage of the virtual set and the motion capture system have been of interest to numerous broadcasters. The combination of these systems is expected to be an attractive tool for realizing a diverse new type of content for television broadcast programs.

Utilizing the latest computer technologies, we at NHK have recently developed a real-time computer graphics production system which combines our "virtual set" and motion capture system. The virtual set creates three dimensional computer images which are synchronized with camera motion or zoom. These three dimensional images can be composited into live video images. The motion capture system maps actual real-time human body motion onto a computer generated human character using data collected from magnetic sensors attached to the body.

We describe our recent works in various broadcast program productions such as the 1995 Japanese House of Counselors Election Coverage and the NHK special series TV programs and discuss solutions for the various problems regarding hardware and software systems and real-time three dimensional production methods. We also discuss what new talents and skills for these new types of productions need to be fostered.

# 1. Introduction

Computer Graphics has a wide range of applications in television broadcast programs, from three dimensional visual simulations using scientific data to three dimensional character animation representing lifelike human motion.

We at NHK Tokyo naturally have a great deal of experience in computer graphics image production for television programs. We have created various three dimensional computer graphics animation to meet diverse on-demand programming needs using our own original computer graphics software and applications. They are running on SGI graphics workstations networks and can create images both for NTSC and HDTV ( Hi-Vision ) standards.

With the latest computer technologies, we at NHK Tokyo have recently developed a real-time computer graphics production system which combines our "virtual set" and motion capture systems. The virtual set creates three dimensional computer images which are synchronized with camera motion or zoom and can be composited into live video images. The motion capture system maps real-time human body motion onto a computer generated human character using data collected from sensors attached to the body.

This new system enables the use of real-time interactive three dimensional graphics production in live TV programs, such as an interview program with a computer generated actor on screen with a human guest, together in a computer generated virtual set environment. We are now preparing to use this new production system in the practical creation of broadcast programs for both NTSC and HDTV standards.

In this paper, we describe our recent work using the real-time three dimensional computer graphics production system prototype, some of the problems we encountered, and the solutions we have implemented. We also discuss the need for new talent and skills for creating this new kind of programming.

# 2. TV Program Production Using the Virtual Set System

Last year, for the 17th House of Counselors Election Coverage, we developed a compact version of the real-time virtual studio set system. This system is based on a prototype developed by NHK Science and Technical Research Laboratories in 1993.

For use during the election coverage, we further improved the hardware and software. Hardware improvements were accomplished by stabilizing data detection on the zooming and focusing parameters of the TV camera using a rotary-encoder device. The video delay equipment to compensate for time differences of the output video signals between the TV camera and the computer graphics workstation was also developed. By making the hardware compact enough to put on a portable video rack, we have created a system that is easy to transport to different TV studios.

The software systems were optimized to enable rendering of texture mapped three dimensional scenes at video frame rates. A menu-driven tool for easy adjustment of rendering attributes, such as color and the position of lights and camera in the virtual environment was also added, as shown in Figure 1.

In the 17th House of Counselors Election Coverage, three dimensional graphs to track the number of votes obtained from the Government and the Opposition parties were composited with live images from TV cameras. In this case, as is shown in Figure 2, the three dimensional graphs played an important role as a virtual studio set. Our real-time virtual studio system has been widely used, not only in the election TV program but also other TV programs produced for both NTSC and HDTV standards. It is highly effective for the real-time virtual studio set system to be merged with the live TV programs as shown in Figure 3.

## 3. The Application of Motion Capture Technology to Computer Graphics

One of the major long-standing goals of computer graphics animators worldwide is to create 3D characters capable of representing natural human motions. To achieve this accurate human motion, numerous research projects, from the computation of dynamics to the robotics field have been studied, but many problems still remain. The motion capture technology is another attractive approach to solving these problems in the computer graphics field. Although two kinds of motion capture systems ( optical and magnetic ) are now available for computer graphics production, each system has advantages and disadvantages.

We have selected suitable motion capture systems for the types of applications we want to produce. The following criteria determine which system may be suitable for each application:

- Real-time or non real-time use
- Complex or simple representation of motion
- Interactive or non-interactive use
- The size of the working area for a performer

We have used an optical system, which is good for capturing more complex motion like dance. However, it still has problems in realizing real-time motion capture because captured data have to translate to three dimensional data in the computer before display on the character object. Therefore, the animators often must correct the position and orientation data of human motion from the optical systems using manufacturer's software. But we think that the flexibility of the optical system outweighs its current problems.

The magnetic system can achieve real-time motion capture, but is somewhat limited by the number of polygons that can be displayed. We have recently developed a magnetic system prototype which maps real-time human body motion onto a computer generated human character using data collected from magnetic sensors attached to the body. This system enables us to display the three dimensional character object with human-like motion in real time, allowing us to produce a wide variety of applications in TV programs.

In the following sections, we describe further some actual production examples that illustrate the uses of both of these systems.

## 3.1 Computer Graphics Production Using the Optical Motion Capture System

We recently produced a Hi-Vision special program entitled "We Love LUCY". This program presents a virtual world on the Hi-Vision screen where the heroine "LUCY", children and a teacher live together. LUCY is an ancestor of mankind from about 3.5 million years ago. She is rendered in detail as a young lady, using high resolution HDTV computer graphics.

Important key points in this program were to represent her motion such as dancing and running as accurately as possible. With the optical motion capture system, precise and subtle nuances of her finger motion were represented. Collected three dimensional position data from optical sensors were given to the Wavefront Kinemation software package and LUCY's bone character model was rendered for each TV frame.

Figure 4 shows capturing the performer's motion using the optical motion capture system.
Figure 5 also shows a scene adapted from the captured data to LUCY's character model.

## 3.2 Real-time Computer Graphics Production Combining the Virtual Set and the Magnetic Motion Capture System

We have developed a real-time computer graphics production system which combines our virtual set and the magnetic motion capture system prototype. Since the motion capture system is capable of capturing a performer's motion in real time, we can use this system to mix live actors and computer characters simultaneously in the virtual set. An example is an interview program with an interactive computer generated actor on screen with a human guest together in a computer generated three dimensional studio set environment.

Using this system, we were able to produce, from the specifications of an NHK TV program director, a show in which LUCY, the ancestor of mankind, interacts with each guest in a Hi-Vision variety show program.

Figure 6 shows the block diagram of the real-time computer graphics production system.
Figure 7 shows capturing the performer's motion using the magnetic motion capture system.
Figure 8 also shows the interaction of LUCY with a guest in the virtual studio set environment.

To capture both whole body and lip motion, two professional performers-a dancer and a radio actress-played their roles. A total of seven magnetic sensors were attached to the performer's hands, feet, head, neck and hips to capture the whole body motion. In addition, sensors to capture finger motion were used. Other sensors to capture lip motion were also attached to the radio actress. This enabled us to create the real-time lip animation synchronized with the performer's mouth motions.

Thus, with the combination a small number of sensors and inverse kinematics techniques, we created the real-time three dimensional computer graphics character animation in the computer generated virtual studio set environment. We also recognized that an advantage of our system was that we can easily check and refine the animation of the three dimensional character on the CRT display in real time, since the entire motion capture system is on the set at the TV studio.

## 4. Some Issues with the Systems

As is mentioned before, there is no doubt that the virtual set and motion capture systems are highly regarded as new program production techniques for producing new kinds of effects in TV programs. However, in our program production experience in using these systems, we recognize that we have a lot of practical problems to solve in order to meet the expectations and requirements from directors of varied TV program productions.

In motion capture systems there can be problems caused by differences of figure size between a performer and the computer generated three dimensional character. Our prototype solves this problem by using the transform software function which converts captured data to the joint motions of the three dimensional character's body.

Rendering speed is one of the biggest bottlenecks, especially in real-time Hi-Vision production. It needs very high image quality-twice the quality of that of NTSC standard images. The number and size of the polygons required for realistic rendering is another potential bottleneck. For these scenarios, not only do we need to optimize the rendering process, but we also need good art direction that can work with the limitations and constraints of the hardware and the software.

Another problem is concerns actors in virtual studio sets, and the motion capture performers. They often experience difficulties in positioning themselves or interacting with virtual objects created by computer graphics. We must help teach them how to portray the most suitable movements of their bodies while considering machine rendering speed. To reduce the actor's training time, we show them how to act with natural eye-contact in the virtual studio set. Another problem is that program directors do not always figure out the most effective production techniques that utilize the various sub-systems that exists in our real-time production systems.

## 5. Conclusion-What is Needed for the Future?

Computer graphics TV program production has changed along with the progress of computer power. Up to now, computer graphics images were highlighted in commercials and other TV programs. In recent years, greater realism in rendering has made possible the seamless combination of live actors working in virtual sets. And realistic human character animation has been enhanced by the use of motion capture systems.

At the same time, the number of requirements by TV program directors for novel and attractive productions has been increasing. To meet these desires, new, practical, and efficient production techniques that take into consideration the constraints we mentioned need to be developed.

The various productions we have created using our motion capture and virtual set technologies are helping us to define what techniques need to be developed, as well as the types of human skills that need to be fostered. Figure 9 shows a structure of the project staff in a program production of an NHK one year series special TV program, entitled "Part III of the Universe Within". The artistic technical director in the Figure is a key person who is responsible for computer graphics and other video production, including traditional video editing and compositing live images with computer generated images.

The following are the major skills which the artistic technical director should have:

- Managing and coordinating production schedules and budgets
- Making decisions about suitable facilities-either in-house or outside production
- Making decisions about suitable software-either our own original software or manufacturers' software applications
- Supervising an art designer, an animator, software programmer and a video engineer, and the resources of in-house and outside production
- Communicating technical and artistic information, such as limitation of the real-time motion capture system, to a program director

For fifteen years, our Computer Graphics Group, a small staff of engineers with software skills, has been creating various three dimensional computer graphics products based on our own original software systems. Work such as the human simulation and scientific visual simulations were utilized as core pieces in NHK TV programs. We are also trying to expand our engineers' skills to include the ability to work with, and be sensitive to the needs of art directors, performers and program directors.

We have described our recent work and some of the advantages and disadvantages of the new system prototypes. We have also mentioned the necessity of new skills and talents for the new types of productions we are creating. In the NHK special TV programs, especially in Hi-Vision (HDTV) programs, more complex new production techniques are becoming similar to the production of SFX movies. In order to meet the new desires and challenges in program production, we are working continuously on developing technical advances in hardware and software as well as trying to improve the skills of our engineers and our production teams.

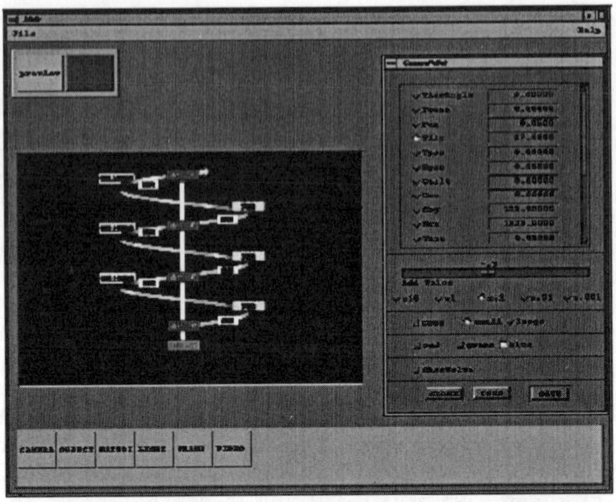

**Figure 1** : A menu for adjusting of rendering attributes.

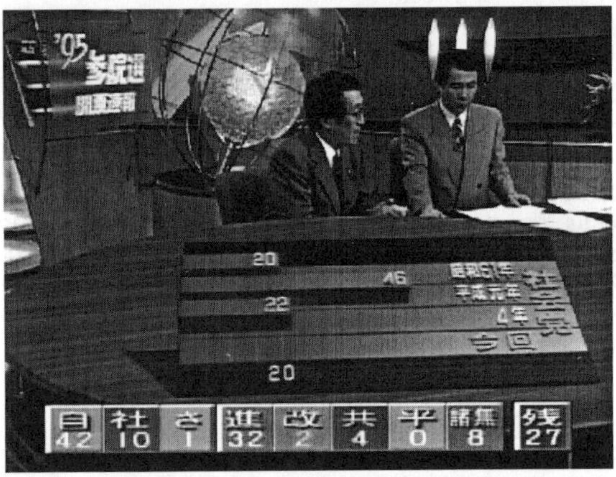


**Figure 2** : An example of application in the live TV programs using the virtual studio set system.

Three dimensional graphs to track the number of votes obtained from the Government and the Opposition parties were composited with live images from TV cameras in the 17th House of Counselors Election Coverage.

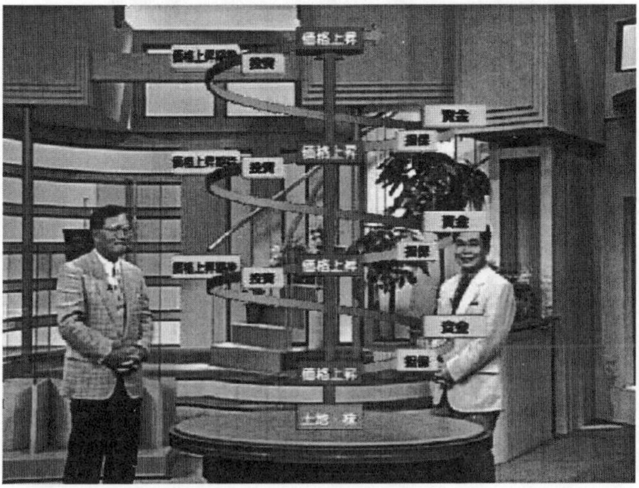


**Figure 3** : An example of application in the information TV programs using the virtual studio set system.

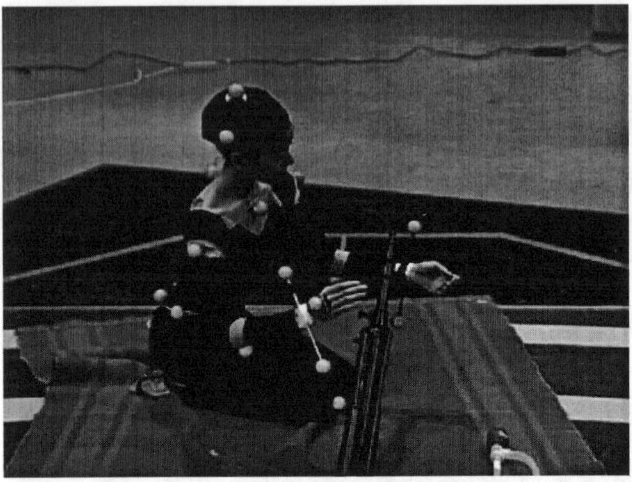

**Figure 4** : Capturing the performer's motion using the optical motion capture system.

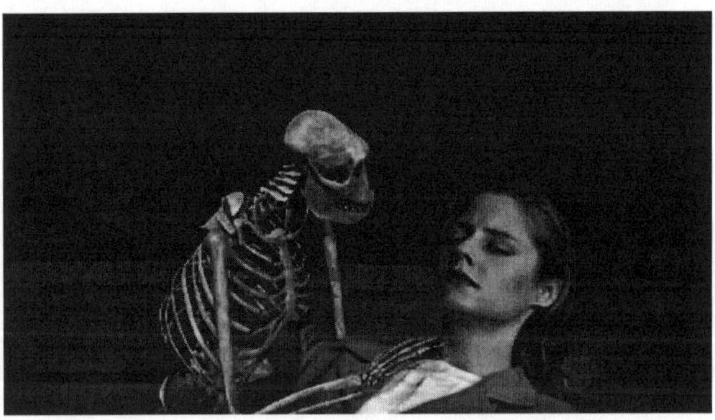

**Figure 5** : A scene adapted from the captured data to LUCY's character model.

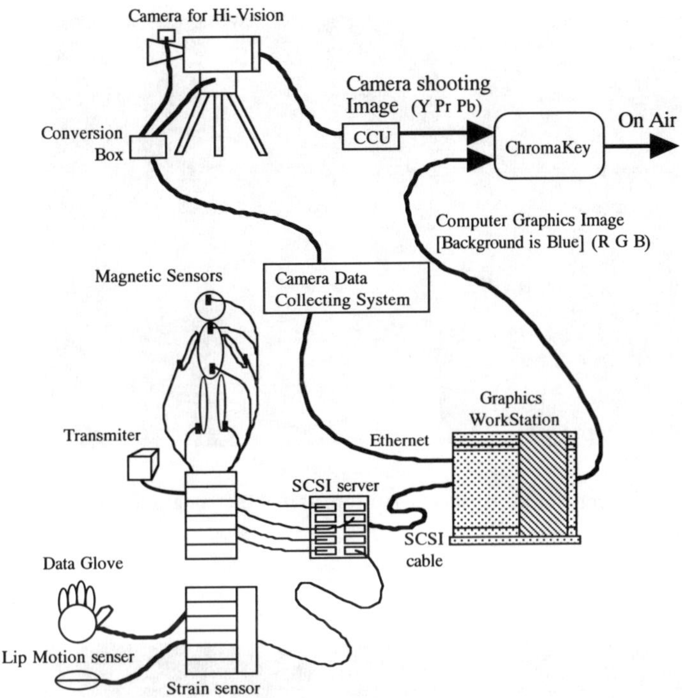


**Figure 6** : Block diagram of the real-time computer graphics production system.

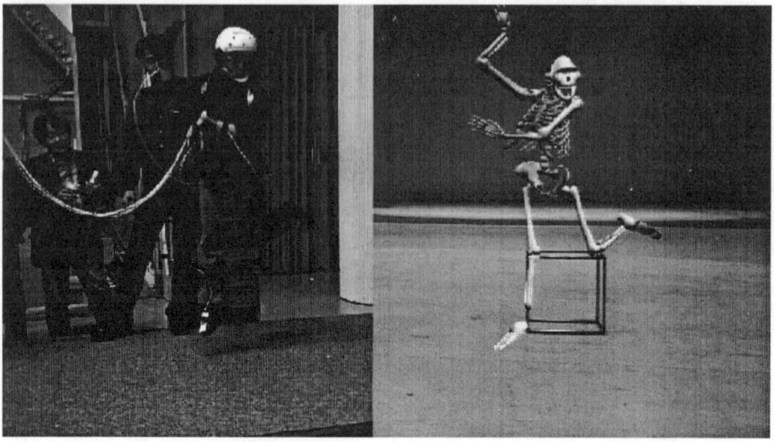

**Figure 7** : Capturing the performer's motion using the magnetic motion capture system.

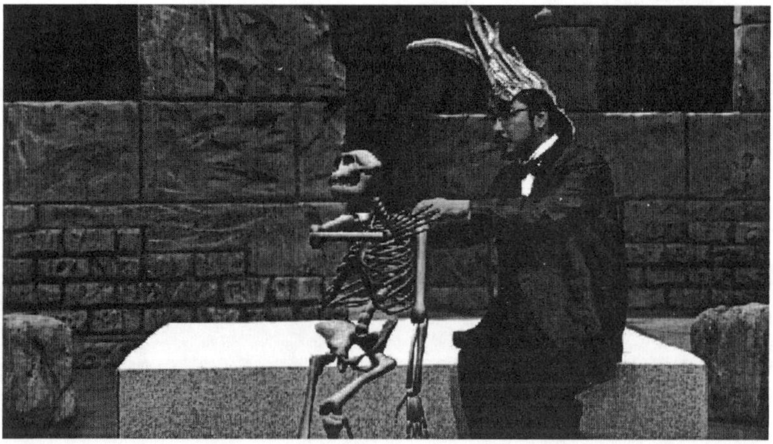

**Figure 8** : The interaction of LUCY with a guest in the virtual studio set environment.

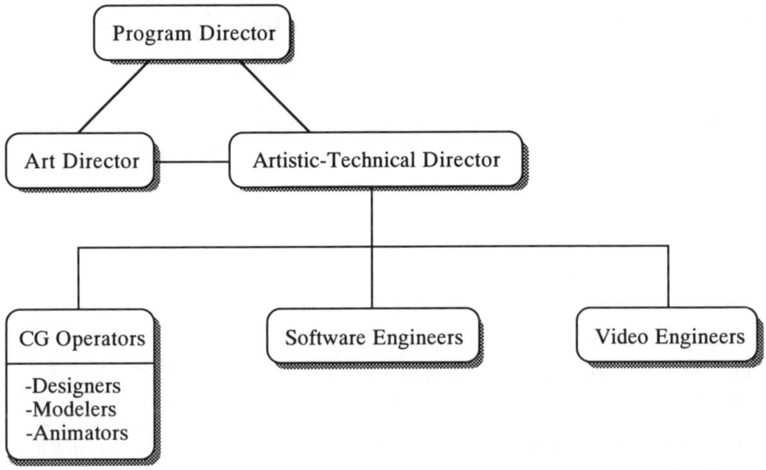


**Figure 9** : A structure of the project staff in a program production of an NHKcoming one year series special TV program

The artistic technical director is a key person who is responsible for computer graphics and other video production, including traditional video editing and compositing live images with computer generated images.

# Practical Studio Productions Using High Quality, Low Cost, Virtual Sets

David N. A. Drew
Radamec Inc.
Scotch Plains, N.J.

## Abstract:

Virtual Studios have been demonstrated at Broadcast Exhibitions since their first showing at IBC in 1994. They created an immediate impact as program producers were excited by both the technology and the potential for enhancing their own productions. Subsequent to the initial euphoria, it was soon realized that not only did these virtual studios require substantial amounts of computing power, but also needed a number of specialist staff to operate and design the virtual sets. Could a lower cost, simpler alternative be found?

The paper will discuss the requirements for operating a low cost 2D virtual studio. It offers a ground up approach on how virtual programs can be designed and produced, starting from a conventional studio or chroma key facility. The vital components for any virtual studio will be introduced and described, as will the potential benefits of using a virtual set

# 1. Introduction

For many years the technique of chroma-keying to super-impose a studio presenter over a background has been used to create special effects and enhance sets. One major limitation of this method becomes apparent when the camera makes any kind of movement, the result is that the presenter appears to 'float' as the background remains stationary. This effect can only be avoided by adjusting or 'moving' the background image synchronously with the movements of the camera. To do this with a three dimensional virtual set requires substantial amounts of computing power to process the movements and reproduce the background *in real time.* With the use of the very latest super-computers it is now possible to control and manipulate three dimensional 'virtual' studio sets provided they are not too complex. (i.e. not too many 'polygons')

In 1994, the first modified pan and tilt head (Radamec Broadcast Systems 435VR) for operation with virtual studios was manufactured. With the addition of precision rotary encoders, the angular position of the pan and tilt head could be monitored to an accuracy of 1/1000 of a degree. This enabled an interface to a powerful computer which could render the set every field, thereby creating possibilities of a virtual studio.

The early virtual studios which used super-computers pushed technology to the limit. At that time the sets were limited in complexity to a specific level of detail, governed by computer processing power. They were also costly and risky to use for on-air transmissions without a backup. Thus was born the drive for a low cost, reliable alternative.

Low cost VR Studio Systems are able to overcome these problems by taking a radically new approach to the hardware requirements for virtual studio productions. By coupling a very high quality purpose designed DVE to a Radamec pan and tilt head, the main limitations of virtual studio production are eliminated. One of the most promising low cost solutions from Radamec Broadcast Systems and the BBC is Virtual Scenario. It can handle high quality, full bandwidth backgrounds or sets; this single card DVE solution is inherently more reliable, and the cost is very much lower.

# 2. Production in 2D, enhanced 2D, & 3D

## 2.1 Two Dimensional production

Until Radamec Broadcast Systems unveiled Virtual Scenario, the only commercially available virtual set systems used expensive super-computers which rendered, or redrew the images in real time, 50 or 60 times per second. Alternatively, images could be manipulated in post production.

For the illusion of virtual reality to be complete, the foreground actor must be made to appear as if they were actually within the scene. Traditional chroma key techniques partly accomplish this, but the camera has had to remain locked off with this set up. Virtual Scenario, by zooming into the scene, creates an enlarged image for the action to move over.

Virtual Scenario is in effect a video image manipulator or high quality DVE that allows the camera to moved, enabling pan, tilt and zoom to be fully utilized for enhancing program productions. With a serial component digital picture, Virtual Scenario can change the background image size by up to eight times without introducing the pixellation artifacts normally associated with DVE's when they enlarge an image even slightly. The background merely softens, which is what would be expected in a real set as the camera zooms in to enlarge the foreground.

Because Virtual Scenario accepts a standard digital video input, the range of backgrounds which can be manipulated is unlimited. The background can be live or a still image, increasing production flexibility over systems which must render their own set internally. It is also possible to mix from one background to another without the need for any additional Scenario channels.

As the camera is panned and tilted, Virtual Scenario ensures that the correct visual perspective for the background is maintained. This is implemented by introducing a variable trapezoid distortion into the image, further maintaining the virtual illusion.

In addition to increasing the size of the background image by up to four times from full frame, Virtual Scenario can reduce the background image to one quarter of the original. With the use of live video in this application, back projection or video wall systems may be replaced with Virtual Scenario.

### 2.2 Enhanced two dimensional production

As standard, Virtual Scenario includes a key or matte channel. This allows an additional key/matte to be manipulated as well as the main background image. Actors can therefore be made to appear behind objects within the background such as pillars, desks or other objects as required.

The key or matte channel can also be used to provide a safe working area, particularly if the area of chroma key background is limited. This enables a traditional garbage matte to track with the background and camera moves.

Many popular chroma keyers provide a matte channel, a feature which can easily be included within the virtual studio installation. Alternatively, this keying function can be done within the latest generation of vision switcher, some of which include chroma keying as standard.

Additional DVE channels can be locked to a single camera. Here there are two options. The first is to lock them together with image size and position the same, but with different 'zoom offsets'. This will allow each channel to move at a slightly different rate when the camera is panned or tilted, creating an effect similar to tracking the camera. This can enhance realism. The second is to lock them together but with different sizes and positions. A typical situation for this setup is replacing two or more back projectors. This allows the camera to zoom into the 'back projected' image with no loss in picture quality.

### 2.3 Three dimensional production

Using enhanced 2D, Virtual Scenario is capable of creating programs which have a three dimensional look. For true 3D, additional processing is required. To date, true 3D productions have all used the Onyx super-computer which can render a new background in 1/50th sec. (625 lines) or 1/60th sec. (525 lines).

These systems are very expensive and are not best suited to handling live video inputs, which are only 2D.

Radamec are able to supply the RP2VR robotic camera pedestal, which has already been integrated into true 3D systems. Its additional X, Y and height data allow a 3D system to create the necessary parallax changes which are seen during a camera track. Other solutions use a crane on rails with each joint, and the wheels fitted with sensors, or a full motion control rig such as the type manufactured by Mark Roberts.

Many 3D systems currently use the Radamec 435VR pan and tilt head. Therefore an existing Virtual Scenario Studio System can be used as the basis for a full 3D studio. The Virtual Scenario 2D unit can then be used to provide a backup video manipulator in the event of a super-computer failure.

## 3. The Benefits from Virtual Sets & 'VR' Productions

### 3.1 Which programs can benefit?

It is generally accepted that 2D virtual reality is ideally suited to News, Sport, Weather and Current Affairs programs where the presentation format is not only known in advance, but where consistency and repeatability of production are essential. However, the BBC during their early trials explored a wide range of options including light entertainment and Drama [D. Allen - BBC Executive Producer, 1995].

Subsequent to these trials, two new productions were commissioned for BBC Education and BBC Natural History. 'This Multi-media Business' set out to provide a 12 part series of 15 minute programs to introduce viewers to the benefits of multi-media for both the home and business. The set used was a Gothic Temple which would simply not have been afforded if the set had had to be built [G. Aukland - BBC Producer, 1995]. 'The Web' was a children's program about wildlife. The set was a huge web which would have been impossible to construct in reality, even if the largest studio in the world had been available [D. Wallace - BBC Producer, 1996].

Additional use for the replacement of costly back projection systems enables large screen TVs (projectors) to be placed in positions which would be impossible in real life. For example, huge screens could be made to appear on famous monuments and landmarks, or perhaps more practically, made to appear in the foyer or atrium of the TV station itself.

### 3.2 The cost benefit

At first sight it is easy to see that there are many potential savings from the use of a virtual set. The obvious include the ability to change sets almost instantaneously, thereby reducing the down time of a studio while the set is being struck or installed. This could impact on staff requirements, as no scene shifting or upkeep is necessary. Others include the ability to make a small studio appear very large, and the flexibility to alter a set should the need arise.

For a one-off program, it is unlikely that any cost savings could be made, for the moment anyway. Where virtual productions really save money is when a series of programs are commissioned, all using the same background sets and camera shots.

### 3.3 Production Benefit

The program production team will have a far greater range of options available to them when they consider the format design. There will be no limitation as to how large the set can be, except that any movement made by the talent requires the actual amount of space required for that movement. An example would be if a presenter was required to walk amongst and around a number of virtual objects on the floor; for instance a number of bar graphs that come up out of the floor.

Small studios are ideal where a News presenter remains seated behind a desk. The presenter can be keyed over a virtual set which makes the studio seem very much larger.

There is no technical limit as to the number of cameras that can be used in a 2D VR program. However most productions, even fairly large ones, will not require more than three camera channels. If additional camera positions are required, it is a simple matter to prepare a virtual background for that camera position, then use it while the camera is at that location. Backgrounds or sets can be changed in an instant as required.

There is no necessity to use the same studio for every production. It is possible to store the backgrounds and keep them on a disk in your top pocket [D. Popkin - BBC Manager, 1995], broadcasting from wherever is most convenient.

Each camera channel is totally independent from any other. The camera, Virtual Scenario and chroma keyer are all operated independently. Not only is this reassuring from the 'fault tolerant' viewpoint, but also each composite (combined camera & background) image can be previewed in the production gallery in the usual way.

## 4. Set Design and Production Planning

### 4.1 Design

The design of a virtual set will require the same time, skills and effort as needed for a conventional constructed set. A substantial advantage of the virtual set is that of increased flexibility and freedom. Once the set is designed, different views of the set can be rendered in order to fine tune the overall production. The transportation, construction and storage costs associated with conventional set design do not apply to the virtual set.

The designers who create computer generated sets have a range of specialist skills which combine studio planning expertise with a knowledge of computer modeling and image generation techniques. In addition, real sets or locations may be used and incorporated into productions using the Virtual Scenario Studio System.

A wide range of graphic design tools are available to the designer. The lowest cost platforms are PCs which can be purchased complete with 3D modeling software for less than $10,000 Adding a still store and a disk based video recorder creates a most powerful tool for relatively little outlay.

Of course, the more powerful and feature rich packages require faster and more powerful super-computers. These can be used to create the very highest quality backgrounds of immense detail. As a 2D VR studio does not rely on a super-computer to draw and redraw the image 50 or 60 times a second, there is absolutely no limit as to the number of those infamous polygons which can be used when creating the set.

4.2 Studio Size

Any virtual set requires a studio space equipped with an area of chroma key of suitable size to accommodate the shots and action required by the director. Studio size requirements do not necessarily change, because if an actor has to walk 5 or 10 yards towards the camera, then this is still the distance to be walked.

Matching foreground and background perspectives demands an appropriately sized studio. When considering lighting and keying requirements, the actors should ideally be placed no less than 2 yards from the cyc. However, where the program requirements are for fixed position actors and presenters, virtual sets can be used to create an illusion of a much larger set.

Programs such as News, Sports and Current Affairs are ideally suited to using small studios where virtual sets create an apparently larger set. Other ideal applications include continuity suites and weather presentations to name but two.

It is important to match as accuratly as possible the virtual background and foreground camera angles of view. While a different background/foreground camera angle of view discrepancy will not stop the system from working, it will reduce the distance the presenter will be able to move in the virtual set. If the foreground camera uses a wide angle lens, as the presenter moves towards the camera, they will get larger more quickly than they should, spoiling the overall realistic effect.

4.3 Lighting

Virtual set design must take into account the finished combined model and foreground lighting. There is little point designing a virtual set with long shadows if the actor cannot cast the same length of shadow in the studio

Lighting provides the necessary realism, and must be used carefully to prevent the cartoon cut-out appearance that is a feature of many chroma key shots. The virtual set must be lit to ensure that these same conditions can be created in the live studio.

The lighting director must work closely with the set designer to achieve the desired results. A larger and fully equipped studio lighting grid will always make the final lighting task easier and quicker.

4.4 Sound

All real time virtual set systems have a video delay of between four and ten frames. Virtual Scenario adds the shortest delay of only 4 fields which must be compensated for by adding a similar delay to the audio signals.

When incorporating additional DVEs into a production, extra delays need to be included to ensure that correct lip sync is maintained. Two way interviews conducted in a virtual reality environment also require audio delays. This is a known feature which has been resolved over the years due to experience using video synchronizers on incoming feeds.

## 4.5 Planning

Complex computer generated sets cannot be changed quickly as rendering shots from different camera positions can take considerable time. The scenes must be story boarded before the studio days, and each shot well documented.

Where Virtual Scenario is used for repetitive daily or weekly programs using the same format and the same set, considerable savings will be made because sets can be changed quickly. Careful initial planning will prevent problems occurring during the early programs in a series, and will reduce the time required to re make any parts of the virtual set.

## 4.6 Number of Cameras

a. Single Camera Operation.

This is the simplest system configuration and it allows the single camera to be zoomed, panned and tilted within the background. This feature alone adds considerable realism to shots which have hitherto had to remain locked off. With the inclusion of the key/matte channel, z-axis keying further enhances the realism of interaction with the background. The combined image can be monitored and distributed with the advantage of full preview.

Simple single camera sequences could be edited together during post production to give the program an appearance of being a multi-camera shoot.

b. Multi camera operation.

There are no inherent system limitations as to the number of camera channels that can be used at any time in a studio. Each additional camera channel is a straightforward step and repeat of the first. However, each camera requires a separate background and key/matte image associated with its position and relative angle to the virtual set. If the position of a camera is moved significantly, a separate background and key/matte will be required.

Integration with a fully robotics multi-camera system can have the benefit of automatic background selection when used in conjunction with a Touch Control Panel (see Robotics brochures and application notes). An interface with a stills store will be able to automatically recall the appropriate background for the camera's current position.

# 5. The Technical Requirements for a Virtual Production:

## 5.1 Overview

A Virtual Studio is a stage or studio covered with a suitable chroma key color, usually blue or green, a lighting rig, and technical equipment for combining foreground images with a background. The correct view of the background is derived from data obtained from sensors on the camera. These combined images, which may include a background key/matte, create the illusion of reality on the main studio output.

Any normal studio can be used, but it will generally be best to use a fully equipped digital video studio which will incorporate the following basic elements:

## 5.2 Cameras & Camera Head Sensors

Virtual studios use video cameras mounted on pan and tilt heads which incorporate precision rotary encoders. In addition, precision sensors are added to the lens to read zoom and focus data.

These precision positional sensors (for pan, tilt, zoom and focus) work entirely independently of any robotic system, allowing either manual or robotic virtual studio operation as required. These data are combined at the camera head and are passed, via a standard RS422 serial datalink, to the user workstation.

Other methods of establishing the position of the camera are pattern recognition systems. Such a system was developed by Orad [Tamir, 1996]. These require a mathematically calculated pattern, using two slightly different shades of the same color, to be placed in the set immediately behind the camera. They have the advantage that full camera movement is possible, even using hand held cameras. For the moment these system are quite expensive and introduce a considerable video delay.

## 5.3 Image Manipulation

Any high quality image processing (HQIP) system must be capable handling full bandwidth serial component digital video, minimizing any resolution loss as the background image is enlarged. Careful attention has been paid to the design of each module, ensuring the highest possible image quality, even when zoomed in by up to four times. This is optimized because no processing is required for spins flips and tumbles normally provided, and expected, on a conventional Digital Video Effects unit used in today's TV studios. As with conventional DVEs, the processing delay through this module is about 3 TV fields.

The focus of a 2D HQIP must therefore be not towards fancy effects but towards the highest image quality. Two measures must be taken to ensure this high quality of image. Firstly, the HQIP must work with complete television frames combined as non interlaced images which are refreshed every 60th of a second, as against just the single field of a DVE. This enables the system to interpolate between vertically, as well as horizontally-adjacent pixels. Secondly, the processing must look at the coefficients of a larger group of pixels. An array of 15 x 13 coefficients compared with 4 x 4 or 4 x 8 which are more typical of a conventional DVE is preferred. The more pixels that are used in the predictive processing, the greater the precision of the prediction and the further the image can be enlarged before the information available becomes insufficient to create a clear and artifact-free image.

## 5.4 Operational Interface

The key to any successful system is the user friendliness of the operational interface. A touch screen interface has become the accepted norm for robotic camera installations, and is therefore the natural choice for a straightforward system which will integrate seamlessly into existing studio operations.

The main purpose of the operational interface, which combines a PC based computer system, is to process the raw data received from the camera pan tilt zoom and focus axes, and provide control data to the HQIP. Two basic functions are essential: the ability to engage and disengage the background image from the foreground: and to force the background to full frame. This enables the foreground to be correctly aligned to the background prior to locking the two together to create the illusion of a virtual production.

A user interface should not normally require a full time operator, the exception being when initial line-up functions are undertaken such as lens calibration, data routing and diagnostics. However, where the system is used in multiple camera studios with robotic cameras, the camera operator may set up shots calling up the appropriate virtual background from within the control system.

## 5.5 Chroma Keyers

It is not intended to cover the principles of chroma-keying in any great depth, however as this method of keying a foreground over a background is such an integral part of he virtual Studio, it warrants a brief consideration here. For the moment, chroma-keying is the only solution, however a number of other techniques are being investigated which may be able to use pattern recognition as a blue or green-less alternative.

Using a plain, evenly illuminated color (usually green or blue), an electronic signal is derived that enables the foreground to be distinguished from the background. This signal can then be used to change the background to a different one, other than the plain color. With linear keying systems, foreground shadows can be picked out and added to the background.

Ideally, the chroma key system will have digital inputs and outputs and will include a matte channel for enhanced 2D operation. Perhaps the best known system is 'Ultimatte', however there is an increasing choice of competent systems available on the market, expanding because of the perceived increase in market size for high quality chroma keying, brought about by the significant interest in virtual productions.

## 5.6 Video & Audio delays

Real time virtual set systems have a video delay upwards of 4 fields. This delay is made up from three distinct delays. The delay in processing the raw data from the camera and head sensors takes about half a field, the delay in processing the pan, tilt zoom and focus data in the user interface (PC) takes about one and a half fields, and the remaining delay in the image processing.

---

A 2D image processor will take about 2 fields to output the correctly sized and positioned image, whereas a real time rendering engine will take significantly longer. Because of this unavoidable delay, it is necessary to add a delay to foreground or camera output. This ensures that the movement of the foreground is time coincident with that of the background.

Audio delays must be inserted to ensure that the sound cannot arrive at the viewers ears earlier than the video. Early audio is very much more objectionable that late audio.

While many questions do get raised regarding audio delay, the practical problems generated are in fact little greater than those understood will by news studios who always have to add audio delays into their incoming feeds as they as timed using frame synchronizers.

Virtual Scenario adds the shortest delay of only 4 fields which must be compensated for by adding a similar delay to the audio signals.

When incorporating additional DVEs into a production, extra delays need to be included to ensure that correct lip sync is maintained. Two way interviews conducted in a virtual reality environment also require audio delays. This is a known feature which has been resolved over the years due to experience using video synchronizers on incoming feeds.

The digital video delay module delays the foreground video by four fields. This is necessary in order to ensure co-timed foreground, background and key/matte video signals. It allows for the time taken to process the control data received from the camera via the user workstation.

# 6. Considerations when Integrating a VR System into a Studio

## 6.1 Overview

The Virtual Scenario Studio System provides all that is required to convert an existing chroma key studio for 'VR' productions. This assumes that all the relevant video signals are in serial digital form, and that separate chroma keyer(s) with a matte channel is available.

The system is straightforward in both operation and installation. The camera is mounted onto the new 435VR pan & tilt head, but do ensure that your existing pedestal will accept the 435VR. The lens mounted encoders (for zoom and focus) will usually be installed at the factory or, alternatively, by one of Radamec's fully trained installation engineers.

Both the Virtual Scenario chassis and the User Workstation Scenario Control Unit (SCU) are rack mounting (2U and 4U respectively). The Touch Screen should normally be positioned close to the camera operator in the gallery, however, once the system is operational, it does not require constant use. Essential controls are remoted to the camera head.

The SCU is connected to the Virtual Scenario via a RS485 serial datalink. All computations are done within the SCU for control of up to 4 camera channels. For normal operations, the control signal for the background and background key/matte channels are joined. The system can be configured so that they are separate, giving the possibility for differential image moves between two different backgrounds.

### 6.2 Additional equipment

Chroma keyer: This is the most essential component for any high quality chroma key shoot. A number of manufacturers produce units, with a range of prices: you can expect an increasing number of choices in this market because of the increased use of chroma keying for VR applications. Some existing vision switchers already contain this facility.

Video stills store: A good quality picture store is required to provide background and background matte images to the Virtual Scenario. Modern stills stores are capable of storing many hundreds of high quality images at a reasonable cost. Indeed some mixers now have hard disk options specifically to store images which can be output on the Aux busses directly to Virtual Scenario.

ENG camera and lens: Currently only lightweight (ENG) lenses have been adapted to include the precision sensors need for VR productions. These encoders are mounted onto the lens and engage with the zoom and focus rings. It is hoped that it will shortly be able to provide modifications to studio lenses.

Camera pedestal: A suitable unit must be able to carry up to 75kg which is the combined weight of the 453VR pan & tilt head equipped with a maximum payload camera. These are readily available from leading manufacturers.

Blue background: Traditionally a blue cyc is constructed when programs using chroma keying are considered. This can take the form of a specially shaped blue wall and floor, or where a less permanent solution is required, by using a large blue suspended cloth. Alternatively a light box can be used which can either have a pure blue 'film', or, where the background may occasionally be seen in shot, a heavily blue tinted picture.

Graphics computer: To generate original backgrounds for VR productions, a computer with a graphics package is essential. Contrary to popular belief, this need not be an expensive super computer. The latest generation of fast PCs, when equipped with sufficient RAM, are capable of rendering suitable backgrounds.

Other equipment: Additional analogue to digital and digital to analogue converters may be necessary if the current studio is not fully digital.

## 7. Future upgrades and advanced Production Concepts.

### 7.1 Adding 3D to the Installation

Once a studio has acquired pan & tilt heads fitted with encoders, it is possible to upgrade the studio to full 3D animation by the addition of a super-computer e.g. Silicon Graphics Onyx or its derivative. As the cost of such an upgrade is likely to remain relatively high, at least in the medium term, adding 3D to one of say, a three camera system could prove an attractive option. As the production team gain experience working with VR, the attractions of a full 3D system, even if only part of the studio is thus equipped, will be difficult to resist.

Additional sensors for Ped X, Y and height would enable to camera to be moved on-shot, a most desirable feature if the power of a 3D system is available on-line.

## 7.2 Animated sets

An interesting idea, which is an extension of what the BBC currently do with their opening sequence for the main evening news, is to animate the set and play it from a laser/disk player.

There is no limitation as to the type of video which can be used as the set background with Virtual Scenario It is therefore possible to animate a set with moving objects and input this directly as a background. A laser or disk based player would be ideal.

## 7.3 Advanced Virtual Scenario configurations

The Virtual Scenario control system is able to address up to four different outputs. These can have size or position offsets, enabling multi-layered productions. Additional keying and mixing of the images is however required. This can be achieved, in the case where images do not overlap (blue windows in the set) by mixing 100% of each image together. The resultant video being used as the key fill when creating the composite camera output.

# 8. References


1. Allen D. (1995), Virtual Reality, The Story so Far...... BBC video.
2. Aukland G. (1995), BBC News.
3. Wallace D. (1996), Virtual Reality, BBC video.
4. Popkin D. (1996), BBC Guide to Virtual Stuidio Productions in 2D & 3D.
5. Tamir M. (1996), The Orad Virtual Set

# THREE-WAY LOUDSPEAKER SYSTEMS FOR MOTION PICTURE USE

John Eargle, JBL Incorporated and JME Consulting Corporation,
Los Angeles, CA
Mark Mayfield, JBL Professional, Northridge, CA, and
David Gray, Dolby Laboratories, Los Angeles, CA

**Abstract:**

Digital sound tracks have the potential of delivering lower distortion signals with flat power bandwidth capability in the motion picture theater. Traditional 2-way theater loudspeaker systems are presently being pushed far beyond their original performance limits with digital sound tracks, and 3-way systems are now being considered as their future replacement. The authors have developed such systems for both small and large venues and will discuss the many observations, measurements, and decisions made during the engineering phase of development.

The chief option available to the loudspeaker designer is to redesign the system as a set of bandpass sections with matching radiation characteristics and mutually compatible power handling capability. The authors describe a three-way system from the following points of view:

1. Choice of crossover frequencies and slopes; electrical drive requirements.
2. Directional control.
3. System layout; effect of multiple sources and delay adjustments.
4. Driver performance, LF, MF, and HF.
5. Distortion and related quality issues.

**1. Bandpass Analysis:**

Frequency division in theater loudspeaker systems normally takes place approximately at frequencies representing geometric mean ratios relative to the overall system bandwidth. Typical early 2-way theater systems covering the range from 50 Hz to 6.3 kHz generally had a crossover frequency of 400 or 500 Hz, as shown in Figure 1a. Later system improvements extended the LF cutoff down to about 40 Hz, while the HF bandwidth was extended to about 12.5 kHz.

A similar approach to frequency division may be applied to a 3-way system as shown in Figure 1b. Here, the overall response of the system is assumed to extend from 40 Hz to 16 kHz. This is a total range of nine octaves, and the nominal network dividing frequencies may be set at the equally spaced ISO preferred frequencies of 315 Hz and 2.5 kHz. With this design goal, actual crossover frequencies may be adjusted up or down within a one-third octave range.

**1.1 Power Response Considerations, Two-way Systems:**

The second generation two-way systems designed by Lansing and Hilliard (1944) made use of ported horn systems and multicellular HF horns. The LF ported horns had a characteristic shelf in their LF response at the frequency below which horn loading was effective and vented enclosure effects took over. This is shown in Figure 2a. The falloff in HF response was generally ignored, inasmuch as the increase of directivity with rising frequency more or less corrected for it, at least along the major axis of the HF horn.

## 0. Introduction:

Loudspeaker systems for motion pictures have traditionally been of two-way design, with frequency division between HF (high frequency) and LF (low frequency) sections taking place in the range of 400 to 500 Hz. During the 1980's, subwoofers were added in theaters which regularly screened multichannel films, but the screen channels themselves remained as two-way designs. With few exceptions, two-way systems have continued to the present time.

The introduction of digital sound in the motion picture theater during the early 1990's provided transmission channels with flat power bandwidth from 20 Hz to 20 kHz. This development has led to a nominal dubbing level standard for presentation at an average level of 85 dB(C) in the theater, referenced to a recorded level of -20 dBFS (dB *re* full scale). Nominal dialog level is generally in the range of 82 to 85 dB(C).

By comparison, music and sound effects have the additional capability of reaching levels of 105 dB(C) (0 dBFS). While dialog is not normally a problem in the theater, the demands of modern music forms and sound effects have pushed the performance envelope to much higher levels, placing increased demands on the HF sections of conventional loudspeakers.

Since the acoustical power output of present-day HF compression drivers rolls off 6 dB per octave above the diaphragm's mass break point (normally in the range of 3 kHz), flat acoustical output above this frequency requires a 6-dB/octave boost of the drive signal. This in turn results in a "derating" of the compression driver at high frequencies, both in terms of power handling and distortion, which limits the overall system's capability of handling a flat bandwidth input signal.

Options in HF driver design are limited, inasmuch as many current models are already operating within 2 dB of their theoretical mid-band efficiency. In addition, the mass break point is largely determined by the density of the diaphragm material and saturation of the magnetic structure in the range of 20 teslas, neither of which factor offers a substantial range for future development.

The third generation two-way systems of the early eighties removed the LF shelf through the application of high output transducers in simple ported enclosures that could deliver full power output down to 40 Hz, as shown in Figure 2b. At high frequencies, the general use of uniform coverage horns mandated the use of power response correction, shown here by the crosshatching. As a result of ongoing transducer development over the years, HF compression drivers since the middle eighties can be equalized for flat response out to 16 kHz, a technique that requires careful monitoring of program input signals (Engebretson and Eargle, 1982).

The maximum acoustical power output of these two-way design approaches are shown in Figures 3a and 3b. (For making meaningful comparisons, we are assuming that both of these systems are outfitted with a pair of identical modern LF transducers.) The older ported horn system exhibits a mid-bass rise and subsequent step-down in power output capability at its upper response limit, as shown at 3a. The later design, with its ported direct radiating LF transducers maintains flat power response up to the crossover frequency, as shown at 3b. In both cases, the maximum power output capability at mid-low frequencies is 25 acoustical watts, which translates roughly to peak sound pressure levels of about 110 dB at a distance of 10 meters from the loudspeakers.

Both old and new 2-way systems shown here have many of the same difficulties in terms of power handling, but there is no question that the newer system offered considerable improvements in terms of spectral balance and uniformity of coverage in the theater, primarily through the use of ported LF enclosures and uniform coverage HF horns.

**1.2 Power Response Considerations, Three-way Systems:**

When the spectrum is divided into three sections of roughly equal percentage bandwidth, a number of benefits can be realized:

1. The LF system operates essentially within its so-called piston band range, over which on-axis pressure response and power response are both uniform with respect to frequency (40 - 400 Hz).

2. The MF (mid-frequency) section operates essentially over a range where its power response and on-axis response are both uniform without the need for added equalization (300 - 3000 Hz).

3. The HF section operates with its present mass break point limitation and must be boosted above 3 kHz as before. However, since it operates only above about 3 kHz, more of its total power capability is available for the upper two and one-third octaves.

4. The requirements for both MF and HF horns present the opportunity to use new horn/driver hardware designed specifically for the frequency regions at hand. JBL's new Optimized Aperture™ horns and matching rapid flare compression drivers offer considerable improvements in 2nd and 3rd harmonic distortion, as compared to the traditional horn hardware.

Thus, while the three-way system does not provide flat power bandwidth capability beyond 3 or 4 kHz, it does provide spectral capability that matches the normal program rolloff traditionally observed with music and dialog (Eargle 1989). Digital sound effects are another matter, in that they may, on an instantaneous basis, require full bandwidth up to 20 kHz. Such instances are rare, but when they do occur they have the potential for taxing the system beyond its normal performance limits. Fortunately, the normal program duty cycle at very high frequencies is short enough so that this is not a significant problem.

Many of the active dividing networks used in multi-way systems include some degree of user selectable HF limiting, so the potential for damage is considerably reduced. In most professional installations limiting is not normally employed, but it can be considered a fallback for difficult installations.

Maximum on-axis sound pressure level at 10 meters and maximum acoustical power output for a typical three-way system using modern transducers are shown in Figures 4a and b. A 3-way system intended for a large theater would normally have 4 LF transducers per screen channel. Smaller screening rooms may be designed with only a pair of LF transducers per screen channel, and review rooms may need only a single LF transducer per channel.

While MF and HF transducers will normally be the same for all three applications, the horn hardware itself may be scaled downward for the smaller rooms if mounting space is at a premium.

### 1.3 Crossover Frequencies, Network Slopes, and Drive Requirements:

There are two primary considerations here: minimizing of system lobing in the vertical plane and matching of pattern control at the crossover frequency. Higher order dividing networks generally result in less lobing in the vertical plane inasmuch as the region of overlap between adjacent elements is minimized. On the other hand, sharp transitions at crossover frequencies may exaggerate irregularities in power response if there are serious mismatches in the radiation patterns of adjacent elements.

Since theater loudspeakers are normally intended to cover a 30 degree range of vertical listening angles as well as a 90 degree range of horizontal listening angles, a final assessment of crossover frequencies and slopes can be made only after detailed *in situ* listening tests and measurements.

Virtually all high performance theater loudspeaker systems are multi-amplified, often with frequency division, delay correction, and power response equalization carried out in the digital domain. Figure 5 shows an electrical flow diagram for a typical three-way system. Delay settings are often varied from installation to installation in order to optimize smoothness of coverage in critical portions of the theater.

Maximum power allocation for driving the system is generally made on the basis of a 6-dB (x4) increase over the steady state power rating of each section of the system. This "over-rating" of the system takes into account the ability of theater quality components to handle such momentary peaks in stride, but it also makes the assumption that the system is properly set up, well maintained, and operated "by the book."

### 2. System Physical Layout:

In many ways, today's new three-way systems resemble earlier theater systems, as can be seen in Figure 6. The traditional two-way horn system in general use from the forties through the seventies is shown at *a*.

The chief problems with this design were response smoothness in the range from 40 to 160 Hz, the disparity between power response and axial response, which made it impossible to achieve smooth response over a wide listening area in the theater, and high frequency "fingering," or lobing, in the response of the multicellular horn.

The system shown at *b* set new performance standards when it was introduced in the early eighties. The major improvements were extended smoothness of both axial and power response in the LF section up to 500 Hz. In the form shown here, the signal for the lower LF enclosure was rolled off above 315 Hz in order to minimize vertical lobing effects in the 400-500 Hz range. Above 500 Hz the uniform coverage horn, equalized for flat power response, provided an unprecedented degree of uniformity in both on- and off-axis response in the theater. This system continues to be the reference standard in a great many theaters in the world, but the inexorable march of digital, with its increased demands at high frequencies, points to the need for extending the horn coverage consistency and crossover point lower, and providing dedicated coverage of the top three octaves.

The system shown at *c* represents the preferred embodiment of a three-way system for large theater use. Here, horn loaded sections cover the upper six octaves, while a direct radiator section covers the bottom three octaves. Modern Optimized Aperture™ Bi-Radial® horn designs can be adapted to any size and are shown here as new models for MF (mid-frequency) and HF coverage.

By their sheer size, these systems should be auditioned no closer than about two times their maximum vertical dimensions. For application in smaller spaces, such as dubbing theaters or review rooms, a smaller HF horn may be used and may be mounted coaxially with the MF horn. Additionally, in smaller spaces, single or dual LF transducers may be used rather than the four shown in the figure. Thus, the systems can be easily scaled for specific applications.

**3. Directional Response:**

Figures 7a and b show respectively the directional response of the most recent two-way model and the new three-way model. In these figures, vertical and horizontal -6-dB beamwidth and directivity index plots are shown on one-third octave intervals. Note that the three-way design has smoother vertical pattern control in the 500 Hz range than the two-way design.

The two-way design shown here attained its success largely on the basis of its uniform horizontal directivity and smooth frequency response in the theater. The new three-way design combines the advantage of smooth directional response with the extra advantage of higher output capability.

### 4. Recent Developments in MF and HF Compression Driver Design:

Extending the discussion presented in Section 1, we will now describe the mechanical and acoustical aspects of new drivers and horns engineered for specific three-way applications.

#### 4.1 MF Considerations:

The development of the JBL 2490 midrange driver during the early nineties provided solutions to power bandwidth problems in the critical frequency decade from 300 Hz to 3 kHz. By limiting the required response to a single frequency decade, the driver and matching horns could be optimized for both smooth axial and power response and for lowest distortion. The loading factor, or compression ratio, was set at 4-to-1 and the exit diameter was set at 76 mm (3 in) in order to minimize distortion (Bie, 1992). A new family of Optimized Aperture horns, the 2390 series, was developed to take advantage of these performance improvements in both general sound reinforcement as well as in cinema applications.

#### 4.2 HF Considerations:

The new rapid HF flare drivers and Optimized Aperture horns take advantage of a number of JBL developments made during the last fifteen years. The Diamond Surround™ (Murray and Durbin, 1980; U. S. Patent 4,324,312) and Coherent Wave™ phasing plug have contributed to extended HF output by broad-banding the driver's response in the upper octave and by equalizing the multiple output paths from diaphragm to the driver exit, respectively. Additional improvements have been made in the driver diaphragm, through the use of either ribbed titanium or smooth, damped titanium, depending on the specific application of the driver.

Significant improvements in distortion have been accomplished by shortening the fore-aft profile of the driver through the use of thin magnet structures, allowing the driver to accommodate a rapid throat expansion into a new family of horns. Details here have been discussed by Gelow, et al., (1994) and in a paper to be delivered at the 101st Audio Engineering Society Convention in New York, 1996 (Eargle and Gelow, 1996).

**5. MF and HF Distortion Measurements:**

In order to determine the optimum crossover points for the 3-way system, we will compare the traditional 2-way system with the 2392/2490 MF horn system in terms of distortion and compare the older HF hardware with the new Optimized Aperture hardware. We will analyze:

A. Second and third harmonic distortion data over the frequency interval from 250 to 3000 Hz, and

B. Second harmonic distortion data over the range from 1 kHz to 16 kHz.

**5.1 MF Distortion Data:**

The measurements shown in Figure 8 were made over the frequency range from 250 to 3000 Hz at a distance of 4 meters at a nominal level of 112 dB. The on-axis fundamental level was equalized for approximate flat response, and the second and third harmonic values have been raised 20 dB for ease in reading. Because of the 20-dB offset between the fundamental and distortion curves, when those curves appear to intersect, the actual level of the distortion is 20 dB lower, indicating 10% harmonic distortion.

The 2-way system is shown at Figure 8a. Here, we are observing the combined output of LF cone drivers in the range from 250 to 500 Hz and the output of the JBL 2360/2446 combination above 500 Hz. At the output level of 112 dB at 4 meters, 2nd harmonic distortion reaches 10% slightly above 1 kHz. However, below 400 Hz, where the LF cones are dominant, the distortion is in the 3% or lower range.

Performance of the 2392/2490 MF horn over the same frequency range is shown in Figure 8b. This combination generates 10% second harmonic distortion slightly below 3 kHz. Level for level, there appears to be about an 8-dB advantage for the MF horn in terms of distortion in the range above 800 Hz. However, the distortion below about 400 Hz is greater due to slight suspension non-linearity in the MF compression driver.

Based on these distortion curves, the optimum lower crossover point for the MF horn system was chosen as 380 Hz in order to realize the benefit of the very low distortion of the JBL 2226 LF transducers at frequencies below 380 Hz.

The levels at which these distortion curves have been run are extreme; normal theater levels would be lower than shown here, and normal program input would be wide-band rather than sine wave. Even at these drive levels, the percentages of second and third harmonic remain in the range of 3% or lower.

**5.2 HF Distortion Data:**

HF distortion is shown in Figure 9. Here, we have held the fundamental level at a value of 107 dB-SPL at a distance of 1 meter and plotted the discrete values of second harmonic distortion (again, raised 20 dB). Note that the older hardware (Figure 9a) produces about 8 dB greater second harmonic distortion than the newer, rapid flare driver/horn hardware.

The crossover from the MF horn to the HF horn was chosen as 3 kHz, which is the effective upper limit of the 2392 horn. The value of 3 kHz also restricts the HF section to only the upper two and one-third octaves of the spectrum, where its full power bandwidth can be utilized.

**6. LF Considerations:**

Depending on the selected venue, the LF complement of transducers used in the 3-way system may vary from a single unit up to four. When four transducers are used, they are mounted in a tight, diamond shaped cluster in order to minimize lobing in the crossover region. The concern here is for good horizontal coverage over a range of ±45°, and the curves shown in Figure 10 give an idea of what can be expected. This off-axis data is for a pair of 380 mm (15 in) transducers located side by side and measured in the horizontal plane. Note that for ±45° there is an off-axis null at just above 500 Hz, indicating that our choice of 380 Hz as the crossover frequency between LF and MF will work well.

Figure 11 shows 2nd and 3rd harmonic distortion for a pair of 2226 LF transducers with a swept sine wave input of 100 watts. The performance of four such transducers with a total input of 100 watts would be approximately 3 dB higher in all regards, but with diminished output above about 500 Hz. As in the other distortion measurements presented in this paper, the harmonics have been raised 20 dB.

The performance of the JBL 2226 LF transducers benefits from their Vented Cap Cooling (VGC™) construction (Button, 1992; U. S. Patent 5,042,072). Through the use of VGC these transducers maintain thermal equilibrium under normal conditions with an input of 600 continuous watts, exhibiting dynamic power compression due to voice coil heating of only 4 dB.

Summarizing, the target crossover frequencies in the 3-way system have been chosen based on the following observations:

LF Section: Crossover at 380 Hz into the MF horn. Operation of the LF section from 35 Hz to 380 Hz ensures that the LF section will exhibit both flat power response and axial response with extremely low distortion. Excellent directivity matching with the MF section is also assured.

MF Section: Crossovers at 380 Hz and 3 kHz. Operation over this band will ensure the lowest possible MF distortion at maximum operating levels with minimum equalization for flat response. Excellent directivity matching with the HF section is also assured.

HF Section: By restricting the 2352/2451 to the band above 3 kHz, we are assuring that the full power bandwidth of the combination can be brought to bear on HF program demands. The reduction of diaphragm displacement demands here will result in greater system reliability at high frequencies.

## 7. Notes on System Installation:

### 7.1 Screen and Air losses:

The vast majority of high-end motion picture loudspeaker systems and those located in professional studios are installed in a floor-to-ceiling baffle, which simulates ideal half-space ($2\pi$) mounting conditions for the loudspeaker systems. Under these mounting conditions, a system that has been adjusted for flat power response will produce on-axis response in the theater that is proportional to the directivity index along that axis, modified only by screen losses and air losses over distance. While there are certain broad parameters of the system in terms of crossover frequencies and slopes, there may be slight adjustments of these values based on local acoustical conditions, height of the loudspeakers behind the screen, and the rake of the seating area.

The nature of screen losses can be seen in the data of Figure 12. The data shown at *a* is for a JBL 2451/2352 driver/horn combination, without screen, measured with flat signal input at a distance of 4 meters at bearing angles of 0°, 15°, 30°, 45°, and 60°. The data clearly shows near ideal polar response for a horn with nominal 90° horizontal coverage.

The data shown at *b* was run under similar conditions but with a Stewart 8% perforated screen placed at a distance of 50 mm (2 in) from the damping material surround the horn mouth. Note that the effect of the screen is to "square up" the polar response of the horn for off-axis positions, in effect creating a horn with a nominal horizontal angle of 120° or greater.

Moving the screen to a distance of 200 mm (8 in) from the damping material (shown at *c*) results in diminished output at frequencies above 10 kHz, indicating that best HF response results when the horn-to-screen distance is minimum. Under this mounting condition, the effect of horn mouth-to-screen reflections can be seen. These are well within the normal range of system on-site equalization procedures.

Air losses are quite predictable and manifest themselves as excess attenuation in addition to inverse square losses. At 50% relative humidity, air losses at 10 kHz are in the range of 0.2 dB per meter, so the cumulative effect over a distance of, say, 15 meters in a large cinema would be 3 dB in addition to the screen losses at 10 kHz.

### 7.2 System Setup and Alignment:

The first step in installing a 3-way system is to align all of the elements in time. A number of FFT based measurement systems can be used for making the necessary measurements. Each system must be individually aligned, ideally at the same position in the theater, and this is normally done at a position about two-thirds back in the seating area.

The next step is to perform a rough equalization of each frequency band in the system using the equalizer sections that are normally included in the crossover-controller. The more carefully this is done, the less there will be need for extensive 1/3-octave equalization.

Final equalization of the systems to match the required ISO2969 curve may then be done using a distributed microphone array with their outputs multiplexed for determining a spatial average. If care has been taken in the initial stage of system equalization, there may be no need at all for further one-third octave fine tuning.

Then comes the time for serious listening to a wide variety of program material, with minor changes made as needed.

## 8. Performance Data: Dolby Laboratories Screening Room

The Larry Umlang Presentation Theater at the Los Angeles offices of Dolby Laboratories was the first professional installation of a JBL 3-way system. Since the space is fairly small (25 seats), the three screen channels were configured each with a single JBL 2226H LF transducer; a JBL 2490/2392 driver/horn combination, with the horn mouth reduced in size; and a HF system comprising the 2451 driver and the small format 2332 horn. Two JBL model 4645B subwoofers complemented the screen installation. Stewart Microperf™ vinyl screen material was used.

Using only the equalizer sections in the BSS FDS388 Digital Controller, the response of each screen channel is as shown in Figure 13*a*, *b* and *c*. These curves were taken with a four microphone multiplexed array and show excellent conformance with the ISO 2969 recommended response curve out to 16 kHz. The response of the subwoofer system in this installation is shown in Figure 13*d*.

Figure 14 shows the electrical drive levels for LF, MF and HF sections of one screen channel. The degree of equaliza.ion employed here is in the range of ± 3 dB and was accomplished entirely with the equalizer sections built into the active dividing network.

**9. Credits and Acknowledgements:**

The authors wish to acknowledge the contributions to this complex project made by Douglas Greenfield, of Dolby Laboratories, Rick Kamlet and William Gelow, JBL Professional, members of the Theater Standards Committee of the Academy of Motion Picture Arts and Sciences, and above all, the late John Bonner of Warner-Hollywood Studios.

References:

D. Bie (1992), "Design and Theory of a New Midrange Driver," preprint number 3429, presented at the 93rd AES Convention, 1 - 4 October 1992, San Francisco.

D. Button (1992), "Heat Dissipation and Power Compression in Loudspeakers, *J. Audio Engineering Society*, volume 40, number 1/2.

J. Eargle (1989), *Handbook of Sound System Design*, Elar, Commack, NY

J. Eargle (1994), *Electroacoustical Reference Data*, Van Nostrand Reinhold, New York.

J. Eargle and W. Gelow (1996), "Performance of Horn Systems: Low-Frequency Cut-Off, Pattern Control, and Distortion Trade-Offs," to be presented at the 101st AES Convention, 8-11 November 1996, Los Angeles.

M. Engebretson and J. Eargle (1982), "Cinema Sound Reproduction Systems: Technology Advances and System Design Considerations," *J. Society of Motion Picture and Television Engineers*, volume 91, number 11.

M. Gander (1994), "Loudspeakers for Studio Monitoring and Musical Instruments," Chapter 9 in Borwick (ed.) *Loudspeaker and Headphone Handbook,* Butterworths, London.

W. Gelow, M. Gander, and J. Eargle (1994)," An Integrated Digital Concept in Studio Monitoring," *Proceedings of International Radio Symposium,* 9 - 11 June, Montreux.

J. Lansing and J. Hilliard (1945), "An Improved Loudspeaker System for Theaters," *J. Society of Motion Picture Engineers,* volume 45, p. 339.

F. Murray and H. Durbin (1980), "Three-Dimensional Diaphragm Suspensions for Compression Drivers, *J. Audio Engineering Society,* volume 28, number 10.

Figure 1. Basic frequency division. Early 2-way system (a); modern approach to a 3-way system (b).

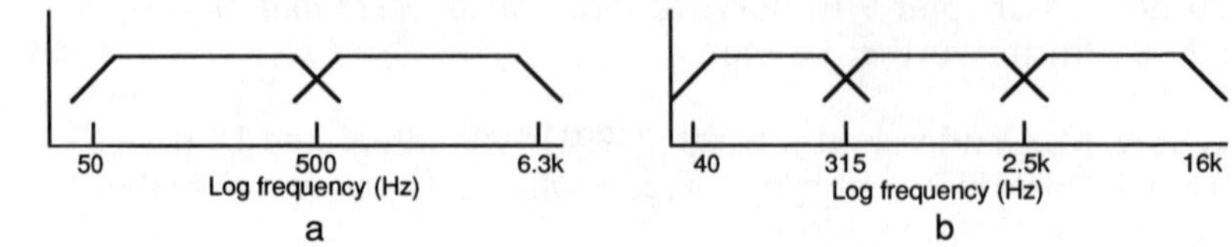


Figure 2. System response, 2-way designs. Lansing/Hilliard design (a); early 1980's design (b).

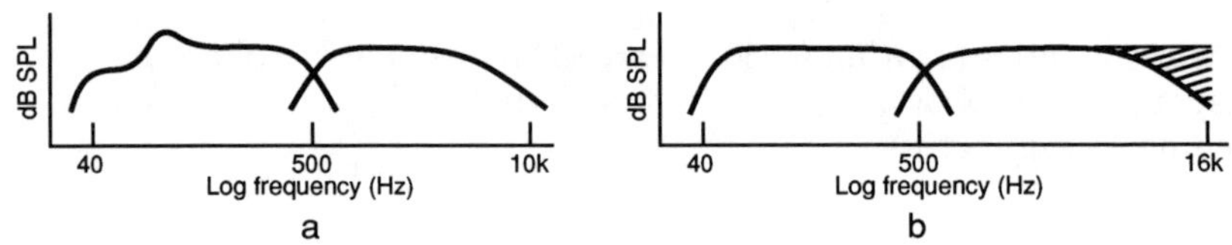


Figure 3. Maximum acoustic power output. Lansing/Hilliard design (a); early 1980's design (b).

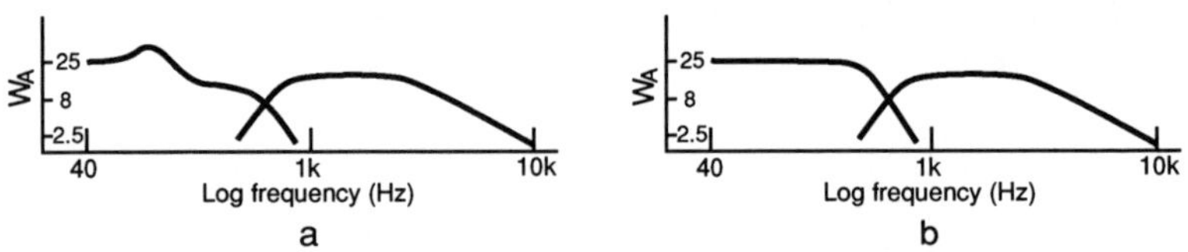

Figure 4. Maximum acoustical power output (a) and maximum sound pressure level at 10 meters (b) for a 3-way design (4 LF transducers)

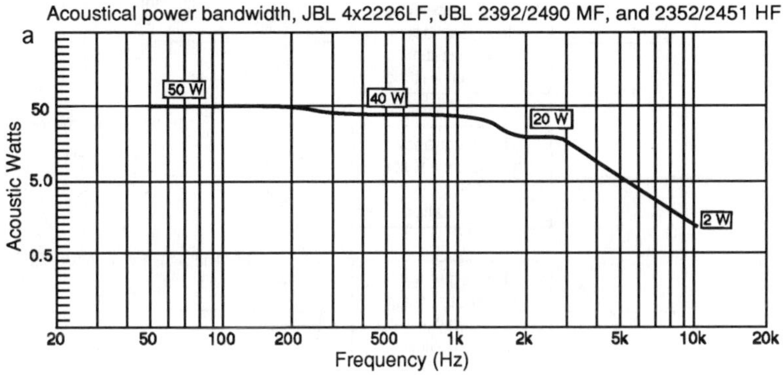


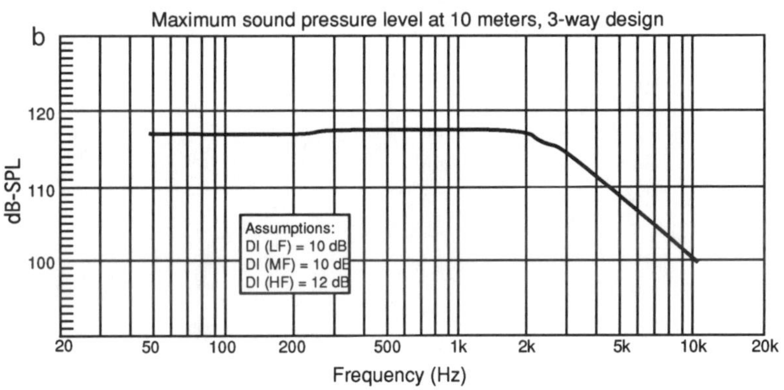

Figure 5. Typical B-chain for a 3-way theater system.

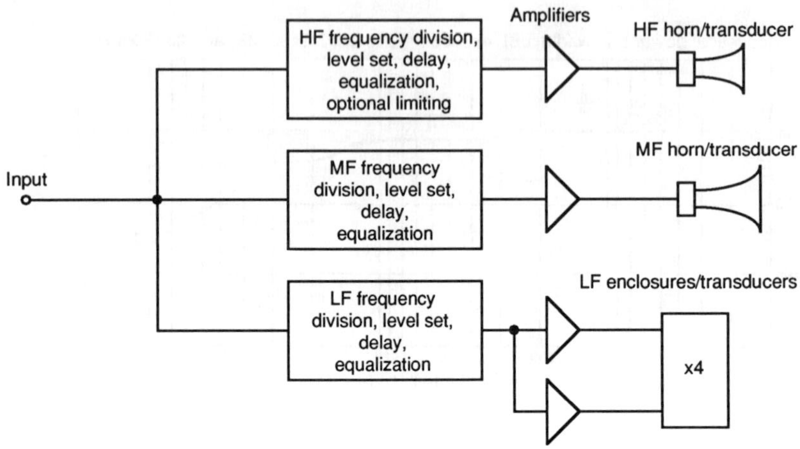

Figure 6. 2-way and 3-way theater systems. Older 2-way (a); later 2-way (b); new 3-way (c).

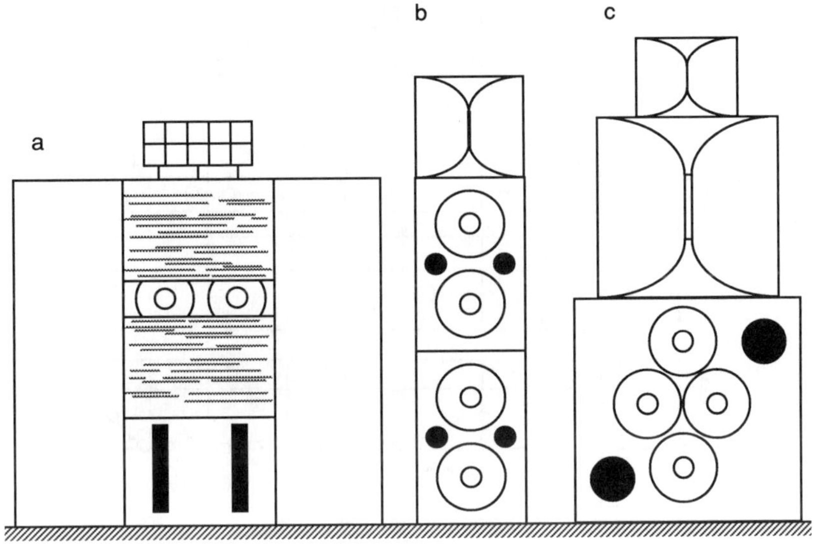

Figure 7. Beamwidth and directivity for standard 2-way system (a) and for new 3-way system (b).

a

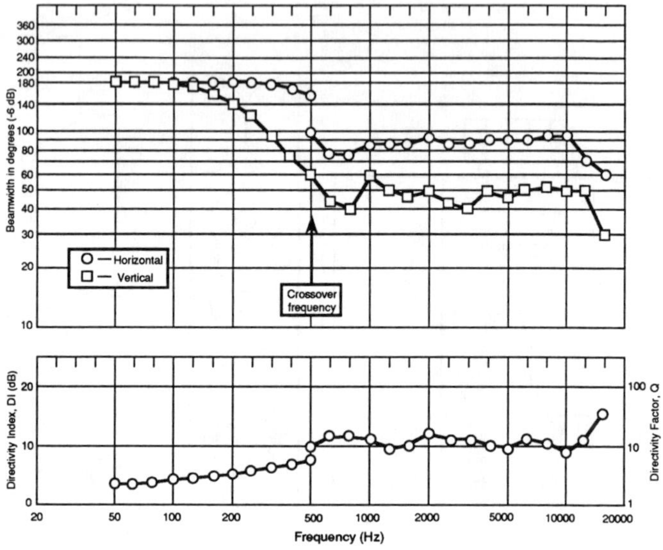


b

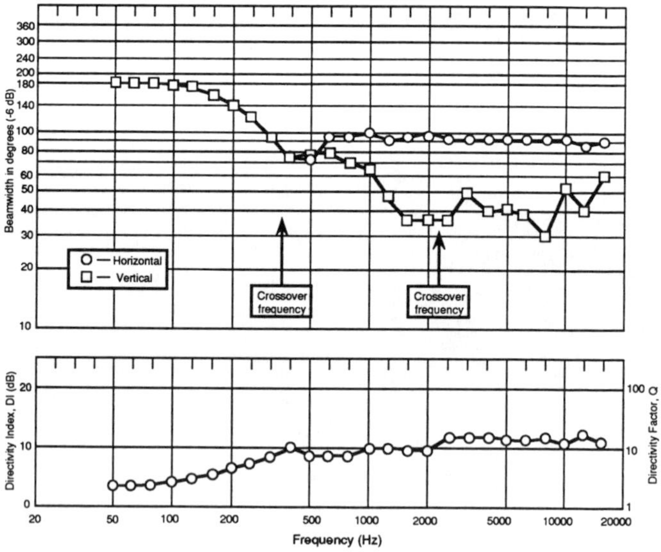

Figure 8. Midrange distortion, 112 dB SPL at 4 meters (2nd harmonic, dashed line; 3rd harmonic, dotted line). Standard 2-way system (a); JBL 2392/2490 MF system (b).

a

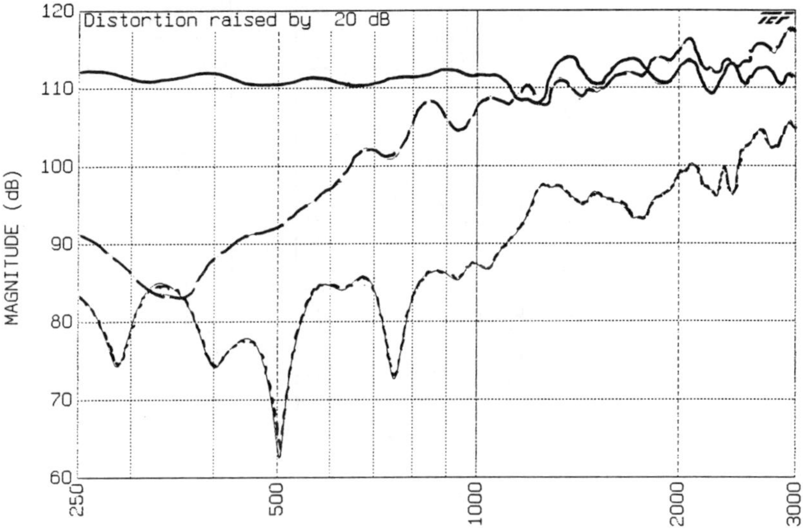


b

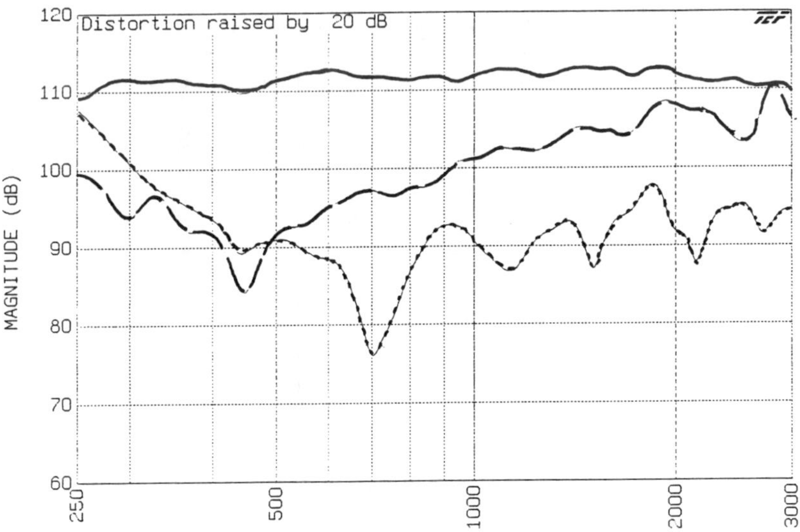

Figure 9. Comparison of 2360/2450 (older hardware) and 2352/2451 (new hardware) 107 dB at a distance of 1 meter.

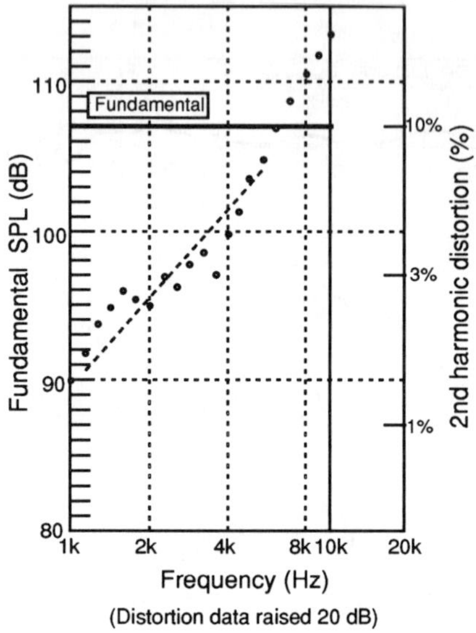


A. 2360

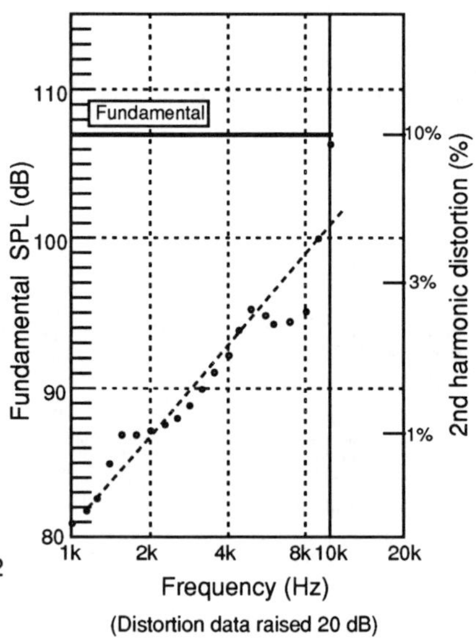


B. 2352

Figure 10. On- and off-axis response of two 380 mm (15 in) LF transducers.

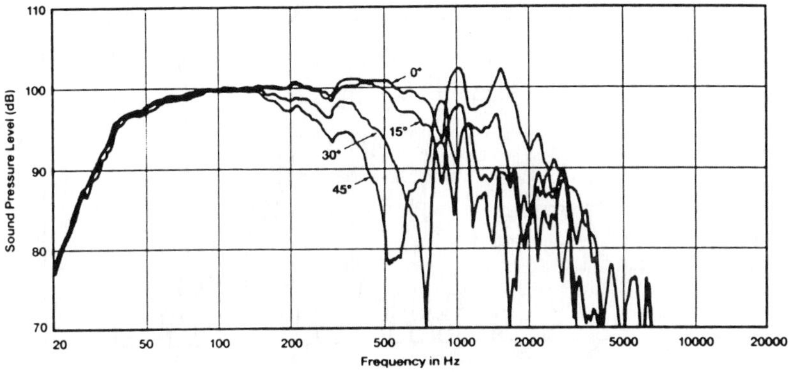

Figure 11. Second and third harmonic distortion, two JBL 2226H transducers, 50 watts per transducer (distortion raised 20 dB).

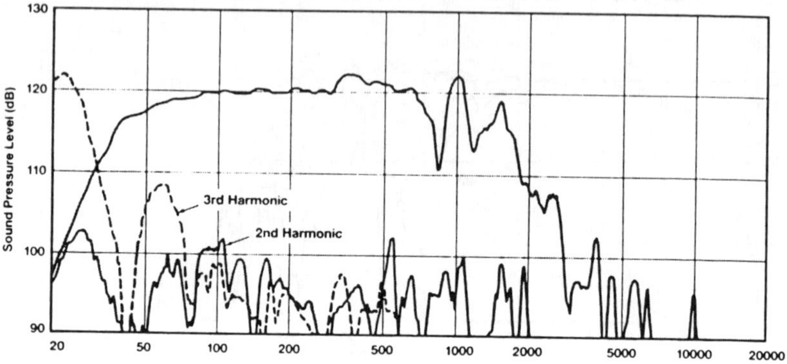

Figure 12. Off-axis response with and without screen (0, 15, 30. 45, and 60°).

a. No screen

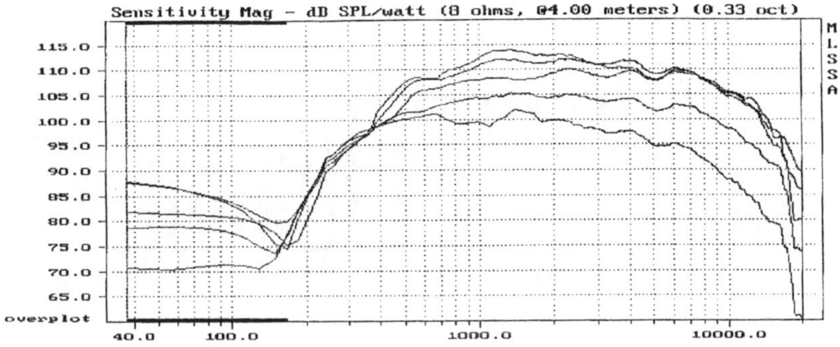


b. Screen 2 inches from foam damping material

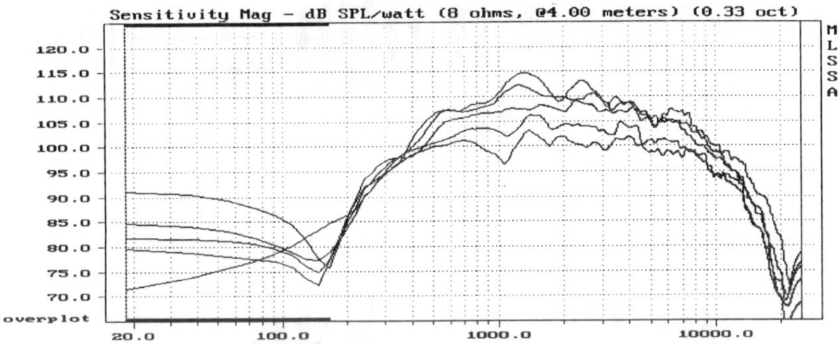


c. Screen 8 inches from foam damping material

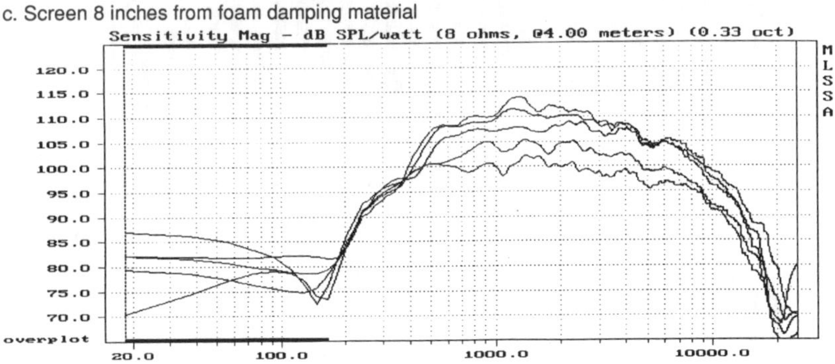

Figure 13. One-third octave acoustical response in the Umlang Presentation Theater (four microphones multiplexed).

a. Left channel

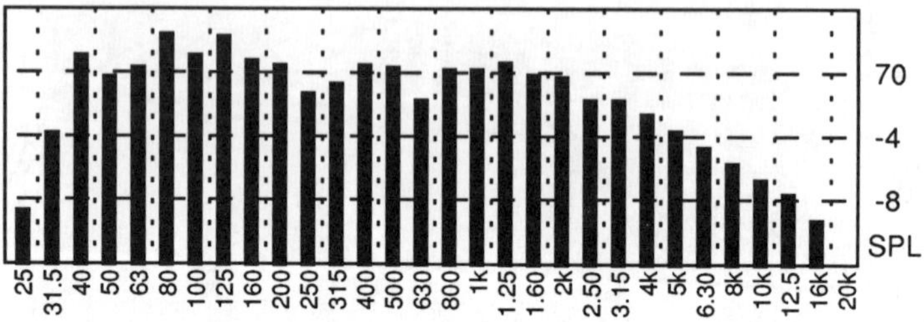


b. Center channel

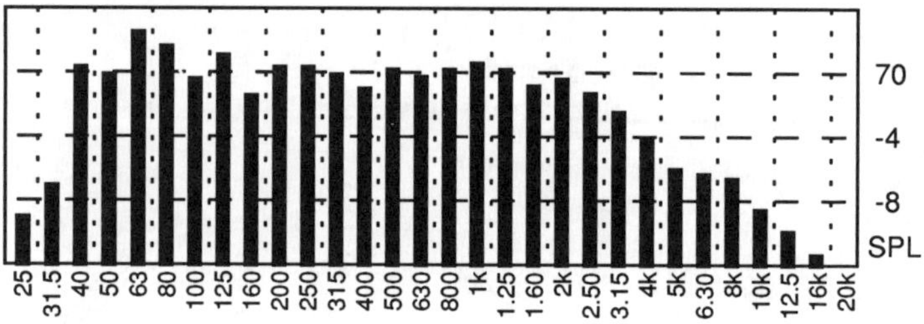


c. Right channel

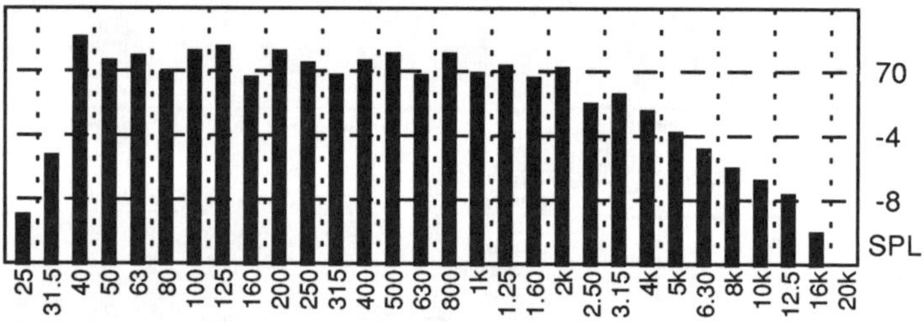


d. Subwoofer channel

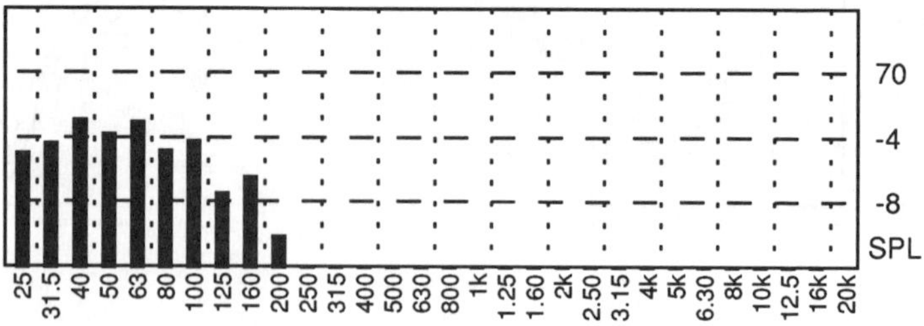

Figure 14. Relative drive voltage levels for a single screen channel, Umlang Theater.

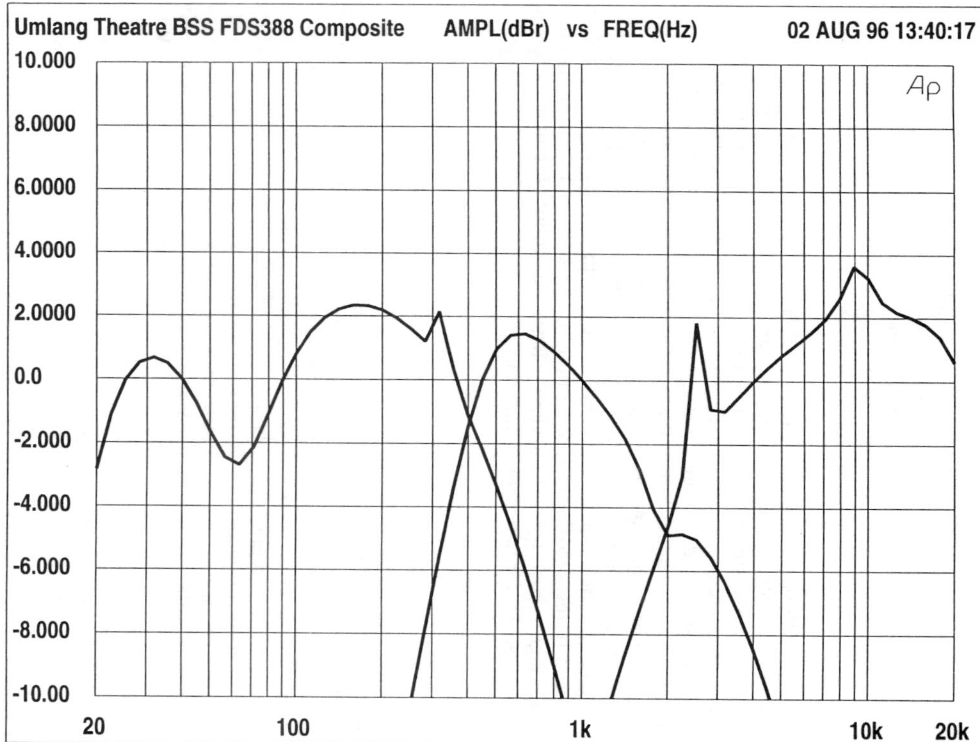

# Monitoring Sound in the One-Person Environment

Tomlinson Holman
University of Southern California
School of Cinema-Television
and TMH Corporation

*Abstract*
With the growth of personal computers as display devices for media has come the need to monitor sound accompanying images on these systems. Many of the same parameters that constitute the capabilities of large-scale systems also need to be addressed in small-scale ones in order to produce similar experiences of the program material. These include frequency range and response over the range, dynamic range, and stereo imaging capabilities. In addition, some new problems also arise, such as those brought about by being so close to the loudspeakers, and the difficult acoustical environment faced by the loudspeakers. Several methods are described which make the desktop environment useful in making professional judgments of sound usually reserved for calibrated monitoring systems in motion-picture dubbing stages. Having such a system extends the utility of digital audio and video workstations. Performance data is given.

## *Background and Environment*

### *Film monitoring standards*

The film industry employs standardized monitor conditions in dubbing stages to ensure interchangeability of program material in theaters[1]. It has been shown conclusively that errors in monitor response result in competent mixers taking corrective action *for what they hear over the monitor* , but in so doing they affect the program material which, if subsequently played over a system lacking the error, reveals the correction as an mistake. Thus it is important to have and to meet monitoring standards so that program material is made for a universal condition that can exist in many places. Published, or under consideration, are SMPTE standards or recommended practices for speaker arrangements for multi-channel monitoring, sound pressure level calibration, frequency response of monitors, control of reverberation time and discrete acoustical reflections, and background acoustic noise. When all these standards are met, along with some de facto industry practices such as directivities of loudspeakers for certain applications, interchangeability is good from dubbing stage to dubbing stage and from dubbing stage to theaters. These standards have evolved over many years, and many engineers have worked to make them have a balanced combination of good performance in preserving interchangeability and relative ease in application. Many dubbing stages and mixing rooms more or less meet all of the existing documented standards and practices.

---

[1]Parts of the television industry also employ standardized response and levels as described for film, although the standards are somewhat different, but the use of such standards in television production is not so wide-spread as it is in the film industry.

*Discrete reflections*
Among these standards and practices probably the least well known and practiced is control over discrete reflections. Such reflections have been shown to be important by a number of experimenters including F. Toole[2], then at the National Research Council of Canada, S. Bech[3], then at the Technical University of Denmark, and R. Walker[4] at the BBC. In a "Report on Mixing Studios Sound Quality" published in the *Japan Audio Society Journal* (Fall, 1994), I showed that in rooms that met all other SMPTE standards and practices, lack of control over early reflections is the largest contributor to a lack of uniformity in monitoring among the rooms. Rooms with a high level of early reflections (exceeding –15 dB spectrum level re the direct sound for the first 15 ms) sounded "colored" compared to those that did not have these same early reflections. Robert Walker at the BBC made the same finding at about the same time with regard to control rooms for radio production.

In professional environments, there are several dominant sources of such early reflections, depending on the venue. For conventional film dubbing, the largest reflections occur between the screen and the high-frequency horns behind the screen, since the screen is increasingly reflective as frequency goes up, and no treatment of the horn is possible to absorb reflections without destroying the waveguide properties that made the horn valuable to directivity control in the first place[5]. See Fig. 1. The console, which could be considered at first glance to be a significant source of reflections for mixers sitting behind it, is in fact not so important, probably because the reflection at grazing incidence over the top of the console is not nearly so prominent as a more direct reflection. For instance, in conventional music control rooms with the monitors located above the studio window, the largest source of reflection is the console located between the monitors and the listening position. See Fig. 2. In this case, the reflected spectrum level lies between 0 and –20 dB re the direct sound depending on frequency. Such an intense reflection contributes to a very strong timbral signature in such spaces due to the resulting comb filter. While the reflection level has been measurable with a variety of techniques for many years, relevant psychoacoustics really were not available to correctly weight the results until more recently. As a good example, Toole's experiment used speech as a test signal, certainly of great interest to film sound, and was performed in the late 1980's and reported in 1990.

*Near-field monitoring*
A solution to these problems in theory is near-field monitoring. The idea behind this is to reduce the effects of room acoustics to inaudiblity, since the monitor speaker is so close to the listener that he is completely dominated by the direct field of the loudspeaker. One primary problem for this approach is that these so-called

---

[2]Reported in the proceedings of the 1990 AES Washington Conference.
[3]Reported to the 13th International Congress on Acoustics.
[4]Reported to the Amsterdam AES convention in 1994.
[5]A new, more transparent (for sound) screen has recently become available that solves this problem, albeit at high cost. The element which makes the screen more acoustically transparent is to use more, finer, perforations than typical, which permits greater high-frequency transmission.

near-field loudspeakers are usually placed on top of the console meter bridge. There they suffer from several acoustic effects due to their local acoustical environment. First is that there is a very strong reflection off the console. See Fig. 3. Second, there is the fact that the meter bridge and console act to constrain the radiation of the speaker, forming in effect a larger baffle face of the loudspeaker than planned, boosting mid-bass frequencies. While it may be possible to design a speaker deliberately for the environment of the top of the console for this effect, it is not possible in the conventional speaker to compensate for the reflection off the console. An "acoustic barn door" (in the same sense as barn doors on studio lights) can be used, on the other hand, to shade the console from direct radiation from the loudspeaker. A relative thin but absorbent sandwich such as 1" of absorptive material on a piece of Masonite can be placed under the loudspeaker and made to stick out from the bottom of the speaker towards the listener. The idea is to absorb high-frequency energy directed towards the console, thus greatly reducing the reflected sound off it. See Fig. 4. This very inexpensive solution is not employed however. It does not solve the radiation load problem of the speaker which is due to the unintended extension of the baffle face, for which the speaker design must be modified, but it significantly alters the "splash" off the console. (The operator can still see everything because he looks at the barn door on edge: he has a clear line of sight to the speaker above, and the meters below, the barn door.) Of course, mid- and low-frequency sound diffract around the barn door and reflect off the console still, but fixing the high-frequency regime is nevertheless useful with this simple trick.

Another difficulty with "true near field monitoring," if you will, is that the small loudspeakers usually used are two-way designs with a physically separated woofer and tweeter. When such a speaker is used well away from reflecting surfaces such as the console in order to produce a direct field dominate sound at the listener's ear, say hung in more or less free space, another problem surfaces. Strong radiation pattern changes often occur in such designs at crossover, so while it is possible to choose one precise position for the direct sound to make flat through the crossover region, altering that position just a little often results in non-flat direct sound, as the amplitude and phase matching through crossover matters a great deal. See Fig. 5. Since listening position becomes so critical, typical small two-way speakers are not really terribly well suited to a near-field type condition. Coincident designs where the tweeter radiates from the center of the woofer do not show radiation pattern lobing through crossover so could be better suited perhaps, but they have the difficulty that the acoustic load on the tweeter is the woofer cone, which, along with the inevitable discontinuity between the woofer cone and the tweeter element, often causes response aberrations on axis. Why not therefore design a loudspeaker with a one-way driver? While this could be an attractive proposition, practical manufacturing difficulties in making drivers flat over many octaves while doing everything else that must be done usually leads one to reject it as a possibility. Furthermore, such a driver if round would inevitably beam excessively at high frequencies, making it critical in use, and would provide no directivity control at low frequencies.

Finally, near-field monitoring, even where it is truly practiced by hanging the loudspeakers well clear of reflecting surfaces, suffer yet another problem. While it is possible in this condition to listen with direct field dominance for middle and high frequencies, room modes still exist for low frequencies, and it only takes a round trip of the sound, at the speed of sound, to form a standing wave. Thus the low frequency response of such systems is still subject to room acoustics, and the inevitable low-frequency variations that they cause.

*The desktop environment*

Digital non-linear editing based on computer storage of picture and sound has become increasingly prominent in professional filmmaking circles recently. Listening at these stations, which are typically set up in ordinary editing rooms, constitutes a new type of listening environment for professionals. The current problem with this environment is that the director will hear one thing on a digital workstation and pass on it as adequate, but then find that it is inadequate when the elements come to the dubbing stage, since the full character of the sound has not been reproduced over the workstation monitoring system.

It is important to distinguish here between two items: the quality of audio stored within the workstation, and the sound reproduction system attached to the workstation over which the tracks are heard. Often, poor quality audio and video dubs are used as input to the workstation process, since such editing is an "off line" activity. The picture quality is not up to the standards of the source film, as it does not need to be to make editorial decisions, and storing video at high resolution to make a high-quality picture is very expensive. Often, this process is extended to the audio, which although it may be stored in the workstation as a 16-bit linear PCM word, with a professional sample rate, may be a copy of a 3/4" video tape copy of the production sound. Without fully realizing it, the source quality has been very substantially downgraded by the intervening video stage, which has much poorer audio quality than an audio cassette (the primary purpose being video). For instance, the low frequency headroom available above 0 VU (100 nW/m) on 3/4" tape is actually negative in deciBels! The tape saturates fully before 0 dB is reached at the lowest audio frequencies. Audio which has been through such a video tape generation should be considered to be the equal of the low-bit-rate picture: an off line sketch of what the sound content is to be, rather than a usable element in a dub.

The generally poor sound reproduction systems used along with workstations consist on the low end of computer monitors with responses shown in Fig. 6 and 7, and on the high end of professional near-field monitors. Neither of these is adequate to the task since the computer monitor lacks the frequency range and smoothness needed to reproduce the sound quality, and the near-field monitor is mis-applied in an environment which alters its output significantly due to reflections off the other equipment and work surfaces around it, and at low frequencies the standing wave problem is dominant. Either of these approaches produces sound that does not translate well to hearing the same recording on the dubbing stage. Furthermore, they both may well obscure problems with the sound quality of the recording that only become audible after the job has been transferred to the dubbing stage. The cry "it sounded all right on the workstation" has to be one of the most frequent heard in post production today, where just the basic frequency range and smoothness of the poor monitoring obscured problems.

*A new system*

With the above problems in mind, a set of solutions to the problems perceived was developed for one person sitting at a workstation, and allowing monitoring which sounds much more like a competent dubbing stage than has heretofore been possible. Among the strategies to solve the unique problems of small-space monitoring at a computer workstation are:

1. Direct-path dominant design. For most of the frequency range, the listener is close enough to a directional enough source of sound that the direct sound dominates reflected sound and reverberation. See Fig. 8. The degree of dominance required is set by psychoacoustic knowledge of the effects of reflections and reverberation. The listener hears a sound field that is uncolored by the effects of such reflections and reverberation, to the extent that the experience sounds fundamentally different from other types of small-room monitoring, including near-field monitoring. The decisions for the direct-path dominant design are made in context of the contribution of the associated picture monitor to extending the baffle face of the loudspeaker, while reducing the effect of the keyboard work surface to below audibility through directivity control. See Fig. 8.

2. Low-frequency correct response. Small rooms suffer greatly in low-frequency response uniformity about the space, and in frequency response at a point in the space, due to the prominence of standing waves in such spaces—their large frequency spacing yielding response errors up to ±15 dB in real rooms! However, with a given loudspeaker location, and a known listening location, it is possible to equalize the response for such a condition and produce very smooth low frequency response, despite the small room size. A limitation is that the area of good equalization is a sphere of several feet diameter from the center of the listening area. This limitation is a fundamental one in the room acoustics of such spaces, so does not represent a limit on this system, but on any in such a room, and with such specific equalization, the response can be corrected for one or for two listeners seated very close together.

3. Custom surround solution. We have found through the installation of this system in many rooms that one type of surround or another does not suffice, but rather the type of surround must be matched to the room. This is due to the wide variety of treatment by acoustic materials found in editing rooms. Basically, lively rooms can make use of diffuse-field dominant surround loudspeakers to produce an enveloping sound field, while rooms that are dead acoustically may use direct radiating types.

*Equalization*

One of the largest problems faced in the development of this system is the equalization method for it. This is because conventional room equalization is not appropriate, since we are not in conventional rooms which are typically equalized by 1/3-octave-band constant Q equalizers.

The reason that conventional 1/3-octave band equalization is not appropriate is that it is based on the critical band theory of hearing. Under this theory, frequency components of program material close to one another in frequency are evaluated for loudness and timbral contribution differently than frequency components further away. So for certain important characteristics it is possible to consider a frequency band as being significant, rather than a single spot frequency, due to this resolving power which can be compared to the bandwidth of a filter (although the center frequency of a critical band filters is not fixed but rather adapts to the signal). However, the problem with this theory comes in applying it to a system that includes not only a listener, for which it is appropriate, but also a room, for in some frequency regions the theory fails due to the strong effects of the room on the transfer function from the loudspeaker to the listener.

In particular, at low frequencies, standing waves dominate the sound fields in rooms, and more so to a higher frequency in smaller rooms than in larger ones. So this is a problem associated particularly with small rooms. Above a certain frequency, dependent on room volume and called the Schroeder frequency, the number of standing waves per 1/3-octave is so high that a diffuse field exists, and critical band theory works. But below the Schroeder frequency a diffuse field does not exist, and it is possible for the fundamental of one low frequency note to be reproduced at a widely different level from the next note to it one-half step away on a source instrument, even though the two notes lie within one critical band of each other. This note-by-note lack of uniformity is not covered by critical band theory, and the notes are heard at different levels. Thus low frequency equalization of small rooms is not well served by 1/3-octave equalization.

Another fact of life in small room acoustics is that the standing waves arise very quickly in time, due to the speed of sound, and since it only requires a round trip for the standing wave to start: there is no build-up time like that seen in large rooms for reverberant properties. A commonplace worry is that by equalizing the steady-state sound that the first-arriving transient sound will be made worse. In small spaces there is such a short time difference between the direct sound and the standing wave response to it that the two fields that they are evaluated as one insofar as perception is concerned. So equalizing the steady-state for flat response at low frequencies is adequate to produce optimal response in small spaces. Fig. 9 shows the frequency response of the system in a head-sized spatial average with 1/5-octave frequency smoothing.

*Center channel reproduction*

All film sound originated sound sources have a center channel. In the case of workstation monitoring, this center channel is most often delivered by means of a phantom image between two loudspeakers located left and right of the monitor, in the manner of conventional two-channel stereo. There is an improvement over two-channel stereo imaging however, simply because by the nature of the keyboard and monitor setup, the user is most likely to occupy a fairly small range of listening positions, and this helps center the phantom image on the picture. Problems do arise from center channel phantom images even in two-channel stereo. These include the fact that instead of one sound from one loudspeaker, there are actually two sound sources carrying one signal, and each one addresses each ear. The left and right loudspeaker speak simultaneously, and the sound arrives at the respective left and right ear at the same time for a centered listener facing the screen. But the sound from each loudspeaker also reaches the opposite ear, about 200 μs later than the direct sound from the same side loudspeaker. The response of the acoustic signal around the head is modified by diffraction and reflection effects, and the result combined with the time delay is a frequency response error for phantom center sound that would not be present with a center loudspeaker. This problem has been studied for years in two-channel stereo and solutions have been found such as first by Atal and Schroeder. Some commercial equipment such as the Lexicon CP-3 and DC-1 have crosstalk canceling schemes to produce an equal and opposite signal at the ears to eliminate the crosstalk, and this must be done in several iterations (canceling the signal intended to cancel the crosstalk...) for complete cancellation.

***Conclusion***

A system for monitoring sound in relatively small spaces having the full frequency range of a film sound track, the full dynamic range capacity, and in particular, dealing with the acoustical problems that arise in room acoustics of such spaces has been described. The primary solution to the room problem is to make dominant the direct sound field at the listener's ears over much of the frequency band, and to employ narrower band equalization than conventional 1/3-octave equalization in low frequency ranges where the room modes are dominant. Performance curves of this system have been given, along with other common situations.

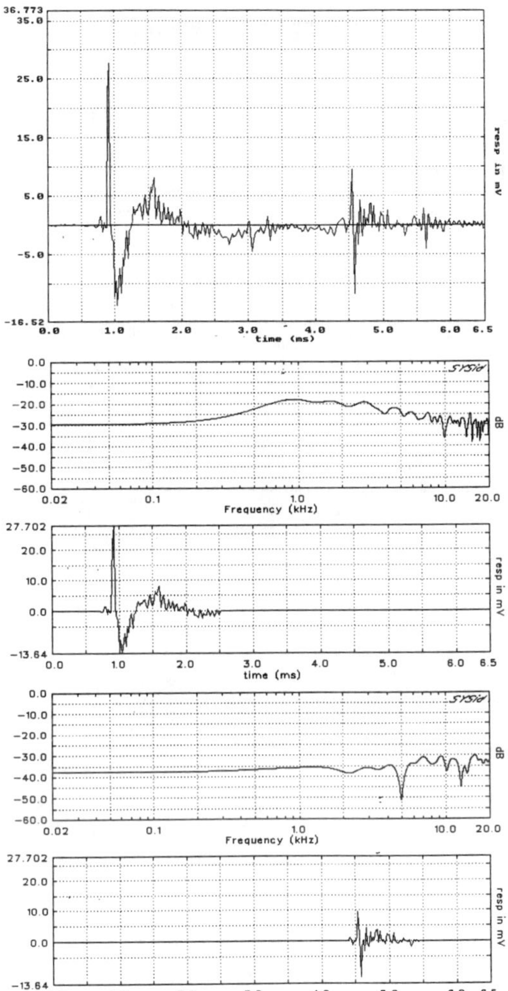


Fig. 1 a-e. a) time response of dubbing stage monitor system showing reflection from screen-to-horn-through screen. b) frequency response of direct sound. c) time response of direct sound. d) frequency response of reflection. e) time response of reflection. Note the level of frequency response of the reflection reaches levels equalling the direct sound at high frequencies where the screen is most reflective.

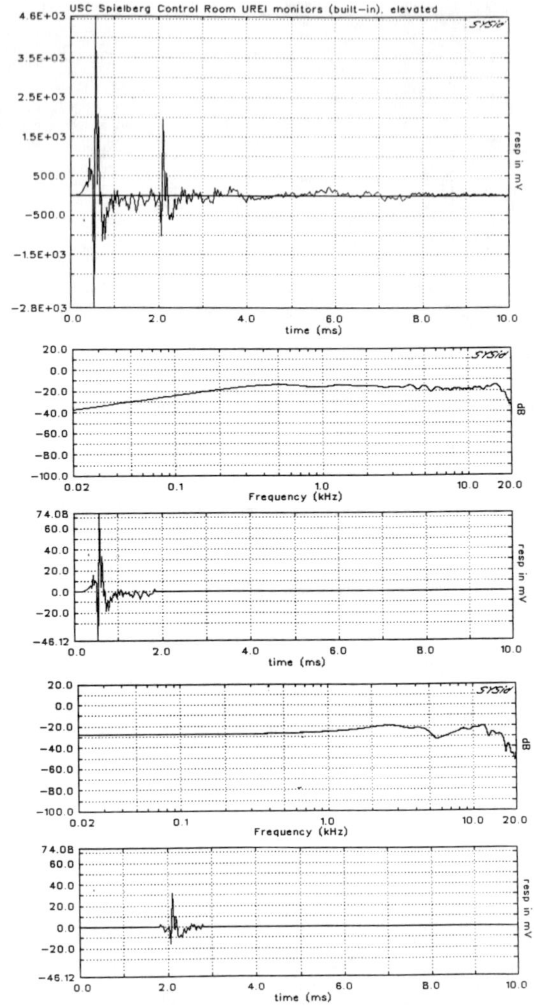


Fig. 2 a-e. a) time response of a conventional music control room with monitors located above a studio window; the prominent reflection is off the console. b) frequency response of the direct sound. c) time response of the direct sound. d) frequency response of the reflection. e) time response of the reflection.

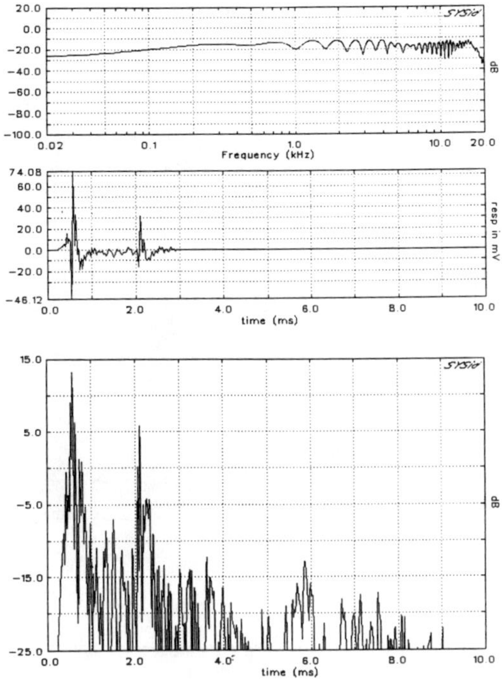


Fig. 2 f-h. f) frequency response of the combined direct sound and console reflection. g) time response of the direct sound and console reflection. h) log envelope time response.

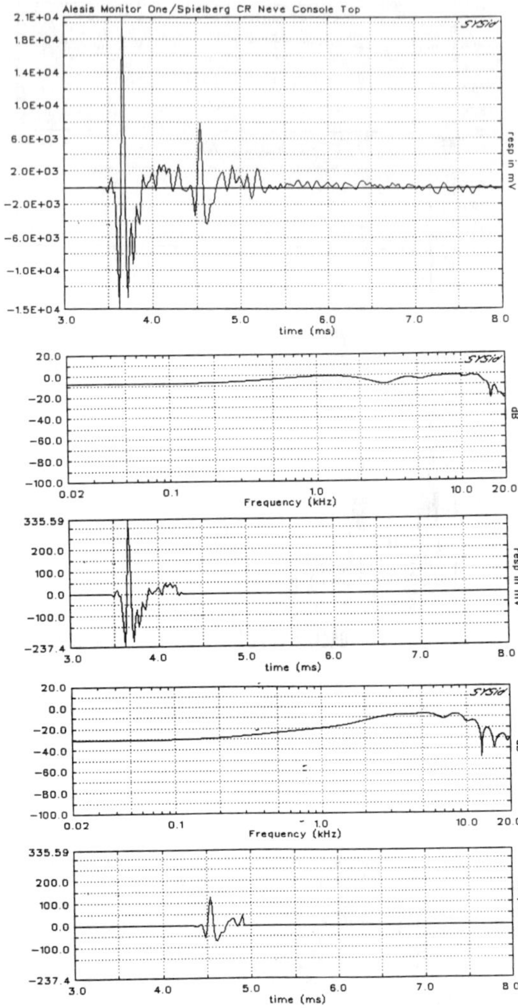


Fig. 3 a-e. a) time response of a near-field monitor set on a console meter bridge measured from a normal operating position. b) frequency response of the direct sound. c) time response of the direct sound. d) frequency response of the console reflection. e) time response of the console reflection.

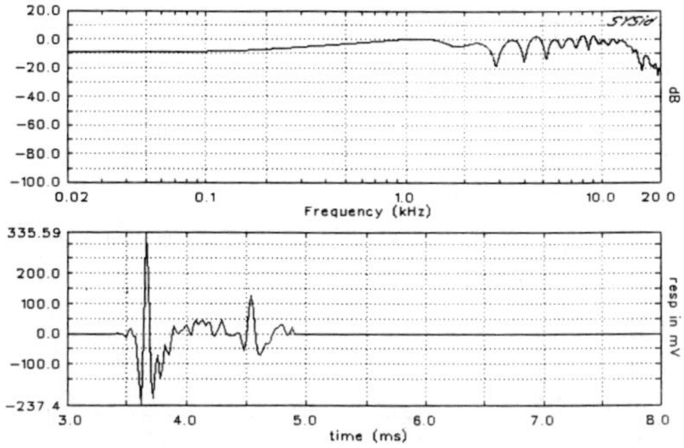


Fig. 3 f-g. f) frequency response of the combined direct sound and console reflection. g) time response of the combined direct sound and console reflection.

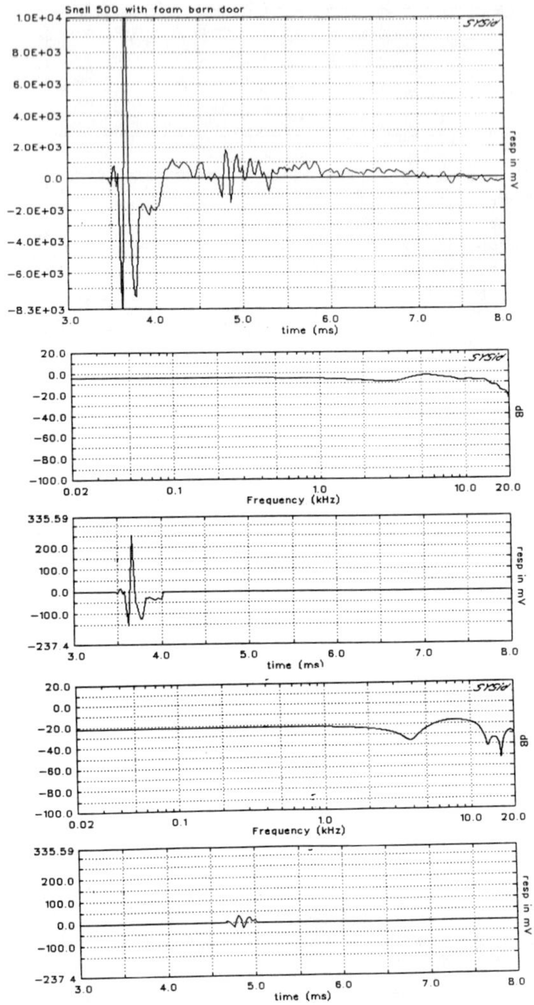


Fig. 4 a-e. a) time response of console top monitor with controlled vertical directivity and acoustic barn door described in the text. b) frequency response of the direct sound. c) time response of the direct sound. d) frequency response of the console reflection. e) time response of the console reflection.

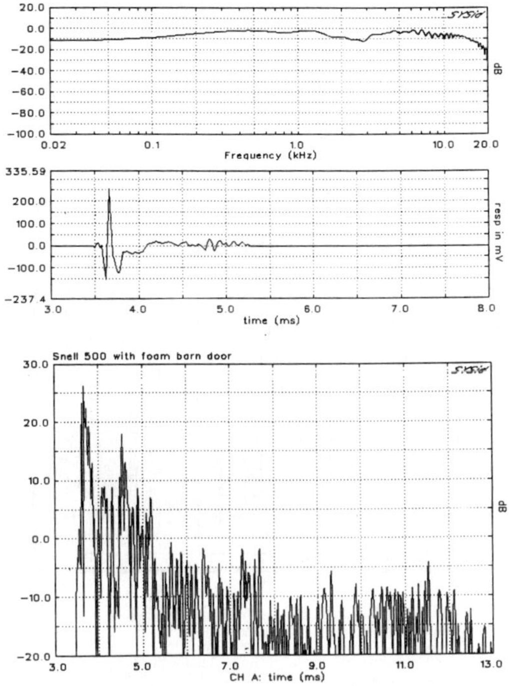


Fig. 4 f-h. f) frequency response of the combined direct sound and console reflection. g) time response of the combined direct sound and console reflection. h) log envelope time response.

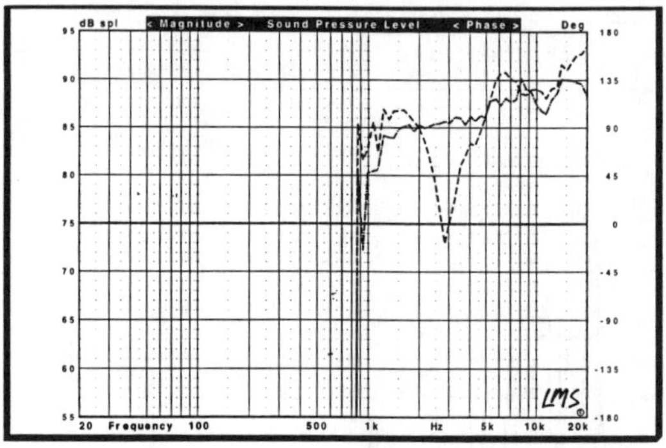


Fig. 5 Frequency response of the high-frequency range of a near-field loudspeaker measured at 1 m and on its central axis vs. a few inches lower along one side representing the real range over which the speaker may be used.

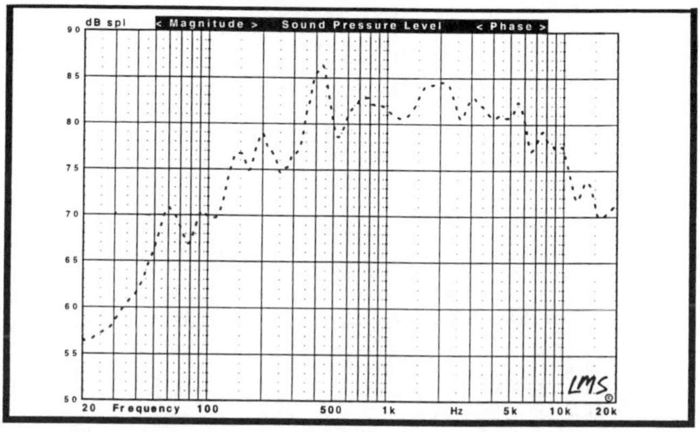


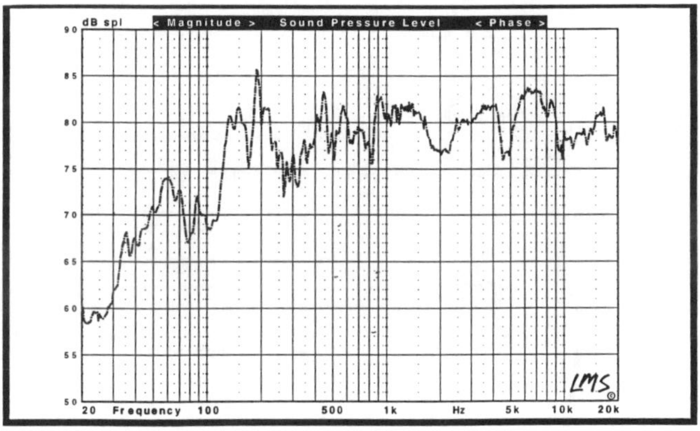


Fig. 6 and 7. 6) Frequency response in situ of a satellite-subwoofer multi-media monitor system. 7) Frequency response in situ of a small powered two-way high-end multi-media monitor system.

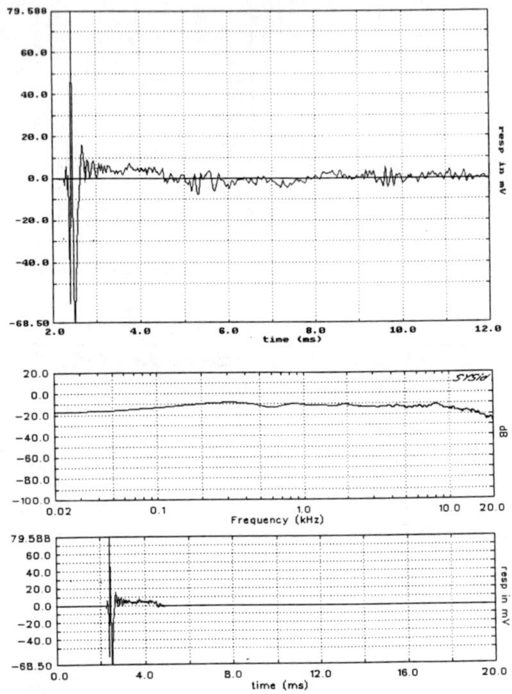


Fig. 8 a-c. a) time response of the monitoring system described in this paper. b) frequency response of the direct sound. c) time response of the direct sound.

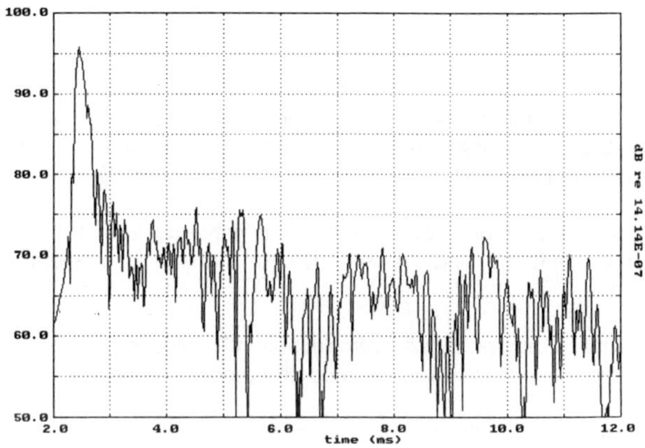


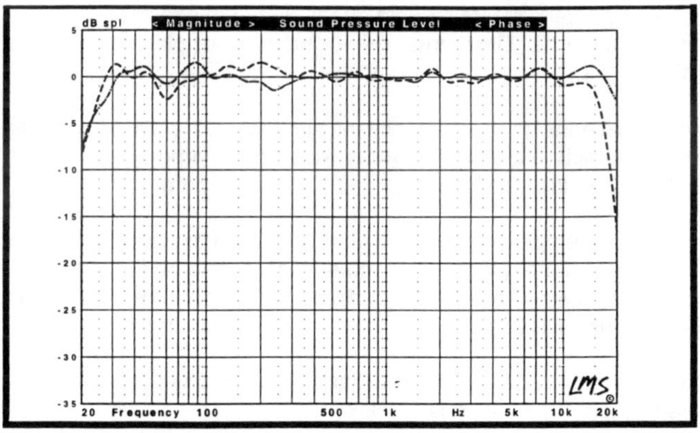


Fig. 8 d-e. d) log envelope of the time response of the new system described in this paper. It meets not only the criteria of –15 dB for 15 ms, but a more stringent one proposed by R. Walker of the BBC as desirable, if not likely to be reached, of –20 dB for 20 ms of reflection spectrum level re the direct sound. e) frequency response in situ of the system proposed in this paper equalized in place.

# Elements of a New Authoring System for Digital Video Disk (DVD)

Kenji Sugiyama
Victor Company of Japan
Yokosuka, Japan

Neil Neubert
JVC Professional Products Company
Elmwood Park, New Jersey

**Abstract**

The realization of DVD, Digital Video (Versatile) Disk, requires an authoring system to process the video, audio, sub-picture, and other program material before a disk can be made. Special DVD program material such as sub-picture, and the functions of a new DVD authoring system are presented.

The authoring system is composed of four functional elements; scenario converter, source encoder, pre-mastering, and checker. The functions of these elements are described in the paper.

The scenario converter element permits introduction of "navigation" data to program material so the viewer may interact with, and control program playback.

The source encoder element utilizes various compressed and non-compressed coding methods to encode video, audio and sub-picture.

The pre-mastering process creates a data stream conforming to compression system, and DVD format standards. Data stream checking includes playback emulation and verification of the data.

DVD offers new presentation display functions such as multi-point of view selection, and "pan and scan" picture area selection for wide screen programs. The authoring system permits these functions to be included in the DVD data.

The authoring system employs a new rate control method for variable bit rate encoding that yields both best picture quality and optimal fit of all data on the DVD disk. A two pass video encoding method has been developed to first analyze the program material, and then optimize the VBR rate control during the final encoding process.

The authoring system includes processes that thoroughly check and verify the data stream before it is recorded on the DVD disk.

## 1. Introduction

The new Digital Video Disk offers enhanced capabilities for mass-storage media recording and playback. DVD permits new functionality and features to be included along with recording and playback of high quality video and audio. The authoring system is a fundamental process that permits combination and integration of all of the possible functions and features to be recorded with any program material on DVD. DVD is thus, more attractive media than that of its predecessors.

The authoring process includes video, audio, and sub-picture data encoding. Most important, this authoring system provides for variable bit rate video data encoding, necessary to yield constant, good picture quality within media of limited, fixed data capacity. Bit rate control technique is emphasized in the discussion and an improved, two-pass encoding rate control system for VBR video data is described. In addition, the authoring system incorporates a "navigation" function to permit a viewer to be interactive with the program material, and to select among other features and functions such as multi-lingual audio. Data checking is important and included to assure media compatibility with all relevant standards, and DVD players of all makes and models. This authoring system for DVD is considerably improved from predecessors designed for CD-ROM and Video-CD.

## 2. An Authoring System for DVD

### 2.1 Overview of the Authoring System

The authoring system that is the subject of this paper is composed of four parts; scenario converter, source encoder, pre-mastering, and checker.

Figure 1 shows the functional system composition:

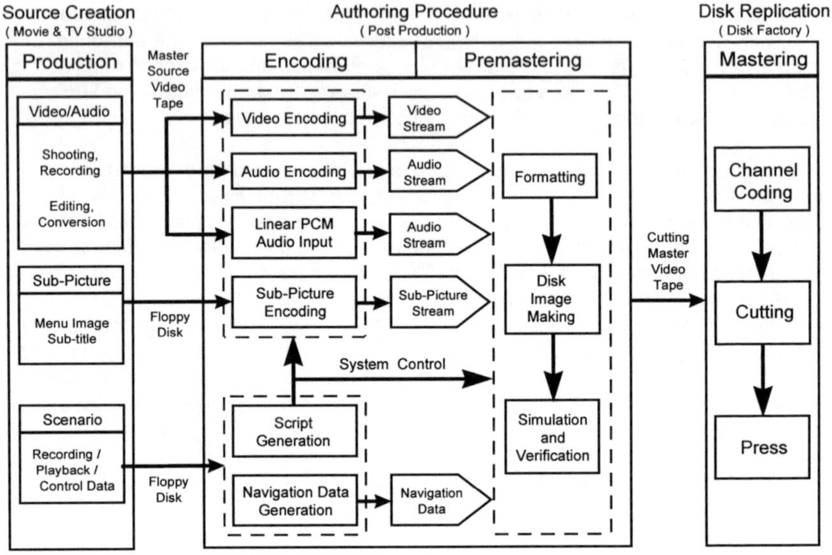


Figure 1 - Overview of DVD Authoring Procedure

The scenario converter is an interactive element that permits a director or editor to develop and introduce "navigation" data to the process of authoring as he observes the playback and display of original program material.

The source encoder section encodes three specific signals that will be part of the DVD. Main program video is encoded by MPEG-2, program audio by the AC-3 process, and a sub-picture. The sub-picture is a new encoding format for DVD that accommodates simple captions, titles, and other text elements that might be added to the final picture.

The pre-mastering process creates a data stream that satisfies the requirements of the MPEG-2 system standard, as well as fitting the DVD format. The checking section includes an emulator and verifier.

Figure 2 shows the hardware system configuration. In this initial authoring system, original audio and video program material is assembled and edited in the traditional manner in television post-production facilities. Consequently, an edited master source tape can be prepared to include only the basic, original DVD navigation functions. Future authoring systems might include the first edit process, as well, to permit integration of all DVD functions and features more efficiently. Digital media is used to store and transport the encoded output data to the mastering process. It is anticipated that the format and media on which it is recorded will be standardized in the future. Figure 2 shows a data tape recording format and media as one such possibility.

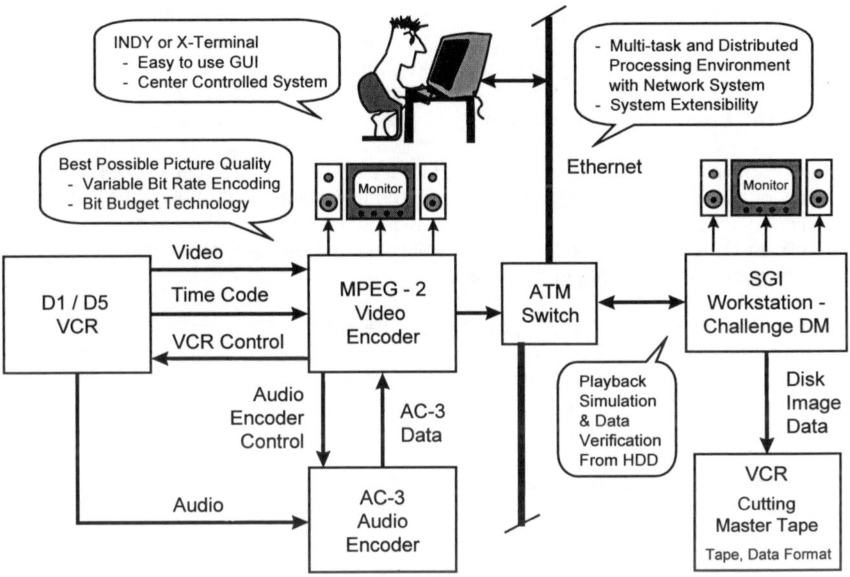


Figure 2 - Configuration of DVD Authoring System

### 2.2 The Multi-Media Encoder

The source encoder section encodes three specific signals that will be part of the DVD. Main program video is encoded by MPEG-2, program audio by the AC-3 process, and a sub-picture. The sub-picture is a new encoding format for DVD that accommodates simple captions, titles, and other text elements that might be added to the final picture.

#### 2.2.1 Video Coding

The MPEG-2 compression method is utilized to encode video at main profile, main level (MP@ML). The MPEG-2 standard is recognized and accepted internationally and is quickly being chosen for a majority of compressed digital video storage and distribution applications including proposed digital broadcasting systems. The authoring system possesses a hardware based, real time, MPEG-2 encoder.

### 2.2.2 Audio Coding

The AC-3 method is used to encode audio for 525 line, 60 field per second television systems in areas that use NTSC encoding for analog television transmission. AC-3 can be selected for 5.1 audio channels, or normal two channel stereo sound. MPEG-2 stereo audio encoding is used for 625 line, 50 field per second television systems in areas that use PAL encoding for analog television transmission.

### 2.2.3 The Sub-Picture and Coding

The sub-picture is a useful new encoding format for DVD that accommodates a wide variety of captions, titles, and other multi-colored text elements that might be added to the final picture. The sub-picture uses a run-length coding data compression technique. It is usually encoded utilizing software processing because it does not require rigorous processing in real time.

Simple text elements can be composed within the authoring system at the same time that encoding takes place using the sub-picture capabilities. Titles and text elements that require special artistic content will continue to be made by graphic artists in television production studios. Such titles resemble actual pictures and necessarily are encoded within the video encoding process.

The data streams for these three signals are multiplexed by using the MPEG-2 system (program stream) method. Finally, the data streams are formatted to conform to the DVD format.

## 2.3 New Presentation Display Functions

DVD offers some new presentation features such as multiple camera angle view selection. The authoring system provides the tools necessary to incorporate these and other new features as part of a finished Digital Video Disk.

### 2.3.1 Multiple Camera Angle View

A multi-view disk provides the viewer with different point of view choices for individual scenes within a program. Figure 3 illustrates multiple point of view data streams and how the viewer can skip between them during playback. These are multiplexed together during relatively short intervals. The time length should be equal for each point of view in a single scene to assure seamless playback as the viewer switches between them.

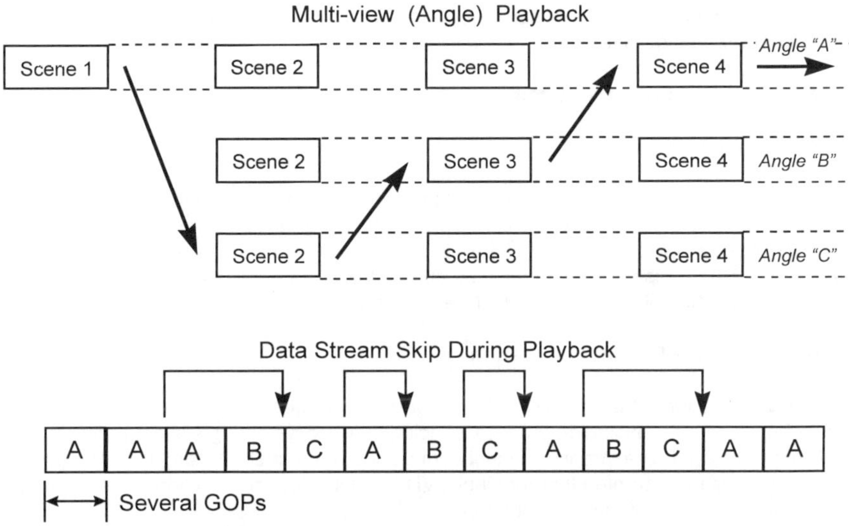


Figure 3 - Multi-angle Picture Playback Processing

### 2.3.2 Pan and Scan Function

DVD also offers "pan and scan" picture area selection for wide screen programs that are displayed on television sets with traditional aspect ratios (4x3). An MPEG-2 function makes it possible to assign a center of picture location for playback during the authoring process. The authoring system does not determine the center of picture information itself, but accepts it from an operator during the authoring process. The center of picture information is multiplexed into the encoded data stream. During playback, the selected picture center is automatically located in the center of the display and the left and right edges of the picture are truncated accordingly. Alternatively, the viewer can select a "letter-box" display mode that shows the entire wide screen picture but with black areas at the top and bottom of the picture.

### 2.3.3 Navigation Function

The quick view function for rapid picture search, and convenient chapter change feature are useful in DVD. The DVD data stream possesses information revealing the location of MPEG-2 "I" frames in both the forward and reverse play directions so that these functions occur quickly and conveniently on command of the viewer. "I" frames are the only frames that are intra-frame coded (coded independent of picture information contained in adjacent frames) in an MPEG-2 group of pictures (GOP). Consequently, these are the only frames that can be decoded rapidly for quick and convenient search and chapter change operation.

## 2.4 Check of the Data Stream

### 2.4.1 Emulation Playback

An emulation function is included in the authoring system to determine that the picture and sound, to be reproduced from playback of the DVD, have been optimally processed and encoded prior to the very final authoring process for the DVD itself.
A magnetic hard disk drive is applied as an emulator and provides quick and convenient virtual playback of the picture and sound.

### 2.4.2 DVD Data Format Verification

The DVD data format is complicated, and careful management of the data stream is very important. A verification process is included in the authoring system to thoroughly examine the final data stream for strict compliance with the DVD standard. The goal of verification is to guarantee that the final DVD disk will play and function perfectly in all players, regardless of make and model.

# 3. Bit Rate Control

## 3.1 Variable Bit Rate for MPEG-2 Coding

MPEG-2 compression utilizes inter-frame prediction and variable length coding techniques. These methods provide very efficient video compression at a high compression ratio and low video data bit rate. Nevertheless, constant good picture quality requires a relatively high video data bit rate, even using MPEG-2 compression. Constant bit rate encoding requires a rate for good picture quality that is determined by the part(s) of the program that is the most difficult to compress (encode). A 6 to 8 Mbs rate is considered the minimum bit rate required to compress difficult pictures while retaining good picture quality.

DVD has an advantage that it can operate at a variable a bit rate. Variable bit rate for video in DVD makes it possible to allocate many bits to encode difficult pictures, and few bits to encode simple pictures. Since typical program material is composed of both difficult and simple pictures, the overall result can be satisfactory picture quality at an average bit rate of only 3 to 4 Mbs. An average rate of 3 to 4 Mbs yields picture quality almost as good as that of CBR at 6 to 8 Mbs and permits lengthy feature movies to be contained on just a single DVD disk.

A two pass encoding method has been developed for VBR in packaged media. The very best picture is achieved by first searching the entire program to determine the required bit rates for each of the many short segments contained in the program.

Interim processing establishes target bit rates on a frame by frame basis. Finally, actual encoding takes place and it is controlled to match the established target bit rates. The result is the best possible picture quality in an amount of data that best fits the available disk space of DVD.

### 3.2 Control of Total Data Amount

| | *VIDEO* | *AUDIO* | *SUB-PICTURE* |
|---|---|---|---|
| *CODING METHOD* | MPEG - 2 (MP@ML) | AC - 3 (MPEG - 2) | Original |
| *VBR / CBR* | VBR | CBR | VBR |
| *RATE CONTROL* | Possible | Not Necessary | Difficult |
| *TYPICAL RATE RANGE* | 1 to 10 Mbs | 384 kbs | 0 to 3 Mbs |
| *TYPICAL AVERAGE RATE* | 4 Mbs | 384 kbs | 100 kbs |

Table 1 - Digital Signal Characteristics

The total amount of all data that can be recorded on a single layer DVD disk is fixed at 4.7 GByte. Maximum data transfer rate can be no greater than 10 Mbits/second. Table 1 describes the fundamental parameters of Video, Audio and Sub-Picture data for DVD, and each possesses a different set of data parameters. To fit all of the data on the DVD disk, the authoring system employs a new rate control method which encodes the sub-picture before main video since the sub-picture data rate is difficult to control. The main video signal is encoded last and its bit rate is varied as necessary to satisfy the picture quality requirements, and the space available on the DVD disk.

Figure 4 illustrates this concept of total data amount control.

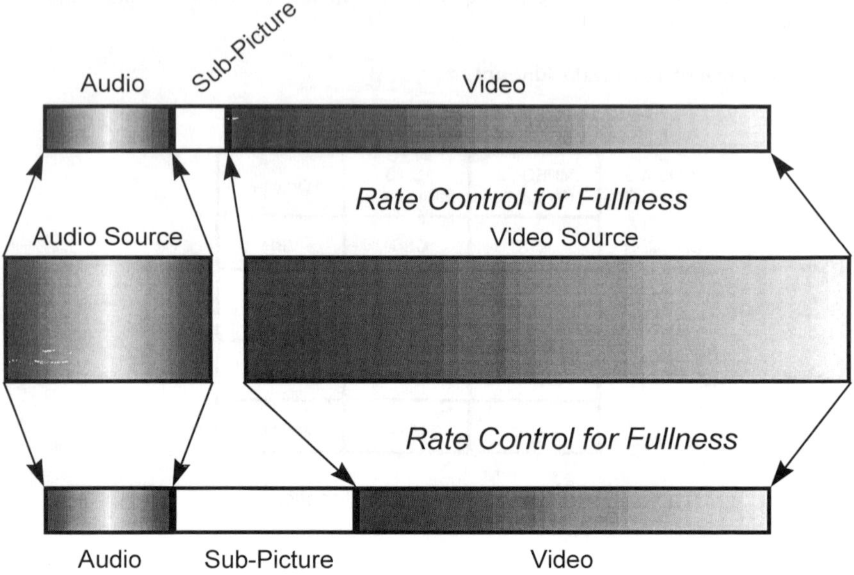


Figure 4 - Total Data Amount Control: Video, Audio, Sub-Picture

Audio is encoded at constant bit rate, independent of the sub-picture and video. Bit rate for the sub-picture varies depending on its complexity but it cannot be controlled easily. Finally, the amount of video data is controlled and adjusted as necessary to consume the remaining data space available. The amount of data space available for video depends on the amount of space required for the sub-picture. Consequently, the video encoder has to be part of the main authoring system since it must be aware of the data space committed to the sub-picture. While this is necessary to fit the most data possible on fixed disk space, the total amount of sub-picture data is typically small and has little effect on the video picture quality.

Figure 5 shows actual bit rate variation for audio (CBR), sub-picture, and video:

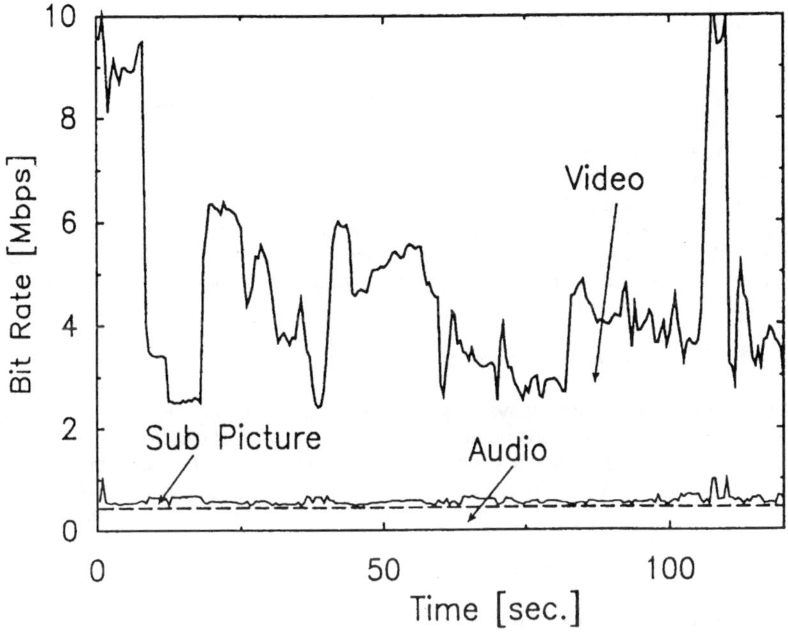


Figure 5 - Bit Rate Variation - Video, Audio, and Sub-Picture

### 3.3 Rate Control for the Multi-Angle View Multi-Angle View Function

Multi-angle view requires that the data corresponding to several different versions of the scene, be multiplexed together. The MPEG-2 program stream cannot be multiplexed easily, however, and care is required because large differences in bit rate between each view angle version can compromise seamless playback. The authoring system permits control of the data rates so that they are about the same for each view angle to permit seamless playback.

## 4. High Picture Quality Coding

MPEG-2 decoding is strictly specified and standardized, but the encoding process offers modest design freedom. MPEG-2 picture quality is therefore influenced by the quality of the encoding technique. The authoring system employs some special techniques to yield the best possible picture quality.

### 4.1 Picture Quality Control

MPEG-2 should allocate many bits to parts of the picture (macro blocks) where compression artifacts and degradation are most apparent. The authoring system calculates a parameter based on the subjective picture quality anticipated from picture activity, and employs the parameter to change the quantization step size as necessary to optimize picture quality. The parameter is calculated by measuring both spatial and temporal activity in the picture. Spatial variance is measured by observing variation between sub-blocks in specific neighborhoods within the picture. Temporal variance is measured by observing variation between frames of the picture. Manual picture quality adjustment is provided so that picture quality may be further controlled and optimized by viewers during the authoring process.

### 4.2 Optimum Processing Techniques

MPEG-2 can utilize many adaptive picture processing techniques. Picture quality is of paramount importance for DVD authoring and an optimal set of picture processing techniques is selected to yield the best possible picture quality. The additional processing cost to do this is more acceptable for DVD authoring than for other MPEG-2 encoding applications. To realize this, thorough information about the picture is gathered during the first virtual coding and used later for basic VBR control. Further discussion follows in the next section.

### 4.3 Pre-Processing Techniques

Pre-processing is generally not used for original source pictures that are of satisfactory picture quality. Pre-processing may be applied to source pictures that are of unsatisfactory quality. For example, pictures that possess excessive noise might have noise reduction processing applied to them before they begin the DVD authoring process.

## 5. An Advanced Two Pass Video Encoder

An advanced two pass encoder has been developed to achieve both the best rate control and picture quality. Figure 6 shows a block diagram of this two pass processing:

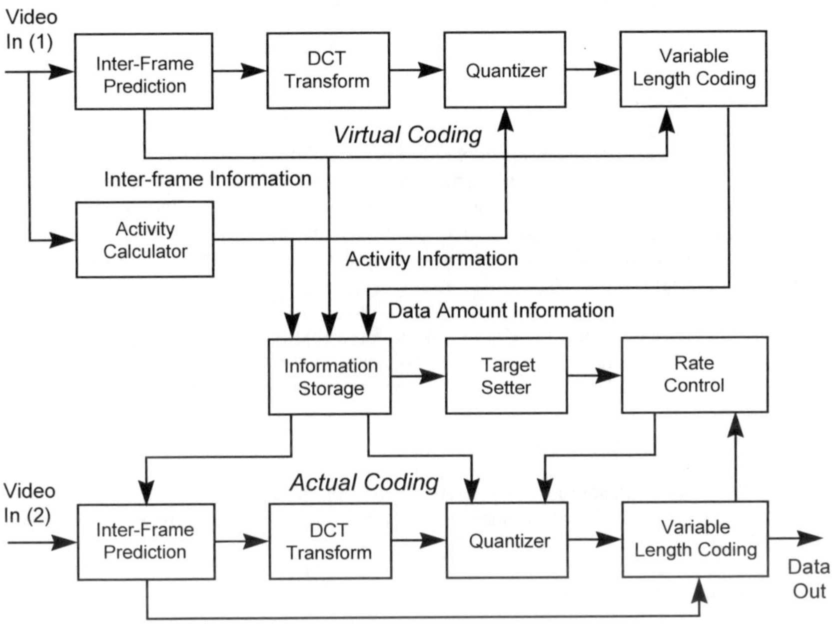


Figure 6 - Block Diagram - Advanced Two Pass Encoder

Many parameters of the picture are searched, analyzed, and used for establishing the target data rate and selecting the adaptive mode during the actual coding process. The constraint parameters for MPEG-2 must be kept within the maximum values listed in table 2. The length of the interval between MPEG-2 reference "I" frames (GOP) should be kept as short as practicable to assure rapid and smooth picture search and random access.

| | |
|---|---|
| Picture Size | 720 (704) x 480 |
| Picture Rate | 29.97 Frames / Second Maximum |
| I Frame Interval (N) | 18 Frames Maximum |
| Bit Rate | 9.8 Mbs Maximum |

Table 2 - MPEG-2 Constraint Parameters for DVD

## 5.1 Virtual Coding (Pass 1)

The first pass is a virtual coding process that is very similar to the actual, final coding process. Utilization of coding conditions similar to those of the final, actual process is very important and yields the most possible, useful information to affect the final, actual encoding process. The rate control process is necessarily inactive during this first pass encoding. The following data is searched, analyzed and retained to affect the coding during the second pass;

- The total amount of generated data for each macroblock (16x16 pixels).
- The amount of data that represents inter-frame prediction information.
- The amount of data that results from DCT transformation of the picture.
- Data associated with motion vector and adaptive processing mode information.
- Data associated with scene change information.

Frequently, it is beneficial to control information contained in larger picture units (picture area or group of picture). Information to effect this is gathered from analysis of macroblocks.

## 5.2 Target Rate Setting

The GOP target rates are determined by non-linear conversion of the observed GOP rates. A non-linear conversion function that yields full data recording is used. The relation between the inter-frame amount of data, and the amount of data resulting from DCT transformation is considered.

## 5.3 Actual Encoding (Pass 2)

During the second pass actual coding, the rates are controlled to follow the target rates. As a result of this control, the total amount of data just fits the capacity of the disk, and is of nearly constant, good picture quality. The searched, analyzed, and retained information obtained during first pass virtual coding, is used to achieve optimal encoding during the second pass. Motion vector and prediction information is used to select the exact quantization, and the inter-frame processing mode.

## 6. Conclusion

These are the elements of a first generation authoring system for DVD. Picture quality is considered to be the first priority in this system. Emphasis has been placed on rate control methods and their total management, and the highest quality two pass encoding processes. The scenario converter for interactive navigation data development, and the checker (emulator and verifier) satisfy only the minimum requirements of the DVD concept. Future generations can offer improved interactivity that will permit greater creative and artistic content to be included on DVD.

## References

1. Kenji Suguyama, M. Fujiwara, K. Yokouchi, "Video Disk System using Variable Bit Rate," *IEEE Transactions on Consumer Electronics, 41*, 504-509, August 1995

2. Kikuchi Sugiyama, "An Authoring System for Digital Video Disk," 1996 IEICE General Conference, TC-2-7, March 1996

# Compression to Disc Building: DVD for Movies

Jerry A. Pierce
Director
Digital Video Compression Center
Universal Studios

## Abstract

The process of building a DVD movie disc requires a new set of skills. In addition to the traditional skills required to assemble a Laserdisc title, the DVD production process requires knowledge of audio/video compression, man-machine interface, and the intricacies of the DVD Navigation specification.

This paper discusses the various issues involved in the total production of a DVD movie. It will discuss the choices for a DVD design, the assembly of original content, the design of a "standard" user interface, and an overview of the compression/ authoring process.

## Introduction

A DVD movie can be as simple as a Laserdisc or as complex as a full interactive CD-ROM. The complexity will be transparent for most consumers since the movie will be a seamless presentation of the appropriate choices for that consumer, primarily due to the language and version choices that the consumer makes. With the convenience of DVD in both functions, physical size, and familiarity with the CD package, DVD has a good chance of making significant market penetration.

The production of a DVD movie is a convergence of two industries: Video Post Production that understands audio/video and the needs of the content providers and CD-ROM production where the computer is the tool of choice. Both industries must modify their traditional methods of working to meet the challenges of DVD. DVD is just the beginning. Other new digital distribution methods will also need to learn from the production methods of DVD and hopefully will share the same files as those created for DVD.

The first challenge is to understand the total process of making a DVD. This includes the design of a DVD movie, the processing steps for the audio/ video/ subtitles, the assembly process for the multiplexed streams, the authoring of the various elements to create a disc image and finally the emulation of disc image for testing of a final product.

### Key Goals for a DVD Movie

To achieve success in the delivery of video to the home, packaged media such as DVD must differentiate itself though a variety of benefits for the consumer. These include:

- High quality video: DVD has already proven higher quality over Laserdisc technology. Maintaining this high quality is essential for DVD.
- High quality audio: The digital 5.1 audio on DVD significantly adds to the enjoyment of watching a movie on DVD.
- Language selections: A unique feature of DVD is the ability to include multiple languages for the customer.
- Attractive, easy to use menu screens: Random access is a major differentiation for DVD over all other forms of video distribution.

### Basic Design of a DVD Movie

As a DVD Movie title is being designed a number of choices are available to the producer. These include:

Video: All MPEG video encoders encode digital component signals (some encoders accept composite signals and internally convert to component). The best results for DVD is video that is of the best quality which, in general, is component digital video. The selection of wide-screen material, full frame, or letterbox must be also made. DVD offers the ability to record wide-screen material (anamorphic 16x9) for full-frame presentation on 16x9 TV's and automatic letterbox creation on standard screen 4x3 TV's.

Audio: The DVD format can hold up to 8 different audio streams conforming with the video. A typical movie may have three or four languages and might contain one or two auxiliary streams of director's comments or descriptive language for the visually impaired.

Each Audio stream may be mono, stereo, surround sound stereo, or full 5.1 channel surround. The encoding can be uncompressed PCM, AC3 on NTSC discs, or MPEG PAL discs. The encoding rate must also be specified.

Subtitles: A new industry is being formed for the creation of subtitles and captions[1] for DVD. These are called subpicture streams and are bit mapped files for an overlay generated by the player. This gives us full control of the font, size, style, and positioning on the screen. We have limited, but sufficient, control over the colors on the screen for subtitles.

A DVD title can have up to 32 subpicture streams. These can be computer file (i.e. TIFF files) with SMPTE Timecode identifiers for display control. The files must be conformed to the video and will need critical control for overlay for "forced" titling for locale identifiers.

Navigation Design: The DVD format allows the use of Menu Screens with Buttons and a navigation language allowing use of "jump" statements, conditional branching, and control of audio, subpicture, and video streams during playback.

It is critical at this early stage to build a common method of presenting movies to the customer. Controls in consistent places between movies will make a user-friendly environment.

The start-up procedure is part of the design and can set the language, check for locale, check for parental control, etc. It is possible to present status messages to the user and/or begin playing of the movie. As an industry we should agree on common ways of operation to make the total system user friendly.

Added Value Material: Laserdiscs have set the standard for additional material for consumer presentations. This can include trailers for the movie, out-takes, the making of the movie, and a variety of story board still frames. DVD can present this material in the "standard" way and offers new opportunities for new methods of presentation.

## A User Interface Philosophy

Much like a computer operating system, there will be many ways to accomplish the same task. There are two main methods:

- Control via a GUI and/or
- Remote Control Keypad dedicated buttons.

---

[1] We define "Subtitles" as titles for hearing viewers of a foreign language; "Captions" are designed to assist the hearing impaired — i.e. a ringing phone will be described; and "Closed Captions" are captioned text on line 21 of the video.

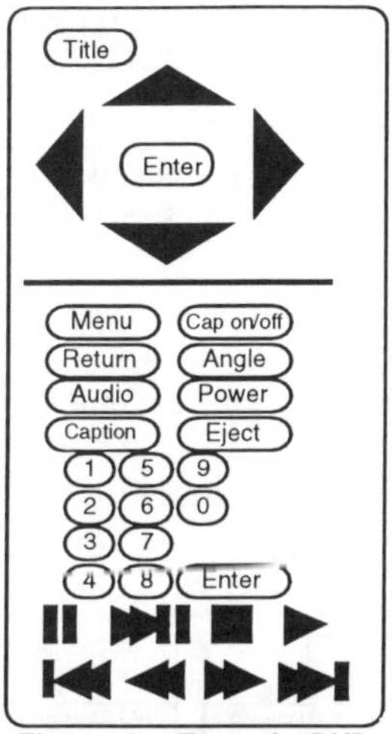


**Figure 1 - Example DVD Remote Controller**

Figure 1 shows a candidate remote controller. Many hardware companies will have multifunction remote controllers and the placement and presence of the keys is up to the hardware company.

It is important to allow hardware companies the ability to build simplified remote controllers. A candidate navigation system is being proposed where all features and functions can be reached with six buttons: Up/Down/Left/Right/Select/Title.

Other buttons can add significantly to the ease of use. Buttons such as Return, Captions on/off and the "standard" control functions (Play, stop, pause, etc.).

The buttons Title and Menu can be confusing to the user, one possible proposal is to merge these to perform the same function.

The general navigation of a movie could take the form shown in Figure 2:

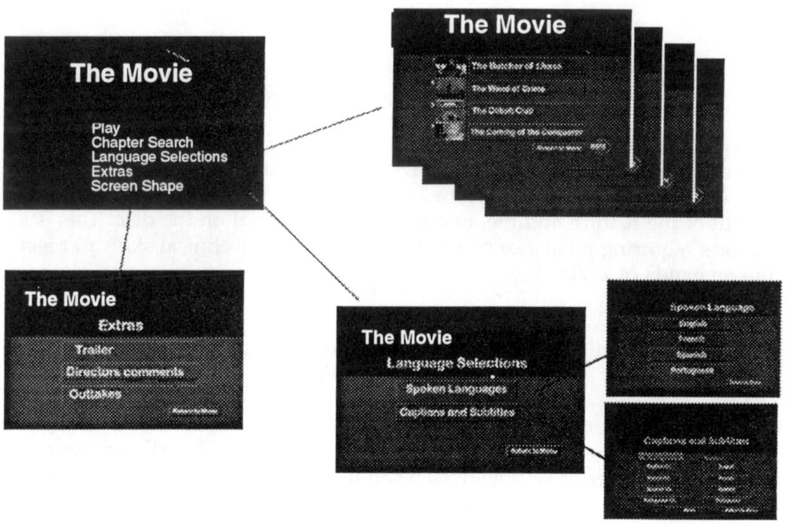


Figure 2 - Candidate Movie Layout

The Main Menu Screen can lead the user to the other screen of the disc. A typical movie would have "Play," "Chapter Search," "Language Selections," "Extras," and might have "Screen Shape" submenus.

In a Multi-language DVD it may be appropriate to build a sets of these menu screens for each language. In one disc under development there are four of these sets for English, Spanish, French, and Portuguese.

## End-to-end Process

Figure 3 shows a general view of the overall process steps for the creation of a DVD disc. Each of these steps will be briefly described below.

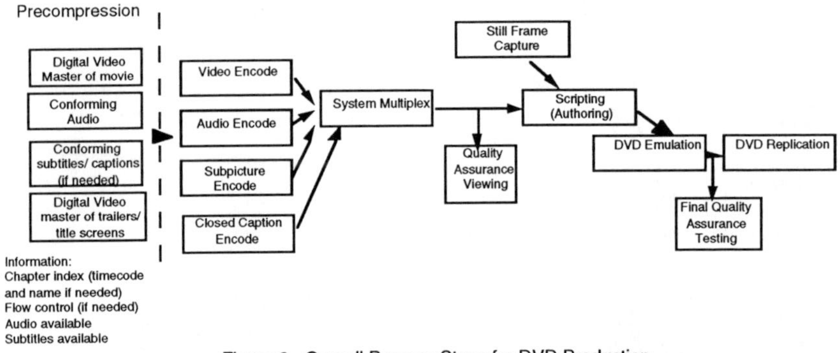


Figure 3 - Overall Process Steps for DVD Production

Video Encoding: The process of video encoding is one of reducing the incoming source bit stream of approximately 170 Mb/s to the encoded stream of variable bit rate of an overall average from 2.5 Mb/s to 4.5 Mb/s, depending on the length of the feature and the amount of extra material on the disc. This is a process requiring a balance of artistic judgment and technical skills to meet the demands of DVD.

Video encoding is the most visible of the various steps in preparing of a DVD disc. Video encoding is not the most time consuming step. Video encoding is under 20% of the process time to create a DVD.

Audio Encoding: The audio encoding process reduces the bit rate from a 5.1 channel system at 4.5 Mb/s to an encoded stream of 0.384 Mb/s. An AC3 encoder requires a number of settings which can include instructions in the bit stream for dynamic range reduction and the equations for Dolby Pro Logic surround sound.

Subtitles/Captions Encoding: Typical subtitles for DVD are created as TIFF files. The DVD format is a 2 bits per pixel run length encoded stream. Other methods include starting with the ASCII text and directly rendering into the DVD encoded stream format. These are computer intensive procedures using developed tools.

System Multiplex: The assembling of all the elementary streams is the role of the System Multiplexer. This computer program creates the presentation time stamps for all streams and maintains stream number assignments as well as handles the variable bit rate issues associated with the video. The result is a stream suitable for testing to confirm lip sync, video and audio quality.

Navigation and Scripting: The design of the user interface for a variety of skills of users is the goal of the navigation system. Most systems use a GUI tool and a skilled programmer to construct the final disc instructions. These include the design of seamless video presentations, the functions of all the buttons, and the presentation of all menu screens. The DVD navigation system also is responsible for creating all the buttons themselves and the graphic overlays for the buttons.

DVD Building and Emulation: The final step for DVD construction is the actual assembly of a disc image. This computer intensive process creates the final image and loads the image onto a DVD emulator for testing. The final approved image is sent to the Disc Replicator for making of the DVD discs.

## Conclusions

DVD is a spectacular format! The quality we are seeing from the prototype consumer players is sensational and lives up to the hype of "almost studio masters." The convenience factors of no-rewind, ease of storage and one-sided movies, are certainly going to be attractive to consumers. The variety of languages, subtitles, menu screens and added value material will set it apart from laser disc and VHS. We should have a winner on our hands.

The production of DVD discs provides new challenges to two established industries: Video Post Production and CD-ROM. Working together these groups can exercise the DVD capabilities to their utmost and create both excellent packaging of existing movies as well as new multimedia entertainment on a consumer device.

Jerry Pierce is Director of the Digital Video Compression Corporation located at Universal Studios. DVCC is actively preparing movies for the upcoming introduction of DVD.
818-777-6300 FAX 818-866-3313 EMail JAPierce@aol.com

# *Picture Quality Editing for Variable Rate Compressed Video*

**Jay Yogeshwar, Mikhail Tsinberg**
**Toshiba Advanced Television Technology Center**
**Princeton, NJ, USA.**

## Abstract

This paper discusses a novel video encoding system in which a user controls the quality of the encoded video. It uses an algorithm for re-allocation of target bits to the segment selected for editing or quality change. The algorithm is based on the availability of a log file containing statistics pertaining to the original run that produced the compressed video. A key aspect of the bit allocation is that subjective input from the user is used to alter the picture quality of the edit segment. Bitstream splicing is carried out to complete the process of edit.

The video is initially encoded according to an automatic process without user intervention. An operator then reviews it manually, and indicates that the quality of specific time periods or regions that is to be altered. A numeric value for picture quality is assigned in the range [-5, 5]. First, a common bit pool is created by removing a percentage of bits from the time periods or regions for which quality priorities have been specified. These are then redistributed as a function of the user selected priority. The bit assignments are adjusted such that buffer under-flow condition is avoided. Also, the buffer occupancy at the trailing edge of the edit segment is maintained at its original level.

After the assignment of new target bits, the average quantizer scale value is determined using a previously determined rate quantizer function. The video is then re-encoded with the new set of target bits to achieve the desired quality change. Bitstream and log files are updated by proper splicing.

## I. Background

Variable Bit Rate (VBR) coding of video affords the possibility of large changes in bit rates among the different sections of video, as compared to Constant Bit Rate (CBR) operation. Further, it affords the possibility of re-assigning data rates to some user defined sections of video, in a scale not possible with

CBR operation. Three major constraints have to be met in Temporal Editing or the re-allocation of bits among the various sections of an Edit Segment. These are:

1. The total bits for the movie/video that is edited does not exceed the allocated capacity.
2. There is no buffer under-flow within the edit segment.
3. There is no buffer under-flow outside of the edit segment.

This variety of human assisted compression is very different from those for CBR, primarily because of the degree of change in bit-allocation from the original allocation.

In VBR operation of an encoder, a modified version of the Video Buffer Verifier (VBV) model is used. This is different from the corresponding model for CBR operation. In the VBV model for VBR, the buffer in the decoder may remain full, but is restricted from under-flowing. In addition, the buffer fills up at a constant rate, $R_{max,}$ until the buffer is full. At every frame interval, the bits required to decode one frame is removed from the buffer.

In the VBR encoder, target bits are assigned to each frame of video, such that it is conformant with the buffering model described above. Objective measures of quality is used as the basis for allocating frame target bits, when the "Auto" mode is used, i.e., when no user preferences are indicated. The aim is to maintain a constant quality of compressed video. These objective measures do not necessarily translate to consistent subjective quality. Hence it is important to take corrective action on sections of compressed video, via some manual/operator input.

The notion of manual editing and temporal re-allocation of bits thus arises. Typically, the operator input is via specification of temporal priority of sections of video within the edit segment. The priority is relative among the sections, and specified in the range of (-5, 5), and a special character'P' denoting 'Protected'. The protected section is not affected by the re-allocation of bits.

Several issues need to be addressed in temporal bit re-allocation. Among these are:

1. How many bits may be removed from a section of video within the edit segment
2. How many bits may be added to a section
3. How is user priority input used to calculate the amount of bits re-allocated
4. What is the buffer occupancy constraint at the boundary of edit segment such that the VBV model is not violated in subsequent frames.
5. After re-allocation, is the VBV satisfied? If not, what procedure is used to modify the re-allocated bits to make it VBV conformant

These issues are addressed in the next section, and an approach is suggested for solving the problem of temporal bit re-allocation.

## II. Bit Budget for Sections of Video within Edit Segment

**Amount of bits that may be added or taken away from a section of video:** This depends on the effective bit rate of the section of video under consideration. The effective rate, R, is calculated as:

$$R = (\text{Total Allocated Bits} / \text{Number of Frames}) * \text{Frame\_Rate} \quad \textbf{(EQ 1)}$$

Assuming that a guaranteed minimum rate is applied to any section of video, say $R_{min,}$ then, the maximum number of bits that may be taken away from section 'i' is

$$T_i = (R_i - R_{min}) * N_i / \text{Frame\_Rate} \quad \textbf{(EQ 2)}$$

where $N_i$ is the number of frames in section 'i', and Ri is the effective rate of same section. The guaranteed minimum is required in order to assure some minimum quality level for the section. Similarly, the maximum number of bits that may be added to a given section 'j' is calculated as

$$T_j = (R_{max} - R_j) * N_j / \text{Frame\_Rate} \quad \textbf{(EQ 3)}$$

where $R_{max}$ is the maximum rate, or rate at which the buffer fills up when not full.

## III. Priority Allocation Algorithm

**Re-allocation of bits as a function of user specified priority:** To implement the effect of priority on the redistribution of bits, an exponential relationship of the general form **exp(-priority/k$_3$)** is used. The term $k_3$ in the exponential is referred to as the **Dynamic Range Factor (DRF)**, as this determines the shape of the exponential curve. The curve gets steeper for larger values of DRF, effectively increasing the disparity in bits re-allocated among the sections with varying priorities. This negative exponential means that as the absolute value of the priority is increased (lower priority section), the bits allocated to that section will decrease, i.e., priority value of 1 has the highest priority, and increasing number means lower priority. The priority specified by the user is in the range (-5, 5), and this is inversely mapped to be in the range (0,10). Priority of 5 is mapped to 0, and -5 is mapped to 10. The mapped priorities of 0 and 10 are considered as special cases, and not used in the exponential function described above. In practice, first, a fixed percentage of bits is taken away from the bits assigned to each section, and put in a common pool. This fixed fraction is referred to as the **Redistribution Depth**. Sections marked *Protected* are not affected by this process. Bits from this pool is redistributed based on the exponential relation described above. In addition, they are normalized by the size of the section of video (number of frames in that section) in proportion to the whole. After re-distribution, the number of bits assigned to each section is checked against the constraint represented by Equations 2 and 3. If the constraints are not satisfied, the above is repeated by taking out a smaller fraction of bits from each section of video. The ratio of the final allocation to the initial allocation is the scale factor. The scale factor is further split into two varieties, one for Intra frame type and the other for Non-Intra frame type. The initial bit allocation when multiplied by these scale factors, on a frame by frame basis, results in the final bit allocation for each frame. The split in the scale factors is such that the sum of newly assigned target bits is still equal to the final bit allocation on a section by section basis. The intra scaling is more conservative compared to non-intra, since the bits consumed by the intra frames are generally much larger than that of the non-intra frames. The entire procedure described above is referred to as the Priority Allocation Algorithm. A more detailed explanation of the same is as follows. It is assumed in the following description that the user has already reviewed the Edit Segment, and has assigned priorities as well as the Min. allowable bit rate. The Max. bit rate used is the same as that for the Automatic Encoding mode.

**Step 1**: Pick a value for the Redistribution Depth ($k_1$) $k_1$=0.4 is used in the current algorithm implementation. This means that 40% of bits from each non-protected and non-special-case section will be used to form a common pool of bits for later redistribution. If a larger value is used, it will mean greater bits depletion, and hence a greater chance that the lower bound on the bit rate will be reached. The algorithm automatically reduces this value if the data rates for any section of the edit segment reaches either the Min. or the Max. allowed bit rate. This value is changeable in software if needed, based on feedback from usage in the field.

**Step 2**. Pick/compute the following other parameters:

1. Dynamic Range Factor ($k_3$). $k_3$= 1.0 is used in the current algorithm. A larger value for the DRF would mean that a small change in priority would result in a large change in bit allocation. Similarly, making DRF smaller would give a finer control over the redistribution of bits. This value is also changeable in software. Next compute the following other parameters as below:

Let

$$E_i = \exp(-p_i / k_3) \qquad \textbf{(EQ 4)}$$

$$k_2 = \sum E_i \qquad \textbf{(EQ 5)}$$

$$R_i = E_i / k_2 \qquad \textbf{(EQ 6)}$$

In the above equations, $k_2$ is the priority normalization factor, and $p_i$ is the priority of the $i^{th}$ section of the edit segment after mapping on a [0, 10]. The priority normalization factor is needed to ensure that the sum of all bits reassigned according to the priorities, always sum up to the available common pool of bits. $R_i$ is the relative priority fraction for the $i^{th}$ section. Note that $R_i$ always sums to unity over all sections.

**Step 3.** Compute the Size Normalization Factor, $k_4$.

$$k_4 = \sum (T_i * R_i) \qquad \textbf{(EQ 7)}$$

where $T_i$ is the fraction of the Edit Segment frames in the $i^{th}$ section, and computed as $T_i = N_i / N$. Here $N_i$ is the number of frames in the $i^{th}$ section, and N is the total number of frames in the Edit Segment.

**Step 4.** Compute common pool of bits, and new target bits allocation by section:

$$C = \sum (k_1 . B_i) \qquad \textbf{(EQ 8)}$$

$$F_i = C * T_i * R_i / k_4 + (1 - k_1) * B_i \qquad \textbf{(EQ 9)}$$

where C is the common pool of bits to be redistributed, and $F_i$ is the Final Target Bits Allocation for the ith section.

**Step 5.** Check for bounds on bit rate.

Check to see if the bit allocation computed in Step 4. above exceeds the Min. / Max bounds on bit rate. If within bounds, proceed to next step. Else, repeat Step 4. with a reduced value of $k_1$. In our implementation, we have reduced $k_1$ by 0.01 with each iteration.

**Step 6.** Compute Target Bits for each frame within each section.

In order to carry forward from new target bits for each section to new target bits for each frame, a Bits Scale Factor is first computed for each section. Further this is separated into an Intra and Non-Intra Bits Scale factor. The original bits for each frame is multiplied by the appropriate scale factor based on its picture type. The various scale factors are computed as shown below:

For each section, compute the Bit Scale Factor, $S_i$

$$S_i = F_i / B_i \qquad \textbf{(EQ 10)}$$

Let $I_f = 0.8$. This number is used to limit the variation in the bit assignment of the Intra pictures to 20%. Large intra frame bits can potentially cause buffer under-flow, and hence If provides a safety net. Let $S_i' = S_i - 1.0$. Then the Intra and Non-Intra Bit Scale Factors ($SI_i$ and $SN_i$) are computed as:

$$SI_i = S_i - (I_f * S_i') \quad \textbf{(EQ 11)}$$

$$SN_i = S_i - (-I_f * S_i' * BI_i / BN_i) \quad \textbf{(EQ 12)}$$

where $BI_i$ and $BN_i$ are the total Intra and Non-Intra bits summed over the $i^{th}$ section by picture type.

**Re-allocation of bits for sections with priorities of -5 and +5:** Target Bit Assignment for the sections with priorities of +5 and -5 are handled differently from others. Sections with -5 are assigned Min. bit rate, while sections with +5 priority are assigned Max. bit rate. However, such an assignment might be unrealistic, since other sections may be left with either too few or too many bits. This will result in these sections violating the Min. / Max. bit rate bounds.

In order to prevent this, an iterative procedure is used. If insufficient bits exist to code the non-special-case sections, the Min. bit rate bound is increased, while the Max. rate bound is lowered, and bits re-assigned to the special case sections. The iterations are repeated until sufficient bits remain for the non-special sections. The Min. and Max. rates are also adjusted to ensure that the 'Protected' sections always receive the same target bit assignment as before.

Note that the Special Case Allocation always precedes the Priority Allocation Algorithm based target bit assignment. The bits remaining over from special case and protected area allocation are assigned to each of the remaining sections in the ration of their original distribution.

## IV. Buffer Occupancy Constraints

**Video Buffer Verifier (VBV) Model for VBR encoding of Video:** The simple modified VBV model for the DSM is assumed. And if the system layer is used, then correct time stamp should be multiplexed on the system encoder. The simple modified VBV model for VBR [1] is as follows:

1. bit_rate field at sequence_header represents the "max_bit_rate".
2. The VBV is initially empty. After filling the VBV buffer up to the full (i.e. VBV buffer size) at the rate of "max_bit_rate", the decoding process begins. The picture data is immediately removed and decoded like CBR's VBV model defined in MPEG2 DIS.
3. The Bitstream is placed into the VBV buffer at the rate of "max_bit_rate" until the VBV buffer is full. If the VBV buffer occupancy is full, then the bitstream transmission to the VBV buffer is immediately stopped. And after the next picture data is removed, the bitstream transmission immediately starts.
4. The VBV buffer shall not under-flow
5. Each of the "vbv_delay" field is set to FFFF.

**Buffer occupancy constraints at the trailing edge of video edit segment:** In VBR mode operation, it is possible for the buffer occupancy at the trailing edge of the edited video segment to be different from that of the run that was modified, even if the edit segment is replaced by exactly the same number of bits. This arises from the idiosyncrasy of the VBV model for VBR. Hence it is important to examine buffer occupancy constraints. It is fairly straightforward to show that no problem exists if the buffer occupancy at the trailing edge of an edit segment is exactly the same or higher. If the buffer occupancy is exactly the same as before, then that of subsequent frames also remain exactly the same as the previous run, which was already checked for VBV violations. If the occupancy is higher than before, there is the possibility of the buffer becoming full during subsequent frames, and that is a perfectly allowable condition. It does not affect buffer under-flow. A third case arises when the buffer occupancy is lower at the trailing edge, compared to the previous run. This has the potential for creating buffer under-flow in subsequent frames. We shall avoid this situation by maintaining buffer occupancy level either equal to or greater than that prior to edit. However, it is possible to determine analytically the smallest allowable level for which no buffer under-flow will occur in subsequent frames. This requires knowledge of buffer occupancies of all future frames beyond the endpoint of edit.

**VBV conformance check:** After temporal re-distribution of bits, there exists a possibility of buffer under-flow within the edit segment. These under-flow conditions have to be remedied by removing bits from frames leading to under-flow condition, and adding them to those frames that would not cause subsequent frames to have under-flow. The steps used in the algorithm for the detection and correction of buffer under-flow is as follows:

1. Scan the final target bit allocation. Use Buffering Model to determine buffer under-flow and buffer full points. Maintain a list of the buffer full and buffer under-flow points and call them o_list and u_list respectively. Also for each entry in the u-flow list, note the amount of under-flow in bits, call this the u_val list. If there are no entries in the u_list, there is no buffer under-flow problem - exit.
2. Check the buffer occupancy at the trailing edge of the edit segment. If this value is less than the minimum allowed value, add this to the u_flow list and the u_val list. Essentially, the problem of buffer fullness value at the trailing edge being smaller than that prior to edit, is treated as an under-flow problem. For the sake of simplicity of implementation, the minimum allowed value of buffer occupancy at the trailing edge of the Edit Segment is taken to be the same as occupancy prior to the edit.
3. Create an 'L' section for each point in the u_flow list. An 'L' section is a collection of all frames to the left of the u_flow point, up to and including the nearest o_flow point.
4. Sum up the u_val for all points in the u_list. Distribute (add) these bits to all frames not in any 'L' section or any section with priority "Protected", equally.
5. Repeat steps 1 through 4 until no entries remain in the u_list.

## V. Rate Quantizer Model

To estimate the picture by picture basis Rate-Quantizer Function (RQF), two data points for each picture is required. The RQF [2] is as follows:

$$R = X \,.\, Q^{(-g)} + H \qquad \textbf{(EQ 13)}$$

where R: Bits used to code one picture Q: quantizer scale X, g, H: are the picture by picture basis modeling parameters.

H is the bits which is independent of quantizer scale. So, H is the bits consumed by the. header, the Motion Vectors (MVs), DC coefficients, etc. And X, g are estimated from a pair of data points corresponding to AC coefficients bits used to code the picture for a given quantizer scale.

The first run of the encoder may be used to generate the two data points for each coded picture in the video sequence. This may be done by using a pair of alternating quantizer scale values used for each Macroblock in the picture. These are processed to compute the Rate Quantizer Model parameters (X, g). These two parameters along with the Value of H may be stored in a file, one per frame of coded video.

In order to determine the Quantizer Scale which will produce the Target Bits assigned to a particular coded frame of video, the above equation is used with 'R' representing the target bits, and the values of (X, g, H) read from the stored data file. The value of 'Q' that best fits this equation, is the desired quantizer scale.

## VI. Results

Figure 1 shows the Toshiba's MPEG-2 video encoding system that allows picture quality editing for variable rate compressed video. The top down solution approach for Temporal Manual Editing, as discussed above, is presented via the flow chart in Fig. 2. Figure 3 depicts the graphical user interface for Temporal Manual Editing. Finally, figures 4 and 5 show two example results of changes in bit-rates as a result of setting priorities for various sections of an Edit Segment.

The bottom half of figures 4 and 5 show the Temporal Priority settings made by the user. The Edit Segment, and the Sections within the Edit Segment are delineated by Start and End Time Codes. The background priority applies as a default to those sections within the Edit Segment not specified by the user.

The top half of figures 4 and 5 show the Data Rate (or Bit Rate) corresponding to every half a second of video (One Group of Pictures or GOP in this example contains 15 pictures, which is about half a second of NTSC video). The solid line denotes the automatic allocation by a computer program that analyzes the picture statistics from the first run of the encoder. The dashed line indicates the data rate after priority based allocation is done.

Note that the relatively high priority areas show an increased data rate, which could cause improved picture quality. In addition, no buffer under-flows were noticed. These results provide intuitive verification of the Temporal Manual Editing Algorithms.

## VII. Conclusion

A system and algorithm has been presented to improve the picture quality of variable rate compressed video. The quality improvement is based on delineating an edit segment and making subjective judgments on where more resources need to be allocated, and where less. The re-allocation of target bits and the suggestions for quantizer scale values that will result in coded bits close to the suggested target, are performed off-line. As a result, only the edit segment needs to be re-compressed. The method presented in this paper may be easily extended to quality improvements within a single picture, or used as a combination of spatial and temporal quality improvement.

## Acknowledgments

We would like to thank Dr. Sakurai and his group at Toshiba Multimedia Lab., Yokohama, Japan, Mr. Odaka and his group at the Toshiba Corp. R&D Center, Kawasaki, Japan for all their assistance. We would also like to thank Andrew Rosen, formerly at the Time Warner CVC facility for his feedback on the manual picture quality editing procedures. Finally, we would like to thank Adam Lesh and his dedicated group at the Time Warner CVC facility for their ideas on improving the editing system.

## References

[1] ISO/IEC JTC1 CD 13818. Generic Coding of Moving Pictures and Associated Audio. International Organization for Standardization (ISO), 1994.
[2] Koto, Odaka, et. al., Toshiba R&D Center, Kawasaki, Private exchange.

# TAZ Encoder System in TOSHIBA

Fig 1

EWS1 Video Encoder Control
EWS2 TAZ Formatter
EWS3 System Control

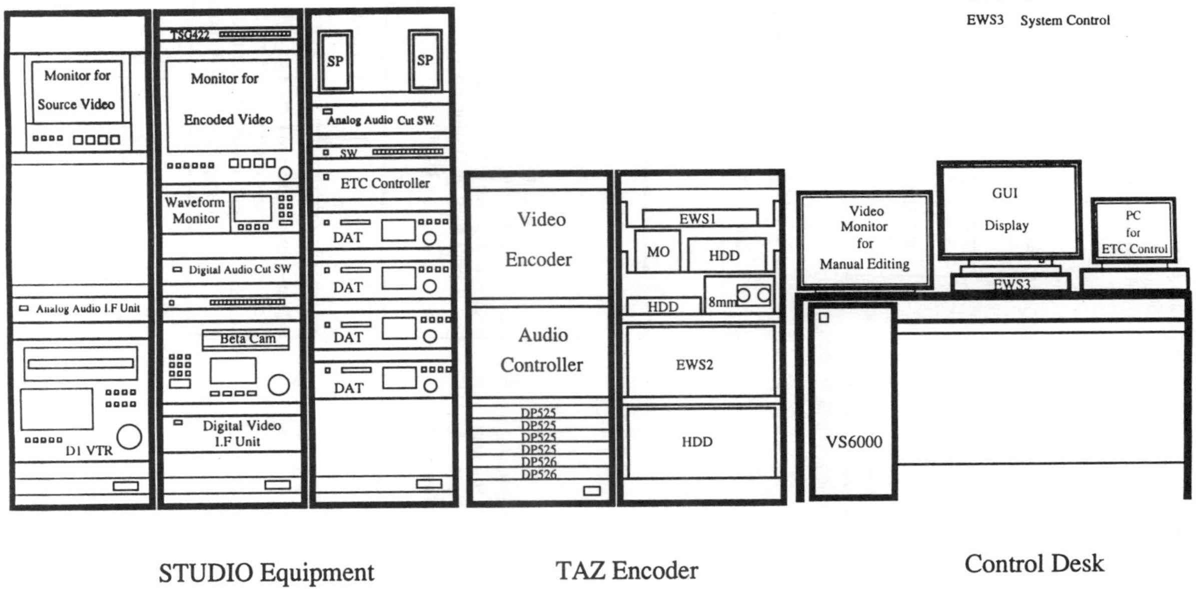

**Top Level Drawing**

## TEMPORAL MANUAL EDITING OF COMPRESSED VIDEO

Jay Yogeshwar

**PURPOSE:**

To Re-allocate Target Bits and Average Quantizer Scale Value to Each Frame of the Edit Segment, Based on User Assigned Priority and Available Picture Statistics from the First Run of the Encoder.

**FLOW CHART OF THE OVERALL PROCEDURE:**

*Model: Parameters defining a relationship between quantizer scale and bits consume

*VBV: Video Buffer Verifier models the way the buffer fills up and empties at the decoder.
*VBR: Variable Bit Rate

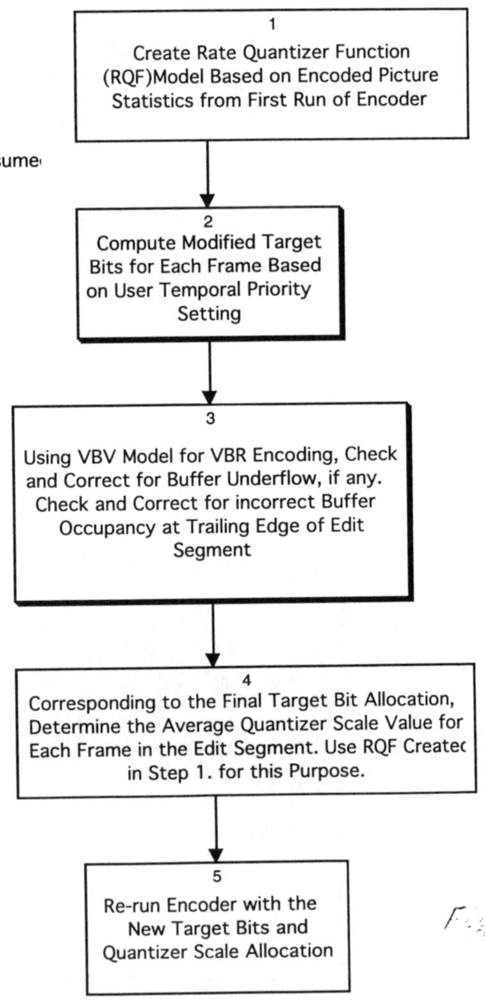


Fig. 2

FIG. 3

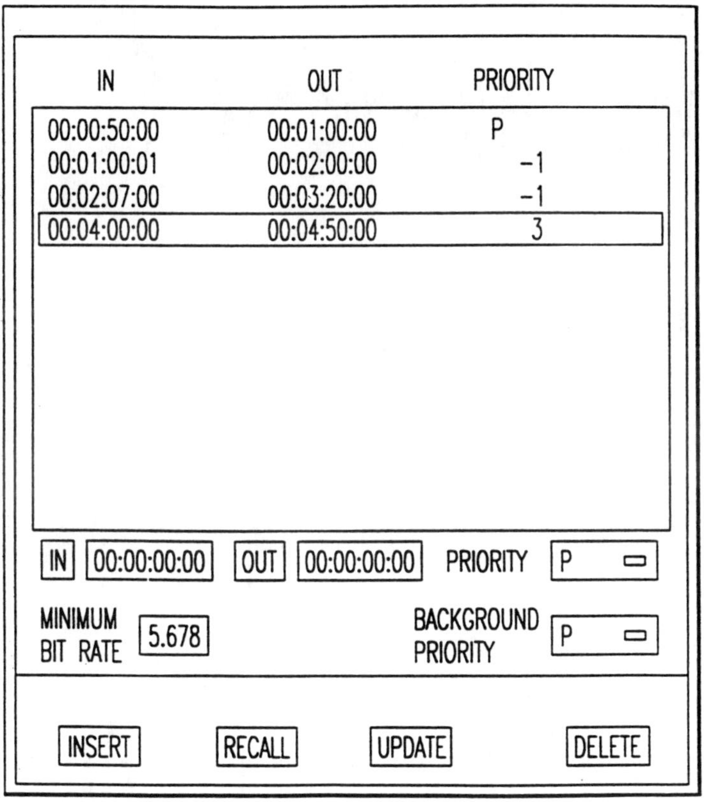
IN
OUT
PRIORITY
00:00:50:00
00:01:00:00
P
00:01:00:01
00:02:00:00
-1
00:02:07:00
00:03:20:00
-1
00:04:00:00
00:04:50:00
3
IN
00:00:00:00
OUT
00:00:00:00
PRIORITY
P
MINIMUM BIT RATE
5.678
BACKGROUND PRIORITY
P
INSERT
RECALL
UPDATE
DELETE

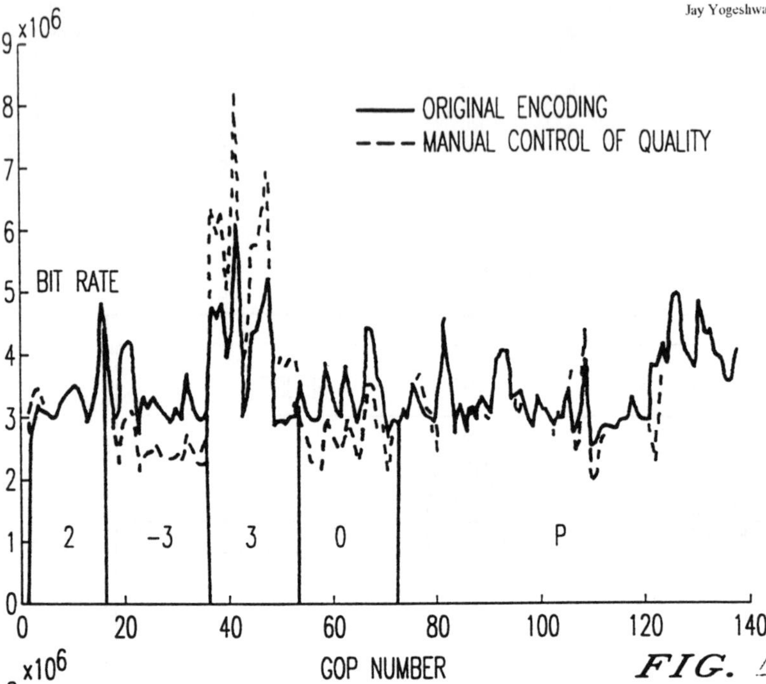
x10^6
ORIGINAL ENCODING
MANUAL CONTROL OF QUALITY
BIT RATE
2
-3
3
0
P
GOP NUMBER
0 1 2 3 4 5 6 7 8 9
0 20 40 60 80 100 120 140

FIG. 4

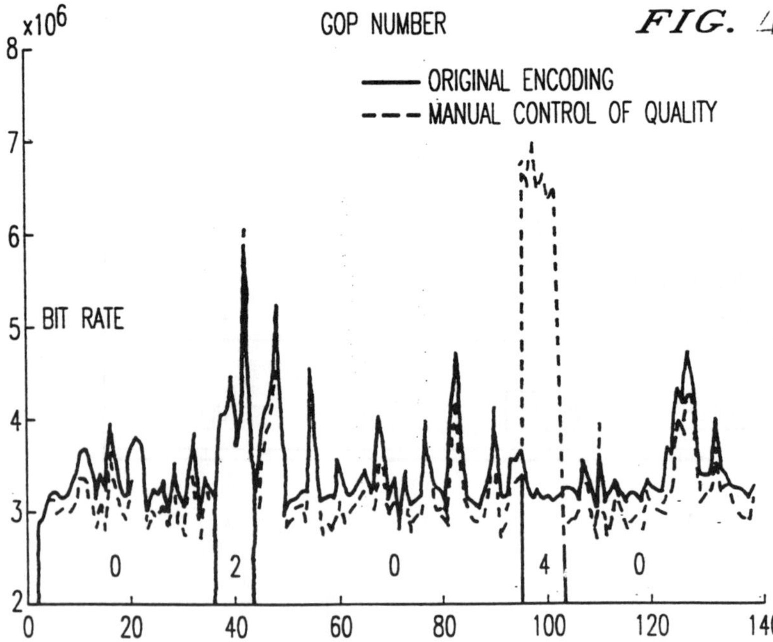
x10^6
ORIGINAL ENCODING
MANUAL CONTROL OF QUALITY
BIT RATE
0
2
0
4
0
GOP NUMBER
2 3 4 5 6 7 8
0 20 40 60 80 100 120 140

FIG. 5

# *Captions*

Fig.1: Toshiba MPEG-2 Video Encoding System Capable of Picture Quality Editing.

Fig. 2: Temporal Manual Editing Flow Chart

Fig. 3: The Graphical User Interface for Temporal Manual Editing. Priorities may be selected in the range [-5, 5] and 'Protected' for the time periods specified by the IN and OUT fields.

Fig.4,5: Effect of Priority Setting on Bit Rate of Coded Video.

# DVD Premastering: A Facility's Perspective

C. Bradley Hunt
All Post, Inc.
Burbank, California

## Abstract

Digital Versatile Disk Video (DVD-Video) is a revolutionary, new consumer video system. The expected demand for DVD programming represents a huge opportunity for the studios and content producers to profit from the sale of movies rereleased in this new format. Due to the richness and complexity of features and the image and sound quality of the format, content producers will need to work closely with DVD authoring facilities in the mastering of their movies to this new high-quality medium. From the facility's perspective, there are many steps involved in the DVD-Video authoring process. This paper will focus on the critical steps of element preparation, telecine transfer, video preprocessing, and compression which greatly influence the quality of the DVD-Video product.

# Introduction

Digital Versatile Disk Video (DVD-Video) represents a totally new consumer video format. Its high quality video and audio playback capabilities will deliver an exciting new home theater experience. The format's specification was developed with an eye towards the future and its use in various applications. It has a number of important features and customer benefits which should accelerate its successful market introduction and acceptance. DVD-Video is the first consumer video format to playback component digital video at D1-video resolution. A single-sided, single-layer DVD-Video can store up to 133 minute movie using MPEG-2 Variable Bit Rate (VBR) video compression.

DVD-Video players will also have the capabilities to playback both widescreen 16:9 and standard 4:3 aspect ratio programming. The player's remote control will allow the conversion of full-frame, "anamorphic" 16:9 programming to be played out as a 4:3 letterbox program. The MPEG-2 compression also allows film-originated programs to be encoded at 24 frames per second with the 3:2 pulldown reinserted by the decoder to produce the 60 Hz playback. DVD-Video also has a number of interesting audio features. It can carry multiple streams of Dolby Digital (AC-3) 5.1-channel surround sound to enable up to 8 separate language tracks to be carried with the video. The DVD-Video Book B specification defines several other player features. The format allows full interactive branching capabilities. This enables the inclusion of a parental lock feature which prevents playback of an "R" rated movie by a child. This branching also facilitates the authoring of a DVD-Video title that carries multiple rating versions of a movie on one disk. The branching capability can also be used for creating programs with multiple camera angles, multiple running times, or the development of interactive movies where the viewer steers the plot.

With all of these capabilities, the premastering of a DVD-Video by a facility involves many steps. The process, outlined graphically in Figure 1, starts with a review of the customer requirements and continues with work on the film, audio, and graphics preparation and then compression. It finally finishes with DVD-Video authoring, formatting, and then output to computer tape.

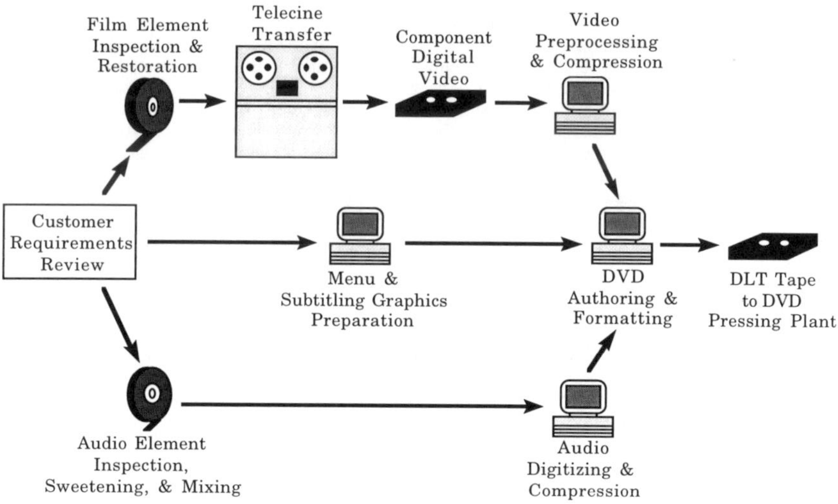


**Figure 1: DVD-Video Premastering Process**

The premastering of material for release on a DVD is not as simple as laying down audio and video to a videotape master. There are many new issues for a facility getting involved in premastering DVD-Videos. Because of the limited data capacity and bit rate of DVD, the authoring process involves compromises constrained by the length of the program, the picture quality, the quality and number of audio tracks, the number of subtitles, and the level of interactivity and branching. The 4.7 Gigabytes "bit budget" data capacity of a single-sided, single-layer DVD-Video allows the playback of a 133-minute movie at an average data rate of 4.69 Megabits per second. If the movie is shorter, a higher average bit rate can be used to improve the image quality. On the other hand, if the movie has several audio language tracks, multiple rating versions, and multiple language subtitles, then the average bit rate allocated to the video images must be reduced. It is a authoring facility's responsibility to discuss these tradeoffs with their clients to insure that the best DVD-Video product is delivered.

All Post decided to enter the DVD-Video premastering business because it was a natural extension of our service offerings provided to the studios. Cinetech, our specialty film laboratory subsidiary, provides film restoration and wet-printing services used for the creation of new interpositive elements. At All Post's video operation, we operate 10 telecine suites transferring feature films and episodic TV programs to digital video masters. We provide digital and analog, multistandard video dubbing services. The company also has a complete audio department having full audio layback, sweetening, foreign language dubbing, music and effects filling, and 5.1 channel surround sound mixing capabilities. Establishing a DVD authoring operation within the company was part of our strategic plan to provide a comprehensive portfolio of services at the highest level of quality, from film restoration, telecine transfer, video and audio dubbing, and finally compression and DVD premastering. We believe a full-service operation has the most control in assuring that a client's movie title is converted to the DVD-Video format at the highest quality possible. After evaluating the available technology in early 1996, we invested in Sonic Solution's DVD Creator System for authoring and audio encoding and Minerva's Compressionist 200 MPEG encoder for video compression.

The introduction of the DVD-Video format will raise the consumer's quality demands and thus impact the industry's quality requirements for feature film transfers. With the format's rich feature set and the use of compression, there will be differences from one facility's DVD-Video master compared to another. Because DVD is based on MPEG-2 Variable Bit Rate (VBR) encoding, the allocation of the "bit budget" is critical to maximizing the subjective image quality of the DVD master. A large determinant of this quality is based on: 1) the quality of the facility's original film to component digital telecine transfer and 2) the methods of video image preprocessing that is done just before compression. Processing to eliminate film grain, telecine noise, dust and dirt artifacts, and image unsteadiness is absolutely essential in order to avoid using the bit rate allocation to unnecessarily encode these artifacts. Significant testing of preprocessing techniques have been investigated by All Post's technical team in order to optimize its DVD premastering process. This includes proprietary techniques used in the facility's film-to-tape transfer and compression operations. However, the first step begins with the film and audio elements being carefully inspected and prepared for encoding.

## Film, Audio, & Graphic Element Preparation

The initial client requirements review is critical at the beginning of a DVD-Video premastering project. This is especially true when an older title from the library is being premastered. In this review, important decisions must be made concerning the tradeoffs between image quality, program length, number of language and subtitle tracks, degree of interactivity and branching, and cost. In addition, the format's superior sound and video playback capabilities and consumer's high quality expectations may require content owners to consider producing new film elements, new remixed and sweetened audio masters, and/or the production of new telecine transfers prior to compression and authoring.

After the requirements review and decision on the content and feature set of the title, the client and facility must review the film and audio elements available for making the DVD-Video title. Some of the questions about the elements which need to be answered are:

1) what age, film type, and in what condition is the film element;
2) is a mono, a stereo, a 4-channel LCRS, or a full 5.1-channel surround audio track available;
3) does a fully-filled music and effects track exist for making foreign language tracks; and
4) do any foreign language subtitling files exist.

Prior to telecine transfer and video compression, the film elements must be inspected. This includes the feature program, the studio's opening logo, and any trailers that will be included on the disk release. At our film laboratory, Cinetech, we examine the elements and advise our client whether a new interpositive needs to be printed from the conformed camera originals. On an older film, the scene-to-scene timing is checked by making an answer print. Then we make a fully-timed, wet-gate, slow-speed printed, Estar interpositive. Many times we find that the interpositives produced for the theatrical release have subtle color nonuniformities produced at frames where color timing changes occur. These are not visible in theatrical screening but are picked up in the telecine transfer. This is more of a problem with Cinemascope films since they use the entire height of the film frame. Slow-speed printing insures that large, scene-to-scene timing changes do not create these intraframe color artifacts. Slow-speed, wet-printed interpositives are also sharper and eliminate much of the visibility of dirt and scratches on the original conformed negatives. Because of the significant granularity improvement in today's intermediate stocks, such as EASTMAN EXR Color Intermediate Film 5244, we always recommend a new Estar interpositive be made when the existing interpositive is more than 15 years old. This is not only an investment in making today's DVD master but also for making tomorrow's HDTV master.

Because of the digital quality and the diverse audio possible on a DVD-Video, the audio mastering for an older movie is a particularly complex area. This requires a thorough review of the audio options with the client including an evaluation of the audio elements available. Given the elements, decisions need to be made on the different types of audio mixes which will be created and mastered for the DVD-Video release. The standard, for example, allows up to 8 different audio streams to be multiplexed with the video. All 525-line/60 Hz DVD-Video disks must contain a Dolby Digital (AC-3) audio bitstream and/or a Linear Pulse Code Modulated (LPCM) bitstream. All 625-line/50 Hz DVD-Video disks must contain an MPEG-2 audio bitstream and/or a Linear Pulse Code Modulated (LPCM) bitstream. Due to data rate constraints, most DVD-Video disks will be released with the more compact Dolby AC-3 or MPEG-2 audio. The players are only required to produce a full reconstruction of a Stereo Left and Right audio program. More expensive players will output the full 5.1-channel Dolby Digital AC-3 audio.

A Dolby Digital AC-3 audio bitstream can be encoded as one of seven different audio modes: 1) Mono; 2) Left & Right Stereo; 3) Left-Center-Right; 4) Left & Right Stereo with Mono Surround; 5) Left & Right Stereo with-Left & Right Surround; 6) Left-Center-Right with Mono Surround; and 7) Left-Center-Right with Left & Right Surround. The Low Frequency Effect Channel is a bandwidth-limited subwoofer track (the ".1" in "5.1") which can be optionally added to any of the above. With the variety of audio options available, the client needs to determine the most appropriate audio program content for the title and the geographical markets being pursued.

When remastering older movie titles to DVD-Video, the audio elements may come in a number of different forms. It might be come in as a 3-track magnetic fullcoat with mono dialog, music, and effects. It might come in as a 6-track mag with stereo dialogue, stereo music, and stereo effects. It may come in as a 6-track mag Left-Center-Right-Surround mix with stereo music, stereo effects, mono surround, and mono dialogue. In order to create foreign-language-dubbed versions, separate music and dialogue tracks at a minimum must be supplied. Effects sounds in both the front and surround channels can be folied and filled for the foreign language audio masters. In addition, older audio masters sometimes need to re-equalized, de-noised, and peak limited to make them suitable for a digital audio home cinema release.

In addition to reviewing the various audio program release options available to the client, the facility must review the options concerning parental control features, subtitle graphics, chapter stops, program navigation capabilities, and the associated menu graphics. A DVD-Video title can be released as both an "R"-rated Director's cut and a "G"-rated family version if the client supplies additional replacement scenes with matching audio or can specify offending scenes to be navigated around in the "G"-rated version. Plans for including foreign language subtitles need to be specified up front in the customer requirements review. Standard subtitling files can be converted to TIFF files for overlaying as subpicture graphics during the authoring step. Chapter stops need to specified as well as any particular requirements for the control menu graphics. Although complex DVD-Video titles can be produced, we believe that in the beginning of the market, most titles produced will be simple, linear titles without complex branching or no more than a few language and subtitling tracks.

Once the DVD-Video program specifications have been agreed and the audio and film elements inspected and prepared, then the audio tracks can be digitized and the film elements transferred in the telecine operation.

## Telecine Transfer

Because DVD-Video has such high video image quality, it is critical that the very best film transfers are used for DVD-Video premastering. Older videotape masters of films which were good enough for the broadcast or the VHS home video market may not be adequate for use as a master for DVD-Video. To determine a video master's quality after compression, the client may request the facility to do a short MPEG-2 compression evaluation. A few minutes of the movie are encoded and reviewed with the client prior to making a decision to retransfer. Clients should be aware that with DVD-Video's ability to handle squeezed, full-frame 16:9 video playback, many more letterbox-transferred movies will need to be retransferred to the full-frame 16:9 format. When a new film transfer is required, there are a number of details surrounding the transfer operation which are crucial to obtaining the very best MPEG-2 compression results.

First, it is important to transfer the film to a component digital video master to optimize the MPEG compression process. Composite video masters make encoding more difficult and produce noticeable compression artifacts. Although composite masters can be MPEG-2 encoded, the best results are achieved when starting with a component digital video master. It should be clarified that DVD-Video premastering does not require a separate film transfer optimized for DVD premastering. A good, high-quality film transfer to a component digital video format will serve both DVD and the TV broadcast, VHS home video, and laserdisk markets.

Another area of critical importance in the noise level in the film transfer. Noise is a big problem for compression systems. Noise in a film master consists of the film related noise associated with the film grain, dirt, and scratches and the electronic noise introduced by the telecine, image processing, and recording systems. Since noise represents random information, this creates a problem for MPEG compression systems which look to eliminate the redundant information between frames. It is important to make sure that the telecine system is performing optimally to obtain the best signal-to-noise performance. A slight amount of film grain noise reduction is also recommended, especially if an older film element is being used. In addition to film grain, film-related noise can also come from dirt and scratches. Adequate ultrasonic cleaning combined with particle transfer rollers will insure that dirt defects are kept to a minimum. There are also digital image processing hardware such as the Philips BTS MNR-11 and the Digital Vision DVNR 1000 which can be used to digitally eliminate dirt and scratch artifacts during the transfer or in a tape-to-tape correction suite. It is critical not to use excessive amounts of noise reduction, especially recursive noise filtering, as this can create its own set of unnatural image artifacts which can make the video harder to encode. The idea is to use the bits to encode picture information and not to waste them on encoding noise or artificial image processing artifacts.

Image steadiness is also an important aspect of the film transfer process which can impact the efficiency of video compression. If a picture is moving due to mechanical unsteadiness introduced at the printing or telecine transfer stage, then the MPEG-2 encoder will not be able to detect redundant frame-to-frame image information. This will cause it to use its precious bits inefficiently. The use of a real-time steadiness improvers like the Rank Cintel JumpFree, the VP&T Meta-Speed Digital Servo and the Steadi-Film RTS Steadigate can make a real improvement in the vertical and the horizontal steadiness of film transfers. These steadiness improvements at the telecine stage can save significant amounts of encoding data that can subsequently be used for encoding picture information.

The amount of aperture correction used to enhance the high frequency detail in a film transfer can also create problems during video compression. High levels of aperture correction can create ringing artifacts on the edges of objects. These ringing artifacts and the over-enhanced scene details can again unnecessarily use precious bits of data. The general rule of thumb is to use a realistic level of aperture correction so that the resulting film transfer is pleasing to the eye and does not create visible artifacts. If an over enhanced film transfers is encountered, some of the unwanted effects can be eliminated at the video preprocessing step prior to compression. However, the best DVD-Video masters will be obtained by starting with the cleanest, most natural-looking, artifact-free film transfer for encoding.

Finally, the last area of the telecine operation that can have beneficial results is in oversampling the image and spatially interpolating the image back to standard, interlaced CCIR 601 video. Today, there is a number of different ways to do this. The film transfer can be made on an HDTV telecine and then down-converted in a standards converter to D1 video. One can also use an 8:4:4 telecine, like the Advanced Video Designs' HR1440 telecine or the Philips BTS Spirit Datacine, to scan and then down-convert in the frame store/interpolator. The Philips BTS telecine is a rather interesting telecine in that it has a spatial interpolator that takes the nearly 2K by 2K progressively-scanned image and spatial interpolates it in both the vertical and horizontal directions to a standard CCIR 601 interlace video image. Another more cost effective way to eliminate aliasing artifacts is the use of DAV's Clrview System. This box is designed for use on a Rank Cintel Mark III telecine where it oversamples in the vertical direction and uses this increased, progressively-scanned information with some sophisticated interpolation to produce standard, interlace CCIR 601 video output. The system is cost-effective and virtually eliminates the aliasing and the interlace flicker artifacts that occur around the sharp vertical edges such as car grills or venetian blinds and on the edges of diagonal lines.

Again, it is important to reemphasize that DVD-Video premastering does not require a completely different type of film-to-video transfer. The quality of the format and the compression used however does put real demands on the film transfer in order to get the very best DVD-Video image quality. Once the film transfer is made, the next step of video preprocessing is important as it prepares the video master to further optimize the compression process.

## Video Preprocessing & Compression

DVD-Video utilizes MPEG-2 Variable Bit Rate (VBR) compression process. This allows the encoding bit rate to vary form a low of 1.5 megabits per second to as high as 9.8 megabits per second based on scene content and complexity. The nominal video bit rate will average about 3.5 Megabits per. A simple, static scene with a talking head will require fewer bits to encode than a scene with moving areas of fine detail. Because of the limited data capacity and bit rate of DVD-Video, a good video master needs some video preprocessing before compression to make the best use of the bits. The idea of preprocessing is to modify the image to allow encoding to be as efficient as possible. The limited data should be used for encoding only visually-important picture information. Preprocessing can make a significant improvement in the encoding results especially when starting with less-than-optimum video masters. There are several types of video preprocessing that are used in order to optimize MPEG-2 compression.

One of the more important steps of preprocessing is noise reduction of the video signal prior to compression. The same comments hold here as they do for noise reduction at the telecine stage. Because MPEG encoding is based on looking for redundant image information, noise's random nature has a large impact on the efficiency of encoding. Noise reduction during video preprocessing is much more subtle than that which is used during telecine transfer. The idea is to remove only the noise which has no visual impact but would unnecessarily use bits during encoding. A subtle amount of noise reduction should be used which produces no image artifacts. Because preprocessing noise reduction can sometimes help simplify encoding but also create artifacts if incorrectly applied, a skilled video compressionists with a trained eye must closely monitor the compression process to optimize the level of preprocessing noise reduction.

Another form of preprocessing to improve MPEG-2 compression involves elimination of the frame redundancy associated with the 3:2 pull-down of film-to-tape transfers. When film-originated programming shot at 24 frames per second is transferred to 30 (29.97) frame per second video, the telecine creates redundant fields of video. During telecine film transfer, 24 frames of film are used to create the 60 (59.94) individual video fields. This is done by a process known as 3:2 pull-down whereby the first frame of film is used to make 2 fields of video, the second frame of film is use to create the next 3 video fields, the third frame is used to produce the next 2 video fields, etc. The order of the video fields results in a unique pattern that repeats itself every five frames.

MPEG-2 decoders have the ability to accept a 24 frame per second MPEG video stream and turn it back into a standard 29.97 Hz video signal. This ability to do frame rate conversion at the decoder allows 29.97 Hz film-originated video to be converted back to its original 24 frame per second film image sequence. This removal of the 3:2 pull-down redundant fields is called "inverse telecine" processing. By eliminating the redundant fields of video, the compression system can allocate more bits to encoding the original film image frames. This is especially important with the encoding of long movies with multiple language tracks where the data capacity is limited. Inverse telecine preprocessing will always provide better looking MPEG-2 video streams.

Finally, another technique used in improving the process of MPEG-2 VBR encoding is the process of "forcing" I-frames during encoding. There are three types of frames in an MPEG-2 video stream: Intra or I-frames which are encoded using only information present within the frame; Predicted or P-frames which are computed based on forward prediction using the nearest previous I or P frames; and Bi-directional or B-frames which use both a past and a subsequent frame as a reference to calculate the compressed frame. I-frames carry the most image data and are the basis for creating the standard sequence of frames of I-B-B-P-B-B-P-B-B-P-B-B-P-B-B -I which is known as a Group of Picture (GOP) of 15. Fifteen represents the number of frames between I-frames. If during encoding, a scene has excessive motion or many rapid scene cuts, the compression operator can modify the I-B-P sequence by adding additional I-frames at scene cuts. This forces more bits to be used to encode a larger number of high-quality I-frames which should improve the reproduction of these difficult scenes.

## Summary

The Digital Video Disk (DVD) represents a revolutionary, new consumer video format. For studios and content producers considering releasing movie titles in this new format, a number of recommendations can be made. First, due to the richness and complexity of features and the image and sound quality of the format, content producers need to work closely with their DVD authoring facility in the requirements clarification and in the mastering of their movies to this new high-quality medium. Second, the format's superior sound and video playback capabilities will raise consumer's quality expectations. This may require content owners to consider producing new film elements, new remixed and sweetened audio masters, and new component digital telecine transfers to deliver DVD-Video titles which meet these higher consumer expectations. Finally, many steps can be taken by the facility in the telecine transfer stage, in video preprocessing, and in compression that can dramatically improve the quality of the end product.

Not all DVD-Video masters will be created equal. By working with a knowledgeable DVD premastering facility with the broadest range of in-house experience across multiple disciplines of audio, film, and compression, the client has the best chance of introducing their DVD movie title to the marketplace with the highest quality possible.

# Video Testing in Modern Television Systems

David K. Fibush
Tektronix, Inc.
Beaverton, OR

**Abstract**

Measurement of picture quality has been high on the list of television engineering priorities since video compression became a practical reality. This paper examines the modern television system outlining its elements and the appropriate levels of testing. The need for continuation of traditional analog and digital testing methods is emphasized as a prerequisite for both effective video compression and the measurement of resulting pictures. Proposed picture quality measurement methods and possible limitations of their application are discussed.

## INTRODUCTION

In the days of composite analog television systems a very limited set of video signal types were used throughout the production and distribution chain. There were component red/green/blue (RGB) signals in the camera and display device with the composite PAL, SECAM or NTSC signals predominant in most of the processing chain. Such systems are basically linear which means that simple test signals can be used to characterize a portion of the processing chain providing good correlation with picture quality results. Concatenation of measurement results from a series of processes also maintains that correlation. A modern television system is much more complex often requiring conversion of the video signal into a variety of signal types including non-linear compressed forms.

A simplified block diagram of a modern television system is shown in Fig. 1. Analog RGB video is produced in the camera and processed into one or more of several possible formats; analog composite, digital composite, analog component or digital component. Full-bandwidth digital video is an extremely important part of the television system today. Program production process must be full-bandwidth digital (or analog) in order to manipulate the audio and video to produce desired artistic results.

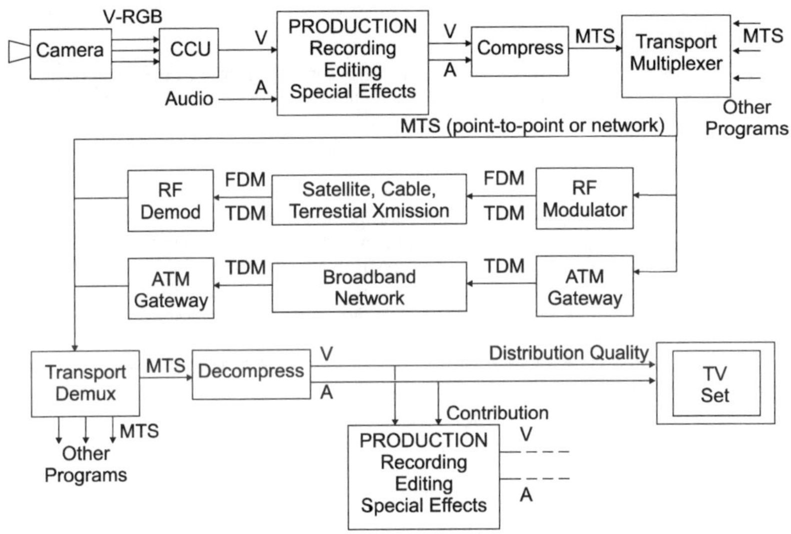


Figure 1. Modern television system

Following program production the television signal may be compressed for storage, efficient transmission or intra-facility interconnection in digital form. Typically this will be MPEG compression resulting in an MPEG transport stream (MTS) which is then multiplexed with other MPEG transport streams for transmission or interconnection.

Many radio frequency (RF) transmission systems still use frequency division multiplexing (FDM) for transmission of television signals. As new systems are installed the preferred choice will be time division multiplexing (TDM) which is generally more robust for the same transmitted power and provides the digital channel for compressed television signals. It is important to note, even compressed digital video broadcasting to the home starts with full-bandwidth digital video to drive the bit-rate efficient statistically multiplexed compression system.

The broadband telecommunication system provides a variety of transmission methods. Traditionally these have been voice channel oriented with special data mapping for digital television signals. Use of asynchronous transfer mode (ATM) hides such formatting from the user. At the receive end of a transmission system the desired program is demultiplexed from the MTS and the program data is decompressed. One of the advantages of compression is the capability of providing different video picture quality levels based on bit rates. Distribution quality to the home may be adequate with bit rates of 2 Mb/sec to 8 Mb/sec for standard definition television (SDTV) and 20 Mb/sec for high definition television (HDTV). Contribution quality is required if further production processing is planned for the received signal. In that case bit rates of 18 Mb/sec to 50 Mb/sec are required for SDTV and 270 Mb/sec to 400 Mb/sec for HDTV.

Video testing in this modern television system is not just a matter of developing new techniques for the difficult non-linear compression process. A significant portion of the system still uses analog and full-bandwidth digital signals requiring application of traditional analog and recently developed digital test methods.

## ANALOG VIDEO TESTING

Video systems are intended to display a picture which accurately represents the scene being scanned by the camera. With today's special effects capabilities the displayed pictures may differ in an artistically defined manner from the original. None-the-less, at some point in the processing, where the artistic changes are complete, the resulting pictures are to be accurately transmitted to the final display device. In order to test the video system a logical sequence of tasks must be performed generally starting from the basic camera/display combination and working towards the more complex parts of the signal processing system. An experienced video engineer recently stated "First align the camera and display in monochrome, add and adjust color and then test the more complex digital parts of the system. After everything is tested to be within specifications a human observer should still have a look to make sure nothing important or unusual was missed". This view is even more critical for compressed video systems because the input to a video compression codec must be accurate, in compliance with appropriate standards, and of as high a quality as possible to provide for efficient encoding. Hence there is a strong requirement for testing of the analog and full bandwidth digital portions as well as the sophisticated compression and transmission systems.

Measurement practices for analog television systems are well defined[1,2] and very reliable. They are based on the linear system premise that video distortions produced in a system may be accurately determined by passing suitable test signals through the same system. However, a series of different tests are required to verify that the system will produce acceptable pictures. One test will not do the job.

Fig. 2 is a block diagram of an analog system and the associated functional testing layers. Although there are three functional layers to test, only two types of equipment are required. The physical layer (coax, connectors, patch panels) can be verified with a time domain reflectometer (TDR). The other two layers can be tested with a single specialized oscilloscope looking at the one integrated waveform which combines the video signal and the synchronizing signal. A minimum set of tests for an analog system might be: luminance amplitude, rise/fall times, bandwidth, group delay, signal-to-noise ratio, and waveform non-linear distortions. For composite systems (PAL/NTSC) chroma amplitude, chroma phase, differential phase and differential gain are also important. A matrix of tests and specifications can be associated with different qualities of video signal transmission[3] but no one number or mathematical combination of parameters will describe the resulting system operation. If adjustments are made there is quite often interaction between processing elements resulting in changes of several measurement parameters. A television engineer must evaluate the combined results of the various tests as well as observe the resulting picture.

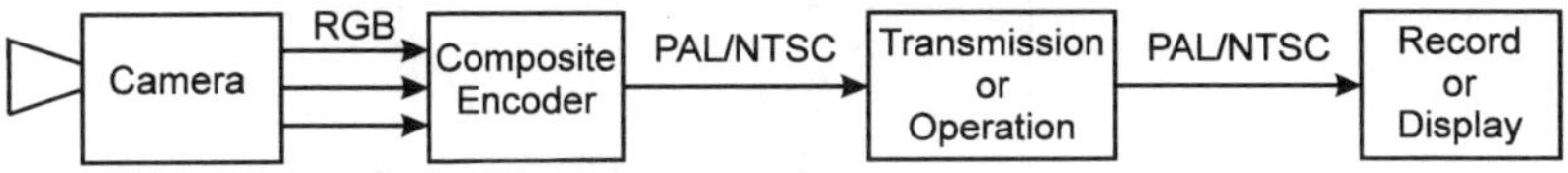


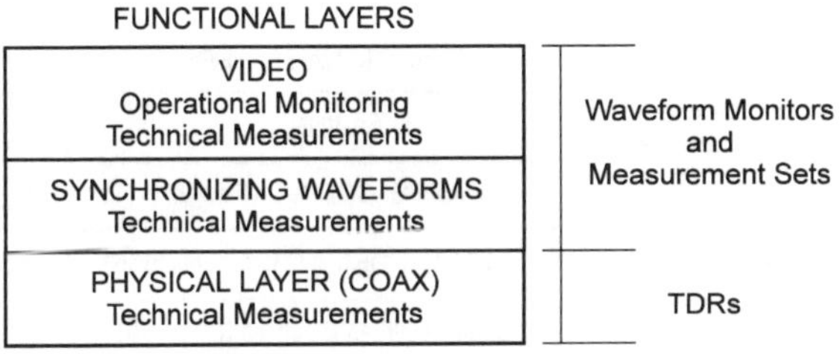


Figure 2. Analog system and functional layers

**FULL-BANDWIDTH DIGITAL VIDEO TESTING**

Even with the rapid rise in the use of compression techniques, full-bandwidth digital television will continue to be a major element in television systems. Processing and interconnecting video in a digital form eliminates most of the signal quality loss problems of an analog system. However it introduces a new set of distortions in the analog-to-digital (A/D) and digital-to-analog (D/A) conversions requiring modification of signal-to-noise-ratio and differential phase/gain analog test methods.[4] Fig. 3 is a block diagram showing the digital additions to the previous analog system. As the television industry transitions from analog to digital video, combinations of composite and component systems are being used however the preference is for all-component video operation. Transmission to the home viewer of this higher quality digital signal has generally been accomplished by *compression* back to the composite analog domain while still providing a picture quality improvement over an all-analog system. With the advent of digital compression techniques the final picture quality is now a variable leading to further testing requirements discussed later in this paper.

The component analog signal is converted to digital in accordance with the sampling standard, ITU-R BT.601 (Rec 601) [5]. Formatting and studio interconnection of the digitized signal follow a related standard, ITU-R BT.656 (Rec 656) [6], leading to additional functional layers and a variety of tests[7] to be performed.

For operational purposes, the monitoring of equivalent analog video signal properties is still key with this signal processed from the digital data. Where testing of the analog signal required only that various parameters be measured on a single waveform digital testing requires three types of analysis: digital signal coding, digital data formatting and parameters relating to the digital waveform. Although all three of these measurement types can be performed with a single instrument, such as the Tektronix WFM 601M, there is significant processing between each pair of layers with different analysis methods for each layer as well.

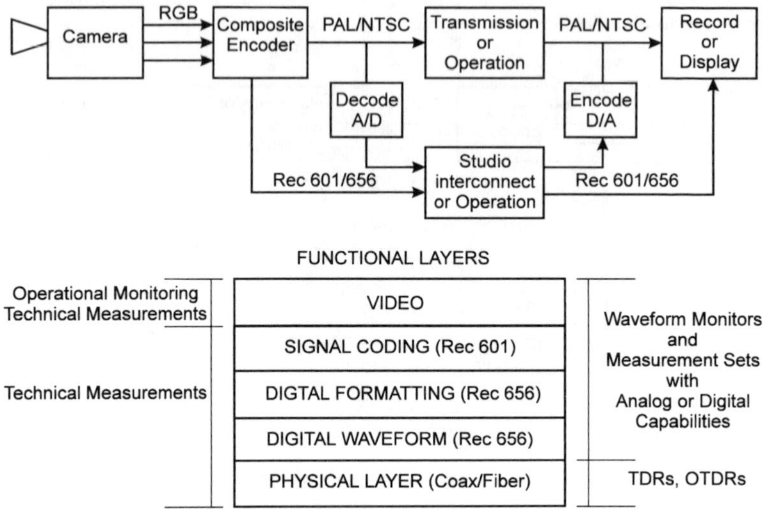


Figure 3. Digital system and functional layers

Correct coding of the signal, with respect to the standard, can be determined by a waveform display of the resulting analog signal and a readout of the corresponding digital values in defined areas such as, black, peak white, zero-color, maximum color excursions, and non-use of certain excluded digital values. Direct generation of a digital video signal in operational equipment, such as a character generator or production switcher, leads to another coding consideration. The digits must represent a band-limited signal such as those defined by the filter parameters of Rec 601 or excessive ringing will result in the analog domain[(8)]. Digital signal monitoring equipment will not only show the resulting analog artifacts but will allow precise determination of the sample values causing undesired effects.

Digital formatting of the non-video part of the signal can be quite complex particularly when digital audio is embedded in the digital video signal[(9)]. Measurement includes displaying an analog rendition of the formatting digits, cursor selection of each sample for a readout of the digital value, as well as a logic-analyzer type display of a selected group of digital words. Included in the digital formatting are error detection cyclic redundancy check (CRC) words that can be used in monitoring or operational equipment to determine if the digital signal at a receiver exactly matches that of the sending equipment where the CRCs were inserted[(10,11,12)]. Called EDH, for error detection and handling, this method provides an accurate way to determine the onset of errors when a stressing method is used to measure operational headroom in the virtually error free environment of serial digital video.

Analysis of the serial digital waveform (which is really an analog signal) may be the most complex of the three measurement types. An eye pattern display is used to measure basic parameters such as amplitude, risetime and overshoot. The eye pattern can also be used to measure jitter if the clock used to produce the eye pattern is carefully specified[(13,14,15)]. In a typical serial digital television waveform monitor, eye pattern determination of jitter would require setting of cursors to make the measurement, however numeric measurement values may be quickly obtained using a demodulator method. In many cases operational headroom for a serial digital video signal is simply related to the amount of coax in the transmission path and the amplitude of the launch signal. A measurement of these parameters can be derived at the receiver end based on an assumed type of coax thereby providing some important headroom information.

## TESTING LAYERS

Three key testing layers can be defined for the modern television system as shown in Fig. 4. Each has its own subset of more detailed testing layers, the signal quality layers having been described in the previous sections. Quality measurements at the uncompressed level now consist of two parts, signal quality and picture quality. *Signal quality* measurements are made with a suite of test signals whose resulting distortions will determine transmission channel or video processing parameters.

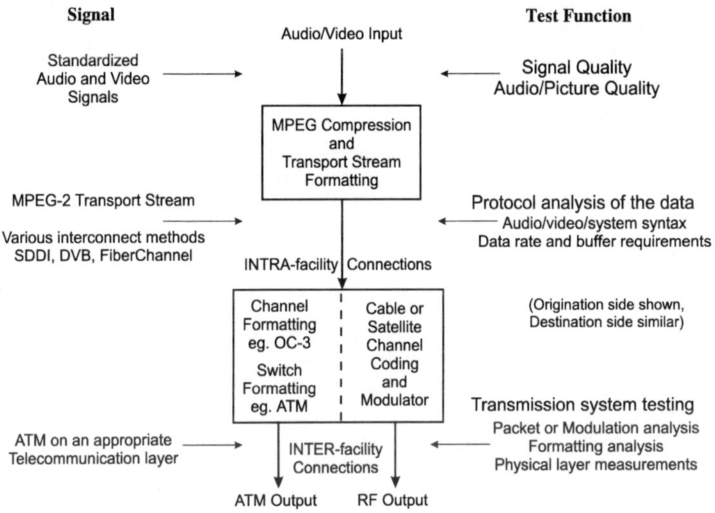


Figure 4. Video Testing Layers

These test signals can be very short, as an example, one line in the vertical interval. In a completely uncompressed system such testing will give a good characterization of picture quality (with the exception of helical-scan videotape recorders). This is not true for the compression encoder/decoder part of the system as has been described in numerous recent articles[16,17,18,19,20]. Traditional test signals are relatively simple compared to a natural scene and are easily compressed with little distortion or loss. However, due to the ease of compression, these signals do not evaluate the encoder/decoder process. Therefore *Picture Quality* measurements require natural scenes, or an equivalent thereof, which are much more complex than traditional test signals. These complex scenes stress the capabilities of the encoder resulting in non-linear distortions that are a function of the picture content.

Once the picture has been compressed, the resulting data is formatted for intra-facility connections. Examples for the use of such connections are: program interchange between video disk servers or several video/audio encoders sending single program transport streams to a multiplexer to produce a multi program transport stream for satellite broadcasting. This is an appropriate layer for

*Protocol* testing because the data formatting can be quite complex and is relatively independent of the nature of the uncompressed signals or the eventual conversion to inter-facility transmission formats. Typical protocol testing equipment will be both a source of known valid, or specifically invalid, signals and an analyzer which locates errors with respect to a defined standard and determines the value of various operational parameters for the stream of data.

In order to send the television data to a remote location, one of many possible digital data transmission methods is used. This might be by cable or satellite using a suitable modulation system or by the broadband network using a telecommunications method possibly carrying ATM packets. *Transmission System* testing, although much older than analog television testing, is still a rapidly growing technology.

The emphasis in this paper is picture quality and signal quality testing of the full bandwidth video. There are a number of competing compression methods for video most of which use discrete cosine transform (DCT) based coding. Other methods, such as fractiles and wavelets, are used for some applications. Picture quality testing should be designed to be coding method insensitive whereas protocol testing is very much dependent on the coding and transmission methods.

## PICTURE QUALITY TESTING

Today, measurement of picture quality is accomplished by subjective methods, people evaluating the displayed video. In its more scientific forms this takes a large amount of time and resources. The widely used ITU-R BT.500 was originally developed for non-compressed video systems and has been updated in recent years. None-the-less some researchers consider it to be inadequate for compressed video so there is significant work under way to expand subjective testing methods(22,23). In an operational broadcast environment the subjective evaluation is generally accomplished only by expert observers, is still not calibrated in any meaningful manner and is certainly not automatic.

Although the term "picture quality" is used in this paper, what is actually measured, by either subjective or objective methods, is picture degradation. A reference motion sequence is compared to an impaired motion sequence producing a difference value as the output of the measurement system.

Much effort has been expended in research laboratories to develop objective quality measurement methods and determine their correlation with subjective results(24). A set of measurements has been standardized by the American National Standards Institute as ANSI T1.801.03(25). Some of the parameters measured by the standard are: Average gain, offset level, Active video area, Spatial shift, Spatial information, Temporal information, Radial average of spatial frequencies, Added/Lost motion energy, Added/Lost edge energy, Added/Lost spatial frequencies, and Peak signal to noise ratio (PSNR). Most of these measurements are calculations of picture content properties, the exception being PSNR which is the only measurement requiring a full copy of the reference scene for comparison with degraded scene at the point of calculation. PSNR is a very intuitive comparison method being a calculation based on simply taking the absolute difference between video frames. Although PSNR can give misleading results in some situations it is still a benchmark measurement and can be useful for controlled experiments. In one recent example PSNR was used to compare the down-sampled to SDTV results of certain encoder constraints for HDTV compression against the results from an unconstrained decoder(26). It was possible to identify I, P and B-frames as well as get a general idea of picture quality degradation.

A combination of several T1.801.03 measurements was evaluated extensively for correlation between objective and subjective results(27). Unfortunately the results of experiments did not show a high enough correlation to be included in the standard. Therefore, in the scope of the standard it states "Experimental results indicate that the objective measures presented here are insufficient to predict viewer responses with the accuracy needed to discriminate similar systems." It further states in the purpose "This standard is intended to be especially useful as a basis for comparing the present operational readiness of a system with the same system's past performance." Although there are examples where a system is more or less invariant the general case is change, either in the characteristics of the system such as changing the compressed bit rate or simply the concatenation of an uncontrolled variety of compression schemes during program production or transmission.

What is needed for picture quality measurement is a metric that is based on the human visual system. A review article compared thirty two such models that have been published over the past twenty four years(28). It states that all but one of "the models can be regarded as simplified versions of the Lubin (1993) model" (29). Dr. Lubin, a researcher at the David Sarnoff Research Center in New Jersey, has extended that work to cover the broader category of picture quality measurements(30). The Sarnoff visual discrimination model is shown in Fig. 5. The luminance portion of digitized input images are processed through several stages representing specific characteristics of the human eye. This processing takes into account the optics of the eye, retinal cone mosaic, contrast sensitivity verses retinal angular frequency, response to edges for various orientations, and the dipper shape of contrast discrimination functions. Following those processes the resulting data for the two images is compared for differences (distance) providing a map whose intensity is related to the human perception of the differences between corresponding areas of the two pictures. This map is called a JND map for just noticeable differences. Single-number results of picture quality differences can be derived from the distance data using such things as peak or mean values. It is expected that extensions of this type of picture quality metric to include temporal response of the eye and human judgment in response to the resulting human perception will lead to an objective measurement method providing good correlation to subjective measurements.

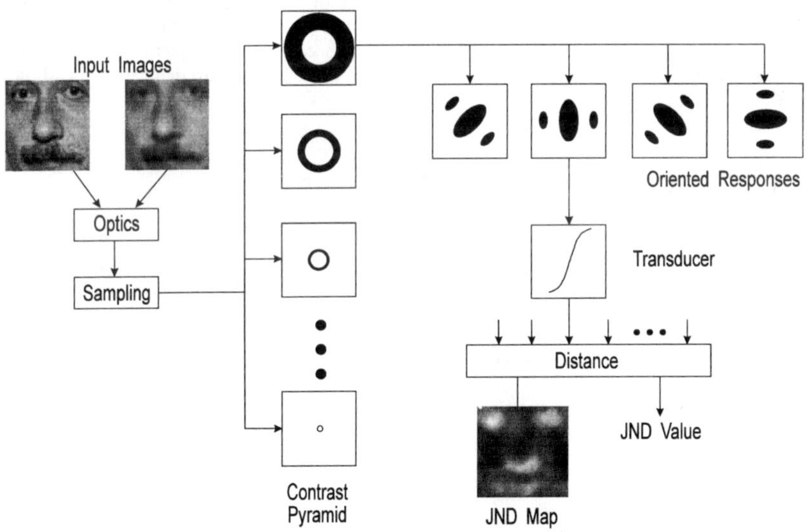


Figure 5. Sarnoff visual discrimination model

In order to make objective measurements of picture quality it is necessary to insure the two video sequences are presented to the instrument in much the same manner as required for subjective tests. That is, gain and dc level of both the luminance and chrominance must be closely matched.

In addition there must be temporal alignment and very accurate spatial alignment. These latter two requirements are due to the need to do some sort of a differencing process between video frames as done with PSNR and the Sarnoff model. Results of experiments conducted at Tektronix indicate picture quality measurement methods that use full comparisons of both images at the measuring device provide the best correlation between subjective and objective measurements. Another requirement is that the test material be such that the system being measured is working at or near the limits of its capabilities. This has always been done with traditional analog measurements (an example would be use of the 2-T pulse) and is even more important to stress the non-linear characteristics of video compression systems. Again, as has been true in the past, one test sequence (signal) will not be sufficient. Therefore a number of difficult test sequences must be used to test video compression systems. These sequences will represent a variety realistic scenes, an example being the ANSI T1.801.01[31] video test scenes which were derived primarily for video conferencing system evaluation.

Use of specific test scenes which must occupy most or all of the active picture area means that testing will be out-of-service. This paradigm for video testing will not be popular with those who have, for many years, used vertical interval test signals (VITS). Although in-service testing with the actual program material would be logistically possible in some applications (monitoring a direct broadcast satellite system at the up-link location) it might not provide meaningful results for a majority of the program material which does not stress the system. Beyond that there is an operational parameter that may not be satisfactory with general program material. Time to make the measurement is an important feature in test equipment. If the picture matching; gain, spatial alignment, etc., is to be done on program material a large amount of compute time will be required to make correlation calculations. This is in addition to the time required to just make the measurement after the two video scenes are correctly matched. Therefore, it is proposed that some known alignment signals be added to the video sequences for rapid picture matching again requiring out-of-service operation. A possible approach to such a measurement system is shown in Fig. 6.

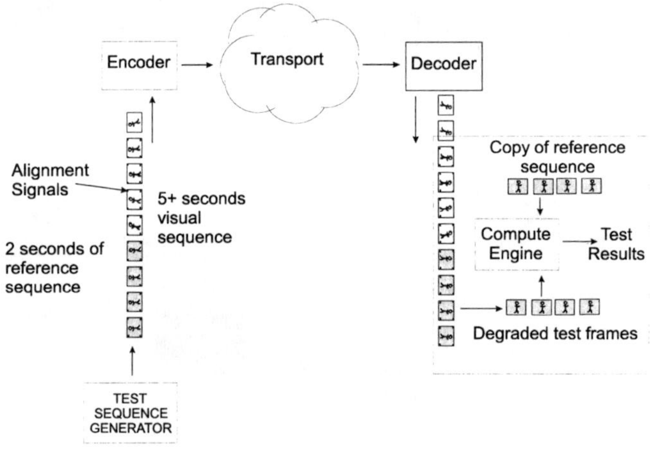


Figure 6. Picture quality test method

Objective measurements of picture quality including temporal aspects of the human visual system should be possible with about two seconds of video sequence. However, subjective assessment by an expert viewer may also be desired so the test sequence source should provide five or more seconds of continuous video which may be repeated or palindromed for longer viewing. The video source could be a tape recorder of suitable quality, however a test signal generator would be much more cost effective. Included in the video are suitable alignment signals to speed the measurement. After the video has passed through the system under test the appropriate two seconds are captured by the measurement instrument. Within the instrument is a copy of the reference sequence thereby allowing end-to-end testing of a system where the source and destination are a great distance apart. Because of the compute power required for a temporal analysis, results are likely to take up to a minute or more to calculate.

## CONCLUSION

As much as we would like to measure the absolute quality of a picture, that is probably not possible. What we can do is measure picture degradation in a manner similar to the way a human perceives the difference between a reference picture and a degraded output picture. When considering the complexity of video compression methods and their non-linear characteristics it might be appropriate to forget all the testing methods for analog and full bandwidth digital systems.

The truth of the matter is compressed video systems are always a subset of a larger system which include traditional analog and digital video processing. In fact, it is the non-compressed part of the system that must be attended to first and with great care because the quality of the input and output video processing can obscure a measurement of picture quality. Even more important the conformity to a standard and quality of video input to the compression system has a great affect on its ability to effectively perform its task.

A picture quality (degradation) measurement instrument is not yet available. There is work going on in research laboratories and we can expect to see a picture quality measurement method which has good correlation to subjective measurements in the not too distant future.

## ACKNOWLEDGMENT

The concept of Figure 5 is reproduced with the permission of the David Sarnoff Research Center.

## REFERENCES

1. Tektronix Inc., "Television Measurements for NTSC Systems," Tektronix Inc., Beaverton, Oregon, 1994, Lit No. 25W-7049-3.
2. Tektronix Inc., "Television Measurements for PAL Systems," Tektronix Inc., Beaverton, Oregon, 1994, Lit No. 25W-7075-1.
3. ANSI T1.502, "System M-NTSC Television Signals - Network Interface Specifications and Performance Parameters."
4. Correspondence to "Video Services Industry Forum" from David Fibush, Nov 30, 1994.
5. Recommendation ITU-R BT.601, "Encoding Parameters of Digital Television for Studios."
6. Recommendation ITU-R BT.656, "Interfaces for Digital Component Video Signals in 525-line and 625-line Television Systems Operating at the 4:2:2 level of Recommendation 601."
7. Tektronix Inc., "A Guide to Digital Television Systems and Measurements," Tektronix Inc., Beaverton, Oregon, 1994, Lit No. 25W-7203-1.
8. Dan Baker, David Fibush and Bruce Penney, "Digital to Analog Conversion — Data and Filter Requirements", SMPTE Journal, 104:124, Mar. 1995.
9. David Fibush, "Integrating Digital Audio into the Serial Digital Video Signal", SMPTE Journal, 103:574, Aug. 1994.

10. Bob Elkind and David Fibush, "Proposal for Error Detection and Handling", SMPTE Journal, 100:940, Dec. 1991.
11. SMPTE RP 165, "Error Detection Checkwords and Status Flags for use in Bit-Serial Digital Television Interfaces"
12. David Fibush, "Error Measurements in Studio Digital Video Systems", SMPTE Journal, 102:688, Aug. 1993.
13. David Fibush, "Jitter Effects and Measurements in Serial Digital Television Signals", SMPTE Journal, 102:693, Aug. 1993.
14. SMPTE RP 184, "Specification of Jitter in Bit-Serial Digital Systems"
15. SMPTE S17.121-6, "Jitter Measurement Procedures in Bit-Serial Digital Interfaces"
16. C.P. Cressy, G.W. Beakley, "Computer-based Testing of Digital Video Quality", IS&T/SPIE Symposium on Electronic Imaging Science and Technology, February 6-10, 1994, San Jose, California.
17. M. Schubin, "Testing: Zero, One", Videography, Vol 19, No 12, p 18, 1994.
18. D. Wood, "Television Picture Quality, What does it mean? What does it matter?", EBU Diffusion, Spring 1995, pp 46-51.
19. G.M. Drury, "Picture Quality Issues in Digital Video Compression", IBC Broadcasting Convention, September 14-18, 1995, Conference Publication No. 413.
20. G. Beakley, C. Cressy, J. VanPelt, "Video Compression: The Need for Testing", SMPTE Journal, Vol 104, No. 11, pp 742-750, November 1995.
21. ITU-R BT.500, "Method for the Subjective Assessment of the Quality of Television Pictures".
22. N. K. Lodge, "Picture Quality Assessment and Optimisation Methods for Advanced Television Systems", Image Technology - Journal of the BKSTS, September 1994, pp 147-154.
23. N. K. Lodge, "A Method for the Subjective Assessment of Low Bit-rate Picture Quality", in the PhD thesis "Interpolative Coding Methods for Digital Transmission of Conventional and High Definition Television", Heriot-Watt University Edinburgh, March 1993, pp 179-203.
24. S. Voran and S. Wolf, "An Objective Technique for Assessing Video Impairments", Proceedings of IEEE Pacific Rim Conference, 1993.
25. ANSI T1.801.03, "Digital Transport of One-way Video Signals, Parameters for Objective Performance Assessment".
26. J. Boyce and L. Pearlstein, "Low-cost All Format ATV Decoding with Improved Quality", Paper 11, 30th SMPTE Advanced Motion and Imaging Conference, Feb 1996.
27. A.W. Webster et al, "An Objective Quality Assessment System Based on Human Perception", SPIE International Symposium on Electronic Imaging: Science and Technology, June 1993.
28. A.J. Ahumada, Jr, "Computational Image Quality Metrics: A Review", SID Digest, vol. 24, pp. 305-308, 1993.
29. J. Lubin, "The use of Psychophysical Data and Models in the Analysis of Display System Performance", A. Watson (ed.), Visual Factors in Electronic Image Communications, Cambridge, MA: MIT Press, 1993.
30. J. Lubin, "A visual discrimination model for imaging system design and evaluation, in Vision Models for Target Detection and Recognition", E. Peli, ed., World Scientific Publishing, 245-283, 1995.
31. ANSI T1.801.01, "Digital Transport of Video Teleconferencing - Video Telephony Signals - Video Test Scenes for Subjective and Objective Performance Assessment".

# The Unified World Environment

## Using 3-D Databases as an Aid to Visual Effects Production

Joel Hynek and John Gaeta
Mass.Illusion
Lenox, Massachusetts

## Abstract

As we move steadily into the world of the digital backlot, methods of visual effects production that can efficiently integrate the vast array of required image elements become necessary. One such method, the unified world environment, answers the call.

This paper will present the unified world environment as developed at Mass.Illusion focusing on the role of pre-visualization and 3-D databases as the skeleton that holds the body of visual effects disciplines together.

## The Visual Effects Process - The Problem

There is a problem that lies in the very definition of a visual effect:

> A visual effect is an image that is produced by separately created elements.

The problem is that, usually, the separately created elements are produced on different camera systems, in different locations, or on different software platforms. Getting meaningful information from one system to another is often tedious and sometimes not possible.

Every visual effects shot begins with a plan, usually in the form of a storyboard, diagram, blueprint and/or pre-visualization. As the process moves forward various elements are created based on the plan that relate to each other in order to build the final image. In the final step of compositing, all the elements come together. Here you discover whether or not all the elements conform to the plan. Generally, due to the fact that the real world does not correspond exactly to the planned world, the elements vary to some degree from their intentioned aim. Significant time must then be spent adjusting or re-doing the elements so that they will fit together correctly.

## The Solution

The idea of the unified world environment is to provide a central storehouse of accurate real world information that all departments can draw upon, allowing for the almost automatic coordination of CGI, live action, and model photography. This method increases production efficiency and insures better integration of visual effects elements. It relies heavily on the use of pre-visualization and the creation and continual updating of central 3-D databases.

## 3-D databases and Pre-visualization

The key to this approach is that every shot has a 3-D database associated with it. These databases are updated all the way through the process and are accessed at every step from design to compositing.

Each shot's 3-D database begins its life in the pre-visualization department and is comprised of design and geometry input from the art department. Next comes geometry data from the motion control stages and from the live action stages. Also incorporated are the limitations of the camera systems. Armed with this data, the models, stage set-ups, and shot designs are accurately visualized.

Once the shot pre-visualizations are approved by the director, the design data goes to the model shop as Autocad information where it directly drives the model making process through Lasercamm cutting of the model parts and through Autocad generated blueprints. The design data is also used to drive a CNC milling machine which cuts complex 3-D shapes out of a solid block. The model placement data and stage set-up plan, generated in pre-visualization, are used to position the models on the stages.

The camera movement data goes to the motion control stages where it drives the camera, at least as the initial move. Usually the move is modified for a variety of reasons. Once the shot is in the can, the set and the models are surveyed with any one of a variety of survey tools. The camera is also surveyed. This data is then used to update the database in the Pre-Visualization department. It now becomes an accurate record of what was shot and how it was shot. CGI and other model elements can now be easily and accurately coordinated.

## Data Capture devices:

We have used a variety of survey/data capture devices. Depending on how you use them their accuracy can be more than adequate.

1). Laser Theodilite. Some come with software that not only capture a cloud of points but also build a 3-D database as you survey with a PC laptop. That database then transfers into Softimage. Laser theodilites are not fast and time must be set aside to accomplish the task. Range is relatively great (approx. 500 feet).

2). Infared Emitter Tracking. This motion capture device can capture data in real time. It is a system that measures position with a three headed infared sensor array. Infared emitters can be built in to a model, set, or camera. For surveying where there are no emitters, a digitizing marker probe is used. Range is limited to about 75 feet.

3) Active Photogrammetry. This survey tool uses two high resolution digital cameras to track passive markers placed on a subject. Position data is calculated instantaneously. A digitizing marker probe is also used to survey objects that do not have markers on them. Range is limited to about 100 feet.

4) Passive Photogrammetry. This system uses photographs or digital images taken from different positions of an object or building to build a 3-D database. This method cuts time on stage but requires considerable analysis off stage. Range is essentially unlimited but accuracy will vary according to intelligent placement of the still cameras.

## CGI (Computer Generated Imagery)

CG elements are given a head start during the design phase because the design databases used in pre-visualization accurately reflect the geometry of the stages that will be used. Also the database driving the model construction is the same database driving the creation of CG elements. For instance if a building is being built as a physical model and as a computer generated model (physical for close-up and CG for everything else) both versions will have a good chance of looking the same. Further down the production trail, after the as-built model survey data has been incorporated into the central database, the CG model can now look exactly the same as its physical cousin.

## Compositing

In compositing things come together needing little if any adjustment. However, the need to access the 3-D databases does not stop here. We continue to draw upon the databases to:

1) Create 3-D mattes that move automatically with the shot, thus eliminating the need to rotoscope or pull density mattes.

2) Add CG reflections or alter the lighting of a physical object with a CG element through knowledge of its position and shape.

3) Move an object around in 2-D simulating a move created in 3-D. In other words, create a move in 3-D based on knowledge of the already filmed elements and use that information to automatically drive the 2-D manipulation of scanned film elements. Specifically, use Softimage (a 3-D based CG package) to drive Cineon (a 2-D based compositing program.)

## Conclusion

Our philosophy is to accurately gather data up front so that you know as soon as possible where everything is rather than waiting to get to post to figure it out afterwards. With some shots, of course, you have no choice but to work out the geometry and motion after the fact.

The end result of this approach is a more streamlined production flow that can significantly cut production time on stage. It also results in less time spent fudging and tweaking the mechanics of production and more time spent tweaking the creative aspects of visual effects. And this, hopefully, results in better looking and more effective images.

# CONTEMPORARY TECHNIQUES FOR DIGITAL COMPOSITING IN MOTION PICTURES

Michael Kanfer
Digital Domain
Venice, Calif.

## Abstract

In this paper, I will discuss my experiences as Digital Composite Supervisor for Digital Domain on the motion picture, *Apollo 13*. During the production of *Apollo 13,* it was my responsibility to maintain the look of the principal photography, practical effects elements, and computer generated (CG) elements throughout the digital process. Much of our work involved studying all available NASA footage. Everything was re-created from scratch. Not a single frame of NASA motion picture footage was used in our composites. We analyzed various phenomena that occurred in the NASA films, and made our work match it as closely as possible. Motion controlled model photography of the spacecraft was integrated with live action photography, digital paintings, and practical effects. Computer generated elements such as ice, condensation gas, vapor, engine blast, explosions and debris were synthetically created to complete the illusion. Camera shake was added to the shots using a special program that maintained natural motion blur between frames. The resulting composites had the look and feel of the NASA documentary films that we all remember. Yet, the superior image quality, unique camera angles, and continuity of lighting gave our footage the added drama necessary to re-create some of the most exciting and harrowing moments of the flight of *Apollo 13.*

## CREATING AND COMPOSITING THE ELEMENTS

The most challenging sequence to portray photorealistically was the launch. During background plate photography at the Kennedy Space Center, Visual Effects Supervisor Rob Legato took detailed measurements of lighting ratios for every shot. This information was then used for lighting all of the models photographed on the Digital Domain stages. The contrast ratios derived from this information were passed along to Digital Effects Supervisors Mark Lasoff, Karen Goulekas and John McLaughlin to ensure that the CG elements for condensation gas, ice and debris had matching contrast values. Digital Effects Art Director Kevin Mack and Digital Matte Artist Martha Snow Mack also made use of the lighting information when creating various paint extensions of the launch pad and clouds. With the help of my co-supervisors Price Pethel and Gray Marshall, I was able to set up a compositing paradigm that enabled our shots to blend seamlessly into the movie.

Many of the elements used in Apollo 13 were generated entirely inside the computer for several reasons. Since the extreme range of the camera moves precluded filming in real time, the model photography of the rocket during the launch had to be filmed by undercranking. Motion controlled repeat passes of practically shot ice or vapor could not be used, since everything would look way too fast. Doing it in CG gave us infinite control over the speed and look of the vapor, ice, and engine blast for the launch. Explosions, re-entry fire trails, engine blast, helmet and window reflections, thrusters, debris, and even some urine crystals fill out a heavy CG palette. In all cases, natural photographic phenomena such as the lighting, granularity, motion blur, and color of these synthetic elements were critical to their believability in the composites. For every model shot needing a CG element, Supervising Digital Artist Judith Crow derived matching 3D camera moves from the motion control data. This enabled our 3D artists to create elements for the compositors which matched the movements of the practical photography.

A crucial element of the launch sequence was the ice falling off of the rocket. In reality, on the launch pad, up to four inches of ice can form on the Saturn V skin due to condensation of the moist air that gets frozen by the refrigerated propellants inside the fuel tanks. Supervising Digital Artist Dennis Blakey was responsible for one of the most difficult CG effects. Using a program called Prisms, Dennis created a cylinder that wrapped around the rocket, tracking the motion controlled model. He then broke the cylinder up into 5,000 pieces to create the shapes of ice. Each piece is a single surface, transparent polygon, which can conform to the surface of the rocket. Dennis was able to control the individual patches so that he could trigger portions of the ice to crack off at just the right moments. As the ice falls off the rocket, pieces of it hit and bounce off the gantry arms. To achieve this effect, Dennis simulated the arms with 3D boxes that act as collision objects within the computer that split specific polygons upon impact. For enhanced photorealism, Dennis gave each color layer of the CG ice image files a different amount of grain and sharpness, just like real film would have done if the elements were shot practically. The red layer was the softest and least grainy, followed by the green layer appearing sharper and less grainy than the blue layer. Dennis was also the creator of CG smoke trails during the launch, and of the trailing fire plume upon re-entry.

Prisms 3D software was also used by Supervising Digital Artist David Isyomin to create the engine exhaust blast during the launch. The initial look of the exhaust was created by using two ellipsoidal shapes and two shaders that he wrote using Renderman. A shader can make shapes or particles look like an infinite variety of real life textures, and in this case it was a fiery blast plume. By adding noise, and animating the geometry, the shaders create an inner core of fast moving, streaky fire surrounded by an outer layer of fiery glow. Prisms particle systems and Renderman software were also put to use for the creation of condensation gases, urine crystals, and jet exhaust. In all cases, the ages, size, decay rate and turbulence of the particles can be controlled to achieve the desired effects. Supervising Digital Artist Robert Small perfected the particle techniques in his creation of the condensation gas which looked photorealisitic, even though it was computer generated.

After the oxygen tank explodes during the flight of Apollo 13, mylar insulation debris is all over the place outside the ship. Supervising Digital Artist Neville Spiteri adapted Dennis Blakey's ice program to animate thousands of tiny pieces of mylar. The actual size of the panel that got blown off the command module during the explosion was divided up into a polygonal mesh. Points along its surface were joined to produce the thousands of pieces that it would separate into. Neville defined the force and velocity that shatters the polygonal mesh. A shader which gave the mylar its shiny and reflective qualities was also written to accurately describe the look of the particles as they were illuminated by the sun and the explosion itself.

Shots that were part of the explosion sequence had numerous elements in addition to the mylar. Among them were: multiple passes for the spacecraft, multiplaning greenscreens of astronauts inside the windows, two layers of CG mist created by the escaping oxygen, CG starfields, CG venting gas, CG earth and moon elements. In one instance, a sunflare behind the moon was created by Digital Artist Randall Rosa, using Alias software. Practical fireballs and liquid nitrogen vapor were supplied by pyrotechnics specialist Joe Viskocil.

The rendition of stars in the space sequence proved to be quite challenging. Digital Effects Supervisor John McLaughlin procured a NASA database of stars. He then wrote a program that enabled him to generate moves on the starfield that matched the motion controlled moves from the model shots. The stars were rendered as spheres in the computer using a Renderman shader. After numerous tests and wedges, Digital Effects Supervisor Mark Lasoff and Supervising Digital Artist Judith Crow came up with an intensity and size for the point source light of the stars.

We ran various wedges on our digital negative, throughout each step of the Super 35 optical process. Anamorphic internegative was created from an interpositive, and then release printed. The final analysis of various release prints enabled us to choose the best settings for the stars. We made sure the stars were not too dim and small or too bright and big. The stars required the tightest spec out of all of the elements, which meant that the exposure and contrast ratios of the earth, moon, and spaceship had to be just right since they were locked into the settings that were specific to the stars. The sharpness and fine grain characteristics of 5244 intermediate stock exposed by the Cineon Laser film recorder enabled the stars to be tack sharp, point light sources. This result cannot be achieved using traditional CRT film recorders.

While viewing footage of rocket launches, we observed an intensely luminous glow that surrounded the engine blast. Originally, we attempted to create the glow as a purely CG element, but there were some problems. In addition to long rendering times, the CG glow was almost too clean and the intense highlights in the core of the glow did not taper off realistically. Rob Legato decided that a much simpler approach might be in order. A pin registered Mitchell camera with various fog and diffusion filters was set up to re-photograph the original CG glow elements off of the screen of a computer monitor. The film was then scanned back in to the digital realm. The result was a glow element which could be mixed with just a little bit of CG blast element to create a realistic flare coming from the engine blast. At times, the flare would obliterate the image for a few frames, just like the original NASA footage.

Impossible situations such as the insertion of a 1970's Saturn V rocket into a modern day helicopter plate of the Vehicle Assembly Building (VAB) required specialized forms of computer tracking. First, a 3D camera move was derived from a Wescam live action plate that circled from above the building to reveal the rocket inside the gigantic front door. Since there was absolutely no motion control data, a 3D wireframe blueprint of the modern day VAB was digitally pinblocked to the existing plate. The result yielded camera position data which was scaled down by Supervising Digital Artist Judith Crow to create data for a motion controlled camera move. A 1/96 scale model of the Saturn V was shot using this move at the Digital Domain stage. With special software that reconciles the slight inconsistencies between plates, and some careful massaging by Digital Compositor Pablo Helman during the composite, the resulting shot looks as if we really flew by the vehicle assembly building in 1970 and saw the Apollo 13 spacecraft during construction. To make things even more difficult, we had to do some serious roto to open up the front door of the VAB, since it could not be open during the original plate photography.

This same technique was also used to create a shot that shows the Saturn V inching its way down the road to the launch pad atop the heavy duty crawler transport vehicle. The real life crawler was photographed from a helicopter without any cargo. Once the camera move was derived from the plate, a scale model rocket, launch pad, and gantry were then tracked and composited by Lead Compositor, Adam Stark.

Traditional 2D tracking was used to composite the rocket in a shot at night before the launch. A wild plate was shot by the first unit at night in a parking lot, sans rocket and spotlights. Lead Compositors Steve Scott and Gary Walker masterfully tracked and composited the elements, including several paintings of beams by Martha Snow Mack. In a simple, yet elegant signature shot of the film, Lead Compositor Mark Forker combined a studio plate of the Saturn V with a sunrise plate shot in Florida by Rob Legato. Condensation gas can be seen pouring slowly down the side of the rocket in the distance. Here is a case where less is more.

Erik Nash, our Visual Effects Director of Photography, worked closely with the compositing team on every aspect of the process. It was decided early on that all of the model photography would have a beauty pass shot against black, followed up by multiple passes in sections for green or red screen silhouettes. (For practical reasons, simple, one pass greenscreen photography of the command module would have yielded unworkable plates. The command module is essentially a mirror that would reflect any color screen right back into the camera). At times, separate key and fill passes had to be shot to create some of the beauty elements. Unfortunately, the studio lights for the fill would reflect off of the mylar command module surfaces right into the camera. To accomplish this, the reflective sections of the model were wrapped in black velvet during the fill pass. Key passes were shot separately, allowing only one source, the sun, to reflect as it would naturally. The key and fill passes could ultimately be combined in camera, which saved time in scanning and compositing.

To complete the matte we also had to use an ultra-violet (UV) pass. The normally invisible ultra-violet lacquer that was sprayed on to all of the models was illuminated by UV light, causing it to glow bright blue. Using this method, stubborn reflective areas that showed color spill in the silhouette passes would now appear as a self matting image. This pass was then selectively combined with the other mattes into one master *"combo matte,"* to be used by the animators and compositors.

With the beauty pass against black, and combo matte passes at hand, we developed a process whereby all natural photographic effects could be preserved in the composited image. Specular highlight glows, flares and kicks that occur on bright or highly reflective surfaces were seamlessly blended into all model shots, through *additive mixing*. Many of the launch sequence shots used large shutter angles that yielded beauty passes with lots of motion blur. Using a technique devised by Price Pethel, we were able to integrate every bit of the motion blur with the subject's matte, so that even in broad daylight, the spaceship looked photorealistic while it was moving.

## SCANNING, COLOR CORRECTION AND RECORDING

One of the most important aspects of photorealistic digital compositing is the preservation of the tonal integrity of the original camera negative. Assuming the cinematographer has provided a good negative, the digital process has the capability to return images back to film that exactly reproduce the look and feel of the original photography within a multi-layered composite.

Negative shot for Apollo 13 was scanned on Kodak's Lightning Scanner and on our custom built Oxberry/Photometrics Scanner. At Digital Domain, we convert the logarithmic density data of a digital scan into the familiar, linear representation of the video world. We call this process *color grading*. Under my supervision, Digital Artist Craig Halperin meticulously color graded every shot in the film. If a composite only involved simple layering without major color correction, the sam formula that was used to convert it to linear data was also used to send it back to film. This process is the safest method to use for working in the digital realm. As long as highlights and shadows are not compromised the resulting negative can be color timed to be a perfect match of the camera original. There has been absolutely no harm done to the contrast ratio inherent to the original film. In back to back projection, one would be hard pressed to pick the original from the digital version.

The limitation of the above process is that it is difficult to do major color corrections. So, in cases where the contrast and color of a scene need to be drastically altered, we prefer to use a fixed output conversion where the image is wedged to deliver a suitable negative. All the space shots were locked into values that enabled the stars to print properly, thus, extra care had to be taken to preserve the contrast ratio between key and fill sources on the spacecraft and all CG elements.

## COMPOSITING HARDWARE AND SOFTWARE

During peak production times, we had nine Discrete Logic Flame workstations running 24 hours a day, and in addition, over 30 more Digital Artists working on Indigo2 workstations using our in house, scan-line based compositing software, called *NUKE*. During the genesis of *FLAME*, Price Pethel consulted with Discrete Logic on the development of the color correction and keying software. As a result, we were able to translate his approach to compositing into our in house software, so that both FLAME and NUKE worked similarly. Thus, when the real-time interactivity of the Flame was not necessary, we were able to achieve identical and therefore interchangeable results with our in-house software.

## COLOR TIMING THE FINAL PRINTS

The final color timing sessions took place at Deluxe Labs with colorist Bill Pine. Todd Hallowell made sure that Rob Legato, Price Pethel, and I were able to work with Director of Photography

Dean Cundey to preserve the look of our shots. Bill Pine was able to effortlessly color time our negative into the show so that none of the effects shots stood out from the principal photography. Our job was done.

## ACKNOWLEDGEMENTS

Having worked on several shots for Rob Legato on last year's *Interview With The Vampire*, I was honored when he asked me to be the Digital Composite Supervisor for Apollo 13. From the beginning, I knew this was going to be the challenge of a lifetime. I am especially grateful to Price Pethel, my co-supervisor, for his wisdom and experience which guided me through the project. In retrospect, I can only say that I have never had more fun and learned so much during a job than I did with Rob Legato and our crew on this movie.

# The Studio of The Future - The Future of the Studio

Michael Van Himbergen
Jeffrey A Diamond
MediaFusion Inc
San Mateo Ca & Great Barrington. MA

## Abstract

This paper explores "next generation" media studios and considers how traditional process methodologies and physical infrastructure requirements must adapt to an emerging media context.

The characteristics of the near future studio are evolving to operationally address the goal of an "end-to-end" process solution (from creation to distribution) in a more effective, networked manner. Applications of integrated production, post production, and electronic distribution will shape the studio's capabilities and alter its function in the creative community. Services including image processing, digital effects, rendering, film scanning and recording, distribution formatting, variable-term archiving and media asset management are being offered in much the same way that film lab services are today

Advanced studio solutions being designed and constructed as part of modernization and/or futurization initiatives for some of today's traditional studios. Such a "next generation" studio is already under construction: High Tech Center Babelsberg in Potsdam, Germany. High Tech Center is an advanced studio whose operational model is based on an innovative service provider axiom.

Another advanced technology and media content facility combines the development of technology with media content and features the distribution and warehousing of such content and software tools. This entertainment technology enterprise resembles what Gistics Group has defined as a 21st Century Asset Foundry.

# I. Overview

This paper explores "next generation" media studios and considers how traditional process methodologies and physical infrastructure requirements must adapt to an emerging media context.

The characteristics of the near future studio are evolving to operationally address the goal of an "end-to-end" process solution (from creation to distribution) in a more effective, networked manner. Applications of integrated production, post production, and electronic distribution will shape the studio's capabilities and alter its function in the creative community. Services including image processing, digital effects, rendering, film scanning and recording, distribution formatting, variable-term archiving and media asset management are offered in much the same way that film lab services are today

The operational fusion of preproduction, production and post production processes is now being accelerated due to advancements underway at numerous hardware and software companies. As these tools are improved, and the human interfaces become better adapted to creative methodologies, physical studio real-estate as a production site will be made more efficient and require less space.

As information from preproduction to post production becomes critical to the media capture process, the need to "wire" studios for broadband connectivity is undeniable. A common project knowledge base creates the ability to rapidly format and distribute electronic 3-D storyboards, camera pathing, staging setups, motion-control programming, raw footage, audio elements, and management information amongst distributed departments and vendors. Consequently, during production, actual data is collected directly from stage, describing camera, lighting, objects, and actors position and other attributes which accelerate and inform the post production process.

Captured film, video or digital media is delivered to an on-lot digital service center to be posted and prepared for distribution. Formatting of materials film, Video, Digital media) for direct electronic distribution is then implemented.

Electronic commerce will have significant impact on future studio environments. The digitization of all production elements and finished products necessitates the utilization of robust media asset management systems to catalogue, re-format, store and distribute content. This capability will enable studios to distribute content directly from studio servers or via data "warehouses" over broadband pipelines, the Internet, World Wide Web, and direct broadcast satellite.

Advanced studio solutions are being designed and constructed as part of modernization and/or futurization initiatives for some of today's traditional studios. Such a "next generation" studio is already under construction: High Tech Center Babelsberg in Potsdam, Germany. High Tech Center is an advanced studio whose operational model is based on an innovative service provider axiom. A client base of producers directors, technical talent and other vendors delivering finished media or segments of media process.

Another advanced technology and media content facility combines the development of technology with media content and features the distribution and warehousing of such content and software tools. This entertainment technology enterprise resembles what Gistics Group has defined as a 21st Century Asset Foundry.

## II. Future Media Forms - Context Creation

The convergence of entertainment and technology defines new distribution platforms creating a rich mixture of products and experiences for the consumer.

These emergent media forms are defining a dynamic commerce context which studios need to plan for and adapt to. Future media studios will address a broad spectrum of digital media production in addition to today's dominant forms of film, television, and specialty venue attractions. Emerging future media forms will become increasing important as both ancillary and autonomous entertainment products. Examples of such platforms will define the type of media and data that must be produced and utilized across a which spectrum of product application.

### *A. Digital Cinema*

Electronic distribution of feature films from studio and third-party host server farms will become possible as technical and economic developments mature. Key developmental areas include:

1. laser video projection
2. broadband telecommunications distribution
3. compression/decompression
4. security encryption
5. digital watermarking

### *B. Digital Television*

Digital television offerings are rapidly taking hold as the success of Direct Broadcast Satellite systems expand the broadcast domain. Key developmental considerations for future media studios will include:

1. combined digital television and World Wide Web offerings
2. interactive cable and satellite offerings
3. Internet and web-based desktop video studio offerings

### *C. Cybercasting*

Multipoint World Wide Web "cybercasting" of interactive entertainment offerings will increase as developments in the following areas become widely available:

1. 3D world creation/interaction
2. streaming audio and video
3. bandwidth-on-demand
4. electronic credit/debit transaction
5. intelligent digital agents

### *D. Specialty Venue*

Location-based and specialty venue attractions will become increasingly sophisticated as consumer expectations evolve and technical capabilities increase. Key developments include:

1. real time, high resolution virtual environments
2. networked content distribution
3. personalized audience interaction
4. take-home and follow-on media ancillaries

### *E. Live Performance*

Musical, theatrical, and other live performance offerings will provide the setting for unique, hybrid applications of multimedia content. Technology-assisted performances will evolve as primary, core entertainment events which are augmented and extended through the incorporation of:

1. real time virtual worlds
2. broadband telecommunications links
3. interactive audience participation
4. take-home and follow-on media ancillaries

## III. Future Media Studio Characteristics

Given the emergent media forms outlined above and the evolution of a new dynamic commerce context, future media studios are anticipated to adopt the following general characteristics:

### A. *Centralized*

This category is represented by large and medium scale studios primarily in the business of creating original content as opposed to providing services to third-party project producers. Examples include Disney, Warner Bros., DreamWorks SKG, and Sony. Universal/MGM is an exception due to its studio services orientation. Key characteristics include:

1. increased strategic alliances with technology and telecommunications providers
2. rapid up-grading or new installations of substantial technical infrastructure
3. increasing adaptation of emerging future media forms initially invented and proven by smaller, more experimental enterprises
4. development of proprietary technical production methodologies and solutions
5. acquisition of strategic or competing companies
6. creation of large-scale digital media asset libraries and repositories which provide a common content pool from which multiple media products can be created from the same audiovisual assets.

### B. *Distributed*

Inter and intra company remote collaboration via broadband communications networks will provide medium and small studio operations with the ability to provide high-quality, fast time-to-market media products. "Virtual Studio" collaboration between producers, multiple creative vendors and service providers will increase as economical methodologies and technical solutions are implemented to provide a competitive advantage over centralized large-scale studio operations.

### C. *Digital Backlot Services*

"Digital Backlot" enterprises will increasingly offer services which provide producers with an economical alternative to expensive investments in technology and/or audiovisual content elements. Example services include:

1. motion capture
2. cyber scanning
3. film scanning & recording
4. MPEG encoding
5. reality capture
6. digital 3D objects
7. 2D image banks
8. audio databases
9. videoconferencing
10. virtual sets

### D. *PC Studio*

The ability to configure digital studios around the WindowsNT platform using low-cost, high-speed microprocessors and hundreds of available software applications will continue to advance the viability of "botique" studios as well as allow large scale studios economically enter the next phase of the digital revolution. A typical configuration of the PC studio may have 10 to 50 NT workstations linked in a high-speed network, utilizing distributed rendering, centralized or out sourced render farm processing. These studio will be ideally suited for creative content authoring. Large-scale projects will be addressed by utilizing the services of Digital Backlot providers and engaging in remote collaboration with other companies via broadband telecommunications.

### E. *Hybrids & Mixtures*

Other studios will develop which constitute a hybrid or mixture of the above enterprises. These studios will operate from a centralized infrastructure location, depend on remote, multi-company collaboration, provide digital backlot services, and and co-produce original content. Additionally, this class of studio may provide limted data warehousing and electronic distribution for its clientele and original content programming.

## IV. High Tech Center Babelsberg

### A. *Business Model*

HTC is a unique, large-scale, digital studio development in, Potsdam Germany. Located in the center of Babelsberg film and television Studios, HTC is designed as a "service provider to service providers" offering advanced technical capabilities to creative content producers. This approach is characterized by the purposeful separation of the technical infrastructure from the creative application, explicitly providing an environment and business model which prevent the studio from competing with its own clientele.

As designed, HTC is a resolution and platform independent digital media facility incorporating a technical and methodological concept described as "INDIWHISE" or Integrated, Networked, Digital, White Box, Service.

### B. *Studio Babelsberg*

HTC will be integrated into the extensive production and postproduction services available at Studio Babelsberg which include:

1) 13 large-scale sound stages
2) 35 & 16mm film lab
3) 32 track mixing studio
4) quad-stage television production center
5) extensive scenery, costume and rigging facilities and more.

### C. *Physical Facilties*

1. shooting stage
2. motion control stage
3. multipurpose stage
4. virtual set stage
5. interactive auditorium
6. motionbase simulation
7. digital authoring suites
8. digital post production suites
9. edit situation room
10. machine rooms
11. public areas
12. dining
13. meeting rooms

### D. *Technical Infrastructure*

The primary components of HTC's technical infrastructure include

1. Network LAN/WAN
2. HTC system block diagram
3. Edit Situation Theatre
4. Multimedia authoring
5. digital post production
6. servers and distribution

# V. RENCEN - Fusion Facility

## A. *21st Century Asset Foundry (Business Model)*

RENCEN is the concept for a combined technology company and media studio enterprise which simultaneously focuses on digital media content and technology asset creation. This model calls for the systematic design, testing and utilization of advanced technology tools and solutions on real-world media projects. The operational structure of RENCEN consists of three primary divisions designed to optimize the fusion of media and technology:

1. applied technology R&D
2. advanced systems design and implementation
3. digital media production and distribution services

## B. *Strategic Advantage:*

1. ownership of applied technological intellectual property tested in a shop floor "research and production" environment which is productized through third-party partners.
2. ownership of and/or service provider for media content created with "first-use" advanced technical solutions.
3. ownership of continuing electronic commerce distribution systems and products.

## C. *Resources and Infrastructure*

1. Physical Facilities
    - a) interior
    - b) exterior
    - c) sky stage
    - d) sea stage
    - e) production offices
    - f) support enterprises
2. Technical Capabilities
    - a) process integration
    - b) media asset management
    - c) electronic distribution
    - d) strategic partnerships

## VI. Key Developmental Areas

### *A. Process Linkage*

1. pre-visualization & simulation
2. pre production
3. production
4. post production

### *B. Media Asset Management*

1. objects,
2. information
3. electronic commerce products

### *C. Enterprise Management*

1. optimizing communication, quality and control

## VI. Conclusions

### *A. Now What?*

Now that digital tools have proven to be necessary and viable in media creation, studios of the future are challenged with second-order issues such as end-to-end fulfillment, digital infrastructure flexibility, and asset creation/management. These considerations will increasingly figure into studio design and implementation strategies.

### *B. Superstorytelling*

Another major force driving the development of future studios is the emergence of a general Global Audiovisual Language. The successful evolution of the studio will enable it to produce film, television, interactive games, virtual reality experiences, theme park attractions and live performances as interrelated "acts" in a multimediographic "superstory".

Ultimately, the fusion of production and distribution will change the very definition of "storytelling" as consumers experience multidimensional content in a multiplicity of contexts.

## Traveling Mattes: Above and Below the Waterline

Jonathan Erland
Kay Beving Erland
Composite Components Company
Los Angeles, California

### Abstract

This paper will discuss the most rapidly proliferating technology in current motion picture production: traveling matte composite photography.

The motion picture industry, and Visual Effects in particular, is undergoing a technological change unequaled since the advent of sound. The impact of computer digitization and manipulation of both sound and images has, during the last decade, profoundly altered the motion picture production process.

Probably the most dramatic impact has been felt in the field of traveling mattes, which have gone from an expensive rarity to becoming ubiquitous and relatively economical across the breadth of motion picture production. We now stand poised on the threshold of the full realization of the virtual set. Wherever a motion picture camera has been required to go in the past, a traveling matte technician must now also be prepared to go.

In the air, on land and even underwater are becoming routine venues for the demanding and complex technology of traveling matte photography. This paper will demonstrate a variety of approaches to the challenges of these new environments and describe advances in the systems for providing backings optimized for digital electronic compositing techniques.

## The Significance of Traveling Matte Cinematography in Modern Motion Pictures

Throughout the last thirty years of the technological history of filmaking, it has been increasingly difficult to overestimate the significance of traveling matte in film production. The following opening paragraphs from my 1984 S.M.P.T.E. paper[1] are illustrative:

> *Blue-Max High-Power Blue Flux Projector*
> *for Large Scale Bluescreen Composite Photography*
>
> *Jonathan Erland*
>
> *In the eight years that have elapsed since the release of the motion picture Star Wars, the compositing technique known as "bluescreen" has enjoyed a phenomenal growth. Greater sophistication in the application of this technique has, in turn, led to greater demand for it. One of those demands, heretofore difficult to meet, has now been satisfied: bluescreen on a large scale - 50' by 150' or larger.*
>
> *BACKGROUND*
>
> *The compositing process known as bluescreen had its beginnings in the work of Messrs Dunning, Pomeroy and Oliver in the late twenties and early thirties. From Dunning's use of a colored backing to distinguish the foreground from the background, through Pomeroy's five separate compositing processes, to Oliver's insightful application of the lithographic color separating process, these pioneering efforts produced a system of traveling matte photography that was to blossom into a rich tapestry of technical wizardry.*
>
> *While traveling matte photography has been in the arsenal of motion picture technology for many years, the refinements that occurred in the years since Star Wars have catapulted it into one of the most important motion picture processes extant. It has been estimated that from Star Wars through the present, motion pictures incorporating traveling matte photography have accounted for approximately $10 billion in revenues. The Academy of Motion Picture Arts and Sciences has acknowledged the importance of this aspect of film technology by granting several technical awards in connection with traveling matte processes including a Technical Achievement Award for the subject of this paper.*

When that paper was presented, there were still a number of respectable professionals who were prepared to regard this as overly strong language in support of a niche activity in the filmaking lexicon. Twelve years later, the language I used then is beginning to look fairly pedestrian, and the revenues are almost incalculable. Even at that time however, it was sufficient to galvanize Eastman Kodak into addressing the issue of traveling matte in the design of film stocks such as EK5295, and new ones still on the drawing boards will hopefully further facilitate this fascinating form of imagery.

Meanwhile, in the intervening twelve years, massive changes have come about in the way we accomplish composite images, and the Academy's recognition has been expanded to include no less than two of its highest honors, an Academy Award of Merit and a Gordon Sawyer Award, to Petro Vlahos for his pivotal contributions to this technology. (While Petro's name did not appear in the excerpt above, he figured mightily elsewhere in the paper and fully half of the references cited were from his writings.) Further, the Academy has expanded its family of Branches to include Visual Effects, for whom of course, traveling matte is the staff of life.

## Digital composites

Of course, the biggest single change in traveling matte technology in recent years has been the advent of digital compositing. The most intense developmental activity has naturally been focussed on the I/O apparatus and the software programs for manipulating the images once they have been digitized. A great deal of this work has been amply reported on in the Journal of this Society.[2 3 4 5]

## Redefining the backings

To some extent, the assumption was made that the image acquisition part of the equation—the original photography—was a fully matured part of the process requiring no further refinement. But the backing requirements for digital compositing are demonstrably different than those for photochemical composites. For example, in the days of photochemical optical composites, blue was essentially the only record available to us for motion picture work. Only the most rash and foolhardy practitioners dared attempt green screen and then only as a desperate measure. With the advent of electronic compositing systems, the whole subject of the backing screens that provided the matte field demanded redefinition.

It is a popular misconception that traveling mattes are simply sophisticated photographically derived rotoscopes, in other words, a switcher that permits either one of two images to appear at a particular place in an image. It's true that the earlier iterations of bluescreen in motion pictures and chromakey in television functioned in much that way. But mattes for the modern digital compositing process can be seen to have gradients which enables them to reproduce translucent images such as shadows or glass objects or smoke. The images, now becoming known as the Alpha channel[6], are continuous tone rather than the hi-con film mattes.

In photochemical film optical composites, this was only possible by employing very pure bluescreens exposed to a precise density and shot "clean" (meaning no garbage mattes), which permitted the use of either a very thin or even no cover matte at all in the composite. Such conditions were ordinarily extremely difficult to achieve in normal stage operations.

In Ultimatte (Vlahos) matte extraction logic, as applied to digital film composites today, the process (while still quite similar), is freed from confinement to the Blue record and readily incorporates garbage and window mattes without any compromise of the finely detailed continuous tone feature.

The starting point for a digital blue or green screen color difference composite is a matte generated by subtracting the value of one color from the value of another for each pixel in the image. (Whether this is accomplished through software or through analog video circuitry, the net effect is the same.)

With Blue logic, the raw matte is a grayscale image whose value at each point is simply the amount by which Blue exceeds the higher of the other two colors. The result is a matte which is dead black anywhere Blue is less than Red or Green and some shade of grey wherever Blue is the predominant primary color.

This matte is subjected to a variety of adjustments before it is used to process the foreground and background images, but the crucial point is that the matte is generated from the absolute levels of the color components for each pixel. A pixel having values of 200 Blue, 100 Green and 100 Red will yield a pixel with a value of 100 in the matte while a darker pixel of the same hue with values of 100 Blue, 50 Green and 50 Red will yield a matte value of 50.

In other words the Ultimatte electronic or digital color difference matting process is a function of the luminance or brightness of the backing as well as the chrominance (hue) or purity of its color and the uniformity or consistency of the matte field.

What emerges quite clearly from this description of how the Ultimatte (and other comparable matte extraction programs) work is that chrominance, (the purity of the backing color), luminance (the brightness of the backing color) and uniformity (the lowest possible variations in chroma and luminance) are all crucial to the process of creating a matte and to the subsequent composite image.

**Development of a coordinated series of traveling matte backing materials for digital composites**

A review of the existing traveling matte backing materials extant at the time of the introduction of digital compositing revealed serious inadequacies. A systematic approach was required to redress this situation.

Individual components had been addressed on an ad hoc basis, in some cases with considerable success. The contributions of Stewart Filmscreen and my own work during my tenure as Director of Research and Development at Apogee Productions, as well as that of others, have been well documented in the American Cinematographer Manual[7] and also recognized by the the Academy. What was found to be particularly lacking was a consistency among the various components available for matte backings so that, for example, painted elements could be filmed in conjunction with fabric backings with relatively little difference in chroma and luminance. Also lacking was a luminance level sufficient to ensure that shadows, now much more accessible through digital compositing, could be retained from the backing and carried into the composite scene without noise. This fundamental lack of luminance in the conventional backing materials had confounded many efforts to produce traveling mattes in daylight and other location venues, without expensive supplemental lighting.

Thus we resolved to start again from the very beginning with the goal of developing a suite of materials optimized for current motion picture negative stocks. Working outward, so to speak, from the film emulsion spectral sensitivity curves through the camera lens, we sought to target the requisite dyes and pigments that would yield the maximum actinic effect for a given quanta of illumination.

Previous work with fluorescence and phosphors gained during the development of the Reverse Bluescreen[8] process and with fluorescent lamps for traveling matte illumination indicated that these processes could be helpful. Accordingly dyes and pigments and phosphors were developed that would produce the whole panoply of backing materials: paints and fabrics, and fluorescent lamps to illuminate them. Not all of these elements were new. For example, the design for the blue fluorescent lamps was first produced at Apogee in 1986, and went into service on the film *Spaceballs,* where one thousand such lamps complete with solid state high frequency power supplies illuminated what was probably the largest front lit Tempo bluescreen till that time. What was new was that now all the spectral emmission curves were brought into much closer alignment with the spectral response curves of color film, yielding negatives with the higher color difference ratios preferred by the Ultimatte algorithm.

The physical properties of various fabrics were examined and the traditional Tempo backing material was rejected in favor of a four way stretch nylon fabric. The new fabric permitted the ability to stretch it into an aluminum frame, forming an absolutely smooth wrinkle-free surface. It is far less bulky than Tempo and can be readily laundered to maintain a high level of performance as a matting field. To facilitate both the ability to stretch into a frame and its launderabilty, this screen is not hemmed and grommetted in the conventional fashion, but is provided with garter snaps to which are attached cords for tying. This approach further provides greater flexibility, as the snaps can be relocated on the screen to adjust the size and shape for various situations.

The use of the stretch nylon fabric also facilitated various ancillary devices such as slip covers for flags and sandbags as well as cable sleeves, pipe covers, etc. Additionally, the material is the ideal choice for creating matte costumes, including gloves and hoods. The material provides an extremely smooth, lightweight form-fitting costume, permitting excellent freedom of movement.

The proliferation of traveling matte photography has required that mattes be acquired in a steadily widening range of environments. Day exterior is now commonplace, and underwater mattes are steadily gaining popularity. The nylon fabric screens perform exceedingly well underwater. The fluorescent dyes exploit the underwater phenomena by which the longer wavelengths of light are progressively absorbed during passage through water. Thus the green screen is able to absorb the predominantly blue light and transform these shorter wavelengths into the longer wavelengths of green. The corresponding red screen will effect a similar conversion, and may be employed as a means to restore some red component to underwater ambient light by deploying it as a bounce.

In yet another underwater application, these backings are provided as a segmented floating raft. The segments are provided as small hexagonal shaped pads of plastic such as polypropylene, incorporating matching dyes and pigments. When an appropriate quantity of these floats are deployed on a water surface, they conglomerate into a continuous raft and form a backing field for traveling matte filming from either above or below the waterline. Among the advantages of this approach is that the raft remains permeable to air rising to the water surface which would otherwise be trapped against a solid membrane screen and form ever larger bubbles having the optical property of mirrors and destroying the backing field. Of course, the segmented screen also permits the ready ingress and egress of people and equipment directly through the raft. The raft can also serve to either reflect light (white floats) or exclude light from the tank (black floats).

Based as they are on fluorescent dyes and pigments, these backings will illuminate under Blacklight radiation and thus lend themselves to blacklight matting processes such as Reverse Bluescreen.

While the design goal laid out for this traveling matte backing system was principally aimed at producing superior quality mattes and composite imagery, there are collateral benefits in the form of quite substantial cost savings. This stems from the significantly lower light levels required for such high luminance materials. We have reports of many cases where the backing lighting package was reduced to a third or less of the package required for conventional backings. Since the lighting package is by far the greatest expense for traveling matte shoots, the consequence is that these screens frequently save several times their own rental cost.

We feel that the degree to which the goals have now been met results in a very substantial advance for composite photography, although, of course, the process of refinement of this system is ongoing.


1. Erland, Jonathan; "Blue-Max High-Power Blue Flux Projector for Large Scale Bluescreen Composite Photography"; *SMPTE Journal*; November, 1995, Volume 94, Number 11.

2. Kennel, Glenn, Digital Film Scanning and Recording: The Technology and Practice tutorial, SMPTE Journal, 103:174, Mar. 1994

3. Kennel, Glenn, et al., Digital Moving-Picture Exchange: File Format and Calibration, SMPTE Journal, 102:712, Aug. 1993

4. Kennel, Glenn, Hunt, B. et al., High-Resolution Electronic Intermediate System for Motion-Picture Film, SMPTE Journal, 100:156, Mar. 1991

5. Kennel, Glenn, and Snider, D., Gray Scale Transformations of Digital Film Data for Display, Conversion, and Film Recording, tutorial, SMPTE Journal, 102:1109, Dec. 1993

6. Porter, Thomas, and Duff, Tom; *Computer Graphics*, July, 1984, Vol. 18, No. 3, p 254,.

7. Ryan, Rod, Ed., American Cinematographer Manual, Seventh Edition, The ASC Press, Hollywood, California, 1993, pp 430-460.

8. Erland, Jonathan; "Reverse or Negative Bluescreen Traveling Matte Process"; *SMPTE Journal*; March, 1993, Volume 92, Number 3.

# Second Generation HDTV Switcher

Vince Harradine, Alan Turner

Broadcast & Professional R&D Department
Sony Broadcast & Professional Europe
Basingstoke, Hampshire, UK

## Abstract

High definition television systems were first shown at IBC, Brighton, UK in the early eighties but have since had only limited impact in specialist areas due to the size, weight and consequential cost of high definition processing, storage and transmission.

In Japan today at least 12 hours of high definition material are broadcast per day to more than 1 million receivers using a compression technology known as multiple sub-nyquist encoding or MUSE.

There is now a growing demand with Japanese broadcasters and programme producers to capture their original material using high definition systems.

Sony is responding by introducing a new generation of high definition products. The range of products is to include studio cameras, portable cameras, studio VTRs, portable VTRs, digital multi effects and digital switchers all suitable for live, production and post production use.

## Introduction

During 1992~93 the Broadcast & Professional R&D department of Sony Broadcast & Professional Europe developed prototype hardware for a 2ME+DSK high definition (HD) digital video switcher with a specification similar to that of the 525/625 DVS-6000C product.

The video inputs and outputs of that development conformed to the SMPTE 260M standard that defines the digital representation and bit-parallel interface for 1125/60 HD production systems. Therefore, the HD digital switcher processed digital video based on the three primary signals $E_G'$, $E_B'$ and $E_R'$ that are transmitted at the 22:22:22 level of the CCIR digital hierarchy with a nominal sampling frequency of 74.25MHz and 10 bits per sample. Additionally, the standard also defines that the parallel interface uses a 93-pin connector and connecting cable consisting of 31 shielded conductor pairs.

Extensive re-use was made of ASICs originally developed for the 525/625 DVS-8000C digital switcher. These ASICs had been designed for operation nominally at 4fsc PAL (17.734MHz) and therefore the HD digital switcher processor was designed to operate with one quarter rate HD data (18.5625MHz).

Based on the above conditions the processing electronics of the prototype HD digital switcher occupied 7 x 10U chassis with more than 75 chassis to chassis video data interconnecting cables. As a product this would have really made its use prohibitive in space conscious applications such as outside broadcast vehicles.

To meet with the introduction of Sony's next generation of HD equipment suitable for live, production and post production use, the Broadcast & Professional R&D group of Sony Broadcast & Professional Europe are now developing a pre-production HD digital switcher.

The experiences gained during the previous development have been vital to achieving the primary product objectives - a 30 input 3ME HD digital switcher with a specification similar to that of the current 525/625 DVS-7000C product, but occupying just a single 15U chassis.

Extensive and innovative work at the system design phase has produced the product design that is small, low power, low cost and flexible. This has been achieved primarily in three ways:

- by using newly developed HD serial digital interface technology,
- by re-evaluating ASIC function and extending bandwidth to allow video data processing at a clock speed of 74.25MHz, and
- by developing a low power solution to the transfer of video data internally at the full HD data rate.

The focus of this paper will be on our investigation into reliable board to board communications at a data rate of 74.25Msamples/sec.

## HD Digital Switcher Key Features

- All I/O is to be HD SDI
- 30 primary inputs
- Automatic input timing
- 15 external outputs including ME 1 PGM, ME 2 PGM, PGM, PST, CLN and 10 AUX busses
- Colour black & 2 colour backgrounds (1 with wash capability)
- $YC_bC_r$ 10-bit processing (internally conforms to SMPTE 260M)
- 3ME multi-level structure
- ME re-entry
- 2 key processors per ME
- Each key processor has border, drop border, drop shadow and outline
- Key source & fill fed from primary inputs
- 1 chromakey channel per ME
- Processor amp controls for all ME backgrounds & key fills
- Mix, NAM and Super Mix modes
- 1 wipe generator per ME
- 1035/1080 active line operation
- 59.94/60Hz switchable operation
- 16:9/4:3 switchable operation
- Frame memory system
- Fully functional and assignable colour corrector
- Signal processor to occupy 1 x 15U chassis
- DME Link supported
- RS-422 editor interface

## System Input/Output

Although ratified as part of the SMPTE 260M standard, the 93-pin interconnect system for bit parallel interface of HD data has not been accepted by the limited number of HD equipment manufacturers. This is due to a number of reasons and in particular its physical size, cost and potential unreliability.

Remember the early days of CCIR-656 interconnects where the original standard defined the use of the slide/lock connection for those awful 25-way D-Sub connectors? Many installations did in fact make use of the parallel digital interface for CCIR-656 but it was not really until the advent of the serial digital interface (SDI) as defined in SMPTE 259M that digital system installations really took off in a big way.

Since 1993, the Development group of Sony's Broadcast division have been working on a HD version of the serial digital interface (HD SDI). The result of this work is a chipset suitable for the transmission of full bandwidth 10-bit luminance (Y) and colour difference ($C_bC_r$) video data over a regular coaxial cable at a data rate of 1.485Gbits/second.

The HD SDI technology is available as a 2 circuit board set, one for transmitting the other for receiving. Each of the 2 circuit boards measures 100mm x 70mm with the HD SDI connection being made via a SMA type RF connector. The parallel 74.25MHz Y and multiplexed $C_bC_r$ data is input and output via a low profile 100-pin surface mount connector.

The key enabling technology for the HD SDI is a Gallium Arsenide (GaAs) ASIC which performs the serial to parallel/parallel to serial conversion. This ASIC is housed in a 124-pin package incorporating a 3 metal fin heatsink.

This HD SDI technology is now generally available and is being used by a large number of manufacturers developing HD products for the Japanese market. Indeed all of the next generation of Sony HD products currently under development will make use of this HD SDI technology with the HD digital switcher being no exception.

As can be seen from the above feature list, the system supports up to 30 primary inputs, 15 outputs including 10 Aux outputs. This has only been made possible by using the HD SDI boards thus allowing the system to occupy only a single 15U chassis. The 2 input boards of the HD digital switcher each house 15 of the HD SDI input modules with the output board similarly housing 15 of the HD SDI output boards.

Once the input video data has been de-serialised, subsequent processing is on the 10-bit parallel data bus at 74.25Msamples/sec.

An important ASIC which has been developed for the new switcher is the so-called I/O processor. This device comprises a full HD line FIFO which can be operated in both synchronous and asynchronous modes making it suitable, for example, as the input line synchroniser. In addition, this ASIC provides all commonly required input/output processing functions such as:

- EAV/SAV detection and correction of single bit errors in the TRS word,
- FIFO write reset generated from input SAV words,
- Black and white hard and soft variable clipping,
- Hard and soft blanking insertion,
- EAV/SAV insertion,
- Delay/line delay function.

This very useful ASIC has been developed for operation at 74.25MHz using a 0.5μm technology and is housed in a 68-pin PLCC package.

## The HD System Design Challenge

When designing large digital video processing systems whose I/O conforms to, for example, CCIR-601, such a system will typically consist of a number of individual daughter printed circuit boards (PCBs) which plug into and communicate with one another using a motherboard. In a CCIR-601 based system, the processing speed of the video data will be dependent on whether processing is on demultiplexed Y and $C_bC_r$ data, in which case the speed is 13.5MHz per data path, or multiplexed $C_bYC_rY$ data, where the frequency of operation is 27MHz.

Generally such systems are designed to be synchronous with a single master clock. The master clock will drive every board in the system providing a data-only channel between cards. Subsequently, data transfers between PCBs must complete within the clock period of either 74nsec or 37nsec. Although one must be careful when designing at such speeds, issues such as propagation delays down motherboards or even extender boards (used during testing) are rarely considered. However, in designing a system to allow video data processing and board to board data communications to operate within the full HD clock period of 13.468nsec, these are factors which now have to be taken into account.

An alternative approach to data transfers is to use a completely asynchronous solution where the transmit clock is also sent with its data bus to the receiver. At the receiver the data is synchronised to the local board clock in a FIFO memory.

A major part of the new switcher system design involved investigating solutions to the problems of clock distribution and board to board data transfers. These are serious problems, considering that the majority of processing is at the full HD rate of 74.25MHz, including board to board data transfers.

## Synchronous Data Transfer Approach

Firstly, the synchronous data transfer timing will be analysed to determine the constraints placed on component choice and system design.

Next, techniques to improve operating margins will be considered and the effect on the timing of the data transfer analysed.

Finally, a comparison of Emitter Coupled Logic (ECL) and Transistor-Transistor Logic (TTL) implementations is made.

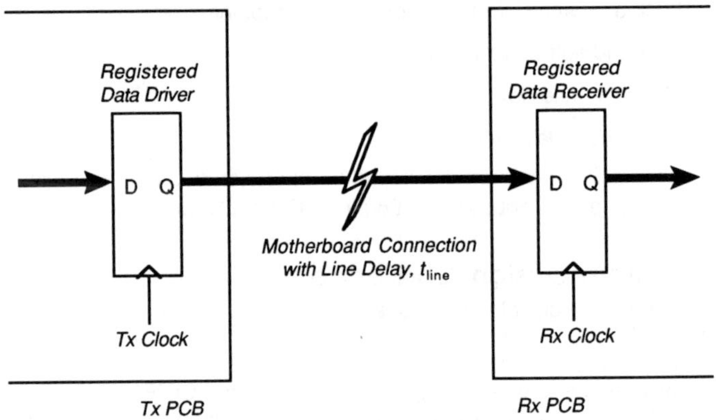


**Figure 1** **Synchronous Data Transmission Between Tx and Rx Boards Along the Motherboard**

### Basic Analysis

Clock skew and inter-board delay are the factors that ultimately set the maximum data transfer rate as both erode the fundamental clock cycle time available. Ideally there should be zero phase error between clocks across all daughter PCBs.

It is possible to optimise the clock distribution for minimum skew as we are dealing with only a few signals. However, for the data, the variation in distances between daughter PCBs means skew is unavoidable. This is not a problem provided that the transfer with the longest delay (PCBs furthest away from each other) can be completed in the cycle time. Delays are kept to a minimum by limiting this distance and using registers with low propagation delay.

The speed at which a motherboard data transmission scheme will operate is determined by:

- system clock period, $T$,
- transmit and receive device parameters; set-up time, $t_{su}$, hold time, $t_h$, clock skew, $t_{skew}$ and minimum and maximum propagation delay, $t_{pd}$,
- physical separation of the transmitting (Tx) and receiving (Rx) PCBs causing a transmission line delay, $t_{line}$, and
- other physical characteristics (such as variation in PCB dielectric constant, mechanical track tolerances, connector boundaries, etc.) largely of minor significance.

Transmit and receive clocks will be skewed creating problems in meeting both the set-up and hold time of the Rx data receiver (Figure 2 and Figure 3).

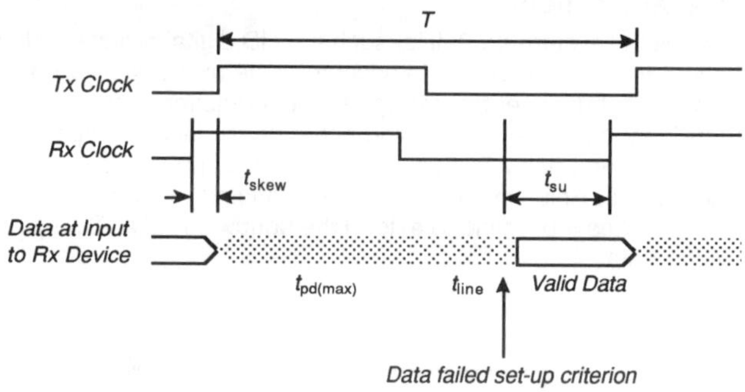


**Figure 2 Clock Skew Causes Problems Meeting Rx Device Data Set-up Time**

Referring to Figure 2 with a negative value of $t_{skew}$, data at the receiving device will meet the set-up time if:

$$T > t_{su} + t_{pd(max)} + t_{line} - t_{skew} \qquad \textit{Equation 1}$$

and, from Figure 3, it will meet the hold time if

$$t_{skew} + t_h < t_{pd(min)} + t_{line} \qquad \textit{Equation 2}$$

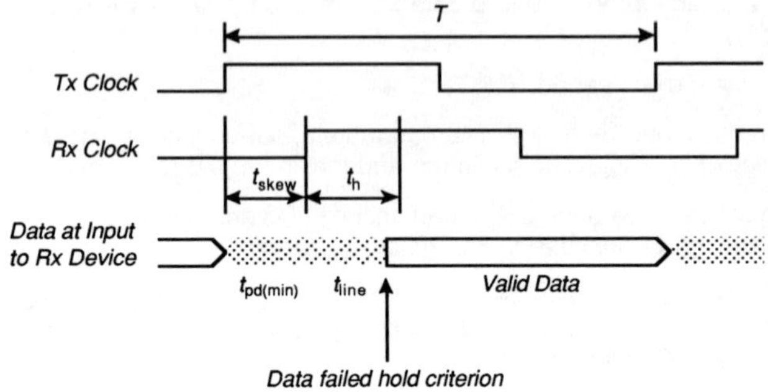


**Figure 3 Clock Skew Causes Problems Meeting Rx Device Data Hold Time**

## Clock Phase Adjustment

In a high speed digital system (>50MHz) such the HD digital switcher, clock phase adjustment may be necessary to accommodate excessively large or small line delays and thus meet the set-up and hold requirements (Figure 4). This adjustment may be achieved by using either phase locked loops with output phase adjustment, delay line devices in the clock path or possibly a combination of the two. Adjustment such as this, coupled with suitable bus interface devices makes it possible to extend the bandwidth of a TTL system to full rate HD video data.

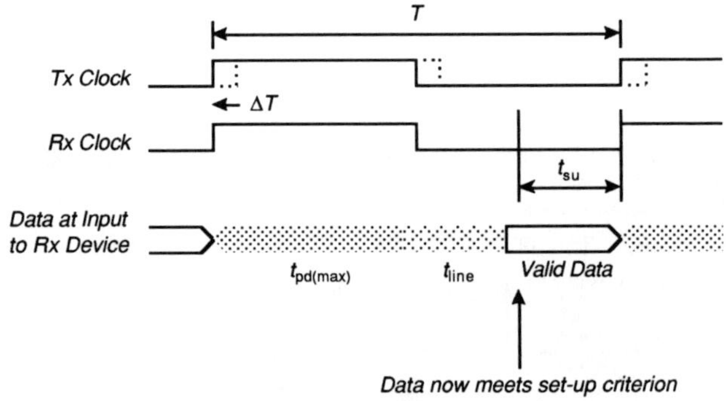


**Figure 4 Clock Phase Adjustment Helps Meet Timing Specifications**

A graphical representation of how clock phase adjustment can ease the timing constraints set out in equations 1 and 2 is shown in Figure 5. For zero clock phase adjustment ($\Delta T = 0$) successful data transfer takes place only if the line delay between Tx and Rx devices lies in the range $C2 < t_{line} < C1$. However, by retarding or advancing the transmit clock by $\Delta T$, the effect of a long, or short, line delay can be respectively reduced thus bringing the data timing into the region of operation.

$$C1 = T - t_{skew} - t_{su} - t_{pd(max)} \quad \textit{Equation 3}$$

$$C2 = t_{skew} + t_h - t_{pd(min)} \quad \textit{Equation 4}$$

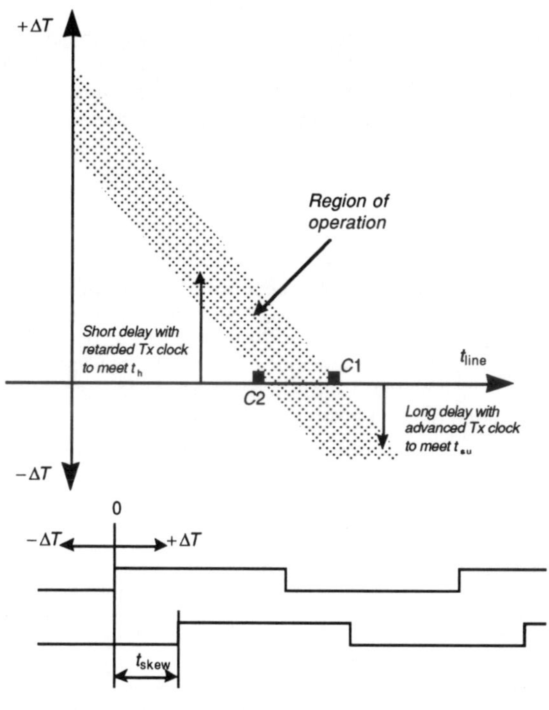


**Figure 5 Operating Region for Data Transfer Employing Clock Phase Adjustment**

## Margin of Operation

The margin of operation, (size of the operating region) can be calculated by combining equations 3 and 4:

$$Margin = C1 - C2 = T - (2 \times t_{skew}) - t_{su} - t_h - t_{pd(max)} + t_{pd(min)} \quad \textit{Equation 5}$$

if and only if the following criterion is met:

$$t_{pd(min)} < t_{skew} + t_h \quad \textit{Equation 6}$$

i.e. $C2 > 0$ in Figure 5.

If Equation 6 is not met, all Tx clocks must be advanced, regardless of transmission distance (i.e. for all values of line delay).

Whatever scheme is used for clock phase adjustment (e.g. phase locked loops, tapped delay lines, etc.), there will almost certainly be a minimum phase adjustment increment, $\Delta T_{min}$. Clearly, a compensating phase adjustment must be able to bring a non-operational data transfer into the operational region. Hence:

$$Margin > \Delta T_{min} \quad \textit{Equation 7}$$

## TTL versus ECL Implementation

Using the above analysis it is possible to compare full rate data distribution using TTL with an ECL approach to demonstrate the good reasons for choosing an advanced TTL solution. Figures 6 and 7 illustrate examples of TTL and ECL solutions to the synchronous data transfer which can be analysed using the above criterion. In addition other factors such as power consumption and PCB real estate used can be and are taken into account.

The table below shows the main results of the TTL/ECL comparison.

| Criterion | TTL | ECL |
|---|---|---|
| Interface I/O power consumption | 34mW/bit | 435mW/bit |
| Clock buffering power consumption | 124mW/clock | 158mW/clock |
| Timing margin of operation | 3.5nsec | 7nsec |
| Crosstalk (edge rate of change) | 1V/nsec | 0.8V/nsec |
| Interface I/O board area | 0.025sq. in/bit | 0.094sq. in/bit |
| Clock buffering board area | 0.105sq. in/clock | 0.131sq. in/clock |
| Interface I/O cost | $0.32/bit | $2.18/bit |
| Clock buffering I/O cost | $5.89/clock | $1.22/clock |

**Table 1 Main findings of TTL verses ECL**

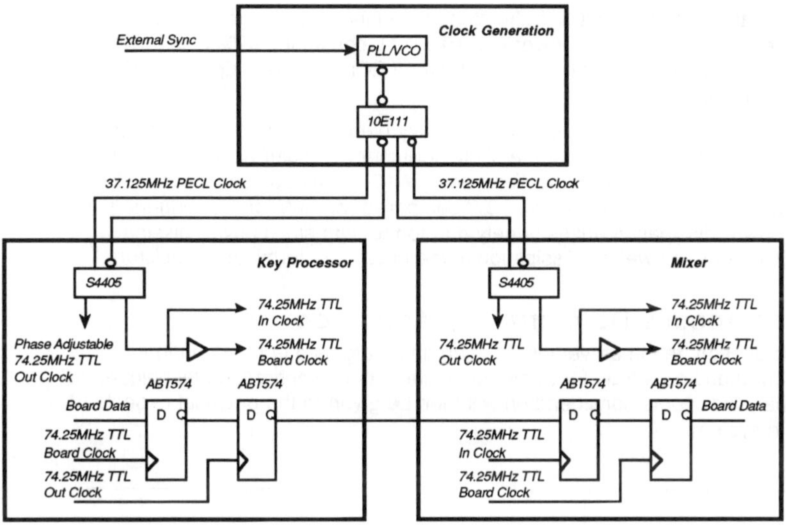


**Figure 6 Board to Board Data Transfer - The TTL Solution**

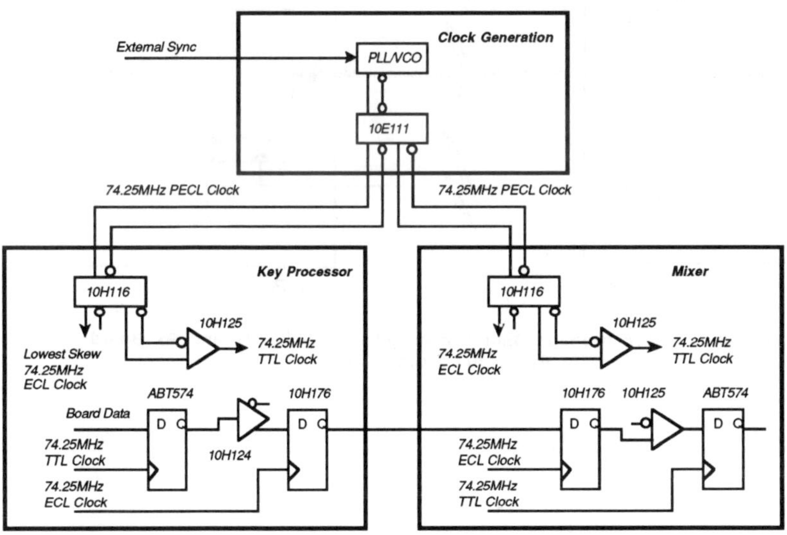


**Figure 7 Board to Board Data Transfer - The ECL Solution**

Since both solutions meet with the stringent timing criteria, the main differences between technologies are power and size. TTL consumes 92% less power in the board to board data transfer circuitry than ECL and takes up over 73% less board space.

The use of ECL components places a heavy bearing on the power dissipation of individual circuit boards. In the digital switcher the mixer board with some eleven 10-bit video bus connections and six 12-bit key bus connections, ECL data buffering will consume over 79W compared with 6W for TTL buffering. This high power dissipation arises largely due to the high static power dissipation of the ECL parts, as well as dissipation in the necessary termination resistors.

## Asynchronous Data Transfer Approach

In this section, the improvement in operating margins due to adopting an asynchronous data transfer approach, instead of a synchronous technique, will be analysed. Some consideration will then be given to the practical aspects of such a system.

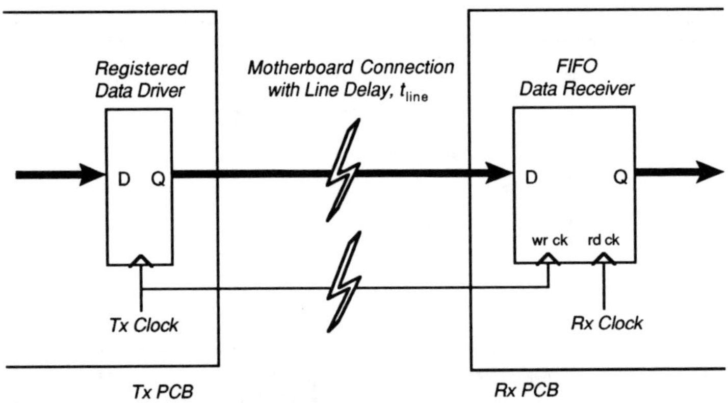


**Figure 8 Asynchronous Data Transmission Between Tx and Rx Boards Along the Motherboard**

### Basic Analysis

Using equations 1 and 2 from the basic analysis of the synchronous data transfer, it can be shown that the asynchronous approach increases the margin for set-up time, $t_{su}$, and hold time, $t_h$.

From Equation 1 as $t_{skew} = t_{line}$ then data at the receiving FIFO will meet the set-up time provided:

$$T > t_{pd(max)} + t_{su} \quad \text{Equation 8}$$

Similarly from Equation 2, as $t_{skew} = t_{line}$ then the hold time requirement at the receiving FIFO will be met if:

$$t_{pd(min)} > t_h \quad \text{Equation 9}$$

This clearly increases the margin to allow reliable data transfer by effectively removing the variables $t_{skew}$ and $t_{line}$.

### Other Considerations

- The same arguments regarding TTL versus ECL implementation equally applies to the asynchronous approach.
- The data bus together with its associated transmit clock must follow the same path on the motherboard.
- Additional overhead of requiring receive FIFO for re-synchronisation.
- Potential increase in crosstalk due to transmit clock with every data, particularly significant in the HD digital switcher.

## Conclusions

With adequate devices to satisfy the timing criteria of the synchronous approach, as would be expected TTL looks to be the best implementation when dealing with many video data buses.

However, considering the critical timing requirements, such a system is judged to be impractical to implement in mass-produced equipment. Also there would be concern over data transfer reliability during test and debug, where it is necessary to use extender boards.

Consequently an asynchronous data transfer approach has been adopted for the HD digital switcher. The advantages of this being:

- relaxed timing tolerances for board-to-board data transfer, and
- removal of the need for tight control otherwise placed on a centrally distributed clock.

## Acknowledgements

We like to particularly thank our colleagues from A/V Production Products Department No. 3 of the Image & Sound Communications Company, Sony Corporation for their invaluable assistance during this development. We would like to thank Sony Corporation for their permission to publish this paper.

# Optical Restoration of Faded 35mm Color Negative

Peter Kuran
VCE, Inc.
Sylmar, Calif.

**Abstract**

Since 1950, color negative film has become the standard on which millions of motion picture and television films have been photographed. Since the early 1970's, it has become apparent that the color negative film stock on which these images were recorded was not entirely stable and was fading with time. Digital technology is beginning to offer solutions to saving these records but will continue to be unavailable to most of these records due to cost. Optical (Photo-chemical) restoration offers a cost effective alternative to preserving many film records that may be lost by the time digital technology is affordable.

# Optical Restoration of Faded 35mm Color Negative

## History

35mm Eastman Color Negative Film 5247 was introduced in 1949. This camera film quickly replaced the Technicolor 3-strip camera system for the origination of high quality color motion pictures. Other companies have produced a Color Negative Film including Fujicolor and Agfacolor.

Unlike black-and-white negative films, early color negative films kept under even the most ideal conditions demonstrate fading of their color dyes. These color negative films, many over 40 years in age, generally exhibit strong fading. Even films produced as recently as 20 years ago can exhibit signs of fading. Also, the older intermediate films and color reversal intermediate films (CRI's) exhibit different fading characteristics, causing opticals to stand out from original negatives which may not exhibit fading.

Some studios have taken the precaution of protecting their original negative investment in the past by making Red, Green and Blue Separations.

But even under the best conditions, many separations made in the 1950's and 1960's suffer from varying amounts of white dirt, dust and scratches enhanced by optical systems before wet gate printing became possible. In addition, differential support shrinkage between the three separations can cause fringing problems when they are recombined.

## Symptoms of faded Color Negative

During prolonged storage many factors effect the dye stability of color negative films, including the composition of the original film itself, storage temperature, humidity, tightness of winding, and the original processing of the color film. The yellow dye layer is particularly vulnerable to these factors. Computer analysis of the dynamic range of a faded color negative image (Figure 1) generally shows significant loss in the yellow dye layer and to a certain extent, the magenta layer . Yellow dye loss can be as much as 75%.

Upon visual inspection of the original color negative, the film will appear to have a strong magenta cast to the emulsion. A standard LAD print from this negative will yield an overall green appearance. Creating a timed print from faded color negative will exhibit a "crossover" effect -- i.e., very blue shadows and very yellow highlights.

Trying to correct for this condition on serverly faded color negative with printing-timing changes is essentially impossible.

When one attempts to time out the yellow in the highlights, the shadow areas become even bluer and more unnatural. When one attempts to time out the blue in the shadows, the whites become even more yellow and sick looking.

**Existing Techniques of restoring color**

Other techniques in attempting to restore the color of faded color negative may yield results which range from good to unacceptable depending on the faded condition of the original.

In situations where the negative has been well kept and preserved, and depending on the subject matter, a good film timer knowledgeable in the problems of faded negative may time a new print to near perfect acceptability. This however will not work on severely faded negatives and demanding subject matter.

Making red, green and blue separations and greatly increasing the gamma of the blue record (e.g., 4X in the case of 75% dye loss) through development, while excellent in theory, often results in a very grainy blue record unusable for recombining.

If the original faded negative or best new print from this negative were telecined, current video technology is able to bring these crossover discrepancies into range, but these results are only at video resolution (less than one quarter the resolution of 35mm motion picture film) and do not address the long term solution of restoring the material back to a film master with a higher resolution.

Digital technologies have advanced the most promise to create a new negative at film resolution with good color dynamic range. But, the cost is high though, and even with the present trend of computer costs dropping, the ability to provide this technology to all faded motion picture color negatives is unlikely.

**The RCI Processes**

The RCI (or Restored Color Image) Process offers two choices of different optical (photo-chemical) processes. Each process utilizes intermediate elements generated from the original negative and then combined with the original negative to produce a matte which is then combined with an Interpositive to create a new Internegative.

The most easily reproduced process utilizes existing industry standard film processes to restore color by creating a mask which is combined with an Interpositive to create a new internegative. This process is easily implemented because of the use of existing film processes and currently available off-the-shelf stocks.

The original negative is printed to an Interpositive and an Autopositive. The Interpositive is made using Kodak LAD standards and no attempt is made to correct the color at this stage. Attempts to correct the color on the interpositive appear to reduce the success of the final image later on at the final step.

The Autopositive is generated from available film stocks (such as Kodak 5360 Direct MP) and processed in conventional D-97 processing. The image created on the Autopositive stock is very light and is used only to boost the contrast of the original color negative for the next intermediate step. This element is recombined on an optical printer with the faded original negative to create a yellowish color mask onto registered color print stock (Bell and Howell perf, .1866 pitch) such as Kodak's 5384 or 5386.

The resulting color print intermediate element is recombined on a two projector head optical printer and fit against the Interpositive to create a new internegative. Our research shows that this intermediate mask requires fine incremental adjustments for scene to scene color correction when it is being made.

Hopefully, advances in color analyzing technology will follow this process and provide a special color analyzer to meet the requirements of this new technology to make the process an extremely cost effective one.

This process however, is successful about 70% of the time depending on the contents of the scene. The results range from astonishing to mediocre; but when compared to a timed print off an extremely faded original negative, there is no question that the results are far superior for theatrical projection.

The problems of this process arise from the fact that the Autopositive stock, which provides most of the objectives required (i.e. microfine grain and a direct reversal of the image) also provides a limitation in that it is only sensitive to green and blue (hence orthochromatic). This creates the appearance of a slightly lower saturation in the green values.

Our second process is the most reliable from the standpoint of accuracy of color reproduction, but requires non-standard processing of intermediate elements for the process to work. Our research has shown that to provide the most accurate color balanced reproduction, the Autopositive would have to be sensitive only to red or be panchromatic and exposed with a red separation filter (such as a 29 or 70 red).

Since it is impossible to manufacture a film stock which is only sensitive to red (let alone an Autopositive film stock with microfine grain) the choice would have to be a panchromatic film stock which is exposed with red filtration. Current ly researched black and white stocks would add additional grain to the resulting image.

Experimentation with an Ilford black and white stock has shown the most promising results, especially since it works well with reversal processing and hence would replace the autopositive step. However, this is not a standard process and would require substantial investment of a film lab and additional work to modify a black and white film stock.

## Conclusion

The results of our process has been substantial, used primarily to fix the color of extremely faded Eastman color negative originally shot in the 1950's which was used in a recently released documentary film finished in the 35mm format. This footage was so faded that it otherwise could not have been used. This footage was also classified until recently and would never have been seen by anyone.

Even with recently enhanced awareness that motion picture color negative is fading, only a chosen few films and records will be saved using expensive, state of the art digital techniques to restore their images to near perfect reproduction at film resolution. The others, not so fortunate but equally as important, whose value is judged solely against this expense will continue to fade into obscurity and will be lost forever.

The RCI process provides the only optical (photo-chemical) technique to restore color images at film resolution at costs well below those of current digital technology and create the ability to save these records for future generations before further deterioration occurs.

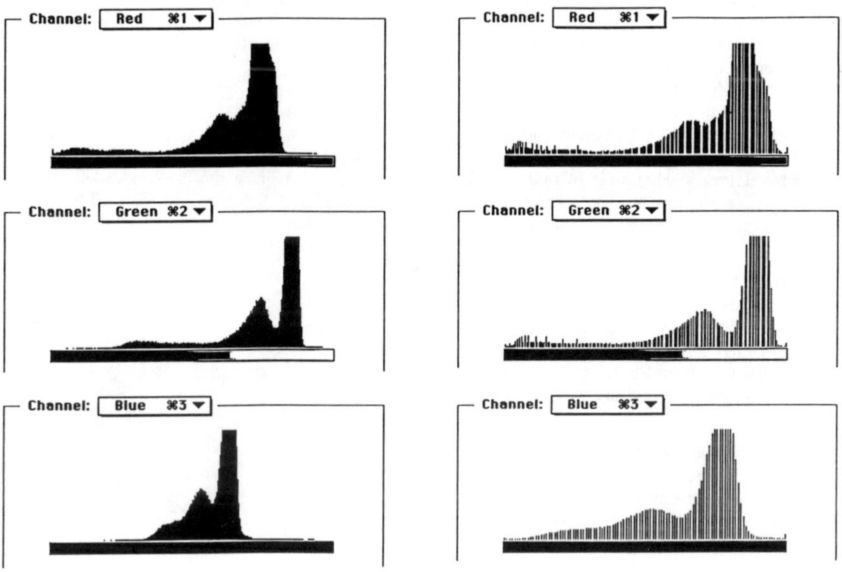


**Figure 1**. Histogram of information created by sampling a faded color negative frame scan using Photoshop (Left column). The Right column displays the corresponding histogram with the data stretched into the proper values. Each square reveals the dark to light values of the negative. The histogram shows the fading especially noticable in the Blue (yellow) channel.

# Film Storage • What's Coming?

by
Morten Jacobsen
Dancan
Denmark

## Abstract

Motion picture film has been with us for over 100 years. Very few of the original negatives from that period or for that matter any period are preserved.
35mm film is the only moving media that has kept its physical properties unchanged. A film from that time can in principle be screened to-day.
35mm film has always been stored in the tin in which the raw stock manufacturer supplied it in, nearly and in principle, yes. Tins have from time to time been changed to new ones when they were too rusty and bumbed, but basically no.

## Status Quo

This means in fact that 98% of all film is still kept in the metal tin and the condition as such is not known. Metal tends to rust even if kept under dry conditions, but has any film ever had that chance from day one?

## Storage Conditions

Film should ideally be kept at 35% RH and below 16°C for black and white and 2°C for color with good ventilation.

## Lost Film

The major enemy used to be nitrate lost in fires. That is still the case and the Henderson fire in London a few years ago proved the point. Do not work on film in the daytime and put it back in the vault in the evening! Put it in a separate safe.
The second enemy is perhaps the "Vinegar Syndrome" which is a base decay where acetic acid is released and no wonder, the film is made of it.
This will come to all acetate film sooner or later. Especially film manufactured from 1950 to 1980. Then the manufacturers started to realize they had to fight it in the laboratory.

## It is your problem

to keep control of the situation. Your vaults may smell of vinegar all over the place and you don't stand a chance of checking it on a day-to-day basis unless you begin to open your tins, that is if you can open them.

## Indicating

There are two ways of doing it. The IPI way and my way. Image Permanence Institute in Rochester have made som excellent strips called A-D Strips and referred to as film base deterioration monitors. You have to open every single can to perform this operation, twice.

## Danchek

This is my way

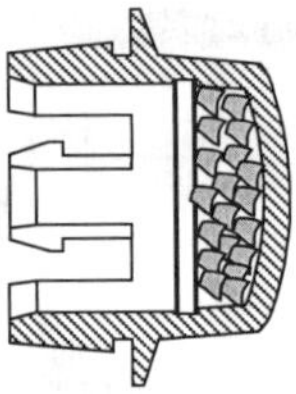

The indicator is seen from the side.
It is pretty small, actual size

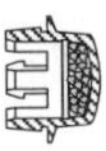

and it fits into a 11mm hole in the side of the can. The chemistry is the same as with IPI in principle, but it is time stable. It keeps it's color blue as long as the film has it's basisity intact. Once the acetic acid is released it turns over green to yellow. It is very easy to see when you walk along the iles in your vaults. By the way it is also light stable.

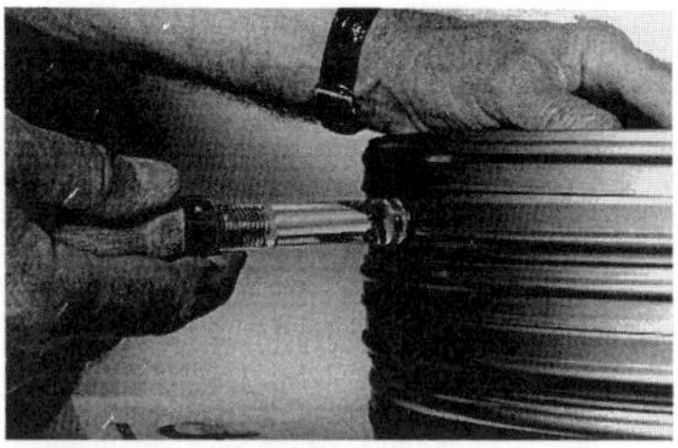

## Things in perspective

Now you can see what we are talking about, but before you can put it into the hole you have to make a hole.

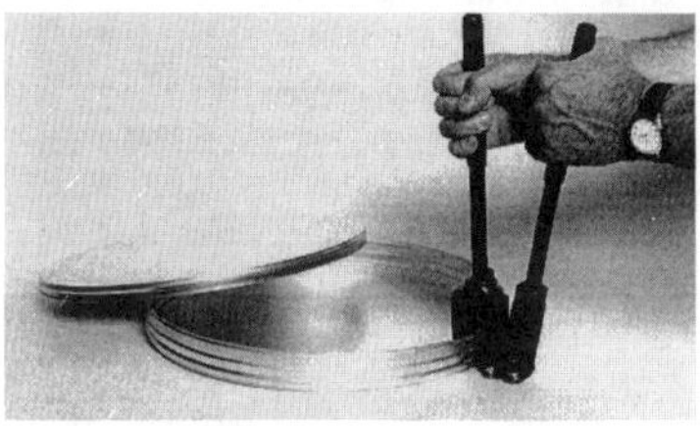

## Danlock

It is easy to punch a hole in any can with this tool and the process can be automated.

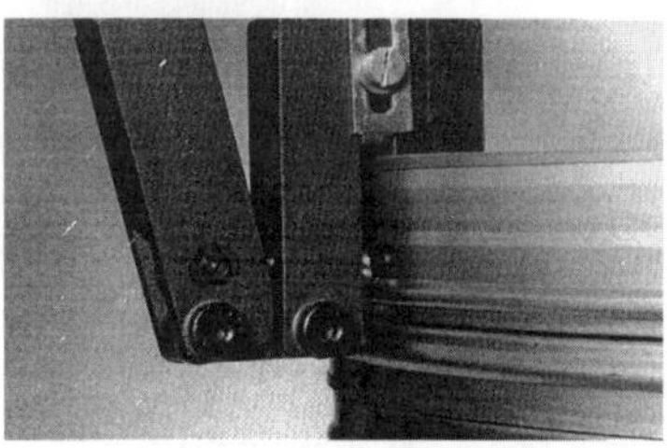

## Danchek • Acetate

Danchek is an indicator for acetate film. It shows a color shift from blue to yellow. All of the transitional green shades in between are created purely as a function of the relative proportion of the indicator in the blue state versus indicator in the yellow state.
Therefore the colors form a continuum from blue through green to yellow as the amount of acidity increases.

| | |
|---|---|
| **Level 0** | Blue indicates an acidity roughly 0,1 free acidity and below. |
| **Level 1** | Green is about 0,2. |
| **Level 2** | Green,yellow is about 0,5. |
| **Level 3** | Yellow is 1,0 and above. |

Most of the values are at or below the critical 0,5 level because at levels above 0,5 an archivist doesn't need an indicator to tell him that they have a problem. At this level the film will smell of vinegar, but it may not have any other symtoms of degradation and will be perfectly usable. Film above level 2 should be stored separately.

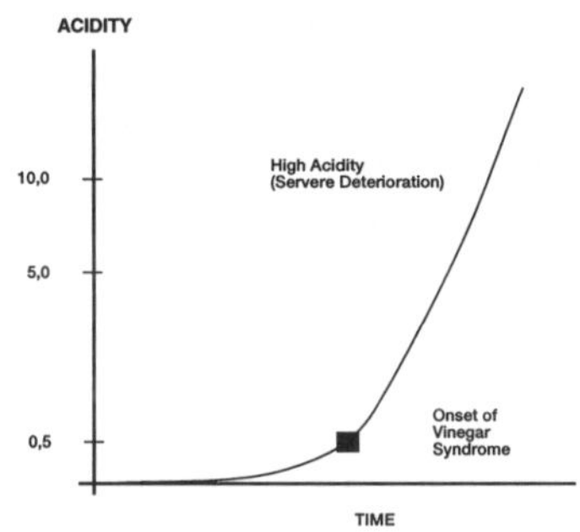



Reference:
IPI Storage Guide for Acetate film by Image Permaence Institute
Rochester. NY 14623-0887. USA.
ANSI Standard IT9.1-1992


## Danchek • Nitrate

Deteriorating nitrate film is a different ballgame. Where reaction with acetate can take place within 24 hours then this takes weeks.
The basic color is yellow and that is very confusing. However I did not make up the chemistry, I just obey the laws of mother nature.
Color shift is to red. The reading is in contrast not great but sufficient and you can completely forget the alyzerin test if you are using it and it is more sensitive. This test takes a laboratory and is labour intensive and the worst part of it, it costs you a foot of film every time you perform it.

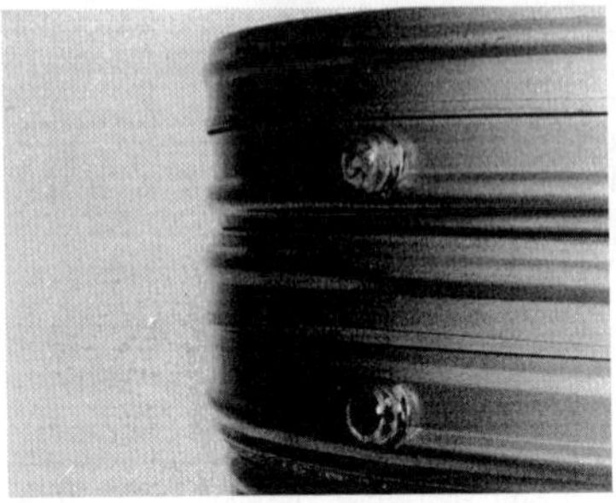

## Finale
Once Danchek is permanently on your filmcan, just walk up and down the iles of the archive and watch for Danchek.
If the color has changed – removed it for inspection and storage elsewhere.

## Storage Materials
I have for the past decade recommended filmarchives to change their storage materials to plastic.
That has been an uphill struggel.

## Plastic
Plastic film cans come all over the place, they are manufactured mainly for the purpose of feature film distribution, made to meet price and sufficient protection.
Easy to understand. Hopefully not too many reaches the archive because they are manufactured in the cheapest possible polypropylene, often recycled.
Still excellent for its purpose in film distribution. But beware Mr. Archivist!

## Dancan
has always been made to the stringest specifications in polyethylene or polypropylene. (PE or PP)

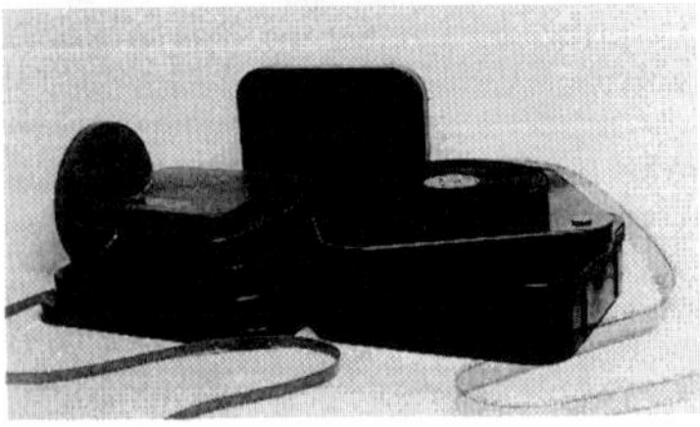

## Research
I have spent time and money in research at Manchester Metropolitan University in England, where the behaviour of plastic versus metal has been investigated and where significant improvements has been the result of it.
The techniques are wellknown in the plastic industry when escpecially outdoor usage conditions are tough.

## Additives
is the magic word to prevent the film from being degraded by the filmcan. It is still claimed that ordinary plastic releases peroxides that are more harmful to the film than metal. We add it at a cost in Dancan.

## The best of two Worlds
is perhaps back to metal, but not raw metal, only coated metal. We have chosen enviromentally safe production methods based on powder coatings specifically designed for the protection of your film.

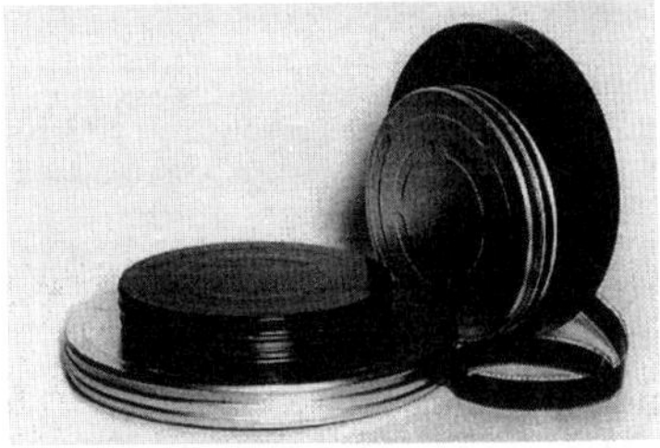

## Dancan • Metal
Advantages are that they do not burn, they don't rust and the coating prevents the metal from acting as a catalyser to the vinegar syndrome. How about that?

Thank you for your attention.

# Contrast, Color & Light in Film and Video Projection

Glenn M. Berggren
Sigma Design Group
854 Guanajuato Drive
Claremont, CA, 91711

**Purpose:** This technical paper is to further explore areas of immediate improvement of the image on the "big" screen. In this case, "Contrast, Color & Light". In addition, a transition, or crossover of these three prime factors between film projection factors, and video projection factors will be summarized. These three factors are included in a single SMPTE document, as each is intertwined with the next. For instance contrast is directly involved with color saturation, and light level is directly involved in contrast.

The core of non-home entertainment is display of moving pictures on the big screen! Although the camera negatives and intermediates have improved dramatically during the past decade, the image transfer losses in large screen projection have not kept pace. There are solutions for Contrast, Color and Light, which apply equally to film and video projection The visible image on the "big" screen has yet to be scientifically defined for optimum image quality, although SMPTE separates the screen image playback standards into four major areas as follows:

**1. Resolution** [or fine line detail of image or printing.]
**2. Light Level & Uniformity**, [before application of the feature image material]
**3. Color of white light** [before application of the feature image material]
**4. Contrast** [as a ratio of light to dark before application of the image details.]

Color & contrast investigation is an old topic for this author who provided an SMPTE paper on it 27 years ago! Factual in 1969, it's reality upset a number of film studio people. For this and related reasons, it was not offered for publication. However, it remains valid! Its conclusions have been buttressed during the passing years, with some original details having already been written into SMPTE #196-1995. This work is done with thanks to Gorton Lilgegren of Disney, Colin Mossman of DeLuxe Labs, and others in the theatre and studio arena, where tests and modifications were made.

**Curtain of Light**: The screen image for film and video is a "curtain of projection light" which has a set of characteristics as to light, colorimetry, and contrast factors. These playback characteristics in a screening room or movie theatre may or may not equal the SMPTE standards, and all too often do not. This work is done to call for support for higher standards for color, light & contrast for projection of film & video .

**Color:** The current SMPTE #196 standard includes Section #7-Spectral Distribution, which lists, in color temperature terms: 5400°K +600-200, or a range of 5200 to 6000°K, tested without film in the projector. There is a paragraph regarding precise color matching for color labs, and special screening rooms, to be done in x, y chromaticity, not color temperature, and lists the typical chromaticity readings being D5500 or $x=0.332$ and $y = 0.347$. The proposal from 1969 was almost identical, but related to the older 5400°K nominal rather than the higher nominal now in force. It is recognized that the almost universal use of xenon arc, and its associated heat filters has caused an upward drift everywhere as to color temperature so that the 5400°K is no longer valid for showing motion pictures, but is closer to the 5600 to 5900°K area for cinemas and studios with newer equipment.

The major point in color description of white light is recognition of the chromaticity chart in which the color temperature curve is shown. In general terms, the x factor relates to color temperature, but the y factor is the green-to-magenta axis which color temperature does not recognize, so it is missing in the color temperature specification. It is possible to have an 'acceptable' color temperature reading with green at an erroneous level. Defective coatings can and have caused this problem. It becomes even more serious in video projection. The use of Color Temperature in this industry is antique, and it should be abandoned in favor of chromaticity readings, especially in studio screening rooms and color labs, plus the setting of standards.

The color temperature measurement is rooted in physics. It's measurement assumes a radiant solid, such as a metallic filament, which is the "black-body" described by Kelvin, but which, in fact, does not exist in the use carbon or xenon arcs! As pointed out in 1969, and demonstrated with newly designed equipment, both then and now, the actual color of white light for film is not on the black body line, and never has been with either xenon arc or carbon arc light sources using modern lens and mirror coatings. It is commonly above the "black-body" line into the green zone, which is where most color mismatches arise in color labs and similar special inspection locations; and also in movie theatres.

**Color matching:** The color labs have the challenge of conducting color matching and approvals for customers, using at least two projectors which are different. During 1995, at DeLuxe Labs, it was found that not only could the mirrors, coatings and lenses be swapped to achieve exact color temperature, but that with only a little extra work, the x, y chromaticity figures could become identical, for the same format on two different projectors in a screening room. At that point, the well-trained eyes of the color timers could no longer see differences in the "curtain of white light". Their eyes agreed with the chromaticity meter, in this case a CS-100 Minolta. Both DeLuxe and Technicolor already own and use the CS-100 instrument for x, y readings.

**Color in Video:** The use of color temperature for projection video becomes almost useless, because there are three separate light and color sources, whether three-gun, or single lens, or liquid crystal types. Without x, y chromaticity readings from the screen, the separate color readings can be anything! A seemingly OK color temperature can be obtained with the green source off. In larger video situations, there are often two stacked units, and if one takes readings for chromaticity or color temperature across the width of the screen, the fact that the three "guns" have an RGB color-tube location can be read in the color figure differences. Video projection often uses gain screens, in some cases much higher than 1.5, and if so, the color variation can become a problem from left to right. One solution is to have the stacked unit have the tubes reversed, RGB above and BGR below, so that they compensate for each other, providing uniform white light color across the screen. For projection video, the color and chromaticity specifications for public viewing should be the same as for film, regardless of the fact that the usual TV sets and monitors seem to be aimed toward D6500 which has a higher "blue" content. For feature film viewing in the future Electronic Cinema, using D6500 would be an error, and there should be a film industry review of actual studio and first run locations to determine the optimum x, y values, and those same standards be applied to Electronic Cinema!

**Color Summary:** The film and video industries should abandon color temperature, totally, as an antique and mostly mis-leading color measurement, not much better than semi-trained eyes. The

SMPTE specifications should be changed from the 5200 to 6000°K range to a similar, but much more accurate chromaticity nominal of x= 0.332, with y = 0.347, [but subject to further analysis]. The color readings should be taken at three points across the horizontal center line, and three on the vertical centerline of the screen. In the future, we can measuring color saturation in a repeatable way, but the present holds the possibility of improved color accuracy on the screen, and precise color matching at the color labs and studio screening rooms.

**CONTRAST:** The topic has been studiously ignored over the years, but the arrival in 1978 of multi-coated projection lenses in matched groups improved the projection part of getting the image to the screen. Multi-coating permitted more light through the lens, [perhaps 99+% rather than 82%] so that stray light in the lens was reduced by a factor of ten. Thus the darkest area of a screen image, perhaps a black shadow could actually be darker than with the previously utilized Kollmorgen or Bausch & Lomb lenses. If the whitest part were the same, and the darkest part were darker, then the overall contrast ratio potential was expanded, and it could be seen.

**Contrast Ratio:** The usual tests for contrast ratio in a projection system, including auditorium stray light is based on the work in the 1950's by Ray Estes of Kodak. The concept is an irregular black & white pattern with places to take readings. Of course, the lightest readings might be in the 8 to 30 foot-Lamberts range, so the usual Screen Brightness meter of the 1° type can be used, however, for the darkest reading, a meter is required that can read reliably in the 0.010 foot-Lamberts region. The meter previously mentioned, the Minolta CS-100 can do exactly this, and contrast readings were taken in places where color measurements were taken.

For example, if blank film is installed in a projector previously providing 16 foot-Lamberts on the screen, the remaining light level would be in the 10 to 11 foot-Lamberts region, which would be the highest light level possibly seen in an actual outdoor-scene, perhaps very white clouds. The darkest area on the screen includes the density of the film, [perhaps 2.8], plus the scatter remaining in the newest lenses, the scatter in the port window, and the collected ambient light on the screen. If the white light with blank film is 10 foot-Lamberts, and the darkest spot on the screen, all things in the running mode is 0.010, then the contrast ratio is 10/ 0.01 = 1000 to 1, which would be excellent, but rare even in Hollywood.

The dark reading is based on several controllable factors, including whether the port window is coated, whether the projection lenses are multi-coated, whether the xenon system is designed and aligned properly, and the gain & shape of the screen. the gain of the screen becomes a major factor, because it can reject the ambient light of the auditorium. With the numerous government regulations, there is some light in the auditorium for safety purposes, much of which can damage the contrast of the scene on the screen. If the screen is very low gain and flat, then any ambient light can and will reduce contrast ratio. However, if the screen is properly curved or compound curved to focus the projected light at the audience, then lights of exits or overhead safety lighting at the sidewalls will not be reflected from the screen, but "bounced" to some remote auditorium location.

**Video Projection:** When the light-starved HDTV projection system are utilized for public viewing, the screen size can dictate that a much higher screen gain be used, perhaps between 2 and 3. For example, the SONY High Definition Screening Room in Culver City has a compound curved high gain [3] screen of a metallic surface, and with updated contrast measuring patterns, the contrast ratio was 600 to 1, with the double stack set on the pattern having a center white or black hole and segmented at the sides. The white was just over 10, and the black was between 0.01 and

0.02. The usual concept that projection video is between 75 and 150 is simply false, as proven by John Galt of SONY. It was also found that a high gain white was inferior to a high gain metallic. With the high gain metallic, it was found that the screen image looked quite well with all auditorium lights on, while in other locations, the house lights on simply destroyed the picture.

**The Pattern:** In conjunction with several film and video specialists, a black and white pattern was created, of a 9 by 5 square pattern, with white corners, and alternate white and dark squares all around the perimeter, with a large black area on each side of the center, and a single white square in the center in which to take a reading. The comparison was completed by the white center reading with corners to assure that uniformity were present, still with either film or video, the overall area was about 60% dark, yet with sufficient light at the perimeter to test the corner light and the lens contrast factors at the same time. For video, the center white square is compared to each side black area. For film, the center white square is compared vs. an opaque light barrier, either in the gate, or before the port window, to test the center darkness, to obtain the optimum ratio.

With the latest of film emulsions, and the latest of projection lenses, with multi-coating, all other contrast factors, can be controlled, as follows:

**1. Port Window coated with anti-reflection coatings**--this is more important to the screen image than whether it is optical glass, the favorite of the studios.

**2. Xenon Lamphouse Design & Alignment:** The mis-alignment of the lamphouse mirror to the lens optical axis can cause stray light, and contrast reduction. Having a xenon mirror of excessive f/number as compared to the lens f/number can create excess stray light in the lens, which further reduces the contrast ratio. This was proven in the variety of tests and modifications at DeLuxe Labs in 1995.

**3. Screen Gain & Shape:** With the very low gain and flat screen apparently the worst, the proper selection of screen gain and curvature of the screen becomes quite important to preserve screen image contrast ratio. This has been proven in tests with AMC cinemas, where this has been given increasing attention during the past 10 years.

**4. The availability of sufficient light:** The practice of utilizing insufficient light in a screening room or more-so in a public cinema destroys the original contrast ratio of the scene created by the Director and Cinematographer. The opposite has been proven by AMC cinemas, where many auditoriums function with 18 to 20 foot-lamberts, with excellent control of auditorium lights to yield excellent color saturation, excellent contrast ratios, and overall screen images equal or superior to studio screening rooms, for the same film reel. Those cinemas who choose to utilize screen light levels of 5 to 10 foot-Lamberts can not possibly achieve the existing SMPTE contrast ratio of 400 to 1 minimum (par. 10 in #196), and 600 to 1 for better theatres and screening rooms.

In summary, there are no mysteries in the color, light and contrast region, only the refusal to change obsolete thinking so that the best of the film image can be seen in studios and cinemas. Because the most important factors have already been proven, there is little reason not to adopt the final tests and specifications for color, contrast and light values for this growing industry, and apply they equally to Projection Video.

# Implementing Server-Based Systems in the Broadcast Environment

Lionel Hightower
Avid Integrated Solutions
Avid Technology, Inc.
Tewksbury, Massachusetts

## Abstract

This presentation will focus on the practical considerations of implementing a server in a broadcast facility. Beyond the selection process of the hardware and software involved, a successful installation and operation of a server-based solution involves a number of factors to be taken into consideration. A discussion of these factors and a real-world case study will be presented as illustration.

Broadcasters moving into the server-based production and playback arena also need to be cognizant of the impact a server will have on the daily operation of their facility. Usually there is an impact on the way work is accomplished, primarily to take advantage of the new capabilities that a disk-based server offers to the broadcast facility. A reevaluation of job functions and work flow is usually an integral part of the planning process prior to a server implementation. This presentation will offer a framework for this process, as well as offering a case study for examination.

## Introduction

### *Today's Broadcast Environment*

Broadcasters today find themselves at a significant technical crossroads: the transition from videotape to hard disk-based infrastructures. Paradigms that have been deeply ingrained in the broadcast industry over the last 40 years are now suddenly nonapplicable to implementations of hard disk server/client models for capture, edit, and playback. Installation, training, and maintenance issues involved are all new and unfamiliar. Even the fundamental business issues underlying the justification of the jump to server-based systems are new and different from the usual issues that presented themselves in the videotape format change period of the last two decades. The convergence of the broadcast and computer industries produced server/client based systems for broadcasters. A successful implementation and operation of a server-based infrastructure in a broadcast facility requires that Broadcasters familiarize themselves with computer and network technologies that formerly were completely within the computer information systems realm.

### *Broadcast Model Vs Computer Model*

Broadcasters comfortable with 8281 video cable, 75 ohm terminations, and VTRs are now examining systems that involve hard disks, Local Area Networks, multiple operating systems and hardware platforms. Computer technologies providing word processing, E-Mail, and spreadsheets are now at the heart of the on air broadcast infrastructure. Technology leveraged by the consumer and corporate computer markets now is intimately involved in the bread and butter tasks in television facilities across the world.

## Business Considerations

### *Evaluation Process*

Beyond the technical and operational issues involved in choosing a server system, how does one build a convincing business justification for a large outlay to acquire this new technology? What are the expected cost savings and what is the total cost of ownership over its expected lifetime?

An evaluation for acquiring a server-based system is based on a complex multivariate equation that varies from broadcast facility to broadcast facility. There are many factors to consider, some easy to quantify and some more difficult to gauge.

The process used to evaluate the acquisition of a server-based system should include consideration of the following aspects:

### *Cost Reductions*

Elimination of some number of VTRs will result in the reduction of tape stock and the replacement costs (both parts cost and maintenance effort) of heads, pinch rollers, guides and other mechanical subsystems.

### *Productivity/Efficiency Gains*

Servers offer the opportunity to accomplish "more with less." Numerous server sites have taken advantage of the ease of nonlinear editing to create a multitasking environment that allows personnel to change duties depending on the workload and time of day. Additionally, nonlinear editing in the server environment allows multiple versions of stories to be quickly and easily created, as well as last minute changes accommodated without a complete re-edit session.

### *Functionality/Competitive Advantage Issues*

Because server-based systems can easily multiversion, re-edit at the last minute, and allow more to be done with less, a value should be attributed to the competitive advantage that this provides the broadcast facility. Although difficult to quantify, there is value that needs to be included in the overall equipment acquisition formula.

### *Acquisition Costs*

Server system solutions will provide new operational functionality, introduce large amounts of new computer systems and software into the facility, and require ongoing upgrades. Because of these factors, you must consider a number beyond just the actual hardware costs. Budgeting for the installation of the system (including local area networks), training for large numbers of operations and maintenance personnel, and long-term software maintenance agreements must be planned and budgeted if a successful implementation is to occur.

Once these factors are assigned a weighting, a comparison of the alternatives available to a broadcast facility can be accomplished. Obviously, other internal station factors such as the position on the replacement cycle of the majority of the stations hardware, outside competitive pressures, and new service/station launch timeframes contribute to the overall decision equation.

## Technical Considerations

### *Power*

Servers and disk drives require large amounts of power, especially during initial powerup. Many systems require three phase power at 220v or higher. Uninterruptable Power Supplies are highly recommended. Restart times from a power loss are not instantaneous. Additionally most operating systems used in servers, such as UNIX, require an orderly shutdown for disk file management. A hard shutdown may require a rebuild of the disk files system on restart, causing major delays before the system is operational.

### *Space*

A suitable space that is large enough to long term expansion of storage will be required for a server installation. Because of the networking connections involved, close proximity to the client systems will minimize network cable connections and will facilitate troubleshooting. Because of the multi-user environment that a server will required to support, physical access to the server may be a concern.

### *HVAC*

Computer equipment typically requires large amounts of air to stay at a safe operating temperature. Large numbers of internal cooling fans typically are used to facilitate air flow through the various system components. Disk drives will require a relatively clean environment to operate without excessive failure rates.

### *Station Interface*

A server system will provide audio, video, and control "ports" that will connect to the rest of the broadcast facility to interface with routers, automation systems, etc. At what point is the facility in the transition to a digital infrastructure? Should the server system I/O be analog or digital? What is expected from the automation control and what changes need to occur to take advantage of new capabilities?

## Organizational Considerations

### *Cross Departmental Responsibilities*

Because server systems are comprised of computer components and networking, there may be a need to draw expertise from the MIS side of the broadcast facility if computer expertise does not reside in the Broadcast Engineering group. Networking, client/server trouble shooting, and data maintenance are areas that the MIS staff has considerable experience.

## Human Resource Considerations

### *Training*

Introduction of a server-based system or any new major system will require a carefully planned training program to assure a smooth transition and to maximize the new capabilities offered by the system.

Because of the multitasking opportunities, many sites have trained the majority of the staff on all client systems, resulting in a complex training scheduling scenario. For both start-up operations and transition facilities, this is a problem that takes many by surprise.

For maximum utilization of the training sessions, experience has shown that grouping classes into various levels of experience and computer skills is highly desirable. Students with no computer skills should not be grouped in a class with experienced editors with nonlinear experience, for example.

### *Personnel*

Because server-based systems are computer based, it would be tempting to assume that perfect candidates for a start-up server-based facility would be those with advanced computer skills. However, editing requires effective story-telling skills rather than pure mechanical technical proficiency. Experience has shown that experienced editors, producers, and reporters who have the ability to tell a story in an interesting way can learn nonlinear editing easily and become very productive quickly. Facilities have found that it easier to teach nonlinear editing than to teach the journalistic ability to communicate a story to the audience.

## Operational Considerations

### *Workflow*

Because of the management services required by server-based production systems, new roles are being created in the broadcast environment. Two important ones are the *Media Managers* and *Systems Administrators*. Media Managers control the recording of media to the server and deletion of media from the server and Systems Administrators keep the clients, servers, and network maintained. The coordination of these roles requires a new level of integration between engineering and computer services or requires that the engineering department take on the role of systems administration. In the most successful implementations, these two groups work closely to define training requirements, resource allocation, and workflow definition.

If we look at the broadcast information and resource flow we get to a model that begins to look much like a assembly line:

- <u>Acquisition:</u> Video tape capture, record to server or client, add catalogue data (name conventions)
- <u>Production:</u> Editing, nonlinear access to all resources data and video, production management
- <u>Transmission:</u> Processes taken from edit decisions, production management with automation

The workflow is the relationship between all of these procedures, as well as the coordination between human and technical resources. To begin implementation of a server-based system it is important that you understand the strengths and weaknesses of your current workflow and can identify which operations compliment performance and which are hindrances. It is also important to recognize that no two installations will benefit from the exact same workflow. While many operating processes can be shared between similar operations, just as many procedures and naming conventions will be unique from site to site. The operational flow in an affiliate creating one hour of original newscasts a day in a "wheel format," for example, will be dramatically different from a station that is primarily repurposing feeds.

The process of defining workflows for a server-based environment will also depend on whether the site is a new facility or a transitioning newsroom. New facilities have no established processes and a totally new staff. On the down side, that means there are no existing procedures from which to build the optimal workflow. On the upside, however, pre-air date rehearsals afford ample opportunity to fully refine new procedures.

In the transition site, you will find existing processes and workflows from which to build. The challenge there, however, is freeing people for training and migrating to the new working procedures without affecting current transmission.

Although this paper does not cover the elements of a successful training program in detail, it is worth noting the general three stage plan used at most Avid sites:

1. Nonlinear editing training on the stand-alone client
2. General training on the basics of server technology
3. Site-specific training, such as naming conventions and workflow

Stage three training comes only after in-depth research and workflow analysis so that operators can be trained on their very specific procedures.

## Case Study

Given a basic understanding of the importance of workflow in the server-based environment, we can now examine two different types of implementations: a cable news operation and a network affiliate.

### Server-Based Technology Applied to Repurposing of Feeds Model

The repurposing broadcast model is one in which a network location receives edited material via satellite or fiber line from numerous bureaus. The finished material may or may not be mixed with live or locally-produced pieces. In this model, the following flow is generally used:

1. Feeds are recorded directly to the central storage library
2. The server processes requests and manages access to central storage
3. Nonlinear editors are used for editing locally-produced pieces and finishing fed pieces
4. A playback client plays back material directly from the central storage
5. A newsroom computer system is used for scripting and program management

In one server site, the following roles and responsibilities have emerged:

1. Producers and their staff edit their own material on the nonlinear editors
2. Feeds technicians, primarily union personnel, handle all tapes and feeds and quality control
3. Directors operate the playback clients
4. Editorial staff members manage the media and operate as a liaison between the other three user groups

Using the assembly line model described above, the following workflow for this repurposing application has emerged.

#### *Acquisition*

Producers scan tape and feed logs to find available media, which is fed via a dedicated fiber link. Regularly-scheduled network feeds, the majority of which are pre-edited, are recorded to disk. They are also recorded to tape at the same time. This provides a backup in case of a server failure, as well as an additional copy should both record clients be in use and unable to take the feed. Incoming tapes are screened and given to the "Feed Technicians" for digitizing.

The feeds staff records to one of two server-based "bins" named for the record client and the date, for example "MR1 3/4/96". (On all Avid systems, a bin is an organizational device somewhat like a folder in the Macintosh software user interface or a directory in the Windows interface.) These two bins function as a repository for all of the raw media. There are two individual bins so the record clients can operate independently of the server. The date allows the Media Manager to clearly identify outdated media. The media is named according to a three-field naming convention. The first field is the story slug/topic, the second is the reporter name, and the third identifies the type of media (package, voice-over, or soundbite). Examples would be "ibm.pilgrim.pkg," "ford.exterior.vo," "economy.brusca.sot."

## *Production*

*Reading In/Reading Wires*
Producers look for most of their information from feeds and locally-produced material in the newsroom computer system. This system contains queues where producers can see tape logs, feed logs, and scripts. Producers submit requests to the Media Managers, who then make the media available.

*Writing Scripts*
Producers put their rundowns together and write scripts on the newsroom computer system. The scripts can be called up on the TelePrompTer in the control room.

*Editing Feed Material*
In the repurposing model, most of the feed material is complete requiring only the countdown at the beginning and, possibly, the trimming of extraneous material from the end. Media management staff trim most of the elements and put them in a daily archive. Producers can then pull air-ready elements from the archive rather than recutting the same material again.

Each show has its own Playback client bin containing elements for air. Producers are responsible for assigning individual ID numbers. The ID numbers contain a three-letter show abbreviation, one-letter element abbreviation ("P" for package, "V" for voice over, "S" for sound on tape), and 4-number unique ID number. The ID number is entered into a field in the rundown to create a correlation between media on the server and the script on the newsroom computer system.

*Graphics*
All graphics systems operate independently of the nonlinear editing systems. A graphic identifier is entered into a field on the rundown in the newsroom computer system. Titles (lower thirds) that are needed on an edited item are produced on the final output (transmission) by sending the graphic identifier to a character generator where they are superimposed by a video switcher to air.

*Creating a Rundown on the NewsRoom Automation System*
When scripts have been written and the producers are ready to construct the show they build their own rundowns. The rundowns contain command information for: the character generator, the AirPlays, the TelePrompTer, and the Still Store.

## *Transmission*

Once all the production work has been completed, the Director loads both the playback clients with media located on the server. Once the media is on both playback clients, the director can set them up to immediately produce an effects transition between two elements.

## *Archiving the Media/Media Management*

All media is saved for 48 hours. After that, producers can put anything they would like to save for a longer period in an "HFR" (hold-for-release) bin. Each producer is allocated 30 minutes. There is also a bin that holds the regularly used elements like opens and closes, which is never deleted. Everything else is manually deleted from one of the nonlinear editing systems.

As the shows are airing, they are recorded to digital tape. Presently, these airchecks are recycled in a 30-day cycle. The individual tapes of all the feeds are kept for 48 hours at which point they are recycled.

## Server-Based Technology Applied to the Affiliate Mode

Another server-based example is an affiliate station that creates 2.5 hours of news a day. The news team uses a fairly typical format for the news shows creating programming from a combination of edited feeds, live microwave links, locally-produced items, and the news studio.

The major groups of users within this affiliate include:

1. Video Journalists who shoot stories and edit on the nonlinear editing systems
2. Editors who cut up-to-the-minute news, bumps, donuts, and trails
3. Producers who are in charge of the show production and building rundowns
4. Directors who operate the playback clients
5. Media Manager who maintains the media on server

While the affiliate workflow is different the repurposing feeds model, it can be viewed in the same four assembly line stages:

### *Acquisition*

Ten video journalists shoot, write, and edit local stories. Approximately five hours of news feeds and one hour of sports are recorded daily. First they are recorded to tape for backup and archiving and then items that are to be used in transmission are digitized to the server. Some breaking news items are recorded directly, but the majority is via tape-on-its way. Only items to be used are digitized into the server.

### *Production*

*Reading In/Reading Wires/Writing scripts*
The news producers are able to read AP and other news wires on their newsroom computer system. They are also able to review and compose scripts for air. This material is transferred to the TelePrompTer for the anchors to read.

*Editing Feed Material*
From the six hours that feed the station each day, producers choose which items they wish to select for transmission. The material is then edited as air-ready items (voice-overs and packages) on the nonlinear editing system. When an item is completed, it is assigned a unique ID number. This is entered into a field on both the NewsCutter and the newsroom computer system.

*Editing Field Acquired Material*
Material shot by the VJ (video journalists) is digitized to the local drives on the nonlinear editing system and then consolidated to the server. The consolidation process copies only the parts of the source material that are required for the edited item. In this process up to 70 percent of the source material can be discarded and only the valuable 30 percent transmission media need remain on the server.

*Promo Material*
An high-end post-production nonlinear editing system is used to edit any material that requires more "post production," such as promotional material or title sequences.

*Graphics*
All the graphics systems operate independently of the nonlinear editing system. A graphic identifier is entered into a field on the newsroom computer system rundown. Titles (lower third) that are needed on an edited item are produced on the final output transmission by sending a graphic identifier to a character generator and then superimposing the graphic by video switcher to air.

*Creating a Rundown*
When scripts have been written and the producers are ready to construct their show they build a rundown. Rundowns contain command information for the character generator, playback clients, TelePrompTer and the DVE.

*Transmission*

Once all the production work has been completed, the Director is able to select the required items located from their ID numbers as referred to in the rundown. With the media on both playback clients, the Director can transfer immediately between two items (AB roll). The Director rescans the rundown for any late additions. Occasionally, some items are introduced so late in the production process that they are played out directly to air from the nonlinear editing system. On average, between 20-40 items are played out of the server per half hour newscast.

*Archiving*

Feed recordings and field-acquired material are reused depending on their content. If these tapes and recordings contain long-term newsworthy material it is then archived in the library for later use. Media is usually kept on the server for a three-day period. Individual items that are used in the newscast are compiled on a nonlinear editor and archived to tape. These tapes are made with split track audio and without graphics, so they can be used with re-editing, if required at a later date. Air check masters are kept of transmitted newscasts.

## Summary

The advantages of shared media and immediate playback access require consistency in the area of naming conventions and structure in the area of data management. Because of full shared media access, users need to know on a newsroom-wide basis where items are located and how they are named. An additional advantage of the server environment is the ability to create multiple versions of the same media. This also requires planning to locate which edited version needs to be aired.

Since the inception of ENG taped based news acquisition, the operational model has been well institutionalized by the broadcaster. Server-based news production offers operational improvements, however, it requires some change in the familiar workflow model. The new model generated by this technology is no more difficult to implement, only a different approach.

Successful implementation of a server-based system requires careful consideration of more just than the obvious technical considerations. Because of the sweeping changes to workflow, job responsibilities, and exciting new capabilities, the entire organization will be effected and this change must be managed.

The move to computer-based solutions is a major, yet exciting, transition. Broadcasters who adapt quickly will give their organization a edge in today's highly competitive marketplace.

# A Studio Compression Format for HDTV Applications

**Mahesh Balakrishnan, Kiran Challapali, Hayder Radha**
**Philips Research, Briarcliff Manor, NY 10510**

**ABSTRACT**

This paper presents a video compression format for HDTV video to be used in studio applications. Digital HDTV signals need to be compressed in order to be routed or stored within a studio. The bitrates targeted support the use of viable networking technologies such as SMPTE-259 and OC-3. The requirements of a studio are considered in the choice of the format. These requirements include excellent picture quality, good quality even in the presence of cascaded coding, adequate sampling of the chroma signal, support for studio operations such as chroma-keying, and frame or field accurate editing. We will also examine techniques for switching between highly compressed video signals, a requirement in the studio, both for production purposes and for transitioning between programs or commercials.

**Keywords:** HDTV, studio, compression, splicing, switching, editing, MPEG, 422 profile, cascaded, multi-generation, ATV

## 1.0 Introduction

The process of establishing a standard in the United States for the transmission of digital high-definition television (HDTV) is nearing completion. In Europe, the Digital Video Broadcasting (DVB) specifications provide a standard for the broadcast of digital video over satellite and cable. In order to enable broadcasters to utilize digital transmission of compressed video, it is essential that television studios be capable of generating, storing and processing compressed video. This paper is based on work done in the authors' organization and is part of a bigger cross-industry program involving multiple companies. The goal of this US government funded multi-company program is to develop the technology necessary for a digital studio supporting digital television broadcast. This consortium of companies is known as the Digital Studio Alliance.

In Section 2 of this paper we will examine some of the challenges inherent in using compressed video in a studio. We will also discuss the reasons why compression is necessary in a production environment. In section 3, the choice of a compression format for use in a studio is discussed. In section 4, we look at the issues behind switching compressed video and presents possible solutions. The conclusions are given in Section 5.

One of the goals of the Digital Studio Alliance project is to use ATM technology as the switching fabric in the intra-studio network. This will allow all of the kinds of data that need to be transported within the studio, namely, video, audio, speech, text and auxiliary data to be carried within the same pipe. As we shall see later in this paper, this has ramifications on the choice of certain parameters in the studio video compression system.

# 2.0 Compression in the Studio

## 2.1 Need for Compression

Uncompressed HDTV is at a data rate of over 1 Gbps. If all of the video processing within the studio were done at these rates, it would imply that all studio devices would connect to the intra-studio network at over 1 Gbps. This would preclude the use of either OC-3 (155 Mbps) or OC-12 (622 Mbps) in the network. Another factor to consider is that many existing studios are upgrading their facilities to SMPTE-259 which is at 255 Mbps. Taking all of this into consideration, it was determined that a requirement for the studio video format be that it supports data-rates less than 622 Mbps. In fact, we see great advantage in being able to compress video to less than 255 Mbps while meeting the quality requirements of a studio, since this would enable continued use of the

SMPTE-259 switching fabric while handling studio-quality HDTV. If the appropriate quality can be met at 155 Mbps, then OC-3 technology also becomes viable.

An additional advantage of compressing video within the studio is that the costs associated with storing or archiving decreases [1]. For one, the amount of storage media (tape or disk) that is required is less. A second improvement is in the reduction of the output bandwidth that needs to be supported on a video server for playing out a video stream. Alternately, for the same bandwidth supported on a video server, there is an increase in the number of output channels or streams that can be simultaneously supported.

## 2.2 Requirements for the Compression Format

As we have seen, there are advantages to using compression within the studio. However, any compression format that is chosen for use within the studio has to meet certain requirements. In this section, we shall briefly look at the principal requirements.

**Picture Quality -** The quality of the compressed and decompressed video is of paramount importance for studio applications. There is a strong likelihood that many of the video processing operations that take place in the studio today in the uncompressed domain will migrate into the compressed domain as the required technology becomes available. However, at least in the near future, there will be many video production related operations that will continue to be done in the uncompressed domain, since technology is not available to perform them in the compressed domain. For this reason, it will be necessary to decompress an already compressed video sequence prior to performing these operations. Subsequent to the required processing, the video will be re-compressed. This set of operations imply that video sequences can go through multiple generations of compression and decompression within a studio. It is therefore necessary that good quality video be attainable even after multiple generations of compression. In our experiments, we required that the video quality be adequate after 8 generations of coding.

**4:2:2 Color sampling -** Many operations within a studio rely on the color signals being sampled at a frequency higher than what is supported by typical broadcast compression systems. For instance, the MPEG-2 Main Profile supports only 4:2:0 color subsampling. An example of a studio operation that needs high fidelity color is chroma-keying. Thus, another requirement on the studio compression format is that artifact-free chroma-key operations be possible on video that has gone through multiple generations of compression.

**Editability -** High quality video production requires the ability to edit the video sequence to single-frame accuracy. Although in certain video-production applications it may be sufficient to edit at two or four frame intervals, it is never-the-less necessary that the studio compression format allow for single-frame accurate edits. Although, it is always possible to edit compressed video by decompressing, editing and then re-compressing, we deemed it a requirement that it be possible to do edits without going through such a process, since edits are among the most common procedures in a studio.

**Switching -** It should also be possible to switch between two compressed streams at pre-defined points, thus enabling the stitching together of a video program from separate and distinct video-clips.

**Ease of transcoding -** The finished product from the studio has to be converted to a format suitable for broadcast to the end viewer. For television stations in the United States, that format will be the ATSC specification which is based on MPEG-2 and is the Main Profile version of MPEG-2. For studios in Europe following the DVB specification, it will also be the MPEG-2 Main Profile. The studio compression format should, therefore, be such that it is easy to transcode from the studio format to the transmission format (MPEG-2 Main Profile).

**Low Delay -** It should be possible to do low delay encoding of video since the production of television programs involving conversation can greatly benefit from it.

**Bitrate Flexibility -** The studio format should be capable of supporting multiple as well as both constant and variable bit-rates. This would enable different applications to choose the bit-rate that is required by them up to a defined maximum rate.

**Ease of implementation -** Finally, ease and cost of implementation are issues that need to be addressed. The compression format should lend itself to reasonable implementations of encoders, decoders and other studio devices that process compressed video.

## 3.0 A Studio Compression Format

The MPEG-2 4:2:2 profile is a compression format that has been defined for studio applications. It is, however, a specification that exists only for standard-definition video. We have extended the 4:2:2 profile to higher resolutions including the 1920x1080 format specified for HDTV. The performance of such an extended 4:2:2 profile encoder was then compared to a non-DCT based algorithm.

In our simulations, we adopted the MPEG-2 Transport Stream packetized structure for the delivery of the video elementary streams. The transport stream structure has a 2.13% overhead associated with it's headers. These transport stream packets were then encapsulated in ATM cells using AAL-5. The ATM and AAL layer add an additional 11.32% overhead. In total, the overhead was 13.21% of the total bandwidth.

Simulations were performed at the two data rates of interest - 155 and 255 Mbps total bandwidth. After accommodating for the packetization overhead discussed above, and the audio, which is potentially uncompressed, these bitrates corresponded to 129 Mbps and 225 Mbps for the elementary video stream. The video data was coded to conform to the MPEG-2 4:2:2 profile using no motion compensation, i.e., all I-frame coding [2]. This was done in order to determine the lower bound on the video quality scale since the use of motion compensated frames can only increase the quality at a given bitrate. The use of the 4:2:2 profile without motion compensation also implied that the streams generated would lend themselves to frame accurate editing with minimal or no processing.

Simulation of multi-generation coding was done by coding each generation completely independent of the previous generation. Furthermore, two spatial shifts were introduced in the eight generations. Between the first decoding and the second encoding of the sequence, the video sequence was shifted spatially one pixel to the right and one (field) line down. Between the fifth decoding and the sixth encoding of the sequence, the pictures were shifted spatially in the opposite direction, i.e., one pixel to the left and one line up.

In the simulations using three test sequences, the non-MPEG technique failed to outperform the MPEG 4:2:2 profile. The 4:2:2 profile was therefore chosen as the studio format for the following additional reasons. It is an established standard and is likely to therefore result in cost advantages that are derived from a larger user base. A second advantage of using the 4:2:2 profile within the studio is that it is MPEG-2 and DCT based which makes it easier to transcode to the broadcast format which is also MPEG-2 based (Main Profile).

Our simulations did show, however, that there is a quality loss in multiple generation coding. The loss in SNR from the first generation to the eighth generation varied from 3 to 4 dB for the luminance and about 1-2 dB for the chrominance. There is room for improvement here and it is the subject of ongoing work.

## 4.0 Switching Compressed Video

In this section we will briefly discuss the obstacles to switching between compressed video streams and will then present a candidate solution. Although we will use MPEG-2 as an example, the fundamental problems are common to almost any video compression system.

The MPEG-2 4:2:2 profile as well as the Main Profile use video encoding algorithms that are inherently variable-rate in nature. In the majority of cases, an encoder-decoder buffer pair is utilized to smooth out this variation, thereby resulting in a constant bit rate stream that is transmitted over the communications channel. However, since the encoder is variable-rate in nature and the communication link is typically a constant-rate channel, this results in encoder and decoder buffers that have varying states. When the encoder is producing data faster than the channel can absorb, the amount of data in the encoder buffer increases and vice-versa. Similarly, data gets buffered in the decoder buffer prior to when it is decoded. Real-time video compression systems are also constant delay systems where the delay between the input to the encoder and the output from the decoder is constant. This also implies that the total delay experienced by a datum in the encoder and decoder buffer put together is a constant.

The varying state of the encoder and decoder buffer is the root cause of the difficulty associated with switching between compressed bitstreams. In MPEG-2 transport streams, decoders are synchronized through the use of program clock reference (PCR) timestamps and decode timestamps (DTS). The PCRs allow decoders to recover the encoding clock used by the encoder while the DTS indicates to the decoder the time at which a particular picture is to be decoded. The DTS is given in terms of the clock that would be recovered through PCRs.

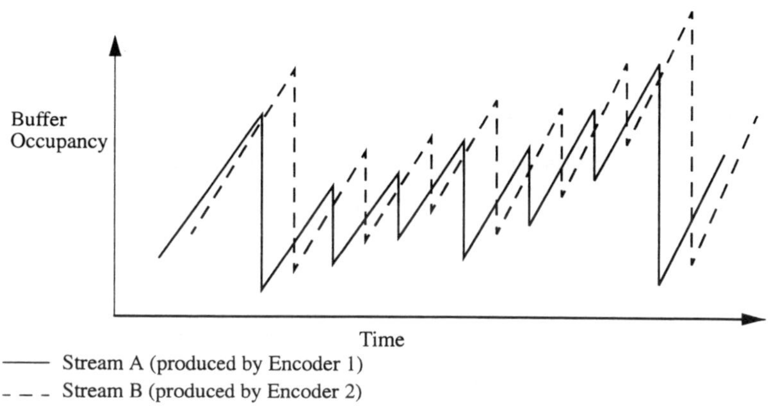


**Figure 1: Typical variation in decoder buffer occupancy**

Figure 1 provides a typical buffer occupancy curve which illustrates the variation in decoder buffer occupancy. The solid line indicates the decoder buffer occupancy curve as a function of time that is associated with the output of one encoder while the dashed line indicates the decoder buffer occupancy associated with a second encoder. For the purposes of the switching operation that we are considering, we can assume that Stream A is the stream that is being switched out of, while Stream B is the one being switched into. As Figure 1 shows, the two curves are not identical which is the case in general. In fact, it would be extremely rare for two independent encoders to have the same decoder buffer occupancy curve.

Using Figure 1 we can illustrate the buffering problem associated with switching between compressed video streams. If one switches a decoder from Stream A to Stream B (of Figure 1), the decoder would do one of two things. One possibility is that it will lose synchronization since the decoding times of the stream produced by Encoder 2 are not equal to the decode times of Encoder 1. A second possibility is that the decoder will maintain synchronization by synchronizing to Encoder 2, in which case, in the vicinity of the switch point, the time interval between two consecutive "decodes" will not be equal to a frame period. This can result in a visible artifact and is therefore not acceptable. Perhaps a more important objection to such a switching operation is that the resulting stream as perceived by the decoder is not MPEG-2 compatible.

A solution to this problem is as follows. The MPEG-2 stream can be constructed so as to satisfy certain constraints at those points in the stream where switching is required to be supported. These constraints enable switching to be then implemented as primarily a packet switching operation with minimal processing. The constraints also enable the construction of the stream that is to be switched to. For instance, knowledge of the constraints enable Stream B to be designed so that the stream resulting from the concatenation of Stream A up to the switch point, and Stream B starting from the switch point, is a compliant datastream.

These constraints are essentially in the form of two parameters. The first, termed splice_decoding_delay enables the calculation of the decoder buffer delay that is to be undergone by the last picture that precedes the switch point. If this parameter is known to Encoder 2, it can construct Stream B so that the decoder buffer delay of it's first frame following the switch point is such that it will be decoded exactly one picture period after the last picture from Stream A that precedes the switch point. This ensures a seamless transition.

A second parameter that is used in MPEG-2 is termed max_splice_rate. Encoder 1 constructs Stream A so that it can be switched with any stream at rates that are no greater than that given by max_splice_rate. All that Encoder 2 has to do, in this case, is to ensure that Stream B is at a rate lower than (or equal to) max_splice_rate.

## 5.0 Conclusion

We have discussed the requirements for a video compression format for use in studio applications and discussed the suitability of the MPEG-2 4:2:2 profile for such a purpose. We have also elaborated on the reasons why switching between compressed video streams is complicated and have presented a solution for performing such switching with minimal processing.

## 6.0 Acknowledgment

This work was carried out within the HDTV Broadcast Technology program which is partially funded by the National Institute of Standards and Technology's Advanced Technology Program under Award No. 70N1NB5H1174. The NIST Technical Program Manager is Ms. Florina Hoffer.

## 7.0 References

1. M. Ostlund, "Multichannel Video Server Applications in TV Broadcast and Post Production", 136th SMPTE Technical Conference and World Media Expo, October 12-15, 1994, Los Angeles.

[2]. "Generic Coding of Moving Pictures and Associated Audio: Video", ISO/IEC 13818-2, 1994.